"This volume covers an amazing amount of territory in both biblical and scientific studies relevant to the question of the historical Adam and Eve. The author's wide reading, amazing erudition, and carefully articulated judgment shine through. One does not need to agree with every point the author makes, every step in his argument, or his conclusions to gain a great deal from reading this volume. He faces the issues squarely, explains them clearly, and carries the reader along with him well. Those who seek to contribute to this discussion going forward must pay careful attention to what this highly accomplished scholar has set forth so well in this book."

— **RICHARD E. AVERBECK**
professor of Old Testament at Trinity Evangelical Divinity School

"This book truly is a 'quest,' an intellectual journey, beginning with Scripture and ending in a meaningful exchange with science. Craig's quest brings him into an ancient and growing conversation about human origins, a storied exchange between many theologians, philosophers, and scientists. In this conversation, many fear that it is only by compromising our core commitments that space is made for evolutionary science. This book demonstrates, to the contrary, an account of human origins that makes space for evolution without capitulating to a science-only view of the world. Craig shows us not only that constructive dialogue between theology and science is possible, but also that theological questions can sharpen our understanding of science. The scientific content in this book will be surprising to many, but it is sound, even as it gives a much-needed pushback on overreach by evolutionary creationists. We find that many scientists misunderstood, and even overstated, the scientific evidence against Adam and Eve, ancestors of us all. Craig's explanation of how genetic evidence does, and does not, delimit human origins is true to our current scientific understanding. In so clearly making this scientific corrective, this book promises to be a landmark, a gift to the church, with reverberating significance to the conversation. His telling of the science makes space for many ways of understanding everything together, so the conversation should not end here. May we together be drawn deeper into the mystery, enticed to explore with one another what science is discovering about when and how 'humanness' arises in our past. Could sacred and natural history entwine, telling us something important about who we are and what it means to be human?"

— **S. JOSHUA SWAMIDASS**
associate professor of laboratory and genomic medicine
at Washington University in St. Louis

"This is a book for those who want to pursue the truth. Here William Lane Craig combines thorough research and judicious weighing of the arguments to show that the biblical picture of human origins, rightly understood, can match very well with the best results of the sciences—again, rightly understood. He holds all of these disparate disciplines accountable to the requirements of sound reasoning. Craig's honesty and bracingly relentless logic make it a pleasure to follow his detailed discussions and allow us to feel the attraction of his proposed location of Adam and Eve. He challenges and equips us to engage these issues at his own high and responsible level, for which I thank him."

— **C. JOHN COLLINS**
professor of Old Testament at Covenant Theological Seminary

"There has been a great deal of recent scholarly debate and discussion concerning the historicity of Adam and Eve. However, few treatments of the subject are able to bring together biblical, theological, philosophical, and scientific perspectives simultaneously. In this volume, Dr. Craig does just that—weaving these threads together in ways that respect orthodox Christian doctrine and incorporate our best current understanding of the origins of our species. All Christian scholars wrestling with this topic will benefit from Craig's deep and learned treatment."

— **MICHAEL J. MURRAY**
senior visiting scholar of philosophy at Franklin and Marshall College

In Quest of the Historical Adam

A Biblical and Scientific Exploration

William Lane Craig

William B. Eerdmans Publishing Company
Grand Rapids, Michigan

Wm. B. Eerdmans Publishing Co.
4035 Park East Court SE, Grand Rapids, Michigan 49546
www.eerdmans.com

Published 2021
Printed in the United States of America

27 26 25 24 23 22 21   1 2 3 4 5 6 7

ISBN 978-0-8028-7911-0

Library of Congress Cataloging-in-Publication Data

Names: Craig, William Lane, author.
Title: In quest of the historical Adam : a biblical and scientific exploration / William Lane Craig.
Description: Grand Rapids, Michigan : William B. Eerdmans Publishing Company, 2021. | Includes bibliographical references and indexes. | Summary: "An interdisciplinary investigation into the historicity of the biblical figure of Adam, drawing upon Old and New Testament studies and a wide range of scientific disciplines"—Provided by publisher.
Identifiers: LCCN 2021013206 | ISBN 9780802879110 (hardcover)
Subjects: LCSH: Adam (Biblical figure) | Bible. Genesis, I–XI—Criticism, interpretation, etc. | Theological anthropology. | Paleoanthropology.
Classification: LCC BS580.A4 C73 2021 | DDC 222/.11092 [B]—dc23
LC record available at https://lccn.loc.gov/2021013206

Biblical quotations follow the Revised Standard Version unless otherwise noted.

To our grandson

Oliver,

whose quantal vowels would be
the envy of any Neanderthal

CONTENTS

FIGURES

PREFACE

Old Testament scholar Richard Averbeck has cautioned, "No matter what you say (or write) about the early chapters of Genesis, you are in a lot of trouble with a lot of people."[1] As I offer this book to the reading public, I am acutely conscious of Averbeck's words. People on both the left and the right can be expected to be upset with this book and, unfortunately, its author. All I can do is plead that they give an honest and open-minded reading of the case I make for my conclusions. I assure my readers that this book is the result of a genuine struggle on my part with the evidence, both biblical and scientific, concerning the historical Adam.

This book is not a scholarly treatise, though it draws on high scholarship to make its case. Neither is it a superficial popularization, though I make an effort to explain technical terms to readers outside the many specialist disciplines featured in this book. My target audience is people like myself, persons who are Christian philosophers, theologians, and other academics but who are neither Old Testament scholars nor scientists—though I hasten to add that Old Testament scholars will profit greatly from the discussion of the scientific evidence for human origins in this book, and specialists in the various scientific disciplines relevant to human origins will likewise profit greatly from the discussion of the biblical issues to be found in these pages. By thus simplifying the material for nonspecialists, I make the book useful as well to intelligent laymen who are not academics, for we are all laymen when it comes to areas outside our areas of specialization.

The reader will soon notice quite lengthy footnotes attending the main text. These provide a sort of running discussion of the text, where considerably more detail can be provided without interrupting the flow of the text.

1. Richard E. Averbeck, "The Lost World of Adam and Eve: A Review Essay," *Themelios* 40, no. 2 (2015): 226.

By this means I am able to streamline the main text, keeping it succinct and moving forward at a good pace. Readers who want more detail are advised to consult the accompanying notes.

The book comprises two principal parts with some introductory remarks and closing reflections. The first main part deals with the biblical data pertinent to human origins and the second with scientific evidence for the same. The order of the two parts is important. We want first and foremost as Christians to know what the Bible has to say about human origins independent of modern science. We want to know what our biblical commitments are concerning the historical Adam, and we can know those only insofar as our hermeneutical approach to Scripture is not shaped by modern science. After all, if biblical teaching is at odds with the deliverances of modern science, then we want to know that and act accordingly. In light of our study of Scripture, only then do I turn to an examination of the deliverances of modern science to see if the findings of modern science are compatible with the historicity of Adam and Eve.

In discussing various points of view, I have tried to avoid labels like "liberal," "progressive," and "conservative" because these politically charged terms are prejudicial. Still, one needs some terms to characterize competing viewpoints, and so I have adopted the labels "traditional" and "revisionist" as the least problematic. There is, after all, a traditional view of Adam and Eve that has dominated church history, and there are various revisionist views, usually relatively recent, that modify the traditional view to different degrees. In the traditional interpretation of Adam and Eve, they are the original human pair, miraculously created *de novo* by God a few thousand years before Christ. They are the parents of the entire human race, so that every human being who has ever lived on the face of this planet is descended from them. They lived in the paradisaical Garden of Eden somewhere to the east of the Levant, whence they were expelled by God for yielding to the temptation of the serpent and disobeying God, thereby bringing misery on themselves and their descendants.

Further with regard to terminology, I should explain that I shall use the phrase "the historical Adam" as convenient shorthand for "the historical Adam and Eve," a more cumbersome, if more accurate, expression. When it comes to scientific nomenclature, I shall use species terminology like *Homo sapiens* to denominate either the particular class of a hominin or a concrete member of that class. In some cases we can distinguish easily between a class name like *Homo neanderthalensis* and the word for a member of that class, "Neanderthal." Unfortunately, such differentiation is not easy to find for other species terms like *Homo erectus* or even *Homo sapiens.* I am confident that the reader will not mind my avoiding frequent use of pedantic expressions like "members of *Homo erectus.*"

I have profited from conversations with too many fellow scholars to mention by name. But I do want to single out S. J. Swamidass as an invaluable guide to the challenge discussed in part 3 issuing from population genetics to the historical Adam. I am also grateful to Old Testament scholars Richard Hess and Richard Averbeck for their comments on my discussion of the biblical material in part 2. I heartily thank my research assistant Timothy Bayless for procuring for me numerous research materials from often recondite sources, as well as for his preparation of the bibliography and indexes. I am deeply indebted to Gabriel Jones and James Urban for their creative work with most of the figures illustrating the text. I thank editor Andrew Knapp for securing the permissions for many of the figures, as well as for his close reading of and comments on the text. I am grateful to the eagle-eyed Kevin Whitehead for his help in proofreading the galley proofs. As always, I am thankful for my wife Jan's interest in and support of this research.

WILLIAM LANE CRAIG
Atlanta, Georgia

ABBREVIATIONS

General

ANE	ancient Near East(ern)
bk.	book
ca.	*circa*, about
EQ	encephalization quotient
ESA	Early Stone Age
et al.	*et alii*, and others
frag(s).	fragment(s)
HLA	human leukocyte antigen
kya	thousand years ago
LSA	Later Stone Age
MIS	Marine Isotope Stages
MR	metabolic rate
MSA	Middle Stone Age
mya	million years ago
NT	New Testament
OT	Old Testament
pt.	part
SVT	supralaryngeal vocal tract
TMR4A	time of the most recent four alleles
TMRCA	time of the most recent common ancestor

Bibliographic

AnBehav	*Animal Behavior*
ACPQ	*American Catholic Philosophical Quarterly*

AJPA	*American Journal of Physical Anthropology*
AMM	*American Mathematical Monthly*
AO	*Aula Orientalis*
ARA	*Annual Review of Anthropology*
Aramazd	*Aramazd: Armenian Journal of Near Eastern Studies*
ARL	*Annual Review of Linguistics*
AS	Assyriological Studies
AYB	Anchor Yale Bible
BAR	*Biblical Archaeology Review*
BBS	*Behavioral and Brain Sciences*
BDAG	Danker, Frederick W., Walter Bauer, William F. Arndt, F. Wilber Gingrich. *A Greek-English Lexicon of the New Testament and Other Early Christian Literature*. 3rd ed. Chicago: University of Chicago Press, 2000.
BN	*Biblische Notizen*
BSac	*Bibliotheca Sacra*
BZABR	Beihefte zur Zeitschrift für altorientalische und biblische Rechtsgeschichte
BZAW	Beihefte zur Zeitschrift für die alttestamentliche Wissenschaft
CA	*Current Anthropology*
CAJ	*Cambridge Archaeological Journal*
CB	*Current Biology*
CBQMS	Catholic Biblical Quarterly Monograph Series
CD	Damascus Document
CENTJ	*Creation Ex Nihilo Technical Journal*
COBS	*Current Opinion in Behavioral Sciences*
CPF	Contemporary Philosophy in Focus
CR	*Clergy Review*
CSEL	Corpus Scriptorum Ecclesiasticorum Latinorum
CSR	*Christian Scholar's Review*
EA	*Evolutionary Anthropology*
EBC	Expositor's Bible Commentary
EPSL	*Earth and Planetary Science Letters*
EvQ	*Evangelical Quarterly*
FC	Fathers of the Church
FJB	*Frankfurter Judaistische Beiträge*
FP	*Frontiers in Psychology*
GB	*Genome Biology*
JANESCU	*Journal of the Ancient Near Eastern Society of Columbia University*

JAOS	*Journal of the American Oriental Society*
JAS	*Journal of Archaeological Science*
JBL	*Journal of Biblical Literature*
JHE	*Journal of Human Evolution*
JICA	*Journal of Island and Coastal Archaeology*
JP	*Journal of Phonetics*
JPSTC	JPS Torah Commentary
JSL	*Journal of Symbolic Logic*
JSOTSup	Journal for the Study of the Old Testament Supplement Series
JSPSup	Journal for the Study of the Pseudepigrapha Supplement Series
JTS	*Journal of Theological Studies*
JTVI	*Journal of the Transactions of the Victorian Institute*
KAR	Keilschrifttexte aus Assur religiösen Inhalts
LHBOTS	Library of Hebrew Bible/Old Testament Studies
LI	*Linguistic Inquiry*
NAC	New American Commentary
NACG	*Newsletter of the Affiliation of Christian Geologists*
NCBC	New Cambridge Bible Commentary
NICNT	New International Commentary on the New Testament
NICOT	New International Commentary on the Old Testament
NIGTC	New International Greek Testament Commentary
NTA	Neutestamentliche Abhandlungen
OTL	Old Testament Library
PBR	*Psychonomic Bulletin and Review*
Philos. Christi	*Philosophia Christi*
PNAS	*Proceedings of the National Academy of Sciences*
PRS	*Proceedings of the Royal Society*
PSCF	*Perspectives on Science and Christian Faith*
PTRSB	*Philosophical Transactions of the Royal Society B: Biological Sciences*
QI	*Quaternary International*
RGRW	Religions in the Graeco-Roman World
RSR	*Religious Studies Review*
SA	*Science Advances*
SAIPS	Stone Age Institute Publication Series
SANE	Sources from the Ancient Near East
SBT	Studies in Biblical Theology
SBTS	Sources for Biblical and Theological Studies
Sci. Am.	*Scientific American*

SCL	Sather Classical Lectures
SGBC	Story of God Bible Commentary
SJA	*Southwestern Journal of Anthropology*
SR	*Scientific Reports*
TEE	*Trends in Ecology and Evolution*
TL	*Theologische Literaturzeitung*
TM	*Time and Mind*
VIBS	Value Inquiry Book Series
VT	*Vetus Testamentum*
VTSup	Supplements to Vetus Testamentum
WBC	Word Biblical Commentary
WTJ	*Westminster Theological Journal*
WUB	*Welt und Umwelt der Bibel*
YES	Yale Egyptological Studies
ZAW	*Zeitschrift für die alttestamentliche Wissenschaft*

PART 1

The Importance of the Historical Adam

Chapter 1

WHAT IS AT STAKE

Introduction

Before embarking on a quest of the historical Adam, it is appropriate that we ask ourselves what is at stake in this endeavor. After all, if the question is of little significance, one may think it not worth the time and effort to embark on the quest in the first place but decide instead to devote one's resources to more important projects.

On the one hand, it is tempting to view the question of the historical Adam as a peripheral concern, hardly at the heart of Christian theology. It has never been addressed by an ecumenical council, and the church's insouciance cannot be written off wholly as a result of the doctrine's being universally accepted, since church fathers like Origen and Augustine showed themselves to be open to figurative interpretations of the Genesis narratives.[1]

1. In his systematic treatise *On First Principles* Origen asked incredulously,

> What man of intelligence, I ask, will consider it a reasonable statement that the first and the second and the third day, in which there are said to be both morning and evening, existed without sun and moon and stars, while the first day was even without a heaven? And who could be found so silly as to believe that God, after the manner of a farmer, "planted trees eastward in Eden," and set therein a "tree of life," that is, a visible and palpable tree of wood, of such a sort that anyone who ate of this tree with bodily teeth would gain life; and again that anyone who ate of another tree would get a knowledge of "good and evil"? And further, when God is said to "walk in the paradise in the evening" and Adam to hide himself behind a tree, I do not think anyone will doubt that these statements are made in scripture in a figurative manner, in order that through them certain mystical truths may be indicated. (4.3.1; trans. G. W. Butterworth [New York: Harper & Row, 1966], 288–89)

Augustine worried that a literalistic interpretation of the Genesis creation story would invite the mockery of unbelievers and thus prove to be an obstacle to saving faith. In his *Literal Commentary on Genesis* he writes, "I fear that I will be laughed at by those

The doctrine certainly does not have the centrality that doctrines concerning justification and sanctification do, not to speak of such core doctrines as the Trinity, incarnation, and atonement.

Many traditional theologians would think the historicity of Adam crucial for hamartiology, or the doctrine of sin. For if Adam was not a historical person, clearly there was no historical fall into sin in the traditional sense. In particular, the doctrine of original sin must go by the board if there was no historical Adam and hence no fall. For in the absence of a historical Adam, there is, or was, no sin of Adam that can be imputed to every human being. It should be obvious that we cannot be held guilty and hence deserving of punishment for an infraction that never occurred. By the same token we cannot be heirs of a corrupted human nature as a result of Adam's sin if no such sin ever occurred. Thus, in the absence of a historical Adam the traditional doctrine of original sin cannot be maintained.

In virtue of Paul's contrasting Adam and his sin with Christ and his atoning death, some theologians have gone so far as to assert that the denial of the historical Adam undermines in turn the doctrine of the atonement. Dyson Hague wrote in *The Fundamentals*, "So closely does the apostle link the fall of Adam and the death of Christ, that without Adam's fall the science of theology is evacuated of its most salient feature, the atonement. If the first Adam was not made a living soul and fell, there was no reason for the work of the Second Man, the Lord from heaven."[2] Such a consequence would

---

who have scientific knowledge of these matters and by those who recognize the facts of the case" (1.10; cf. 1.19.39; FC 41:30). He therefore expressed openness to figurative interpretations of the text when the literal sense would be untenable: "Certainly, if the bodily things mentioned here could not in any way at all be taken in a bodily sense that accorded with truth, what other course would we have but to understand them as spoken figuratively, rather than impiously to find fault with holy scripture?" (8.1.4; CSEL 28:1, 232). Augustine's principle, derived from Origen, that any text which, taken literally, implies falsehood or impurity should be interpreted figuratively was widely accepted in both Western and Eastern exegesis through the Middle Ages (Richard Swinburne, "Authority of Scripture, Tradition, and the Church," in *The Oxford Handbook of Philosophical Theology*, ed. Thomas P. Flint and Michael C. Rea [Oxford: Oxford University Press, 2011], 16). For illuminating discussion, see Gavin R. Ortlund, *Retrieving Augustine's Doctrine of Creation: Ancient Wisdom for Current Controversy* (Downers Grove, IL: IVP Academic, 2020).

2. Dyson Hague, "The Doctrinal Value of the First Chapters of Genesis," in *The Fundamentals*, ed. R. A. Torrey and A. C. Dixon (Grand Rapids: Baker Books, 2003), 1:285, cited in Matthew Barrett and Ardel B. Caneday, eds., *Four Views on the Historical Adam*, Counterpoints (Grand Rapids: Zondervan, 2013). Concurring with Hague is William D. Barrick, "A Historical Adam: Young-Earth Creation View," in Barrett and Caneday, *Four*

eviscerate Christianity. Hence, some traditional theologians have claimed that the historicity of Adam is, in popular parlance, "a gospel issue"—that is to say, an issue on which the Christian faith stands or falls.[3]

The attempt to make the doctrine of original sin a necessary condition of the doctrine of the atonement is, however, an overreach. Nowhere in the New Testament (NT) is Christ said to have died for original sin. Rather, the gospel proclaimed by the apostles was, in the words of the traditional kerygmatic formulation quoted by Paul, that "Christ died for *our sins* in accordance with the scriptures" (1 Cor 15:3). Never mind Adam's sin; ours alone are quite sufficient to require the atoning death of Christ for salvation! Interpreting Adam as a purely symbolic figure, a sort of Everyman, that expresses the universality of human sin and fallenness would not undercut the gospel of salvation through Christ's atoning death. Therefore, denial of the doctrine of original sin does not undermine the doctrine of the atonement.

We may nonetheless agree that the historicity of Adam is entailed by and therefore a necessary condition of the doctrine of original sin. But this conclusion is indicative of the importance of the historical Adam only if the doctrine of original sin is itself of vital importance. It is, however, dubious that the doctrine of original sin is essential to the Christian faith.[4] The doctrine enjoys slim scriptural support, to put it mildly; not to be found in the ac-

Views on the Historical Adam, 222. From a less alarmist but revisionist point of view, Daniel Harlow thinks that the reformulation of the doctrine of original sin mandated by Adam's nonhistoricity "requires that we now favor theories of the atonement like the *Christus victor* model or the moral influence theory" ("After Adam: Reading Genesis in an Age of Evolutionary Science," *PSCF* 62 [2010]: 192).

3. See, e.g., Donald Carson's warning: "If Paul's insistence on the historicity of Adam, on his individuality and representative status, on the nature and consequences of the fall, on the links between these things and the person and work of Christ, and on their typological place with respect to the new creation—if this all be allowed to tumble into disarray, the foundations of *Christian* theology (not just *Pauline* theology) are threatened. The church is left only with disparate but scarcely related truths, diversely interpreted, or with systems of theology which are Christian in name only, but not deeply and essentially biblical" (D. A. Carson, "Adam in the Epistles of Paul," in *In the Beginning . . . : A Symposium on the Bible and Creation*, ed. N. M. de S. Cameron [Glasgow: Biblical Creation Society, 1980], 41).

4. For the opposite view, see the treatment of Matthew Levering, *Engaging the Doctrine of Creation: Cosmos, Creatures, and the Wise and Good Creator* (Grand Rapids: Baker Academic, 2017), chap. 6. As a Catholic theologian, Levering is guided in his theologizing principally by the teaching of the magisterium rather than Scripture, which takes a decidedly subordinate role in his discussion. By contrast, for me as an evangelical Protestant, the teaching of Scripture is paramount; hence, our strikingly different treatments of the importance of the historical Adam.

count of Gen 3 of the curses following the fall, the doctrine depends entirely on one biblical passage, Rom 5:12–21, and that passage is vague and open to multiple interpretations. Paul does not teach clearly that either (1) Adam's sin is imputed to every one of his descendants or (2) Adam's sin resulted in a corruption of human nature or a privation of original righteousness that is transmitted to all of his descendants. That Christianity can get along without (1) is evident from the example of the Orthodox Church, whose doctrine of original sin affirms only (2). Even (2) can hardly be said to be essential: not only is it not clearly taught in Rom 5, but the mere universality of sin among human beings is sufficient to require Christ's atoning death for our salvation. "Since all have sinned and fall short of the glory of God, they are justified by his grace as a gift, through the redemption which is in Christ Jesus" (Rom 3:23–24). The attempt to explain the universality of human sin by postulating a corruption or wounding of human nature inherited from Adam is a theological add-on to which the Christian theologian need not be committed.[5]

Thus, while the doctrine of original sin depends crucially on the fact of a historical Adam, Christianity need not embrace the traditional doctrine of original sin but may content itself with affirming the universal wrongdoing of human beings and their inability to save themselves.

Before we dismiss the question of the historical Adam as a theological sideshow, however, we must consider whether other considerations might not justify its importance to Christian faith. It seems that there are, indeed, such considerations. If the Scriptures clearly teach that there was a historical Adam at the headwaters of the human race, then the falsity of that doctrine would have a reverberatory effect on the doctrine of Scripture with regard to Scripture's truthfulness and reliability. The Scriptures would then be convicted of teaching falsehoods. Peter Enns is right to emphasize that "Paul's Adam in Romans is not a 'plain reading' of the Adam story but an interpretation of that story for theological purposes that are not rooted in Genesis." The difficulty, however, is that, given scriptural inspiration, Paul's interpretation is God-breathed and therefore authoritative in all that Paul means to teach. Enns insists that it is not modern science that needs to be

5. As Cornelius Plantinga reminds us, "Although, partly because of the silence of Scripture, Christians of various theological orientations differ on central issues in the doctrine of original sin—for example, how a child acquires the fateful disposition to sin, whether this disposition is itself sin, how to describe and assess the accompanying bondage of the will—they agree on the universality, solidarity, stubbornness, and historical momentum of sin" (Cornelius Plantinga Jr., *Not the Way It's Supposed to Be: A Breviary of Sin* [Grand Rapids: Eerdmans, 1995], 33).

grafted onto the Bible; rather, "the truth . . . is that our readings of Genesis and Romans are what need to be adjusted to allow the graft to take."[6] But how can they be adjusted if we are confident that we have rightly interpreted the teaching of the divinely inspired author, in this case Paul, as Enns seems to acknowledge? If such an adjustment is not possible for the honest exegete, then a major revision of the doctrine of inspiration would be required, such that the teaching of error would be consistent with Scripture's being divinely inspired.

Worse still, if, as seems plausible, Jesus himself believed in the historicity of Adam and Eve (Matt 19:4–6), then even if Jesus were not guilty of teaching doctrinal error, he still would have held false beliefs concerning Adam and Eve, if there were no historical Adam, which is incompatible with his omniscience. Notice that the concern here is quite different from Jesus's having limited knowledge. Traditional Christology recognizes that Christ had a human mind or consciousness that was limited in knowledge and that developed throughout his lifetime.[7] That is why we are not committed to the monstrosity of the baby Jesus lying in the manger contemplating the infinitesimal calculus or quantum mechanics. Rather, Jesus possessed at every point during his lifetime a typical human consciousness. But it is a very different thing to say that Jesus possessed false beliefs. Even if in his human mind or consciousness Jesus was not aware of or did not have access to the full contents of the mind of the Logos, the second person of the Trinity, still the person who Christ is had the full knowledge proper to an omniscient being with respect to his divine nature. Since there is according to orthodox Christological confession but one person who is Christ and since that person is divine, that person is omniscient.

6. Jim Stump et al., "*Adam and the Genome*: Responses," *BioLogos* (blog), January 30, 2017, https://biologos.org/articles/adam-and-the-genome-responses.

7. Thus, the concern expressed by Jud Davis is quite inappropriate to a Chalcedonian Christology: "I wonder if Jesus thought the earth was flat as he, in the unity of his person, held the molecules of the universe together, or when he, lying helpless in a manger, brought out the stars one by one and called each by name" ("Unresolved Major Questions: Evangelicals and Genesis 1–2," in *Reading Genesis 1–2: An Evangelical Conversation*, ed. J. Daryl Charles [Peabody, MA: Hendrickson, 2013], 212). Davis fails to appreciate that despite the unity of his person, Jesus had a human consciousness that was not the full consciousness of the Logos. So just as the omnipotent Logos could be "lying helpless in a manger," so the omniscient Logos could be ignorant of many facts, including the date of his second coming—in both cases with respect to his human nature. Davis's understanding of the incarnation seems to be along the lines of Superman disguised as Clark Kent. NB that Davis's citations of Wayne Grudem do not at all say what Davis imagines.

But by definition an omniscient person cannot possess false beliefs. According to the standard definition, a person *S* is omniscient iff for any proposition *p*, if *p*, then *S* knows that *p* and does not believe not-*p*.[8] Kenotic theologians notwithstanding, it is plausible to think that omniscience is an essential attribute of God, entailed by his being the greatest conceivable being.[9] Therefore, Jesus must have been and is omniscient. It does no good to say that a typical human consciousness is error-prone and therefore Jesus could have held false beliefs according to his human nature during his so-called state of humiliation (his state from conception through his burial). For beliefs are held by a person, not by a nature, and the only person in Christ is a divine person, who therefore could not hold false beliefs, period.[10] The person Christ is is divine and therefore is omniscient and therefore believes every truth and no falsehoods. Thus, as crazy as it sounds, denial of the historical Adam threatens to undo the deity of Christ and thus to destroy orthodox Christian faith.

Our Options

Now many contemporary theologians would simply embrace such consequences, denying that the Scriptures are in any way more authoritative for human existence than comparable ancient Near Eastern (ANE) myths, and perhaps even affirming that Jesus was merely human. These positions are not, however, acceptable to any theologian who wants to maintain some semblance of orthodox Christianity. What, then, are our options as orthodox Christians (fig. 1.1)?

We might try to avert the disastrous consequences mentioned above by arguing that the existence of the historical Adam is in fact compatible with the scientific evidence, properly interpreted, concerning human origins,

8. A brief account of divine omniscience, and of the many questions it raises, may be found in my and J. P. Moreland's *Philosophical Foundations for a Christian Worldview*, 2nd ed. (Downers Grove, IL: InterVarsity Press, 2017), 524–30.

9. For a critique of kenotic Christology, see Moreland and Craig, *Philosophical Foundations*, 601–5.

10. It would be logically absurd to say that Christ believed *p* and that *p* was true according to his divine nature but false according to his human nature. If *p* is a historical statement like "Pontius Pilate is the Procurator of Judea," it would be a self-contradiction to say that this statement is true according to Christ's divine nature and false according to his human nature—similarly with "Adam was a historical person."

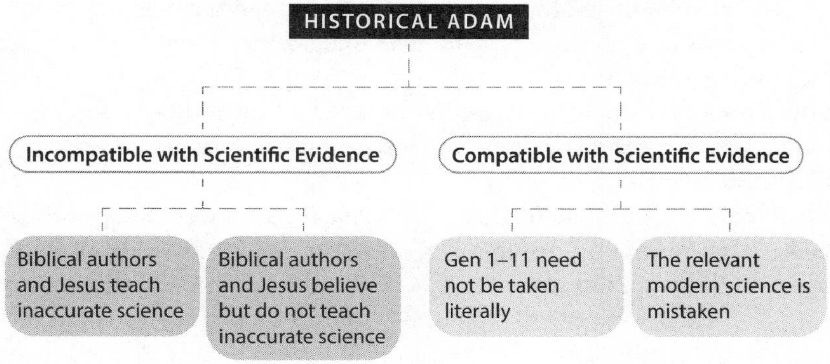

Figure 1.1. Options for orthodox Christians concerning the alleged conflict between modern science and the historical Adam.

as indicated on the right-hand side of our diagram. But it is often useful in weighing challenges to Christian faith to consider first a worst-case scenario and to ask what our options are in such a case. Assuming, then, that the scientific evidence is incompatible with the existence of the historical Adam, as depicted on the left-hand side of the diagram, how might the orthodox Christian theologian respond, short of embracing the consequences mentioned above?

Assuming that we want the Scriptures still to be in some way authoritative, even though the historical Adam did not exist, one option is to affirm that the Scriptures do teach, however erroneously, the existence of a historical Adam but—on the assumption that inspiration guarantees truth—to restrict inspiration and hence the guarantee of truthfulness to the spiritual or theological content of Scripture. A good many revisionist theologians have taken this option. Ironically, perhaps, they are thus hermeneutical bedfellows with traditional literalists, who argue that the plain interpretation of Scripture is that the world is a recent creation by God in six consecutive days, that there was an original human pair living in the Garden of Eden who sinned by eating the fruit of the tree of the knowledge of good and evil, that there was a worldwide flood that destroyed all terrestrial life save that aboard the ark built by Noah, that the world's languages resulted from the confusion of tongues at the Tower of Babel, and so on. The revisionist agrees with the young earth creationist that the Scriptures teach all these things, but unlike the young earth creationist, the revisionist regards all these teachings as falsehoods. They are therefore not part of divine revelation, for

God has accommodated himself to speaking through the often erroneous thought forms of a culture, embedding theological truths within the husks of scientific and historical errors taught by Scripture. This option will involve an overhaul of the doctrine of inspiration and biblical authority, forcing us in some way to discriminate between inspired theological truths and uninspired cultural husks.

Alternatively, we might maintain that while the authors of Scripture may well have *believed* in a six-day creation, a historical Adam, a worldwide flood, and so on, they did not *teach* such facts. Since inspiration's guarantee of truthfulness attaches only to what the Scriptures teach, we are not committed to the truthfulness of the authors' personal beliefs. A good many contemporary scholars have embraced this option in order to deal with such elements in the Genesis narrative as the three-decker cosmos, the firmament, and the waters above it, and some have extended this approach to include belief in a historical Adam as the progenitor of the human race. Such beliefs are supposed to be adventitious to the teachings of Scripture, which are true and authoritative. This option differs from the first in that it denies that the Scriptures teach the objectionable doctrines. The challenge of this option is to make the distinction between what the author believed and what he taught a plausible one. This approach can seem a bit too convenient, allowing us disingenuously to exclude from the teaching of Scripture anything that we find scientifically unacceptable and to relegate such obsolete science to merely the author's beliefs.

If there was no historical Adam, then along with the doctrine of inspiration we shall also need an overhaul of the doctrine of the incarnation in order to allow Jesus to entertain false beliefs. Distinguishing, as above, between what he believed and what he taught is of no avail, since the problem posed by his deity is precisely his inability to believe falsehoods. Perhaps the best way of attacking this problem is to distinguish between *accepting* a proposition and *believing* a proposition. This distinction plays an important role in the philosophy of mathematics with respect to the ontological commitments of mathematical language.[11] Some thinkers hold that belief in the truth of even simple arithmetic statements like 2 + 2 = 4 commits one to the reality of mind-independent Platonistic entities like the number 4. Belief in the axioms of Zermelo-Fraenkel set theory allegedly commits us to the reality of an infinite set, an extravagant metaphysical commitment.

11. See discussion in my *God and Abstract Objects: The Coherence of Theism; Aseity* (Berlin: Springer, 2017), 312, 316–17, 344–45; cf. 256–57.

Most practicing mathematicians and scientists would probably not consider themselves to have made such metaphysical commitments by means of their assumptions or assertions. So it is common to distinguish between *accepting* a mathematical statement and *believing* a mathematical statement. Philosopher of mathematics Penelope Maddy, for example, distinguishes between what she calls "believing the axioms" and "defending the axioms."[12] Although such an apologetic concern seems at first blush to assume that the axioms are true and that it is the truth of the axioms that is to be defended, what Maddy is in fact talking about is defending *the use* of the axioms, regardless of their truth. Indeed, her aim is to "shift attention away from . . . elusive matters of truth and existence."[13] In Maddy's view, what justifies the use of set-theoretical axioms is fruitfulness: axioms are properly adopted that are rich in mathematical consequences, or what Maddy calls "mathematical depth."[14] Thus, accepting the axioms of set theory does not imply belief in the axioms of set theory.

Such a distinction does not imply any disingenuousness on the part of the mathematician or scientist; indeed, he may never have even thought about his ontological commitments. This sincere acceptance of set-theoretical axioms leads Platonist philosophers John Burgess and Gideon Rosen to complain that "to assent verbally to a claim without conscious, silent reservations, to rely on it in both theoretical and practical contexts, just *is* to believe that it is true."[15] They thereby testify to the sincere acceptance of the axioms on the part of mathematicians and scientists. But the anti-realist may plausibly challenge the Platonist to prove that the majority of mathematicians and scientists, in giving verbal assent to and relying on mathematical existence theorems, really believe that there are mathematical objects such as the Platonist asserts there are. Burgess and Rosen do acknowledge indirect evidence in favor of the view that practitioners have less than belief in

12. See Penelope Maddy, "Believing the Axioms I," *JSL* 53, no. 2 (1988): 481–511; Maddy, "Believing the Axioms II," *JSL* 53, no. 3 (1988): 736–64; and her later *Defending the Axioms: On the Philosophical Foundations of Set Theory* (Oxford: Oxford University Press, 2011), ix. The question will be whether the intrinsic and extrinsic justifications she surveys really provide grounds for believing the axioms to be true rather than for entertaining or accepting the axioms without believing them.

13. Maddy, *Defending the Axioms*, 1.

14. Maddy, *Defending the Axioms*, 82.

15. Gideon Rosen and John P. Burgess, "Nominalism Reconsidered," in *The Oxford Handbook of Philosophy of Mathematics and Logic*, ed. Stewart Shapiro (Oxford: Oxford University Press, 2005), 517.

mathematical objects—namely, the *lightheartedness* with which novel mathematical entities are introduced, the *indifference* when it comes to questions of identifying mathematical objects such as the number 2 with other objects such as {{Ø}} or {0, 1}, and the *varying reactions* of mathematicians when pressed by philosophers about the ontological commitments of their theorems. *Pace* Burgess and Rosen, these do seem to supply strong grounds for suspecting that statements of mathematical existence are often not understood by mathematicians and scientists as equivalent to a statement that the Eiffel Tower exists. The overriding point is that a sincere acceptance of the axioms can be meaningfully distinguished from believing the axioms.

Similarly, perhaps we could distinguish between Jesus's *accepting p* and his *believing p*. In his finite human consciousness perhaps Jesus accepted *p*—that is to say, verbally assented to *p* without conscious, silent reservations and relied on *p* in practical contexts—without believing *p*. For what the person of Christ believed is what the divine Logos believed, since the Logos, not the human mind of Christ, is the person Christ is, and the Logos believes no falsehoods. Such a view might even seem to yield a more plausible view of the incarnation, not requiring silent reservations on Jesus's part when he said of the mustard seed that "it is the smallest of all seeds" (Matt 13:32), or of the moon that "the moon will not give its light" (Matt 24:29), thereby implying that the moon is luminous, or of the eye that it is "the lamp of the body" (Matt 6:22).[16] Such a view might also yield a more realistic account of Jesus's human experience. By way of illustration, did Jesus as a lad never hear a noise in the next room and think, "James has dropped something," when it was in fact Joses who made the noise? Or see someone in the distance and think, "Miriam is coming," when it turned out to be Elizabeth? Would not Jesus have naturally thought that, say, the sun moves across the sky or that the moon is luminous? We could perhaps similarly maintain that Jesus, while not believing that Adam was a historical person, nevertheless as a condition of his incarnation accepted this and many other false beliefs of his countrymen.

The options considered thus far show that even in the worst-case scenario, according to which Adam did not exist, the situation is not hopeless. Still, these options would involve us in pretty extensive theological revisions of the doctrines of Scripture and the incarnation. So we need to consider

16. It is commonplace to say that Jesus did not teach such things, but the suggestion here is that neither did he believe such things.

how Scripture's teaching that there was a historical Adam is or might be compatible with the scientific evidence.

I mentioned above that certain revisionists and young earth creationists are united in the conviction that the Scriptures do teach the existence of a historical Adam. Where they differ is that young earth creationists argue that the scientific evidence, when properly interpreted, is compatible with the literal truth of Genesis. Young earth creationism thus involves both a hermeneutical claim and a scientific claim. Hermeneutically, the claim is that Genesis is intended as a historical account that is to be interpreted basically literally. Such a straightforward interpretation of the text does not exclude the use of figures of speech like "the eyes of both were opened" (Gen 3:7), but it does affirm that the accounts are basically nonfigurative. Scientifically, the claim is that some sort of "creation science" is the correct view of the world in opposition to the current scientific consensus.

Although young earth creationism is widely despised, its hermeneutical claim is eminently plausible and deserves to be taken seriously by the biblical scholar. Not a few revisionist scholars agree that the young earth creationist has rightly interpreted the text.[17] The difference between them is that the young earth creationist believes that the text, so interpreted, is a true account of origins, while the revisionist believes that the account is false, though perhaps embodying deep truths.

On the other hand, young earth creationism's scientific claim is wildly implausible. By its proponents' own admission, young earth creationism places Genesis into massive conflict with mainstream science, not to mention history and linguistics.[18] In defense of their view, creation scientists

17. See, e.g., Gerhard von Rad, *Genesis: A Commentary*, rev. ed., OTL (Louisville: Westminster John Knox, 1972), 47–48; James Barr, *Fundamentalism* (Philadelphia: Westminster, 1978), 42; John Day, *From Creation to Babel: Studies in Genesis 1–11*, LHBOTS 592 (London: Bloomsbury, 2013), 2. For discussion of James Barr and his nineteenth-century predecessor Benjamin Jowett's championing a "plain" reading of the text, see C. John Collins, *Reading Genesis Well: Navigating History, Science, Poetry, and Truth* (Grand Rapids: Zondervan, 2018), 18–24.

18. Harlow lists the following areas of conflict: Gen 1: astronomy, atmospheric science, and evolutionary biology; Gen 2–5: genetics, palaeoanthropology, and cultural anthropology; Gen 6–9: biogeography and geology; and Gen 10–11: palaeoethnography and linguistics ("After Adam," 193). Even if some of these conflicts can be resolved, the conflict of modern science with young earth creationism remains massive. I can therefore regard only as very naive the view expressed by Donald Carson: "The problem, I contend, belongs neither to the age, nor to science, nor to theology, but to certain scientists, to cer-

tend to focus on anomalies within the current scientific paradigm, failing to appreciate that the presence of anomalies serves neither to overturn the overwhelming weight of the evidence nor to establish a credible alternative paradigm. Thus, Bible-believing Christians had better hope that the young earth creationist's hermeneutical claim is also false, lest we be thrown back onto the worst-case scenarios.

We therefore need to consider the option that Gen 1–11 need not be taken literally. One cannot help but suspect that precisely fear of young earth creationism motivates many of the novel and sometimes bizarre interpretations of the text of Genesis aimed at bringing it into line with contemporary science.[19] Rather than taking the text at face value, scholars have proposed many elaborate schemes in order to make Genesis compatible with the history of the earth as we know it. Th. P. van Baaren observes that myths, including ancient myths, exhibit an extraordinary amount of flexibility, which enables them to adapt to changing situations, so that they are "armed to withstand a new challenge." He then remarks, "We are reminded of the way in which various theological schools of the last 150 years have treated the creation myths in the first chapters of Genesis."[20] At first blush, van Baaren's comparison might seem like a category mistake: the "myths" of Genesis have not changed, just biblical theologians' interpretations of them. But van Baaren goes on to make the following points by way of summary, which clarify his meaning:

---

tain spirits of the age, and to certain theologians. . . . It might prove helpful if theologians would stop appealing to modernity as the basis for their particular brand of skepticism and tell us, without using any form of the word 'modern,' exactly why they cannot believe this or that notion. The discussion might then proceed with more profit" ("Adam in the Epistles of Paul," 40).

19. There is no use denying Todd Beall's contention that "many scholars propose non-literal interpretations of Genesis 1–2 in order to harmonize the biblical text with current scientific theory" ("Reading Genesis 1–2: A Literal Approach," in Charles, *Reading Genesis 1–2*, 56). In all fairness, however, in many cases scholars claim that the role of science was simply to lead them to look again at the text with fresh eyes to see if they had misunderstood it, an entirely legitimate reaction, since in such a case scientific findings serve merely as the *occasion* for a reinterpretation rather than as *grounds* for it. Moreover, even in cases where a scholar revises his interpretation on scientific grounds, the attempt to invalidate that interpretation by exposing such an illegitimate procedure is guilty of the genetic fallacy, since the truth of a view is independent of a person's motivations for arriving at that view.

20. Th. P. van Baaren, "The Flexibility of Myth," in *Sacred Narrative: Readings in the Theory of Myth*, ed. Alan Dundes (Berkeley: University of California Press, 1984), 218.

1. In this conflict-situation between mythical and worldly reality one force must give in and change, or disappear.
2. The character of myth is opposed to disappearance, but not, in view of what we have said about its plasticity, to change.
3. The reality of this world is only rarely open to sufficiently fundamental change; therefore, in case of conflict, as a rule it is the myth which will change.
4. In this situation the invention of writing has wrought havoc, because this invention has made it possible to fix the text of a myth more or less permanently.
5. History of religions teaches us that in this situation the flexibility of myth is transferred to its exegesis. This explains the important function of this branch of theology in all religions based on sacred texts. It is well-known that in primitive religions a large number of versions of one and the same myth exist and that it is not possible to point out one of them as the generally authoritative and original version. In the same way do we encounter in the book-religions a large variety of exegeses of which, *mutatis mutandis*, the same can be said.[21]

According to this profoundly disturbing analysis, the mythical traditions of Genesis, if still transmitted orally, could change in the face of genetic and palaeoanthropological evidence concerning human origins so as to adapt to the new situation; but with their being concretized in an authoritative text, that function has been taken over by exegesis, which, to put it bluntly, concocts new interpretations of the text in order to bring it into accord with modern science.[22]

21. Van Baaren, "Flexibility of Myth," 223–24.

22. Van Baaren's analysis raises the interesting possibility espoused by Wolfhart Pannenberg that the author of Gen 1, by seeking to integrate theology with the science of his day, has legitimized a similar project for us (Wolfhart Pannenberg, "The Doctrine of Creation and Modern Science," in *Toward a Theology of Nature: Essays in Science and Faith*, ed. Ted Peters [Louisville: Westminster John Knox, 1993], 45–46). Rather than rest content with the obsolete science of Genesis, we are authorized by Scripture to integrate the science of our day with biblical teaching. We thereby retain the flexibility of the original text to change in the face of changing circumstances in order to meet new challenges. On this view God has inspired in Gen 1 a type of literature that is inherently flexible and so should not be regarded as frozen in time. The limitation of Pannenberg's hermeneutic is that it seems to apply only to Gen 1 and not to the remainder of the primaeval history of Gen 1–11, which does not evince the integrative interest ascribed to P, the author of Gen 1.

Such a hermeneutic is fundamentally misconceived. By employing contemporary science to guide one's interpretation of the text, it represents one of the worst forms of concordism. Following Denis Alexander,[23] we may distinguish three ways in which the word *concordism* has been used: (1) the attempt to extract modern scientific information from scriptural passages—for example, taking Gen 1:1 to teach big bang cosmology; (2) the attempt to interpret scriptural texts in light of modern science—for example, day-age and gap interpretations of Gen 1; and (3) the attempt to integrate the independently discovered findings of contemporary science and biblical theology into a synoptic worldview. Concordism in the first two senses is a flawed hermeneutic because it runs roughshod over the way in which the original author and his audience would have understood the text and because each successive generation would be justified in reading its own science (for instance, Aristotelian physics) into the text. While (1) and (2) are an illicit imposition of science onto the biblical text, however, (3) represents an important and vital project of the systematic theologian, who seeks to formulate an integrative view of the world based on all our sources of knowledge. In what follows I shall use the term *concordism* to refer to hermeneutical concordism rather than to the task of systematic theology.

If van Baaren is right that the original flexibility of the stories of Genesis has been lost by their enscripturation, so that exegesis has assumed the function of adapting the text to new challenges and changing situations, then the danger of concordism becomes acute. For it is difficult to face with open eyes the terrifying possibility that the young earth creationist hermeneutical claim may in fact be right. The temptation to come up with new interpretations of the text that are scientifically acceptable may prove irresistible to those committed to biblical authority. We should nonetheless resist such concordist impulses in favor of trying to understand the text as the original author and his audience would have understood it. When we do, we may well find that Gen 1–11 belongs to a literary genre that does not support a literal interpretation.

Modern literary criticism has served to deepen our understanding of ancient texts and to shed new light on them. Jud Davis demurs, cautioning that if our interpretation of the relevant biblical texts was not advocated by any

23. Denis Alexander, "The Various Meanings of Concordism," *BioLogos* (blog), March 23, 2017, http://biologos.org/blogs/guest/the-various-meanings-of-concordism. For discussion, see Andrew Loke, *The Origin of Humanity: Science and Scripture in Conversation* (forthcoming).

church father, then in all probability we have misinterpreted the passage in question.[24] Such a hermeneutical guideline is, however, far too simplistic to be reliable. For no church father may happen to advocate a particular biblical interpretation that we should today reasonably accept. For example, the church fathers interpreted the scriptural passages about the motion of the sun literally, in line with Greek geocentric cosmology. I am not aware of any church father who believed in heliocentrism or the rotational movement of the earth. But an interpretation that does not take literally biblical passages describing the sun's motion is not therefore precluded to us. Numberless commentators, including young earth creationists, have pointed out quite plausibly that the biblical authors' statements are phenomenal in character, just as ours are when we, despite our knowledge of modern astronomy, speak unreflectively of the sunrise and sunset.

Denis Lamoureux disputes this, claiming that the ancients uniformly interpreted their phenomenal reports to be literal descriptions of the world.[25] What the biblical writers saw with their eyes, they believed to be real, like the literal rising and literal setting of the sun. Lamoureux's claim is, however, patently false. In the first place, ancient people fully realized that phenomena may not correspond to reality. They knew, for example, that the observed shrinkage of objects as they receded into the distance was not real but mere appearance. When a caravan gradually disappeared from sight, they did not think that the people and animals were literally shrinking until they vanished. After all, they themselves were sometimes the travelers and could observe the same diminution in size of the city they had left. We actually have a wonderful illustration of the phenomenal shrinkage of objects with increasing distance in the Sumerian myth of *Etana*, where Etana's ascent to heaven on the back of an eagle is vividly described:

> [The eagle] took him upwards for a mile.
> "My friend, look at the country! How does it seem?"
> "The affairs of the country buzz (?) [like flies (?)]
> And the wide sea is no bigger than a sheepfold!"
> [The eagle took him] up a second mile.
> "My friend, look at the country! How does it seem?"
> "The country has turned into a garden [ ],

24. Davis, "Unresolved Major Questions," 215.

25. Denis O. Lamoureux, "No Historical Adam: The Evolutionary Creation View," in Barrett and Caneday, *Four Views on the Historical Adam*, 46.

And the wide sea is no bigger than a bucket!"
It took him up a third mile.
"My friend, look at the country! How does it seem?"
"I am looking for the country, but I can't see it!
And my eyes cannot even pick out the wide sea!
My friend, I cannot go any further towards heaven.
Retrace the way, and let me go back to my city!" (*Etana* III)[26]

The story of Etana's ascent toward heaven shows clearly that the ancients understood that phenomenal reports should not be uncritically equated with literal descriptions.

Second, ancient peoples may have been unconcerned to give a realist interpretation of celestial phenomena. Lamoureux fails to reckon with the instrumentalist nature of Babylonian astronomy, as we shall see later in some detail.[27] Babylonian astronomers were able to predict with great accuracy the motions of the sun, stars, and planets using two systems that if taken literally were incompatible with each other. No matter, however; for the motions charted by the systems were purely phenomenal, and no attempt was made to offer a literal cosmological description of the heavens. Thus, Lamoureux is demonstrably mistaken in thinking that ancient phenomenal descriptions of the sun's motion must be and were understood literally.

With all due respect to the church fathers, they did not enjoy the benefits of modern scholarship with respect to genre analysis and interpretation of ancient texts. Old Testament (OT) scholar Brevard Childs is right to remind us, "To compare the church fathers, or the Reformers for that matter, with modern scholarship in terms of philology, textual and literary criticism, or of historical knowledge and exegetical precision should convince any reasonable person of the undeniable achievements of historical critical scholarship in respect to the Old Testament."[28] In interpreting Gen 1–11, we should be foolish, indeed, to disdain such achievements.

Our interest in examining the biblical materials concerning the historical Adam is not in source- or tradition-historical analysis of the biblical text, seeking, for example, to determine the sources or traditions that lay behind the "creation" accounts in Gen 1 and 2 or the sources and traditions that were

26. Stephanie Dalley, ed., *Myths from Mesopotamia: Creation, the Flood, Gilgamesh, and Others*, rev. ed. (Oxford: Oxford University Press, 2000).

27. See pp. 179–83.

28. Brevard S. Childs, *Introduction to the Old Testament as Scripture* (Philadelphia: Fortress, 1979), 40.

combined to give us the canonical flood story. In biblical studies since the 1980s, there has been a reappreciation of the value of studying the canonical text, a movement sometimes known as canonical criticism to differentiate it from source, form, and tradition criticism. Childs draws attention to "the enormous hiatus" that exists between the critically constructed development of the text and the actual canonical text as we have it.[29] David J. A. Clines, in his pioneering study of the theme of the Pentateuch, points out that biblical scholarship belongs firmly in the tradition of humanistic studies and thus has more in common with literary analysis than with the scientific search for new data.[30] Hence, he indicts biblical scholarship for its "geneticism" and "atomism" to the neglect of the final form of the text. Complaining of "the fragile nature of much of the traditio-critical work on Genesis" as well as its "speculative results,"[31] Childs points as an example to Claus Westermann's massive commentary on Gen 1–11, in which "all the problems inherent in the tradition critical method reached their zenith, but in a complexity which threatened to devour exegesis."[32] Despite its brilliance, Westermann's com-

29. Childs, *Introduction to the Old Testament*, 40.

30. David J. A. Clines, *The Theme of the Pentateuch*, 2nd ed., JSOTSup 10 (Sheffield: Sheffield Academic Press, 1997), 11.

31. Cf. the comments of a pessimistic Richard Averbeck:

> All agree that critical method in the study of the composition of the Pentateuch has become an increasingly "pluralistic" affair. There is very little agreement between those who hold opposing theories or even between scholars who follow the same basic approach, whether source or redaction as outlined above. . . . The fact of the matter is that none of the paradigms currently in place are likely to produce a consensus. They have gone too far beyond the available verifiable data, found problems where there are none, propounded competing theories that they often treat as if they are verified, used them to build up other theoretical constructs that easily collapse when the previous arguments cannot bear the weight, and so on. The multiple, and increasingly multiplying, dissections and reconstructions do not inspire confidence that any of these approaches will ever yield results that can stand the test of time and scrutiny. (Richard E. Averbeck, "Reading the Torah in a Better Way: Unity and Diversity in Text, Genre, and Compositional History," in *Paradigm Change in Pentateuchal Research*, ed. Matthias Armgardt, Benjamin Kilchör, and Markus Zehnder, BZABR 22 [Wiesbaden: Harrassowitz, 2019], 23)

See the remarks cited by Averbeck from David Carr: "I am evermore struck with just how fraught and difficult it is to us to know anything secure and detailed about the undocumented prehistory of any text. The field is littered with the carcasses of dead theories by once-prominent pentateuchal scholars, and I suspect that many theories advanced today will fare no better" (Averbeck, "Reading the Torah," 27).

32. Childs, *Introduction to the Old Testament*, 142.

mentary does not aid greatly in understanding the meaning of the text before us. "The significance of the final form of the biblical text," explains Childs, "is that it alone bears witness to the full history of revelation."[33] Tradition-critical questions are for us of interest only insofar as they shed light on the interpretation of the final form of the text.

Our interest lies, then, in what the canonical text teaches, if anything, about the historical Adam. The reason for focusing on the canonical text is not that historical-critical questions are uninteresting or unimportant but that the canonical text is, after all, the basis for a Christian doctrine of man. So in this study I shall adopt a canonical approach to the question of the historical Adam, proceeding from the biblical text as we have it.

It may turn out as a result of a careful genre analysis of Gen 1–11 that no novel reinterpretations of the text are necessary in order for the systematic theologian to integrate its teachings with the data of contemporary science, history, and linguistics. To resist the sirens of concordism, we shall in this book pursue the hermeneutical task first and independently of an examination of the scientific evidence pertinent to human origins and then, only after coming to some conclusions concerning the genre of Gen 1–11 and what Scripture teaches concerning the historical Adam, turn to an examination of the scientific data.

Contextualizing Adam and Eve

The stories of Adam and Eve are largely confined to but two chapters of Scripture, Gen 2–3. But these chapters should be read not in isolation but in the context of the pre-patriarchal narratives of Gen 1–11, often called the primaeval history, of which they are a part. The primaeval history, however, needs to be understood within the context of Genesis as a whole. The book of Genesis is in turn part of a larger work, the Pentateuch, which comprises the first five books of the Bible, Genesis, Exodus, Leviticus, Numbers, and Deuteronomy. What initially appeared to be a narrowly defined and tractable task thus threatens to balloon out of proportion, making our quest all the more difficult. Nonetheless, such a wider perspective is necessary if we are to do our job responsibly.

33. Childs, *Introduction to the Old Testament*, 76.

The Pentateuch

In considering the Pentateuch as a whole and the relationship of Genesis and the primaeval history to it, we may profit from the seminal and influential work of David J. A. Clines on the theme of the Pentateuch. In attempting to determine the "theme" of the Pentateuch, Clines is asking for the rationale of the content, structure, and development of the work.[34] He thinks that there can be little doubt that the impetus for the movement in the Pentateuch is God's threefold promise to the patriarchs, especially Abraham, of a posterity, of a relationship with God, and of land. The promise to Abraham in Gen 12:1–3 comprises all three elements: "Go from your country and your kindred and your father's house to the land that I will show you. And I will make of you a great nation, and I will bless you, and make your name great, so that you will be a blessing. I will bless those who bless you, and him who curses you I will curse; and by you all the families of the earth shall bless themselves." The theme of the Pentateuch, then, is the partial fulfillment of the promise to or blessing of the patriarchs.[35] The posterity element is dominant in Gen 12–50, the relationship element in Exodus and Leviticus, and the land element in Numbers and Deuteronomy.

This statement of theme for the Pentateuch obviously leaves Gen 1–11 out of account. Clines thinks that this section demands a separate treatment of its theme. For not only is it temporally prior to the first statement of the theme of the rest of the Pentateuch in Gen 12:1–3 and therefore not subsumed under it, but its tendency is in a quite different direction from that of the remainder of the Pentateuch.[36] In determining the theme of Gen 1–11 Clines looks for a rationale that will cover not only the narratives but also the genealogies and the Table of Nations in chapter 10. Clines argues that any adequate total statement of the theme of Gen 1–11 should allow for both the theme of the spread of sin/spread of grace, as God's judgment of mankind's worsening sin is consistently tempered by mercy,[37] and the theme of

34. Clines, *Theme of the Pentateuch*, 23; cf. 20.

35. Clines, *Theme of the Pentateuch*, 30.

36. Clines, *Theme of the Pentateuch*, 15.

37. See von Rad, *Genesis*, 24, 152–53. Clines considers the objection that the Tower of Babel story does not represent an intensification of mankind's sin in comparison to the sin prompting the flood. His answer, that the pre-flood sin was not worse than the tower builders' sin and that the punishment of the tower builders was in some ways worse than the flood, is implausible. A better answer is that the tower story could not be put before

creation-uncreation-recreation, as the flood and the confusion of languages reverse the direction of creation.

Two overall themes of Gen 1–11 present themselves, depending on where the emphasis is put: either that humankind tends to destroy what God has made good or that no matter how drastic human sin becomes, God's grace never fails to deliver humankind from the consequences of sin. Clines thinks that although the primaeval history viewed in isolation from the rest of the Pentateuch is "utterly ambiguous in its central statement," since it ends ambiguously with the Tower of Babel story, nevertheless, by considering it in relation to the remainder of the Pentateuch, it is possible "to opt decisively" for one of these two alternatives.[38]

Since the patriarchal history unfolds the fulfillment of the divine promise, it is most likely that the positive reading of Gen 1–11 is appropriate. The primaeval history flows smoothly into the patriarchal history. Since we find between the primaeval history and the patriarchal history a developed transitional passage (Gen 11:27–32), it is improbable that the two units are meant to be seen as opposed to each other thematically. So despite the destructive consequences of human sin, God finds a way of deliverance and blessing. Clines concludes that the divine promise to the patriarchs, then, demands to be read in conjunction with Gen 1:26–28 as a reaffirmation of God's original intentions for humanity.[39]

Ancient Near Eastern Mythology

Not only should the primaeval narratives of Gen 1–11 be read within the context of Genesis and the Pentateuch, but they should also be read within the wider context of the literature of the ancient Near East (ANE). OT scholars have been aware for centuries of the resemblance of the primaeval narratives of Gen 1–11 to ancient Mesopotamian myths on the basis of the Babylonian priest Berossus's account of Mesopotamian religion for Greek readers of the third century BC.[40] This awareness became acute with George Smith's publication of the flood account from the eleventh tablet of the *Epic of Gilgamesh* in

---

the flood story because then the present linguistic diversity of mankind would be unexplained, since everyone but Noah's family perished in the flood. So logically the tower incident has to come later than the flood, even if it does not involve an intensification of sin.

38. Clines, *Theme of the Pentateuch*, 83.

39. Clines, *Theme of the Pentateuch*, 85.

40. See Stanley Mayer Burstein, ed., *The "Babyloniaca" of Berossus*, SANE 1/5 (Malibu, CA: Undena, 1978). Berossus did for Babylonian religion what Josephus did for Jewish

1872. Since that time, the ongoing discovery and publication of cuneiform texts (i.e., texts in the wedge-shaped script of the ancient Sumerian and Akkadian languages) from ancient Sumer and Babylon has augmented our knowledge of the literature of the ANE, the earliest literary remains of mankind. OT scholars have remarked on the resemblance of Gen 1–11, in contrast to Gen 12–50, to this literature, both in terms of the structure of the narratives and of the themes treated.[41] Structurally, on the basis of texts like the *Atrahasis Epic*, the so-called Eridu Genesis, and the *Epic of Gilgamesh*, many OT scholars discern a similar structure in Gen 1–11, comprising narratives of creation, humanity prior to the flood, and the flood itself. Thematically, grand themes like the creation of the world, the origin of mankind, and the near destruction of humanity in the cataclysmic flood are shared by both the ancient myths and Gen 1–11.

The structural similarities can be exaggerated, however. The *Atrahasis* and *Gilgamesh* epics contain no creation account, and the Eridu Genesis, a hypothetical narrative compiled of texts of different dates, is merely presumed to have included an account of creation, now missing. None of these myths has anything similar to the story of Adam and Eve, their temptation and fall, so pivotal to Gen 1–11, prior to the flood, nor do we read of anything like the ensuing story of the Tower of Babel. More important than the structure of the narratives of Gen 1–11, then, are the similar themes that these chapters and ANE myths treat. In Gen 12–50, by contrast, the focus narrows sharply to Israel, and no similarity of themes to ANE myths exists. The question then naturally arises as to whether the primaeval narratives of Gen 1–11 should not be taken to be a compilation of Israelite myths.

---

religion: explain the tenets of one's religion in Hellenistic terms that the culturally dominant Greeks could understand and appreciate.

41. See, e.g., Gordon J. Wenham, *Genesis 1–15*, WBC 1 (Grand Rapids: Zondervan, 1987), xxxvii: "When Gen 1–11 is compared with chaps. 12–50, a striking difference emerges: chaps. 1–11 are full of parallels with Near Eastern tradition, so that it looks as though Genesis is reflecting these oriental ideas both positively and negatively." Both the *Atrahasis Epic* and the Sumerian flood story show clearly that "no later than 1600 BC a story of origins was known in Mesopotamia that bears a striking resemblance to Genesis as it now stands. . . . Gen 1–11 does seem to bear witness to an outline of earliest antiquity common to Babylon and Israel" (Wenham, *Genesis 1–15*, xli). "But chaps. 12–50 are quite different. Abraham and his descendants are the exclusive concern of these chapters: there is no suggestion that the patriarchal stories are adaptations of well-known oriental sagas" (Wenham, *Genesis 1–15*, xxxvii). This answers the question of literalist Todd Beall, "What justification does one have for using a different hermeneutic for Genesis 1–2 or Genesis 1–11 than one does for the rest of Genesis?" ("Reading Genesis 1–2," 59; cf. 46). We shall see in the sequel that different genres are in play.

Comparative literary studies in ANE mythology and religion take us into a world that is utterly alien to most of us Western readers. We have some familiarity with the stories of Greek and Roman mythology and are familiar with the names of gods and goddesses like Venus and Mercury, Mars and Jupiter, since the planets in our solar system bear these very names. We feel at home with names like Apollo and Athena and Zeus. The same is true to a lesser extent of Egyptian deities. Most of us have at least heard of gods and goddesses like Isis and Osiris, Horus, and Amun-Re, even if we do not know who they are. But when we are told about Mesopotamian deities like Ninhursag, Enki, Anu, and Nintu, and people like Ziusudra, Utnapishtim, Enkidu, and so on, we are apt to find this bewildering and off-putting. The world of ancient Mesopotamian religion appears to most of us as, frankly, weird.

It will therefore be helpful to include at this point a brief word of introduction to the myths of ancient Mesopotamia and Egypt, the two most relevant areas of comparative studies for Gen 1–11. My goal in so doing is not to provide even a cursory survey of the various myths but merely to help reduce the foreignness of these myths by gaining some initial familiarity with them and some of their characters. Then when we look at them later in greater detail, we shall not have to struggle so in order to overcome their strangeness to us.

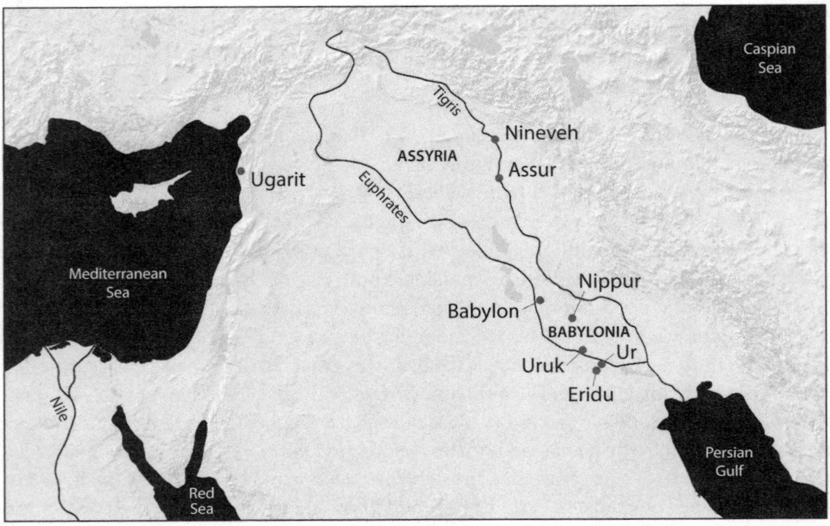

Figure 1.2. Map of Mesopotamia.

Mesopotamia

Let us begin with Mesopotamian religion. Mesopotamia, as its name intimates, is the geographic regionēdrained by the Tigris and Euphrates Rivers, roughly modern-day Iraq (fig. 1.2). Since the beginning of the third millennium BC, the region endured a tumultuous history of rising and falling competing empires, including Sumer, Akkad, Assyria, and Babylon (see fig. 1.3).

Oldest was Sumer, whose principal cities included Eridu, Uruk, Ur, and Nippur, and which dominated what is today southern Iraq from at least the beginning of the third millennium BC until Sargon the Great of the city of Akkad united all of Mesopotamia into the Akkadian Empire (ca. 2335–2154 BC). Babylonia, a region just to the north and centered on the fabled city of Babylon, enjoyed brief periods of domination during the Old Babylonian Empire (1830–1531 BC), whose most famous king was Hammurabi, and the Neo-Babylonian Empire (626–539 BC), especially known to biblical readers as the time during which King Nebuchadnezzar conquered Jerusalem and exiled Jewish people to Babylon. In 539 BC the Achaemenid Empire under Cyrus the Great sacked Babylon, bringing the Neo-Babylonian Empire to an end and leading eventually to Jewish repatriation. Interspersed were periods of regional dominance by the far more powerful Assyrian Empire, famed for giving us the cuneiform library of King Ashurbanipal in Nineveh, which also rose and fell in phases of the Old Assyrian Empire (ca. 2025–1522 BC), the Middle Assyrian Empire (1391–1050 BC), and the Neo-Assyrian Empire (911–605 BC), during which latter phase King Sargon II conquered the Northern Kingdom of Israel in 721 BC.

More important for our purposes than these political realities were the linguistic differences. The Sumerians were a migrant, non-Semitic people speaking a language unrelated to Akkadian, the language of the Semitic peoples in the region. Sumerian literature, the oldest in the world, was unearthed at Nippur inscribed in cuneiform script on thousands of clay tablets. With the ascendancy of Akkad, Assyria, and Babylon, Akkadian came to replace Sumerian, although Sumerian continued to be used among scribes for several centuries. The thousands of cuneiform tablets unearthed at Nineveh from Ashurbanipal's famous library are in Akkadian. Some texts are available in both languages.

Sumerian myths describe a polytheistic worldview involving thousands of humanoid deities who determine man's existence. Chief among these was Enlil, patron god of Nippur. In the Sumerian creation myth the world was

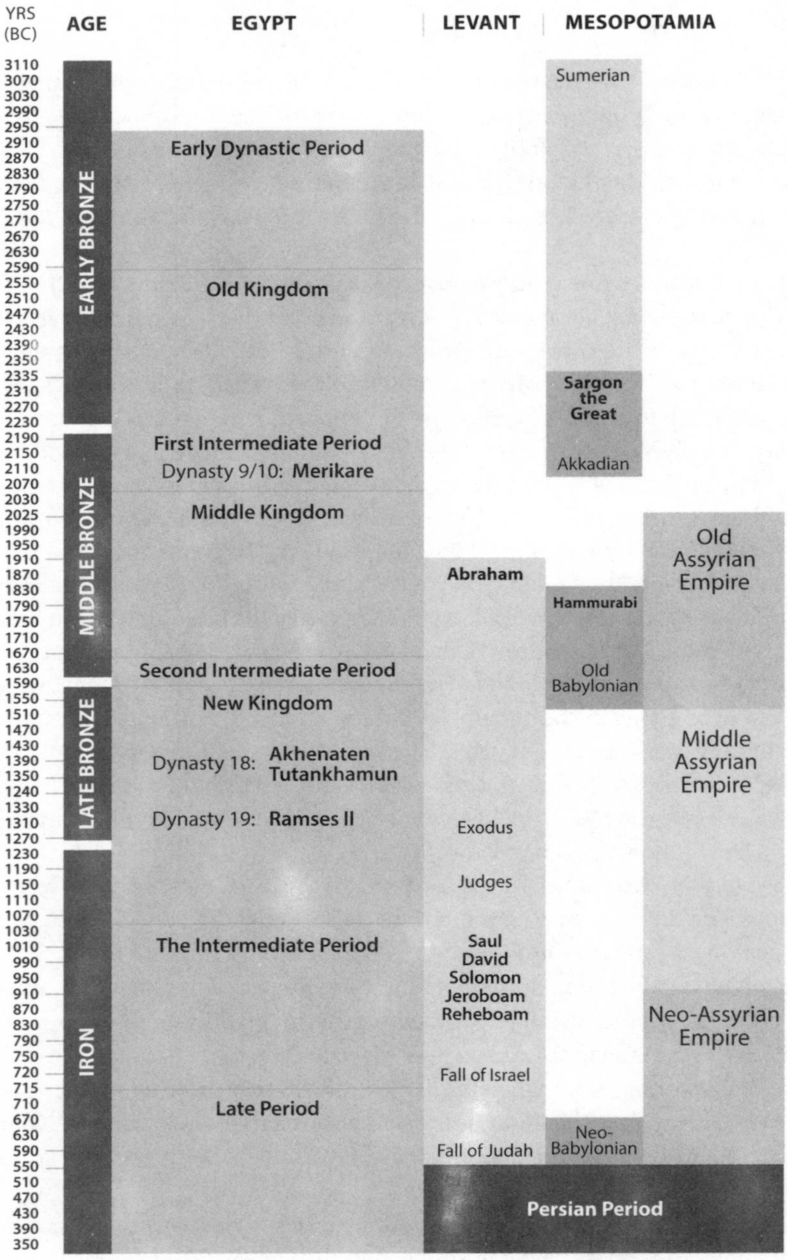

Figure 1.3. Comparative chart of ancient Near Eastern history.

created when the god An (Akkadian: Anu) claimed the heavens and Enlil claimed the earth, thereby separating the heavens and earth. In Akkadian myths Enlil is responsible for sending the flood to destroy mankind, with whom he is annoyed for disturbing his sleep. In the Sumerian myth *Enlil and Ninlil* he is a serial rapist in different disguises of the goddess Ninlil. The god Enki (Akkadian: Ea), patron god of Eridu, was a more beneficent god responsible for bestowing on mankind various technological advances. He inhabited the underground waters (Apsu). In the Akkadian flood story it is Enki who thwarts Enlil's plan to destroy humanity by telling Atrahasis (Sumerian: Ziusudra) to build a boat in which to ride out the storm. Enki's main consort is the goddess Ninhursag, also called Ninmah, Nintu, and Mami. The Sumerian myth *Enki and Ninmah* describes Ninmah's creation of humanity by fashioning figures from pieces of clay, which then gestate within the wombs of birth goddesses until their delivery. An, Enlil, Enki, and Ninmah are "the great gods" of Sumerian mythology.[42]

In later myths from Babylon, Marduk, the patron deity of Babylon, comes to supplant Enlil as head of the pantheon of deities. The *Enuma elish* (Akkadian: "When from above") describes the ascendancy of Marduk over the other gods, largely through his vanquishing the dragon goddess Tiamat. The *Enuma elish* contains an account of Marduk's creating the world out of Tiamat's bisected corpse and a later account of Ea's creation of mankind from the blood of the god Qingu, who was executed for inciting Tiamat's rebellion. The myth concludes with the gods' bestowal of fifty exalted names on Marduk as supreme god.

The following is a selection of the names of Mesopotamian figures with a description of their respective natures:[43]

***Adapa*:** Human son of Ea. He is given the chance at eternal life but misses it when ill-advised by Ea.

Anu (Sumerian: An): Sky god, father of Enlil, head of the older pantheon of gods.

Apsu: Domain of underground waters, the home of Ea. Personified as the male consort of Tiamat and father of the first generation of gods.

Atrahasis: Survivor of the flood; identical to Utnapishtim.

42. In the words of "The Creation of Humanity" (KAR IV), lines 67–69. For this text I use the translation of Richard A. Averbeck in *The Context of Scripture*, vol. 4, *Supplements*, ed. K. Lawson Younger Jr. (Leiden: Brill, 2017).

43. From Dalley, ed., *Myths from Mesopotamia*, "Glossary of Deities, Places and Key Terms," 317–31.

Ea (Sumerian: Enki): God of subterranean waters who bestowed upon mankind various technologies and tools of civilization. He sent the Seven Sages (*apkallu*) in the form of fish-men from the Apsu to teach mankind the use of the technologies.

Ellil (Sumerian: Enlil): Head of the younger pantheon of Sumerian and Akkadian gods. Nature and attributes still uncertain. He is supplanted by Marduk in Babylon.

Enkidu: Wild man of nature created specially by the gods as a companion to Gilgamesh.

Gilgamesh (Sumerian: Bilgamesh): Mighty king of Uruk who embarks on a futile quest of immortality.

Mami: Mother goddess Ninhursag.

Marduk: Patron god of Babylon, slayer of Tiamat and creator of the world, who rose to supremacy among the pantheon of deities.

Nammu: Sumerian birth goddess, mother of Ea.

Ninhursag: Mother goddess, also known as Ninmah, Nintu, Mami, etc.

Ninurta: Sumerian warrior god and son of Enlil.

Qingu: God slain for the creation of mankind as a result of inciting Tiamat's rebellion against the gods.

Tiamat: Female personification of the sea as a ferocious dragon. She begot with Apsu the first generation of gods. She was slain in a titanic struggle with Marduk, who makes the world out of her corpse.

Utnapishtim: Flood survivor by building a boat.

In the sequel we shall have occasion to speak of these deities and people at greater length as we compare the myths of their exploits with the narratives of Gen 1–11.

Egypt

Turn now to the vastly different Egyptian mythology. Over the course of its long history since the beginning of the third millennium BC (see fig. 1.3), Egypt developed a basic metaphysical and religious worldview that came to varying expression in four predominant cult centers: Memphis, near the mouth of the Nile delta; Heliopolis, slightly to the northwest; Hermopolis, to the south, on the boundary between Lower and Upper Egypt; and Thebes, in Upper Egypt, about five hundred miles south of the Mediterranean Sea (fig. 1.4).

The metaphysical worldview underlying all of these religious perspectives was monism, the view that reality is ultimately one, an underlying, undifferentiated unity. Multiplicity emerges from this primordial underlying unity. In various myths darkness and boundless water represent this primordial state. The unfolding of primordial oneness into multiplicity takes form primarily in the process of theogony, the emergence of the gods. The first god, since there is no one to create him, is said to be self-created or to be identical to the primordial waters (personified as the god Nun). The self-created god may be identified as Atum, as is the case in Hermopolis and Heliopolis, or Ptah, as in Memphis, or some fusion of deities like Atum-Re the sun god; it is the god's role, not his name, that matters. In the cult of Hermopolis there

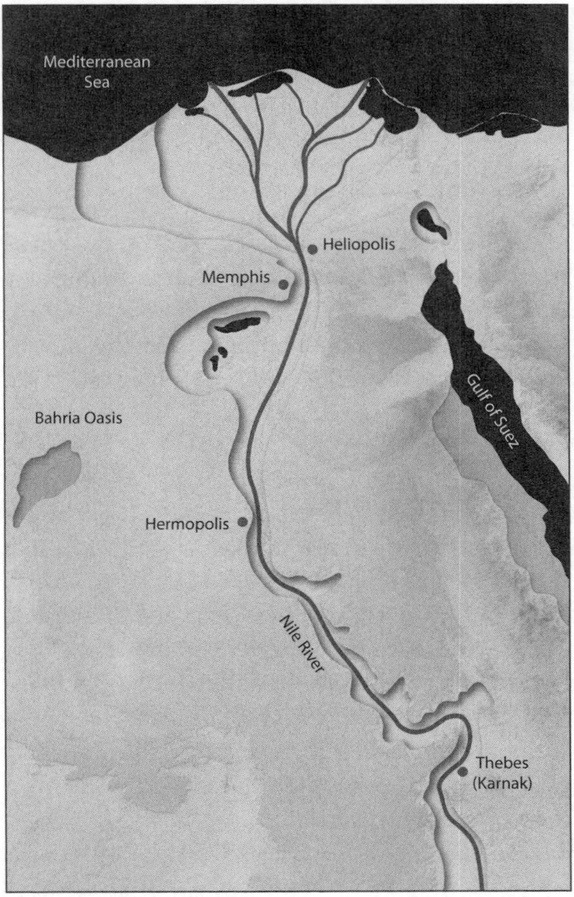

Figure 1.4. Map of ancient Egypt showing cult centers.

is postulated an ogdoad of four gods, Kuk, Nun, Huh, and Atum, with their female doublets, which are identified respectively as the darkness, water, boundlessness, and undifferentiation of the primordial state.

The emergence of the first god is often represented as the emergence of a hillock from the waters. Atum may be seated on the hill or identified with the hill itself. If Atum is alone, he is represented as forming the other deities by acts of sneezing or spitting or, logically it seems, masturbating and self-impregnation. In Heliopolis Atum gives rise to an ennead of five successive generations: the god of dry air, Shu, and the goddess of moisture, Tefnut, who in turn give birth to the god of the ground, Geb, and the goddess of the sky, Nut. Geb and Nut sire four children, Osiris, Seth, Isis, and Nephthys. The apex of theogony is the begetting of the sun god, who since the late Old Kingdom had been worshiped under various names as the most important deity and as the creator and sustainer of all creatures and things. Religiously, then, Egyptian monism is a type of panentheism, according to which all things emerge from the divine One.

The following is a list of some of the principal Egyptian deities and their respective natures:[44]

Amun: "The Hidden One." His cult is attested first in Thebes, though he is mentioned earlier as a primeval deity. In later times he belongs to the Hermopolitan Ogdoad.

Atum: "The Undifferentiated One," both the primaeval being and the creator of the world. He is, paradoxically, both everything and nothing. In Heliopolis he is the head of the Ennead.

Geb: God of the earth or the ground.

Hathor: "House of Horus." The most universal Egyptian goddess, who has the characteristics of a mother but as the "eye of Re" also brings truth to all enemies. She is worshiped as a goddess of the dead, especially in Thebes.

Horus: "The Distant One" (?). Ancient god of the sky and of kingship with close links with the sun god and later with Osiris and Isis.

Isis: Mother of Horus and sister and wife of Osiris. Depicted in countless forms, so that she becomes the "Multiform One" par excellence.

Nun: Personification of the primaeval waters from which everything arose and out of which the sun comes daily anew. Nun is the most important of the Hermopolitan Ogdoad.

44. From Erik Hornung, *Conceptions of God in Ancient Egypt: The One and the Many*, trans. John Baines (Ithaca, NY: Cornell University Press, 1982), "Glossary of Gods," 274–84.

Nut: Ancient goddess of the sky who is depicted as a woman arching over the earth god Geb.

Osiris: The ruler of the realm of the dead, having suffered himself a violent death.

Ptah: A Memphite deity who is worshiped as creator, prior to Atum, and patron of the crafts.

Re: A Heliopolitan deity who is the most important and widespread form of the sun god, pictured as traveling in a barque through the sky by day and through the underworld by night. He is combined syncretistically with many other gods.

Shu: God of the open space between the earth and sky. By separating the earth and sky he takes part in the creation of the world. Often portrayed as supporting Nut.

Tefnut: A goddess who forms with Shu the first divine couple, engendered by Atum alone.

As one would expect, in Egypt the gods are the source of the creatures in the world, including humans. In the *Instruction of King Merikarē* the sun god is portrayed as a benevolent creator of humans, who are his physical likenesses. The god Khnum, associated with the temple at Elephantine, near the boundary of Upper Egypt and Nubia, is pictured in the *Hymn to Khnum* as a potter seated at his wheel fashioning men out of clay. Beyond these vague descriptions there is no specific account of how humanity was created.

Conclusion and Prospect

We have seen that in order to understand the narratives of Adam and Eve, we must read them within the context of the primaeval history of Gen 1–11, and the primaeval history in turn within the context of Genesis as a whole, and Genesis within the context of the Pentateuch. Moreover, we should read the primaeval history within its ANE cultural context. To understand that cultural context, we shall consider the myths of the above-mentioned Mesopotamian and Egyptian deities more closely. But as a preliminary to our discussion it will be necessary to say something about the nature of myth itself.

PART 2

Biblical Data concerning the Historical Adam

Chapter 2

THE NATURE OF MYTH

As we saw in our first chapter, biblical scholars have for centuries been aware of the resemblance of the primaeval narratives of Gen 1–11 to ancient Mesopotamian myths on the basis of Berossus's account of Mesopotamian religion for Greek readers of the third century BC. This awareness became acute with George Smith's publication of the flood account from the eleventh tablet of the *Epic of Gilgamesh* in 1872. Since that time the ongoing discovery and publication of ancient Sumerian and Babylonian cuneiform texts has augmented our knowledge of the literature of the ANE, the earliest literary remains of mankind. OT scholars have remarked on the resemblance of Gen 1–11, in contrast to Gen 12–50, to this literature in terms of both the structure of the narratives and the themes treated. The question then naturally arises as to whether the primaeval narratives of Gen 1–11 should not be taken to be a compilation of Israelite myths.

The Nature of Myth

The exploration of this question requires us to say a word about the nature or character of myth. Originally, the Greek word *mythos* meant simply a story, though it eventually came to designate specifically stories about gods. Biblical scholar J. W. Rogerson observes that today the range of the meaning of the word *myth* is so broad that the word can hardly be wrongly used![1] This

1. J. W. Rogerson, "Slippery Words: Myth," in *Sacred Narrative: Readings in the Theory of Myth*, ed. Alan Dundes (Berkeley: University of California Press, 1984), 66. For a concise yet thorough history of the use of the concept of myth in OT studies, see J. W. Rogerson, *Myth in Old Testament Interpretation*, BZAW 134 (Berlin: de Gruyter, 1974). Rogerson identifies twelve conceptions of myth that OT scholars have employed ("Slip-

leads the eminent folklorist Alan Dundes to complain, "Nothing infuriates a folklorist more than to hear a colleague from the anthropology or literature department use the word *myth* to refer to anything from an erroneous statement to an archetypal theme."[2] Andrew Von Hendy distinguishes four broad views of myth: the romantic, the ideological, the folkloristic, and the constitutive, observing that the consensus view in classical studies is the folkloristic.[3]

On this conception, as Dundes explains, "A myth is a sacred narrative explaining how the world and man came to be in their present form."[4] Some of the features of this disarmingly simple characterization deserve comment. First, a myth is a linguistic composition, either oral or literary. In contrast to common parlance, then, specialists do not take *myth* to be synonymous with *falsehood*. Neither do they use *myth* in the popular sense to refer to some sort of idea, such as "the myth of the noble savage" or "the myth of the self-made man." Rather, a myth is an entity composed of words. Second, it is a narrative; that is to say, it is a story, which will involve characters and a plotline. A myth describes a sequence of events. Third, it is a sacred narrative; that is to say, it has religious significance in the culture in which it is embraced. This implies that it will have something to do with a deity

pery Words," 175–78). These tend to be correlated with the various conceptions of myth surveyed by Robert A. Segal, *Myth: A Very Short Introduction*, 2nd ed. (Oxford: Oxford University Press, 2015). Rogerson observes that half of these are attempts to explain the origin of myths, while the remainder take myth as a given and try to explain its meaning and function. Rogerson thinks that we ought to recognize that there is myth in the OT but to recognize this in such a way that alien interpretations (e.g., polytheism) are not imported into the OT. One way of achieving this, he advises, would be to adopt a literary and functional definition of myth. Myths would be stories that expressed the faith and worldview of a people and so would have much to say about their view of origins and would express their intuitions of transcendent reality (Rogerson, "Slippery Words," 188). This is the approach we adopt.

2. See Alan Dundes's introductory comments to William Bascom, "The Forms of Folklore: Prose Narratives," in Dundes, *Sacred Narrative*, 5. For just such a broad and nebulous understanding of "myth," see William G. Doty, *Myth: A Handbook* (Tuscaloosa: University of Alabama Press, 2004), who treats such things as *Star Trek*, Disney's *The Lion King*, baseball, Elvis, and Madonna as examples of myths. He admits that Dundes "would not find my argument convincing and would probably refer to it as an example of 'the madness in method'" that Dundes rejects (114). Even so, Doty recognizes that "myths are above all but not exclusively narrative" (8).

3. Andrew Von Hendy, *The Modern Construction of Myth* (Bloomington: Indiana University Press, 2002), 11.

4. Dundes, introduction to *Sacred Narrative*, 1.

as one of its principal figures. Fourth, it is assumed that it is a traditional narrative, one that is handed down over the generations, not a recent, free composition. Accordingly, we could improve Dundes's characterization by making this assumption explicit: "a traditional, sacred narrative." Finally, fifth, a myth seeks to explain present realities by anchoring them in the past, understood to mean the prehistoric past. Stories of the origin of the world and stories of mankind are just two examples of narratives grounding present realities in the prehistoric past; the list could be extended.

The term *mythology* is used, in turn, to refer either to the study of myths or to a given body of myths such as, for example, Norse mythology or Greek mythology. Mythology in the sense of a field of study is an interdisciplinary enterprise, engaging the attention of students of folklore, anthropology, ethnology, religious studies, classics, psychology, and philosophy. According to Robert Segal, what unites the study of myth across these disciplines are the questions asked, mainly questions concerning the origin, the function, and the subject matter of myth.[5] The question of origin has to do with explaining why or how a myth or myths arose. The question of function concerns what a myth does in a society that embraces it, what role it plays and how it does so, which typically involves ritual studies. The question of subject matter has to do with what a myth is about, a question involving the interpretation of the myth as literal or figurative. As one might expect in so diverse a field of study, scholars in various disciplines are often engaged with different questions and come at them from different perspectives and so can talk past one another.[6] Our interest will be primarily with myths as the object of religious studies.

Myth, Folktale, and Legend

Ever since the groundbreaking work of Jacob and Wilhelm Grimm, students of folklore have distinguished myths from folktales and legends. The Grimm brothers first collected various German folktales in their *Kinder- and Hausmärchen* (1812–15); their subsequent *Deutsche Sagen* (1816–18) was a collection of German legends; and their *Deutsche Mythologie* (1835) dealt with German myths. Anthropologist William Bascom, writing in the 1960s,

5. Segal, *Myth*, 1–2.

6. See Lauri Honko, "The Problem of Defining Myth," in Dundes, *Sacred Narrative*, 46–47, for twelve angles from which myths are studied today.

held that it was time to return to the categories recognized by the Grimm brothers, along with settled definitions. Accordingly, Bascom distinguished three types of prose narrative studied by folklorists: myths, folktales, and legends (fig. 2.1).[7]

THREE FORMS OF FOLKLORE

FORM	BELIEF	TIME	PLACE	ATTITUDE	PRINCIPAL CHARACTERS
MYTH	Fact	Remote	Different world: other or earlier	Sacred	Nonhuman
LEGEND	Fact	Remote	World of today	Secular	Human
FOLKTALE	Fiction	Anytime	Any place	Secular	Human or nonhuman

Figure 2.1. Three forms of folklore.

According to Bascom, myths are prose narratives that, in the society in which they are told, are considered to be truthful accounts of what happened in the remote past. They are to be believed and may be cited as authoritative. Usually sacred, they are the embodiment of dogma and are often associated with theology and ritual. Their main characters are not usually human beings but deities, heroes, or animals, whose activities are set in an earlier age, when the earth was different than it is today, or in another realm such as the sky or underworld. Myths account for such things as the origin of the world and of mankind and for various phenomena of the natural world.

Folktales, by contrast, are prose narratives that, in the society in which they are told, are regarded as fiction. The events they relate may or may not have happened. They are not to be taken seriously as dogma or history. Although it is often said that folktales are told only for amusement, they can have other important functions, such as teaching moral lessons. They usually recount the adventures of animal or human characters and may be set in any time and at any place.

Finally, legends are prose narratives that, in the society in which they are told, are, like myths, regarded as true but are more often secular than sacred, their principal characters being merely human. They are set in a time

7. Bascom, "Forms of Folklore," 8–9.

considerably less remote, when the world was much as it is today. They are often the counterpart in oral tradition of written history.

Although, according to Dundes, Bascom's definitions are today shared by most folklorists,[8] they are not unproblematic.[9] It is puzzling, for example, why Bascom restricts himself to prose narratives.[10] Restricting myths to prose narratives would prevent our classifying such epic poems as Homer's *Illiad* or *Odyssey* and the *Epic of Gilgamesh* as myths, despite the fact that they are paradigm examples of myth. While such a restriction would not affect the classification of Gen 1–11, since the biblical primaeval narratives are prose, such exclusion of narrative poetry is unjustified. Moreover, Bascom's characterization of myths as "truthful accounts of what happened" is potentially misleading, since the sense in which myths are taken to be truthful is ambiguous. Are they to be taken as literally true or as expressing deep truths in figurative guise? That remains to be seen. Similarly, in figure 2.1 the use of the word *fact* as opposed to *fiction* is misleading. Fiction is not opposed to fact, since a fictional narrative, by Bascom's own lights, may or may not be true, and many, if not most, contemporary theorists of fiction do not think that falsehood is a necessary condition of fiction.[11] Neither is it apparent that myths are believed to be factually true (whatever that means). "For myth may constitute the highest form of truth, albeit in metaphorical guise."[12] A more accurate designation under the heading "Belief" would be "to be believed" for myths and legends and "not to be believed" for folktales. Finally, under the heading "Principal Characters" in figure 2.1, the appropriate designation for myths is not merely "nonhuman" but "divine," since deities are the main characters in such narratives. Myths that feature *prima facie* animal characters may actually be about deities represented by the animal figure.

The Finnish folklorist Lauri Honko offers the following "descriptive and concise definition" of myth:

8. See Alan Dundes's introductory comments to Bascom, "Forms of Folklore," 5.

9. See comments by Lauri Honko, "Der Mythos in der Religionswissenschaft," *Temenos* 6 (1970): 53–54.

10. He writes, "These three forms are related to each other in that they are narratives in prose, and this fact distinguishes them from proverbs, riddles, ballads, poems, tongue-twisters, and other forms of verbal art on the basis of strictly formal characteristics" (Bascom, "Forms of Folklore," 7).

11. See, e.g., Kendall L. Walton, *Mimesis as Make-Believe: On the Foundations of the Representational Arts* (Cambridge, MA: Harvard University Press, 1990), 74.

12. Dundes, introduction to *Sacred Narrative*, 1.

> Myth, a story of the gods, a religious account of the beginning of the world, the creation, fundamental events, the exemplary deeds of the gods as a result of which the world, nature and culture were created together with all parts thereof and given their order, which still obtains. A myth expresses and confirms society's religious values and norms, it provides patterns of behaviour to be imitated, testifies to the efficacy of ritual with its practical ends and establishes the sanctity of cult.[13]

Honko explains that his definition involves four factors: form, content, function, and context.[14] In terms of its *form* a myth is a sacred narrative of origins. Notice that for Honko a sacred narrative is taken to be a story about the gods. As for *content*, myths generally contain information about decisive, creative events in the beginning of time. Cosmogonic descriptions are not just central to myth but isomorphic with other stories that a society accepts as the ultimate source of its identity. As for *function*, myths provide an ex-

13. Honko, "Problem of Defining Myth," 49; cf. Honko, "Der Mythos," 40–41. Honko's definition is accepted by Hagar Salamon and Harvey E. Goldberg, "Myth-Ritual-Symbol," in *A Companion to Folklore*, ed. Regina F. Bendix and Galit Hasan-Rokem (Oxford: Wiley-Blackwell, 2012), 125. Cf. what Mircea Eliade calls the least inadequate definition of myth:

> Myth narrates a sacred history; it relates an event that took place in primordial Time, the fabled time of the "beginnings." In other words, myth tells how, through the deeds of Supernatural Beings, a reality came into existence, be it the whole of reality, the Cosmos, or only a fragment of reality—an island, a species of plant, a particular kind of human behavior, an institution. Myth, then, is always an account of a "creation"; it relates how something was produced, began to *be*. Myth tells only of that which *really* happened, which manifested itself completely. The actors in myths are Supernatural Beings. They are known primarily by what they did in the transcendent times of the "beginnings." Hence myths disclose their creative activity and reveal the sacredness (or simply the "supernaturalness") of their works. In short, myths describe the various and sometimes dramatic breakthroughs of the sacred (or the "supernatural") into the World. It is this sudden breakthrough of the sacred that really *establishes* the World and makes it what it is today. Furthermore, it is as a result of the intervention of Supernatural Beings that man himself is what he is today, a mortal, sexed, and cultural being. (*Myth and Reality*, trans. Willard R. Trask [New York: Harper & Row, 1963], 5)

These definitions emphasize the way in which myths are foundational for a society, or, as Doty puts it, "'originary,' a term identifying the ongoing fruitfulness of some early materials, rather than arguing that such and such is 'the earliest formulation' of something now held dear" (*Myth*, 19).

14. Cf. his somewhat different account of these four factors in Honko, "Der Mythos," 41–44.

planation of the world, at the basis of which lie the creative activities of the gods and models for behavior. Finally, the *context* of myth is in normal cases ritual or cult. The proper context of myth is thus implied to be religion.

G. S. Kirk, a British classicist, objects to the folklorists' definition of myth as a "sacred tale" or a tale involving "supernatural elements."[15] Rather, he proposes "traditional oral tale" as the only safe basis for a broad definition of myth. Kirk thus consciously collapses the distinction between myths and folktales, since they are both traditional oral tales. But why does he have misgivings about taking myths to be, as Honko says, stories about the gods? Kirk thinks that restricting the scope of myths in such a way will exclude some traditional tales that clearly are myths and will include some that are not. He explains,

> It is true that many traditional tales are "sacred" in that they concern gods or spirits—for example most cosmogonical myths, a well-known class, are sacred in that sense. But other tales are not primarily about gods at all, and have no ancillary implications of sanctity or tabu. It is not helpful to regard many of the tales about Heracles as sacred, even if he is persecuted by Hera or helped by Athena. Deucalion's re-creation of men by throwing stones over his shoulder is not usefully specified as a sacred tale, even though the action is suggested by a god, is set in the early days of the world, and is the result of a divinely-caused flood. Most traditional tales in non-literate societies (which are usually highly religious) contain supernatural elements and often "supernatural" will mean "divine" in these circumstances. But not everything that is supernatural is sacred. . . . In short, although many myths in many different cultures concern gods and other sacred beings, or the period of creation, not all do so in any essential way and therefore it can be misleading to focus on this quality as primary.[16]

A close reading reveals that Kirk does not deny that the gods are "sacred beings" and that therefore stories concerning them are sacred. Since these

15. G. S. Kirk, "On Defining Myths," in Dundes, *Sacred Narrative*, 57. Similarly, Doty, *Myth*, 117. Doty does not want to include in the definition of "myth" the sacred or religious because for anyone fully immersed in contemporary Western consciousness and praxis myths are often secular, deriving from arbitrary external influences like the mass media. But Doty is working, not with the folklorists' understanding of myth, but with an extremely broad notion, as mentioned above in note 2. Still, Doty does want to include a phrase like "intervention of suprahuman entities."

16. Kirk, "On Defining Myths," 57.

"highly religious" societies worship and serve such beings, it is only logical that stories about these deities should count as sacred. But Kirk contends that not everything that is supernatural is divine and therefore sacred. What does he have in mind here? Elsewhere he explains that the presence of supernatural elements in a tale cannot serve as a criterion for myth because "there are often fantastic, magical or miraculous elements in folktales. . . . In ordinary folk tales . . . witches, giants, ogres and magical objects represent the supernatural."[17] This is a sweeping conception of what it means to be "supernatural," for giants and ogres would not usually qualify as supernatural, a term that is normally reserved for the miraculous and therefore indicative of divine intervention in the world. Magic, such as practiced by witches and wizards, might be characterized as in a sense supernatural, though nonmiraculous.[18] Folktales featuring witches and magicians could be said to involve supernatural elements that are not divine and therefore not sacred, so that such tales should not count as myths.

But Honko's definition did not concern the supernatural in such sweeping terms but rather specified that the stories are about the gods, which provide the basis for a society's religious values and norms, establish patterns of behavior, and ratify the cult. Folktales such as Kirk envisions would not and ought not to qualify as myths under Honko's definition.

Kirk also contends that reference to the gods is not a necessary condition of myth. For stories about Greek heroes such as Heracles are not primarily about the gods and yet are surely myths. "The prominence of the heroes in Greek myths is itself a standing refutation of the contention . . . that all myth is primarily concerned with gods, that it is a facet of religion."[19] But, Kirk

17. G. S. Kirk, *Myth: Its Meaning and Functions in Ancient and Other Cultures*, SCL 40 (Cambridge: Cambridge University Press, 1970), 37.

18. Honko suggests "supernormal" ("Der Mythos," 53); "paranormal" also comes to mind.

19. Kirk, *Myth*, 178. Kirk admits, however, that "the Greeks are a special case. In the mythology of most other peoples, heroes (in the sense of superior mortals placed in the not indefinite past, some of whom acquired a cult and certain supernatural powers after their death) are either inconspicuous or altogether absent" (179). Kirk exhibits a curious aversion to taking the proper context of myth to be religion. See, by contrast, Lesley A. Northup, "Myth-Placed Priorities: Religion and the Study of Myth," *RSR* 32, no. 1 (2006): 6, who argues persuasively that "if we make any attempt to distinguish myth from epic, fable, fairy tale, urban legend, and simple fiction, we come inevitably to its root in some elemental and ultimate belief system. That places it squarely within the study of religion." Northup complains that too few academics are willing to acknowledge the elephant in the room—viz., "the reluctance of scholars to concede the centrality of religion to the study of myth" (9).

notwithstanding, these stories *are* about the gods, even if the gods are not the protagonists in the story. The heroes are men who had a god (or goddess) as one parent. They receive power and aid from the gods to carry out their feats. If the gods were deleted from the stories, the tales would cease to make sense. In any case, the gods and goddesses are not in fact absent but are among the tales' *dramatis personae* who intervene in human affairs on behalf of the heroes. Moreover, even leaving aside the gods, the heroes themselves could be the object of a cult, in which case the element of the sacred intrudes.

Family Resemblances among Myths

All this is, however, somewhat beside the point. The lines between myth, folktale, and legend are apt to be blurry, so that it is probably impossible and unprofitable to lay down necessary and sufficient conditions for each of these narrative types. In that sense, the search for a strict definition of myth is a misguided and rather surprising pursuit.[20] Instead, what we ought to be looking for is what Ludwig Wittgenstein called "family resemblances" among stories regarded as myths.[21] Using the illustration of games, Wittgenstein observed that given the diversity of games—board games, card games, athletic games, guessing games, and so on—it is impossible to lay down necessary and sufficient conditions for what it is to be a game. Rather, games exhibit family resemblances, features that are shared by different games with no feature sufficient for being a game common to all.

It was precisely to such family resemblances that NT scholar Richard Burridge turned in his revolutionary and influential work on the literary genre of the Gospels.[22] Burridge was able to identify a considerable number

20. Doty complains, "The nub of the problem has to do with traditional modernist definitions . . . in which rationalist outlines of what delimited one item from another were absolute, and never flexible." But "today most postmodernist definitions acknowledge that slippage between one or another genre or definition is simply to be expected" (*Myth*, 116). What Doty fails to perceive is that the problem can be solved through the "family resemblances" approach rather than a postmodernist approach to myth that is so nebulous as to be unmanageable.

21. Ludwig Wittgenstein, *Philosophical Investigations*, trans. G. E. M. Anscombe, ed. G. E. M. Anscombe and R. Rhees (Oxford: Blackwell, 1953), §§65–66.

22. Richard A. Burridge, *What Are the Gospels? A Comparison with Graeco-Roman Biography*, 2nd ed. (Waco: Baylor University Press, 2018), 38, 41. Burridge appeals to the work of literary theorists Alastair Fowler, "The Life and Death of Literary Forms," in *New*

of family resemblances among ancient biographies that were also shared by the Gospels, including both external features of form and structure and internal features of content. That some of these features go missing for some ancient biographies is not problematic because one is not trying to define "ancient biography" but trying to identify ancient biographies via characteristics shared to various degrees by them. "It does not matter if a particular work does not have all the features or fit the genre exactly. What is important is that it has *sufficient* features for the family resemblance to be recognized."[23] As a result of Burridge's work, the consensus among NT scholars has come to be that the Gospels belong to the genre of ancient biography.

Similarly, we can examine myths to determine what family resemblances exist among them. It might be objected that this approach suffers from vicious circularity because to determine family resemblances among myths one must have already settled on a class of myths.[24] But this sort of problem will attend any inductive, as opposed to a merely stipulative, approach to determining genre and may be resolved, as James Barr advises,[25] by beginning with paradigmatic examples of myths and then looking for family resemblances among the paradigms in order to then determine further instances. We have in ancient Mesopotamia, Egypt, and Greece just such paradigmatic examples of myths.

On the basis of our discussion thus far, we have already seen a number of characteristics typical of myths. Kirk would add that one of the distinguishing characteristics of myths is their "free ranging and often paradoxical fantasy."[26] He even compares myths to dreams in this respect.[27] Kirk makes the significant observation that "this lack of ordinary logic operates quite apart from supernatural components."[28] Additionally, Barr thinks that "the centre

Directions in Literary History, ed. Ralph Cohen (London: Routledge & Kegan Paul, 1974), 77–94, and E. D. Hirsch Jr., *Validity in Interpretation* (New Haven: Yale University Press, 1967), who emphasize that genre is best identified by describing the common elements in a narrow group of texts.

23. Burridge, *What Are the Gospels?*, 42.

24. Such an objection was raised by Helen K. Bond, "What Are the Gospels? And Why Does It Matter?" (paper presented at the Annual Meeting of the Society of Biblical Literature, Synoptic Gospels Section, Denver, CO, November 17, 2018).

25. James Barr, "The Meaning of 'Mythology' in Relation to the Old Testament," *VT* 9, no. 1 (1959): 2.

26. Kirk, *Myth*, 39.

27. Kirk, *Myth*, 268–69.

28. Kirk, *Myth*, 39–40.

of mythology, or at any rate its characteristic which is specially significant in relation to the Biblical material, is its doctrine of correspondences. Myth always maintains a secret correspondence or hidden harmony of some kind between gods and man, gods and nature, man and nature, the normative primeval and the actual present."[29] The degree to which myths express a correspondence between the gods and nature is quite controversial, as we shall see,[30] but it would be a mistake to deny that a good many myths do in some way express such a correspondence, so that, even if not the center of mythology, such a relation does count as one of the family resemblances. Kirk, while cautioning that universalistic theories like those of the nineteenth-century nature-myth school (all myths are allegories of natural processes) can be negated by citing many obvious instances of myth that do not accord with the assigned origin or function, adds that this does not imply that the universalistic theories are wrong in all respects. "It is possible to accept that they may be substantially right for some classes of myths, while being misleading for others. . . . It is only the theory that all myths have this function which is incorrect."[31]

Summary

In sum, family resemblances among myths include the following:

1. Myths are narratives, whether oral or literary.
2. Myths are traditional stories handed down from generation to generation.
3. Myths are sacred for the society that embraces them.
4. Myths are objects of belief by members of the society that embraces them.
5. Myths are set in a primaeval age or another realm.
6. Myths are stories in which deities are important characters.
7. Myths seek to anchor present realities such as the world, mankind, natural phenomena, cultural practices, and the prevailing cult in a primordial time.

29. Barr, "Meaning of 'Mythology,'" 5–6.
30. See *infra*, pp. 166–72.
31. Kirk, *Myth*, 54–55, 59–60.

8. Myths are associated with rituals.
9. Myths express correspondences between the deities and nature.
10. Myths exhibit fantastic elements and are not troubled by logical contradiction or incoherence.

It remains now to examine Gen 1–11 in light of these earmarks of myth.

Chapter 3

ARE THE PRIMAEVAL NARRATIVES OF GENESIS 1–11 MYTH? (PART 1)

In our last chapter we observed ten family resemblances among myths. Many of these family resemblances among myths will be shared by folk-tales and legends as well as other kinds of literature, and so the presence of one of these characteristics will not be very helpful in classifying Gen 1–11. On the other hand, the absence of one of these characteristics would count against taking Gen 1–11 as myth, even if not decisively. Consider, then, our list in numerical order.

1. Narrative

Narrative is clearly the correct description of Gen 1–11 as a whole, not merely of its individual units. These chapters tell the story of primaeval events in roughly chronological succession. Although there may be flashbacks, as it were, in the story of Adam and Eve's creation in Gen 2 and in the story of the Tower of Babel in Gen 11, nonetheless it is indisputable that, for example, the fall of mankind occurred according to the story after the creation of mankind, the flood occurred after the fall, and the confusion of languages at the Tower of Babel occurred after the flood. That we have here a chronological narrative is the lesson learned from the famous *tôlədôt* formulae ("these are the generations [*tôlədôt*] of") that punctuate the narrative. The genealogies serve to order the stories into a narrative. Although it is constantly and carelessly repeated that the *tôlədôt* formulae determine the structure of Genesis,[1] including its primaeval narrative, what is true is that the sequence of these formulae with their named descendants constitutes a timeline on which the

1. See discussion in chapter 5.

individual stories are ordered. The genealogies are like the string on which a necklace is strung. While the string does not determine the structure of the necklace, it provides at least a linear ordering of its elements. The primaeval narrative thus encompasses the entire sweep of prehistoric events from the creation until the call of Abraham, a period of at least 1,948 years according to the given life spans of pre-Abrahamic ancestors.

Moreover, it is worth noting that the primaeval narrative is a prose narrative. Although snippets of Hebrew poetry appear in Adam's exultant cry upon seeing Eve (Gen 2:23) and in Lamech's boast (4:23–24), the overwhelming bulk of the narrative is prose. The prose of Gen 1 is certainly highly stylized, bordering on poetry, but is prose nonetheless, what OT scholar John Collins aptly calls "exalted prose."[2] Unlike most biblical scholars, Collins finds it unhelpful to speak of the "genre" of Gen 1–11 because the term is ambiguous and tends to collapse important distinctions between literary form, style/register, language level, and social function, so that the term's ambiguity actually impedes sound analysis of the text.[3] In Collins's view, the main literary form of Gen 1–11 is prose narrative, and that prose varies throughout in its style and register and, hence, in its language level.[4] The narrative's social function is to serve Israel as "prehistory" and "protohistory"—namely, "to tell the story of the distant past as part of the worldview story that gives the community its distinctive identity and values."[5] In Collins's scheme, myth would not be a literary genre but a social function, having to do with how the text functions "to shape the beliefs, practices, and dispositions of the target communities," in this case Israel.[6]

2. Traditional Narrative

Genesis 1–11 is also universally recognized to comprise *traditional stories*. This conclusion is the legacy of more than two hundred years of source, form, and tradition criticism of the Pentateuch and of Genesis in particular. Source criticism seeks to detect and delimit literary sources used by the redactor of the canonical text. Form criticism seeks to push further back

2. C. John Collins, *Reading Genesis Well: Navigating History, Science, Poetry, and Truth* (Grand Rapids: Zondervan, 2018), 155.

3. Collins, *Reading Genesis Well*, 285.

4. Collins, *Reading Genesis Well*, 148.

5. Collins, *Reading Genesis Well*, 123.

6. Collins, *Reading Genesis Well*, 44.

beyond literary sources to identify the preliterary oral traditions that were reshaped by the later authors. Tradition criticism seeks to reconstruct the trajectory assumed by the developing traditions and sources to yield the canonical text.

The so-called Documentary Hypothesis of Julius Wellhausen (1844–1918) remains the paradigm of contemporary source theories. Wellhausen posited four main sources behind the Pentateuch, labeled, in order of their composition, J (Jahwist = Yahwist), E (Elohist), D (Deuteronomist), and P (Priestly). Their final redaction into the Pentateuch allegedly took place after Israel's return from exile in Babylon. Since neither E nor D comes into play in Gen 1–11, these chapters are typically divided between J and P as follows:

P = 1:1–31; 2:1–4a; 5:1–28, 30–32; 6:9–22; 7:6, 11, 13–16a, 17a, 18–21, 24; 8:1–2a, 3b–5, 13a, 14–19; 9:1–17, 28–29; 10:1–7, 20, 22–23, 31–32; 11:10–27, 31–32

J = 2:4b–25; 3:1–24; 4:1–26; 5:29; 6:1–8; 7:1–5, 7–10, 12, 16b, 17b, 22–23; 8:2b–3a, 6–12, 13b, 20–22; 9:18–27; 10:8–19, 21, 24–30; 11:1–9, 28–30

J is traditionally thought to have been written around the time of King Solomon (950 BC), while P was composed after the return from the Babylonian exile around 550–450 BC. Genesis 1–11 is a fusion of these two sources by a postexilic redactor. Given standard source theories, then, it is clear that we are dealing with traditional stories in Gen 1–11.

The Documentary Hypothesis has been subjected to much criticism and has continued to evolve since the time of Wellhausen,[7] but no scholar seems prepared to give it up entirely.[8] There is considerable skepticism concerning

7. For concise, accessible accounts of the history of source criticism, see Victor P. Hamilton, *The Book of Genesis: Chapters 1–17*, NICOT (Grand Rapids: Eerdmans, 1990), 11–38; B. T. Arnold, "Pentateuchal Criticism, History of," in *Dictionary of the Old Testament: Pentateuch*, ed. T. Desmond Alexander and David W. Baker (Downers Grove, IL: InterVarsity Press, 2003), 622–31. For a seven-point critique of the Documentary Hypothesis, see Richard S. Hess, *Israelite Religions: An Archaeological and Biblical Survey* (Grand Rapids: Baker Academic, 2007), 46–59.

8. Claus Westermann provides a sensible assessment of the evidence for the use of literary sources by the final redactor of Gen 1–11 (Claus Westermann, *Genesis 1–11: A Continental Commentary*, trans. John J. Scullion [Minneapolis: Fortress, 1994], 576–84): (1) *Style and language*. The parts of the Pentateuch attributed to P show a unified, rigidly concise style that can be demonstrated by stylistic characteristics. The result is "a certain and clear argument for the literary unity of this series, the P layer" (577). But as for J, this argument proves nothing more than that other texts in Genesis do not belong to P. (2) *Different*

scholars' ability to identify the specific boundaries and contents of the hypothetical sources, as done above. Others challenge the dating of the sources, even reversing the chronological priority of J and P.[9] Some would venture to dispense with either the P source or the J source altogether, metamorphos-

---

names for God. When one finds that in Gen 1–11 the name *Elohim* is employed throughout passages that have already been identified as belonging to P on the basis of style, then the use of differing names for God confirms the argument from style. It is difficult to conceive that the same writer who says in Exod 6:3 that the name *Yahweh* had not been previously revealed is the same author who has people referring to God as Yahweh already in Genesis. And it is scarcely imaginable that the same writer could say in Gen 4:26 that people at that time first began to call on the name of Yahweh, whereas that statement would be unproblematic for J. Thus, "the criterion of the different names for God in Gen 1–11, taken with the two passages Gen 4:26 and Ex 6:3 has retained its full force despite all opposition" (579). While not proving the existence of two literary sources, this argument proves that two voices are being heard. By contrast, none of the competing explanations for the variation of the divine names has been convincing. (3) *Contradictions and discrepancies*. Westermann agrees with the critics of source criticism that this argument is inconclusive and has proven to be untenable in very many cases. Rather than indicate different literary sources, contradictions may evince simply the incoherence of the narrative or the fusion by one author of prior, independent oral traditions. Thus, this argument can be used only in conjunction with other criteria. (4) *Doublets and repetitions*. Westermann also regards this criterion as inconclusive and incapable of standing alone, for one cannot exclude that a single author has woven together or even juxtaposed different oral traditions in his writing. (5) *Theological differences*. Again, this argument is indecisive. For once we recognize the independent paths of oral tradition that the individual units followed before being incorporated into the written work, we cannot use this argument independently. None of the hypothesized authors presumed to be a creator of his own theology. "All of them, without exception, are first and foremost mediators of tradition. They propose what their ancestors have said" (584). Thus, in Westermann's assessment, all the arguments for literary sources depend ultimately on the first, the uniqueness of P's style. Still, his discussion serves to highlight the importance of the preliterary oral traditions, which only underlines our point that these are traditional narratives handed down over generations.

9. For a concise summary of the issues, see Benjamin Kilchör, "Challenging the (Post-) Exilic Dating of P/H: The Most Important Issues" (paper presented at the Annual Meeting of the Society of Biblical Literature, San Diego, CA, November 22, 2019). He presents three arguments against an exilic/postexilic date of P: (1) According to diachronic linguistics, P is written in Classical Biblical Hebrew, not in Late Biblical Hebrew, and therefore originates in the preexilic period. Kilchör thinks that this consideration alone "will put an end to the tendency to date large parts of the Pentateuch's origin in the exilic and especially the post-exilic periods." (2) Given the total absence of Zion theology in the Pentateuch and given the recent archaeological findings on the temple in Shechem, it is difficult to envisage the pro-northern Pentateuch as written in postexilic times. (3) Since we do not have a single, undisputed Hebrew inscription from the exilic or the Persian periods, it is questionable whether these periods can be the most important epochs for

ing one of them into the final redactor who reworked the other remaining source. Nonetheless, the existence of the J and P sources behind Gen 1–11 remains widely accepted.[10] Since our interest is primarily in the canonical text rather than in its sources, we need not take a position on the various source-critical theories. Even scholars still holding to Mosaic authorship of the bulk of Genesis acknowledge that "sources were probably used in the writing of Genesis—sources that were brought by ancestors from Mesopotamia, sources and records of the ancestral families kept by the patriarchs, genealogical records, and the like."[11]

Hermann Gunkel (1862–1932), the pioneer of form criticism, accepted Wellhausen's Documentary Hypothesis but went beyond it in seeking to detect nonliterary sources of individual textual units of Gen 1–11 embedded even more deeply in the past. Gunkel was convinced on the basis of texts of Mesopotamian myths discovered only in the late nineteenth century that Israelite authors had borrowed extensively from pagan mythology for the primaeval history. But the Hebrew tradents, offended by the crass polytheism of these pagan myths, are thought to have thoroughly revised these mythic poems so as to make them theologically acceptable. For example, Gunkel thought that the use of the word *təhôm* (deep) in Gen 1:2 is a distant echo of the name of the goddess Tiamat, described in the Babylonian cosmogonic account *Enuma elish*, indicating that Gen 1:1–3 had its origin in a pagan myth of *Chaoskampf*. Since the oral sources were so thoroughly recast by the Hebrew tradents, the form critic must seek to imagine the original story in its own setting (*Sitz im Leben*) and to discern how it has been recast by its being taken up into an Israelite context. Because the stories of Gen 1–11 have been so thoroughly demythologized, Gunkel referred to them, not as myths, but as "faded myths," or *Sagen* (legends).[12]

---

the formation of the Pentateuch. In light of these considerations, it would be imprudent to make one's interpretation of P passages in Gen 1–11 dependent on an exilic/postexilic date.

10. For a recent assessment, see Jan Christian Gertz, "The Formation of the Primeval History," in *The Book of Genesis: Composition, Reception, and Interpretation*, ed. Craig A. Evans, Joel N. Lohr, and David L. Petersen, VTSup 152 (Leiden: Brill, 2012), 107–35. He reports, "Despite the rather confusing current state of research, . . . historical-critical scholarship agrees that we can distinguish and differentiate two groups of texts in Genesis 1–11, which can be delineated because of their linguistic profile and content and that are internally linked by several cross references. . . . In this sense the consensus formed by Witter, Astruc, and Eichhorn during the eighteenth century remains valid" (113).

11. Allen P. Ross, *Creation and Blessing: A Guide to the Study and Exposition of Genesis* (Grand Rapids: Baker Books, 1998), 35.

12. Hermann Gunkel, *The Legends of Genesis: The Biblical Saga in History*, trans. W. H.

As with source criticism, there has been a considerable evolution of form criticism over the past century. When the Babylonian texts were first unearthed and published in the late nineteenth century, they caused a tremendous stir known as the Babel-Bible controversy, after the title of a public lecture by Assyriologist Friedrich Delitzsch in 1902.[13] It seemed that the stories of Gen 1–11 were merely pale versions of Mesopotamian myths. In time, however, it came to be realized that the Genesis narratives could not, in general, plausibly be thought to be derived from the Mesopotamian myths. Gunkel's famous etymology for *təhôm*, for example, was shown to be spurious, and the Genesis account of creation unrelated to the *Enuma elish*. The one exception was the flood story in the *Epic of Gilgamesh*, with its remarkable parallel to Noah's release of birds from the ark in order to test the conditions of the land after the flood.[14] In recent years scholars have expressed a great deal of skepticism about the project of form criticism because of its highly conjectural and unverifiable nature. But obviously our inability to retrieve the original oral narratives with their *Sitz im Leben* does not imply that they did not exist. Indeed, as Westermann's arguments noted above so poignantly illustrate, the presence of oral traditions behind the Genesis narratives tends to undermine the case for separate literary documents.

Tradition criticism is an extension of form criticism that seeks to retrace the history of transmission of tradition. As Westermann explains, it begins at the end point when the oral traditions were incorporated into the written sources (J and P) and then works backward to reconstruct the paths along which the individual blocks of material were transmitted.[15] One discovers that the text of Gen 1–11 has a different history of tradition than Gen 12–50 and the rest of the Pentateuch. One then examines individual textual units within Gen 1–11 to see if they reveal anything about the way in which they were handed down. One discovers that the genealogies are a distinct literary type that have been incorporated into the narrative text. The narratives, too, form groups like the creation stories, which follow different paths of

---

Carruth (New York: Schocken Books, 1964), 14–15. This book is the English translation of Gunkel's introduction to his influential Genesis commentary *Genesis: Übersetzt und erklärt* (1901). Gunkel distinguished between the primitive legends (faded poetic myths) and the patriarchal legends (which are not rooted in myth).

13. Friedrich Delitzsch, *Babel und Bibel: Ein Vortrag* (Leipzig: Hinrichs, 1902). For a historical retrospective, see Bill T. Arnold and David B. Weisberg, "A Centennial Review of Friedrich Delitzsch's 'Babel und Bibel' Lectures," *JBL* 121, no. 3 (2002): 441–57.

14. See discussion in chapter 4.

15. Westermann, *Genesis 1–11*, 588.

tradition. Finally, one broadens the inquiry to take account of ANE parallels in both the early and late cultures. The conclusion for Gen 1–11 is that the authors of J and P took over traditions that link Israel's understanding of the world and mankind with that of the early and late ANE cultures. "One is dealing with a tradition which has had a long and varied history, which grew and was adapted for hundreds of years in Israel before it took written form under J and P, and of which every single part had a prehistory outside Israel."[16]

A good illustration of this method is Gordon Wenham's treatment of the text of Genesis.[17] He observes that when Gen 1–11 is compared with Gen 12–50, a striking difference emerges: Gen 1–11 is full of parallels with ANE traditions such that these chapters appear to reflect these Oriental ideas both positively and negatively, whereas Gen 12–50 is devoid of such parallels. Within Gen 1–11 certain sections stand out as quite different: for example, the genealogies in chapters 5 and 11 and the Table of Nations in chapter 10. It seems likely that they come from a source different from the surrounding materials. Prebiblical accounts of primaeval history such as the *Atrahasis Epic* and the *Sumerian Flood Story*, all dated to 1600 BC or earlier, include features from both the J and P parts of Gen 1–11. Thus, no later than 1600 BC a story of origins was known in Mesopotamia that bears a striking resemblance to Genesis as it now stands. This makes it unlikely that the Genesis account was created by some later editor who knitted together two independent Hebrew versions of origins, J and P. Wenham therefore believes that the final editor had before him an outline of primaeval history, an abbreviated version of our present Gen 1–11, which he reworked to yield the present form of the text. Although it is difficult to identify the boundaries of the individual

16. Westermann, *Genesis 1–11*, 65.

17. Gordon J. Wenham, *Genesis 1–15*, WBC 1 (Grand Rapids: Zondervan, 1987), xxxvii–xlv. Unlike Westermann, Wenham thinks that the literary evidence for distinctly P passages points most clearly to P's chronological priority. He observes that throughout Gen 5–11 it appears that comments by J have been appended to P texts. This is recognized by Westermann in the flood story. Clearer still is the evidence of Gen 5, where J has taken a genealogy ascribed to P and added his own introduction and conclusion and inserted a comment about Noah's name. In the Table of Nations in Gen 10, a fairly compact list ascribed to P has been broken up by long interpolations by J reflecting his special interest in Israel's neighbors. This suggests that J is a later writer than P. The P material is often so sketchy that it would be easier to see it as fragmentary. If the J material draws on a variety of fragmentary sources and the material conventionally called P also derives from a diversity of sources, it is possible to see Genesis as basically the work of J, who used a number of relatively short sources to compose the work.

sources, Wenham thinks that the fact that Genesis makes use of multiple sources, both oral and written, is doubtless true. This last conclusion would be today virtually unanimously acknowledged.

3. Sacred Narrative

Again, it is uncontroversial that the narratives of Gen 1–11 are *sacred* for Israelite society. Not only do these stories tell the acts of the God of creation, but more particularly they tell the acts of Israel's covenantal God, Yahweh. Sabbath observance and animal sacrifice, so central to Israel's cult, are already grounded in the early chapters of Genesis. More broadly speaking, the Pentateuch presents itself, as Collins explains, as the authoritative story specifying how Israel ought to see itself. The Pentateuch thus presents itself, in effect, as the constitution of Israel as a church-state nexus.[18] Genesis 1–11 provides the prehistory and foundation for Yahweh's call of Abraham to establish the nation of Israel in order to achieve the end of blessing mankind that was aborted by Adam and Eve's sin. As we saw from Clines's analysis of the theme of the Pentateuch, God's promise to the patriarchs should be read in conjunction with Gen 1 as a reaffirmation of the original divine intention for humanity. Thus, Gen 1–11 is a sacred preamble to the history of Israel.

4. Belief

Similarly, the stories of Gen 1–11 are *to be believed* by members of Israelite society. We see this fact clearly when later passages in the Pentateuch reaffirm statements in the primaeval narrative. For example, in Exod 20:8–11 we have a recapitulation of the creation week: "Remember the sabbath day, to keep it holy. Six days you shall labor, and do all your work; but the seventh day is a sabbath to the LORD your God; in it you shall not do any work . . . ; for in six days the LORD made heaven and earth, the sea, and all that is in them, and rested the seventh day; therefore the LORD blessed the sabbath day and hallowed it." Again we read, "The people of Israel shall keep the sabbath, observing the sabbath throughout their generations, as a perpetual covenant. It is a sign for ever between me and the people of Israel that in six days the LORD made heaven and earth, and on the seventh day he rested, and

18. Collins, *Reading Genesis Well*, 131–34.

was refreshed" (Exod 31:16–17). Such passages imply belief in the creation account of Gen 1.

One might make the same point by appealing to passages outside the Pentateuch evincing belief in the creation story—for example, Ps 104:5–30. But the difficulty is that, given the uncertainty of the dates of the traditions of Gen 1–11, we really do not know whether these extra-pentateuchal passages are dependent on Gen 1–11, in contrast to passages in the Pentateuch itself, where the final redactor certainly knew Gen 1–11, so that subsequent passages refer back to the primaeval narratives.[19] But the genealogies of Gen 1–11 are certainly regarded as authoritative by the Chronicler, who has an indisputedly postexilic date, for 1 Chr 1:1–27 simply sums up the genealogies of Gen 1–11 without comment.

5. Deities

The resemblances mentioned thus far, while characteristic of myths, are not unique to them and so of little help in classifying Gen 1–11. But the fifth characteristic, that myths are stories in which *deities are important characters*, seems to be a more distinctive feature of myths. It is therefore significant that a good many scholars have argued that on the basis of this criterion the primaeval narratives of Gen 1–11 should not be classified as myths. For the striking feature of Genesis is its monotheism, which excludes a plurality of gods. Therefore the stories of Gen 1–11 are not stories in which deities are important characters and so are not myths.

It was precisely on this basis that Gunkel regarded the stories of Gen 1–11 as now faded myths. Gunkel remarked on the difference between the legends of the primaeval narrative and the legends of the patriarchs: the former feature an anthropomorphic God as a principal actor, whereas in the latter the principal actors are human and God is more mysterious and remote. Since myths are stories of the gods, in contrast to legends in which the main actors are human, the primaeval legends have "a more decidedly mythical character."[20] Nonetheless, Gunkel insisted on the plurality of dei-

19. For a forceful argument that Gen 1 is actually dependent on Ps 104, see John Day, *From Creation to Babel: Studies in Genesis 1–11*, LHBOTS 592 (London: Bloomsbury, 2013), 21–22.

20. Gunkel, *Legends of Genesis*, 14.

ties in myth: "For a story of the gods at least two gods are essential."[21] Thus, despite the prominence of an anthropomorphic deity in these stories, the primaeval legends are not technically about *gods* and, hence, not myths.

Gunkel equated Israel's aversion to polytheism with an aversion to myths: "Monotheism [is] hostile to myths."[22] So Gunkel understood the elimination of polytheism from the original stories as the elimination of myth: "In very many legends of Genesis a monotheistic tendency is to be observed, an avoidance of mythology to which we have referred (see pp. 15 and 95)."[23] Intriguingly, what Gunkel actually refers to on pages 15 and 95 is the avoidance of polytheism, not mythology: "The equivalence of the divine beings and the objects or realms of nature, the combat of the gods with one another, the birth of the gods, are some of the features which have disappeared in the version of Genesis."[24] "Naturally these foreign themes were vigorously adapted in Israel . . . , a process to be recognized most clearly in the case of the Babylonian-Hebrew legend of the Deluge. Here the polytheism has disappeared."[25] Hence, "the primitive legends preserved to us are all dominated by this unspoken aversion to mythology."[26]

Now Gunkel appears in this regard to have been guilty of a fundamental category mistake.[27] An aversion to polytheism is not an aversion to a literary function or genre. Israel was deeply averse to polytheism; but with what right can we say that Israel was averse to its stories' playing a certain literary function? With what justification can we say that a plurality of gods is an essential feature of a story's functioning as a myth in a particular culture?[28]

21. Gunkel, *Legends of Genesis*, 15.
22. Gunkel, *Legends of Genesis*, 15.
23. Gunkel, *Legends of Genesis*, 103.
24. Gunkel, *Legends of Genesis*, 15.
25. Gunkel, *Legends of Genesis*, 95.
26. Gunkel, *Legends of Genesis*, 16.

27. Making the same category mistake as Gunkel, confusing content with function or form, is Beall, who demands, "If the perspective of Gen 1–11 is so contrary to the ANE worldview, then why should one assume that it was written according to that same worldview?" (Todd Beall, "Reading Genesis 1–2: A Literal Approach," in *Reading Genesis 1–2: An Evangelical Conversation*, ed. J. Daryl Charles [Peabody, MA: Hendrickson, 2013], 52).

28. Rogerson draws attention in this regard to an inconsistency in Gunkel's treatment of myth. On the one hand myths were stories about gods, but on the other they were stories that answered questions of universal concern. "Thus on the one hand, there were no myths in the *Urgeschichte* because there were no stories about gods. . . . However, in so far as stories in the *Urgeschichte* explain matters of universal concern, they *were* myths" (J. W. Rogerson, *Myth in Old Testament Interpretation*, BZAW 134 [Berlin: de Gruyter, 1974], 63). Rogerson reports that, at the time of his writing, Gunkel's definition of myth

Following Gunkel's lead, many contemporary scholars who deny that the stories of Gen 1–11 are myths equate the elimination of polytheism with demythologization. To take one example, Gerhard Hasel, in an oft-cited article, argues that the creation story in Gen 1 is a polemic against polytheism, which he equates with an anti-mythical polemic. He claims that "the author of Gen 1 rejected explicitly contemporary mythological notions by using the term *tehôm* . . . in such a way that it is not only non-mythical in content but antimythical in purpose. Thus there comes to expression with *tehôm* an antimythical polemic which can be observed also in other parts of the creation account of Gen 1." Again, in discussing God's separating the waters, Hasel equates an anti-polytheistic polemic with an anti-mythical polemic: "Inherent in the separation of heaven and earth is an antimythical polemic. Separation takes place without struggle whatever. . . . In this instance Gen 1 is again opposed to pagan mythology."[29] In denying that the sun, moon, and stars are astral deities, "the Hebrew account of the creation, function, and limitation of the luminaries is another unequivocal link in the chain stressing that in Gen 1 there is a direct and conscious antimythical polemic."[30] We could agree that the author polemicizes against polytheism and therefore against pagan mythology;[31] but with what right can we say that his polemic is against mythology as such?

There seems to be a confusion among these scholars between demythologization and what we might call the desacralization of nature.[32] What the author of Gen 1 did was to desacralize nature, in the sense that the objects and phenomena in the world were stripped of their divinity and regarded as mere creatures created by a transcendent God. They were neither deities nor indwelt by deities and in that sense purely natural. This desacralization of nature was an astounding achievement, especially if the traditions behind Gen 1 are early. For the conception of God in Gen 1 is so staggeringly different from

as stories about the gods had been widely accepted and so little room had been found in the OT for myth (145).

29. Gerhard F. Hasel, "The Polemic Nature of the Genesis Cosmology," *EvQ* 46 (1974): 85.

30. Hasel, "Polemic Nature," 116.

31. But see the cautionary note by Bill Arnold that the primary purpose of Gen 1 is not polemical. Pagan positions are not directly attacked. Rather, "as an entirely new worldview, Gen 1 includes polemic but transcends competing theologies by presenting a new paradigm altogether" (Bill T. Arnold, *Genesis*, NCBC [Cambridge: Cambridge University Press, 2009], 32).

32. Or, alternatively, what John Day calls the "monotheization" of ANE polytheistic traditions (*From Creation to Babel*, 111).

anything else in the ANE.[33] Nahum Sarna encapsulates the concept of God in Genesis thus: "The God of Genesis is the wholly self-sufficient One, absolutely independent of nature, the supreme, unchallengeable Sovereign of the world, who is providentially involved in human affairs."[34] The dominant tenet of Hebrew thought, state Henri Frankfort and H. A. Frankfort, is the absolute transcendence of God.[35] Yahweh is not in nature. Neither the earth nor the sun nor the stars is divine; even the most potent natural phenomena are but creaturely reflections of God's greatness. Moreover, as William Irwin reminds us, Israel's monotheism was an ethical monotheism, according to which God is good and acts consistently with his character.[36] The deities of Israel's neighbors are primitive and, frankly, vile by comparison.[37]

It is customarily said that the sixth-century BC Ionian philosophers were responsible for desacralizing the world described by pagan mythology and thus for preparing the way for a scientific understanding of nature. But equal credit should be given to Israelite thinkers—and perhaps even pride of place if the traditions behind Gen 1 are preexilic. For like the Ionian philosophers, they, too, opposed the polytheism of ANE mythology and articulated a desacralized view of nature. As a result, one must agree with Irwin's judgment, so contrary to conventional wisdom, that Israel's worldview was much more like ours than that of the ANE.[38] As he explains, "The boundary between the ancient world and the modern is to be traced, not in the Aegean or the middle

33. Frankfort and Frankfort, in their survey of ANE mythological thought, conclude that the view that was "universally accepted by the peoples of the ancient world with the single exception of the Hebrews" was that "nature is but the manifestation of the divine" (H. Frankfort and H. A. Frankfort, "The Emancipation of Thought from Myth," in *The Intellectual Adventure of Ancient Man: An Essay on Speculative Thought in the Ancient Near East*, by Henri Frankfort et al. [Chicago: University Chicago Press, 1946], 367).

34. Nahum M. Sarna, *Genesis*, JPSTC (Philadelphia: Jewish Publication Society, 1989), xii; cf. 4.

35. Frankfort and Frankfort, "Emancipation of Thought," 367.

36. William A. Irwin, "The Hebrews: God," in Frankfort et al., *Intellectual Adventure of Ancient Man*, 227.

37. See, e.g., the myth *Enlil and Ninlil*. Lest anyone think such a harsh verdict is merely the expression of modern prejudice, it should be noted that ancient Greek philosophers like Theagenes and Xenophanes in the sixth century BC and, later, Plato criticized Greek myths on similar grounds.

38. Irwin, "Hebrews," 224. Cf. Wenham's judgment that Genesis and the ANE probably have more in common with each other than either has with modern secular thought (*Genesis 1–15*, xlvii). The emphasis here must be on "secular." Wenham takes that description to imply philosophical naturalism. But a modern, scientific view of the world need not commit one to philosophical naturalism.

Mediterranean, but in the pages of the Old Testament, where we find revealed Israel's attainments in the realms of thought, her facility in literary expression, her profound religious insights, and her standards of individual and social ethics."[39] This fact should not really surprise us when we reflect on the determinative influence of Judaeo-Christian thinking on Western culture.

But desacralization is a very different thing than demythologization. The latter is a literary activity, involving a change of function or genre. It is far from clear that desacralization of nature implies literary demythologizing of stories. Certainly Israel was averse to polytheism and hence committed to a desacralized view of nature, but it does not follow that Israel was bent on a literary program of demythologization.

The tacit assumption of these scholars is that there cannot be a monotheistic myth. Logically speaking, that assumption is demonstrably false. For, logically, a story that is about a deity is a story about deities. In quantificational logic, "There is one deity" entails that there are deities. To say "Some deities exist" is just to say that at least one deity exists. If it is true that "There is some x such that x is a deity," then at least one individual, but perhaps many individuals, are values for x. Thus, if one deity exists, then deities exist. So logically, a story about one deity is a story about deities. Logically, then, a myth could be about just one deity; accordingly, there can be monotheistic myths.

Now these OT scholars might be averse to this sort of "logic chopping," insisting that myths are inherently stories of a plurality of gods and that therefore there cannot be monotheistic myths. But such a contention seems highly implausible. How could the literary function of a narrative depend on the numerosity of the gods featured in it? If the number of gods in a myth that serves to explain some present feature of the world in terms of divine activity in the primaeval past were reduced from, say, seven to three, would its mythic character be diluted? Presumably not! And if the number were reduced from three to one, why would its mythic character suddenly disappear? Would it not still function to ground present realities in the primaeval past for members of the society that embraces it?

39. Irwin, "Hebrews," 224. With regard to the contribution of the Ionians, Frankfort and Frankfort observe that "Thales speaks of *water*, not of a water-god; Anaximenes refers to *air*, not to a god of air or storms. Here lies the astonishing novelty of their approach. Even though 'all things are full of gods,' these men attempt to understand the coherence of the *things*" ("Emancipation of Thought," 378). Something similar could be said with equal justice of the author of Gen 1: even though all things have been created by God, he sought to understand the coherence of the *things*.

In the Sumerian myth *Enki and Ninmah* 24–37 we read that Enki enjoins the mother goddess Namma to knead clay so that the birth-goddesses could nip off pieces with which she could fashion human beings. How is the story of God's forming man from the dust of the earth in Gen 2 functionally distinct from such a story simply in virtue of the fact that Yahweh is the sole deity? It is easy to understand why the presence of at least one deity is crucial for a story's being a myth, but it is hard to see why the number of deities assumed in a story is determinative for its being a myth.

Indeed, there are pagan myths in which only a single deity is a character in the story. For example, the African Bushongo have a creation story that describes Bumba, the Creator, as a gigantic white being in human form who existed alone in the beginning, in a universe where there was nothing but water. One day he vomited up the sun, moon, and stars, and then after some time vomited up eight animals, including the leopard, crocodile, eagle, and so on, which in turn gave rise to all the rest. Finally, he produced man.[40] The Hawaiian people have a creation story that features a founding figure Kane, who places a man and his wife in "a fertile garden from which they were driven because of disobedience to the laws of Kane."[41] These stories are no less myths because they feature one deity than their polytheistic counterparts.

Brevard Childs is keenly aware of the implausibility of insisting on the plurality of deities in myth. Reflecting on Gunkel's understanding of myth, Childs muses, "If myth is understood only as 'a story of gods,' then there is no true myth possible in a monotheistic religion, and myth is eliminated by definition from the Old Testament. The defenders of this definition have often failed to reckon with the possibility that the Old Testament faith may have maintained and even developed mythical thinking while merely eliminating the crude polytheism."[42] Childs therefore proposes to redefine myth so as to allow for the possibility of a monotheistic myth: "Myth is a form by which the existing structure of reality is understood and maintained. It concerns itself with showing how an action of a deity, conceived as occurring

40. Alice Werner, "African Mythology," in *The Mythology of All Races*, vol. 7, *Armenian and African*, by Mardiros H. Ananikian and Alice Werner (Boston: Marshall Jones, 1925), 144.

41. Martha Beckwith, *Hawaiian Mythology* (New Haven: Yale University Press, 1940), 308–9.

42. Brevard S. Childs, *Myth and Reality in the Old Testament*, 2nd ed., SBT 1st ser., 27 (1962; repr., Eugene: Wipf & Stock, 2009), 15–16.

in the primeval age, determines a phase of contemporary world order."[43] By "a deity" Childs means "at least one," in line with both quantificational logic and the intention of the folklorists' definition of myth.

6. Primaeval Narratives

The stories of Gen 1–11 are *set in a primaeval age*, if not in another realm. The primaeval age in Genesis runs right back to God's creation of the world "in the beginning" (Gen 1:1). Moreover, the Genesis account narrates the creation of humankind as well as of plant and animal life. The origin of civilization and several of its inventions, such as metallurgy and music, are related. The origin of the world's languages is described. The period described is thus truly the primal age of mankind and the world.

Brevard Childs has claimed, however, that the OT's concept of time is in conflict with mythical time. He argues that "Israel succeeded in overcoming the myth because of an understanding of reality which opposed the mythical."[44] In terms reminiscent of Gunkel's "faded myths," Childs therefore speaks of "broken myths" in the OT.

What, then, is the mythical concept of time? Childs characterizes it as follows:

43. Childs, *Myth and Reality*, 29–30. Unfortunately, Childs departs from the folklorist and form-critical definition of myth by abandoning the notion that a myth is a narrative in favor of construing myths as forms (of thought?). Why does he take this radical step? He explains that on the form-critical definition, "myth is defined too exclusively as a literary product. Although its pre-literary stage is evident to those applying it, the function of the definition is directed primarily to defining limits on the literary plane" (15). This assertion is more than mildly surprising. Form critics, of all people, were interested in studying myths that were transmitted orally, before they were reduced to writing. It is no part of the standard folklorist definition adopted by the form critics that the sacred narratives be written rather than oral. In any case, no justification has here been given for redefining myth as a form (whatever that is) rather than as a narrative (oral or written) that has the function specified. Curiously, Childs thinks that his "phenomenological" redefinition represents the "general consensus of opinion" among scholars of comparative religion and is "in fundamental accord" with the position of James Barr (16, 30), which does not appear to be the case. The general consensus is that myths are narratives, not forms, and Barr's position sees the center of mythology in the correspondences between the gods and nature, a feature that plays no role in Childs's definition.

44. Childs, *Myth and Reality*, 97.

> The concept of time found in the myth is, first of all, characterized by its understanding of time as absolute. Time stems ultimately from the one primeval act of power before which there was no time and beyond which one cannot pass. This dividing line which separates the world of being from that of non-being marks off the beginning of time. There is no actual distinction in mythical time between the past, the present, and the future. Although the origin of time is projected into the past, to the primeval act of becoming, this is only a form in which an essentially timeless reality is clothed. Time is always present and yet to come. . . . In the cultic representation of the myth this act is relived. The power of this event, which fills the content of mythical time, is actualized as the cultic festival becomes the primeval act. The two times sharing the same content are therefore identical.[45]

Now while it is possible that this description accurately represents the mythical understanding of time, the sympathetic interpreter will be reluctant to ascribe such incoherent nonsense to the progenitors of myth. What does it mean to say that time is "absolute," and how is that consistent with saying that reality is "essentially timeless"? Is it really the case that mythical thinking had so sophisticated a grasp of time as to affirm a beginning of time itself and an origination of the world *ex nihilo*? How is that claim consistent with the quite different claim that "mythical thinking grew out of a 'two-stage' understanding of the formation of world reality. There was *initially* a period of non-being. This was *superseded* by the decisive acts of the primeval age at which time . . . the world structure was fixed"?[46] Or are we to understand that the origin of time and, indeed, time itself are illusory projections of consciousness? If there is no actual distinction in mythical time between past, present, and future, then how can time be "always present and yet to come"—and what does *that* mean? In the cultic celebration, is the primaeval act literally *re*lived—that is, experienced *again*? Then the primaeval act and its cultic representation are not numerically identical but temporally related as *earlier than/later than*. But then reality is not timeless, as claimed.

And what of the biblical concept of time? In contrast to the mythical two-stage understanding of the formation of the world, Childs describes

45. Childs, *Myth and Reality*, 73–74. As we have seen (note 43), for Childs "myth" does not refer to a narrative but to a form of some sort.

46. Childs, *Myth and Reality*, 83 (my emphases). The italicized words indicate that time existed prior to the decisive acts of the beginning of the world.

the biblical understanding of reality as three-stage. First, "there was a state of non-being pictured as chaos in the Old Testament." Second, this state "was overcome by God's gracious acts of creation which brought world reality into being."[47] Third, a redemptive history was inaugurated as a result of human disobedience and finds its fulfillment in the eschatological future. Let us overlook Childs's inaccurate description of the first stage.[48] The only difference between the biblical understanding and the supposed mythical understanding of time is the additional eschatological element. "The myth looks to the past, the Old Testament to the future."[49]

This, however, is a difference not in the concept of time—indeed, the differing outlooks assume a real distinction between past and future—but in the concept of history. Incredibly, Childs, while recognizing that the Hebrews registered the passing of successive events in their chronologies and genealogies and that the eschatological view of a future event toward which all history moves cannot be minimized,[50] nevertheless asserts that "the concept of 'linear history,' so frequently employed as the antithesis of cyclic myth, is not itself a Biblical category, but a rationalization of another sort."[51] Of course, linearity is a geometrical concept that may not have been known to ancient Hebrews (in contrast to Babylonians!); but *our* use of that concept to characterize their view of history may be accurate without implying anachronistically that *they* would have employed such a concept to express their view. The commitment to temporal succession and to eschatology in which the future is not identical to the past implies a linear view of history.

The decisive third stage does not figure prominently in the primaeval narratives of Gen 1–11; that is why Clines says that the meaning of the primaeval history is ambiguous until its resolution in Gen 12:1–3 and the remainder of the Pentateuch.[52] So the eschatological hope cannot serve to differentiate Gen 1–11 from ANE myths. Moreover, like Gen 1–11, the ANE myths also could recount "the struggle between reality and the perversion of reality," a "history which is not a continuation of God's creation but a perversion of reality."[53] That perversion is not the result of human disobedience but of human overpopulation and the annoying din, which the gods had failed to

47. Childs, *Myth and Reality*, 83.
48. We shall have more to say of this anon. See *infra*, pp. 68–69.
49. Childs, *Myth and Reality*, 84.
50. Childs, *Myth and Reality*, 77.
51. Childs, *Myth and Reality*, 76.
52. Recall pp. 21–22.
53. Childs, *Myth and Reality*, 83.

foresee and now had to deal with (*Atrahasis Epic* II). The point is that the primaeval history of Gen 1–11 is compatible with the concept of time that finds expression in myth. We shall have more to say on this head in chapter 4 when discussing the interest in history shown by Gen 1–11.

The history of Gen 1–11 is thus set in a primaeval time, a characteristic of myths, especially myths of origination.

Chapter 4

ARE THE PRIMAEVAL NARRATIVES OF GENESIS 1–11 MYTH? (PART 2)

In seeking to determine the genre of the primaeval narratives of Gen 1–11, we have identified ten family resemblances common among myths. We have seen that the stories of Gen 1–11 exemplify the first six such family resemblances. We now come to the seventh.

7. Etiology

The primaeval history of Gen 1–11 seeks to *anchor realities present to the pentateuchal author,* such as the world, mankind, natural phenomena, cultural practices, and the prevailing cult, *in a primordial time.* Here we come to the very heart of myth. In grounding present realities in the primordial past, the primaeval narrative functions as Israel's foundational myth, not, indeed, the founding of Israel as a nation, but even more fundamentally, laying the foundations of Israel's worldview.

Hebrew Borrowing?

The claim here is not that the narratives of Gen 1–11 are derived from ANE myths. Hermann Gunkel and the pan-Babylonian school that followed in his train made such a claim, but few scholars defend the dependence thesis today. Far too many OT scholars fell victim to the "parallelomania" against which Samuel Sandmel warned NT scholars.[1] Sandmel observed that in

1. Samuel Sandmel, "Parallelomania," *JBL* 81, no. 1 (1962): 1–13. Sandmel defined "parallelomania" as "that extravagance among scholars which first overdoes the supposed similarity in passages and then proceeds to describe source and derivation as if implying

order to establish their dependence claims these scholars would need to establish three subsidiary claims: (1) that the relevant passages are indeed parallel; (2) that the parallels are to be explained by a causal connection between them; and (3) that the causal connection is asymmetrical.

When it comes to establishing these claims with respect to Gen 1–11 and ANE myths, one might justifiably complain about what seems to be an extraordinarily low standard of proof that has prevailed among many OT scholars. The sort of evidence often taken to be sufficient to establish various dependence claims would make a scientist blush. In the physical sciences, extraordinarily high standards of evidence are in place and must be met before a hypothetical claim is taken to be established. Alternative explanations of the data must be rigorously excluded. One thinks, for example, of the experimental evidence that is demanded by physicists in order to establish the existence of gravitational waves predicted on the basis of the general theory of relativity. Now, admittedly, OT studies belong to the humanities, not to the physical sciences, and so cannot be expected to meet such rigorous standards of evidence. But that fact provides no justification for credulity in OT studies but only underlines the necessity of a tentative attitude toward one's preferred hypothesis. Given the conjectural nature of many tradition-historical claims, an attitude of skepticism regarding such claims is surely often prudent.

Establishing (1) alone, not to mention (2) or (3), is fraught with difficulty. Two pitfalls deserve to be mentioned. First is the fallacy of *neglecting context*. Entire passages need to be compared, and not just isolated elements of them. Claus Westermann advises,

> A comparison which serves in understanding biblical texts must proceed from and aim at phenomenologically graspable wholes. . . . Drawing mere points of comparison is then no longer sensible. Seeking and finding parallel points . . . in this isolated way can be of little service to biblical understanding. The mere realization that there is—or is not—some such thing in another religion has in itself scarcely any hermeneutical value; such pointlike comparison can very easily lead to failures of judgment. The danger of failures of judgment becomes even greater when one additionally tries to

literary connection flowing in an inevitable or predetermined direction" (1). The terms "inevitable" and "predetermined" are too strong; "flowing in a certain direction" would suffice to capture the claim of the parallelomaniacs.

draw one isolated phenomenon *here* out of another isolated phenomenon *there*. . . . Point-like comparison never leads to parallels; they are possible only where lines on both sides can be shown to be parallel to each other.[2]

Focusing on isolated elements in a text while ignoring context courts the danger of "cherry-picking." To illustrate, we all know about the tragic disaster that occurred when a large airliner, on its way from Massachusetts to New York, crashed into one of New York's tallest office buildings between the seventy-seventh and eighty-fifth floors shortly after 9:00 a.m., setting it afire and resulting in the loss of everyone on board and many office workers. The terrorist attack of 9/11? No, the crash of a B-25 into the Empire State Building on July 28, 1945.[3] By cherry-picking details and ignoring context, one can create the illusion of parallelism where in fact none exists. A full story of the events in this illustration makes it evident that the points of similarity are coincidental.

Peter Enns, to name one example, fails to take account of context when he lists the following "commonly agreed upon similarities" between Gen 1 and the Babylonian epic *Enuma elish*: (1) matter exists independently of the divine spirit; (2) darkness precedes creation; (3) in Hebrew *təhôm* (the deep) is linguistically related to "Tiamat," the name of the goddess symbolizing chaos; (4) light exists before the creation of the sun, moon, and stars; (5) Marduk fillets the body of the slain Tiamat to form a barrier to keep the waters from escaping, while Genesis depicts the sky as a solid dome to keep the waters above where they belong; (6) the sequence of the days of creation is similar, including the creation of the firmament, dry land, luminaries, and humanity; (7) all is followed by divine rest.[4] The problem is not just

2. Claus Westermann, "Sinn und Grenze religionsgeschichtlicher Parallelen," *TL* 90, no. 7 (1965): 490–91; cf. Westermann, *Genesis 1–11: A Continental Commentary*, trans. John J. Scullion (Minneapolis: Fortress, 1994), 6. A notable recent example of such point-like comparisons is John W. Hilber, *Old Testament Cosmology and Divine Accommodation: A Relevance Theory Approach* (Eugene: Cascade, 2020), chap. 1.

3. See Wikipedia, "1945 Empire State Building B-25 Crash," https://en.wikipedia.org/wiki/1945_Empire_State_Building_B-25_crash. I am indebted to Michael Licona for this example. Similar cherry-picking can make the assassinations of Abraham Lincoln and John F. Kennedy look parallel.

4. Peter Enns, *The Evolution of Adam: What the Bible Does and Doesn't Say about Human Origins* (Grand Rapids: Brazos, 2012), 39. Similarly, Kenton L. Sparks lists similarities between the *Enuma elish* and Gen 1 as well as similarities of the Eden/fall narrative to Mesopotamian traditions without consideration of context ("Genesis 1–11 as Ancient

that Enns's alleged parallels are frequently questionable and even spurious[5]

Historiography," in *Genesis: History, Fiction, or Neither? Three Views on the Bible's Earliest Chapters*, ed. Charles Halton [Grand Rapids: Zondervan, 2015], 110–39). Richard J. Clifford, in his *Creation Accounts in the Ancient Near East and in the Bible*, CBQMS 26 (Washington, DC: Catholic Biblical Association of America, 1994), 148–49, actually appears to *endorse* cherry-picking, comparing *details* of narratives without regard to their *context*. For he states, "Such kaleidoscopic reuse of traditional details may seem strange to modern readers, but ancient authors evidently liked to put familiar objects in new contexts." He gives as his example certain details from the *Epic of Gilgamesh*: "The naked and animallike Enkidu acquires wisdom from his seven-day dalliance with a prostitute. Afterward she clothes him and leads him to the city of Uruk and its king Gilgamesh. Genesis rearranges the same traditions to describe the institution of marriage!" This is truly parallelomania and to my mind the *reductio ad absurdum* of the cherry-picking methodology.

5. For example, (1) the claim that matter exists independently of the divine spirit is not true of the *Enuma elish*, which does not even mention the divine spirit but begins with the deities associated with primordial waters. Nor is it clearly true of Genesis, since God has already been said in Gen 1:1 to have created the heavens and the earth in the beginning, a statement that most scholars now recognize to be an independent clause. (For argument, see Westermann, *Genesis 1–11*, 93–97.) *Pace* Westermann, v. 1 is arguably not a title for the creation story, since it is connected to v. 2 by *waw* (and) and, if taken as a title, would be inaccurate, since the ensuing account does not, in fact, describe the creation of the earth (v. 2). (2) For the same reason, it is questionable to claim that in Gen 1 darkness precedes creation, since creation begins in v. 1. Worse, darkness does not feature in the *Enuma elish*, so that the alleged parallel is spurious. (3) Tiamat and Genesis's "deep" (the words for which have been shown to be semantically underived from each other) are actually points of contrast between the accounts, Genesis describing an earthly ocean and the *Enuma elish* an amorphous divine substance that exists prior to the earth's existence and that gives birth to other gods. (4) In the *Enuma elish* Marduk does not create light before creating the sun, moon, and stars. Of course, the primordial events concerning the gods do not take place in the dark, but neither do they take place in the earthly realm, in contrast to Genesis, and so the presence of day and night in the realm of the gods is of no relevance. (5) Tiamat's severed corpse and Genesis's firmament are in stark contrast (wholly apart from the fact that Gen 1 does not depict the sky as a solid dome). (6) This claim is mistaken, since there is no "sequence of the days of creation" in the *Enuma elish*. As for the order of events, Marduk first creates the heavens by stretching out Tiamat's skin to keep back the waters, then the abodes for the various gods, then constellations, then the moon, so important for Babylonian astronomical timekeeping, then clouds and rainstorms, then the Euphrates and Tigris Rivers, then the mountains and springs, then the "great bond" and the supports for the heavens, and then he is done. The creation of men as slaves for the gods is a later incident, related after the story of Babylon's creation. This is scarcely similar to the sequence of events in Gen 1. (7) Marduk does not rest after these works are done. Instead, he attaches guide

ropes and hands them over to the god Ea while he goes to the god Anu to deliver the Table of Destinies. The only time he rests is immediately after slaying Tiamat, before undertaking the works just mentioned. The later celebration of the gods, as John Day points out, is not their resting from creative labors but their relaxing after their toilsome duties have been given over to human beings (*From Creation to Babel: Studies in Genesis 1–11*, LHBOTS 592 [London: Bloomsbury, 2013], 17).

I cannot help but wonder how Enns could have so seriously misread the *Enuma elish*. If we may hazard on the path of tradition-historical analysis ourselves, it appears that Enns has simply followed Alexander Heidel, *The Babylonian Genesis: The Story of Creation*, 2nd ed. (Chicago: University of Chicago Press, 1951), 129 (fig. 4.1).

Enuma Elish	Genesis
Divine spirit and cosmic matter are coexistent and coeternal	Divine Spirit creates cosmic matter and exists independently of it
Primeval chaos; Tiamat enveloped in darkness	The earth a desolate waste, with darkness covering the deep (*tehom*)
Light emanating from the gods	Light created
The creation of the firmament	The creation of the firmament
The creation of dry land	The creation of dry land
The creation of the luminaries	The creation of the luminaries
The creation of man	The creation of man
The gods rest and celebrate	God rests and sanctifies the seventh day

Figure 4.1. Heidel's list of similarities between *Enuma elish* and Gen 1.

What is striking is that Enns reproduces *the errors* in Heidel's table of alleged similarities, such as primordial darkness (which Heidel admits is not to be found in the *Enuma elish* [*Babylonian Genesis*, 101] but derives from Berossus, perhaps under the influence of Greek cosmogony) or divine rest following creation. Interestingly, Richard Clifford makes precisely the same indictment of commentator E. A. Speiser, who "simply adopted A. Heidel's chart of the sequence of acts in *Enuma elish* and Genesis 1, assuming it proved borrowing." In fact, "the sequence of events in the two works [is] not truly parallel" (Clifford, *Creation Accounts*, 140).

Heidel admits that "the divergences are much more far-reaching and significant than are the resemblances, most of which are not any closer than what we should expect to find in any two more or less complete creation versions (since both would have to account for the same phenomena and since human minds think along much the same lines) which might come from entirely different parts of the world and which might be utterly unrelated to each other" (*Babylonian Genesis*, 130). Enns acknowledges that the

but that they are simply listed without any consideration of context and are therefore little better than cherry-picking. When the two accounts are read as wholes, they are far from parallel. The *Enuma elish* is only improperly characterized as a Babylonian creation epic; it is actually a panegyric of Marduk explaining his ascendancy to king of the gods. Hence, while the *Enuma elish* may be indirectly relevant to Gen 1, most scholars have abandoned the claim of direct dependence.[6]

The second pitfall in establishing parallelism is the fallacy of *overgeneralization* or *abstraction*. OT scholars engaged in comparative studies very frequently resort to a high degree of descriptive generalization or abstraction in order to make two elements appear parallel. To illustrate this fallacy, I recall the story of two persons, one of whom believed that there are lizards living in Los Angeles and the other of whom believed that there are snakes living in Los Angeles. It was reported that the two agreed that there are reptiles living in Los Angeles.[7] By resorting to a high level of generalization, their divergent viewpoints are suppressed and a pseudosimilarity constructed in their place. Sandmel emphasizes the importance of minding the difference between "an abstract position on the one hand and the specific application on the other." He insists that "it is in the detailed study rather than in the abstract statement that there can emerge persuasive bases for judgment" of parallelism. "The issue for the student is not the abstraction but the specific. Detailed study is the criterion," and the detailed study, he

---

Babylonian and biblical stories have many significant differences, suggesting that something other than simple borrowing has taken place, but he remains guilty of alleging parallels on the basis of listing isolated elements of the narratives without consideration of context.

6. See Brevard S. Childs, *Introduction to the Old Testament as Scripture* (Philadelphia: Fortress, 1979), 26, who observes that Assyriologists no longer regard the *Enuma elish* as so promising a source of comparisons as they once did. Cf. W. G. Lambert's judgment that the *Enuma elish* "is not a norm of Babylonian or Sumerian cosmology. It is a sectarian and aberrant combination of mythological threads woven into an unparalleled compositum. In my opinion it is not earlier than 1100 BC. . . . The various traditions it draws upon are often perverted to such an extent that conclusions based on this text alone are suspect. It can only be used safely in the whole context of ancient Mesopotamian mythology" ("A New Look at the Babylonian Background of Genesis," *JTS*, n.s., 16, no. 2 [1965]: 291; see further W. G. Lambert, "Mesopotamian Creation Stories," in *Imagining Creation*, ed. Markham J. Geller and Mineke Schipper, IJS Studies in Judaica 5 [Leiden: Brill, 2007], 15–59).

7. I heard this story, as I recall, from Robert Adams, then professor of philosophy at UCLA.

reminds us, "ought to respect the context and not be limited to juxtaposing mere excerpts."[8]

As noted, this fallacy is depressingly common among writers on Gen 1–11. A good example is the parallel often drawn between the aquatic plant that restores youth in the *Epic of Gilgamesh* and the tree of life in the Garden of Eden. The obvious difference between a fruit-bearing tree in a garden and a piece of prickly seaweed is suppressed by resorting to a higher level of abstraction and referring to them both as "life-giving plants."[9] Furthermore, the difference between a snake's taking the plant before Gilgamesh can eat it and God's preventing Adam and Eve from eating the fruit of the tree by expelling them from the garden after their yielding to the snake's temptation is suppressed by the abstraction that the action of a snake prevents the relevant person from eating the plant and becoming immortal.[10] The narrative contexts of these abstracted similarities, moreover, are utterly distinct: one a story of the futile quest for immortality and the other the story of man's temptation and disobedience to God.

Daniel Harlow similarly overgeneralizes when he compares the Adapa myth about Adapa's being wrongly advised to refuse to eat the bread of the gods conferring immortality with the account of the fall in Gen 3 because Adam and Adapa are both "commanded about eating and not eating" and each "misses out on the chance for immortality," which he mistakenly takes

8. Sandmel, "Parallelomania," 2. He continues, "Two passages may sound the same in splendid isolation from their context, but when seen in context reflect difference rather than similarity."

9. See, e.g., Gordon J. Wenham, *Genesis 1–15*, WBC 1 (Grand Rapids: Zondervan, 1987), 52; similarly, Sparks, "Genesis 1–11," 125–26. Interestingly, the aquatic plant in the Gilgamesh story does not confer immortality but enables the one who eats it to become young again (A. R. George calls it a "plant of rejuvenation" [*The Babylonian Gilgamesh Epic: Introduction, Critical Edition, and Cuneiform Texts*, 2 vols. (Oxford: Oxford University Press, 2003), 1:522]) on the pattern of a snake's shedding its skin, a motif also found in myths from Oceania (see Alan Dundes's introductory comments on James G. Frazer's fanciful essay on Gen 3, "The Fall of Man," in *Sacred Narrative: Readings in the Theory of Myth*, ed. Alan Dundes [Berkeley: University of California Press, 1984], 72–74, 88–95). Are we to think on the basis of this parallel that the Oceanic myths and the Gilgamesh story are causally connected?

10. Daniel C. Harlow, "After Adam: Reading Genesis in an Age of Evolutionary Science," *PSCF* 62, no. 3 (2010): 183, calls it "immortality being sought but lost because of a serpent"—an overgeneralization that is not even accurate, since Adam and Eve were not seeking immortality before losing it.

to be "the central theme in Genesis 3."[11] Harlow also misleadingly compares Adapa, just one of the Anunnaki, to Adam as "the special creation of the god Ea" as well as being "clothed by Anu with new garments," when it is just a matter of changing his mourning dress, not covering his nakedness. The level of abstraction becomes almost amusing when Benedikt Otzen says that in the Adapa myth "the hero is at least offered something edible."[12]

Another such example is the surprising claim that Adam's role in tilling and keeping the garden is reminiscent of the work assigned to humans in the Sumerian and Babylonian creation myths.[13] This alleged parallel is purchased only at the expense of a level of abstraction that suppresses the difference between slave labor and a sacred and ennobling responsibility entrusted to humanity. Again, it is no less astonishing to find God's creation of Eve as a companion for Adam compared to the gods' creation of the wild man Enkidu as a counterpart to Gilgamesh,[14] a generalization that collapses on closer comparison. Or again, one is amazed to hear it said that "while the biblical Fall finds no counterpart in Babylonia, the provocation of deity leading to the Flood is comparable in general terms."[15] It is precisely this phrase "in

11. Harlow, "After Adam," 183.

12. Benedikt Otzen, "The Use of Myth in Genesis," in *Myths in the Old Testament*, by Benedikt Otzen, Hans Gottlieb, and Knud Jeppesen, trans. Frederick Cryer (London: SCM, 1980), 47.

13. Sparks, "Genesis 1–11," 125–26; Otzen, "Use of Myth," 42. Harlow, "After Adam," 182, compares agriculture by irrigation with Eden's being watered "by irrigation," the Igigi gods as original laborers with Yahweh as the original laborer (he "plants a garden"), and the Anunnaki gods' enjoying privileges of divine right with Yahweh's having "a private garden with magic trees." On the basis of such comparisons Harlow draws the astonishing conclusion that "virtually all of the narrative details in Genesis 2–8 are borrowed from Mesopotamian mythology."

14. Harlow, "After Adam," 183.

15. A. R. Millard, "A New Babylonian 'Genesis' Story," in *"I Studied Inscriptions from before the Flood": Ancient Near Eastern, Literary, and Linguistic Approaches to Genesis 1–11*, ed. Richard S. Hess and David Toshio Tsumura, SBTS 4 (Winona Lake, IN: Eisenbrauns, 1994), 125. Millard maintains that while an equation of mankind's evil conduct in Gen 6 with mankind's bothersome noise in the *Atrahasis Epic* "may appear improbable, the basic idea of disturbing deity is surely common to both narratives as the provocation leading to the decision to send the Flood" (123). Cf. the claim of Longman and Walton, after surveying the various interpretations of the reason for which the gods sent the flood, that "we need not choose among these, because disruption of order characterizes all of them. . . . [A]ll accounts suggest the situation that motivated the gods to send the flood is increasing disorder" (Tremper Longman III and John H. Walton, *The Lost World of the Flood: Mythology, Theology, and the Deluge Debate* [Downers Grove, IL: IVP Academic, 2018], 68). Such overgeneralization masks crucial differences and hinders comparative studies.

general terms" that subverts the comparison by masking the differences between a holy God's indignation with sin and the humanoid deities' grumpy insomnia caused by their annoying human slaves. Once again, a healthy skepticism toward alleged parallels involving such a degree of abstraction seems to be in order.

Establishing further the claim that the alleged parallels are to be explained by dependence of one account on the other is also fraught with difficulties. One problem is that isolated, even if striking, *similarities may exist between two narratives that are independent of one another*.[16] An instructive illustration of the point is Morgan Robertson's novel *The Wreck of the Titan*, published in 1898, fourteen years before the sinking of the *Titanic*. In Robertson's story a great ocean liner, *Titan*, the largest in the world and said to be unsinkable, one night in April strikes an iceberg on her starboard side in the North Atlantic, four hundred nautical miles off Newfoundland. It sinks, and most of its passengers and crew perish in the icy waters owing to a lack of lifeboats. The points of commonality with the sinking of the *Titanic*—there are even more—are quite uncanny. When read in their literary context, they are part of the story of John Rowland, a young deckhand who survives the wreck, is charged with kidnapping a female passenger, is exonerated, drops out of society, and finally reemerges as a successful government civil servant. If one did not know the date of Robertson's novel, one might well surmise that it was a fictional account based on the sinking of the *Titanic*.

In the same way, for example, scholars often point out the similarities between the Garden of Eden and the island of Dilmun in the Sumerian myth *Enki and Ninhursaga*. It is said that Dilmun, like Eden, is an abundantly watered, paradisiacal land, in which all nature is at peace.[17] These similarities are exaggerated and their contexts are wholly different,[18] but waiving

16. There is an analogy in evolutionary biology in so-called convergent evolution, whereby two causal chains arrive at a strikingly similar end product. For example, the closest eye in the animal kingdom to the human eye is the cephalapod eye, which is also a camera eye. Yet obviously, no genealogical connection exists between octopuses and human beings. Similarity alone does not demonstrate causal dependence.

17. Harlow, "After Adam," 182.

18. What is described in Dilmun (which is a habitat not of humans but of the gods) is not so much a paradise as a situation in which the natures of things have not yet been determined. According to the myth,

> In Dilmun the raven uttered no cries,
> The *kite* uttered not the cry of the *kite*,
> The lion killed not,
> The wolf snatched not the lamb,

that, few scholars would think the similarities that can be drawn are best explained by a dependence of the narrative of Gen 2 on the Sumerian story. One suspects that the appeal to *Enki and Ninhursaga* as a basis for Gen 2 is prompted by the fact that the paradise motif is virtually nonexistent in ANE mythology, so that the story mentioning Dilmun is all that we have for a parallel.[19]

A second difficulty in proving dependence arises from taking *an inadequate inductive sample* of texts. The more restrictive one's data class, the more uncertain the inductive inferences based on that class. For example, positive results of clinical trials of hydroxychloroquine in treating the coronavirus during the 2020 pandemic on too small a group of people may have been aberrations when compared to later studies done on a wider sampling.

Similarly, the frequent claim that the primordial darkness and watery deep of Gen 1:2 show the influence of Egyptian creation stories on biblical tradition is rendered uncertain, not merely by the fundamental difference between them,[20] but by the fact that these motifs are so widely disseminated

---

Unknown was the kid-killing dog,
Unknown was the grain-devouring *boar*,
The bird on high . . . not its *young*,
The dove . . . not the head,
The sick-eyed says not, "I am sick-eyed,"
The sick-headed says not, "I am sick-headed,"
Its old woman says not, "I am an old woman."
Its old man says not, "I am an old man,"
Its unwashed maid is not . . . in the city,
He who *crosses* the river utters no . . . ,
The *overseer* does not . . . ,
The singer utters no wail,
By the side of the city he utters no lament.

The lines about the raven and the kite, in particular, suggest a not-yet-fixed primordial condition (at this point in the myth Dilmun does not even have fresh water).

19. J. H. Walton, "Eden, Garden of," in *Dictionary of the Old Testament: Pentateuch*, ed. T. Desmond Alexander and David W. Baker (Downers Grove, IL: InterVarsity Press, 2003), 202–7, contrary to Harlow's assertion, "The Garden of Eden is Genesis' rendition of a widespread motif in ancient Near Eastern literature" ("After Adam," 182).

20. It is important to understand that in the various Egyptian myths, what is at stake is the ancient problem of the One and the Many, as these myths seek to derive multiplicity from a primal monism. (See Erik Hornung's *Conceptions of God in Ancient Egypt: The One and the Many*, trans. John Baines [Ithaca, NY: Cornell University Press, 1982], 66–67, 174–76, which seeks to explain the Egyptian answer to this problem and whose original title in the German, *Der Eine und die Vielen*, is preserved in the English subtitle.) In these myths water and darkness represent the undifferentiated, unbounded Monad from which all

in creation myths. According to K. Numazawa, myths of the world's origin in which earth and sky were originally combined as one, whether as water alone or as a featureless substance or as a cosmic egg, "can be found among practically all peoples," being found, for example, even among North Amer-

---

multiplicity emerges. The god Atum, Hornung explains, "in the beginning was everything, complete in the sense of being an undifferentiated unity" and yet, paradoxically, "at the same time nonexistent" (*Conceptions of God*, 67). The nonexistent signified, negatively, that which is inchoate, undifferentiated, unarticulated, and unlimited or, affirmatively, the entirety of what is possible, the absolute, the fundamental. In comparison with the nonexistent, the existent is clearly defined and articulated by boundaries and distinctions (Hornung, *Conceptions of God*, 183). "The most important positive description of non-existence is limitless waters and total darkness" (Hornung, *Conceptions of God*, 177). Sarna suggests that water seemed to the ancients the appropriate representation of the primordial substance because of its amorphous nature, which appropriately represented the state of affairs before things were given order and stable form (Nahum M. Sarna, *Genesis*, JPSTC [Philadelphia: Jewish Publication Society, 1989], 6).

In contrast to this monistic picture, the state of the primitive earth in Gen 1:2 is not an undifferentiated unity or chaos (despite the careless statements of many commentators), much less nonexistent, but just a primaeval ocean cloaked in darkness. It is not unbounded but exists on the earth, covering the land that will eventually emerge from it and having a surface over which wind is moving (cf. 7:18; 8:1). It is not characterless but is the same water that will eventually fill the seas, in which marine life will thrive, and that will fall from the sky as rain. It is not unordered or chaotic but has the properties of water with which ancient Israelites would have been familiar, such as liquidity, weight, surface tension, buoyancy, solvency, and potability. The primaeval ocean is no more a chaos than is a ravaged landscape, also described as *tōhû wābōhû* (Jer 4:23), i.e., uninhabitable desolation. Tsumura rightly concludes that the phrase "has nothing to do with primeval chaos" but simply refers to the earth as an unproductive and uninhabited place (David Toshio Tsumura, "Genesis and Ancient Near Eastern Stories of Creation and Flood: An Introduction" and "The Earth in Genesis 1" [1989], both in Hess and Tsumura, *"I Studied Inscriptions,"* 33, 310–28; Tsumura, *Creation and Destruction: A Reappraisal of the* Chaoskampf *Theory in the Old Testament* [Winona Lake, IN: Eisenbrauns, 2005], 9–35). Just how wrongheaded it is to call the primaeval state "chaos" is evident from the story of the flood (Gen 7:17–24), which returns the earth to its desolate condition but is obviously not, *pace* many commentators, a state of chaos.

An ancient Israelite would probably have pictured the state described in Gen 1:2 to be like a pitch-black night out on the Mediterranean Sea when no moon and stars were visible, a condition that both seafaring peoples known to Israel (Gen 10) and, during the monarchy, Israeli sailors themselves (1 Kgs 10:22) would have experienced. This state of affairs is wholly unlike the primal, monadic condition envisioned in Egyptian mythology, which is much more akin to Plotinus's One, which is beyond being and from which all multiplicity emanates. Indeed, the primordial state described in Gen 1:2 more closely resembles the primordial condition of the earth portrayed in North American Indian creation stories than in Egyptian myths.

ican Indian tribes.[21] According to these myths, a formless substance existed in primordial darkness until its separation into the earth and sky, which marked the beginning of the universe. Common to nearly all the myths is the idea of utter darkness before the separation of the sky and earth, when light appeared for the first time.[22] Scholars appealing to Egyptian influence on the

21. K. Numazawa, "The Cultural-Historical Background of Myths on the Separation of Sky and Earth," in Dundes, *Sacred Narrative*, 185; for Native American myths, see Alan Dundes, "Earth-Diver: Creation of the Mythopoeic Male," in Dundes, *Sacred Narrative*, 277.

22. Consult the index of the now dated but still useful volumes in Louis Herbert Gray and John Arnott MacCulloch, eds., *The Mythology of All Races*, 13 vols. (1916–33; repr., New York: Cooper Square, 1964). William Fox draws attention to the Orphic story according to which uncreated *Nyx* (night) existed first, regarded as a great black-winged bird hovering over a vast darkness (Gray and MacCulloch, *Mythology of All Races*, vol. 1, *Greek and Roman*, by William Sherwood Fox, 4–5). John MacCulloch reports that among Scandanavian myths "a pre-existing state of darkness, out of which light and life has proceeded, is . . . very widely presupposed" (Gray and MacCulloch, *Mythology of All Races*, vol. 2, *Eddic*, by John Arnott MacCulloch, 201). Greek myths might be thought to evince the influence of Egypt, but this is less plausible for myths from the Far East. According to Uno Holmberg, the idea of a primordial ocean is common to most Asiatic creation myths, the most prolific myth, in many variants, featuring a being diving into the water to bring up earth matter from the depths. The independence from early Christianity of the more primitive, nondualist versions of the myth is shown by "the innumerable stories of similar content gathered among the Indian tribes of North America" (Gray and MacCulloch, *Mythology of All Races*, vol. 4, *Siberian Mythology*, by Uno Holmberg, 313, 326). One Mongolian story tells how in the beginning, when there was as yet no earth and when water covered everything, a lama came down from heaven and stirred the water, creating the land. A similar Japanese story relates how, in the beginning, one of the seven gods of heaven stirred the water to form the islands of Japan. In Africa the Bushongo have a creation myth unparalleled elsewhere in Africa, which exhibits features "surprisingly suggestive of Genesis 1," such as a solitary Creator existing in the beginning with nothing else but water (Alice Werner, "African Mythology," in Gray and MacCulloch, *Mythology of All Races*, vol. 7, *Armenian and African*, 144). Among South American tribes, we find the myth of the northern Andean Chibcha, who believe that in the beginning all was darkness, since light was imprisoned in the house of Chiminigagua, the supreme Lord of all things, who then created the sun, moon, and the rest of the universe (Gray and MacCulloch, *Mythology of All Races*, vol. 11, *Latin-American*, by Hartley Burr Alexander, 199). Creation myths featuring primaeval darkness or water, or both, may also be found among the Atlantic coastal Guaraní people and their descendants the Guarayú (Alfred Métraux, "The Guaraní" and "The Guarayú and Pauserna," in *Handbook of South American Indians*, ed. Julian H. Steward, vol. 3, *The Tropical Forest Tribes* [Washington, DC: Smithsonian Institution and United States Government Printing Office, 1948], 92–94, 436–38). Even among the South Pacific islanders one finds the myth of primordial darkness (Martha Beckwith, *Hawaiian Mythology* [New Haven: Yale University Press, 1940], 312).

Genesis creation account have often failed to inquire just how widespread the favorite motif is among the world's peoples.

Myths tap deeply into the human psyche, and so we should not be surprised to find that similar myths, whether by polygenesis or convergence, exist among unrelated peoples throughout the world.[23] In order to demonstrate causal connection among myths, it will be necessary to exclude the possibility that similar myths arose independently, which is difficult to do. Minimally, the theorist engaged in comparative studies of Gen 1–11 needs to widen his comparison class beyond the myths that have a possible causal connection with the primaeval narrative so as to be sure that a genealogical connection, rather than mere similarity, truly exists.[24] The need to do so is especially urgent when the similarities are isolated elements in vastly different contexts like monistic Egyptian theogonies.

The final challenge, more tractable than the foregoing but nonetheless worth mentioning, is demonstrating *the direction of asymmetrical dependence*. Palaeoanthropologists confront such a problem in trying to reconstruct the course of human evolution. It is evident that connections exist between the various hominins whose remains have been discovered, but, as we shall see, establishing the lines of dependence between forms is difficult and controversial.

Similarly, the relation of the biblical account of the flood and the flood story in the *Epic of Gilgamesh* (tablet XI) has been a matter of considerable controversy. Forty years after the height of the Babel-Bible controversy, Gerhard von Rad could confidently report that the dossier on the relation of the biblical story to the Babylonian story "is more or less closed. A material relationship between both versions exists, of course, but a direct dependence of

23. Noting that the themes in the biblical story of primaeval events occur in the myths of unrelated African peoples, Westermann comments, "The ways in which people of all places and at all times are going to present the origin of humanity and the universe or of the present state of the world . . . are relatively few. And so there will be many similarities even though direct influence is excluded" (*Genesis 1–11*, 5; cf. 20). Cf. Alan Dundes's observation that "there are not so many myths in the world. . . . In contrast there are many, many more folktales. For every ten myths there are probably several hundred folktales. Yet however many folktales there may be, they do not compare in numbers with the abundance of legends" (introductory comments to William Bascom, "The Forms of Folklore: Prose Narratives," in Dundes, *Sacred Narrative*, 6).

24. See, e.g., Stith Thompson, *Motif-Index of Folk-Literature: A Classification of Narrative Elements in Folktales, Ballads, Myths, Fables, Mediaeval Romances, Exempla, Fabliaux, Jest-Books, and Local Legends*, rev. ed., 6 vols. (Bloomington: Indiana University Press, 1955).

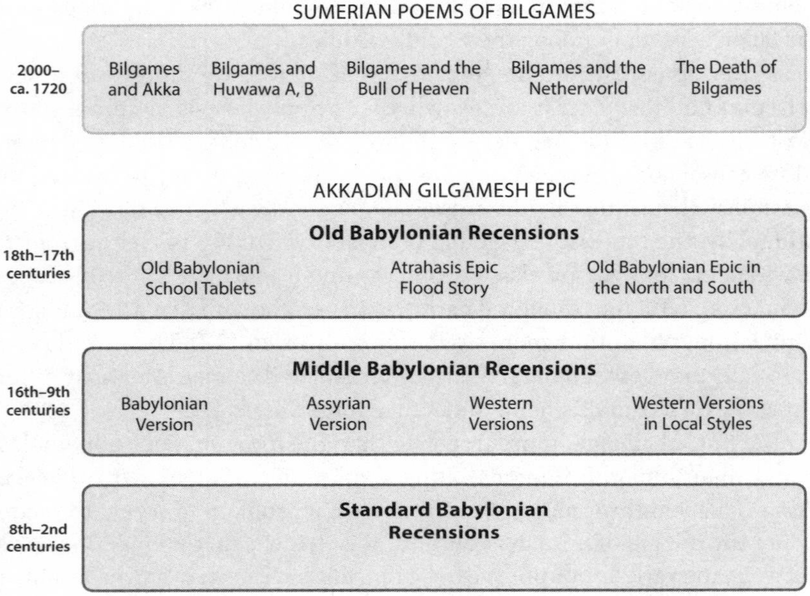

Figure 4.2. Evolution of the *Epic of Gilgamesh*.

the biblical tradition on the Babylonian is no longer assumed."[25] Rather, both versions, he says, are independent arrangements of a still older tradition.

Like many, von Rad thought that the flood story contained in the *Epic of Gilgamesh* may have stemmed from the Sumerian flood story, a story that is wholly independent of the hero Gilgamesh (or, rather, Bilgamesh), who is the subject of several Sumerian epic poems, which reach back to the third millenium BC.[26] None of the five Sumerian poems about Gilgamesh contains the flood story. Indeed, neither did the early versions of the Gilgamesh epic. The *Epic of Gilgamesh* evolved over the course of the second millennium in Akkadian through Old, Middle, and finally Standard Babylonian versions, during which time it absorbed traditions from around the ANE, the sources of which remain largely unknown (fig. 4.2).[27]

25. Gerhard von Rad, *Genesis: A Commentary*, rev. ed., OTL (Louisville: Westminster John Knox, 1972), 123–24.

26. For an account, see George, *Babylonian Gilgamesh Epic*, vol. 1, pt. 1.1: "The Literary History of the Epic of Gilgameš."

27. See the account by A. R. George, the editor of the critical edition of the *Epic of*

Neither the Old Babylonian nor the Middle Babylonian version of the Gilgamesh epic includes the flood story, although the latter version mentions its immortal survivor. The Standard version of the Gilgamesh epic, which does include the account of the flood, was established by a Babylonian redactor named Sin-leqi-unninni of uncertain date but probably somewhere around the turn of the first millenium BC. The flood story of tablet XI has been recognized to be, not a derivation from the Sumerian flood story, but "a straightforward and sometimes verbatim adaptation" of part of the recently recovered Babylonian *Atrahasis Epic*.[28] A. R. George expresses his "subjective view" that it was Sin-leqi-unninni who interpolated the flood story of *Atrahasis* into the Gilgamesh epic and made major changes to the epic. What we do not know is the extent to which the text we read today is Sin-leqi-unninni's or whether further significant changes were made to his text.[29] The existence of textual variants in manuscripts of the Standard version from the first millennium may suggest that other unknown redactors have left their mark as well.

While acknowledging that the flood stories of Genesis and the *Epic of Gilgamesh* need not be connected, W. G. Lambert thinks that the episode of the release of the birds from the ark in Gen 8:6–12 is so close to the parallel passage in the eleventh chapter of the *Epic of Gilgamesh* that "no doubt exists" of a connection between them. There are differences in the two accounts concerning the birds. In the Genesis account Noah sends out two birds: first a raven, which does not return, then a dove on three separate occasions. The third time it fails to return. In *Gilgamesh* Utnapishtim sends out successively a dove, a swallow, and a raven, each bird one time, in that order. The dove and the swallow return, but when the raven does not, he disembarks. Still, despite these differences, the similarities are such that the two accounts are plausibly related.

But is this a case of Hebrew borrowing? The ancient flood story in the *Atrahasis Epic* makes no mention of the release of the birds, although this is a feature of the Standard Gilgamesh epic. Lambert notes that the flood story is a late interpolation into the Gilgamesh epic attested no earlier than 750 BC. Only the Babylonian priest Berossus, about 300 BC, mentions the birds in his account of the flood story.[30] If the biblical traditions of the flood

---

Gilgamesh, "Shattered Tablets and Tangled Threads: Editing Gilgamesh, Then and Now," *Aramazd* 3, no. 1 (2008): 7–30, https://eprints.soas.ac.uk/7497/.

28. George, "Shattered Tablets," 18.

29. George, *Babylonian Gilgamesh Epic*, 32.

30. See *The "Babyloniaca" of Berossus*, ed. Stanley Mayer Burstein, SANE 1/5 (Malibu,

are preexilic, then Hebrew borrowing becomes much less likely. Although Lambert admits that the biblical flood story is older than the earliest surviving testimony to the Babylonian parallel of the birds,[31] he holds that there is "certain dependence" of the Hebrew writers on Mesopotamian tradition.

Lambert provides two reasons for this conclusion. First, we have copies of the earlier Sumerian flood stories from about 1800 BC, "which virtually excludes any possible Amorite influence in the initial formation of the Mesopotamian tradition."[32] The emphasis here seems to be on the word *initial*: given the age of the Sumerian flood traditions, the advent of the Amorites at the end of the third millennium BC comes too late to initiate formation of the Mesopotamian tradition. Thus, Lambert concludes, priority lies on the Mesopotamian side. It is not clear, however, how this argument is relevant to the inclusion of the episode of the birds in the flood story, an episode that came as a much later modification of the Mesopotamian tradition.

Lambert's second reason is simply that "it is inconceivable that the Hebrews as such influenced the development of Babylonian epics."[33] Presumably the point here is that a tiny and primitive nomadic culture could hardly have exerted a significant influence on the literature of a mighty civilization like Babylon. But the Gilgamesh epic is already an agglomeration of traditions from around the ANE,[34] so why could not a borrowing of the episode

CA: Undena, 1978), bk. 2.2.2 (p. 20). Berossus does not specify the kinds or number of the birds and has them released all at once three times.

31. Lambert argues that the traditions codified in Gen 1–11 had been long established in Israel, forcing one back at least to the period of the Judges ("New Look," 299).

32. Lambert, "New Look," 292.

33. Lambert, "New Look," 292.

34. Cf. Lambert's remarks about how widespread Mesopotamian literature became during the Amarna period, with pieces of the *Epic of Gilgamesh* showing up in Megiddo and *Atrahasis* in Ras Shamra, and about the cultural activities of the Hurrians, who were great borrowers from all the peoples among which they moved and settled ("New Look," 299–300). Is it so inconceivable that, as the Mesopotamian traditions migrated westward, there a was a reflex influence of Israelite flood traditions on some of the varying local Babylonian renditions? Cf. George's interesting remarks on the alleged influence of the *Epic of Gilgamesh* on Homer and other Greek literature:

> ancient poets had . . . a fund of familiar episodes and standard passages on which they might draw as they pleased. It is highly probable in a world where musicians, scholars, and other experts are known to have traveled internationally that many staple motifs and patterns of narrative would have been held in common by poets composing in various different ancient Near Eastern languages. . . . The influence of these texts on indigenous culture cannot accurately be gauged, but was certainly considerable enough to generate new versions and paraphrases in some of the

of the birds from Hebrew tradition be possible? Perhaps an influence of Hebrew traditions about the birds on the Babylonian redactor (or redactors) is not inconceivable during Solomonic times, when Israel had extensive international connections.

Noting that Israelites would have better knowledge of maritime customs than the landlocked Assyrians, David Freedman has argued for the priority of the Genesis account on the grounds that the order in which the birds are released supports the priority of the Hebrew account. He cites references in ancient literature to show that mariners used ravens to guide them to land (Callimachus, *Hymns* 2.66; Strabo, *Geography* 17.43; Scholiast to Aristophanes's "Clouds" no. 134, line 123). Doves could be used to guide mariners through straits to the open sea (Appollonius Rhodius, *Argonauticae* 2.317–407, 528–610) or to gauge the weather (Plutarch, *Moralia de Sollertia Animalium* 13.968f). Nautical custom would dictate sending the raven first, as in Genesis. The dove would be better suited for finding out if land is habitable. "The order of the biblical version, therefore, is in complete accord with maritime practice, whereas the Akkadian mention of dove-swallow-raven obscures the original motif."[35]

George, however, claims that M. I. West has supplied evidence from Ceylon and Iceland for mariners' use of doves to find landfall (Pliny, *Natural History* 6.24.83, and the Icelandic saga *Landnámabók* 2).[36] But George has

> languages written locally. A similar outcome was surely seen in oral literature, as Levantine poets assimilated the new forms and adapted them to their own purposes. Influence was also felt in the opposite direction and in other periods. Mythologems stemming from the Levant are already visible in Babylonia of the early second millennium. Some can be detected in the Gilgameš epic (George, *Babylonian Gilgamesh Epic*, 56–57).

It is intriguing that Gilgamesh himself was not forgotten among Jews in the post-cuneiform period. George notes that in the fragments of the Book of Giants from Qumran (4Q530 frags. 2 ii+, 1–2) he surfaces as Gilgamesh (*glgmys*), one of the antediluvian race of evil giants that in Jewish mythology were spawned by the fallen angels described in Gen 6:1–4 (*Babylonian Gilgamesh Epic*, 60). One wonders, then, why, if the Genesis flood narrative is borrowed from the Gilgamesh epic, Gilgamesh is not mentioned somewhere in Genesis.

35. R. David Freedman, "The Dispatch of the Reconnaissance Birds in Gilgamesh XI," *JANESCU* 5 (1973): 124. "Dove(s), swallow(s), raven(s)" are also mentioned in that order, along with other birds, in a nonflood context in the text K. 1520; but Wasserman thinks that the text may well be dependent on *Gilgamesh* XI (Nathan Wasserman, *The Flood: The Akkadian Sources* [Leuven: Peeters, 2020)], 148).

36. George, *Babylonian Gilgamesh Epic*, 517, citing M. I. West, *East Face of Helicon* (Oxford: Oxford University Press, 1997), 492n162.

evidently misinterpreted West's phrase "for this as a practice of sailors" to refer, not to the release of *birds* "to check whether any land was within reach," but to the release of *doves* for that purpose. For Pliny does not speak of doves but more generally of birds (*volucres*); and the Icelandic saga speaks of the release of three ravens by the Viking sailor Floki to lead him to land. These references thus confirm Freedman's argument.

George thinks that more to Freedman's point is the fact that it is in the nature of doves to return but of ravens to fly away, which would mandate releasing the raven before the dove, not afterward. Similarly, Jonathan Sarfati observes that as a carrion feeder, the raven is apt to fly off and not return, since it could find food among the swollen carcasses of animals killed in the flood. So it ought not to be sent out last, as in the Babylonian account; and if sent off first, as in the Genesis account, further reconnaissance with doves would be necessary.[37]

George rejects Freedman's argument for the priority of the Genesis account because he is persuaded that the episode of the birds serves an etiological purpose: doves, swallows, and ravens behave as they do because their habits were conditioned by the different fortunes of the three birds released after the flood. The Western inheritors of the Babylonian story, "missing the etiology entirely," left out the swallow and confused the birds' order and so "failed to appreciate the motif to the full."[38] It is difficult, however, to discern any hint of an etiological motif such as George alleges in the Babylonian account:

> I brought out a dove, setting it free:
> off went the dove. . . .
> No perch was available for it and it came back to [me].
> I brought out a swallow, setting it free:
> off went the swallow. . . .
> No perch was available for it and it came back to me.
> I brought out a raven, setting it free:
> off went the raven and it saw the waters receding.
> It was eating, bobbing up and down, it did not come back to me.
> (XI.148–56)

37. Jonathan D. Sarfati, *The Genesis Account: A Theological, Historical, and Scientific Commentary on Genesis 1–11* (Powder Springs, GA: Creation Book Publishers, 2015), 508.
38. George, *Babylonian Gilgamesh Epic*, 517.

There is no suggestion that the nature of swallows, doves, and ravens is determined by their finding no perch or by finding something to eat.[39] Rather, the Genesis narrative seems to exhibit greater verisimilitude in its account of the release of the birds, just as it does in its description of the configuration of the ark, an apparently viable ship, in contrast to the nautical disaster described in *Gilgamesh*.

Rather, my reservation with this line of argument is that verisimilitude could well be indicative of a later, derivative account, which seeks to improve on the earlier, defective account. Once again, we see how difficult it is to determine lines of causal influence.

Lambert's point conceded, however, he argues that there are only two ways to avoid Hebrew borrowing.[40] The first way is to posit a common source from which both the Hebrew and Babylonian traditions derive, such as an independent Amorite flood tradition. Lambert rejoins, "I can think of

39. It must be said that George evinces a proclivity to finding etiological motifs where none seems to exist—for instance, in seeing in the passage

> At 120 double-furlongs Gilgameš ran out of punting poles,
> then he undid his clothing.
> Gilgameš stripped off [his] garment,
> out of his arms he made a high yard-arm. (X.181–83)

an etiology of sailing ships; or in Gilgamesh's tying weights to his feet to sink down to retrieve the plant of rejuvenation (XI.6) "an etiology of seabed diving"!

40. Cf. John Day's response to the view that the biblical flood account and the Mesopotamian account are both dependent on a common earlier tradition or event. Bearing in mind that the Mesopotamian tradition is much earlier, he says, "This supposition is unwarranted and reflects the logical fallacy known as positing entities beyond necessity" (*From Creation to Babel*, 110). This perfunctory appeal to Ockham's Razor to settle a question of textual dependence is rather startling. Ockham's Razor is but a guideline, and simplicity is not the only or even most important criterion of explanatory adequacy. What NT scholar, for example, would reject the existence of Q merely on the grounds that it posits entities beyond necessity in comparison with the hypothesis that Luke used Matthew? Far more important would be evidence supporting Luke's use of Matthew, such as Mattheanisms in Luke. Similarly, what is wanted in this case is evidence for the biblical traditions' use of *Gilgamesh* or, as Day thinks, *Atrahasis*. Apart from the episode of the birds (which is not extant in *Atrahasis*), the evidence is slim indeed. Ironically, Day's insistence that we compare, not the canonical story, but the separate J and P versions of the flood story to Mesopotamian stories diminishes the best evidence of dependence. For in the J account of the flood a dove is sent out three times, whereas in the P account Noah sends out a raven once, which does not return. Neither of these accounts resembles the episode of the birds in *Gilgamesh* as closely as the canonical account.

no refutation of such a view, though it seems most improbable to me."[41] This is a curious response coming from Lambert, who had earlier complained of such scholarly assertions "as 'it is generally admitted' (which means that no one has ever proved) and 'there is no convincing reason against' (which patently confesses the lack of conclusive reasons for)."[42] Similarly, in the absence of refutation, Lambert's assertion confesses the lack of conclusive reasons against.

Recently, Guy Darshan has claimed that the decipherment of a new Akkadian text from Ugarit (RS 94.2953) published by Daniel Arnaud in 2007[43] disproves the claim of Hebrew borrowing in favor of a common source behind both traditions.[44] The fourteen-line fragment, dated to circa 1250 BC, is a first-person account of how Ea appears at the bedside of the story's protagonist (name unknown) and commands him to cut a window. Arnaud interpreted the text to be an Akkadian version of the story of the installation of a window in Baal's temple known from the Ugaritic Baal Epic (KTU 1.4 vii 14–28), and scholars have tended to accept this suggestion in whole or in part. But Antoine Cavigneaux suggests a number of emendations to the text,[45] which Darshan then translates as follows:

> At the time of the disappearance of the moon, at the beginning of the month, Ea, the great lord, stood at my side (saying:) "Take a wooden spade and a copper axe and make a window at the top. Release a bird and it will find the shore for you!" I heeded the words of Ea, my great lord and advisor. I took a wooden spade and a copper axe. I made a window at the top above me. I released a dove—strong of wings. It went forth and came back. It exhausted her wings. I did the same again and released a water-bird (pelican?).

Following Cavigneaux, Darshan takes the text to be part of a distinctive version of the flood story circulating in western Asia during the second half

41. Lambert, "New Look," 292.

42. Lambert, "New Look," 291.

43. Daniel Arnaud, *Corpus des textes de bibliothèque de Ras Shamra-Ougarit (1936–2000) en sumérien, babylonien et assyrien* (Barcelona: Editorial AUSA, 2007), 201–2.

44. Guy Darshan, "The Motif of Releasing Birds in ANE Flood Stories," TheTorah.com, 2017, https://thetorah.com/the-motif-of-releasing-birds-in-ane-flood-stories. Cf. Guy Darshan, "The Calendrical Framework of the Priestly Flood Story in Light of an Akkadian Text from Ugarit (RS 94.2953)," *JAOS* 136 (2016): 507–14.

45. Antoine Cavigneaux, "Les oiseaux de l'arche," *AO* 25, no. 2 (2007): 319–20.

of the second millennium BC and known by the biblical accounts via oral transmission. Darshan concludes that "the possibility that the bird motif was a late addition to the story can now be put to rest."[46]

This is, however, a bold conclusion. The identification of RS 94.2953 as a fragment of a flood story is predicated on alleged parallels without a context, parallels that depend, moreover, on Cavigneaux's thoroughgoing emendations of the text.[47] Even if we accept that the text speaks of birds rather than temple works with Arnaud's reading, we know that release of birds through windows occurs in other than maritime contexts.[48] Nathan Wasserman finds a parallel in *Epic of Gilgamesh* XI.137, where Utnapishtim recounts, "I opened an air vent and the sunshine fell on my cheek."[49] But Utnapishtim's air hole (*nappašu*; cf. *napāšum* [v.], "to breathe") is not the same thing as a window (*aptum*) in RS 94.2953, nor is the air vent for the release of the birds. Noah has a window in his ark (Gen 8:6; cf. 6:16), but it is not cut as an afterthought but built during construction of the boat. Against the assumption that RS 94.2953 belongs to a flood story rather than the Baal Epic is the fact that a spade and axe, though suitable for a temple's stucco walls, are hardly appropriate for opening a window in a wooden boat. Darshan must construe the expression "spade and axe" (*marra ù ḫaṣṣinna*) as a hendiadys meaning merely "tools," a construal that glosses over the specific nature of the implements as a *wooden* spade and a *copper* axe.[50] Moreover, we might wonder how the disappearance or nonvisibility of the moon could be evident to someone shut inside a boat.[51] It may also be worth noting

46. Darshan, "Motif of Releasing Birds."

47. Cavigneaux's reading is radically different than Arnaud's, which includes no mention of the release of birds at all, not to speak of finding the shore. Even more recently, Nathan Wasserman offers further minor emendations of Cavigneaux's text and takes RS 94.2953 to be a flood story (Wasserman, *Flood*, 87–90). Neither scholar attempts to justify his preferred reading.

48. See text CT 17, 22:140–46, cited in Freedman, "Dispatch of the Reconnaissance Birds," 125.

49. Wasserman, *Flood*, 89.

50. So also Wasserman, *Flood*, 89. Neither Darshan nor Wasserman is able to supply examples in Akkadian of such an idiom.

51. In response to the worry that Noah (NB!), shut inside the ark, would not have been able to tell that it was the time of the new moon, Cavigneaux proposes that he used a sand hourglass to count the days! Wasserman notes that the Old Babylonian versions mention the day of the new moon as the date of *the beginning* of the flood, while RS 94.2953 states that it is the day on which Ea commands Utnapishtim to cut a window to release a bird—i.e., when the flood was *almost over*.

that the release of a water bird (whether a pelican or crane) last in order to find land is even more inept, for obvious reasons, than the sequence of dove-swallow-raven in the *Epic of Gilgamesh*. In any case, if RS 94.2953 is a fragment of a flood story, its genealogical relation to the *Epic of Gilgamesh* and the biblical flood story remains yet to be established, as the case of the Sumerian flood story reminds us. Nonetheless, RS 94.2953 shows that the possibility of a common source behind the Hebrew and Babylonian flood stories is more than mere conjecture.

The second way to escape Hebrew borrowing, Lambert says, is to maintain that the Hebrew and Babylonian accounts go back to the event itself. Lambert finds this alternative "unacceptable," but he does not explain why.[52] By contrast, other scholars have hypothesized that the Hebrew and Mesopotamian traditions could be independent versions originally inspired by a historic flood of great magnitude,[53] though this hypothesis would not explain the late appearance of the episode of the birds in the Gilgamesh epic.

Lambert's final argument for Hebrew borrowing is that the flood stories are connected respectively with the long-reigning, antediluvian Sumerian kings and the long-lived, antediluvian Hebrew patriarchs, also a case of Hebrew borrowing. Again, this argument is curious coming from Lambert, for earlier he had criticized S. R. Driver for claiming that the dependence of the flood story on a Babylonian original lent confirmation to the similar dependence of the creation account: "This amounts to saying that even though the case for the creation narrative is dubious, the better case of the flood can be

52. Lambert, "New Look," 292. Lambert promises to explain the reasons later, but so far as I can tell, he did not return to the topic.

53. For example, Nahum Sarna thinks that the biblical account is "an independent Israelite version that is nevertheless closely related to the Mesopotamian traditions" and that "a single historic event," such as the catastrophic flood known to have occurred in Shuruppak around 2900 BC, "inspired the original composition" (*Genesis*, 48–49). Sparks also thinks that there could be a historical event behind the differing flood stories, such as the deluge that may have flooded the Black Sea area when the Mediterranean broke through the Bosporus Straits around 5600 BC ("Genesis 1–11," 131). Equally provocative is the suggestion that the flood may have occurred when the Indian Ocean submerged the Persian Gulf basin at the end of the last ice age about 10,000 BC, as glacial melting raised sea levels dramatically, sending floodwaters through the Straits of Hormuz (Ward E. Sanford, "Thoughts on Eden, the Flood, and the Persian Gulf," *NACG* 7 [1999]: 7–10). Recent studies among Australian Aborigines and other tribal peoples have shown that oral traditions accurately describing sea level rises that formed offshore islands have been preserved for an astonishing ten thousand years (John Upton, "Ancient Sea Rise Tale Told Accurately for 10,000 Years," *Sci. Am.*, January 26, 2015, https://www.scientificamerican.com/article/ancient-sea-rise-tale-told-accurately-for-10-000-years).

used to prove it, a very debatable procedure."[54] Indeed, and since Hebrew borrowing in the case of the kings and patriarchs is more doubtful than in the case of the flood, Lambert's procedure is even more debatable. In any case, the view that the flood story in *Gilgamesh* derives from the Sumerian flood story is now disfavored, as we have seen.

Whatever one thinks of the question of asymmetrical Hebrew borrowing, our discussion here shows how difficult it can be to establish causal dependence between parallel narratives and the sort of careful argument that needs to be offered.

Common Themes and Etiology

We are inquiring whether Gen 1–11 exhibits the seventh family resemblance of myths that we have identified—to wit, do the primaeval narratives seek to anchor realities present to the pentateuchal author, such as the world, humankind, natural phenomena, cultural practices, and the prevailing cult, in a primordial time? We have seen that the resemblance of the primaeval narratives to myths is not best argued on the basis of their alleged dependence on such myths. Rather, we should explore the degree to which they share an interest in the grand themes of myths and in etiology characteristic of myths.

Genesis 1–11 shares with myths in general and the ANE myths in particular the grand etiological themes of *the origins of the world, of mankind, of certain natural phenomena, of cultural practices,* and *of the prevailing cult.* Of these, Samuel Noah Kramer has observed that "the most significant myths of a given culture are usually the cosmogonic, or creation myths."[55]

54. Lambert, "New Look," 288. Lambert later admits, "The differences are indeed so great that direct borrowing of a literary form of Mesopotamian traditions is out of the question" (299).

55. Samuel Noah Kramer, *Sumerian Mythology: A Study of Spiritual and Literary Achievement in the Third Millennium B.C.*, rev. ed. (New York: Harper & Row, 1961), 30. Westermann agrees, observing that stories of the creation of the world and of mankind are spread over the whole earth, and no other statement about a god or God has such a broad geographical and chronological dissemination (*Genesis 1–11*, 19). After distinguishing between myths of beginning and myths of creation, Westermann identifies four main types of creation myth outside Israel: creation by birth, creation through struggle, creation as fashioning, and creation through utterance. Technically, the first of these are not myths of creation but myths of beginning, typically of the gods themselves. Only the latter two types are found in Genesis.

Origin of the World

Genesis 1 is obviously an etiological account of *the origin of the world* through God's creative activity. As such it is spectacularly different from the cosmic etiologies of Israel's neighbors. In contrast to Babylonian and Egyptian myths, there is neither theogony nor theomachy in Genesis; rather, "In the beginning God created the heavens and the earth" (Gen 1:1). All of physical reality is brought into being by an unoriginate and transcendent Deity.[56] Over the ensuing six days the world is filled out by God's effortless creation of day and night, of the sky with waters above and below, of dry land and seas, of vegetation, of the heavenly luminaries, of marine life and birds, of terrestrial animals, and finally of humans. "Thus the heavens and the earth were finished, and all the host of them" (Gen 2:4). The creation narrative grounds the world with its various familiar creatures and phenomena in the primordial creative work of God.

Origin of Humanity

In Gen 2 we have an etiological account of *the origin of humanity* that supplements the brief notice of mankind's creation in 1:26–27. Contrary to earlier scholarly assertions that we have here a creation account that differs from the creation story in Gen 1, Westermann has rightly distinguished between myths of the origin of the world and myths of the origin of mankind.[57] The latter are plentiful in the ANE and are distinct from cosmogonic accounts.[58] For example, humans are often treated as later creations of the gods for the purpose of relieving the minor deities of the backbreaking labor of digging irrigation canals. In the *Atrahasis Epic* I.1–49 the minor deities are said to have labored for thousands of years before finally rebelling against their overseers, necessitating the creation of man to take over their labors. In the *Enuma elish* Ea does not create man (VI.33–36) until much later than Marduk's creation of the cosmos from Tiamat's bisected corpse (IV.136–V.65). That Gen 2 is not a cosmogony is evident from the fact that it contains no description of God's creation of cosmic features like the sun, moon, and stars. Rather, it seeks to relate God's creation of humanity.

56. See *infra*, pp. 68, 75.

57. Westermann, *Genesis 1–11*, 25–26, 35; so also Sarna, *Genesis*, 16.

58. In Mesopotamia, see, e.g., "The Creation of Humanity"; *Atrahasis Epic* I.204–30; *Enki and Ninmah* 24–37; *Song of the Hoe* 19–20; *Enuma elish* VI.1–44. In Egypt, see *The Instruction of King Merikarē* 130–34 and the *Hymn to Khnum*.

The story in Gen 2 is thus best understood as the pentateuchal author's attempt to supplement the brief notice of mankind's creation in Gen 1.[59] Whereas in Gen 1 we are given a panoramic view of creation, including mankind, in Gen 2 we have a focused account of the creation of humanity on day 6 of Gen 1.[60] Although some scholars have suggested reading the account of man's creation in Gen 2 diachronically or sequentially rather than synchronically in relation to the creation of man on day 6 in Gen 1, such an interpretation is less plausible than the synchronic view. The motivation for the sequential reading is to allow for the existence of a considerable human population prior to and contemporaneous with the specially created couple Adam and Eve. This motivation looks suspiciously concordist, arising from concerns about palaeoanthropology and population genetics. There is little in the text that would lead us to think that the events of Gen 1 and 2 regarding man's creation are nonidentical, much less separated by eons of time.[61]

59. See Sarna, *Genesis*, 16–17, who comments that the passage is not a cosmogonic account but is simply a description of the initial, barren state of the earth after the formation of dry land, which was recorded in 1:9–10. The earth is still a desert, lacking rain, verdure, and humankind.

60. The distinction between a panoramic account and a focused account is suggested by Paul Copan and Douglas Jacoby, *Origins: The Ancient Impact and Modern Implications of Genesis 1–11* (New York: Morgan James, 2019). Similarly, Tsumura, "Genesis and Ancient Near Eastern Stories of Creation and Flood," 27–29, who calls the relationship between the two chapters a "scope change."

61. The only evidence of people not descended from Adam and Eve arises from the old question of where Cain's wife came from (Gen 4:17) and who it was that Cain feared (4:14). But it may be that the pentateuchal author assumed that she was his sister and that his blood avenger (*gōʾēl haddām*) would be a kinsman; or even more plausibly, as Sarna, *Genesis*, 31, suggests, that the pentateuchal author was using an independent tradition about Cain and no more cared to iron out the apparent inconsistency with his earlier story than he did with regard to the creation of the animals and birds after/before mankind's creation in chaps. 1 and 2. "The Yahwist has thus failed to integrate the story properly into its current context" (Day, *From Creation to Babel*, 38; cf. 59). Notice that the apparent inconsistency between chaps. 1 and 2 presses just as hard on a sequential reading of the text, since animals, like other people, would on that account have existed long before Adam and Eve were created and placed in the garden.

John Walton also finds support for a sequential reading in the fact that no precedent exists in the other *tôlədôt* formulae for thinking that the introductory formula in Gen 2:4 is bringing the reader back into the middle of the previous account to give a more detailed description of a part of the story that was previously told (John H. Walton, *The Lost World of Adam and Eve: Genesis 2–3 and the Human Origins Debate* [Downers Grove, IL: IVP Academic, 2015], 66). This argument is misconceived. Virtually all critical scholars agree that the traditions underlying chaps. 1 and 2 were independent, so that the appearance of

On the contrary, there are three reasons for thinking that what is described in Gen 2 is the original creation of mankind. First, the purpose of the primaeval narratives of Gen 1–11 is to portray God's universal plan for and dealings with humankind. Scholars have often asked why the Pentateuch does not begin with the call of Abraham and the founding of Israel in Gen 12. Commentators seem widely agreed that the reason the author prefixes the prehistory to the patriarchal narratives is his universalizing interest.[62] He wants to show that God's original plan was to bless all mankind and that this aim still remains ultimately in mind through the election of Israel, which is now God's means of fulfilling his original intent. "Remove these elements,

---

a recapitulation is the result of the author's conjoining the two accounts. The question is whether in the author's mind the account in chap. 2 gives a more detailed account of the creation of humanity in chap. 1 or is really an account of a later, different act of creation. Walton's appeal to an unprecedented function of the *tôlədôt* formula of 2:4 (1) assumes, improbably I think, that the formula is forward-looking rather than a summary of what has gone before (see *infra*, pp. 134–35); (2) fails to reckon with the diversity of roles played by the *tôlədôt* formulae (see *infra*, p. 135); (3) is diminished in force by the presence of chronological recursions elsewhere in the primaeval history—e.g., in the Tower of Babel story's coming after the *tôlədôt* formula introducing the Table of Nations (see Longman and Walton, *Lost World of the Flood*, 123–24); and (4) fails to appreciate that no precedent also exists in the other *tôlədôt* formulae for a *tôlədôt* that does not concern a personal name, so that 2:4 is unprecedented in any case. The uniqueness of 2:4 is especially unsurprising if, as many think, the original *tôlədôt* book began at 5:1 and the *tôlədôt* of 2:4 is a redactional construction.

62. For example, von Rad comments that in the sacred history beginning with the patriarchs we have "the answer to the unsolved question of primeval history, the question about the relation of God to all peoples" (*Genesis*, 24). Westermann deems it illegitimate to subordinate the universal history to the salvation history of Israel. "As creator, God stands in a relationship to people outside Israel throughout the whole of the history of humankind, in a relationship to the whole world, all of whose being and powers he has created and sustained" (Westermann, *Genesis 1–11*, 605). The attempt to interpret Gen 1–11 in terms of only salvation history must be abandoned, he concludes, because the object of the primaeval event is humankind and the world, whereas the object of salvation history is only the people of God. Wenham points out that the focus narrows progressively throughout Genesis: the origin of the world, the origins of the nations, the origins of Israel. The opening chapters have a universal perspective dealing with all mankind, while chaps. 12–50 deal almost exclusively with Israelite concerns (Wenham, *Genesis 1–15*, xxi–xxii). Wenham identifies two ways in which Gen 1–11 gives the background to the call of Abraham: (1) it discloses the hopeless plight of mankind without the gracious intervention of God; (2) it shows how the promises made to the patriarchs of land, nationhood, the presence of God, and blessing to the nations fulfill God's original plans for humanity (*Genesis 1–15*, li).

and the coherence of the book as a whole disappears."[63] God was not therefore preoccupied with just the offspring of one specially created human couple to the neglect of everyone else, a sort of pre-Israelite election, but with all mankind. Second, a comparison of the story of the creation of man in Gen 2 with other ANE creation stories shows that such stories share an etiological interest in telling how mankind in general came to exist.[64] For example, in the *Atrahasis Epic*, in response to protests and rebellion of the lesser gods over their burdensome labors, the mother goddess decides to create man to take over the labor for them. Humans were created basically as slave labor for the gods. Such stories seek to answer the question of human origins in general. When read against this backdrop, Gen 2 is seen to share a similar

63. L. A. Turner, "Genesis," in Alexander and Baker, *Dictionary of the Old Testament*, 353.

64. Walton claims that pagan narratives about the creation of mankind are not about the creation of the first individual humans but about the origin of archetypal man (*Lost World of Adam and Eve*, 82–91). This claim seems inaccurate on more than one level. In the first place, pagan myths are not about archetypal man as Walton defines that term. He explains that "an archetype here refers to a representative of a group in whom all others in the group are embodied. As a result, all members of the group are included and participate with their representative" (240; cf. 61: "all are embodied in the one and counted as having participated in the acts of that one"). Leave to the side the unclarity of this characterization (what is meant, e.g., by "embodied in the one"?). I can think of no sense in which pagan myths hold that all human beings are embodied in the humans the gods create and participate in their acts as their representatives. Walton, in speaking of the first created humans as "models" for later humans, seems to be confusing the first humans' being *prototypes* of later humans with their being *archetypes* in Walton's representative sense. (Elsewhere he explains that a prototype is the first in a series that serves as a model for subsequent production, whereas an archetype serves as a representative of all other members of the group [John H. Walton, "A Historical Adam: Archetypal Creation View," in *Four Views on the Historical Adam*, ed. Matthew Barrett and Ardel B. Caneday, Counterpoints (Grand Rapids: Zondervan, 2013), 90].) Walton is importing biblical ideas of Adam's representation of mankind into pagan mythology, where it is foreign. Second, the pagan myths are quite clear that the individuals created are the first human beings to have existed. Not only are the first individuals sometimes given proper names (e.g., "The Creation of Humanity," *KAR* IV.52–53), but before their creation there was *no one* to do the labor of the gods for them. Whether archetypal or not, the humans created by the gods are definitely the first humans to have ever existed.

It has also been said that the creation of Enkidu as a companion for Gilgamesh is an exception to the pattern of humanity's creation in the pagan myths, for he is specially created after the creation of human beings in general. This could afford precedent for interpreting Adam as a similarly singled-out creation in a wider human population. But notice that in Gen 2:7–8 "the man" whom God forms is still a generic figure. It is not until 4:1 that "Adam" is used as a proper name. So no reason exists to compare man's creation to Enkidu's creation, as though other men already existed.

etiological interest—but with a very different answer! Third, the account in Gen 2, when read at face value, is about human origins. Employing the typical form of ancient Mesopotamian etiological myths, "When ____ was not yet, then ____," Gen 2:5–7 describes the condition of the earth prior to God's creation of man: "when no plant of the field was yet in the earth and no herb of the field had yet sprung up—for the LORD God had not caused it to rain upon the earth, and there was no man to till the ground; but a mist [stream] went up from the earth and watered the whole face of the ground—then the LORD God formed man of dust from the ground, and breathed into his nostrils the breath of life; and man became a living being." The author states explicitly that there was no man to do the work of agriculture, until God created man. *Adam* is the generic word for man and is not used as a proper name until 4:1. Moreover, woman does not appear until her creation in Gen 2:22. Among all the animals God forms and brings to Adam, "there was not found a helper fit for him" (Gen 2:20). God therefore creates a woman and presents her to the man. Here we have in detail Gen 1:27: "male and female he created them." Prior to their creation there simply was no man or woman. The name later given by the man to his wife, said to mean "the mother of all living" (Gen 3:20), is *prima facie* an affirmation of her (and the man's) universal progenitorship of all mankind.[65] For these reasons the story of man's

65. Walton attempts to avoid this implication by pointing out, first, that the word *living* "can refer to all creatures, yet all animals are not biological descendants of Eve." Second, "the expression 'mother of all . . .' is not necessarily one that pertains to biology," for Jabal was called "the father of all who live in tents" and Jubal "the father of all who play stringed instruments," which shows that this sort of expression has larger associations in mind than just biological descent (*Lost World of Adam and Eve*, 187–88). Are we seriously to think that because the expression "the father/mother of" can take most anything as the object of the preposition, the expression used of Eve in Gen 3:20, "the mother of all living," does not have to do with biological descent or that because *living* can be used of animals, it is not used here to designate Eve's biological descendants?

Walton says that the core proposal of his book is that "the forming accounts of Adam and Eve should be understood archetypally rather than as accounts of how these two individuals were uniquely formed" (*Lost World of Adam and Eve*, 74). NB the "rather than." Walton assumes that being the first human beings to have been created and being the archetypes of other humans are mutually exclusive. "Once the forming accounts are recognized as archetypal, they cease to be meaningful in terms of chronology or history of material human origins, even given . . . that Adam and Eve are historical persons" (200). But like his distinction between so-called material creation and functional creation, this is a false dichotomy that subverts Walton's entire treatment of human origins. Adam can be both the first man and the archetypal man; indeed, being first makes him uniquely suited to be the archetype.

Walton also argues that just as "formed from dust" is a statement of our mortality, not

creation in Gen 2 is not intended by the pentateuchal author as a sequential account distinct from and later than the creation of mankind in Gen 1:26–27, but rather as a focused version of it.

Etiology comes explicitly to the fore in the closing comment on the story, "Therefore a man leaves his father and his mother and cleaves to his wife, and they become one flesh. And the man and his wife were both naked, and were not ashamed" (Gen 2:24–25). The man and the woman are now man and wife. Marriage is thus God's plan for man and woman and is grounded in the primordial creation of man and of woman as his helper. The marriage relationship is taken to be the proper sphere for human sexual activity. This etiological note confirms that the author takes his story to be universal in scope, for marriage is not plausibly taken to be merely God's special provision for this specially created couple but his intention for all humanity.

Natural Phenomena

Etiological motifs concerning *natural phenomena* are also evident in Gen 1–11. Such motifs are especially obvious in the account in Gen 3 of the primordial couple's disobedience to God as a result of their seduction by the serpent.[66] In the punishments pronounced by God on the serpent, the man, and the woman, etiological motifs abound:

> The LORD God said to the serpent,
> "Because you have done this,
> cursed are you above all cattle,
> and above all wild animals;
> upon your belly you shall go,
> and dust you shall eat

of our material origins, "there is no reason to think that it is a statement of Adam's material origins" (*Lost World of Adam and Eve*, 76). But even if we accept that the expression is an idiom for mortality, not physical constitution, presumably the reason we think that we have in Gen 2:7 an account of Adam's material origin is that we have a descriptive account of it: God formed a man from the dust of the ground and breathed into his nose the breath of life and the man came to life! Before this formation event, there was no man (2:5). Again, we see Walton's penchant for dichotomous thinking. Why cannot man be mortal because he is made of dust? When Walton says that would be "flawed chemistry from our vantage point" (73), he lapses into not only concordism but wooden literalism.

66. See commentary by Westermann, *Genesis 1–11*, 256–67.

all the days of your life.
I will put enmity between you and the woman,
and between your seed and her seed;
he shall bruise your head,
and you shall bruise his heel."

To the woman he said,
"I will greatly multiply your pain in childbearing;
in pain you shall bring forth children,
yet your desire shall be for your husband,
and he shall rule over you."

And to Adam he said,
"Because you have listened to the voice of your wife,
and have eaten of the tree
of which I commanded you,
'You shall not eat of it,'
cursed is the ground because of you;
in toil you shall eat of it all the days of your life;
thorns and thistles it shall bring forth to you;
and you shall eat the plants of the field.
In the sweat of your face
you shall eat bread
till you return to the ground,
for out of it you were taken;
you are dust,
and to dust you shall return." (Gen 3:14–19)

Whatever one thinks of the enmity established between the serpent and the woman and their respective offspring,[67] the serpent's slithering on the ground is clearly said to be the consequence of God's judgment for its seduction of the couple.[68] Similarly, however we interpret the woman's subjection to her husband, the explanation for the terrible pain women experience in

67. The enmity might be thought to be an etiological motif concerning mankind's revulsion to snakes; but then the enmity should not be focused on the woman, and the singular in v. 15b would be inapt.

68. The ongoing enmity between the serpent's descendants and Eve's belies Walton's claim that the serpent's going on its belly is a sign of docility, not an etiological motif concerning its locomotion (*Lost World of Adam and Eve*, 130).

childbirth is attributed to the first woman's disobedience. Finally, the toil of farming is attributed to the fact that the land is cursed because of the man's disobedience. Thus, these natural phenomena with which later Israelites would have been all too familiar are explained in terms of our primordial parents' fall into sin.

While the story does not offer an etiology for evil as such—the deceitful serpent simply appears in the garden opposing God—still it does offer an etiology for human misery as a result of sin. In the ensuing narratives, climaxing in the flood story, we have what Gerhard von Rad famously called "an increase in sin to avalanche proportions" as man devolves from bad to worse until God sees "that the wickedness of man was great in the earth, and that every imagination of the thoughts of his heart was only evil continually" (Gen 6:5).[69] Though the story of the fall does not contemplate the later dogma of original sin, still it does portray the disobedience of the first couple as the floodgate through which sin entered into the paradisiacal world created for them by God, leading to their expulsion from the garden to eke out a living from the cursed soil, cut off from the tree of life and so doomed to death.

An apparent etiology for a natural phenomenon also appears at the end of the flood story in the context of God's providing assurance that he will never again destroy the earth with a flood: "And God said, 'This is the sign of the covenant which I make between me and you and every living creature that is with you, for all future generations: I set my bow in the cloud, and it shall be a sign of the covenant between me and the earth. When I bring clouds over the earth and the bow is seen in the clouds, I will remember my covenant which is between me and you and every living creature of all flesh; and the waters shall never again become a flood to destroy all flesh'" (Gen 9:12–15). The phenomenon of the rainbow is apparently explained as a sign given by God of the covenant he has made with the earth never again to destroy it by flood. It has been suggested that there is no etiology here, for rainbows have existed prior to this moment, but now God selects this celestial phenomenon to serve as a sign of the covenant he is establishing. But the repeated use of present-tense verbs, "Behold, I establish my covenant with you. . . . I establish my covenant with you. . . . I set my bow in the cloud" (vv. 9, 11, 13), suggests that we have here performative utterances that actually accomplish the thing pronounced. If so, then we have here an etiological account of rainbows.

69. Von Rad, *Genesis*, 152.

Finally, in the Tower of Babel story we seem to have "multiple aetiologies: not only for human beings having many different languages, but also for the dispersal of humanity throughout the earth, and for the origin of the place name Babel."[70] The story opens with the explanation, "Now the whole earth had one language and few words" (Gen 11:1).[71] In response to human presumption, God decides to "confuse their language, that they may not understand one another's speech" (Gen 11:7). No longer able to communicate with one another, the people leave off building the tower and are dispersed. The author comments, "Therefore its name was called Babel, because there the LORD confused the language of all the earth; and from there the LORD scattered them abroad over the face of all the earth" (Gen 11:9). We thus have an apparent explanation for the different language groups and nations listed in the Table of Nations in the preceding chapter.

It has been suggested that what we have here is not an etiology for the world's languages but just an account of the confusion of speech of the local people who had "migrated from the east" and settled in the plain of Shinar (Gen 11:2).[72] Well and good; but the point remains that in the author's mind the whole earth spoke this people's language, unless by "the whole earth" he means something like "the whole land." If we take the Table of Nations not to be displaced chronologically, then the author knows that there are already different language groups and peoples. He is aware, moreover, of the migration of peoples. The people in Shinar were one such, all speaking the same language. After having confused their language, God scattered them abroad among the other nations. Most commentators, however, take the Table of Nations to be chronologically displaced, in order that the primaeval history might end with the Tower of Babel story.[73] Tellingly, the Table of Nations

70. Day, *From Creation to Babel*, 181.

71. Some scholars have understood the Sumerian myth *Enmerkar and the Lord of Aratta* to describe a time when all people spoke a single language, until Enki changed the speech in their mouths (II.145–46, 150–56) (Samuel Noah Kramer, "The 'Babel of Tongues': A Sumerian Version" [1968], in Hess and Tsumura, *"I Studied Inscriptions,"* 278–82); but other scholars interpret the passage to be a prediction of a future state (see Day, *From Creation to Babel*, 180–81, and the Electronic Text Corpus of Sumerian Literature at http://etcsl.orinst.ox.ac.uk/cgi-bin/etcsl.cgi?text=t.1.8.2.3).

72. So Ross, who says that the story need not envision the creation of new languages but simply such a confusion in the utterance of the old as would naturally lead to discord and division (Allen P. Ross, *Creation and Blessing: A Guide to the Study and Exposition of Genesis* [Grand Rapids: Baker Books, 1998], 246).

73. Von Rad explains that the story about the Tower of Babel concludes with God's judgment but with no word of grace. The question then becomes urgent: Is God's relation-

includes the notice that the name of one of Shem's descendants was Peleg (division), "for in his days the earth was divided" (Gen 10:25), an apparent reference to the confusion of languages and scattering of the people related in the tower story. So if we understand the groups listed in the Table of Nations to result from the confusion of tongues in Babel, then we do have an etiology for the phenomenon of mankind's natural languages.

Cultural Practices

Genesis 1–11 also contains etiological motifs concerning quite a few *cultural practices*. Shepherding originated with Abel, while Cain continued Adam's role as a tiller of the soil (Gen 4:2). Among the descendants of Cain we find the progenitors of three cultural advances: "Adah bore Jabal; he was the father of those who dwell in tents and have cattle. His brother's name was Jubal; he was the father of all those who play the lyre and pipe. Zillah bore Tubal-cain; he was the forger of all instruments of bronze and iron" (Gen 4:20–22). In Sumerian myths the origins of such cultural practices are ascribed wholly to the gods.[74] For example, one is amazed to see so seemingly rudimentary a tool as the hoe or pickax extolled as a gift of the gods in such myths as "The Song of the Hoe."[75] By marked contrast, in

---

ship to the nations finally broken? That question remains open and unanswerable in the primaeval history. But the author does give an answer at the point where sacred history begins. What is promised to Abraham extends far beyond Israel; indeed, it has universal meaning for all generations on earth (von Rad, *Genesis*, 152–54).

74. Sarna comments that this was a widespread motif in ancient mythology:

> Mesopotamian tradition knew of the seven *Apkallu*, or mythical sages, half-fish and half-man, who rose out of the sea to reveal to man the sciences, the social system, writing, and art. Enlil, the air god, created the mattock; Enki-Ea, god of watery chaos, was closely associated with magic, wisdom, the arts and crafts, and music. For Egyptians, it was the god Thot who invented the scales and the balances; Osiris who taught humans agriculture and the arts of life; and Ptah who was the special patron of artists, artificers, and men of letters. In the Ugaritic-Phoenician area, the god Koshar, the divine artisan and smith, was credited with the discovery of the use of iron and the fishing tackle. In the Greek sphere, it was Athena who invented the plough and the rake and who taught both the useful and the elegant arts, while Apollo founded towns and invented the flute and the lyre. (*Genesis*, 35–36)

75. We read that not only did Enlil create the world and mankind with his hoe, but he has bestowed this holy tool on man, who uses it to accomplish great feats in agriculture and construction. "The hoe makes everything prosper, the hoe makes everything flour-

Gen 1–11 cultural advances are treated as human inventions arising from man's natural powers.[76]

The fact that these cultural advances originate in the line of Cain has led some commentators to see them as ambivalent in value,[77] but this is probably reading between the lines. Israel could hardly condemn the nomadic lifestyle, and music was a great good, serving in the worship of Yahweh.[78] There is no reason to think that ancient Israelites, pressed by enemies about them, would not also have seen the ability to forge weapons, not to speak of instruments of cultivation and construction, as a good.

In the story of Noah's drunkenness we have a further cultural etiological notice that viticulture originated with Noah, who first planted a vineyard (Gen 9:20–21).[79] This is in contrast to other ancient cultures' ascribing its origin to the gods.[80]

Religious Cult

Finally, among the most important and obvious etiological motifs in Gen 1–11 are those related to the establishment of *the religious cult*. The creation story ends with God's resting from his work on the seventh day: "And on the seventh day God finished his work which he had done, and he rested on the seventh day from all his work which he had done. So God blessed the seventh day and hallowed it, because on it God rested from all his work which

ish. . . . The hoe, the implement whose destiny was fixed by father Enlil—the renowned hoe!" (*Song of the Hoe* 94, 107).

76. See the very nice discussion in Westermann, *Genesis 1–11*, 56–62. He points out that while the biblical narrative, like the Sumerian myths, finds the foundations of present-day civilization laid in the primaeval period, nevertheless "the motif of the progress of civilization has been radically changed in the biblical primeval story. There is no mention at all of a divine origin. . . . The creator does not bestow ready-made products on people, but gives them the capacity to acquire and to create" (60, 62).

77. See the negative assessment by Tremper Longman III, *Genesis*, SGBC (Grand Rapids: Zondervan, 2016), 95–96, who thinks that Genesis condemns both city dwelling and nomadic herding as evil.

78. See D. W. Baker, "Arts and Crafts," in Alexander and Baker, *Dictionary of the Old Testament*, 49–53.

79. In the same story (Gen 9:25) many commentators also see an etiological explanation for Israel's later conquest of Canaan, though this interpretation seems dubious, since the conquest of the land of Canaan had to be postponed for centuries until the wickedness of the people in the land was complete (Gen 15:16).

80. Sarna mentions the Egyptian ascription of the origin of viticulture to Osiris and the Greek ascription of the same to Dionysus (*Genesis*, 65).

he had done in creation" (Gen 2:2–3). The pentateuchal author is explicit about Sabbath observance's being grounded in the pattern set by God and his hallowing and blessing the seventh day:

> Remember the sabbath day, to keep it holy. Six days you shall labor, and do all your work; but the seventh day is a sabbath to the LORD your God; in it you shall not do any work, . . . for in six days the LORD made heaven and earth, the sea, and all that is in them, and rested the seventh day; therefore the LORD blessed the sabbath day and hallowed it. (Exod 20:8–11)

> Six days shall work be done, but the seventh day is a sabbath of solemn rest, holy to the LORD; whoever does any work on the sabbath day shall be put to death. Therefore the people of Israel shall keep the sabbath, observing the sabbath throughout their generations, as a perpetual covenant. It is a sign for ever between me and the people of Israel that in six days the LORD made heaven and earth, and on the seventh day he rested, and was refreshed. (Exod 31:15–17)[81]

The idea of a seven-day week climaxing in a sanctified Sabbath is unparalleled in other ANE texts. Probably no other etiological motif in Gen 1–11 is so powerfully expressed or so important as the grounding of Sabbath observance in God's own observance of the seventh day as a day of rest in the story of the world's creation.[82]

But other cultic motifs are attested as well. The practice of animal sacrifice, so central to the Levitical cult, is rooted first in Abel's more acceptable sacrifice to God (Gen 4:4) and especially later in Noah's sacrifices offered

81. Sarna, *Genesis*, 354, points out that the vocabulary of Gen 2:2–3 is interwoven with other pentateuchal references to the Sabbath such as Exod 16:5, 22, 26; 23:12; 34:21; 35:2; Lev 23:3.

82. Commenting that the significance of the Sabbath in ancient Israel "can hardly be overstated," Bill Arnold rightly comments,

> Having been a staple of Western culture for so long, it may be difficult for today's readers to grasp the weight of this introduction of the concept of one day of rest in seven. Indeed, our easy acceptance of such an idea may lead us to read 2:1–3 as anti-climactic to what is an otherwise spectacular account of creation. Our difficulty is in reading the institution of the Sabbath as merely a cultic dogma, almost as though it were an afterthought in the creation of the world. On the contrary, by placing it here, at the conclusion of the creation of the world, the author has created an elaborate theology of Sabbath that must not escape us. (Bill T. Arnold, *Genesis*, NCBC [Cambridge: Cambridge University Press, 2009], 50)

after the flood: "Then Noah built an altar to the LORD, and took of every clean animal and of every clean bird, and offered burnt offerings on the altar. And when the LORD smelled the pleasing odor, the LORD said in his heart, 'I will never again curse the ground because of man'" (Gen 8:20–21). "Burnt offerings" are one of the four types of Levitical animal sacrifices (Lev 1:3–17), and the language of "a pleasing odor" is typical for describing their effect (Lev 1:9, 13, 17). A particularly telltale sign of etiological interest is the anachronism of the distinction between clean and unclean animals at this stage (cf. Gen 7:2, 8) and Noah's sacrificing only clean animals to God. Similarly, God's proscription of consuming blood (Gen 9:4) reflects the later, central Levitical rationale for animal sacrifices and the prohibition against consuming blood: "For the life of the flesh is in the blood; and I have given it for you upon the altar to make atonement for your souls; for it is the blood that makes atonement, by reason of the life" (Lev 17:11). In the narrative of the covenant made with Noah, we have the interesting example of an etiological motif identified within the primaeval history itself: "Whoever sheds the blood of man, by man shall his blood be shed; for God made man in his own image" (Gen 9:6). Here the prescription of death for the act of murder is grounded in the creation story of Gen 1.

It is evident, then, that Gen 1–11 is brimming with etiological motifs concerning the origins of the world, of mankind, of certain natural phenomena, of cultural practices, and of the prevailing cult. Even if attempts to show direct borrowing of Gen 1–11 from ANE myths are fraught with conjecture and uncertainty, it cannot be plausibly denied that these chapters treat many of the same themes as ANE myths and seek to ground present realities in events of the primordial past. Even if some of the examples here identified are disputable, the multiplicity and variety of etiological motifs in Gen 1–11 make it difficult to deny that these chapters exemplify this central family resemblance of myths.

8. Ritual

The narratives of Gen 1–11 do not seem to be *associated with rituals*, despite the motif of animal sacrifice. But inclusion of this eighth family resemblance probably reflects the influence of the so-called myth and ritual school, which is now widely rejected.[83] While some myths have ritual associations, such a

83. See Robert A. Segal, *Myth: A Very Short Introduction*, 2nd ed. (Oxford: Oxford University Press, 2015), chap. 4; Lauri Honko, "The Problem of Defining Myth," in Dundes,

connection is missing from many myths. So the absence of ritual associations from the primaeval narratives has little bearing on their status as myths.

9. Correspondences

The primaeval narratives of Genesis likewise do not express *correspondences between deities and nature.* The degree to which pagan myths express correspondences between deities and natural phenomena like the sea, the air, the sun, and so on is a matter of controversy, which we shall take up in the next chapter.[84] But the absence of such correspondences from Gen 1–11 is due to Israel's monotheism, in contrast to the polytheism of its neighbors. Since Israel rejected the existence of the gods, we have in Israel "a very radical departure from the characteristic mythical thought in terms of harmony or correspondence."[85] We can agree with James Barr that this is seen most clearly in the creation story of Gen 1, where a "very sharp distinction between God and his creation" is carried out. But we should not therefore conclude that in Gen 1 "the old creation story is very thoroughly demythologised."[86] For as we have seen, what is going on in Gen 1 is not demythologization but a desacralization of nature, which is required by Israel's monotheism. Simply put, since there are no deities, there can be no correspondences between the deities and nature. So one should not expect to see such correspondences in a monotheistic myth.

10. Fantastic and Inconsistent Elements

Finally, do the primaeval narratives exhibit *fantastic elements* and do they remain *untroubled by logical contradiction or incoherence*? It seems that on both counts the primaeval narratives do share this family resemblance of myths, even if to several orders of magnitude less in comparison to ANE polytheistic myths.

Sacred Narrative, 52; G. S. Kirk, *Myth: Its Meaning and Functions in Ancient and Other Cultures*, SCL 40 (Cambridge: Cambridge University Press, 1970), 11–12.

84. See chap. 5.

85. James Barr, "The Meaning of 'Mythology' in Relation to the Old Testament," *VT* 9, no. 1 (1959): 7.

86. Barr, "Meaning of 'Mythology,'" 7. We leave aside the assumption that Israel borrowed from a polytheistic *Vorlage*, which is questionable. See the next section.

Inconsistencies

Anthropomorphisms

Consider, first, apparent inconsistencies. Despite God's transcendence so dramatically declared in Gen 1, God is portrayed in the story of man's creation in Gen 2 as a humanoid deity worthy of polytheistic myths, as he forms man from the dirt and breathes the breath of life into his nostrils. The same is true of the story of the fall in Gen 3, where God strolls in the cool of the day and searches for the man and woman hiding among the trees; of the story of the flood in Gen 6–9, where God regrets having made man and is pleased with the smell of Noah's burnt offering; and of the story of the Tower of Babel in Gen 11, where God comes down to see the city and tower that the people have built. Such anthropomorphic descriptions of God, if interpreted literally, are incompatible with the transcendent God described at the beginning of creation.[87] Such incoherence could not possibly have escaped the notice of the pentateuchal author, for it is so patent, and yet he felt no need to expunge the anthropomorphic elements. He doubtless assumed that his readers would have understood such anthropomorphic descriptions of God to be just part of the storyteller's art, not serious theology.

Narrative Inconsistencies

Similarly, the author seems untroubled by the apparent inconsistencies that occur in his narratives. It would have been easy for him to bring the account of the creation of man in Gen 2 into accord with Gen 1, rather than leave the apparent inconsistencies concerning the order of creation of man, the vegetation, and the animals.[88] Similarly, the author could have easily eliminated

87. It would be maladroit to interpret these passages as theophanies of God in human form, for (1) God's physical presence is not presented as a theophany (contrast Gen 18:1–2), and (2) God is described anthropomorphically even when not appearing to people (e.g., God's creation of Adam in Gen 2:7 and his creation of Eve while Adam is unconscious in Gen 2:21–22).

88. For a brief list of the alleged contradictions, see U[mberto] Cassuto, *A Commentary on the Book of Genesis*, part 1, *From Adam to Noah: Genesis I–VI 8* [1944], trans. Israel Abrahams (Skokie, IL: Varda Books, 2005), 88–89. He rightly argues that some of these are imagined. Westermann, *Genesis 1–11*, 186, states that one of the most important and decisive results of literary criticism is the acknowledgment that Gen 2–3 was an independent and separate narrative. Although Cassuto denies that the alleged inconsistencies are evidence for the Documentary Hypothesis, still, on Cassuto's own

view, Gen 1 and Gen 2 are based on independent epic poems adapted by the author of Genesis, so that the question of the degree to which he has successfully ironed out the inconsistencies between them remains. Castellino would remove the supposed inconsistency between the aridity of the earth in 2:5 and the garden's being watered by a spring in 2:6 by distinguishing between the earth (*'ereṣ*), the field (*śādeh*), and the ground (*'ădāmâ*) (G. Castellino, "The Origins of Civilization according to Biblical and Cuneiform Texts" [1957], in Hess and Tsumura, *"I Studied Inscriptions,"* 78–79, 94). Averbeck disputes this interpretation because the proximity and seemingly obvious connection with 2:4b, "earth and heavens," "makes the shift in meaning very unlikely in spite of the use of the same term for a particular land later in the passage" (Richard E. Averbeck, "Responses to Chapter Three," in *Reading Genesis 1–2: An Evangelical Conversation*, ed. J. Daryl Charles [Peabody, MA: Hendrickson, 2013], 94). In any case, Castellino's move does nothing to eliminate the inconsistency of chaps. 1 and 2 concerning the presence of vegetation. Cassuto argues that there is no inconsistency concerning vegetation prior to man because Gen 2:5 is not referring to all types of vegetation but specifically to only two: thorns (*śîaḥ*) and grain (*'eśeb*). These came forth from the earth only after and as a consequence of man's sinning and God's cursing the ground (Gen 3:18) (Cassuto, *Book of Genesis*, 101–3; followed by Victor P. Hamilton, *The Book of Genesis: Chapters 1–17*, NICOT [Grand Rapids: Eerdmans, 1990], 154; Kenneth A. Mathews, *Genesis 1–11:26*, NAC 1A [Nashville: Broadman & Holman, 1996], 194). This harmonization seems too clever by half. On this reading the reason given in Gen 2:5 for why the earth had not brought forth thorns and grain should have been "for man had not yet sinned." Since the world was supposedly filled with vegetation, the absence of rain and of any man to till the earth had nothing to do with it. Moreover, man was commanded to till the garden prior to the fall (Gen 2:15), which would imply that the growth of *'eśeb* was not delayed until after the fall. Far more plausible is the view that Gen 2:5 envisions an exhaustive disjunction between uncultivated plants and cultivated plants (Ross, *Creation and Blessing*, 121; Averbeck, "Responses to Chapter Three," 94) and, hence, no vegetation at that time. One cannot plausibly restrict the narrative to concern plants invading the agricultural fields as opposed to the earth in general, since the same phrase used of plants "of the field" (*śādeh*) is used of the beasts and of the serpent in Gen 3:1 as the craftiest animal "of the field," a description obviously not restricted to agricultural fields.

Similarly, with respect to the creation of animals in Gen 2:19, Cassuto says that the redactor must have noticed "so glaring a contradiction" in the order of creation if one exists. He rejects the harmonizing translation "which he had already created" as unworthy of serious consideration. But because Gen 2:19 fails to mention the creation of cattle, or domestic animals, Cassuto assumes that they must have already been with man in the garden, whereas the beasts of the field and the birds of the air, being wild animals, were not. So what 2:19 envisions is the Lord God's forming "particular specimens" of these wild animals in order to present them to man in the garden (Cassuto, *Book of Genesis*, 128–29). We may leave it to the reader to decide whether this is a plausible exegesis of the passage; the overriding point remains that were the author concerned with consistency, he would surely have avoided such a glaring contradiction by making a scenario such as Cassuto imagines a whole lot clearer. It is worth noting that the order of creation of people, vegetation, then animals is the same in the *Sumerian Flood Story* 45–50.

any questions about the provenance of Cain's wife and who the others are that Cain feared would take his life, but he chose not to. Scholars would have dearly liked the author to clarify what he meant in saying, "At that time men began to call upon the name of the LORD" (Gen 4:26), despite his later affirmation that the name "Yahweh" had not been previously revealed (Exod 6:3), but he could not be bothered to iron out the apparent inconsistency. God's instructions to Noah first to take aboard the ark two animals of every kind and then to bring aboard seven pairs of all clean animals (Gen 6:19; 7:3), an apparent inconsistency that has led most scholars to see a weaving together of separate J and P versions of the flood story, could have been so easily straightened out by the author, thus sparing the effort of harmonizers; but he was evidently untroubled by the apparent inconsistency.[89] The seeming inconsistency between the people's different languages in the Table of Nations in chapter 10 and the Tower of Babel story is left to stand without clarification by the author. The point is not whether these apparent inconsistencies are somehow resolvable but that the author is just untroubled by them.

Fantastic Elements

Second, we also find elements in the stories that are fantastic. I take it that fantastic elements are those which, if taken literally, are so extraordinary as

89. In response to Wenham's argument for the unity of the canonical text on the grounds that the supposed J and P versions would be defective because radically incomplete (*Genesis 1–15*, 168–69), Day rejoins that both J and P did have more or less complete accounts but that the redactor felt free to choose an element from one in preference to the other and sometimes even to cite both sources (*From Creation to Babel*, 103). There is a price attached to Day's rejoinder, however. We have to suppose that the redactor deliberately chose to construct from his sources an inconsistent account. Day opines, "Though it might appear strange for a redactor to combine two contradictory sources, it would be far odder for P as a redactor to introduce contradictions into his own account" (103). Day's point seems to be that it is more implausible that P would introduce contradictions into a single consistent source than to combine inconsistently two separate, internally consistent sources. But why think that these are the only two alternatives? It seems more implausible that a redactor would combine two individually consistent accounts into one contradictory account, as Day imagines, than that the redactor had before him a unified account that already contained the alleged inconsistencies and that the redactor was not troubled by these. If that is so, then the inconsistencies could actually be regarded as evidence for, rather than against, a unified story. It is of no avail to respond with Arnold that "we may assume that the sources or traditions underlying the whole had already attained authoritative status, and the editor valued the traditions enough to retain the inconsistencies" (*Genesis*, 97; cf. 102–3), for *ex hypothesi* the redactor has already exercised pick-and-choose from among these allegedly authoritative J and P traditions.

to be palpably false. Here we confront the question of miracles. Naturalistic scholars like Gunkel took the appearance of miracles in the narratives to be indicative of myth. He wrote,

> We believe that God works in the universe in the silent and secret background of all things; sometimes his influence seems almost tangible, as in the case of exceptionally great and impressive events and personalities; we divine his control in the marvelous interdependence of things; but nowhere does he appear as an operative factor beside others but always as the last and ultimate cause of everything. Very different is the point of view of many of the narratives in Genesis. We find God walking about in the Garden of Eden; with his own hands he fashions man and closes the door of the ark; he even breathes his own breath into man's nostrils, and makes unsuccessful experiments with animals; he scents the sacrifice of Noah. . . . We are able to comprehend this as the naïve conception of the men of old, but we cannot regard belief in the literal truth of such accounts as an essential of religious conviction.[90]

Here Gunkel expresses a view of divine action in the world that limits God to being the primary cause of the world but precludes his acting in the series of secondary causes in the world. Gunkel had evidently absorbed the naturalism of nineteenth-century German theology and its rejection of miracles.

Naturalism is a philosophical viewpoint that cannot be simply presupposed. It requires justification. There is a very sizeable literature on divine action among contemporary philosophers of religion, who have offered able defenses of God's ability to act miraculously in the series of secondary causes.[91] Given the existence of a transcendent Creator and Designer of the universe, it is difficult to see why such a being would be unable to act as a cause of events in the world.

Now in the above citation Gunkel conflates anthropomorphisms with miracles. This is a simple category mistake. An anthropomorphic description of God does not imply a miracle: we should not think that the author of Genesis believes that the transcendent Creator of Gen 1 miraculously became incarnate in Gen 2. An anthropomorphism is a literary device. We may agree that the anthropomorphic descriptions of God in Gen 1–11 should not be taken as

90. Hermann Gunkel, *The Legends of Genesis: The Biblical Saga in History* [1901], trans. W. H. Carruth (New York: Schocken Books, 1964), 10.

91. See, e.g., Alvin Plantinga, *Where the Conflict Really Lies: Science, Religion, and Naturalism* (Oxford: Oxford University Press, 2011), chaps. 3–4.

"literal truth," since they are figurative language; but that goes no distance toward justifying rejecting the literal truth of miracle stories. Given that a transcendent Creator of the universe exists, we cannot justifiably classify miracles as fantastic. In determining the genre of a text, therefore, we must prescind from characterizing all miraculous elements as *ipso facto* fantastic.

Moreover, when we deem a narrative fantastic, we presumably mean "fantastic for us." The original author and his audience may not have found the story to be fantastic. But in light of our increased knowledge of the world, we now see that certain elements in the narrative, if taken literally, are palpably false. In so saying, we need to keep in mind that we are looking for family resemblances, not sufficient conditions, of myth. If an ancient scientific or medical text were shown to be fantastic, that would not show it to be mythical. It can be a family resemblance of myths, if not a sufficient condition, that they are characterized by fantastic elements. This indicator will be all the stronger if we can show that the elements identified as fantastic would have been palpably false for the author and his audience as well, if taken literally, for that would tend to show that he did not regard his stories as literal accounts.

Our question, then, is whether there are fantastic, nonmiraculous elements in Gen 1–11. There clearly are. Gunkel, appealing to the "criterion of incredibility" to identify faded myths, lists several fantastic elements in Gen 1–11:

> Thus many things are reported in Genesis which go directly against our better knowledge: we know that there are too many species of animals for all to have been assembled in any ark; that Ararat is not the highest mountain on earth; that the "firmament of heaven," of which Genesis i. 6 ff. speaks, is not a reality, but an optical illusion; that the stars cannot have come into existence after plants, as Genesis ii. 10–14 reports; that the rivers of the earth do not come chiefly from four principal streams, as Genesis ii. thinks, that the Tigris and the Euphrates have not a common source, . . . and so on. . . . The idea that the nations of the earth originated from the expansion of a single family, in each case from a single ancestor, is quite infantile. . . . However cautious the modern historian may be in declaring anything impossible, he may declare with all confidence that animals—serpents and she-asses, for an instance—do not speak and never have spoken, that there is no tree whose fruit confers immortality or knowledge, that angels and men do not have carnal connexion.[92]

92. Gunkel, *Legends of Genesis*, 7–8.

Gunkel's list is something of a mixed bag. We must excise from the list any items deemed miraculous, such as Balaam's ass (not part of Gen 1–11 in any case) and the union of angels and human women.[93] We must also omit items in the list that are not clearly affirmed by the text of Genesis, such as the reality of a solid firmament or the creation of the heavenly luminaries after the creation of vegetation. With respect to the firmament, although many scholars have affirmed that the *rāqîaʿ* is a hard dome covering the earth, the text of Genesis does not say this,[94] and we shall see that the ANE parallels adduced in support of this notion turn out upon examination to be metaphorical, not literal. With respect to the luminaries, while it seems natural to read the creation of the luminaries chronologically in view of the ordinally numbered days, such an interpretation does not force itself on us. For it would have made no sense to an ancient author to affirm the existence of the cycle of day and night, of evening and morning (effectively, sunset and sunrise[95]) on days 1–3 in the absence of the sun. The existence of days prior to the sun's existence might be deemed an incoherence in the text, indicative of a mythical genre. But another possibility is to read the creation of the luminaries nonchronologically. This might be done by taking the days to be merely a literary device for framing the narrative[96] or by taking the creation

93. Given that angels were thought to have the ability to take on human form (Gen 18:1–33), it is hard to see why their siring children with human females should be thought fantastic, unless one regards the existence of angels as fantastic. The danger of anti-supernaturalistic prejudice thus threatens. The possibility of a polytheistic *Vorlage* to Gen 6:1–4 is irrelevant, since the pentateuchal author rejects such an account.

94. Even Westermann, *Genesis 1–11*, 115–16, who thinks that P received the tradition of the heavens as a solid vault over the earth holding back the ocean above, says that we do not know whether the priestly circle shared this view. He notes that the Hebrews developed a more accurate explanation of the formation of clouds and rain (Jer 10:13; Job 36:27; Ps 135:7). See further Vern S. Poythress, "Rainwater versus a Heavenly Sea in Genesis 1:6–8," *WTJ* 77 (2015): 181–91. The fact that Israelites understood the water cycle gives us reason to think that they did not share the older view. Westermann rightly observes that even when ideas change, the old, traditional ways of speaking are retained and not rendered obsolete (e.g., sunrise and sunset). Whether, in fact, the tradition received by the Genesis author assumed that the *rāqîaʿ* was a solid surface will be taken up in the sequel (see *infra*, pp. 189–91).

95. Sarna comments that the Hebrew words *ʿereb* and *bōqer* mean, strictly speaking, the "sunset" and the "break of dawn," terms inappropriate before the creation of the sun on the fourth day (*Genesis*, 8).

96. Ever since the Middle Ages, commentators have noticed a sort of parallelism between days 1–3 and days 4–6. This has led some commentators to adopt what has come to be known as the literary framework interpretation of the days of creation (Henri Blocher,

of the luminaries on day 4 to be out of chronological sequence.[97] In that case

In the Beginning: The Opening Chapters of Genesis, trans. David G. Preston [Downers Grove, IL: InterVarsity Press, 1984]). According to this view, the author of Genesis is not interested in chronology. Rather, the days serve as a sort of literary framework on which he can hang his account of creation. Blocher maintains that on the first three days God forms the domain, or the space, for a certain occupant. Then on the second three days he creates the occupants of the domains. So, for example, on day 1 he creates day and night, and on day 4 he creates the sun, moon, and stars. So the creation week is a literary framework for a nonchronological account of creation.

Although this view has commended itself to a great many interpreters, the parallelism between days 1–3 and 4–6 is not exact. For example, what corresponds to God's creating the lights in the firmament on day 4? Clearly, it is God's creation of the firmament on day 2. On day 2 God creates the firmament, and then on day 4 he places the lights in the firmament. The separation of light and darkness on day 1 is not the creation of a place for the lights; that comes on day 2. Similarly, what corresponds to the creation of the sea creatures on day 5 is God's creation of the seas on day 3. True, the waters were already separated on day 2 into the waters above and the waters below, but the waters were not gathered into seas until day 3, which is the place where the sea creatures were created. Finally, on day 3 God creates not only the dry land and seas but also the vegetation and fruit trees. So God does not create merely the domain; he also creates some of the occupants of the domain on that day. The vegetation can hardly be called the domain for land animals and man, which are created on day 6. So it is not clear that the parallelism is something in the text rather than in the mind of the interpreter.

Moreover, it is difficult to believe that the chronology in the narrative is not to be taken seriously. The chronology is meaningless on the literary framework interpretation; but surely the idea of the ordinal numbering of the consecutive days—second, third, fourth, fifth—and the progression from desolation up through man does seem to have the suggestion of chronology. It is hard to resist the impression that the narrative intends to portray a temporal progression, ending with God's resting from the work of creation on the seventh and final day. Blocher admits that creation over a period of time is a common motif in ANE creation myths. So why think that that motif is here nonchronological? Mere parallelism does not suffice to disprove a chronological interest.

97. John H. Sailhamer, *Genesis: Text and Exposition*, EBC 2 (Grand Rapids: Zondervan, 1990), 33–24; Sailhamer, *Genesis Unbound: A Provocative New Look at the Creation Account* (Sisters, OR: Multnomah, 1996), 129–35, points out that the construction used in 1:14 is not the same as that used for God's previous creatorial decrees in 1:3, 6. The construction here (to be + the infinitive) could be translated, "Let the lights in the firmament be for the separating of the day and night." Unlike the earlier decrees, this clause specifies what something is to be for and thus presupposes that the lights already exist. A problem for this interpretation is that 1:16–18 shows that God has not until that day made the heavenly bodies. This objection, however, ignores the interesting duplex nature of the narrative in Gen 1. Many commentators have observed that Gen 1 seems to combine two types of creation: one by God's creative word (1:3, 6, 9, 11, 14, 20, 24, 26) and one by God's action (1:7, 12, 16, 21, 25, 27). This could be due to the author's interbraiding two traditions. On the other hand, the coherence and unity of the chapter would be more

one does not have the fantastic declaration that the sun was created after the vegetation, not to mention after three previous evenings and mornings.

Six-Day Creation

What is fantastic and therefore mythological in Gen 1 is the creation of the world over six consecutive days.[98] The pattern of evening and morning

---

satisfactorily maintained if we took this duplex pattern to be one of report and comment on the author's part. For example, vv. 4–5, 10 do not describe creatorial acts, nor does v. 12 actually describe something God does; neither is it meant to follow temporally v. 11, for this would seem to be precluded by the phrase "And it was so" concluding v. 11. Rather v. 12, like vv. 4–5, 10, is the author's comment on the report given in the previous sentence. Similarly, v. 15 includes the phrase "And it was so," suggesting vv. 16–18 are the author's comment on God's creation of the heavens, a creation that is not necessarily at that point in time. Indeed, the function of the luminaries "to separate the light from the darkness" (v. 18) suggests that the sun was created by God prior to the fourth day. Hence vv. 14–18 need not indicate God's creation of the luminaries at that time.

98. Wenham adduces three factors showing that in Gen 1 a week of divine activity is being described: (1) the mention of morning and evening, (2) the enumeration of the days, and (3) the divine rest on the seventh day (*Genesis 1–15*, 19). The attempt of John H. Walton, *The Lost World of Genesis One: Ancient Cosmology and the Origins Debate* (Downers Grove, IL: IVP Academic, 2009), to avoid Gen 1's claiming that God brings things into existence over seven consecutive days by taking creation to be merely the specification of functions for already existing objects is itself fantastic. *Pace* Walton, the descriptions of the primordial world in ANE pagan myths are not descriptions of a world of material objects in which plants and animals and buildings and people existed but lacked a function. They are descriptions of a state in which distinct material objects of those sorts do not exist at all. Hence, the creation of an orderly system of functioning objects involved the coming into being of those objects, not just the specification of functions for material objects that were already present.

When it comes to Gen 1, Walton's view differs from Blocher's literary framework view in that days 4–6 describe the creation, not of inhabitants of the realms created on days 1–3, but of things that carry out the functions established on days 1–3. This is an interesting suggestion that seems more plausible than Blocher's view. The sun and the moon in particular seem to be established as functionaries for time measurement. But this does nothing to rule out "material creation" (God's bringing physical objects into being, whether *ex materia* or *ex nihilo*) along with establishment of functionaries. I cannot but agree with John Day when he says, "Although Walton is right to emphasize that there is a functional element in the narrative, he is certainly wrong to understand it wholly in such terms, and it is quite unnatural to deny that Genesis 1 gives us an account of the creation of the material universe" (*From Creation to Babel*, 4).

For Gen 1 to feature *only* functional creation, we must imagine that the dry land, vegetation and trees, sea creatures, birds, and animals, even man, were all there from

shows that ordinary solar days, not long ages, are intended. Moreover, the fact that the successive mornings represent in each case the dawning of the consecutive day shows that no gaps between the days are contemplated. It may be that even the author himself found creation over six literal days fantastic, for he recounts as accomplished in one day events that he well knew could not naturally have happened in twenty-four hours, but that are nonetheless nonmiraculous, such as the draining of the primordial ocean into seas on day 2 (cf. Gen 8:3) or the earth's bringing forth seed-bearing vegetation and fruit-bearing trees on day 3.[99] If so, he may have taken the creation account as mythological, which would also explain his insouciance about the existence of day and night prior to the ostensible creation of the sun on day 4.[100]

---

the beginning but were not functioning in an ordered system. Just how unnatural Walton's interpretation is becomes evident in his statement that the material creation of the biosphere may have gone on for eons prior to Gen. 1:1, and then at some point in the relatively recent past there came a period of seven consecutive twenty-four-hour days during which God specified the functions of everything existing at that time. So Walton affirms that prior to the seven days of Gen. 1 the dinosaurs and hominids were alive and well, waiting only to be given their respective functions (*Lost World of Genesis One*, 169).

Now if we are to adopt a reading of the text which is so at odds with the text's *prima facie* descriptions of the world, we must have very powerful evidence, indeed, for adopting such an interpretation. Walton's principal argument is that the Hebrew word for "create" (*bārāʾ*) concerns functional creation. But, in fact, most of the objects of *bārāʾ* are easily identified as material objects. The three objects of *bārāʾ* in Gen. 1 (heavens and earth, man, and especially the sea creatures) seem clear cases of creation of material objects. Just because they may not be created *ex nihilo* does not imply that they do not come into being at the moment of their creation. Creation plausibly involves both material and functional aspects. So John Collins says, "I agree with almost everyone else that Genesis records some sort of 'material origins,' and I do not grasp exactly why Walton keeps making a disjunction between material and functional" (C. John Collins, "Response from the Old-Earth View," in Barrett and Caneday, *Four Views on the Historical Adam*, 126).

99. Thus, John Day is far too quick when he asserts, "Contrary to what is often said by some popular apologists, there is no reason to doubt that the original writer of Genesis 1 intended his account to be taken literally" (*From Creation to Babel*, 2). Day says nothing by way of analysis of the genre of Gen 1–11, and his expression "the original writer" is ambiguous: Is it P? Or the oral traditions enscripted in P? Or the pentateuchal author? I shall not comment on Day's characterization of OT scholars who advocate a nonliteral interpretation of Gen 1 as "popular apologists."

100. Averbeck's suggestion that the light may be the light of God (Richard E. Averbeck, "A Literary Day, Inter-textual, and Contextual Reading of Genesis 1–2," in Charles, *Reading Genesis 1–2*, 18–19) not only fails to reckon with the fact that in Gen 1 light is a *created* substance but also fails to discern that the real difficulty here is evening and morning (John H. Walton, "Responses to Chapter One," in Charles, *Reading Genesis 1–2*, 43).

Vegetarianism

Another fantastic element of the primaeval narratives is primordial vegetarianism for man and beast alike. "And God said, 'Behold, I have given you every plant yielding seed which is upon the face of all the earth, and every tree with seed in its fruit; you shall have them for food. And to every beast of the earth, and to every bird of the air, and to everything that creeps on the earth, everything that has the breath of life, I have given every green plant for food'" (Gen 1:29–30). Victor Hamilton comments, "At no point is anything (human beings, animals, birds) permitted to take the life of another living being and consume it for food."[101] We do not know when predatory activity among animals is thought to have begun, but humans are given permission to eat animals only after the flood: "'Every moving thing that lives shall be food for you; and as I gave you the green plants, I give you everything'" (Gen. 9:3). The removal of this restriction for humans implies that a similar restriction was in place for the animals in the primordial state. Hamilton muses, "What is strange, and probably unexplainable (from a scientific position), is the fact that the animals too are not carnivores but also vegetarians."[102] This realization is obviously not the result of modern evolutionary theory, however heightened it may be because of it. As Westermann points out, P certainly knew that it was not possible to conceive of all animals as vegetarian. "But P is speaking of primeval time which is not subject to the conditions of present experience."[103] Why the difference? P gives no indication that animal predation is the result of man's fall, and it would be anachronistic to ascribe to him the view that lions and other carnivores familiar to him evolved from animals that were herbivores (Ps 104:21). What makes the primaeval age different is not merely that it was long ago but that it was "long, long ago"—that is to say, mythological in character.

The Snake

In the story of the Garden of Eden we have multiple fantastic elements, wholly apart from God's anthropomorphic appearance. First and foremost, as noted by Gunkel, is the snake, who not only talks but is a conniving and malevolent agent. Although a literal interpretation of this figure might be

101. Hamilton, *Book of Genesis*, 140.
102. Hamilton, *Book of Genesis*, 140.
103. Westermann, *Genesis 1–11*, 164.

purchased by taking the snake to be an incarnation of Satan or a pagan deity, such an interpretation not only reads such a personage into this passage but, more importantly, seems implausible in light of the author's characterization of the snake as "more crafty than any other wild animal that the LORD God had made" (Gen 3:1 NRSV; for similar comparative terms, see 1 Sam 15:33; Judg 5:24).[104] For, as Westermann points out, it seems incredible that the snake, a creature that the Lord God had made, should incorporate a Canaanite fertility god.[105] Elsewhere in ANE myths, such as *The Shipwrecked Sailor* from Egypt, we find snakes portrayed as articulate, intelligent agents. Taking the snake to be just a crafty animal that God had made does not exclude seeing the snake in the story as a symbol of evil or opposition to God.[106] Indeed, ancient Israelites doubtless knew that snakes do not talk

104. Cf. the blasé description of the sea monsters in Gen 1:20. Noting that in Isa 27:1 various monsters, bearing the very same names as in Canaanite poetry, are mentioned as symbols of evil, Cassuto comments that Gen 1 is entirely opposed to such myths, voicing its protest in its own quiet manner: "God created the great sea monsters." "It is as though the Torah said, in effect: Far be it from any one to suppose that the sea monsters were mythological beings opposed to God or in revolt against Him; they were as natural as the rest of the creatures and were formed in their proper time and in their proper place by the word of the Creator" (Cassuto, *Book of Genesis*, 50–51). The snake in the garden, though clearly in revolt against God, remains as natural as the rest of the creatures. Just as the snake is said to be crafty above all (*ʿārûm mikkōl*) animals, so it was said to be cursed above all (*ʾārûr . . . mikkāl*) animals (Gen 3:14). For a critique of recent interpretation of the figure of the serpent, see John Day, "The Serpent of the Garden of Eden: A Critique of Some Recent Proposals" (paper presented at the Annual Meeting of the Society of Biblical Literature, Denver, CO, November 17–20, 2018); cf. Day, *From Creation to Babel*, 25–38.

105. Westermann, *Genesis 1–11*, 238. Cf. Sarna, *Genesis*, 24, who comments that in the ancient world the serpent was an ambiguous figure, being venerated as an emblem of health, fertility, immortality, occult wisdom, and evil, and often worshiped. In Genesis the serpent is, by contrast, simply one of the creatures. The phrase "all the days of your life" (Gen 3:14) underlines its mortal nature. The serpent is reduced to an insignificant, desacralized stature. Its identification with Satan is not encountered before the first century BC in *Wisdom of Solomon* 2.24.

106. Wenham points out that according to the classification of animals found in Lev 11:42, the snake counts as an archetypal unclean animal, so that within the world of OT animal symbolism the snake is an obvious candidate for an anti-God symbol, notwithstanding its creation by God (*Genesis 1–15*, 73). Cassuto also takes the snake to be a symbol, but implausibly finds it to symbolize the craftiness in man himself. The dialogue between the serpent and the woman was in Cassuto's view actually a dialogue that took place in the woman's mind between her wiliness and her innocence. This is why this serpent is said to think and speak; in reality it is the woman who does so in her heart (Cassuto, *Book of Genesis*, 142).

and so would, like us, have found such a description fantastic and therefore understood it nonliterally and perhaps symbolically.

The Trees of Life and of the Knowledge of Good and Evil

Moreover, the trees bearing fruit that, when eaten, convey knowledge of good and evil (whatever that may mean) and immortality would have seemed fantastic to ancient Israelites, as they do to us. It should be emphasized that there is no hint of miraculous action on God's part with respect to the trees, as if God would bestow knowledge of good and evil or immortality on a person on the occasion of his eating. Indeed, quite to the contrary, the fruits seem to produce their effects *ex opera operato*, so to speak, for they act even contrary to God's will to produce knowledge or immortality for the one who eats them. It has been protested that the trees are not magical, since magic, though ubiquitous in ANE literature, was rejected in Jewish religion.[107] Certainly magic involving incantations and ritual manipulation is foreign to Israel, but it remains the case that there is no explanation, natural or miraculous, for the effect that eating the Edenic fruit is said to have and that it is therefore in that sense magical. But we need not stand on the word *magical*; the important point is that the trees of the knowledge of good and evil and of life are fantastic and would have appeared so even to ancient Israelites.

The Rivers of Eden

Then there are the four rivers formed by the unnamed river flowing out of Eden, according to Gen 2:10–14: "A river flowed out of Eden to water the garden, and there it divided and became four rivers. The name of the first is Pishon; it is the one which flows around the whole land of Havilah, where there is gold; and the gold of that land is good; bdellium and onyx stone are there. The name of the second river is Gihon; it is the one which flows around the whole land of Cush. And the name of the third river is Tigris, which flows east of Assyria. And the fourth river is the Euphrates." James Hoffmeier draws our attention to the remarkable fact that while the garden story may contain mythic elements, such as the creation of Eve out of Adam's rib, mystical trees, a talking snake, and so on, still the author goes

107. As emphasized by John D. Currid, *Ancient Egypt and the Old Testament* (Grand Rapids: Baker Books, 1997), 29–30, 48.

to great lengths to place Eden within the known geography of the ANE, which is hard to reconcile with pure mythology.[108] But it is precisely that placement that many scholars have found fantastic. The Tigris and the Euphrates would have been the rivers so known at the time of the pentateuchal author,[109] roughly the same as the rivers so known today. Eden would have to be located in Armenia for these rivers to have a common source, which they, in any case, as Gunkel notes, do not, a fact that was long known to ancient Mesopotamians.[110] Moreover, the Gihon remains unidentified but is said to have flowed around Cush, which is located in Ethiopia or Nubia. Many scholars have therefore thought it to be the Nile. Obviously, it would be fantastic to think that the Nile has the same source as the Tigris and Euphrates. The Pishon, also unidentified, is said to flow around Havilah, which is thought by many to be Arabia. Some interpreters, including apparently Gunkel, take the four rivers as surrounding the known world.[111] There is no reason to take so extreme a view;[112] still, given the traditional identifications, even an ancient

108. James K. Hoffmeier, "Genesis 1–11 as History and Theology," in Halton, *Genesis*, 32–35.

109. Both are mentioned in the *Atrahasis Epic*. Cassuto, like the young earth creationist Sarfati, thinks that the pristine world described in Gen 2 has since suffered a change, so that the text describes a state of affairs that no longer exists. At first the rivers all issued from one place from the ground waters, but now they have become separated and far removed from one another, two flowing in one direction and two in the other (Cassuto, *Book of Genesis*, 117). Cassuto attributes this to man's sin and the advent of rainfall, a view so absurd that were it the intention of the text, it would be evidence that we are dealing here with a nonliteral story. Sarfati's view that the universal flood altered the world's topography (Sarfati, *Genesis*, 316–18) is far more plausible but does not, once more, seem to be contemplated in the text, which assumes that the rivers flowing out of Eden are the same ones that exist at the time of the author's writing.

110. King Sargon the Great (2334–2279 BC) of Akkad's expeditions explored the region (Wayne Horowitz, *Mesopotamian Cosmic Geography* [Winona Lake, IN: Eisenbrauns, 2011], chap. 4), and in both the *Enuma elish* V and "The Creation of Humanity," *KAR* 307 rev. 3, the Tigris and the Euphrates emerge from the slain Tiamat's right and left eyes respectively, not from a common source such as her mouth.

111. Von Rad exclaims, "What an inexpressible amount of water was in Paradise, if the river, after having watered the garden, could still enclose the entire world with four arms and fructify it! All the water outside Paradise, which supplies all civilizations, is, so to speak, only a remainder or residue from the water of Paradise!" (*Genesis*, 79–80). Incredibly, von Rad thinks that this section strives to sketch the real geographical world! On the contrary, so interpreted, its fantastic nature would support a nonliteral authorial intention.

112. The typical prooftexts (Ps 46:5; Ezek 47:1–12) do not speak of four rivers, much less all-encompassing rivers. Walton notes that we have a couple of ancient graphic rep-

Israelite with some geographical knowledge would have found the rivers' description fantastic, since it would have been obvious that the Nile at least does not have the same source as the Tigris and Euphrates.[113]

The very fantasy of these identifications might be taken to suggest, not that they are mythical, but that they have been wrongly interpreted by modern scholars. The most plausible means of interpreting the passage literally would be to take the four rivers as tributaries to the river watering the Garden of Eden.[114] Speiser thinks that when the text says that the river "flowed out of Eden," the author assumes the vantage point of someone in the garden and looking upstream. When Gen 2:10 says that the river of Eden became four "heads" (*rō'šîm*), it is referring to the four distant sources or headwaters of the incoming rivers.[115] As one moves out of the Garden of Eden, the river

---

resentations of gods from whom four streams of water flow (J. H. Walton, "Eden, Garden of," in Alexander and Baker, *Dictionary of the Old Testament*, 204), but it goes far beyond the evidence to infer that these four streams go out to "water the four corners of the earth."

113. E. A. Speiser points out that by the tenth century BC, western Asia, the Nile valley, and the Aegean had long had mutual ties. A millennium earlier there were trade relations between Mesopotamia and the Indus Valley; the same is true of Egypt and Mesopotamia at the very dawn of history. Cf. D. J. Wiseman, "Genesis 10: Some Archaeological Considerations" (1955), in Hess and Tsumura, *"I Studied Inscriptions,"* 254–65, who documents that "before *c.* 2000–1800 BC the flow of trade, and therefore of merchants and their supporting caravans and military expeditions, is abundantly attested by contemporary documents and implies a knowledge of the very area outlined in Genesis 10" (264). Speiser says, "There is a vast difference between drawing a reasonably accurate map of a country and dumping the Nile in the Persian Gulf. The chances are that no ancient caravan ever strayed that far from its intended objective" (E. A. Speiser, "The Rivers of Paradise" [1958], in Hess and Tsumura, *"I Studied Inscriptions,"* 176). The same goes for thinking that the Nile shares a common source with the Tigris and Euphrates. Day's appeal to Pausanias's reporting the story that the Euphrates was said to disappear into a marsh and then to resurface again beyond Ethiopia, becoming the Nile (*Description of Greece* 2.5.3), in an attempt to show people's geographical confusion in the ancient world, goes no distance toward showing that people thought the Nile and the Euphrates might be two rivers flowing from a common source. His assertion that the Pishon represents the Persian Gulf/Indian Ocean/Red Sea, misconceived as a river, makes no sense, since these bodies of water obviously do not originate where the Tigris and Euphrates do (Day, *From Creation to Babel*, 29–30).

114. So Speiser, "Rivers of Paradise," 175–82.

115. In the Sargon Geography "the tail of the Euphrates" refers to its outlet (in our anatomical metaphor, its mouth), so that the river's "head" is its source or headwaters (Horowitz, *Mesopotamian Cosmic Geography*, 85). Kenneth Kitchen states that the author's perspective is that of someone in the garden "looking *out* from where the single stream entered the garden, and looking back just *upstream* to the point where four 'head' rivers

divides into the four named tributaries. Such a reversed point of view would place the Garden of Eden on the ancient coastline of the Persian Gulf, into which the Tigris and Euphrates empty. The Pishon and Gihon could then be variously identified as, for instance, the Kerkha and Diyala Rivers or as the Karun and Kerkha Rivers.

Wenham complains that Speiser does not deal with the text's plain statement that the rivers flow out (*yāṣāʾ*) from Eden, not into it.[116] Hamilton acknowledges that several OT passages use *yāṣāʾ* to describe a river's proceeding from its source (see especially Zech 14:8, which has, like Gen 2:10, *yāṣāʾ mayim* to describe the river's flowing from Jerusalem to the seas). He simply accepts Speiser's claim that the phrase in Gen 2:10 should be translated not "flow from" but "rise in."[117] For his part, Wenham asks whether "the insoluble geography," including the rivers' reversed flow, is not an indication of Genesis's adoption of "old mythological motifs" in the narrative.[118]

The anomaly of a "reversed flow," however, may not be contemplated by the text. For Gen 2:8 speaks of Eden as a geographic area to the east in which God planted a garden. In 2:10 "Eden" still designates this region, not the garden, stating that the river flowed out of Eden into the garden to water it.[119] In a thorough review of the geological and archaeological evidence concerning the geography of the Persian Gulf, Jeffrey Rose explains that from the time of the last ice age in the late Pleistocene epoch (ca. 10,000 BC) until being

came together to form the single stream that entered the garden" (K. A. Kitchen, *On the Reliability of the Old Testament* [Grand Rapids: Eerdmans, 2003], 428–29). On Kitchen's view, the rivers' heads seem not to be their sources but the place of their convergence.

116. Wenham, *Genesis 1–15*, 66.

117. Hamilton, *Book of Genesis*, 168.

118. Wenham, *Genesis 1–15*, 66. Cf. Walton's curious comparison of the "cosmic geography" of Gen 2 to our concept of the Tropic of Capricorn. It is real but not in the same topographical category as the Thames (Walton, "Eden, Garden of," 204). This comparison is strange because the Tropic of Capricorn is a geometrical line and hence an abstract object. The rivers of Genesis are concrete objects, capable of irrigating the land, and so in the same category as the Thames. Walton admits that the four rivers were supposed to be real bodies of water, but he says that their description concerns their "cosmic role." Walton is evidently interpreting the term *cosmic* to mean something like "mythological." On his view the Garden of Eden was the place of God's abode and the source of life-giving water that flowed through the four rivers, benefiting all the earth. Leaving aside the fact that in Genesis Eden is not the place of God's abode—it is not "the garden of God"—but the place of man's abode, the roles designated by Walton are purely mythological, not real. "The geography of the myths is not scientific geography, not even that of the Sumerians" (Castellino, "The Origins of Civilization according to Biblical and Cuneiform Texts," 82).

119. So Kitchen, *Reliability of the Old Testament*, 428–29.

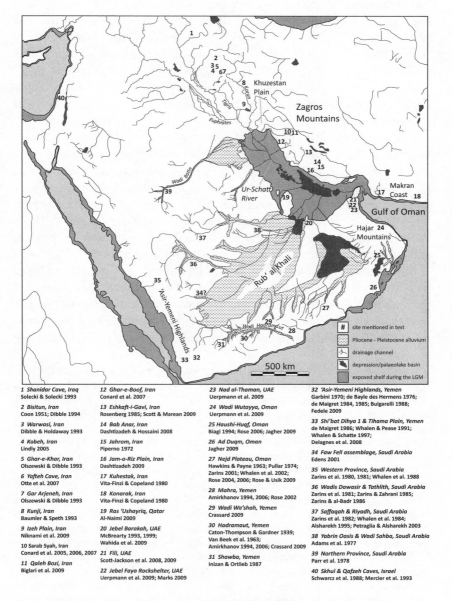

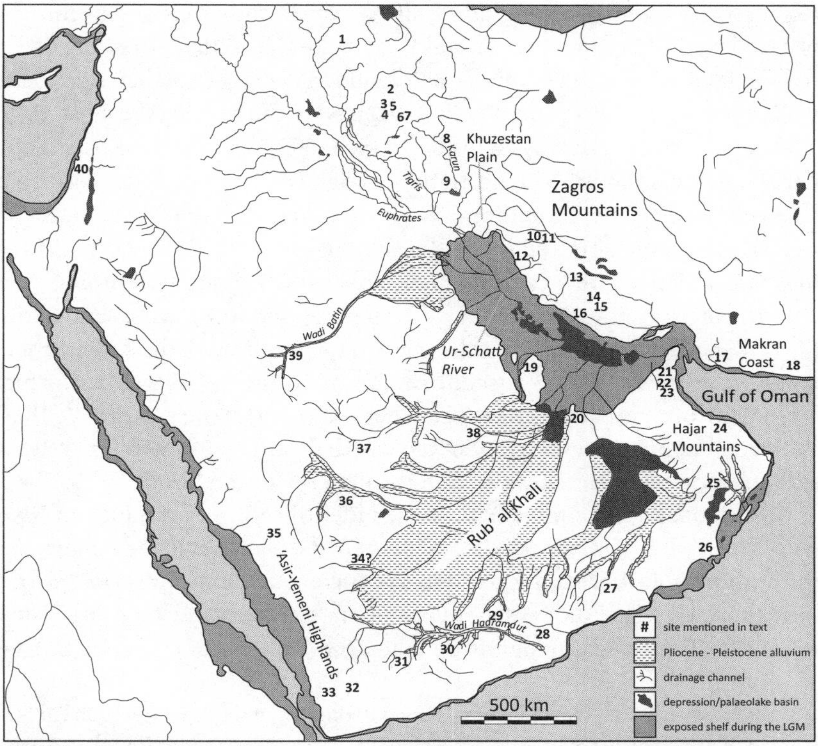

1 Shanidar Cave, Iraq
Solecki & Solecki 1993

2 Bisitun, Iran
Coon 1951; Dibble 1994

3 Warwasi, Iran
Dibble & Holdaway 1993

4 Kobeh, Iran
Lindly 2005

5 Ghar-e-Khar, Iran
Olszewski & Dibble 1993

6 Yafteh Cave, Iran
Otte et al. 2007

7 Gar Arjeneh, Iran
Olszewski & Dibble 1993

8 Kunji, Iran
Baumler & Speth 1993

9 Izeh Plain, Iran
Niknami et al. 2009

10 Sarab Syah, Iran
Conard et al. 2005, 2006, 2007

11 Qaleh Bozi, Iran
Biglari et al. 2009

12 Ghar-e-Boof, Iran
Conard et al. 2007

13 Eshkaft-i-Gavi, Iran
Rosenberg 1985; Scott & Marean 2009

14 Bab Anar, Iran
Dashtizadeh & Hossaini 2008

15 Jahrom, Iran
Piperno 1972

16 Jam-o-Riz Plain, Iran
Dashtizadeh 2009

17 Kuhestak, Iran
Vita-Finzi & Copeland 1980

18 Konarak, Iran
Vita-Finzi & Copeland 1980

19 Ras 'Ushayriq, Qatar
Al-Naimi 2009

20 Jebel Barakah, UAE
McBrearty 1993, 1999;
Wahida et al. 2009

21 Fili, UAE
Scott-Jackson et al. 2008, 2009

22 Jebel Faya Rockshelter, UAE
Uerpmann et al. 2009; Marks 2009

23 Nad al-Thaman, UAE
Uerpmann et al. 2009

24 Wadi Wutayya, Oman
Uerpmann et al. 2009

25 Haushi-Huqf, Oman
Biagi 1994; Rose 2006; Jagher 2009

26 Ad Duqm, Oman
Jagher 2009

27 Nejd Plateau, Oman
Hawkins & Payne 1963; Pullar 1974;
Zarins 2001; Whalen et al. 2002;
Rose 2004, 2006; Rose & Usik 2009

28 Mahra, Yemen
Amirkhanov 1994, 2006; Rose 2002

29 Wadi Wa'shah, Yemen
Crassard 2009

30 Hadramaut, Yemen
Caton-Thompson & Gardner 1939;
Van Beek et al. 1963;
Amirkhanov 1994, 2006; Crassard 2009

31 Shawba, Yemen
Inizan & Ortlieb 1987

32 'Asir-Yemeni Highlands, Yemen
Garbini 1970; de Bayle des Hermens 1976;
de Maigret 1984, 1985; Bulgarelli 1988;
Fedele 2009

33 Shi'bat Dihya 1 & Tihama Plain, Yemen
de Maigret 1986; Whalen & Pease 1991;
Whalen & Schatte 1997;
Delagnes et al. 2008

34 Faw Fell assemblage, Saudi Arabia
Edens 2001

35 Western Province, Saudi Arabia
Zarins et al. 1980, 1981; Whalen et al. 1988

36 Wadis Dawasir & Tathlith, Saudi Arabia
Zarins et al. 1981; Zarins & Zahrani 1985;
Zarins & al-Badr 1986

37 Saffaqah & Riyadh, Saudi Arabia
Zarins et al. 1982; Whalen et al. 1984;
Alsharekh 1995; Petraglia & Alsharekh 2003

38 Yabrin Oasis & Wadi Sahba, Saudi Arabia
Adams et al. 1977

39 Northern Province, Saudi Arabia
Parr et al. 1978

40 Skhul & Qafzeh Caves, Israel
Schwarcz et al. 1988; Mercier et al. 1993

Figure 4.3. Map of the ancient Persian Gulf basin in the late Pleistocene. Reprinted by permission from Rose, "New Light on Human Prehistory in the Arabo-Persian Gulf Oasis," fig. 2.

submerged beneath the waters of the Indian Ocean around 6000 BC, the Gulf region was a fertile oasis extending all the way to the Strait of Hormuz and watered by the Tigris and Euphrates Rivers, the Karun River draining off the Iranian Plateau, and the Wadi Batin River flowing across northern Arabia, as well as by subterranean aquifers that surfaced in the region (see fig. 4.3).[120]

The four rivers converged in the Ur-Schatt River Valley, whose deeply cut channel is still visible beneath the Persian Gulf waters. If the Garden of Eden is conceived by the author of Genesis to lie in the Gulf Oasis, then truly a river (the Ur-Schatt), fed by the four named "heads," flowed out of Eden into the garden. On this view, Cush may be identified not with Ethiopia but with the region of the Kassites in western Iran (Gen 10:8), while association of Havilah with Arabia remains. Moreover, the outflows of the subterranean aquifers, at that epoch exposed, bring to mind the *ʾēd* of Gen 2:6, which "went up from the earth and watered the whole face of the ground."[121] These subterranean rivers, linked to the Rubʿ al-Khali and Zagros aquifer systems, still deliver fresh water into the Gulf through the ocean floor.[122]

In response to Hoffmeier's proposed identification of the Pishon River with the Wadi Batin, Sparks skeptically retorts, "So should we believe that the author spoke of things known to the ancient audience or should we believe that only the author and not the audience knew of the long-lost Pishon River?"[123] The answer depends on when the location of this ancient river

120. Jeffrey I. Rose, "New Light on Human Prehistory in the Arabo-Persian Gulf Oasis," *CA* 51, no. 6 (2010): 849–83, with comments and author's reply. This alternative is also espoused by Hoffmeier, "Genesis 1–11," 32, on the basis of Farouk El-Baz, "A River in the Desert," *Discover*, July 1993; James Sauer, "The River Runs Dry," *BAR* 22, no. 4 (1996): 52–64.

121. One thinks of the land of Dilmun on the shore of the Persian Gulf, of which we are told that "from the mouth of the waters running underground, fresh waters ran out of the ground for her. The waters rose up from it into her great basins. Her city drank water aplenty from them. Dilmun drank water aplenty from them. Her pools of salt water indeed became pools of fresh water" (*Enki and Ninhursaga* 50–62).

122. It has been suggested that this is the "pipe" in the ocean utilized by Gilgamesh to dive down, weighted with stones tied to his ankles, to obtain the plant of rejuvenation (*Epic of Gilgamesh* XI). The Portuguese explorer Pedro Teixeira reported seeing such divers on his visit to the region in 1603: "The chief town of the isle, Manamà, is on the sea shore, and near it, in the depth of three or three and a-half fathoms, are several great springs of fresh, clear, and wholesome water. There are some men who make their living by bringing it up from below in waterskins, which they do very cleverly and easily, where it bubbles up, and sell it cheap" (*The Travels of Pedro Teixeira*, ed. W. F. Sinclair and D. Ferguson [London: Hakluyt Society, 1902], 175, cited by Rose, "New Light," 853).

123. Kenton L. Sparks, "Response to James K. Hoffmeier," in Halton, *Genesis*, 66–67.

was lost to memory or tradition. It is estimated to have dried up between 3500 and 2000 BC, about three thousand years after the rising waters of the Indian Ocean drove the inhabitants out of the Gulf. During that same time, the Sumerian civilization was born. People could easily have preserved memory of that river and perhaps even transmitted earlier traditions of the Oasis's existence.[124]

Even if the location of the garden is an actual region, the garden is still described in ways that would be fantastic if taken literally. What we seem to have here is a commingling of myth and factual geography, just as the real Mount Olympus in Greece served as the location for the home of Zeus and his progeny in Greek myths.[125]

The Cherubim

When God drives the man and his wife out of the Garden of Eden, he stations at its eastern entrance "the cherubim, and a flaming sword which turned every way, to guard the way to the tree of life" (Gen 3:24). What makes this detail fantastic is that the cherubim were not thought to be real beings but fantasies composed of a lion's body, a bird's wings, and a man's head. Nahum Sarna observes that the motif of composite human-animal-bird figures was widespread in various forms in art and religious symbolism in the Fertile Crescent, and the biblical cherubim would seem to be connected with this artistic tradition.[126] The name *cherubim* seems to be related to the *kuribu*, man-headed bulls with eagles' wings that frequently stood outside Mesopotamian temples. Cherubim filled multiple roles in the biblical tradition, such as symbolizing God's presence or sovereignty. Artistic representations of such creatures were to be found in the tabernacle and temple, including the holy of holies (Exod 25:18–22; 26:31; 1 Kgs 6:23–29). Sarna points out that they are the only pictorial representation permitted in an otherwise anti-iconic religion. They do not violate the prohibition against images because they are "purely products of the human imagination" and so "do not represent any existing reality in heaven and earth."[127] Thus, images of them

124. See note 136.

125. Hesiod, *Theogony* 925–30, 950–55, 960–65.

126. Sarna, *Genesis*, "Excursus 1: The Cherubim," 375–76. See James B. Pritchard, ed., *The Ancient Near East: An Anthology of Texts and Pictures* (Princeton: Princeton University Press, 2011), plates 163, 165.

127. Sarna, *Genesis*, 375–76. Cassuto interprets the cherubim and flashing sword to be symbols of storm winds and lightning flashes that guard the way into the Garden of Eden

could be made in ancient Israel without breaking the second commandment prohibiting images of things in heaven (Exod 20:4–5), for the cherubim were not real. Yet here in Gen 3 they are posted as guards at a time and place in history (along with a rotating, flashing sword) to guard for an indeterminate time the Garden of Eden against man's reentry.

The Antediluvians' Life Spans

Gunkel does not mention but certainly might have mentioned the fantastic life spans of the antediluvians (Gen 5:3–32). Von Rad lists some of the incredible implications: "The long lives ascribed to the patriarchs cause remarkable synchronisms and duplications. Adam lived to see the birth of Lamech, the ninth member of the genealogy; Seth lived to see the translation of Enoch and died shortly before the birth of Noah. Lamech was the first to see a dead man—Adam; Noah outlived Abraham's grandfather, Nahor, and died in Abraham's sixtieth year. Shem, Noah's son, even outlived Abraham. He was still alive when Esau and Jacob were born!"[128]

The antediluvians' lives were not prolonged miraculously by God but were to all appearances entirely natural.[129] Commentators have found no explanation of these life spans that commends itself to most scholars.[130] In Sumerian king lists we have examples of antediluvian royal reigns that are even more fantastic, with kingly reigns up to some forty-three thousand years.[131] The life spans of the antediluvians would have appeared fantastic to ancient Israelites, just as they do to us. But persons in myths, even historical persons, can be made to live as long as one likes.

Noah's Flood

We come to the flood story, one of the most fantastic episodes in the primaeval narratives. Gunkel complained that "there are too many species of animals for all to have been assembled in any ark," around 5.8 million terres-

(*Book of Genesis*, 175–76). This is reminiscent of pagan myths in which gods represent forces of nature.

128. Von Rad, *Genesis*, 72.

129. A point emphasized by Sarfati, *Genesis*, 297; cf. chap. 15.

130. Wenham, *Genesis 1–15*, 130–34, has a good discussion of such efforts.

131. Thorkild Jacobsen, *The Sumerian King List*, AS 11 (Chicago: University of Chicago Press, 1939), 73 (col. i 12).

trial animal species today alone.[132] Young earth creationists have responded that the assumption that Noah boarded members of every identified species is gratuitous; the ark would have had ample room to include members of every identified genus of terrestrial animals.[133] But as Hugh Ross rejoins, that answer seems "to trade one implausible hypothesis for another. Animals, especially those as advanced as horses and felines, simply do not—and cannot, by any observed or postulated mechanism—evolve or diversify at such a rapid rate" so as to produce the earth's current 5.8 million land animal species after the flood.[134]

Moreover, it is even more fantastic that the earth suffered a worldwide deluge that wiped out all of humanity not aboard the ark as well as all terrestrial animals. Modern geology and anthropology have rendered such a catastrophe all but impossible.[135] Geologically we have evidence of vast but nonetheless local catastrophic floods, such as the flood that inundated the Black Sea basin when the Mediterranean Sea burst through the Bosporus around 5600 BC or the Missoula floods that inundated the state of Washington at the end of the last ice age from around fifteen thousand to thirteen thousand years ago. But no such evidence exists for a worldwide deluge. Some proponents of a literalist reading of Genesis have therefore claimed that the Noachian flood was also a local catastrophe, perhaps to be identified with the Black Sea disaster or a catastrophic flood in Mesopotamia that occurred around 2900 BC, according to the geological evidence, or even a flood as long ago as the last ice age.

132. Gunkel, *Legends of Genesis*, 7; Hugh Ross, *Navigating Genesis: A Scientist's Journey through Genesis 1–11* (Covina, CA: Reasons to Believe, 2014), 171.

133. Sarfati, *Genesis*, 500–516. Sarfati says that if we take the biblical "kind" to be equivalent to the man-made genus, then since there are around eight thousand genera, including extinct ones, about sixteen thousand individual animals had to be taken aboard the ark. Marine animals and insects did not need to be taken aboard the ark in order to survive the deluge. He calculates on the basis of the ark's dimensions that it would have had a volume of over 340 semitrailer trucks and so could have contained 102,000 sheep-sized animals.

134. Ross, *Navigating Genesis*, 171. Ross is assuming a flood of at least ten thousand years ago. Ross's point becomes especially devastating when one realizes that on a young earth interpretation of Gen 1–11, Noah had to take about one thousand dinosaurs aboard the ark, so that the entire history of dinosaur evolution and extinction had to take place in the roughly three hundred years between the disembarkation from the ark and the birth of Abraham.

135. For a brief but crushing summary of the difficulties, see Ross, *Navigating Genesis*, chap. 17.

We need not dispute that such an event may well have lain at the historical roots of the flood story in its various recensions.[136] But it is quite another

136. An intriguing possibility is that the flood story is a myth rooted in the inundation of the aforementioned Persian Gulf Oasis (see pp. 116–18) that occurred between fourteen thousand and six thousand years ago as a result of sea level rises largely due to glacial melting. See the colorful maps of the gradual ingression of the waters of the Indian Ocean into the Gulf provided by Kurt Lambeck, "Shoreline Reconstructions for the Persian Gulf Since the Last Glacial Maximum," *EPSL* 142, nos. 1–2 (1996): 43–57. By 12,000 BC the Strait of Hormuz had opened up as a narrow waterway, and by about 10,500 BC the incursion into the central basin had started. The western basin flooded about one thousand years later. The present shoreline was reached about 5000 BC and then surpassed, as the relative sea level rose over the next thousand years to more than two meters above its present level, inundating the low-lying areas of southern Mesopotamia. As Teller et al. show, the ingression of the waters occurred in stages, being punctuated by stillstands and relatively rapid advances (J. T. Teller et al., "Calcareous Dunes of the United Arab Emirates and Noah's Flood: The Postglacial Reflooding of the Persian (Arabian) Gulf," *QI* 68–71 [2000]: 297–308; see also Gary A. Cooke, "Reconstruction of the Holocene Coastline of Mesopotamia," *Geoarchaeology* 2, no. 1 [1987]: 15–28).

Teller et al. estimate that because of the varying rate of sea level rise, the waters at times flooded across the flat floor of the Persian Gulf at more than a kilometer per year: "Thus, at several times during the postglacial period, humans living on the exposed floor of the Arabian Gulf would have witnessed rapid inundation along the leading edge of the transgressing sea in only a few decades. Large areas became salinized and submerged within a person's lifetime; settlements, pasture, and cultivated land would have to have been abandoned, navigation along the extended course of the ancient Tigris and Euphrates Rivers changed, and civilization in the region was forever dislocated" (Teller et al., "Calcareous Dunes," 304; see also Douglas J. Kennett and James P. Kennett, "Early State Formation in Southern Mesopotamia: Sea Levels, Shorelines, and Climate Change," *JICA* 1 [2006]: 67–99).

Teller et al. think that the stories of a great flood may be a record of this rapid postglacial flooding of the floor of the Persian Gulf. According to Lambeck, "excavations at Ur and elsewhere have led to evidence of a flooding event at about 4000–3000 BC and it is tempting to associate the Sumerian 'Flood' legend with the peak of the Holocene transgression" ("Shoreline Reconstructions," 56). It deserves to be asked whether there could not have occurred a sudden, massive flooding that was later masked by further ingressions. At least one geologist has proposed such a catastrophic flooding of the Gulf Oasis occasioned by the breaching of a dam at the Strait of Hormuz formed as a result of windblown sand dunes (Sanford, "Thoughts on Eden," 7–10). These sorts of dunes are described in some detail in Teller et al., "Calcareous Dunes."

It might be thought that memory of a flood at the end of the last ice age could not persist until the founding of Sumerian civilization. But fascinating studies among Australian Aborigines have shown that memories of sea level rises covering previously exposed land masses have persisted for nearly ten thousand years since the end of the last ice age (Upton, "Ancient Sea Rise Tale Told Accurately for 10,000 Years"). Researchers have

matter to claim that the text as we have it contemplates a merely local flood, for the text seems clearly to describe a worldwide flood:

> And the waters prevailed so mightily upon the earth that all the high mountains under the whole heaven were covered; the waters prevailed above the mountains, covering them fifteen cubits deep. (Gen 7:19–20)

> The ark came to rest upon the mountains of Ararat. And the waters continued to abate until the tenth month; in the tenth month, on the first day of the month, the tops of the mountains were seen. (Gen 8:4–5)

> The dove found no place to set her foot, and she returned to him to the ark, for the waters were still on the face of the whole earth. (Gen 8:9)

Even the mountaintops were submerged beneath the floodwaters, to a depth of fifteen cubits, which is impossible for a local flood.

Even more indicative of the worldwide nature of the flood are its effects; all humanity and all terrestrial life on earth are destroyed:

> I will bring a flood of waters upon the earth, to destroy all flesh in which is the breath of life from under heaven; everything that is on the earth shall die. (Gen 6:17)[137]

> And all flesh died that moved upon the earth, birds, cattle, beasts, all swarming creatures that swarm upon the earth, and every man; everything on the dry land in whose nostrils was the breath of life died. He blotted out every living thing that was upon the face of the ground, man and animals and creeping things and birds of the air; they were blotted out from the earth. Only Noah was left, and those that were with him in the ark. (Gen 7:21–23)

---

identified eighteen Aboriginal stories that accurately describe geographical features that predated the rising of the seas after the end of the last glacial maximum. Intriguingly, these memories are mingled with native myths, for example, of an old woman who crawled between the islands, followed by a flow of water, or of the ancestral figure Ngurunderi, who marooned his wives on an island. Similar accurate memories are said to persist among coastal Native American tribes.

137. Similarly, in the *Epic of Gilgamesh* the flood is conceived to all but wipe out the human race, as evident from Enlil's angry reaction upon learning that Utnapishtim has survived: "No man was to survive the destruction!" (XI.170; cf. 130).

The flood in the mind of the Genesis writer had to be extensive enough to wipe out every human being on earth not aboard the ark, not to mention every terrestrial animal, lest some escape God's judgment.[138]

Ross argues that, despite appearances, the text does teach a merely local flood.[139] He notes first that in Gen 41:57 "all the countries" are said to come to Egypt to buy grain because the famine was severe "in all the world," even though it was limited to nations within Egypt's sphere of influence.[140] Such an argument is of little force, however, since it merely illustrates the logical point that one's quantifiers are relative to a domain of objects. In order to know what objects are comprised by universal quantifiers like "all," we have to look at the context of use to determine the domain of quantification. In contrast to the restricted domain of Gen 41:57, the domain of quantification in Gen 6–8 seems to be all the earth under the sky and all living terrestrial animals and humans. Of course, the world known to the author was much smaller than the known globe today, but his expressions make it plausible that he took his domain of quantification to be unlimited with respect to the earth's surface.

Ross also infers from the Tower of Babel story that the author of Genesis thought that mankind had failed to disperse, as God originally commanded (Gen 1:28). But even if the author thought that mankind remained localized after the flood, that gives no basis at all for inferring that he thought antediluvian mankind inhabited only the Persian Gulf region. (If he did so think, we now know on the basis of palaeoanthropology that such an assumption

138. Sarfati, *Genesis*, 528–29, notes that the expression "all the mountains under all the heavens" precludes taking "all" in a relative sense. He poses a number of penetrating questions to advocates of a local flood: Why not have Noah just walk to the other side of the mountain to escape the flood? Why send every kind of animal to the ark? Why make the ark big enough to hold all the land vertebrate animals? Why would birds have been sent aboard the ark? How can the waters rise to fifteen cubits above the mountains? Sarfati also points out that a Mesopotamian flood would have flowed toward the south, opposite the Ararat mountains. Local floods do not last 150 days or take so long to dry out. People not living in the vicinity would not have been affected by a local flood and so not judged by God. God would have broken his promise never to send such a flood again because there have been many local floods.

139. Ross, *Navigating Genesis*, chap. 16.

140. Ross also appeals to texts outside Genesis, but these are irrelevant to the way in which the pentateuchal author uses his quantifiers. Ross's attempt to turn back the force of the mountains' being covered with the floodwaters by appealing to the range of meanings of "cover" (*kāsâ*) is futile, not merely because the meaning of the word will be determined by context, but also because even a flood that merely swept over but did not submerge the mountains would not for that reason be local.

is fantastic.)[141] There is no way of knowing from place-names in Gen 2–6 how widely dispersed the author may have thought (if he thought about it at all) antediluvian mankind was. However this may be, the author doubtless did not think that animals had disobeyed God's command to be fruitful and multiply and so would have thought that they were much more widely dispersed than the Persian Gulf area. Yet they all perished in the flood. Even if the author describes hyperbolically a flood that he thought to be merely local, still he thought it was extensive enough to wipe out all human beings and land animals, for that is what God's judgment required. If the story is not fantastic in presupposing a worldwide flood, then it is fantastic in presupposing that a local flood could annihilate all humanity and animals.

The only positive evidence that Ross adduces for thinking that the text contemplates a local flood is that the dove released from the ark is able to return with an olive leaf, which suggests a low altitude tree not destroyed by the flood. The argument has force but may indicate no more than the author's belief that the several months' time during which the waters receded was sufficient for the sprouting of new olive leaves. It does not serve to overturn the author's use of universal quantifiers with respect to the earth, the heavens, land animals, and humanity.

Positive evidence that a local flood is in view might also be adduced from Num 13:33, where the Anakim are said by Israelite spies to be descended from the Nephilim, a race sired by illicit unions prior to the flood, a belief that contradicts the universal destruction wrought by the flood. But it is plausible that the pentateuchal author regards the spies' report as exaggeration inspired by cowardice ("we seemed to ourselves like grasshoppers, and so we seemed to them"). Despite a poetic text like Amos 2:9–10, there is no account of Joshua's having encountered giants in his conquest of the tribes of Canaan (Josh 11:21). The report of the spies does show that belief in descendants of an antediluvian race might exist in Israel, despite the flood story, though such belief is consistent with the spies' not being particularly acute. John Day hypothesizes that a redactor, conscious of the fact that the Nephilim were still around later, added the phrase "and also afterward" to Gen 6:4.[142] But that would be to introduce a contradiction into the flood

141. See David Reich, *Who We Are and How We Got Here: Ancient DNA and the New Science of the Human Past* (New York: Pantheon, 2018), which charts the course of human migrations out of Africa and across the globe.

142. Day, *From Creation to Babel*, 86. Day thinks that we must assume that the story of the sons of God originally involved a postflood setting. But that hypothesis sits ill with the suggestion that a later redactor added the phrase "and also afterward" to the story in

story rather than resolve a problem. And it would seem strange that an especially wicked race of people should be thought to have been spared God's judgment. We have already seen in any case that the pentateuchal author is unconcerned about ironing out inconsistencies between separated narratives, such as Gen 6 and Num 13.

Ross also fails to appreciate the general point that the flood is portrayed as returning the earth to its primaeval condition before the dry land appeared, which requires a worldwide flood. Commentators have often remarked on the linguistic connections between the creation story and the account of the denouement of the flood. Matthieu Richelle, for example, writes,

> In a striking way the subsiding [of the waters] (Gen 8) appears as a renewal of the Creation. The wind which God made to move over the water (8.1) recalls the breath of God circulating over the waters (1.2), just as the common mention of the "deep"; the "windows of heavens" (8.2) evoke the imagery of the "firmament" (1.6–8); the appearance of the summits of the mountains during the recession of the waters (8.5) repeats the initial emergence of the solid land (1.9); the lists of animals are deliberately similar (1.24–25; 8.17–19). Next the discourse about man is manifestly conceived to appear as a renewal of the one at the beginning of Genesis, recalling the motif of the "image of God" (9.6; cf. 1.26–28), the blessing and original mandate (8.1–2; cf. 1.28), and the assignment of food (8.3; cf. 1.29).[143]

The mention of dry land in 7:22 recalls the dry land that first appeared in 1:9–10. The universality of the flood is why creation begins anew, as it were, with a creation mandate to Noah and his family similar to that issued to the first couple.

But is myth the best explanation of the worldwide nature of the flood story? We do need to reckon with the possibility of hyperbole. In the Sar-

its new antediluvian setting. A surprising number of scholars interpret "and also afterward" to refer to the postflood existence of the Nephilim, which on pain of inconsistency requires a merely local flood. See, e.g., Ronald Hendel, "Genesis 6:1–4 in Recent Interpretation" (paper presented at the Annual Meeting of the Society of Biblical Literature, Genesis Section/Pentateuch Section, San Diego, CA, November 24, 2019). The presence of megaliths throughout ancient Israel, noted by Hendel, has no demonstrated connection with Gen 6:1–4.

143. Matthieu Richelle, "La structure littéraire de l'Histoire Primitive (Genèse 1,1–11,26) en son état final," *BN* 151 (2011): 13–14. See his clear tableau of similarities on 14.

gon Geography 6–32, Sargon the Great boasts that he had "conquered the totality of the land under heaven," an expression very much like Genesis's, but he also knows the geographic limits of his empire as well as unconquered nations with whom the empire had trade relations.[144] Tremper Longman III and John Walton, appealing to ANE texts describing military conquests in hyperbolic language, interpret the flood story to be the description of a local flood in universalistic terms. They even suggest that ancient readers would have themselves realized this fact: "The description truly is that of a worldwide flood, not a local flood. Though some modern readers don't see it, the original audience would've understood that such a description is hyperbole."[145] That seems dubious. Militaristic and royal use of hyperbole is really a matter of boasting, but in the case of the flood, the political context that promotes such self-aggrandizement is wanting. Longman and Walton point to the unprecedented and unrealistic dimensions of the ark as evidence of hyperbole, which ancient readers would have recognized as a figurative description. The point is well taken but does not support recognition of a local flood.[146]

The question is, what lies at the root of such figurative descriptions? Is it that the ancients were simply prone to hyperbole? Or is it, more plausibly, that we are dealing here with the language of myth? Longman and Walton compare the flood account to apocalyptic literature in which a sociopolitical cataclysm can be rhetorically described in cosmic proportions.[147] Exactly; and the comparison suggests that in the flood story we are dealing not just with exaggeration but with the genre of myth. Later Longman and Walton identify the genre of Genesis as "theological history."[148] "This story was passed down orally and then eventually in written form through the

144. Taking Sargon's hyperbolic claims literalistically draws Horowitz into an attempt to calculate the area of the earth's surface as reckoned at that time, leading to an absurd result (*Mesopotamian Cosmic Geography*, 95).

145. Longman and Walton, *Lost World of the Flood*, 48. They even assert that Jesus and the NT authors "were sophisticated enough to understand that [the account is hyperbolic] (even if some modern readers are not)" (99).

146. Longman and Walton themselves later acknowledge that more than hyperbole is involved in the description of the dimensions of the ark (*Lost World of the Flood*, 75–76), which again suggests myth.

147. Longman and Walton, *Lost World of the Flood*, 36–37; cf. 178.

148. Longman and Walton, *Lost World of the Flood*, 85. This nomenclature is apparently Longman's (Longman and Walton, *Lost World of the Flood*, 111; Tremper Longman III, "What Genesis 1–2 Teaches (and What It Doesn't)," in Charles, *Reading Genesis 1–2*, 110), for Walton prefers "imagistic history." See *infra*, p. 155.

generations, and it became a very important vehicle to deliver a significant theological message."[149] The problem with this classification, they acknowledge, is that the patriarchal history of Gen 12–50 is also theological history, and yet the primaeval history of Gen 1–11 has "a significantly different feel to it," particularly in its use of figurative language to describe the deep past and its similarity to other ANE flood stories. What Longman and Walton are describing is a genre that others have identified as mytho-history, which distinguishes Gen 1–11 from Gen 12–50.[150] This classification better explains the description of a worldwide flood than mere hyperbole.

The Table of Nations

Gunkel ridiculed the idea that after the flood "the nations of the earth originated from the expansion of a single family." Indeed, the Table of Nations of Gen 10 is fantastic. Although the table presents the various persons and nations as descended from Noah's sons, Shem, Ham, and Japheth (Gen 10:1), the peoples listed are not necessarily connected by blood but represent eclectic groupings based on geographical, linguistic, racial, and cultural similarities.[151] For example, some of the peoples that modern linguists and anthropologists would classify as Semitic—that is, as sons of Shem—are listed in the table as sons of Ham instead. Because the descendants of Ham are under God's curse (Gen 9:24–25), Israel's greatest enemies are listed as Ham's descendants. "Their classification as Hamites indicates that the table of nations is not really so uncommitted as it may first appear."[152] Moreover, this feature of the table is not a modern discovery; the ancient compiler would himself have been aware of how eclectic his groupings were. For ex-

149. Longman and Walton, *Lost World of the Flood*, 86.

150. See *infra*, pp. 152–54. Although the subtitle of their book is *Mythology, Theology, and the Deluge Debate*, Longman and Walton have unfortunately little to say about myth. They deny that the flood story "is myth" (*Lost World of the Flood*, 145), thereby using *myth*, not in the folklorist's sense, but as in the vernacular.

151. Sarna comments, "On the surface, the use of verbs expressing birth and of terms like 'son,' 'father,' 'first-born' suggest straightforward genealogies of the kind already encountered in previous chapters. In actual fact, these recapitulations disclose that the terminology is not meant to be taken literally." He points out, "Many of the personal names listed here are otherwise known to be those of places or peoples. Ten names have plural endings, nine others take the gentilic adjectival suffix *-i*, which indicates ethnic affiliation, and they also have the definite article, which is inadmissible with personal names in Hebrew" (*Genesis*, 68).

152. Wenham, *Genesis 1–15*, 243.

ample, he collects Mesopotamian, Ethiopian, and Arabian ethnicities together under Cush. He could not have failed to notice that Sheba and Havilah are listed as descendants of both Ham and Shem (Gen 10:7, 28–29). All this suggests that he did not understand the genealogy to be a straightforward historical account.

The Tower of Babel

The primaeval narratives close with one last apparently fantastic story, according to which the world's languages owe their origin to the confusion of tongues that God wrought at the Tower of Babel.[153] As a result of modern linguistic studies, we know that such a sudden, unitary origin of the world's languages is palpably false. Defenders of a literal interpretation of the text resort to the same device employed with respect to the flood—namely, treating the story as purely local.[154] Such an interpretation is doubtless more plausible with respect to the tower story than the flood story. But as we have seen, the connection with the Table of Nations suggests a more international perspective on the part of the author.[155] The various languages spoken by these nations seem to be the result of the tower incident. The tower story may have been chronologically displaced in order to close out the primaeval history with God's judgment on sin, leaving an unresolved problem going into the patriarchal narratives of Israel's election.

153. This point is underlined by the ostensible recency of the tower event. The story refers to the typically Babylonian building materials of bricks instead of stones and bitumen for mortar and describes the tower in terms of a Babylonian ziggurat "with its top in the heavens," indicative of a date no earlier than the second millennium BC. See Day, *From Creation to Babel*, 170–78.

154. Hamilton recognizes that if we take the story to account for the origin of a polyglot from a monoglot world, then "Genesis 11 provides a most incredible and naïve explanation of language diversification" (*Book of Genesis*, 358). Hamilton instead suggests that in addition to the local languages alluded to in Gen 10, there may have been a lingua franca spoken by all the listed peoples, which was then dissolved by God. This proposal stands in tension with Hamilton's earlier point concerning the flood that when Genesis speaks of the earth without qualification (e.g., Gen 11:1: *kol-hāʾāreṣ*; cf. 11:2), the reference is universal (273). Thus, just as all humanity had been destroyed in the flood, so all humanity is thought to have spoken this alleged lingua franca, which would require the fantastic conclusion either that at this time in human history people did not live outside the ANE or that Australian Aborigines and South American Indians also spoke this language.

155. Sarna, *Genesis*, 81, opines that the emphasis on involvement of the totality of humankind in the offense is crucial to the understanding of the episode as the climactic event in the universal history of Gen 1–11.

The Age of the Earth

Finally, we should be remiss if we did not mention the most fantastic element of the entire primaeval history—namely, the ostensible claim that the entire world was less than two thousand years old at the time of Abraham's birth. Only 1,656 years elapsed from the time of Adam's creation until the flood, and another 292 years separate the flood from Abraham's birth. The genealogy of Shem in Gen 11:10–26 is so tightly constructed by means of the ages at which fathers bore sons that generational gaps are difficult to interpolate.[156] Noah would thus have been a contemporary of Abraham, and Shem would have even outlived Abraham by thirty-five years, an embarrassment that the Samaritan Pentateuch and the Septuagint both try to avoid by revising the patriarchs' ages.[157] Even if we allow for gaps in the genealogies of Gen 1–11, at most a few thousand years can be reasonably interpolated. As creation scientists themselves recognize, this puts a literal interpretation of Gen 1–11 into massive conflict with modern science, history, and linguistics.[158] In order to explain how we can even see the stars, some of which are billions of light-years away, creation scientists have been led to radically reinterpret modern cosmology.[159] Since Noah was contemporaneous with the age of the dinosaurs, he is said to have taken dinosaurs aboard the ark, two of every one of the five hundred genera. Upon disembarking, he released these dinosaurs into the world, where they spread throughout the earth and evolved into all the known species of dinosaur. Since Noah disembarked only 292 years prior to the birth of Abraham, the entire history of dinosaur evolution and extinction must be compressed into the space of less than three hundred years (unless, that is, dinosaurs were still about at the time of Abraham). In

156. A point emphasized by Sarfati, *Genesis*, 464. See the interesting chart of overlapping life spans of the antediluvians on 449. For the attempt to insert gaps, see *infra*, pp. 144–45.

157. See the helpful comparative chart in Mathews, *Genesis 1–11:26*, 495.

158. See the commentary by Sarfati, *Genesis*, 216–17, 530–33, 559, 569, 581, 596–97, 652, 668, 670.

159. See, e.g., D. Russell Humphreys, *Starlight and Time: Solving the Puzzle of Distant Starlight in a Young Universe* (Green Forest, AR: Master Books, 1996), who proposes a cosmological model according to which the universe is an expanding, rotating ball of matter in empty space with our solar system located at its center. For an irenic but devastating critique of such a cosmology, see Samuel R. Conner and Don N. Page, "*Starlight and Time* Is the Big Bang," *CENTJ* 12, no. 2 (1998): 174–94, who show that even given Humphreys's maverick model, the age of the universe is identical to that in standard big bang cosmology.

order to explain how most all the marsupials, like koala bears and platypuses, crawled all the way from modern-day Turkey to Australia, plate tectonics is held to have not yet separated the primordial supercontinent into the world's continents; this tectonic activity is said to have also taken place within about three hundred years following the end of the flood, while at the same time mountain-building crustal movements were forming the Himalayas and Mount Everest, with remains of the marine life of the flood on its heights. On and on the revisionism must go. Truly, young earth creationists are living in a different universe than the rest of us.

I want to say once more that none of the above has anything to do with a naturalistic bias or a prejudice against miracles. Biblical literalists are far too facile in dismissing such observations as based on anti-supernaturalism. I trust that it is clear that this allegation is false. The fantastic elements in the narratives that we have identified have nothing to do with miracles, which we accept. Rather, they concern nonmiraculous features of the story that, if taken literally, are palpably false.

Conclusion

In summation, the narratives of Gen 1–11 exhibit, sometimes dramatically, the family resemblances that mark the folklorist's genre of myth. They are traditional, sacred narratives set in a primaeval age, featuring a deity as a central character, that seek to anchor realities present to the pentateuchal author in a primordial time. Sometimes fantastic, but untroubled by inconsistencies, they were objects of belief for ancient Israelites.

Chapter 5

IS GENESIS 1–11 MYTHO-HISTORY?

We have seen that the narratives of Gen 1–11 share enough of the family resemblances of myths to qualify as myths. The foregoing is not, however, the whole story. For there is an additional feature of Gen 1–11 that must now be taken into account: the narratives' apparent interest in history. This interest comes most clearly to expression in the genealogies that order the narratives chronologically.[1]

Genealogies

A genealogy may be defined as a written or oral expression of the descent of a person or persons from an ancestor or ancestors.[2] A *linear* genealogy is a genealogy that expresses only one line of descent from any given ancestor. A *segmented* genealogy is a genealogy that expresses more than one line of descent from a given ancestor. The narratives of Genesis are interspersed

1. Sarfati appeals to the *wayyiqtol* verbal pattern of Genesis—i.e., the use of *waw* + the perfect tense of the verb + a subject—to justify seeing a historical interest in the accounts (Jonathan D. Sarfati, *The Genesis Account: A Theological, Historical, and Scientific Commentary on Genesis 1–11* [Powder Springs, GA: Creation Book Publishers, 2015], 48). But this argument is fallacious, since such a form indicates at most a narrative genre, which may be myth, legend, or fable, rather than history. Thus, the crucial consideration will be the genealogies, which connect to personages that are indisputably taken by the pentateuchal author to be historical.

2. This is the definition employed in Robert Wilson's influential *Genealogy and History in the Biblical World* (New Haven: Yale University Press, 1977). It allows even brief notices of the form "____ son of ____" to count as a genealogy. This might seem to lack sufficient depth to count as a bona fide genealogy, but fortunately the Genesis genealogies involve greater depth and so are indisputedly genealogies.

with genealogical notices that include the principal characters of the narratives. These are introduced by a standard formula, "these are the generations [*tôlədôt*, literally "begettings"] of," which punctuates the narratives throughout the book (Gen 2:4; 5:1; 6:9; 10:1; 11:10, 27; 25:12, 19; 36:1, 9; 37:2). By ordering the principal characters in lines of descent, the *tôlədôt* formulae turn the primaeval narratives into a primaeval history. We do not have in Gen 1–11 a cluster of unordered prehistoric stories but a chronological account beginning at the moment of creation and carrying through to the call of Abraham.[3]

But here a word of caution is in order. It is repeatedly said that the *tôlədôt* formulae determine the structure of the book of Genesis. This careless statement is at best misleading and at worst grossly mistaken. As anyone can tell, the book of Genesis falls naturally into three parts: the primaeval history, the patriarchal narratives, and the story of Joseph and his family. The large-scale structure of Genesis is thus tripartite. As a brief consultation of the table of contents of any commentary on Genesis reveals, virtually no OT commentator structures his commentary according to the *tôlədôt* sections.[4] Doing so would divide the book into eleven sections with an introduction, thereby suppressing the large-scale structure of the book:

1. Introduction (1:1–2:3)
2. The *tôlədôt* of the heavens and the earth (2:4–4:26)
3. The *tôlədôt* of Adam (5:1–6:8)
4. The *tôlədôt* of Noah (6:9–9:29)
5. The *tôlədôt* of Noah's sons, Shem, Ham, and Japheth (10:1–11:9)
6. The *tôlədôt* of Shem (11:10–26)
7. The *tôlədôt* of Terah (11:27–25:11)
8. The *tôlədôt* of Ishmael (25:12–18)

3. Westermann contrasts this situation with the primaeval myths of Egypt, Sumer, Babylon, and primitive cultures, in which the motifs of the primaeval event form a pool and can be used arbitrarily in a quite kaleidoscopic manner. By contrast, the biblical primaeval story is arranged in a strict order; it is prefaced to a history and in such a way that there is a succession of generations from a primaeval pair leading up to Abraham (Claus Westermann, *Genesis 1–11: A Continental Commentary*, trans. John J. Scullion [Minneapolis: Fortress, 1994], 64).

4. See the curious comments of Longman that even though Genesis can be structured according to the *tôlədôt* formulae, he will follow in his commentary the tripartite structure of the book, which even the reader of the English Bible can detect (Tremper Longman III, *Genesis*, SGBC [Grand Rapids: Zondervan, 2016], 11).

9. The *tôlədôt* of Isaac (25:19–35:29)
10. The *tôlədôt* of Esau (36:1–8)
11. The *tôlədôt* of Esau (36:9–37:1)
12. The *tôlədôt* of Jacob (37:2–50:26)

Taking this to be the structure of the book of Genesis not only flattens its large-scale structure but wreaks havoc with its substructure as well.[5] It would be literarily obtuse to place the flood story (Gen 6:9–9:29) or the novella of Joseph's life (37:2–50:26) on the same level as the brief notice about Ishmael (25:12–18). The *tôlədôt* of the heavens and the earth (2:4–4:26) is not about the generations issuing from the heavens and the earth but consists of the stories of humanity's creation and fall into sin. Genesis 2:4a is better regarded as a summary of the unfolding of creation that began in 1:1 than as the *de novo* beginning of a new section.[6] It has been displaced to the end

5. See Matthieu Richelle, "La structure littéraire de l'Histoire Primitive (Genèse 1,1–11,26) en son état final," *BN* 151 (2011): 3–22. While preserving the structure of the *tôlədôt* formulae, Richelle identifies various "subsections" within the *tôlədôt* sections, such as the stories of Cain and Abel, the sons of God, and the Tower of Babel. These define more plausibly the literary structure of Gen 1–11, and Richelle's retaining the *tôlədôt* structure in his scheme is a useless concession to customary treatments.

6. Although most scholars regard 2:4a as belonging to the P source and, hence, a summary of chap. 1, I have little confidence in arguments based on such tradition-historical analyses, since the final pentateuchal author could have adapted the traditions he received as he saw fit. Similarly, there is the oft-repeated argument that because 2:4a and b form a chiasmus,

a heaven
  b earth
    c created
    c' made
  b' earth
a' heaven,

the verse marks the beginning of a new section. This argument strikes me as uncertain, not only because the chiasmus is not very tight (no divine name appears in 2:4a, nor any mention of the day of creation, nor are the verbs of creation even the same in 2:4a and b), but also because, once again, the pentateuchal author was free to create a chiasmus if he wanted to that would summarize the creation story and form a bridge to the story of humanity's creation. Rather, the most important consideration determining the function of the *tôlədôt* in 2:4a is the simple fact that while chap. 1 could be described as detailing the generations of the heavens and the earth created in 1:1, the ensuing stories of Adam and Eve's creation, their fall, and Cain and Abel are not the generations of the heavens and the earth (John Day, *From Creation to Babel: Studies in Genesis 1–11*, LHBOTS 592 [London: Bloomsbury, 2013], 18–19). See the comments of Cassuto, who combines these views by

of the creation story by 1:1 at its beginning. Genesis 4:17–26 provides the genealogy of Cain but *without* the *tôlədôt* formula. In 6:1–8 the story of the mating of the sons of God with women hardly belongs to the generations of Adam, and the ensuing flood story is not about Noah's descendants but about Noah himself. The Tower of Babel story gets lost in the *tôlədôt* of Noah's sons, though it is a quite distinct story, plausibly displaced chronologically. Esau's *tôlədôt* appears twice, and Jacob's *tôlədôt*, while serving to launch the story of Joseph, does not really appear until 46:8–27. Kenneth Mathews rightly comments on the *tôlədôt* formulae:

> At times the superscription appears to relate more to the preceding material (e.g., Adam, 5:1); at other times the person named is the subject of the section (e.g., Noah, 6:9); and still at other places the superscription names the father of the descendant who is the subject of the subsequent material (e.g., Terah, 11:27). Its placement does not always seem to be at the most reasoned junctures. What has been segregated by the rubric at points cuts across what seems to belong together (e.g., Esau's genealogy twice, 36:1 and 36:9) and what would appear to belong to separate sections are found under the same heading, such as the narrative conclusion (6:1–8) to the Sethite genealogy (5:1–32). Also the contents of the *tōledōt* sections vary considerably in length and character. For example, some comprise primarily genealogy (e.g., 5:1; 11:10) and others narrative (2:4; 37:2).[7]

Literary analysis, not the *tôlədôt* formulae, should determine the structure of Gen 1–11.[8] We find successive stories of creation, of the origin of humanity, of

arguing that the *tôlədôt* of 2:4a begins a new section by referring back to the creation account: 2:4 "serves to connect the narrative of the first section to that of the second; and its meaning is: *These*—the events described in the previous portion—constituted *the history of the heavens and the earth*, when they were created, that is, when the Lord God made them; and now I shall tell you in detail what happened at the conclusion of this Divine work" (U[mberto] Cassuto, *A Commentary on the Book of Genesis*, part 1, *From Adam to Noah: Genesis I–VI 8* [1944], trans. Israel Abrahams [Skokie, IL: Varda Books, 2005], 99).

7. Kenneth A. Mathews, *Genesis 1–11:26*, NAC 1A (Nashville: Broadman & Holman, 1996), 28.

8. Genesis "can be read as a coherent whole, with detailed correspondences between its parts, but in the main this is achieved through a detailed study of its plot development and repeated themes and motifs rather than through occasional parallel or concentric structures that might occur" (L. A. Turner, "Genesis," in *Dictionary of the Old Testament: Pentateuch*, ed. T. Desmond Alexander and David W. Baker [Downers Grove, IL:

the fall, of Cain and Abel, of the Nephilim, of the flood, the Table of Nations, and the story of the Tower of Babel.

What the *tôlədôt* formulae do accomplish is to help order the primaeval narratives chronologically. Gordon Wenham calls the genealogies "the backbone of Genesis 1–11."[9] The metaphor is apt. The *tôlədôt* formulae no more determine the structure of the book of Genesis than a backbone determines the structure of a vertebrate. Having a backbone does not determine what sort of bodily structure the vertebrate has, whether it has legs, arms, flippers, wings, or any limbs at all. The *tôlədôt* formulae help to order the stories of Gen 1–11 chronologically from beginning to end without determining the literary structure of the history. In contrast to Mesopotamian lists of successive kings, which list the kings in an ascending order from the present into the past, the biblical genealogies list names in a descending order, thus driving the narratives forward in time.[10]

Notice that so understanding the genealogies makes no assumption as to whether the genealogies served as the author's primary sources, which he then fleshed out with various narratives, or whether the narratives were primary and then ordered by means of the genealogies. Since such tradition-historical conclusions are so uncertain, any probabilistic inferences based on such assumptions will become even more uncertain. Taking the text as we have it, we may say that the genealogies imply that the narratives have a roughly chronological order, since a person's descendant could not have lived prior to him in time.

Mere chronology, however, is not sufficient to indicate a historical interest. The *Enuma elish* contains chronologically arranged stories (Marduk

InterVarsity Press, 2003], 352; cf. V. J. Steiner, "Literary Structure of the Pentateuch," in Alexander and Baker, *Dictionary of the Old Testament*, 544–56).

9. Gordon J. Wenham, "Genesis 1–11 as Protohistory," in *Genesis: History, Fiction, or Neither? Three Views on the Bible's Earliest Chapters*, ed. Charles Halton (Grand Rapids: Zondervan, 2015), 77. It is worth noting that when Wilson in his influential work states, "Genealogies were apparently never used as the skeleton of the narratives" (*Genealogy and History*, 135), he is talking about genealogical notices like "son of" in a list of names. Rather, "the list forms the skeleton of historical works" (132). Wilson's conclusion is consistent with holding that the biblical genealogies are the backbone of the primaeval history, since the genealogical connections are inherent to the list, not adventitious.

10. As emphasized by Richard S. Hess, "The Genealogies of Genesis 1–11 and Comparative Literature," in *"I Studied Inscriptions from before the Flood": Ancient Near Eastern, Literary, and Linguistic Approaches to Genesis 1–11*, ed. Richard S. Hess and David Toshio Tsumura, SBTS (Winona Lake, IN: Eisenbrauns, 1994), 67. This does not exclude that on occasion a *tôlədôt* formula is used to continue or conclude a section (2:4a; 10:32; 25:13; 36:9).

conquers Tiamat before ascending to the position of supremacy among the gods), but hardly has a historical interest. What makes Gen 1–11 different is that the genealogies move seamlessly into the historical period of the patriarchs, where the historical interest is obvious and not in dispute. Just as Abraham is presented as a historical person, so his ancestors are presented as historical persons.

That is not to imply the accuracy of the primaeval history. It is important not to confuse an interest in history with historicity. Since it is possible to write bad history, one cannot justifiably deny a historical interest in Gen 1–11 on the grounds of its historical inaccuracy.[11] The question is not whether the author has succeeded in writing accurate history but whether the author intended to be writing or transmitting a historical account. The lack of differentiation between Abraham and his successors and his predecessors supports the view that Gen 1–11 is intended to be a primaeval history.

That being said, the relation between Genesis's genealogies and historical interest is not as straightforward as it might appear. Robert Wilson's ground-

11. To illustrate the confusion, each of the contributors to *Genesis: History, Fiction, or Neither?* was asked by the editor, Charles Halton, to identify the genre of Gen 1–11 and to justify his position. Claiming that there is no inherent conflict between history and myth, James Hoffmeier argues that the *tôlədôt* formulae organize the book of Genesis and are a key to identifying the genre of Genesis as historical (James K. Hoffmeier, "Genesis 1–11 as History and Theology," in Halton, *Genesis*, 28–31). In response, Kenton Sparks accuses Hoffmeier of evading questions concerning "which images are mythic symbol and which are closer to historical representation. . . . Why does he not answer these questions when the historicity of Genesis 1–11 is the main theme of our discussion?" (Kenton L. Sparks, "Response to James K. Hoffmeier," in Halton, *Genesis*, 64). Sparks has evidently conflated the question of genre with the question of historicity, for the historicity of Gen 1–11 was not the main theme of their discussion. Hoffmeier's genre identification does not depend on his ability to specify which parts of the purported history are accurate or inaccurate. Again, Sparks complains that Hoffmeier "recognizes the obvious parallels between the genealogies and those from the ancient world, but he errs when he infers from this the historical accuracy of the genealogies in Genesis" (65), thereby failing once again to see that genre, not historical reliability, is at issue in such comparisons. Again, Sparks claims that Hoffmeier assumes that the author's historical intention must yield historical accuracy. "Why should we assume this? From what we find in Genesis and similar ancient near Eastern texts, it is clear that the authors did not have access to dependable historical sources for the earliest periods of human existence" (65). But Sparks himself errs in thinking that a failure of historical accuracy implies no historical intent on the author's part. Wenham has a better grasp of the question, explaining that whether a text should be classified as history or something else depends on the intentions of the writer. If the text contains historical inaccuracies, that does not necessarily make it nonhistorical, only bad history (Gordon J. Wenham, "Response to James K. Hoffmeier," in Halton, *Genesis*, 62).

breaking work on the function of genealogies has been pivotal in scholarly understanding of the role of genealogies in general and in the biblical text. Wilson seeks to address the fundamental question: Are the genealogies a historiographic genre? Were they constructed for the purpose of making a historical record?[12] In an effort to answer this fundamental question, Wilson examines both the data collected by anthropologists on how genealogies function in tribal societies and the comparative literary evidence from the ANE.

With respect to the first, ever since the heyday of J. G. Frazer and other "armchair anthropologists,"[13] scholars have been acutely aware of the uncertainties involved in the collection, interpretation, and application of anthropological data. Contemporary anthropologists have therefore been much more careful in the collection and interpretation of data. Wilson collects data showing that oral genealogies often involve different domestic or political functions, sometimes resulting in conflicting genealogies, each of which is considered valid in its own sphere. Wilson summarizes the anthropological findings:

> The data we have collected so far casts considerable doubt on the proposition that oral genealogies function *primarily* as historical records. Nowhere in our study of genealogical function did we see genealogies created or preserved *only* for historiographic purposes. Rather, we saw that oral genealogies usually have some sociological function in the life of the society that uses them. Even when genealogies are recited as part of a lineage history, they are likely to reflect domestic, political, or religious relationships existing in the present rather than in the past. The purpose of the recital is not to provide the sort of accurate historical account that is the goal of the modern historian but to legitimize contemporary lineage configurations.[14]

12. He observes, "In reality, the question of the historiographic function of genealogy has never been examined systematically, and one might well ask whether ancient Near Eastern peoples regarded genealogy as a historiographic genre in the same way that we do today" (Wilson, *Genealogy and History*, 7).

13. See this characterization by Alan Dundes in the introduction to *Sacred Narrative: Readings in the Theory of Myth*, ed. Alan Dundes (Berkeley: University of California Press, 1984), 3, and his introductory comments to Bronislaw Malinowski, "The Role of Myth in Life," in *Sacred Narrative*, 193. He also refers to Frazer as a "library anthropologist" in his introductory comments to James G. Frazer, "The Fall of Man," in *Sacred Narrative*, 72–73.

14. Wilson, *Genealogy and History*, 54 (my emphasis).

The emphasis here is on "primarily" and "only." It is hardly surprising that tribal societies do not pursue history for its own sake. That does not imply an absence of historical interest. But that interest is subordinated to contemporary needs:

> Even though oral genealogies are not created or preserved for strictly historiographic purposes, the genealogies that are accepted by a society are nevertheless considered to be accurate statements of past domestic, political, and religious relationships. A society may knowingly manipulate genealogy, and rival groups within the society may advance conflicting tendentious genealogies, but once the society agrees that a particular version of the genealogy is correct, that version is cited as historical evidence to support contemporary social configurations.[15]

This is much the same concern that drives myth, as we have seen. However interesting this data from contemporary anthropology may be, its application to ancient Israel must be fraught with uncertainty in light of the inaccessibility of data concerning Hebrew oral traditions. More relevant will be comparative literary evidence concerning ANE genealogies.

In considering Sumerian and Akkadian genealogies, Wilson turns to an examination of Sumerian, Assyrian, and Babylonian king lists of successive rulers. He finds that genealogical connections were actually incidental to the lists, which were primarily concerned with the succession of cities or dynasties through which kingship passed or the antiquity of kingship in a city. In some lists the formula "____ son of ____" is imposed on names in the list by the scribe whether it applied or not. Thus, in the Mesopotamian king lists the genealogies have "no role in the overall function of the lists. The genealogies were simply part of the additional information that the compilers of the lists added to them." Wilson concludes, "As a rule, ancient Near Eastern genealogies seem not to have been created specifically for the purpose of writing history. They seldom have strictly historiographic functions, but they usually function sociologically in much the same way as the oral genealogies that we have examined."[16] Nonetheless, "they are still valuable historical sources provided their nature and functions are taken into account."[17]

15. Wilson, *Genealogy and History*, 54–55.
16. Wilson, *Genealogy and History*, 132.
17. Wilson, *Genealogy and History*, 133.

If Wilson is right about the role of genealogical notices in the Mesopotamian king lists, then these lists are hardly comparable to the biblical genealogies, which are not incidentally but essentially genealogical. While a segmented list like the Table of Nations might be only incidentally genealogical, the linear genealogies could not even exist if the genealogical connections were removed, making them utterly different than the Mesopotamian king lists. The Assyrian king Sargon II was likely not the son of his royal predecessor in the king list, for example, but Seth is supposed to be the third son of Adam.

In dealing with the genealogies of Gen 1–11, Wilson considers only the genealogies of 4:17–26 (NB not a *tôlədôt* section) and 5:1–32. Unfortunately, Wilson's analysis is predicated on tradition-historical assumptions that lead him to treat these passages as contradictory versions of the same genealogy. Wholly apart from the narrowness of his sampling, the uncertainty attending these assumptions and inferences renders Wilson's conclusions about the function of biblical genealogies less compelling. For example, his claims about the fluidity of the names in the middle of this genealogy can be equally taken as evidence that they are not the same genealogy.[18]

In dealing with the question of why the author would allow contradictory genealogies to remain side by side with no apparent attempt at harmonization, Wilson gives a twofold answer. First, it is possible that he may have wanted to draw a correlation between the traditions of the antediluvian kings and the *apkallu* who worked during their reigns. The *apkallu* were fish-men whom Babylonian tradition regarded as the benefactors who gave technological advances to mankind. Wilson's idea seems to be that J reflects the

18. See the cautionary note of Hess, "Genealogies of Genesis 1–11," 64–65. He points out that both of the comparison classes—the *apkallu* and the Sumerian King List; the Hammurabi and the Assyrian King List—are understood to preserve the names of different individuals, despite the similarities of names between the groups. Concerning the biblical genealogies, Mathews comments,

> Of the names on the lists, only two are actually the same spelling (Enoch and Lamech, excluding Adam). The genealogies show different numbers and sequences of names. More important, however, are those divergences that cannot be attributed to confusion or fluidity between two lists. Chapter 4 does not exhibit knowledge of the flood and stops short of the parade descendant of Adam's line, "Noah." Absent in chap. 5 are the segmented genealogy of names after Lamech and the woman "Naamah." Also the biographical information clearly distinguishes the "Enoch" and "Lamech" of Seth from that of Cain. Additionally, chap. 4 does not use the stereotypical language of Seth's family record in chap. 5, especially the important feature of the patriarchs' ages. (*Genesis 1–11:26*, 281–82)

apkallu tradition in 4:17–26 while P reflects the king lists in chapter 5. So the author wants to keep both in order to draw a correlation between them. Here Wilson's conjectures, in my opinion, have become too fanciful to be credible.[19] Why the biblical author would have any interest in such a correlation is not explained. Second, the anthropological evidence shows that the form of a genealogy frequently changes when its function changes. The different versions are not viewed as contradictory by the people who use them, for they know that each version is correct in its particular context. This second answer is more credible and would be an important conclusion if established by the evidence; but here it is merely hypothesized as an answer to a contradiction generated by Wilson's tradition-historical analysis.

Wilson concludes, "Our work on biblical, as well as extrabiblical, genealogies indicates that genealogies are not normally created for the purpose of conveying historical information. They are not intended to be historical records. Rather, in the Bible, as well as in the ancient Near Eastern literature and in the anthropological material, genealogies seem to have been created and preserved for domestic, politico-jural, and religious purposes, and historical information is preserved in the genealogies only incidentally."[20] It is a shame that this conclusion—which could well be correct—has not been established by the evidence but depends on a narrow sampling of biblical material and uncertain assumptions and inferences about that sample. Wilson has not established that in Gen 1–11 "genealogies seem to have been created and preserved for domestic, politico-jural, and religious purposes." For, according to Wilson's terminology, "Near Eastern genealogies function in the *domestic sphere* when they are part of personal names. They function in the *politico-jural sphere* when they are used to legitimate royal and professional officeholders. They function in the *religious or cultic sphere* when they are part of an ancestor cult."[21] It is striking that none of these functions applies to the genealogies of Gen 1–11. Although Wilson thinks that the linear genealogies in Gen 4 and 5 function in the religious sphere, there is no trace of any ancestor cult.

Aside from the fact that Wilson has not shown that the genealogies of Gen 1–11 were created and preserved for domestic, politico-jural, or religious purposes, what is far from clear is that the recitation of a biblical linear ge-

19. See the symptoms of parallelomania showing at Wilson, *Genealogy and History*, 154, 166.

20. Wilson, *Genealogy and History*, 199.

21. Wilson, *Genealogy and History*, 132 (my emphasis).

nealogy for such purposes does not involve a historical interest on the part of the tradent or author.[22] To infer that because biblical genealogies were not created for the purpose of conveying historical information they are not intended to be historical records is a non sequitur. One comes to realize that Wilson's statement of his fundamental question—Are the genealogies a historiographic genre? Were they constructed for the purpose of making a historical record?—is actually two different questions, and a negative answer to the second does not imply a negative answer to the first. Just as a fictional work might be composed for, say, a politico-jural purpose, so a historical work might be composed for a similar purpose.

Still, Wilson's work reminds us that ancient genealogies were not the work of disinterested historians but can serve other ends. For example, as mentioned earlier, the segmented genealogy that constitutes the Table of Nations in Gen 10, despite its notices "sons of" and "begot," is not about blood relations but lists peoples on the basis of political, linguistic, geographical, and similar factors—and the author of Genesis knew it. It is a showcase example of Wilson's claim that segmented genealogies serve mainly domestic, political-jural, and religious purposes.

With respect to linear genealogies, telescoping and fluidity are common features. Wilson draws attention to a royal inscriptional genealogy of Esarhaddon that calls him "Esarhaddon . . . son of Sennacherib . . . son of Sargon . . . of the everlasting royal line of Belu-bani son of Adasi." The first three names refer to the king, his father, and his grandfather; but on the basis of an Assyrian king list we know that sixty-two kings of Assyria have been omitted between Sargon II and Belu-bani. Another inscriptional genealogy of Adad-nirari III has a gap of fifty-one kings between his predecessors Enlil-kapkapi and Shalmaneser I, and a total of seventy-one omitted names between Enlil-kapkapi and Adad-nirari II. Gaps in the Sumerian, Assyrian, and Babylonian king lists are common. Nonetheless, as John Walton points out, there is no evidence that ancient genealogies included individuals who

22. This point becomes especially clear when we realize, as Wilson emphasizes elsewhere, that the placing of a traditional genealogy into a new literary context may modify the purpose served by the original genealogy (Robert R. Wilson, "Genealogy, Genealogies," in *Anchor Bible Dictionary*, ed. David Noel Freedman [New York: Doubleday, 1992], 2:929–32). Wilson opines that P's use of the *tôlədôt* formula in Genesis is "the clearest example" of literary reuse of earlier genealogical material (2:932). Accordingly, our question needs to be, how does the pentateuchal author intend the genealogies of Gen 1–11 to be understood? Wilson notes that because *tôlədôt* is associated with sequencing and progression, it sometimes takes on the extended meaning *story* or *history*.

were not believed to have existed.[23] Indeed, with respect to many of the kings in these lists, we are confident that they did exist.[24] "Consequently there would be no precedent for thinking of the biblical genealogies differently. By putting Adam in ancestor lists, the authors of Scripture are treating him as a historical person."[25]

Do the genealogies of Gen 1–11 permit long gaps in a literal history? When the *tôlədôt* of Adam in 5:1–32 is conjoined with the *tôlədôt* of Shem in 11:10–26, there is a succession of descendants from Adam to Abraham that seems to permit no missing generations because of the form used throughout: "When X had lived *n* years, he became the father of Y; and when Y had lived *m* years, he became the father of Z." By stipulating the father's age at the time of his progeny's birth, gaps seem to be excluded.

This conclusion was, however, disputed by W. H. Green in a seminal article.[26] In support of his contention that the genealogies of Gen 5 and 11 need not be taken to be complete, Green adduces five lines of evidence: (1) In numerous other biblical genealogies there is incontrovertible evidence of abridgment. (2) The author nowhere sums the ages of the persons listed nor deduces any chronological statement concerning the time that elapsed from the creation or from the deluge, as is done from the descent into Egypt to the exodus (Exod 12:40) or from the exodus to the building of the temple (1 Kgs 6:1). (3) The closest parallel to the time span of the primaeval history is the period of Israel's enslavement in Egypt, which is bridged only by a genealogy extending from Levi to Moses and Aaron (Exod 6:16–26), a genealogy that cannot have recorded all the links in that line of descent and could not, therefore, have been intended to be used as a basis of chronological computation. (4) Insofar as the records and monuments of ancient Egypt show that the interval between the deluge and the call of Abraham must have been greater than that yielded by the genealogy in Gen 11, they

23. John H. Walton, "Response from the Archetypal View," in *Four Views on the Historical Adam*, ed. Matthew Barrett and Ardel B. Caneday, Counterpoints (Grand Rapids: Zondervan, 2013), 69.

24. Jacobsen writes, "Our conclusion concerning the historical value of the King List must thus be that while the arrangement, the succession of the various dynasties, can be considered a later construction of no significance, we possess in the actual material of that document a historical source of high value, from which only some exaggerated reigns occurring with the earliest rulers should be segregated" (Thorkild Jacobsen, *The Sumerian King List*, AS 11 [Chicago: University of Chicago Press, 1939], 167).

25. John H. Walton, *The Lost World of Adam and Eve: Genesis 2–3 and the Human Origins Debate* (Downers Grove, IL: IVP Academic, 2015), 102.

26. William Henry Green, "Primeval Chronology," *BSac* 47 (1890): 285–303.

count against the assumption that this genealogy was intended to supply the elements for a chronological computation. (5) The symmetrical structure of the genealogies in Gen 5 and 11 favors the belief that they do not register all the names in these respective lines of descent.

All these points are well taken.[27] Contemporary commentators are especially struck by the artificial symmetry of ten antediluvian ancestors from Adam through Noah followed by ten postdiluvian ancestors from Shem though Abraham (see fig. 5.1).[28]

A similar ten-name genealogy appears in Ruth 4:18–22 and in various Sumerian, Assyrian, and Babylonian king lists. Nahum Sarna comments, "The conclusion is unmistakable: we have here a deliberate, symmetrical schematization of history, featuring neatly balanced, significant segments of time as a way of expressing the fundamental biblical teaching that history is meaningful."[29] Also striking is the author's failure to sum the ages of the persons listed, suggesting an indifference to the overall time span. One may contrast in this regard the Sumerian King List, which provides totals and subtotals of antediluvian and postdiluvian reigns.[30]

It is quite a different matter, however, to suggest that gaps that might have spanned tens of thousands of years each would be permitted by such genealogies.[31] Moreover, the longevity of the antediluvian patriarchs seems

27. Young objects that Green failed to reckon with the fact that inserting gaps of tens of thousands of years into the genealogies would make the primaeval history hopelessly anachronistic, since farming, metallurgy, musical instruments, etc., are of more recent origin (Davis A. Young, "The Antiquity and the Unity of the Human Race Revisited," *CSR* 24, no. 4 [1995]: 380–96). But this objection would be a problem for a literal historical intent on the author's part only if we assume that it was known to the author of Genesis that these advances and technologies are of relatively recent origin. Since doubtless he did not, he would have had no problem ascribing them to persons in the distant past.

28. It is true, as Sarfati notes, that symmetry is achieved only by adding Abram to the *tôlədôt* of Shem, rather than ending with Terah (Sarfati, *Genesis*, 464). But Abram, not Terah, is clearly the pivotal figure here.

29. Nahum M. Sarna, *Genesis*, JPSTC (Philadelphia: Jewish Publication Society, 1989), 40.

30. Jacobsen, *Sumerian King List*, col. i 35; col. ii 43.

31. Theoretically, one could insert small gaps by interpreting "father" to mean something like "grandfather" (cf. Gen 46:12, 25; 46:16–18): "When X had lived *n* years, he became the grandfather of Y; and when Y had lived *m* years, he became the grandfather of Z." But such gaps are limited because the progenitor must still be a certain age when the descendant is born. Moreover, a few notices in the genealogies connect successors closely—e.g., Lamech's commenting on the meaning of Noah's name. This theoretical suggestion is, in any case, *ad hoc* and therefore implausible. Hamilton's suggestion that "X fathered Y" may

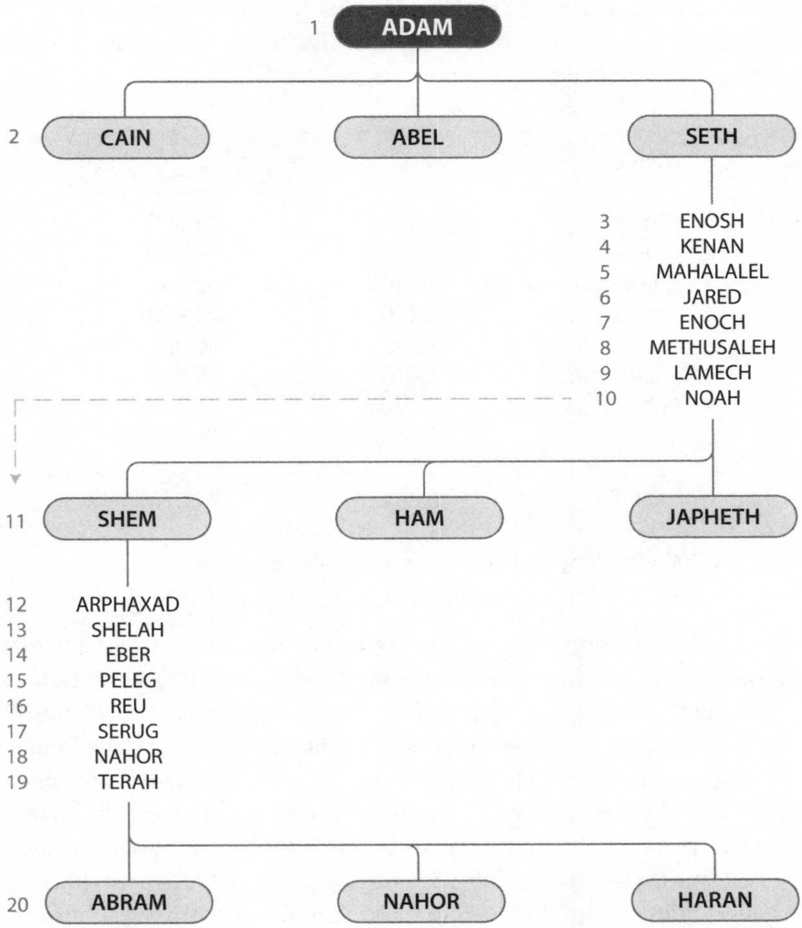

Figure 5.1. Symmetrical ancestral genealogies of biblical antediluvians and postdiluvians.

unlikely to be intended to be literally construed. In the Sumerian King List, the antediluvian kings also have fantastically long reigns, as long as 43,200

mean "X fathered the line culminating in Y" (Victor P. Hamilton, *The Book of Genesis: Chapters 1–17*, NICOT [Grand Rapids: Eerdmans, 1990], 254) is equally implausible, since the genealogies imply that X is still alive when the line culminates in Y. One must agree with Wenham that it requires special pleading to postulate long gaps in the genealogy (Gordon J. Wenham, *Genesis 1–15*, WBC 1 [Grand Rapids: Zondervan, 1987], 153).

years for an individual reign, with the lengths of the reigns diminishing after the flood (see fig. 5.2). Are we seriously to think that ancient Sumerians and Babylonians took such absurdly long reigns literally?

KING	CITY	LENGTH OF REIGN IN YEARS
1. Alulim	Eridu	28,800
2. Alalgar	Eridu	36,000
3. Enmenluanna	Badtibira	43,200
4. Enmengalanna	Badtibira	28,800
5. Dumuzi	Badtibira	36,000
6. Ensipazianna	Larak	28,800
7. Enmenduranna	Sippar	21,000
8. Ubartutu	Shuruppak	18,600
8 KINGS	5 CITIES	241,200 YEARS

Figure 5.2. Sumerian king list featuring fantastically long reigns.

In Genesis the flood similarly interrupts the genealogies in 5:32 and 9:28, and fantastically long life spans are ascribed to the antediluvians, even if less extravagant than the reigns of the Mesopotamian kings, and diminished life spans following the flood. As mentioned earlier, these abnormally long life spans lead to difficulties if taken literally (unless we posit gaps); for example, Noah is still alive when Abraham is born, and Shem outlives Abraham by thirty-five years. The author of Genesis would himself have been aware of how fantastic these ancestral life spans are, which gives reason to think that the genealogies are not intended to be straightforward history. There is no consensus among OT scholars concerning the reason for or meaning of the fantastic life spans attributed to the antediluvians.

Multiple schemes for calculating the ages of the antediluvians have been suggested, usually appealing to the Babylonian sexagesimal (base sixty) number system.[32] But the very multiplicity of such schemes undermines

32. Why a sexagesimal number system helps explain the inflated ages of Gen 5 is unclear. In a sexagesimal system, sixty units of one kind are written as one unit of the next higher order. So to write "70" one would write "1, 10"—which is 60 + 10 = 70 (Otto Neugebauer, *The Exact Sciences in Antiquity*, 2nd ed. [New York: Dover, 1969], 3–28). How does use of this number system lead to inflated life spans?

TABLE 2. Ages of Patriarchs and Corresponding Sexagesimal and Preferred Numbers

Patriarch	Age (yrs) when first son born	Sexagesimal and Preferred Numbers	Re-main-ing years of life	Sexagesimal and Preferred Numbers	Total years	Sexagesimal and Preferred Numbers
Adam	130	60x2yrs + 60x2mos	800	60x10x10mos + 60x60mos	930	60x3x5yrs(60mos) + 6x5yrs(60mos)
Seth	105	60x10x2mos + 60mos	807	60x10x10mos + 60x60mos + 7yrs	912	60x3x5yrs(60mos) + 5yrs(60mos) + 7yrs
Enosh	90	(6+6+6) x 60mos	815	60x10x10mos + 60x60mos + 60x3mos	905	60x3x5yrs(60mos) + 5yrs(60mos)
Kenan	70	7x2x5yrs(60mos)	840	60x10x10mos + 60x60mos + 60x8mos	910	60x3x5yrs(60mos) + 2x5yrs(60mos)
Mahalalel	65	60yrs + 5yrs(60mos)	830	60x10x10mos + 60x60mos + 60x6mos	895	60x3x5yrs(60mos) – 5yrs(60mos)
Jared	162	60x6x5mos + 5yrs(60mos) + 7yrs	800	60x10x10mos + 60x60mos	962	(60+60+60+6+6)x60mos – 5yrs(60mos) + 7yrs
Enoch	65	60yrs + 5yrs(60mos)	300	60x5yrs(60mos)	365	60x6yrs + 5yrs(60mos) = 1 solar year
Methuselah	187	60x3yrs + 7yrs	782	60x10x10mos + 60x60mos – 6x3yrs	969	(60+60+60+6+6)x60mos – 5yrs(60mos) + 7yrs + 7yrs
Lamech	182	60x7x5mos + 7yrs	595	60x10yrs – 5yrs(60mos)	777	7x10x10 + 7x10 +7yrs
Noah	500	60x10x10mos	450	40x2x5yrs(60mos) + 10x5yrs(60mos)	950	60x3x5yrs(60mos) + 10x5yrs(60mos)
Flood						
Shem	100	60x10x2mos	500	60x10x10mos	600	60x10yrs
Arphaxad	35	7x5yrs(60mos)	403	40x2x5yrs(60mos) + 3yrs (6x6mos)	438	40x2x5yrs(60mos) + 60x6 + 60 + 6x6mos
Shelah	30	60x6mos	403	40x2x5yrs(60mos) + 3yrs (6x6mos)	433	40x2x5yrs(60mos) + 6x(60+6)mos
Eber	34	60x6mos + 6x8mos	430	40x2x5yrs(60mos) + 6x60mos	464	40x2x5yrs(60mos) + 60yrs + 6x8mos
Peleg	30	60x6mos	209	40x5yrs(60mos) + 5yrs(60mos) + 6x8mos	239	40x5yrs(60mos) + 6x6yrs + 6x6mos
Reu	32	60x6mos + 6x4mos	207	40x5yrs(60mos) + 5yrs(60mos) + 6x4mos	239	40x5yrs(60mos) + 6x6yrs + 6x6mos
Serug	30	60x6mos	200	40x5yrs (60mos)	230	40x5yrs(60mos) + 60x6mos
Nahor	29	60x6mos – 6x2mos	119	60x2yrs – 6x2mos	148	60x10x2mos + 6x8yrs
Terah	70	7x2x5yrs(60mos)	135	60x2yrs + 60x2mos + 5yrs(60mos)	205	40x5yrs(60mos) + 5yrs(60mos)
Abraham	100	60x10x2mos	75	5yrs(60mos) x 3x5yrs(60mos)	175	60x10x2mos + 15x5yrs(60mos)

Figure 5.3. Ages of antediluvians computed using sexagesimal numbers. Reprinted by permission from Carol A. Hill, "Making Sense of the Numbers of Genesis," table 2.

confidence in the correctness of any one of them. Some of the ways of reckoning the ages are so complex as to strain credulity.

For example, in Carol Hill's helpful chart (fig. 5.3) we find right at the start that Adam's age of 130 at the birth of Seth is said to be calculated by multiplying 60 years × 2 years = 120 years, and then, to get 10 additional years, adding 60 months × 2 months = 120 months = 10 years. We wonder by what principle we are to blend years and months in this way. Kenan's age at his firstborn is reckoned by multiplying 7 × 2 × 5 years (or 60 months) = 70 years. One wonders why his age was not calculated, like Adam's, as 60 years plus 60 × 2 months. Or why was Adam's age not reckoned, like Kenan's, as 7 × 2 × 5 years plus 60 years = 130 years? In order to arrive at Mahalalel's age at death, we are supposed to introduce subtraction into our calculations, first multiplying 60 × 3 × 5 years = 900 years, which is too large, so we subtract from that 5 years to arrive at 895 years of age. If we are allowed subtraction as well as multiplication and addition, then why not also division? Then Enosh's age at the time of his firstborn can be easily reckoned as 60 × 2 = 120 years minus 60 ÷ 2 = 30 years. When we get to Jared's age at death, the calculations become dizzying: to find his age at death we are to add 60 + 60 + 60 months = 180 months and then add 6 + 6 months [6 being, one supposes, justified as one-tenth of 60] to get 192 months, then multiply that total by 60 to get 11,520 months = 960 years (if we neglect leap years), which is not quite enough, so we subtract 5 years to get 955 years, then add back in 7 years—*et voila!*—962 years. When we get to Methuselah's age at death, the calculations are even more complicated. We once again add 60 + 60 + 60 + 6 + 6 months and multiply that by 60 months to get 960 years, then we subtract 5 years to get 955 years, and this time we add back 7 + 7 years to get 969 years. Marvelous contrivance! Is it not more plausible that Methuselah's age was mandated by the necessity of getting him off the scene, lest he be drowned in the flood?

These calculations have all the appearance of cherry-picking, contrived after the fact to arrive at the target age. Moreover, these calculations leave unanswered the question, Why in the world would a Hebrew tradent come up with such arithmetic formulas using a number system foreign to Israel? Kenton Sparks thinks the numbers are based on Babylonian astronomical and mathematical figures.[33] But a reading of the literature he cites reveals

33. Kenton L. Sparks, "Genesis 1–11 as Ancient Historiography," in Halton, *Genesis*, 121. In support he cites C. J. Labuschagne, "The Life Spans of the Patriarchs," in *New Avenues in the Study of the Old Testament*, ed. A. S. van der Woude (Leiden: Brill, 1989),

that the authors' proposals are inconsistent with one another. D. W. Young plumps for the influence of Babylonian sexagesimal mathematics, whereas C. J. Labuschagne thinks that the life spans of three antediluvians (Lamech, Jared, and Mahalalel) correspond to the synodic periods of five known planets. He notes that if we subtract a supermaximum life span of $7 \times 120 = 840$ years from the antediluvians' ages, we arrive at normal life spans. For the postdiluvians he can find no principle governing these numbers except a chronological one—namely, to fill the gap between the prehistoric antediluvian patriarchs and the historic figure of Abraham. Donald Etz thinks that the ages of Methuselah, Jared, and Lamech have been adjusted downward to make room for the flood. He notes that of the many complicated arithmetic schemes proposed to calculate the ages, including Dwight Young's and Umberto Cassuto's, none has been generally accepted. Undeterred, he proposes that the numbers we have in the text, while not random, were derived by arithmetical operations from originally random numbers. He proposes that an original set of ages was invented (randomly?), then 300 years were added to every life span but Enoch's, and finally all the numbers were multiplied by 2.5 and rounded down to whole numbers where necessary. Such a multiplicity of contradictory proposals hardly supports Sparks's claim that the numbers were derived from Babylonian astronomical and mathematical figures, much less that they are symbolic.

Scholars are at a loss to find any symbolic significance in the ages themselves, much less in formulas like $60 \times 10 \times 10$ months + 60×60 months. Sparks suggests that the genealogies are an instance of "elite emulation" on Israel's part, constructing genealogies on the pattern of the Mesopotamian king lists. "It appears the Jewish scribes responded to Mesopotamian ideology by composing texts that imitated one of Babylon's most powerful expressions of power: the king list. I and other scholars suspect that the biblical author's motive was to help Jews resist the assimilating pressure of Mesopotamian culture."[34] Not only is this suspicion conjectural, but it depends on an exilic or postexilic date for the genealogies, an assumption that reduces the probability of the conjecture.[35] Moreover, the hypothesis

121–27; Donald V. Etz, "The Numbers of Genesis V 3–31: A Suggested Conversion and Its Implications," *VT* 43, no. 2 (1993): 171–89; Dwight Wayne Young, "The Influence of Babylonian Algebra on Longevity among the Antediluvians," *ZAW* 102 (1990): 321–35; Young, "On the Application of Numbers from Babylonian Mathematics to Biblical Life Spans and Epochs," *ZAW* 100 (1988): 331–61.

34. Sparks, "Genesis 1–11," 121.

35. See as well note 9 of chapter 3.

does nothing to explain the specific ages of the antediluvians, much less the calculations used to arrive at them. Is it not more plausible that the ages were determined by the need to fill the antediluvian period with people going back to the presumed time of Adam?

Sparks offers a quite independent reason based on probability considerations for thinking that the ages of the antediluvians are symbolic:

> If we look closely at the chronological figures in Genesis 5, we'll find that these are certainly symbolic rather than literal. The final digit for each number is 0, 2, 5, or 7 in all cases but one. Given that the probability of random ages like this is on the order of .000 000 06%, it is clear that these numbers are not chronological in the usual sense.*
>
> *The math is relatively simple. One takes the probability of randomly selecting any of the four digits used (i.e., ".4") and raises it to the power equivalent to the number of random selections (18). This yields $.4^{18}$, or 6.87×10^{8}.[36]

What shall we make of this argument? In the first place, we might wonder why Sparks considers only the third digit of each number. Why not the first or second? Could it be that he is here presupposing Benford's Law, according to which the first digit in many naturally occurring numbers is probably small?[37] The same is true to a lesser extent of the second digit. But once one reaches the third digit, the distribution of the numbers approaches a uniform distribution of 10 percent for each of the ten numbers, ranging from 10.2 percent for 0 to 9.8 percent for 9. That would favor using the third digit, though even here one wonders whether a difference of 0.4 percent in the distribution of the numbers could skew the odds. One wonders as well about the applicability of the law to Hebrew, where words, not numerals, are used to express numbers and the number of words used does not correlate to the number of Arabic numerals used in translation.

Be that as it may, there are nine persons whose ages are given in Gen 5. Why Sparks mentions eighteen selections is not explained. Further, the

36. Sparks, "Genesis 1–11," 120.

37. There is a very nice Wikipedia article on the law at https://en.wikipedia.org/wiki/Benford%27s_law. See further Arno Berger and Theodore P. Hill, "Benford's Law Strikes Back: No Simple Explanation in Sight for Mathematical Gem," *Mathematical Intelligencer* 33 (2011): 85–91; also available at Digital Commons @ Cal Poly, https://digitalcommons.calpoly.edu/cgi/viewcontent.cgi?article=1074&context=rgp_rsr; Theodore P. Hill, "The Significant-Digit Phenomenon," *AMM* 102, no. 4 (April 1995): 322–27. I am grateful to Joshua Swamidass for these references.

final digits involved are not four in number but five: 0, 2, 5, 7, 9. If we take their ages at death, the probability, on Sparks's method, of each number's final digit being 0, 2, 5, 7, or 9 is $0.5^9 = 0.002$, which is about one chance in five hundred, hardly outrageously improbable. If we include Noah, then we have $0.5^{10} = 0.001$, or one chance in a thousand. On the other hand, Hill takes all three ages mentioned per person for a total of thirty numbers, in which case the probability of all thirty numbers ending in one of five digits is $0.5^{30} = 9.31^{10} = 0.0000000009$, which Hill apparently rounds to one chance in a billion.[38] But if we take the genealogies of both the ten antediluvians and the ten postdiluvians through Abraham, we have a total of sixty numbers, each ending in 0, 2, 3, 4, 5, 7, 8, or 9, which has a probability of $0.8^{60} = 0.0000015$, which Hill apparently rounds to 0.000002, or one chance in 500,000.

Sparks's method assumes that the numbers associated with the people's ages is random, as though selected from an urn by a fair randomizing device with each number having an equal probability of being selected and each selection probabilistically independent of the others. That is, however, clearly not the case, for a person's age at death is a function of his age when begetting the firstborn and the number of years he lived afterward. So the numbers selected are not independent. Thus, one can pick only one vertical column in Hill's chart for calculating probabilities, not two or three columns as Sparks and Hill do. Then the odds become quite tractable. Moreover, symbolism is not the only alternative to randomness. Sparks unjustifiably equates being literal with being random. Rounding of numbers will subvert randomness without entailing symbolic meaning, as will a simple preference for some numbers over others. What one comes to see, then, is that Sparks's dichotomy between literal (= random) and symbolic is far too simplistic. The numbers may be nonrandom without being symbolic.

We have reason, then, to interpret the genealogies in their narrative context as evincing a historical interest but not relating straightforward history, even if we do contemplate or permit gaps in the genealogies. Mathews plausibly suggests that in general the genealogies serve the theological purpose of showing the interconnectedness of all mankind and the hope of universal blessing.[39] Our objective is to make sense of the points adduced by Green without imagining enormous gaps in a literal historical record.

38. Carol A. Hill, "Making Sense of the Numbers of Genesis," *PSCF* 55, no. 4 (2003): 245.
39. Mathews, *Genesis 1–11:26*, 295–96.

The Genre of Genesis 1–11

On the basis of comparative studies of Sumerian literature, the eminent Assyriologist Thorkild Jacobsen proposed that we recognize a unique genre of literature that he dubbed "mytho-history." Jacobsen had assembled a Sumerian story out of three fragments of different dates, which he called the Eridu Genesis, dealing with the creation of man, the institution of kingship, the founding of the first cities, and the great flood. He thinks that Genesis similarly describes the creation of man and animals, lists of the leading figures after creation, and then the flood. His reflections on this sort of literature are worth quoting at length:

> These three parts, moreover, are in both traditions combined simply by arranging them along a line in time and not according to the most usual device for connecting separate tales or myths: grouping them around a single hero. . . . In the "Eridu Genesis" moreover the progression is clearly a logical one of cause and effect: the wretched state of natural man touches the motherly heart of Nintur, who has him improve his lot by settling down in cities and building temples; and she gives him a king to lead and organize. As this chain of cause and effect leads from nature to civilization, so a following such chain carries from the early cities and kings over into the story of the flood. The well-organized irrigation works carried out by the cities under the leadership of their kings lead to a greatly increased food supply and that in turn makes man multiply on the earth. The volume of noise these people make keeps Enlil from sleeping and makes him decide to get peace and quiet by sending the flood. Now, this arrangement along a line of time as cause and effect is striking, for it is very much the way a historian arranges his data, and since the data here are mythological we may assign both traditions to a new and separate genre as mytho-historical accounts.[40]

It might be seriously questioned whether the condition identified by Jacobsen for a narrative's qualifying as even quasi-historical in nature—namely, arranging causally connected events in chronological order—is sufficient for a genuine historical interest. By this standard the *Enuma elish* ought to qualify as mytho-historical, since the story of Marduk's conquest of Tiamat most certainly relates chronologically ordered, causally connected

40. Thorkild Jacobsen, "The Eridu Genesis" (1981), in Hess and Tsumura, *"I Studied Inscriptions,"* 140.

events; this seems absurd. But Jacobsen is talking about an ordering in real time, not in merely the fictional time of a myth or fable. The second part of the Eridu Genesis is modeled on the Sumerian King List, and Jacobsen credits the inclusion of this section in the tale to "pure historical interest on the part of its composer."[41] The interest in genuine chronology sets the stories apart from pure myth: "This interest in numbers is very curious, for it is characteristic of myths and folk tales that they are not concerned with time for all. . . . No!—interest in numbers of years belongs elsewhere, to the style of chronicles and historiography. In Mesopotamia we find it first in date-lists, lists of reigns, and in the Kinglist, later on in the Chronicles, but to find this chronological list-form combined, as it is here, with simple mythological narrative, is truly unique. . . . The assignment of the tale to a mytho-historical genre is thus further confirmed."[42]

A good example of the mytho-historical genre more familiar to Western readers would seem to be Homer's account of the Trojan War in the *Iliad*. According to classicist G. S. Kirk, "much of the *Iliad* is obviously historicizing in content. . . . Even those least confident in the existence of a 'Trojan War' concede that some attack took place and that some Achaeans were among the attackers. . . . The story is based on some kind of memory of the past and . . . its progress is described in largely realistic terms."[43] The prime exception is the role of the gods in the story. But Kirk believes that, far from being "a mythopoeic jungle," many of the *Iliad*'s and *Odyssey*'s personifications of physical phenomena and psychological impulses "are more likely to be part of a longstanding and archaistic literary convention than to represent the state of Homer's assumptions on causation."[44] Greek myths thus provide an example of "mythical history."[45]

While the genealogies of Genesis evince an interest in history on the part of the author and his audience, it is important to keep in mind that it is a mytho-history that is being narrated. Chronological calculations become

41. Jacobsen, "Eridu Genesis," 139.

42. Jacobsen, "Eridu Genesis," 141. Jacobsen attributes Genesis's interest in chronology mainly to the P source, or in other words, to the genealogies.

43. G. S. Kirk, *Myth: Its Meaning and Functions in Ancient and Other Cultures*, SCL 40 (Cambridge: Cambridge University Press, 1970), 32. Even the *Odyssey*, Kirk notes, is largely set in the purportedly historical world. Cf. G. S. Kirk, "On Defining Myths," in Dundes, *Sacred Narrative*, 55.

44. Kirk, *Myth*, 240.

45. Kirk, *Myth*, 254. Kirk points to Hesiod's poem *Ehoeae* as one of the clearest instances of this genre. It traces the descendants of eponymous ancestors through more specialized local eponyms down to the heroes and heroines of the full heroic age.

inappropriate for such a genre. Kenneth Kitchen observes that in the ANE people were already aware that the world was extremely old.[46] The Sumerian King List indicates that kings had reigned in Sumer for 241,200 years prior to the flood, which was followed by another 26,997 years of royal rule. According to the Babylonian priest Berossus, kings had reigned in Babylon for 432,000 years prior to the flood.[47] Yet the biblical genealogies famously total to a scant 1,656 years from Adam until the flood, with another 367 years from the flood to the call of Abraham. Genesis presents a mythological history of the world that is extremely short by ancient standards, bound tightly by father-son genealogical notices that seem to contemplate no gaps of tens of thousands of years between them. We should not imagine that the genealogies contemplate the enormous leaps that would be necessary to bring them into harmony with what we know of the history of mankind; but neither should we think them to comprise purely fictitious characters. We can avoid these polar opposites by taking the brief history they relate to be a mytho-history that is not meant to be taken literally.

Evangelical laymen would probably be surprised at how widely accepted Jacobsen's classification of Gen 1–11 as mytho-history is among evangelical scholars. The case of Gordon Wenham, a highly respected commentator, is instructive. Of Jacobsen's classification Wenham remarks, "This is a sensitive analysis of both texts; but myth is a loaded term which leads to misunderstanding. That is why I prefer Proto-history. It is Proto in that it describes origins and sets out models of God and his dealings with the human race. It is historical in that it describes past realities and the lessons that should be drawn from them."[48] This is a distinction without a difference.

46. K. A. Kitchen, *On the Reliability of the Old Testament* (Grand Rapids: Eerdmans, 2003), 439.

47. Stanley Mayer Burstein, ed., *The "Babyloniaca" of Berossus*, SANE 1/5 (Malibu, CA: Undena, 1978), 48. For some perspective, this would place the first kings in the Palaeolithic Age in the middle of the Pleistocene epoch just before the emergence of modern *Homo sapiens*.

48. Wenham, "Genesis 1–11 as Protohistory," 87; cf. Wenham, *Genesis 1–15*, 54. The reader is advised that Wenham's use of *proto-history* is different from that of Kenneth Kitchen, who uses the term to characterize the earliest glimmerings of oral tradition and historical writing, in contrast to the prehistoric era (*Reliability of the Old Testament*, 444). Still, Kitchen classifies the Sumerian King List, the *Atrahasis Epic*, the Eridu Genesis, and Gen 1–11 as "Primeval Protohistories" (424). These are to be distinguished from pure myth because of their historical interest. Similarly, Bill Arnold uses the term *protohistory* to designate, not the primaeval history, but the ancestral history commencing with Abraham (Bill T. Arnold, *Genesis*, NCBC [Cambridge: Cambridge University Press, 2009], 2).

Wenham's characterization of proto-history aptly describes mytho-history. Wenham says, "The genealogical framework of this chapter [4] as well as the introductory formula in 2:4 . . . shows that the editor considers his account proto-historical: he is describing real individuals from the primeval past whose actions are significant for all mankind."[49] The narratives put profound theological truths "in vivid and memorable form in an absorbing yet highly symbolic story."[50] If we take these stories as straightforward history, "we may be forced to conclude that Genesis is trying to relate history but not succeeding, which would be a rather negative conclusion."[51] It is evident, I think, that there is no material difference between Wenham's proto-history and mytho-history. Wenham simply declines to use the word *myth* because of the connotations that the word has in popular parlance.[52]

49. Wenham, *Genesis 1–15*, 116–17.

50. Wenham, *Genesis 1–15*, 55.

51. Wenham, "Response to James K. Hoffmeier," 62. Hoffmeier himself makes the curious assertion, "Fortunately, the Christian committed to Scripture need not commit intellectual suicide by embracing the historicity of the events described in early Genesis, for the text itself is written in such a way to reinforce this view" ("Genesis 1–11," 58). One should have expected him to say, "The text itself is *not* written in such a way to reinforce this view"—i.e., the text does not require us to embrace the historicity of the events described. But upon reflection, I think Hoffmeier means to say, "The text is written in such a way as to reinforce the historicity of the events described, and therefore the Christian need not commit intellectual suicide in embracing their historicity." This assertion does not take with sufficient seriousness the many fantastic elements in the narrative that we have discussed (e.g., a worldwide flood).

52. Similarly, in a brief excursus on myth/mythology, Walton confesses that "I am uncomfortable applying the genre label 'myth/mythology' to these biblical narratives. The designation has too many definitions, and therefore the words lose their ability to communicate clearly" (*Lost World of Adam and Eve*, 136). He observes that some might suggest that the Israelites were historicizing myth—i.e., presenting real events using imagery as a rhetorical means to capture the full range of truth as it was commonly conveyed in the world in which they lived. "Since the concept of myth (mythic/mythical/mythological), however, is so volatile and diversely understood, we need to use it in connection with other qualifying terms" (137). Walton does not consider Thorkild Jacobsen's term *mytho-history*. Instead, he recommends the word group "image/imagery/imagination/imaginative," which unfortunately does not include the word "history." But he says that Genesis preserves "imagistic history." "Some might consider the trees, the garden and the snake to be examples of imagistic thinking without thereby denying reality and truth to the account" (138). This makes all the more bewildering the sort of wooden literalism characterizing much of Walton's exegesis—for example, his view of six literal days of functional creation in the recent past or his bizarre interpretation of Eve's formation by God's splitting Adam in two—which he takes to be a vision given by God to Adam (78–80). If Walton is right that we can recognize language as figurative by how hard interpreters

Precisely the same sort of reservations make C. John Collins hesitant to use the word *myth* with respect to the primaeval history, despite the fact that his notion of "a worldview story," used to characterize Genesis, is not materially different from a myth.[53] He asks, then, "Could it be that 'myth' is the right category for the kind of stories we find in the ancient world, whether from the Egyptians, Mesopotamians, or even the Hebrews? The difficulty is that the word 'myth' has so many different meanings; in popular usage, the term implies a judgment that the story is not true."[54] Collins thinks that the author of Genesis wanted his audience to believe that the events recorded really happened, so that the narratives can be said so far forth to be "historical," but this does not imply that the account has no figurative or imaginary elements.[55] Indeed, Collins appeals to Homer's *Iliad* to illustrate the kind of literature that Gen 1–11 is.

Bill Arnold is an evangelical OT scholar with more temerity. He opines, "These chapters are no simple history or example of ancient historiography. At most, we may say that mythical themes have been arranged in a forward-moving, linear progression, in what may be considered a historicizing literary form, using genealogies especially, to make history out of myth."[56] Not

---

have to work to provide a nonfigurative reading of a passage (Tremper Longman III and John H. Walton, *The Lost World of the Flood: Mythology, Theology, and the Deluge Debate* [Downers Grove, IL: IVP Academic, 2018], 25), then just as Adam's creation is deemed "patently figurative" (28), so should Eve's. By neglecting myth, Walton is forced into such desperate expedients.

53. C. John Collins, "Adam and Eve as Historical People, and Why It Matters," *PSCF* 62, no. 3 (September 2010): 150. He explains, "A worldview is instilled by means of the grand story, which tells a community where it came from, what went wrong, what has been done about it (whether by gods or by humans, or some combination), where it now is in the whole process, and where the whole world is headed. One missiologist suggests that tribal peoples learn their worldviews through the sacred stories their culture tells; but this is true of all peoples, not just of tribal ones" (149). Collins goes on to tie the notion of a worldview story with the sense of "myth" in C. S. Lewis's essay "The Funeral of a Great Myth."

54. Collins, "Adam and Eve," 150; similarly, C. John Collins, *Did Adam and Eve Really Exist? Who They Were and Why You Should Care* (Wheaton: Crossway, 2011), 28.

55. Collins affirms, "If, as seems likely to me, the Mesopotamian origin and flood stories provide the context against which Genesis 1–11 are to be set, then they also provide us with clues on how to read this kind of literature. These stories include divine action, symbolism, and imaginative elements; the purpose of the stories is to lay the foundation for a worldview, without being taken in a 'literalistic' fashion. We should nevertheless see the story as having what we might call a 'historical core,' though we must be careful in discerning what that is" ("Adam and Eve," 151). These comments anticipate the subject of our next chapter.

56. Bill T. Arnold, "The Genesis Narratives," in *Ancient Israel's History: An Introduction to Issues and Sources*, ed. Bill T. Arnold and Richard S. Hess (Grand Rapids: Baker Academic, 2014), 31.

that myth has been lost: rather, myth is combined with history. Accordingly, Jacobsen's nomenclature should be adopted:

> The Primeval History (Gen. 1–11) addresses the origins of the universe, the creation of humanity, and the first institutions of human civilization. We retain the term "history" in the title of this first unit of the Bible—the Primeval History—because, on the one hand, it arranges themes along a time continuum using cause and effect and generally uses historical narrative as the literary medium for communication. On the other hand, those themes themselves are the same ones explored elsewhere in the ancient Near East in mythological literature. . . . The Primeval History narrates those themes in a way that transforms their meaning and import, and for these reasons we may think of these chapters as a unique literary category, which some have termed "mytho-historical."[57]

Although Wenham is doubtless correct that the classification of Gen 1–11 as mytho-history is prone to misunderstanding, I do not think that we should revert to vague euphemisms that tend to conceal rather than elucidate the literary character of Gen 1–11. Scholars simply need to be careful to explain our meaning to laymen.

Conclusion

In sum, the many striking family resemblances between Gen 1–11 and ANE myths lead one to think of the primaeval history as comprising Hebrew myths. Their primary purpose is to ground realities present to the pentateuchal author and important for Israelite society in the primordial past. At the same time, the interstitching of the primaeval narratives with genealogies terminating in real people evinces a historical interest on the author's part in persons who once lived and wrought. Even these genealogies, however, are carefully constructed so as to share in the character of the myths they order, contributing to the overall etiological purpose of the primaeval history.

57. Arnold, "Genesis Narratives," 31. Elsewhere he states, "The literary genre 'mytho-historical' in no way identifies these chapters as myths or mythical, but rather draws attention to the way in which themes previously regarded simply as mythological are arranged along an historical time line using cause and effect" (Arnold, *Genesis*, 7).

Chapter 6

ARE MYTHS BELIEVED TO BE TRUE?

The question of this chapter's title is ambiguous. By whom are myths believed to be true? Doubtless, the question concerns members of the society for which the myths are determinative, not outsiders. We have already said that it is characteristic of myths that they are objects of belief by members of the society that embraces them. But one might believe in a myth in the sense of accepting it, relying on it for determining one's values and practices, embracing it as central to one's identity as a member of one's society, without believing it to be true.[1] No doubt some members of a society believe the myths of the society to be true. But our question is whether belief in the truth of the accepted myths is somehow expected or intended.

Even with that clarification, our question remains ambiguous. For what is meant by "true"? Figurative discourse can be true even if it is literally false. Were the myths of the ANE intended to be taken as literally true? The question is not easily answered because we do not have direct access to the adherents of ancient myths so as to probe their attitudes toward the myths they embraced. As in the case of the genealogies, we must turn to comparative anthropological studies and to comparative ANE literature in order to try to find an answer.

Comparative Anthropological Data

In distinguishing between myths and folktales, William Bascom points out that "factual and fictional narratives are clearly recognized as separate

1. As Michael Rea has emphasized, there is a clear distinction between something's being authoritative and something's being true (Michael C. Rea, "Authority and Truth," in *The Enduring Authority of the Christian Scriptures*, ed. D. A. Carson [Grand Rapids: Eerdmans, 2016], 872–98).

categories in many societies."[2] Granted, but it is not in dispute that myths are not taken to be fictitious by members of the society in which they are embraced or that they are different from folktales. Alan Dundes crucially distinguishes between *analytic* and *native* categories in dealing with folklore genres.[3] Analytic categories are those delineated by modern scholars; native categories are distinctions made by the native members of a particular culture. Sometimes analytic and native categories are congruent, but sometimes they may differ. Native distinctions between truth and fiction may be too coarse-grained to provide accurate answers to our questions. The myths may be regarded as "the absolute truth,"[4] but are they intended to be taken as literal truth? To the extent that myths are part of organized religions, Dundes thinks they are "usually believed to be true—even if only metaphorically or symbolically so."[5] So, Dundes reminds us, "myth may constitute the highest form of truth, albeit in metaphorical guise."[6]

In an oft-cited article,[7] Raffaele Pettazzoni draws on anthropological data similar to those adduced by Bascom to show that North American Indian tribes "differentiate 'true stories' from 'false stories.' . . . In the 'true' stories we have to deal with the holy and the supernatural, while the 'false' ones on

2. William Bascom, "The Forms of Folklore: Prose Narratives," in *Sacred Narrative: Readings in the Theory of Myth*, ed. Alan Dundes (Berkeley: University of California Press, 1984), 19. See the abundant examples he provides from around the world (13–24).

3. Alan Dundes, introductory comments to Bascom, "Forms of Folklore," 5. Cf. Wenham's distinction between taking an *emic* approach (the view of the original author) and an *etic* approach (a definition in modern categories) to the genre of Gen 1–11 (Gordon J. Wenham, "Genesis 1–11 as Protohistory," in *Genesis: History, Fiction, or Neither? Three Views on the Bible's Earliest Chapters*, ed. Charles Halton [Grand Rapids: Zondervan, 2015], 74).

4. Bascom, "Forms of Folklore," 16.

5. Alan Dundes, introductory comments to Raffaele Pettazzoni, "The Truth of Myth," in Dundes, *Sacred Narrative*, 98.

6. Alan Dundes, introduction to *Sacred Narrative*, 1. In his provocatively titled book *Did the Greeks Believe in Their Myths?* Paul Veyne says that Greek myths "were accepted as true in the sense that they were not doubted, but they were not accepted the way that everyday reality is. . . . A Greek put the gods 'in heaven,' but he would have been astounded to see them in the sky. He would have been no less astounded if someone, using time in its literal sense, told him that Hephaestus had just remarried or that Athena had aged a great deal lately" (*Did the Greeks Believe in Their Myths? An Essay on the Constitutive Imagination*, trans. Paula Wissing [Chicago: University of Chicago Press, 1988], 17–18).

7. E.g., by Mircea Eliade, *Myth and Reality*, trans. Willard R. Trask (New York: Harper & Row, 1963), 8–9. In turn, Eliade is cited uncritically, along with Pettazzoni, by Kevin Schilbrack, "Introduction: On the Use of Philosophy in the Study of Myths," in *Thinking through Myths: Philosophical Perspectives*, ed. Kevin Schilbrack (London: Routledge, 2002), 9.

the other hand are of profane content"—for example, antics of the trickster and accomplished rogue Coyote.[8] Sometimes the latter are differentiated from "true tales" as "'funny stories,' mere inventions, having no real substance."[9] It goes without saying, however, that members of a society that embraces foundational myths would never regard such sacred stories as profane or merely funny. Of course, "myth is not pure fiction"; "it is a 'true story' and not a 'false' one."[10] But it is a non sequitur to infer that "it is not fable but history,"[11] since truth comprises much more than history and so cannot be equated with it.

The deeper question raised by these anthropologists is what conception (or conceptions) of truth is held by these various tribal peoples. The predicate *true* has a wide range of meanings, as is evident in such expressions as "true gold," "a true friend," "a true line," "the true path," "a true statement." Why should we think that these tribal societies' conception of truth with respect to myths is the philosopher's notion of truth as correspondence?

Curiously, Pettazzoni himself admits,

> Myth is true history because it is sacred history, not only by reason of its contents but also because of the concrete sacral forces which it sets going. The recital of myths of beginnings is incorporated in cult because it is cult itself and contributes to the ends for which cult is celebrated, these being the preservation and increase of life. . . .
>
> That is why myths are true stories and cannot be false stories. Their truth has no origin in logic, nor is it of a historical kind; it is above all of a religious and more especially a magical order. The efficacy of the myth for the ends of cult, the preservation of the world and of life, lies in the magic of the word, in its evocative power.[12]

Theodor Gaster complains that Pettazzoni's explication confuses truth with efficacy. Truth is a quality inherent in the myth itself, independent of its being effectual.[13] He cautions,

8. Pettazzoni, "Truth of Myth," 99.

9. Pettazzoni, "Truth of Myth," 100.

10. Pettazzoni, "Truth of Myth," 102.

11. Pettazzoni, "Truth of Myth," 102.

12. Pettazzoni, "Truth of Myth," 102–3.

13. Theodor H. Gaster, "Myth and Story," in Dundes, *Sacred Narrative*, 133. Remarkably, the editor of *Numen*, in which Gaster's article originally appeared, intervenes at this point with a footnote, stating that while the truth of a myth and its efficacy are admittedly

> Before any general deductions can be drawn, it would seem necessary to determine exactly the meaning and frame of reference of the native terms rendered "true" and "false." Does "true" mean, in this context, accurate, or historical, or real, or valid, or authenticated? Conversely, does "false" mean untrustworthy, or unhistorical or unreal (fictitious), or futile, or spurious? A story might, for example, be valid functionally—that is, fully serve a ritual purpose—yet be invalid historically, or it might be valid historically, yet futile and inefficacious as a cultic recitation. Again, it might be a genuine tradition, yet in itself fictitious, or, conversely, it might relate an actual, historical fact, yet be a modern product and no genuinely traditional composition. . . . Obviously, then, until we know precisely what words the primitive employs, and in what sense he employs them, it is precarious to deduce from his distinction between "true" and "false" stories anything concerning the fundamental "truth" of Myth.[14]

The dichotomy drawn by native peoples between true stories and false ones is not sufficient proof that members of the society are expected to believe that the myths are literally true.

The fact that myths, while accepted as true and authoritative, are not necessarily taken to be literally true is evident from examples of myths that seem to be clearly metaphorical or figurative. For example, William Doty relates a creation myth belonging to the Chukchee people of northeastern Siberia that is surely metaphorical:

> The self-created Raven and his wife live together where there are no humans, nor any other living creature. The wife says to Raven that he should try to create the earth. When he protests that he cannot create the earth, she says that she will try to create companions for them. She falls to sleep

not the same, this distinction is made by us. For a primitive thinker the truth of the myth is also the necessary and sufficient condition of the myth's efficacy. Therefore, in practice, ideal truth and functional efficacy coincide. It seems to me that this editorial intervention defending Pettazzoni's conflating truth and efficacy is in contradiction to Pettazzoni's distinguishing historical truth from religious truth. Moreover, it begs the question in favor of attributing to natives the philosophical view of truth as correspondence, which is just what Gaster is questioning.

14. Gaster, "Myth and Story," 133–34. Cf. G. S. Kirk, *Myth: Its Meaning and Functions in Ancient and Other Cultures*, SCL 40 (Cambridge: Cambridge University Press, 1970), 32, who expresses his suspicion that the native terms translated as "true" have a variety of meanings, none of which quite corresponds with our word, even if it is extended to mean "significant," thereby confusing many modern critics, including Pettazzoni.

and her black feathers become human and her talons turn into fingers. Her abdomen enlarges, and before she awakes from sleep she has created three human children.

Raven says, "There, you have created humans! Now I shall go and try to create the earth." He flies away and asks all the benevolent beings such as the Dawn, Mid-day, and Sunset for advice, but no one gives it. At last he comes to the place where the sky meets the horizon and sees a tent full of men. Raven learns that they have been created from the dust resulting from the friction of the sky meeting the ground. They are to multiply and become the first seed of all the peoples of the earth.

They ask Raven to create the earth for them, and he agrees to try. As he flies, he defecates, and every piece of excrement falls on water, grows quickly, and becomes land. Then he begins to urinate, and where a drop falls, it becomes a lake, and where a jet falls, it becomes a river. Then he defecates a very hard substance, which becomes the mountains and hills.

When the men complain that they need food, Raven flies off and finds many kinds of trees. He takes his hatchet and begins to chop, throwing the chips into the water, which carries them into the sea. The various kinds of woodchips become walruses, seals, whales, polar bears, reindeer, every kind of sea and land creature. He says, "Now you have food!"

But the men still could not multiply, for there were no women yet. However, a Spider-Woman comes and gives birth to four daughters, who grow fast and become women. One of the men takes one woman as a companion. The next day Raven goes to visit them and finds them sleeping separately in opposite corners of the room. Realizing that they will not multiply, Raven calls a woman to him and treats her to sexual intercourse, which she finds quite pleasant. So she soon teaches the man how to multiply. That is why girls understand earlier than boys how to copulate.[15]

The attribution of both avian and human features and activities to Raven seems to require that this myth was not taken literally. Gods and goddesses are frequently represented in myths as animals. As we shall see, ANE myths exhibit such metaphoricalness.

Not only so, but there are two additional anthropological data that suggest that something other than literal truth may be attributed to a society's myths: the *plasticity* and *flexibility* of myths. Plasticity has to do with the

15. Paraphrased from William G. Doty, *Myth: A Handbook* (Tuscaloosa: University of Alabama Press, 2004), 44–45.

degree of synchronic variability of a myth, and flexibility with the degree of its diachronic variability. Dundes observes that there may be as many different versions of an oral myth as there are tellers of that myth.[16] Although he contrasts oral myths with written myths, which he regards as fixed and stable, the stability of written myths is in fact only a matter of degree, as the evolution of the *Epic of Gilgamesh* so clearly demonstrates.[17] The plasticity of myth is demonstrated by the variability of contemporaneous oral tellings of it, since that shows that the very tellers of the stories did not take them to have a rigidly fixed form; and a myth's flexibility is demonstrated by its evolution over time, its mutability and adaptability to new situations and challenges.

Social anthropologist Raymond Firth shares an example demonstrating both the plasticity and flexibility of myths from the Polynesian people of Tikopia in the Solomon Islands.[18] The example concerns two versions of a remarkably flexible myth about the building of the heavenly Rarofiroki temple, a sacred Tikopian site. The actual temple was built around 1700 and was supposed to be modeled on the heavenly temple built by God. In the contemporary myth God calls on men to pass up to him iron nails to build the temple, but they refuse, passing up only coconut husks and cord. In one version of the story, God, disgusted with them, departs with the iron nails to the land of the white men, leaving the Tikopians to make do with their inferior construction materials. In another version, the model temple is actually being built *in England* and God calls down to the workers *in English* for the nails. Failing to understand English, the Tikopians kept handing up coconut materials, until God in disgust banishes them to Tikopia, keeping the iron nails in the land of the white men. Firth reflects that the story is clearly an etiological myth designed to explain why Tikopians have the construction materials that they do. Now the knowledge of iron implements did not come to Tikopia before 1800. Thus, this feature of the story of the temple building must have been a later adaptation of the myth. We see therein not only the

16. Alan Dundes, introductory comments to Raymond Firth, "The Plasticity of Myth: Cases from Tikopia," in Dundes, *Sacred Narrative*, 207. Cf. Th. van Baaren's comment: "It is well-known that in primitive religions a large number of versions of one and the same myth exist and that it is not possible to point out one of them as the generally authoritative and original version" (Th. P. van Baaren, "The Flexibility of Myth," in Dundes, *Sacred Narrative*, 224).

17. See J. H. Tigay, *The Evolution of the Gilgamesh Epic* (Philadelphia: University of Pennsylvania Press, 1982).

18. Firth, "Plasticity of Myth," 208–12.

flexibility of the original myth but also the permitted variability in its telling. Either version, despite their different locations and explanations, is acceptable in Tikopian society.

Th. P. van Baaren shares several examples to illustrate the flexibility of myths. In precolonial Tahiti there existed a line of kings whose genealogies were part of the myths recited by the priests on the occasion of important festivals. It was so important that the myths be recited accurately that failure to do so could result in execution. Nevertheless, there were sometimes changes of dynasty, in which case the old genealogies were no longer applicable. The priests solved this problem by slowly introducing unobtrusive changes into the myths until accommodation was made to the new situation. But officially no changes had been made to the myths at all. In Borneo there existed among the Dayak the practice of offering a human sacrifice on the occasion of the construction of a new building, a practice that the colonial Dutch banned. The result was a change in the primaeval myth of the sacrifice: the myth sanctioning such a sacrifice was changed, so that it was no longer a human being that was sacrificed but a water buffalo. This change in the myth made it possible now to sacrifice a water buffalo instead of a human being. The Papuans of northeast New Guinea tell myths of origin in which it is related that they sprang from clumps of bamboo, each tribe having its own bamboo clump. With the coming of the white man the myth was adapted so that he also had his own clump of bamboo from which he originated, and during the Second World War the Japanese were also assigned their own clump of bamboo. These examples illustrate changes to myths as a result of external pressures, but myths may also change because of internal factors, such as syncretism.

Van Baaren cautions that if one asks members of the society whether their myths have changed, they will typically deny it. "If asked, the answer of the informants as a rule will be that things are as they used to be since immemorial times. This is self-evident, because within their cultural frame this is the only fitting answer. . . . In this way there resulted an inexact image of primitive cultures as static and stagnant ones."[19] For the same reason, I think,

19. Firth, "Plasticity of Myth," 221. One is reminded of Wilson's finding that when a new genealogy is created to fit a new function, the new genealogy will be in conflict with the older one; but the people who use the genealogies will understand that the written one no longer functions, *even though they may dogmatically assert that it still does* (Robert R. Wilson, *Genealogy and History in the Biblical World* [New Haven: Yale University Press, 1977], 47). He cites the fieldwork of Ian Cunnison among the Baggara Arabs: "It should be stressed that the Humr see no contradiction between the domestic version of the genealogy . . . and the political version. . . . Each is considered accurate in its own context and each may therefore be regarded as 'true'" (54).

we must be cautious about native claims that their myths are absolutely or completely true—what else could they say?

Van Baaren thinks that changeability is actually one of the specific characteristics of myth.[20] The character of myth, he says, is opposed to disappearance but not to change. He explains, "The occurrence of changes in a myth as such does not mean that the myth in question is beginning to lose its function and will probably disappear in time; on the contrary, changes in myth occur as a rule to prevent loss of function or total disappearance by changing it in such a way that it can be maintained. By changing it, a myth is adapted to a new situation, armed to withstand a new challenge."[21] When reality in the world comes into conflict with myth, it is myth that must and does change.

The plasticity and flexibility of myths lend support to the notion that what is at stake in believing a myth is not belief in its literal truth. The different versions of the myth that are believed by contemporaneous members of the society may be logically incompatible with one another; nonetheless, a fundamental religious truth is communicated by the various versions of the myth, so it does not matter which version one relates. One does not bother to correct someone telling a different version of the myth, for it, too, expresses that fundamental truth. If myths were interpreted literalistically, they could not be changed in response to new challenges in ways that are incompatible with the earlier version. But if both versions continue to express the same fundamental truth, then they can both be regarded as absolutely true, despite their differences.

Ancient Near Eastern Literary Evidence

As already mentioned in our discussion of the function of genealogies, contemporary anthropological data will always be of uncertain applicability to

20. Van Baaren, "Flexibility of Myth," 222.

21. Van Baaren, "Flexibility of Myth," 218. With a certain barbed irony, he adds, "To mention one example from our own culture, . . . we are reminded of the way in which various theological schools of the last 150 years have treated the creation myths in the first chapters of Genesis" (218). This example concerns the history of interpretation, however, not a change in the myths, which remain stable. Later in his piece van Baaren makes the provocative claim that the invention of writing has wrought havoc because it has made it possible to fix the text of a myth more or less permanently. In this situation the flexibility of myth is transferred to its exegesis. That would explain the change in the history of interpretation regarding Gen 1–11. Unable to alter the myth, exegetes alter their interpretation of it.

the stories told by ancient Israel; rather, literary evidence from ANE mythology will be more relevant. When we examine the myths of Mesopotamia and Egypt, we find the same use of figurative language, plasticity, and flexibility disclosed by the anthropological data.

Metaphoricalness of Ancient Near Eastern Myths

First, it is evident that ANE myths are often highly metaphorical rather than literal. Here we encounter a scholarly debate concerning how these ancient myths are to be properly interpreted, a debate that finds such eminent Assyriologists as Samuel Noah Kramer and Thorkild Jacobsen on opposite sides of the divide. Fortunately, we need not presume to adjudicate this debate because we shall find that on either interpretation myths tend to be written in highly figurative language that should not be taken literally.

Interpreting Ancient Near Eastern Myths

According to the first interpretation, the referents of the terms, including proper names, for various deities in the myths are the actual gods themselves, who are conceived to be immaterial, humanlike persons active in the world of men. If we were to do an ontological inventory of everything that exists, then gods would be included in our inventory. According to the second interpretation, the referents of the terms for various deities are actually the powers and entities of the natural world. On this interpretation there really are no gods in a sense; rather, an ontological inventory that included the entities and powers of the physical world would have no room for the inclusion of gods because the myths are symbolic or allegorical in employing such terms for divinity. We can say that there are gods if we wish, but what is meant is no more than that there is the sun, the moon, the sea, the wind, the subterranean water, and so on. These physical realities are what men call gods, which have no reality beyond these physical entities.

It is convenient to say something about the second interpretation first. The principal force promoting the second interpretation has been the enormously influential collection of essays by Henri and H. A. Frankfort and others, *The Intellectual Adventure of Ancient Man* (1946). The book features essays by such eminent scholars as John Wilson on Egypt, Thorkild Jacobsen on Mesopotamia, and William Irwin on Israel. In their introductory essay, the Frankforts claim that ancient man personified the powers and objects of the natural world. Lacking much capacity for speculative thought, ancient people engaged in mythopoeic thinking—that is, mythmaking (*mythos* + *poiein*). They thought of the sun, the wind, the sea, and so on as personal beings that confronted them and needed to be dealt with. "The fundamental difference between the attitudes of modern and ancient man as regards the surrounding world is this: for modern, scientific man the phenomenal world is primarily an 'It'; for ancient—and also for primitive—man it is a 'Thou.'"[22] Notice the equation between ancient man and primitive man. Scholars have sharply criticized the Frankforts for helping perpetuate the Comtean fiction of the progressive evolution of mankind from a religious (or mythological) stage to a metaphysical stage and finally to a scientific stage, a view that underlay the theories of myth of nineteenth-century anthropologists like E. B. Tylor and J. G. Frazer.[23] Today this nineteenth-century view of myth has fallen into disfavor, since the evidence does not support the claim that ancient man was intellectually disadvantaged or restricted to mythopoeic thinking (as is evident from Babylonian mathematics and astronomy).[24]

The claim that ancient myths are symbolic or allegorical is independent, however, of the Comtean thesis of mankind's intellectual evolution. In various ANE myths, Anu is obviously closely connected with the heavens, Enlil with the air or wind, Re with the sun, Nut with the sky, and so on and so forth. Could it be that in the view of these ancient mythographers the gods just *are* such natural entities, that they have no reality beyond this? Jacobsen seems to give such an interpretation to the opening lines of the *Enuma elish*:

22. Henri Frankfort and H. A. Frankfort, "Myth and Reality," in *The Intellectual Adventure of Ancient Man: An Essay on Speculative Thought in the Ancient Near East*, by Henri Frankfort et al. (Chicago: University of Chicago Press, 1946), 4.

23. E. B. Tylor, *Primitive Culture* (1913), 5th ed., 2 vols. (New York: Harper, 1958); J. G. Frazer, *The Golden Bough* (1922; reprint, London: Macmillan, 1963). *The Golden Bough* became the best-known anthropological work of the next one hundred years, eventually expanding to twelve volumes in its third edition. Andrew Von Hendy muses that the real puzzle is why this work, which never established its authority within mainstream anthropology and whose faults were so tellingly identified from the start by its professional reviewers, should have had such a significant cultural impact (*The Modern Construction of Myth* [Bloomington: Indiana University Press, 2002], 92).

24. See, e.g., the criticisms of Francesca Rochberg, *Before Nature: Cuneiform Knowledge and the History of Science* (Chicago: University of Chicago Press, 2016), 8–58. She insists that while myth was indeed one of the ways in which what we call the natural was framed in the cuneiform texts, it was not the only way. In fact, on balance, when the divinatory, astronomical, and medical texts are taken into account, hymnic and mythological contexts for defining or explaining physical phenomena are proportionately small (58).

> Then, in the midst of this watery chaos, two gods come into existence: Lahmu and Lahamu. The text clearly intends us to understand that they were begotten by Apsu, the sweet waters, and born of Ti'amat, the sea. They represent, it would seem, silt which had formed in the waters. From Lahmu and Lahamu derive the next divine pair: Anshar and Kishar, two aspects of "the horizon." The mythmaker apparently viewed the horizon as both male and female, as a circle (male) which circumscribed the sky and as a circle (female) which circumscribed the earth.
>
> . . . It is this scene—where the sweet waters of the rivers [Tigris and Euphrates] meet and blend with the salt waters of the sea, while cloud banks hang low over the waters—which has been projected back into the beginning of time. Here still is the primeval watery chaos in which Apsu, the sweet waters, mingles with Ti'amat, the salt waters of the sea; and here the silt—represented by the first of the gods, Lahmu and Lahamu—separates from the water, becomes noticeable, is deposited.[25]

Never mind the credibility of Jacobsen's interpretation; it effectively illustrates how proponents of the second interpretation construe myths: they are really about physical aspects of the world.

Given this interpretation of ANE myths, it immediately follows that the myths are not intended to be literally true. The symbolic or allegorical nature of myth is taken to explain the incoherence of Babylonian and Egyptian myths. Jacobsen discerns in the *Enuma elish* two conflicting accounts of the creation of the sky: one the creation of Anu, the god of the sky, through the gods Anshar and Kishar, representing aspects of the horizon; and the other the fashioning of the sky by the wind-god out of half of the body of the sea.[26] Similarly, the Frankforts claim that the mythopoeic mind of primitive Egyptians could represent the sky as the goddess Nut either in human form bending over the earth or as a cow bearing the sun and stars up to heaven. Thus,

> the ancients . . . present various descriptions of identical phenomena side-by-side even though they are mutually exclusive. We have seen how Shū lifted the sky-goddess Nūt from the earth. In a second story Nūt rises by herself in the shape of a cow.

25. Thorkild Jacobsen, "Mesopotamia: The Cosmos as a State," in Frankfort et al., *Intellectual Adventure of Ancient Man*, 170–71.

26. Jacobsen, "Mesopotamia," 180.

> ... Modern scholars have reproached the Egyptians for their apparent inconsistencies and have doubted their ability to think clearly. Such an attitude is sheer presumption. Once one recognizes the processes of ancient thought, their justification is apparent. After all, religious values are not reducible to rationalistic formulas. Natural phenomena, whether or not they were personified and became gods, confronted ancient man with a living presence, a significant "Thou" which, again, exceeded the scope of conceptual definition. In such cases our flexible thought and language qualify and modify certain concepts so thoroughly as to make them suitable to carry our burden of expression and significance. The mythopoeic mind ... expressed the irrational ... by admitting the validity of several avenues of approach at one and the same time.[27]

Examples such as the above could be indefinitely multiplied and serve as fodder for either interpretation. Here they are viewed as alternative but equally valid symbolic descriptions of natural phenomena. So if this second interpretation is correct, it is clear that ANE myths are not to be interpreted literally.

According to the first interpretation, on the other hand, the myths are to be read as referring to gods who are not identical to natural phenomena but who control them. This was the view of nineteenth-century theorists.[28]

27. Frankfort and Frankfort, "Myth and Reality," 19–20. See also John A. Wilson, "Egypt: The Nature of the Universe," in Frankfort et al., *Intellectual Adventure of Ancient Man*, 47, who notes that in the course of a single text these different ideas about the sky might be used.

28. As Robert Segal explains in an insightful essay, paradigmatic nineteenth-century theorists like Tylor and Frazer were literalists about the primitives' myths. They believed that myth and modern science both arise from man's intellectual quest to explain the phenomena of the natural world. But whereas modern science seeks to explain natural phenomena in terms of impersonal, efficient causes, myths advert to personal, divine agents to explain the phenomena. The explanations offered by myth and science are incompatible because "gods operate not behind or through interpersonal forces but in place of them.... One cannot stack the mythic account atop the scientific one, for the rain god, rather than utilizing meteorological processes, acts instead of them" (Robert A. Segal, "Myth as Primitive Philosophy: The Case of E. B. Tylor," in Schilbrack, *Thinking through Myths*, 20). Such an explanatory project requires that the myths were understood literally. As Segal nicely puts it, "Tylor regards primitives as scientists rather than poets" (24). So "there is a double respect in which Tylor, in the name of primitives, interprets myth literally: not only is myth, according to him, really about the physical world rather than about either society or human beings, but it is really about the divine causes of events in the physical world rather than about the physical world itself" (24).

Segal rightly complains that the central weakness of Tylor's approach is his overem-

But, like the second, this first interpretation is independent of the nineteenth century's condescending attitude toward the intellectual ability of ancient people. Samuel Noah Kramer, in a withering review of *The Intellectual Adventure of Ancient Man,* finds it of "utmost importance" to note that the Frankforts' introductory chapter contains a number of statements with regard to the characteristic features of the mind of the Near Eastern man whose validity is "more than doubtful," including the claims that the cosmos always appeared to the ancients as a "Thou" experienced emotionally in a dynamic reciprocal relationship and that therefore, like primitive man, they simply did not know an inanimate world; that in the ANE, as in present-day primitive society, all experience of this "Thou" necessarily takes the form of a story; and that therefore the ancients could only relate myths and were presumably unable to present analyses or conclusions.[29] At least as far as Mesopotamia is concerned, Kramer states, this analysis of the mind of ANE man is "without basis in fact."[30] Admittedly, in myth and fable, prayer and ritual, an inanimate object can be treated as if it were animate; but that is by no means the same as saying that the Mesopotamian mind was unable to conceive nature and the cosmos except as a living "Thou." Rather, the Mesopotamian myths are about the gods: "From as far back as we have written

---

phasis on myth as akin to science and his underemphasis on myth as akin to literature. For him a myth is a quasi-scientific hypothesis that merely happens to take the form of a narrative. Segal points out three failings arising from Tylor's minimizing the literary nature of myth: (1) *Myths are not restricted to explanations of the physical world.* Even if gods are sometimes postulated in order to explain the physical world, they become items of interest in their own right, and many myths describe the goings-on of the gods. Among Mesopotamian myths, we might note, many have little to do with explaining physical phenomena; e.g., the *Enuma elish,* though touching on natural phenomena, is primarily a panegyric for Marduk. (2) *Descriptions of the realm of the gods and their activities are the work of the literary imagination, unconstrained by the limits imposed by the need to explain the world.* Belief in the gods, far from restricting the imagination, spurs it on. (3) *The actual content of myths does not exhibit the regularity associated with natural processes.* In myths the grandest array of things happens, far beyond the regularities associated with natural phenomena.

In general, Tylor's position is not sufficiently nuanced. Even if, as seems plausible, myths are to be understood as postulating the literal existence of the gods, as Kramer holds, it does not follow that the mythical descriptions of the gods themselves were to be understood literally. Indeed, they pretty clearly were not so understood.

29. S. N. Kramer, review of *The Intellectual Adventure of Ancient Man: An Essay on Speculative Thought in the Ancient Near East,* by H. Frankfort et al., *Journal of Cuneiform Studies* 2, no. 1 (1948): 40–41.

30. Kramer, review of *Intellectual Adventure of Ancient Man,* 41.

records to the very end of the Mesopotamian civilization, the fundamental metaphysical concept of the theologians, the concept that was central and axiomatic to all their religious speculations, was the assumed existence of a pantheon consisting of a group of living beings, man-like in form, but superhuman and immortal, who though invisible to mortal eye, guide and control the cosmos in accordance with well laid plans and duly prescribed laws."[31]

Kramer marshals evidence to show that for the ancient Mesopotamians neither the sky nor the earth nor the waters nor the air was alive; alive, rather, were the humanlike beings in charge of these natural phenomena. The physical world was not animate, but it was indwelt with animate beings such as gods, men, and animals. The harmonious functioning of the lifeless cosmos was best explained by attributing it to the control of these powerful deities.[32]

On this interpretation, then, the myths are about gods, who really exist behind the natural phenomena. It is interesting that some scholars, confronted with so fundamental a disagreement between two giants of Assyriology, have opined that Jacobsen's essay is in fact not in line with the Frankforts' view but departs from it. I think, however, that it would be more accurate to say that Jacobsen's essay is simply internally inconsistent. He does clearly endorse the Frankfortian view when he writes concerning the Mesopotamian attitude toward the phenomena of nature, "Out of the repeated experience of the 'I-Thou' relationship a fairly consistent personalistic view may develop. Objects and phenomena in man's environment become personified in varying degrees. They are somehow alive; they have wills of their own; each is a definite personality."[33] After giving examples of incantations addressed to salt and grain, he infers, "Both Salt and Grain are thus not the inanimate substances for which we know them. They are alive, have personality and a will of their own."[34]

31. Kramer, review of *Intellectual Adventure of Ancient Man*, 44.

32. See further Francesca Rochberg, *The Heavenly Writing: Divination, Horoscopy, and Astronomy in Mesopotamian Culture* (Cambridge: Cambridge University Press, 2004), on divination of the will of the gods. Rochberg makes it clear that myths are not merely allegories about the phenomena of nature. Rather, on the basis of divinatory texts, she explains that astronomical phenomena were taken to be a medium of communication of the gods to mankind (4). Though the myths were expressed in metaphorical language, nonetheless the gods were conceived to be real and to be communicating to us through the medium of natural phenomena.

33. Jacobsen, "Mesopotamia," 130.

34. Jacobsen, "Mesopotamia," 131.

But then Jacobsen crucially qualifies the view: "By saying that the phenomena of the world were alive for the Mesopotamian, that they were personified, we have made things simpler than they actually are. . . . It is not correct to say that each phenomenon was a person; we must say that there was a will and a personality in each phenomenon—in it and yet somehow behind it, for the single concrete phenomenon did not completely circumscribe and exhaust the will and personality associated with it." He gives the example of the reeds that grew in the Mesopotamian marshes. "It is quite clear from our texts that, in themselves, they were never divine. Any individual reed counted merely as a plant, a thing, and so did all reeds."[35] But there were mysterious powers that were to be found in every reed and were always the same. "These powers . . . combined for the Mesopotamian into a divine personality—that of the goddess Nidaba. It was Nidaba who made the reeds thrive in the marshes. . . . She was one with every reed in the sense that she permeated it as an animating and characterizing agent; but she did not lose her identity in that of the concrete phenomenon and was not limited by any or even all existing reeds."[36] This view is evidently not essentially different from Kramer's.

So, since on this first interpretation the myths really are about gods, are the myths to be understood literally? Not necessarily, for though the gods are real, they may be described in figurative language. Since the gods are so mysterious, we can only imagine what they are like. Kramer writes,

> Their [i.e., mythographers'] aim was to compose a narrative poem in which they attempted to explain the origin and being of one or another of these notions and practices in a manner that would prove to be appealing, inspiring, and entertaining. That is, they were not concerned with proofs and arguments which appeal to the intellect; their first interest was in telling a story or in describing an event which would appeal primarily to the emotions. They therefore did not resort to logic and reason as their literary tools, but to imagination and fantasy. Consequently, in telling their story or in describing the particular event, these poets did not hesitate to invent motives and incidents patterned on human action which could not possibly have any basis in reasonable speculative thought, nor did they hesitate to adopt legendary and folkloristic motifs that had nothing to do with rational cosmological inquiry and inference.[37]

35. Jacobsen, "Mesopotamia," 131.
36. Jacobsen, "Mesopotamia," 32.
37. Kramer, review of *Intellectual Adventure of Ancient Man*, 50.

An examination of Mesopotamian as well as Egyptian myths makes it plausible that they were often meant to be taken figuratively and not literally.

Mesopotamian Myths

Consider, for example, the story of Marduk's creation of the world from Tiamat's corpse in the *Enuma elish*. Classicist F. M. Cornford once exclaimed, "No one but a lunatic under the influence of hashish could ever arrive at the theory that they [i.e., earth and sky] were originally formed by splitting the body of a dragon in half."[38] No ancient Babylonian looking to the sky expected to see the desiccated flesh and bones of Tiamat overhead, nor did he expect to find the Tigris and Euphrates flowing out of Tiamat's eye sockets. These are figurative images, "acts of imagination and fantasy," as Kirk puts it, not to be taken literally.[39] Similarly, in tablet VI of the *Epic of Gilgamesh*, Gilgamesh and Enkidu's killing the Bull of Heaven (the constellation Taurus) and distributing its meat to the people of Uruk could not possibly be taken literally. It is impossible for a stellar constellation to rampage through the Sumerian town of Uruk, be grabbed by the tail and stabbed, and be butchered and eaten. If all these things literally happened, then the Bull of Heaven should no longer be seen shining serenely in the night sky.

Similarly, in Egyptian mythology the sky could be depicted as the goddess Nut arched over the earth with hands and feet touching the ground.[40] No Egyptian looking at the sky expected to see the body of a naked woman arched above him, nor, we may hazard to say, did any caravan think that it might come upon Nut's giant legs or arms reaching skyward. Though Egyptian myths often depict the sun god Re sailing across the heavens in his barque, chock-full of other gods and animate tools, nobody gazing at the sun thought that he would see such an entourage. It might be said that these were

38. F. M. Cornford, *The Unwritten Philosophy and Other Essays* (Cambridge: Cambridge University Press, 1950), 111, cited by Kirk, *Myth*, 14–15.

39. In disputing Cornford's claim that the story arose from ritual associations, Kirk takes the images symbolically: "Why cannot a dragon itself represent a condition of primeval disorder outside the ritual? If the primeval figure represents water as well as disorder, as Tiamat certainly did, why should not the idea of dividing the waters (as Genesis puts it) assume the form of dividing the dragon itself?" (*Myth*, 15). I should add that the waters, like the dragon, also belong to the imagery of the *Enuma elish*.

40. Even these depictions are inconsistent with one another. See figs. 38, 39, and 47 in Louis Herbert Gray and John Arnott MacCulloch, eds., *The Mythology of All Races*, vol. 12, *Egyptian Mythology*, by W. Max Müller (New York: Cooper Square, 1964), 43–49.

invisible realities behind the phenomena. But, as we shall see, the extreme plasticity of such depictions gives reason not to take them literally. When the sun journeys into the underworld at night and reverts to its pre-creation state, this cannot be intended literally. Did no soldiers on night watch or farmers rising before dawn ever notice that the world failed to revert to a primordial sea? Sometimes the sun is depicted as undergoing rebirth at night within Nut's body. At sunset it enters Nut's mouth, and she becomes pregnant with the sun. During the night, the sun "sails inside her" until at dawn "he parts the thighs of his mother Nut," as "he opens in his splinting and swims in his redness" of "afterbirth" and moves into the daytime sky.[41] Can anyone deny that this is metaphorical language? Equally and obviously metaphorical is the depiction of the sun as a scarab or as a falcon, since a rolling dung beetle and a soaring bird were both considered apt images of the sun. The various depictions of Egyptian gods and goddesses with human bodies and animal heads should not be taken as literal pictures of them; they are, rather, in Erik Hornung's phrase, "pictorial signs that convey meaning in a metalanguage."[42] Hornung affirms that Egyptian religion lived on the fact that the gods really exist. But in order to describe this reality, it had to speak in "metaphorical and representational images" of the gods. "These images . . . serve to express a content that can perhaps be appropriately expressed only in this way."[43]

Unfortunately, many OT scholars, even those emphasizing the importance of ANE studies as an interpretive backdrop to Genesis, have been seriously misled by a wooden literalism with respect to Mesopotamian and Egyptian myths. To give one example, Denis Lamoureux writes, "People in the ancient Near East believed that the earth was a circular island surrounded by a circumferential sea. . . . The ancient geographical idea of a sea encompassing a circular earth appears in a map of the entire world drawn by the Babylonians around 600 BC. . . . Ancient Near Eastern people believed that the earth literally came to an end at the shore of the circumferential sea."[44] While Lamoureux is not an OT scholar, John Walton similarly claims

41. From inscriptions on the ceiling of Seti I's cenotaph at Abydos, cited in James P. Allen, *Genesis in Egypt: The Philosophy of Ancient Egyptian Creation Accounts*, YES 2 (San Antonio, TX: Van Siclen Books, 1988), 6, plate 1.

42. Erik Hornung, *Conceptions of God in Ancient Egypt: The One and the Many*, trans. John Baines (Ithaca, NY: Cornell University Press, 1982), 117.

43. Hornung, *Conceptions of God*, 258; cf. 253.

44. Denis O. Lamoureux, *Evolution: Scripture and Nature Say Yes!* (Grand Rapids: Zondervan, 2016), 92–94. Lamoureux depicts the map as fully intact rather than partially missing; the triangles representing overseas nations he colors black, so that they look like

that the so-called Babylonian World Map and Egyptian sarcophagi confirm that all ANE cultures considered the earth to be a flat disk floating on the underground waters and ringed by the cosmic sea.[45] On this basis it is argued that the biblical authors similarly believed that the earth is a flat disk that comes to an end at the surrounding ocean.

This is a terrible misunderstanding of the Babylonian World Map.

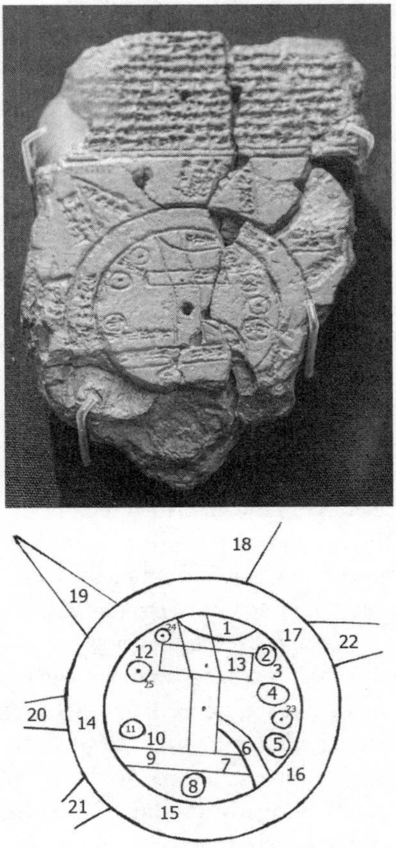

Figure 6.1. The "Babylonian world map."

Objects on the Babylonian world map:

1. "Mountain"
2. "City"
3. Urartu
4. Assyria (Akkadian)
5. Der
6. ?
7. Swamp
8. Susa (capital of Elam)
9. Canal/"outflow"
10. Bit Yakin
11. "City"
12. Habban
13. Babylon, divided by Euphrates

14–17. Ocean

18–22. Outer "regions"

---

mere decorations, and gets their number wrong; and he omits the uncharted regions beyond the circumferential sea, thus giving the appearance that the earth comes to an end on its shores. I can only describe his drawing here because permission to reprint was denied.

45. John H. Walton, *Genesis 1 as Ancient Cosmology* (Winona Lake, IN: Eisenbrauns, 2011), 93; cf. Tremper Longman III and John H. Walton, *The Lost World of the Flood: Mythology, Theology, and the Deluge Debate* (Downers Grove, IL: IVP Academic, 2018), 80. Ironically, Walton also affirms that the earth was believed to be undergirded by pillars or to be supported by the roots of the mountains, which reached down into the netherworld. He muses, "These images must be integrated with the idea that the Earth floated on the underground waters" (*Genesis 1 as Ancient Cosmology*, 96). I have already remarked on the visual metaphors of Egyptian iconography. Yet even James Allen, on the basis of a picture of the world as a rectangle in which the sun is rising, projects the picture to three dimensions and interprets it realistically to prove that ancient Egyptians thought that the world was the shape of a box (*Genesis in Egypt*, 6)!

Consider what this ancient clay tablet, housed in the British Museum, really looks like (fig. 6.1).

What do the triangles on the *other side* of the ocean represent? The cuneiform text on the reverse side of the tablet identifies them as eight regions and speaks of traveling to them. They are lands beyond the sea, places like Dilmun (Bahrain), Magan (Persian Gulf Coast including Oman), and Meluhha (Indus Valley), with which Babylon traded. Between and beyond these regions lies uncharted territory. The closing section of the text explains that the earth's surface extends limitlessly to the north, south, east, and west of Babylon. So to say that the map represents the earth as a flat disk in the midst of a surrounding ocean is a gross misunderstanding.

Indeed, the idea that this diagram is a "world map" is a misnomer. The tablet carries no such inscription. Countries like Egypt, with which Babylon was familiar, do not even appear on it. If it is a map at all, it is a highly stylized map of Mesopotamia with Babylon near the center (naturally!). Overseas countries lie either in the identified regions or in uncharted territory, which is limitless. The circular shape of the ocean should not be taken literally. Babylonian seafarers knew that one could not travel by ship from the Persian Gulf (what they called the Lower Sea) to the Mediterranean Sea (the Upper Sea).

Moreover, it is not even clear that this artifact is a map at all. Wayne Horowitz observes that it is similar to geometrical diagrams in Mesopotamian mathematical texts. According to Horowitz, the map and the text on the reverse side are similar in format to geometric problems that consist of diagrams and procedural instructions in the second person (e.g., "Draw a line from point A . . ."). Similarly, the "map" can be considered to be a diagram, with the text on the reverse repeating the phrase "where you go." Such an interpretation would make good sense of the artificiality of the "map": perfectly circular with a compass hole in the middle and eight symmetrical triangles roughly the same in size, representing regions said to be evenly spaced seven leagues apart.

The further claim that the biblical text also assumes a world geography of a disk-shaped earth surrounded by water is thus unfounded and, given Israel's familiarity with overseas nations (Gen 10:1–31), including seafaring peoples and Mediterranean islands, wholly implausible. In fact, according to 1 Kgs 9:26–28 and 10:22, Solomon owned a fleet of ocean-going merchant ships that sailed from the port of Ezion-Geber on the Gulf of Aqaba and plied the waters of the Red Sea and the Indian Ocean, so they would have been familiar with overseas lands.

But perhaps the most egregious example of unwarranted literalism with respect to ANE materials is the claim that, according to the so-called "cosmic geography" of the ANE, the sky or the heavens are a solid dome over the earth, touching its horizon, in which the stars are engraved.

With respect to Mesopotamian religion, many scholars seem to have been misled by their uncritical reading of Horowitz's oft-cited *Mesopotamian Cosmic Geography*. In his introduction Horowitz makes clear his intention of offering a merely descriptive account of Mesopotamian texts:

> Ancient Mesopotamian authors do not distinguish between cosmographic ideas drawn from direct observation of the physical world (for example, the movement of stars in the sky) and those not derived from direct observation (for example, the geography of the Heaven of Anu above the sky or the fantastic regions visited by Gilgamesh in Gilg. IX–X). The current evidence simply does not allow us to know, for instance, if ancient readers of Gilgamesh really believed that they too could have visited Utnapištim by sailing across the cosmic sea and "the waters of death" or if a few, many, most, or all ancient readers understood the topographical material in metaphysical or mystical terms. Thus, herein I do not attempt to assess the plausibility of ancient cosmographic traditions, to harmonize conflicting traditions, or to flesh out surviving materials by speculation or through comparison with materials from other cultures.[46]

46. Wayne Horowitz, *Mesopotamian Cosmic Geography* (Winona Lake, IN: Eisenbrauns, 2011), xv. Compare Horowitz's nuanced statement concerning our uncertainty about what "few, many, most, or all ancient readers" may have believed with the irresponsible statement by Longman and Walton that "everyone in the ancient world believed in a cosmic ocean suspended above a solid sky" (*Lost World of the Flood*, 9). Contrast Richard Averbeck's cautious statement, "We do not know, for example, whether the ancients really believed things like the embedding of the stars in a solid dome, or if this was just an analogy to them, since they could plainly see that the stars moved in the sky" (Richard E. Averbeck, "A Literary Day, Inter-textual, and Contextual Reading of Genesis 1–2," in *Reading Genesis 1–2: An Evangelical Conversation*, ed. J. Daryl Charles [Peabody, MA: Hendrickson, 2013], 13; cf. 20). In general OT scholars need to quit talking about what ancient Egyptians believed or ancient Babylonians believed about the world, since we are typically in no position to know such things, and instead speak descriptively—e.g., "according to ancient Sumerian myths . . ." or "Egyptian coffin texts portray . . ."

NB as well Horowitz's odd equation of *metaphysical* with *mystical*, terms he views as opposed to *real*. We find the same misunderstanding of metaphysics on Longman and Walton's part, for they associate the metaphysical with the mythical (*Lost World of the Flood*, 19). They compound the terminological confusion by similarly loading the word *cosmic* with mythical connotations, which was not, so far as I can tell, Horowitz's intention, for he seems to understand cosmic geography to have merely a wider scope than terrestrial geography—viz., to comprise the heavens as well as the earth.

Horowitz's purely descriptive account of Mesopotamian cosmic geography is akin to a cartographer's description of Middle Earth in the Tolkien stories. There may be no physical reality corresponding to the geography.

Unfortunately, Horowitz himself often lapses into treating his texts as literal descriptions of the physical cosmos. For example, the mystical-religious text KAR 307, though rich with symbolism, is treated by Horowitz as though it were a literal description of the universe:

> The Upper Heavens are *luludānītu*-stone. They belong to Anu. He settled the 300 Igigi inside.
>
> The Middle Heavens are *saggilmud*-stone. They belong to the Igigi. Bel sat on the high dais inside, in the lapis lazuli sanctuary. He made a lamp of electrum shine inside.
>
> The Lower Heavens are jasper. They belong to the stars. He drew the constellations of the gods on them. (KAR 307.30–33; cf. AO 8196 iv 20–22)

So Horowitz muses that the sky-blue jasper from Persia mentioned by Pliny would be appropriate for the lower heavens—at least on a sunny day. But on a cloudy day, he says, gray jasper would be more appropriate. The problem is that the lower heavens cannot be both, so that a literal interpretation would imply that the mineral substance of the heavens would be constantly changing with the weather. Horowitz muses, "It is not clear, however, how the jasper of the Lower Heavens might have been thought to change from clear to cloudy."[47] Horowitz also indulges in the speculation that because jasper is translucent, the blue stone floor of the middle heavens could be seen through the jasper slab of the lower heavens—a fanciful conjecture that blithely ignores the fact that lapis lazuli, being a favorite mineral of Mesopotamian culture, is said to compose an endless variety of things, including, in the *Epic of Gilgamesh* alone, a tablet on which the entire epic is inscribed (I.27); a chariot (VI.10); minas, each the mass of the Bull of Heaven (VI.162); Enkidu's eyebrows (VIII.71); and a tree (IX.175). In the compendia on plants, stones, and snakes, in the *ṣēru šikinšu* ("The Snake, Its Appearance") we find the following: "The snake whose appearance (is as follows): its scutes are of pappardillu-stone, a snout of red stone, eyes of mušarru-stone, a face of lapis lazuli and gold."[48] No one would have understood such a description of a snake literally.

47. Horowitz, *Mesopotamian Cosmic Geography*, 14.
48. Rochberg, *Before Nature*, 86.

Moreover, since the stars are said to be inscribed on the surface of the lower heavens, this surface would have to be in constant motion in order to explain the rising and setting of the stars in the sky, a cosmic geography incompatible with the heavens' resting on terrestrial supports, be they pillars or mountains or poles or what have you. Since ancient Mesopotamians observed the stars to return annually to the same positions, the lower heavens must somehow revolve with respect to the earth. But a revolving dome is incompatible with that dome's coming into contact with the earth at its horizon. A system of concentric spheres would be needed, as in later Greek cosmology, which is unattested in Babylonian astronomy.

The problem posed by the motion of the fixed stars and planets becomes insuperable for the literal interpretation of the heavens as a hard, stone surface. According to the Babylonian astronomical texts known as the Astrolabes, dating at least to the middle Babylonian period, the stars may be grouped into three "paths" as they move across the sky, each given the name of a deity. The central or equatorial band was called the path of Anu, the northerly band the path of Enlil, and the southerly band the path of Ea. So, are we seriously to think that the ancient Mesopotamians thought that these paths were three stone segments of the celestial dome grinding against each other as they revolved about the earth? Worse problems still are posed by the motions of the planets, as well as the sun and the moon. For the ancient astrologers observed that the planets do not move in tandem with the fixed stars but wander across the heavens, sometimes standing still and even undergoing retrograde motion. Babylonian astronomers thus differentiated the planets (*bibbu*, wild sheep), including, in our nomenclature, Mercury, Venus, Mars, Jupiter, and Saturn, from the fixed stars (*kakkabu*). These planets, along with the sun and the moon, all move in a single band of their own across the sky, but this band *cuts across* the paths of Anu, Enlil, and Ea due to the tilt of the earth's axis. As a result, the planets, as well as the sun and the moon, actually transition from the path of one deity to another, appearing at certain seasons of the year in the path of Anu, for example, and at other seasons in the path of Enlil (see fig. 6.2). These carefully charted observations on the part of ancient Mesopotamians are decisive against the literalistic interpretation of cosmographic texts that describe the heavens as a solid surface on which the stars are engraved.

Historian of science Francesca Rochberg explains that Mesopotamian astronomy was wholly phenomenal or instrumentalist in character. In contrast to later Greek astronomy, "the Babylonian astronomers had no models of planetary motion. What they did have were mathematical schemes for

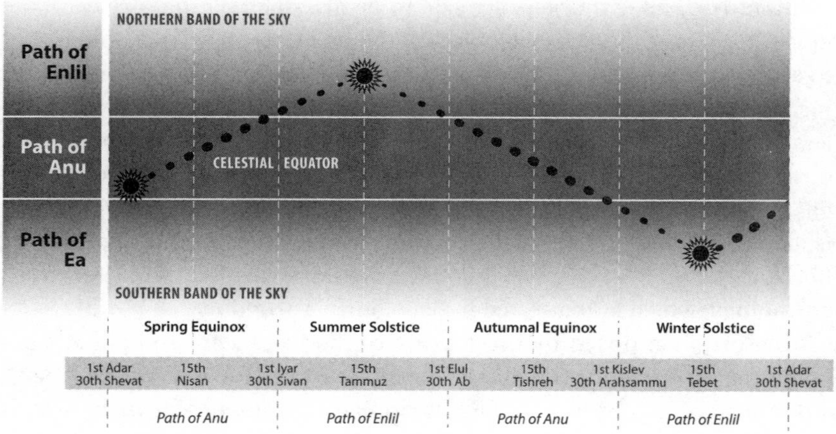

Figure 6.2. The transverse motion of the sun across the paths of Enlil, Anu, and Ea, associated with the fixed stars, as recorded by ancient Babylonian astronomers.

the computation of synodic appearances."[49] Thus, she observes, Babylonian astronomy did not rely or depend on a spherical cosmological framework, nor did it even make use of geometrical models of a celestial body in motion around a central Earth. "The lack of an explicit cosmological model within which Babylonian astronomical theory was to fit was of no consequence in view of the fact that the predictions did not derive from a geometrical conception that attempted to make causal sense of the phenomena, but rather depended on period relations whose purpose was to enable the computation of phenomena either forward or backward in time in an instrumental way."[50]

More recently Rochberg has expanded on this theme, arguing that the Babylonians were not interested in "nature" per se, as opposed to observations of regularities. "Babylonian models all shared a common objective to predict and a disinterest in cosmology or physical explanation. . . . The Babylonians were concerned with periodicity. Theirs was a thoroughly quantitative approach and did not depend upon a physical framework."[51] One important indication of the Babylonians' indifference to physical cosmology is their use of two independent algorithms for calculating the dates and posi-

49. Rochberg, *Heavenly Writing*, 283.
50. Rochberg, *Heavenly Writing*, 32.
51. Rochberg, *Before Nature*, 259, 276; cf. 85.

tions of lunar and planetary phenomena, known as System A and System B. The first described the phenomena by means of a step function, whereas the second used linear zigzag functions.[52] Though empirically equivalent, both systems could not be accurate descriptions of physical reality; neither did either purport to be such. "This theoretical aspect of predictive astronomy seems to have little or no connection to a cosmology, or spatial framework within which to conceive of the planetary or lunar positions," Rochberg concludes. "The coexistence of Systems A and B models further argues against the idea that a physical representation was of any comparative value among Babylonian astronomical models."[53]

Someone might say that the mythological texts had a quite different view of the physical cosmos than the scientific, astronomical texts. But this naive bifurcation has been exploded by the reappreciation on the part of scholars in recent decades of how fully integrated ancient Mesopotamian religion was with their science, including observational astronomy, a fact already evident in the divine names assigned to the three celestial paths. In the *Enuma elish* IV.146 and V.1–46, Marduk organizes the stars, planets, and constellations according to the same pattern described in the Astrolabes, including the paths of Anu, Enlil, and Ea. The traditional celestial omen text *Enuma Anu Enlil* opens with a mythological introduction about how Anu, Enlil, and Ea constructed the heavens so that they can serve as omens. Ancient Mesopotamians were obsessed with divination, which was a massive and lucrative industry, and the reading and interpretation of divinatory signs was the foremost concern of literary and scholarly writings in Babylonia and Assyria.[54] More than half of Ashurbanipal's famous library was devoted to divination, and, of this, 48 percent concerned astrology, 14 percent extispicy, and about 10 percent terrestrial omens. Most historians of science now realize that mathematical and observational astronomy were just as much a part of Babylonian divination as the examination of the liver of a sacrificial lamb. Rochberg has emphasized that the stellar constellations were analogous to a sort of "heavenly writing" by means of which the will of the gods might be discerned. "The image of the heavens as a stone surface upon which a god could draw or write, as a scribe would a clay tablet, complements the

52. For an account, see Otto Neugebauer, *The Exact Sciences in Antiquity*, 2nd ed. (New York: Dover, 1969), 110–14, 129.

53. Rochberg, *Before Nature*, 82, 258.

54. Marc Van De Mieroop, *Philosophy before the Greeks: The Pursuit of Truth in Ancient Babylonia* (Princeton: Princeton University Press, 2016), 98.

metaphoric trope of the heavenly writing."[55] Rochberg sees the following difference between the mythological texts and the astrological texts: whereas Babylonian cosmogonic myths represent the creation of the cosmos as an allegory involving personified cosmic elements, such as sea, earth, sky, and wind, astronomical and omen texts seek to describe the phenomena themselves. Even though celestial phenomena were sometimes described in the latter in metaphorical terms as gods (e.g., "the moon god mourns" serves as a metaphor for the moon's being eclipsed), "the use of metaphorical language in the omens has the force of conveying the appearance of something observed, or potentially observable, and this constitutes suggestive evidence for how the ancient Mesopotamians conceptualized some natural phenomena as manifestations of the gods."[56]

Mythical texts touching on cosmic geography are obviously not intended to be taken literally, on pain of incoherence. In the *Etana* epic, Etana is supposed to fly to the heaven of Anu on the back of an eagle. How he is supposed to get through the solid floors of the lower and middle heavens is not said. In the *Adapa* myth, Adapa walks up the path to heaven. In *Nergal and Ereshkigal*, Nantar climbs a stairway to heaven. In the *Enuma elish*, the metaphor of eastern and western gates with bolts for the astral bodies to pass through (V.9–10), if read literally, presupposes the stars' moving freely rather than being fixed in a revolving solid dome. In the creation story, Marduk filets the body of Tiamat and, with one half of her body, stretches out the heavens and supports them with her crotch (V.61). But no one gazing skyward expected to see the skeleton of a dragon overhead, and no traveler ever expected to find the gigantic crotch of Tiamat propping up the heavens. In the *Atrahasis Epic*, the sea is held in check by a sort of netting (*nahbalu*). This leads to considerable head-scratching on Horowitz's part. He reflects soberly, "Objects made even in part of netting are porous so what is not clear is how a nahbalu could restrain the sea."[57] Is there no poetic license?

In sum, modern Western OT scholars, when they assert that the ancient Mesopotamians thought of the earth as a flat disk in a circumferential sea covered by a solid dome, are thus, despite their claims to understand ANE culture, guilty of importing a wooden literalism that is foreign to the Mesopotamian texts.[58] One is reminded of the remark of J. Stafford Wright

55. Rochberg, *Heavenly Writing*, 2.

56. Rochberg, *Heavenly Writing*, 39.

57. Horowitz, *Mesopotamian Cosmic Geography*, 327.

58. We must guard against such literalism with respect to nonmythic texts as well. For example, Esarhaddon extols the greatness of the temple Ešarra:

concerning the prevalence of metaphorical language in our own scientific discourse—for example, talk in psychoanalysis of the subconscious, the superego, the depths of the psyche, the threshold of consciousness, and so forth. "A critical reader a thousand years hence might well think that the twentieth century held the idea of a three-story solid mind, with doors and gates. We know how wrong he would be; but we would still maintain that these phrases are legitimate metaphors, and indeed almost essential metaphors, to translate non-spatial and comprehensible language."[59]

Egyptian Myths

As far as Egyptian myths are concerned, little more needs to be said. The most important evidence for Egyptian cosmogeography comes from pictures in tombs and their accompanying captions. Othmar Keel and Silvia Schroer caution, however, that "ancient Near Eastern images are conceptual, not photographic."[60] They explain,

> Fundamentally, however, it must be kept clearly in mind just how speculative these ideas of creation are. The thought, pictorial representations, and language of people of that time were generally symbolic—that is, neither entirely concrete nor purely abstract. A cow that bears a calf or the sky-woman who bears the sphere of the sun are not expressions of

---

> I raised to heaven the head of Ešarra, my lord Assur's dwelling.
> Above, heavenward, I raised high its head.
> Below, in the underworld I made firm its foundations.
> . . . .
> Its lofty high head scraped the sky,
> below, its roots spread in the subterranean water.

Such language should no more be taken literally than our talk of skyscrapers in our great cities. Hurowitz comments, "Clearly, descriptions such as this are intent on glorifying the building and the accomplishment of the builder and have no clear desire to present an actual description which would enable the reader to visualize the edifice in any but the most general details" (Victor Hurowitz, *I Have Built You an Exalted House: Temple Building in the Bible in Light of Mesopotamian and Northwest Semitic Writings*, JSOTSup 115 [Sheffield: JSOT Press, 1992], 245).

59. J. Stafford Wright, "The Place of Myth in the Interpretation of the Bible," *JTVI* 88 (1956): 23, cited by Walter C. Kaiser Jr., "The Literary Form of Genesis 1–11," in *New Perspectives on the Old Testament*, ed. J. Barton Payne (Waco: Word, 1970), 61.

60. Othmar Keel and Silvia Schroer, *Creation: Biblical Theologies in the Context of the Ancient Near East*, trans. Peter T. Daniels (Winona Lake, IN: Eisenbrauns, 2015), 79.

> naïve, childlike fantasies regarding the origin of the world but philosophical developments of thought that were able to form and formulate more abstract notions (the coming into being of the world) from concrete experiences (cattle, birth, etc.). This kind of representation is not simple realism but reflects an interest in the powers that operate and appear in the concrete world.[61]

This implies, as John Collins rightly urges, that "the simple citation of pictures and quotations from the other cultures proves nothing. We still must exegete *them.*"[62]

Scholars who believe that ancient Egyptians thought of the sky as a solid dome tend to rely on James Allen's *Genesis in Egypt* (1988). Unlike Horowitz, Allen aspires to "look behind the images for the concepts those images are meant to convey."[63] Unfortunately, Allen constantly conflates images and concepts in his discussion of Egyptian texts. Consider, for example, his discussion of a relief and accompanying inscriptions from the ceiling of Seti I's cenotaph at Abydos (fig. 6.3), in which "the traditional Egyptian concept of the universe is best revealed."[64]

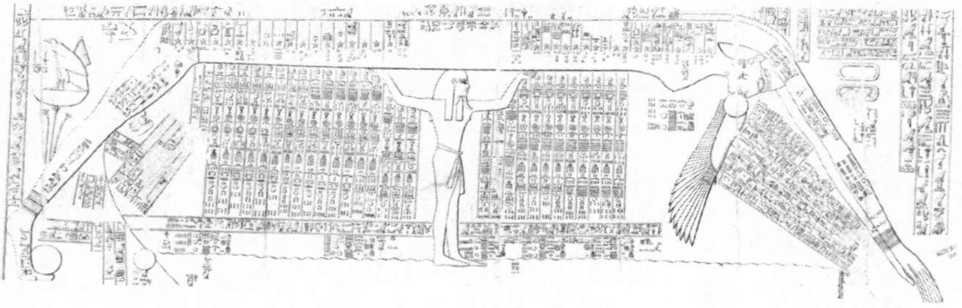

Figure 6.3. Ceiling of Seti I's cenotaph at Abydos displaying the sky goddess Nut as a woman arched over the earth. Drawing courtesy of James Allen.

The relief depicts the sky as the goddess Nut, arched over the earth with her hands and feet resting on it and separated from it by the atmosphere in the form of the god Shu. Stars and the sun are depicted along her body. According-

61. Keel and Schroer, *Creation*, 78.

62. C. John Collins, *Reading Genesis Well: Navigating History, Science, Poetry, and Truth* (Grand Rapids: Zondervan, 2018), 130. Similarly Keel and Schroer, *Creation*, 83, on an iconographic reconstruction of an Israelite image of the world.

63. Allen, *Genesis in Egypt*, ix.

64. Allen, *Genesis in Egypt*, 1.

ing to Allen, "the accompanying texts explain both the illustrations and their relationship to the visible and conjectural universe."[65]

Allen's statement is at best misleading. The texts *describe* what is represented by the various figures in the illustration, but there is no attempt to offer an *explanation* of their relationship to the visible and conjectural universe. Here is the description of Nut:

1.	*Arms*	Her right arm is on the northwestern side, the left on the southwestern side.
2.	*Head*	Her head is on the western horizon, her mouth is the west.
3.	*Mouth*	The western horizon.
4.	*Crotch*	The eastern horizon.

We learn nothing from this description of the reality Nut represents. The inscriptions at her mouth and foot accompanying the winged disk of the sun describe in mythological terms the sun god's entry into Nut in the evening, her pregnancy, and her giving birth to the sun god in the morning:

> When the Incarnation of this god enters is at her first hour of evening,
> becoming effective again in the embrace of his father Osiris, and becoming purified therein.
> When the Incarnation of this god rests from life in the Duat is at her second hour of pregnancy.
> . . . .
> . . . .
> When the Incarnation of this god enters her mouth, inside the Duat,
> it stays open after he sails inside her,
> so that these sailing stars may enter after him
> and come forth after him.
> . . . .
> The Incarnation of this god comes forth from her rear.
> Then he is on course toward the world, apparent and born.
> Then he produces himself above.
> Then he parts the thighs of his mother Nut.
> Then he goes away to the sky.

65. Allen, *Genesis in Egypt*, 1.

These "explanations" are evidently just as mythological as the pictures themselves. They actually portray Nut as the night sky, the sun entering her mouth in the evening and being born anew in the morning. Hence, her image is spangled with stars. Such a portrayal is an alternative to the portrayal of the sun's nightly journey as occurring in the underworld. In those myths the sun's rejuvenating journey may take place, not within Nut's body, but within a gigantic snake or crocodile. Obviously, these portrayals are not to be taken literally.[66] The sky goddess was variously represented in Egyptian iconography.[67] Sometimes she is portrayed as a cow, sometimes as the goddess Hathor. In some representations of Nut she appears to be the daytime sky, the sun sailing above her body, or even in duplicate, the stars located below each body. Hornung emphasizes that none of the divine images—such as frog-headed and snake-headed images of the ogdoad of deities representing the primordial conditions—gives any information about the true form of a deity, which is hidden and mysterious.[68] Hence, multiple images are freely used.

Allen thinks that the reality represented by Nut is the vault overhead that separated our world from the outer darkness and waters. "The sun sails on these waters just as people can sail on the Nile: 'The bark of the Sun courses through the Waters' (CT VI 313p)."[69] Allen's statement conflates mythical imagery and reality. People's sailing on the Nile is an objective reality, but Allen acknowledges that the sun's sailing as a ship on the celestial waters is part of the imagery of Egyptian myth. So why think that the vault belongs to the conceptual content rather than to the imagery? The outer darkness and endless waters are just as much a part of the mythology as Nut or Shu. A ship sailing on the surface of the endless outer waters would be sailing literally upside down, which, apart from being ridiculous, is not the way in which the sun's barque is portrayed in Egyptian iconography. So why think that the vault is a physical reality? The hieroglyph that Allen translates as "vault" means simply "sky." Allen thinks that "in the Egyptian conception, the sky is not so much a solid 'ceiling' as a kind of interface between the surface of the Waters and the dry atmosphere."[70] This characterization would,

66. As Walton nicely puts it, it is not as though one could throw a rock and hit Nut in the knee! (J. H. Walton, "Creation," in *Dictionary of the Old Testament: Pentateuch*, ed. T. Desmond Alexander and David W. Baker [Downers Grove, IL: InterVarsity Press, 2003], 163).

67. See, e.g., the striking images reproduced in Keel and Schroer, *Creation*, 79, 90–91.

68. Hornung, *Conceptions of God*, 124–25.

69. Allen, *Genesis in Egypt*, 5.

70. Allen, *Genesis in Egypt*, 5.

in effect, make the "vault" merely the exosphere or outermost layer of the earth's atmosphere, represented by Shu.

The stars adorn the body of Nut in the portrayal in Seti I's tomb and elsewhere. Like the Mesopotamians, however, ancient Egyptians observed the motion of the stars and planets. As early as the Middle Kingdom, an astronomical system was in place according to which the heliacal stars—that is, the stars that are the last to be seen prior to the dawn—rise over the horizon at ten-day intervals.[71] In the pictures on coffin lids dating 1800–1200 BC, we find the sky represented with thirty-six constellations arranged in their ten-day intervals throughout the year, forming thirty-six columns with twelve lines each for the twelve hours of the night, in effect a star clock. The sun also moves through Nut's body. But the Egyptians observed that the sun has a slow motion of its own, relative to the stars, in the *opposite* direction of the daily rotation of the stars. This eastward relative motion of the sun, completed once in every year, delays the rising of the sun from day to day with respect to the rising of the last stars visible at dawn. As a result, the rising of those stars will be more and more clearly visible, and it will take more and more time before they fade away in the light of dawn. Other stars will replace them as the last stars of the night to be visible. It is this sequence of phenomena that led the Egyptians to measure the time of night by means of stars that we now call the decans: for ten days a star indicated the last hour of the night, then another star was chosen for the next ten days, and so on. On the assumption that a year had exactly 360 days or thirty-six "decades," then thirty-six decans would be required before a given star can once again serve as the decan of the last hour of the night.

The commentary to the inscriptions in the cenotaph of Seti I describes how one decan after another "dies," is "purified" in the embalming house of the netherworld, and is reborn after seventy days of invisibility—a "mythological description" of observational reality.[72] So what is the reality corresponding to these pictures and descriptions? Allen says, "As a vault, the sky rests upon the earth in all directions—as a goddess, she touches the earth

71. See the account by Neugebauer, *Exact Sciences in Antiquity*, 81–89, which I follow here.

72. Neugebauer, *Exact Sciences in Antiquity*, 87. Neugebauer comments that these tomb drawings "demonstrate drastically that artistic principles determined the arrangement of astronomical ceiling decorations. Thus it is a hopeless task to try to find, on the sky, groups of stars whose arrangement might have been the same as the depicted constellations seem to require" (89). Again, we see the imprudence of thinking that the Egyptians took these drawings literally.

with her feet and hands."[73] But given the motion of the sun and stars through the sky (the body of Nut), ancient Egyptians could not have taken the stars or sun to be embedded in a solid vault resting on the earth. Hoffmeier cites various texts according to which the sky is supported by tent poles or staves (Pyramid Texts 348, 360, 1456, 1510, 1559; Coffin Text I, 2641; Book of the Dead 450, 14).[74] A culture responsible for the construction of the pyramids could not possibly have taken such metaphors literally. Wholly apart from being unable to bear the weight of the cosmic dome, such supports would have been ripped from their moorings by the motion of the heavens. A solid vault in which the astral bodies are embedded is no more a part of Egyptian cosmic geography than are Nut or Shu. More plausibly, Nut simply represented the sky.

Keel and Schroer conclude that contemporary scholars who construe the ancients' cosmic geography literalistically have failed to understand them:

> People in the ancient Near East did not conceive of the earth as a disk floating on water with the firmament inverted over it like a bell jar, with the stars hanging from it. They knew from observation and experience with handicrafts that the lifting capacity of water is limited and that gigantic vaults generate gigantic problems in terms of their ability to carry dead weight. The textbook images that keep being reprinted of the "ancient Near Eastern world picture" are based on typical modern misunderstandings that fail to take into account the religious components of ancient Near Eastern conceptions and representations.[75]

It is sobering to reflect that so many OT scholars claiming to inform us of what the ancients believed about cosmic geography should have so seriously misunderstood the relevant texts.

Israelite Myths

So when it comes to the Genesis account of God's creation of the so-called firmament (*rāqîaʿ*), even less needs to be said. With the modern misinterpretation of Mesopotamian and Egyptian cosmogeography exposed, the main

73. Allen, *Genesis in Egypt*, 5.

74. James K. Hoffmeier, "Some Thoughts on Genesis 1 & 2 and Egyptian Cosmology," *JANESCU* 15, no. 1 (1983): 45.

75. Keel and Schroer, *Creation*, 78.

prop for interpreting the *rāqîaʿ* of Gen 1 as a literal, solid dome falls away. Genesis 1 tells us virtually nothing about the nature of the *rāqîaʿ* nor whether the word is used figuratively or literally. All we are told is this:

> And God said, "Let there be a *rāqîaʿ* in the midst of the waters, and let it separate the waters from the waters." And God made the *rāqîaʿ* and separated the waters which were under the *rāqîaʿ* from the waters which were above the *rāqîaʿ*. And it was so. And God called the *rāqîaʿ* Heaven. (Gen 1:6–8)

> And God said, "Let there be lights in the *rāqîaʿ* of the heavens to separate the day from the night; and let them be for signs and for seasons and for days and years, and let them be lights in the *rāqîaʿ* of the heavens to give light upon the earth." And it was so. And God made the two great lights, the greater light to rule the day, and the lesser light to rule the night; he made the stars also. And God set them in the *rāqîaʿ* of the heavens to give light upon the earth, to rule over the day and over the night, and to separate the light from the darkness. (Gen 1:14–18)

> And God said, "Let the waters bring forth swarms of living creatures, and let birds fly above the earth across the *rāqîaʿ* of the heavens." (Gen 1:20)

It is futile to try to determine the meaning of *rāqîaʿ* via etymology, as some have tried to do,[76] since it is use, not etymology, that determines a word's meaning.[77] Outside Gen 1, the word is used to describe a sort of heavenly expanse or backdrop overhead (Pss 19:1; 150:1; Dan 12:3; Ezek 1:22–26; 10:1). The key to the meaning of *rāqîaʿ* as used in Gen 1 comes in v. 8: "God called the *rāqîaʿ* Heaven (*šāmāyim*)." *Šāmāyim* is the word for skies. *Rāqîaʿ* thus denotes the sky or, expressing the notion of breadth, the skies.

76. E.g., Denis O. Lamoureux, "No Historical Adam: The Evolutionary Creation View," in *Four Views on the Historical Adam*, ed. Matthew Barrett and Ardel B. Caneday, Counterpoints (Grand Rapids: Zondervan, 2013), 53. Surprisingly also John Day, *From Creation to Babel: Studies in Genesis 1–11*, LHBOTS 592 (London: Bloomsbury, 2013), 3. Day appeals to the underlying verb *rqʿ*, which means "to beat out" and in the piel and pual forms is used in connection with objects of gold, bronze, and silver—as though the materiality of objects of the verb should determine the verb's meaning and the verb's meaning determine the meaning of the noun!

77. As noted by John H. Walton, "Response from the Archetypal View," in Barrett and Caneday, *Four Views on the Historical Adam*, 67, correcting Lamoureux.

The ancient Hebrews could not possibly have thought that the sky is a solid dome in which the sun, moon, and stars are embedded, for these heavenly luminaries are observed to move through the sky, and that is why they serve to mark seasons and days and years. Birds fly "on the face of" the *rāqîaʿ* (Gen 1:20) and "in the skies" (Deut 4:17). Benjamin Smith has probably given the best characterization of the denotation of *rāqîaʿ* as "*the whole sky, all that can be seen above the Earth from the surface.*"[78] Thus, after fixing the referent of *rāqîaʿ* in v. 8, the author of Gen 1 uses the expression *rəqîaʿ haššāmāyim* (v. 20), indicating the whole expanse of the sky. All this suggests that the *rāqîaʿ* is merely a phenomenal reality. As Walton nicely puts it, "There is a *rāqîaʿ* and it is blue."[79]

As for the role of the *rāqîaʿ* in separating the waters above from the waters below, the waters above are plausibly thought to be the rain that falls from the skies. Although some scholars have alleged that ancient Israelites thought that water fell to the earth through sluice gates of some sort in the solid dome above (the so-called windows of heaven), such a wooden literalism is utterly implausible. Water falling through such an opening would appear as a destructive cataract plunging to the earth, not as rain. But in the flood story we are told, "the windows of the heavens were opened. And rain fell upon the earth forty days and forty nights" (Gen 7:11–12; cf. 8:2). Averbeck points out that in the Ugaritic Baal myth, rain clouds are represented as a window in Baal's palace: "The analogical, metaphorical nature of the referents is clear here: window = rift in the clouds."[80] Elsewhere in the OT the windows of heaven are said metaphorically to deliver barley (2 Kgs 7:2), trouble and anguish (Isa 24:18), and divine blessing (Mal 3:10).

Walton agrees that the *rāqîaʿ* is not a physical reality but thinks on the basis of Job 37:18 that ancient Israelites might have believed that there is *another* reality, *šəhāqîm* (a word also translated "skies"), that is a hard surface.[81] This is a gratuitously literalistic interpretation of a highly poetic text, which may use the metaphor of a molten mirror for the sky to describe the rainless skies during scorching drought (cf. Deut 28:23). In a thorough discussion, Vern Poythress shows that ancient Israelites understood the water cycle and should not be assumed to have believed in a heavenly ocean above a literal,

78. Benjamin D. Smith Jr., *Genesis, Science, and the Beginning* (Eugene: Wipf & Stock, 2018), 240.

79. Walton, "Creation," 159.

80. Averbeck, "Literary Day," 15.

81. Walton, *Genesis 1 as Ancient Cosmology*, 156–57; Walton, "Response from the Archetypal View," 68.

solid dome. He argues that (1) as farmers and herdsmen, Israelites could be expected to have some knowledge of rain; (2) OT passages show that they knew that rain comes from clouds; (3) other ancient peoples were also familiar with rain coming from clouds; (4) the OT nonetheless sometimes describes the rain as coming from "heaven" (e.g., Judg 5:4: "the heavens dropped, yea, the clouds dropped water"); (5) the OT describes the lack of rain as the heavens' being "shut"; (6) "opening the windows of heaven" is used figuratively to describe God's bestowing blessings and the coming of rain; (7) the OT instructs Israelites about things that affect their lives, whereas an alleged heavenly sea closed in by a solid barrier would have no relation to the clouds that were so important for their livelihood; (8) Gen 1 speaks about things relevant to Israelites, so it is not plausible that Gen 1 omits rain from clouds. Poythress concludes that the literalistic interpretation "respects neither ancient knowledge of clouds, nor ancient ability to use colorful images."[82]

In sum, the oft-reprinted drawing of the alleged cosmic geography of ancient Hebrews (fig. 6.4) is a teratological construction formed by cobbling together many different texts conjoined with a wooden literalism. Such a world picture would have been unrecognizable to ancient Israelites, not to speak of the author of Gen 1.[83]

Plasticity and Flexibility of Ancient Near Eastern Myths

All this has been said with respect to the metaphoricalness of many ANE myths. Not only does the metaphorical and figurative language of ANE myths support a nonliteral reading of such myths, but their plasticity and flexibility also indicate that they are not best interpreted literally.

In Mesopotamia we have alternative accounts of Marduk's creation of the world that are significantly different. We have already alluded to the familiar account in the *Enuma elish* of Marduk's fashioning the world out of Tiamat's

82. Vern S. Poythress, "Rain Water versus a Heavenly Sea in Genesis 1:6–8," *WTJ* 77 (2015): 187, in response to Paul Seely, "The Firmament and the Water Above, Part I: The Meaning of *raqia'* in Gen 1:6–8," *WTJ* 53, no. 2 (1991): 227–43; Seely, "The Firmament and the Water Above, Part II: The Meaning of 'the Water above the Firmament' in Gen 1:6–8," *WTJ* 54, no. 1 (1992): 31–46.

83. NB that *pace* Averbeck, "Literary Day," 14, there is no hint in Gen 1 even of a three-decker cosmos, since no subterranean realm is described. We have at most a two-decker cosmos, with the heavens above and the earth below.

corpse. But in the bilingual Sumero-Babylonian creation story there is no such contest. Rather, we read that when all was once sea,

> Marduk constructed a raft on the surface of the waters,
> He made earth and heaped it up on the raft.
> That the gods should be settled in a dwelling of their pleasure
> He created mankind. (17–20)

Though featuring primordial water and Marduk as creator, this serene creation story is vastly different from the agonistic account in the *Enuma elish*.

We also have variable accounts of the creation of humanity out of the blood of slain gods in order to provide workers for the gods. In the *Enuma elish* the

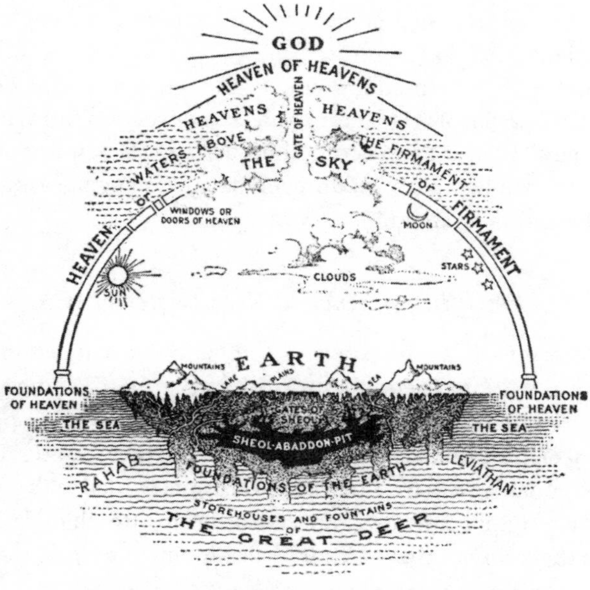

THE ANCIENT HEBREW CONCEPTION OF THE UNIVERSE

TO ILLUSTRATE THE ACCOUNT OF CREATION AND THE FLOOD

Figure 6.4. Teratological composite imagined by some modern interpreters as the world picture of ancient Israelites. Based on George L. Robinson, *Leaders of Israel: A Brief History of the Hebrews from the Earliest Times to the Downfall of Jerusalem, A.D. 70* (New York: YMCA Press, 1907), 2.

god Qingu is executed for inciting Tiamat's rebellion, and "from his blood he [Ea] created mankind, / on whom he imposed the service of the gods, and set the gods free" (VI.33–34). In the story "The Creation of Humanity" in *KAR* IV, the gods Alla and Illa are slaughtered "to grow humanity [with] their blood. Let the labor of the gods become its [humanity's] work assignment" (25–27). In the *Atrahasis Epic* the god Wê-ila is killed, and "from his flesh and blood Nintu mixed clay" (225–26) to fashion man to relieve the gods of their labor. "I have removed your heavy work, / I have imposed your toil on man" (240–41). The central truths of the divine constitutive element in man and the reason for his existence remain constant in these different versions of mankind's creation.

We have already mentioned the amazing flexibility displayed by the Gilgamesh epic. Five ancient Sumerian poems about the exploits of Gilgamesh or Bilgamesh (including two versions of Gilgamesh's fight with the ogre Huwawa) existed prior to the composition of the epic. The epic itself evolved through three stages from the Old Babylonian version through the Middle Babylonian version (neither of which included the flood story) to the now Standard Babylonian version. The Standard version of the epic includes two of the Sumerian poems: *Bilgamesh and Huwawa* and *Bilgamesh and the Bull of Heaven*. The death and funeral of Enkidu in tablets VII–VIII are thought to be based on the poem *The Death of Bilgamesh*. The addition of tablet XII to the epic reproduces the final part of another of the Sumerian poems, *Bilgamesh and the Netherworld*. The account of the flood in tablet XI of the Standard version represents the incorporation into the epic of the *Atrahasis Epic*'s account of the flood. In addition, the Babylonian author drew on other sources for various elements of his story, such as the episode of the birds in the flood account. Not only the Gilgamesh epic but other myths as well, such as *Nergal and Ereshkigal* and *Anzu*, are available in different versions, testifying to the flexibility of Mesopotamian myths.

The syncretism that was pervasive in Egyptian religion can also be found in Mesopotamia. Jacobsen explains that "one god [could] enjoy partial identity with other gods and thus share in their natures and abilities."[84] In "The Creation of Humanity," various members of the god Ninurta's body are themselves said to be the gods Ea, Shamash, and others.[85] Marduk is identified as the god Enlil when the question concerns ruling and taking counsel, but he is the moon god Sin when he acts as illuminator of the night, and so on.[86]

84. Jacobsen, "Mesopotamia," 133.

85. *KAR* IV, line 102.

86. CT XXIV, 50, No. 47406 obverse 6, 8, referenced by Jacobsen, "Mesopotamia," 133.

Jacobsen comments, "As one such 'self' could permeate many individual phenomena, so it might also permeate other selves and give to them of its specific character to add to the qualities which they had in their own right."[87]

It is Egypt, however, that has become famous for the plasticity and flexibility of its myths. John Wilson well epitomizes Egyptian mythology: "The Egyptian accepted various myths and discarded none of them."[88] Over the course of 2,300 years there emerged four major versions of the fundamental myth of origins, each associated respectively with cult centers in Heliopolis, Hermopolis, Memphis, and Thebes, that remained "remarkably consistent" throughout this history.[89] These various versions, despite their differences, enjoyed a harmonious coexistence. The theologians at Hermopolis, for example, who prioritized Amun, affirm,

> All the gods are three:
> Amun, the Sun, and Ptah, without their seconds.
> His identity is hidden in Amun,
> his is the Sun as face, his body is Ptah.
> Their towns are on the earth, fixed for the span of Eternal
> Recurrence:
> Thebes, Heliopolis, and Memphis, according to the pattern of the
> Eternal Sameness. (Leiden papyrus 300.1–7)

The text goes on to affirm, "When a message is sent from the sky, it is heard in Heliopolis / and repeated . . . in Memphis . . . / and . . . answered in Thebes" (8–12). The mutual identification of the gods is an expression of Egyptian syncretism, of which we shall have more to say momentarily. The purpose of the text, as Allen explains, is to show that the three great theological systems of Thebes, Heliopolis, and Memphis are not competing theologies, each attempting to establish its own superiority at the expense of the others, but aspects of the single, consistent understanding of the world and its origins.

According to that understanding, reality is the unfolding of an undifferentiated primordial monistic state represented by water. Out of these waters emerged a hillock, identified or associated with the god Atum, who is self-created. Atum in turn creates the other gods by acts of, alternatively, sneezing or spitting or masturbating. The peak of this creation sequence is the

87. Jacobsen, "Mesopotamia," 134. Recall that for Jacobsen gods are personified powers of nature.

88. Wilson, "Egypt," 50.

89. Allen, *Genesis in Egypt*, 12, 56.

god Re or Amun-Re, whose manifestation is the sun. Every day this creation cycle is repeated as the sun sets in the evening and is reborn at dawn.

Wide variations of this story developed. In Hermopolis the properties of the primordial state were personified as the Ogdoad, four pairs of gods and goddesses, who produce Atum. In Heliopolis Atum creates the first couple, Shu and Tefnut, whose offspring are Geb and Nut, the earth god and the sky goddess; they in turn have four children, Osiris, Seth, Isis, and Nephthys, forming an ennead of deities. But the order of their generations is variable: sometimes Shu and Tefnut are the parents of Osiris, and Seth is the brother of Osiris or Horus.

Egyptian mythology exhibited a syncretism that seems to defy literal interpretation. Hornung characterizes Egyptian syncretism as the view that "the natures of the individual gods are not clearly demarcated so that aspects of one God can be identical with those of another."[90] So Re, for example, was not simply Re, but also Re-Atum at Heliopolis, Amun-Re at Thebes, plus many other combinations, such as Khnum-Re, Sobek-Re, and Montu-Re, at various localities. Hornung differentiates syncretism from an equally difficult notion of a sort of mutual indwelling of different gods, principally Re and Osiris, whereby Re in his daily descent into the realm of the dead becomes Osiris, the god of the underworld. Re does not merely take on the role of Osiris; instead, "he incorporates the ruler of the dead into his own being so profoundly that both have one body and can 'speak with one mouth.'" "This daily reenacted union of two gods is a different phenomenon from the syncretistic combination Amon-Re."[91]

In syncretism the gods involved are not merged together but a new unit is formed of the distinct deities. Syncretism does not therefore imply the identity of the gods involved and can combine into a unit gods and goddesses alike and form even triples or quadruples of deities, like Ptah-Sokar-Osiris and Amon-Re-Harakhte-Atum. Hornung comments, "The Egyptians place the tensions and contradictions of the world beside one another and then live with them. Amon-Re is not the synthesis of Amun and Re but a new form that exists along with the two older gods."[92] The question is how best to make sense of this variability of Egyptian deities.[93]

90. Hornung, *Conceptions of God*, 91.

91. Hornung, *Conceptions of God*, 96.

92. Hornung, *Conceptions of God*, 97.

93. The best sense I can make of the syncretism that Egyptians postulated in their myths is what modern metaphysicians would call mereological fusions of gods. (For an introduction to mereology, see Kathrin Koslicki, *The Structure of Objects* [Oxford: Ox-

Egyptian iconography permitted "an astonishingly rich variety of possibilities" in the representation of a deity.[94] The goddess Hathor, for example, is depicted as a woman, as a cow, as a woman with a cow's head, and as a cow's head with a human face. In addition, she is represented as a lioness, a snake, a hippopotamus, and a tree nymph. Moreover, "we are not observing a historical development in which one form replaced another; at all periods different ways of depicting the goddess simply existed side-by-side."[95] We should not infer that Egyptians thought that Hathor actually had, for example, a human body and a cow's head. Rather, as Hornung explains, the varying images were meant to express different facets of her character—for example, the maternal tenderness of a cow, but also the wildness of a lioness and the unpredictability of a snake. Such images are, as it were, visual metaphors.

We have already alluded to a similar variability in Egyptian representations of the sun and the sky. The sun in its course can be identified with different deities: Khepry in the morning, Re or Harakhte at midday, and Atum in the evening. The sun might be depicted as a boat, as a beetle, as an old man declining in the west, or as a falcon. "These concepts were felt to be complementary not conflicting."[96] The sky was similarly variously depicted. Wilson comments,

> We should want to know in our picture whether the sky was supported on posts or was held up by a god; the Egyptian would answer, "Yes, it is supported by posts or held up by a god—or it rests on walls, or it is a cow, or it is a goddess whose arms and feet touch the earth." Any one of these pictures would be satisfactory to him, according to his approach, and in a single picture he might show two different supports for the sky: the goddess whose arms and feet reach the earth, and the god who holds up the sky goddess.[97]

ford University Press, 2008], chap. 1.) A mereological fusion combines two nonidentical objects into a new, third object without blending them together, so that each retains its distinct character as well as identity. So, for example, one's body might be regarded as the mereological fusion of all the cells of the body. A mereological fusion of distinct gods would involve a very permissive principle of comprehension governing what sort of fusions are possible. I suspect that so construing Egyptian religion would, however, be anachronistic and that it is more plausible to interpret the myths nonliterally.

94. Hornung, *Conceptions of God*, 110.

95. Hornung, *Conceptions of God*, 113.

96. Hornung, *Conceptions of God*, 49.

97. Wilson, "Egypt," 45.

The plasticity that allowed contradictory depictions of the sun and sky is a sure indication of the nonliterality of such representations.

Taken literally, Egyptian mythology is a mare's nest of logical contradictions and metaphysical absurdities. The primal state is said to be an undifferentiated unity, and yet it has fundamental properties. These properties are represented, moreover, as an ogdoad of already existing deities. Atum is said to have created all the deities—including himself! The names, the forms, and the representations of the gods and goddesses are mutually inconsistent. Confronted with the *prima facie* incoherence of Egyptian mythology, Hornung makes the remarkable suggestion that Egyptian myths be understood in terms of a many-valued logic: "A given *x* can be both *a* and not-*a*: *tertium datur*—the law of the excluded middle does not apply. . . . We should not exclude the possibility that the Egyptians had special cases in which a particular given *x* was always *a*. For the Egyptians two times two is always four, never anything else. But the sky is a number of things—cow, baldachin, water, woman—it is the goddess Nut and the goddess Hathor, and in syncretism a deity *a* is at the same time another not-*a*."[98] While acknowledging that this question is beyond the competence of an Egyptologist to decide, Hornung appeals to the formulation of quantum logics for dealing with the apparent paradoxes of quantum mechanics as justification for his proposal.

This astonishing suggestion is not only culturally inept—Are we seriously to suppose that any culture, especially one that could build the pyramids, assumed the principle of excluded middle only in "special cases"?—but also futile. Quantum logic has proven to be a dead end in discussions of quantum mechanics.[99] Moreover, the denial of excluded middle would not in any case resolve all the logical problems of Egyptian mythology, which often involve vicious circularity. For example, the first god who created all the remaining gods is also supposed to have created himself. "Paradoxically too, the sun can be understood not only as the source of the Ennead (in his identification with Atum) but also as the product of the Ennead, in his identification with the god Horus."[100]

Fortunately, Hornung does espy a better solution: we should not assume that Egyptians took their myths to be literally true. Hornung repudiates the condescending attitude of nineteenth-century anthropologists

98. Hornung, *Conceptions of God*, 240–41.

99. Tim Maudlin, "The Tale of Quantum Logic," in *Hilary Putnam*, ed. Yemima Ben-Menahim, CPF (Cambridge: Cambridge University Press, 2005), 156–87.

100. Wilson, "Egypt," 11.

toward ancient man. The logical problems endemic to a literal interpretation of Egyptian mythology should not lead to a wholesale characterization of Egyptian thought in general: "The fact that in Egyptian thought myth is not considered to be contradictory is not sufficient cause for us to term the thought as a whole 'mythical' or 'mythopoeic'; myth is one mode of discourse among many and it is in any case not a form of thought."[101] Exactly, and given its metaphorical and representational images, myth is a special case. Hornung declares,

> I maintain, in opposition to the widespread prejudice against metaphorical and representational images in modern scientific research, that images are among the legitimate systems of signs with which we are provided in order to describe the world.
>
> . . . For the Egyptians the gods are powers that explain the world but do not themselves need any elucidation because they convey information in a language which can be understood directly—that of myth.[102]

The language of myth is figurative and therefore need not be taken literally.

Application to Genesis 1–11

If Gen 1–11 functions as mytho-history, then these chapters need not be read literalistically. Some of the accounts, such as the origin and fall of man, are clearly metaphorical or figurative in nature, featuring as they do a humanoid deity incompatible with the transcendent God of the creation story. Others, as we have seen, would be fantastic, even to the author himself, if taken literally. Since all we have of the primaeval history is the one written account, it is very difficult to know, given the lack of consensus concerning the tradition history of these accounts, the degree to which these narratives exhibit the plasticity and flexibility characteristic of myth. Most scholars take the treatment of the flood account to be the prize example of the success of tradition-historical analysis, construing the account as a combination of two flood accounts, one from J and one from P, in which case we should have a good example of the plasticity and flexibility of the Hebrew story. But the objections raised by critics like Wenham to

101. Hornung, *Conceptions of God*, 240.
102. Hornung, *Conceptions of God*, 258.

the usual tradition-historical analysis of the flood story are enough to temper one's confidence in such hypothetical reconstructions.[103] On the other hand, the *prima facie* inconsistencies between the order of events in the creation account and the account of the creation of mankind suggest that the pentateuchal author would not have been overly concerned about relating events in a somewhat different order, so long as the central theological truths are faithfully expressed. Perhaps the author did not even take his own account to be static and final, but rather saw it as a plastic and flexible account, capable of retelling in different ways and capable of adapting to new challenges.

When we consider the narratives that are at the heart of our quest—namely, the creation and fall of Adam and Eve in chapters 2 and 3—a nonliteral interpretation seems very plausible. First and foremost, as mentioned, is the humanoid deity that appears in these chapters in contrast to the transcendent Creator of the heavens and earth in chapter 1.[104] The anthropomorphic nature of God, merely hinted at in chapter 2, becomes inescapable in chapter 3, where God is described as walking in the garden in the cool of the day, calling audibly to Adam, who is hiding from him. Read in this light, God's creation of Adam in chapter 2 takes on a clear anthropomorphic character. Here God is portrayed, like Nintur shaping bits of clay or Khnum at his potter's wheel, as forming man out of the dust of the ground and then breathing into his nostrils the breath of life, so that the figurine thus formed becomes alive. We are not told whether God similarly formed all the animals when "out of the ground the LORD God formed every beast of the field and every bird of the air" (Gen 2:19), but we cannot help but wonder. When God takes one of the sleeping Adam's ribs, closes up the flesh, and builds a woman

103. Gordon J. Wenham, *Genesis 1–15*, WBC 1 (Grand Rapids: Zondervan, 1987), 156–57.

104. The anthropomorphic descriptions of God in chaps. 2–3 are not plausibly taken to be a theophany of God in human form, such as we have in God's appearance to Abraham in Gen 18, as suggested by John D. Currid, "Theistic Evolution Is Incompatible with the Teachings of the Old Testament," in *Theistic Evolution: A Scientific, Philosophical, and Theological Critique*, ed. J. P. Moreland et al. (Wheaton: Crossway, 2017), 858. For (1) the language of theophany is missing from chaps. 2–3, in contrast to Gen 18, which begins, "And the LORD appeared to him by the oaks of Mamre, as he sat at the door of his tent in the heat of the day. He lifted up his eyes and looked, and behold, three men stood in front of him" (vv. 1–2). And (2), crucially, God is described anthropomorphically in chaps. 2–3 even when *not* appearing to Adam, as in the story of God's fashioning Adam from the dust of the earth and breathing into his nostrils the breath of life, or as in the story of God's building Eve from Adam's rib while Adam is unconscious.

out of it, the story sounds like a physical surgery that God performs on Adam followed by his building a woman out of the extracted body part. Similarly, given God's bodily presence in the garden, the conversations between God and the protagonists in the story of the fall read like a dialogue between persons physically present to one another. God's making garments for Adam and Eve out of animal skins and driving them out of the garden sound like physical acts by the humanoid God. Given the exalted, transcendent nature of God described in the creation story, the pentateuchal author could not possibly have intended these descriptions to be taken literally. They are in the figurative language of myth.

Moreover, we have seen that many features of these stories are fantastic—that is to say, palpably false if taken literally. Previously, we used this fact as an earmark to identify narratives as myths. But now we limit our consideration to features of the narrative that the author himself would have plausibly thought fantastic. In light of chapter 1's affirmation that God had separated the waters above from the waters below, it is hard to believe that the author thought that there was ever a time when the earth was devoid of rain. Just as the waters below took the form of seas and rivers and springs, so the waters above took the form of rain. So an earth replete with seas and rivers and springs, but without rain, seems fantastic, even for an ancient Israelite, given his knowledge of the water cycle. In addition, the idea of an arboretum containing trees bearing fruit that, if eaten, would confer immortality or yield sudden knowledge of good and evil must have seemed fantastic to the pentateuchal author. Recall that we are not dealing here with miraculous fruit, as if God would, on the occasion of eating, supernaturally impose on the eater immortality or knowledge of good and evil against God's will. The Garden of Eden may have been described as existing in a real geographical location, the Persian Gulf Oasis, but, like Mount Olympus, that site may have been employed to tell a mythological story concerning what happened at that site. Then there is the notorious snake in the garden. He makes for a great character in the story, conniving, sinister, opposed to God, perhaps a symbol of evil, but not plausibly a literal reptile such as one might encounter in one's own garden, for the pentateuchal author knew that snakes neither talk nor are intelligent agents. Again, the snake's personality and speech cannot be attributed to the miraculous activity of God, lest God become the author of the fall. When God drives Adam and Eve from the garden and posts cherubim and a flashing sword at its entrance to block their reentry, this is doubtless not intended to be literal, since cherubim were regarded as creatures of fantasy and symbol. It is not as though the author thought—what realism requires—that the cherubim remained at the entrance of the garden for years on end until it was either overgrown with weeds or swept away by the flood.

Then there are the aforementioned inconsistencies in the narratives, which were apparently of no concern to the author, such as the order of the creation of plants, animals, and man, and the curiosity that is Cain's wife. Why was the author so insouciant about these difficulties? Plausibly because he did not intend his stories to be read literalistically. Together all these features of the narratives of Adam and Eve make it plausible that they are not to be taken literally. The author has given us a story of mankind's origin and rebellion against God that embodies important truths expressed in highly figurative language.

Since the pentateuchal author has an interest in history, he intends for his narrative to be at some level historical, to concern people who actually lived and events that really occurred. But those persons and events have been clothed in the garb of the metaphorical and figurative language of myth. As Henri Blocher nicely puts it, "The real issue when we try to interpret Genesis 2–3 is not whether we have a historical account of the fall but whether or not we may read it as the account of the historical fall."[105] It is probably futile to try to discern to what extent the narratives are to be taken literally, what parts are historical and what parts not.[106] Therefore, I think that the objections of Kenton Sparks, for example, to taking the primaeval history to be a combination of history and theology are unfair. If the author of Genesis uses mythical imagery, Sparks demands, then which images are mythic symbol and which are closer to historical representation? Did a serpent speak in the garden? Was the first woman made from Adam's rib? Was there a worldwide flood?[107] I see no reason to think that the viability of a genre analysis of Gen 1–11 as mytho-history should imply the ability to answer such questions. The author does not draw such clear lines of distinction for us.

What are, then, some of the central truths expressed in the primaeval history? The following come readily to mind:

105. Henri Blocher, *Original Sin: Illuminating the Riddle* (Grand Rapids: Eerdmans, 1997), 50.

106. This would amount to literary nephelococcygia, to borrow Speiser's wonderful metaphor.

107. Kenton L. Sparks, "Response to James K. Hoffmeier," in Halton, *Genesis*, 64–65.

1. God is one, a personal, transcendent Creator of all physical reality, perfectly good and worthy of worship.
2. God has designed the physical world and is the ultimate source of its structure and life-forms.
3. Man is the pinnacle of the physical creation, a personal, if finite, agent like God, and therefore uniquely capable of all Earth's creatures of knowing God.
4. Mankind is gendered, man and woman being of equal value, with marriage given to mankind for procreation and mutuality, the wife being a helper to her husband.
5. Work is good, a sacred assignment by God to mankind to steward the earth and its creatures.
6. Human exploration and discovery of the workings of nature are a natural outgrowth of mans' capacities, rather than divine bestowals without human initiative and effort.
7. Mankind is to set apart one day per week as sacred and for refreshment from work.
8. Man and woman alike have freely chosen to disobey God, suffering alienation from God and spiritual death as their just desert, condemned to a life of hardship and suffering during this mortal existence.
9. Human sin is agglomerative and self-destructive, resulting in God's just judgment.
10. Despite human rebellion against God, God's original purpose to bless all mankind remains intact, as he graciously finds a way to work his will despite human defiance.

These are a few of the fundamental truths taught by the primaeval history of Gen 1–11. Such truths do not depend on reading the narratives literalistically.

Summary and Conclusion

Genesis 1–11 exhibits quite a number of the family resemblances characteristic of myths, especially the prominent and abundant presence of etiological motifs. At the same time, the chapters' interest in history, most evident in their genealogical notices that chronologically order the narratives, reveals that we are dealing here, not with pure myth, but with a sort of mytho-history. Comparative studies of both contemporary and ANE myths show that mythological stories need not be read literalistically. The many fantastic elements and inconsistencies of the primaeval history of Gen 1–11 strongly suggest that this is also the case for these chapters. With these results in hand, we now turn to an examination of the NT materials relevant to the historical Adam.

Chapter 7

ADAM IN THE NEW TESTAMENT

Remarkably, for all his importance in Christian theology, Adam is scarcely mentioned in the remainder of the OT outside the primaeval history of Gen 1–11. His name appears again only in 1 Chron 1:1–24 at the head of a genealogy of Abraham that the chronicler constructed via scissors and paste from the genealogies of Gen 4 and 11.[1] In extracanonical Jewish literature, by contrast, the narratives of Adam and Eve are often put to work to serve varying theological interests.[2] We find Adam the paradigmatic moral man of *Sirach* and Josephus, Adam the model of faithful Torah observance of *Jubilees*, Adam the archetypal sinner of *4 Ezra*, Adam the image of the divine Logos of Philo of Alexandria, and so on. It is noteworthy that despite the various theological uses to which Adam is put, all the texts concur in assuming Adam to be a historical person, the first human being to be created.

When we come to the NT, we find the figure of Adam widely deployed, most importantly by Paul. Here are the principal texts:[3]

> Jesus, when he began his ministry, was about thirty years of age, being the son (as was supposed) of Joseph . . . the son of Enos, the son of Seth, the son of Adam, the son of God. (Luke 3:23, 38)

1. "Adam" is used, apparently as a place-name, in Josh 3:16; Hos 6:7.

2. These texts have been ably surveyed in John R. Levison, *Portraits of Adam in Early Judaism: From Sirach to 2 Baruch*, JSPSup 1 (Sheffield: JSOT Press, 1988); Felipe de Jesús Legarreta-Castillo, *The Figure of Adam in Romans 5 and 1 Corinthians 15: The New Creation and Its Ethical and Social Reconfiguration* (Minneapolis: Fortress, 2014), chap. 2; and Dennis R. Venema and Scot McKnight, *Adam and the Genome: Reading Scripture after Genetic Science* (Grand Rapids: Brazos, 2017), chap. 7.

3. Other relevant but more peripheral texts concern episodes of the primaeval history such as Cain's murder of Abel (Matt 23:35 // Luke 11:51; Heb 12:24; Jude 11; 1 John 3:12) and Noah and the flood (Matt 24:37–38 // Luke 17:26–27; Heb 11:1–7; 2 Pet 2:25).

[Jesus] answered, "Have you not read that he who made them from the beginning made them male and female, and said, 'For this reason a man shall leave his father and mother and be joined to his wife, and the two shall become one flesh'? So they are no longer two but one flesh. What therefore God has joined together, let not man put asunder." (Matt 19:4–6)

[God] made from one every nation of men to live on all the face of the earth, having determined allotted periods and the boundaries of their habitation. (Acts 17:26)

(For man was not made from woman, but woman from man. Neither was man created for woman, but woman for man.) (1 Cor 11:8–9)

For as by a man came death, by a man has come also the resurrection of the dead. For as in Adam all die, so also in Christ shall all be made alive. (1 Cor 15:21–22)

Thus it is written, "The first man Adam became a living being"; the last Adam became a life-giving spirit. But it is not the spiritual which is first but the physical, and then the spiritual. The first man was from the earth, a man of dust; the second man is from heaven. As was the man of dust, so are those who are of the dust; and as is the man of heaven, so are those who are of heaven. Just as we have borne the image of the man of dust, we shall also bear the image of the man of heaven. (1 Cor 15:45–49)

I am afraid that as the serpent deceived Eve by his cunning, your thoughts will be led astray from a sincere and pure devotion to Christ. (2 Cor 11:3)

Therefore as sin came into the world through one man and death through sin, and so death spread to all men because all men sinned—sin indeed was in the world before the law was given, but sin is not counted where there is no law. Yet death reigned from Adam to Moses, even over those whose sins were not like the transgression of Adam, who was a type of the one who was to come.

But the free gift is not like the trespass. For if many died through one man's trespass, much more have the grace of God and the free gift in the grace of that one man Jesus Christ abounded for many. And the free gift is not like the effect of that one man's sin. For the judgment following one trespass brought condemnation, but the free gift following many

> trespasses brings justification. If, because of one man's trespass, death reigned through that one man, much more will those who receive the abundance of grace and the free gift of righteousness reign in life through the one man Jesus Christ.
>
> Then as one man's trespass led to condemnation for all men, so one man's act of righteousness leads to acquittal and life for all men. For as by one man's disobedience many were made sinners, so by one man's obedience many will be made righteous. Law came in, to increase the trespass; but where sin increased, grace abounded all the more, so that, as sin reigned in death, grace also might reign through righteousness to eternal life through Jesus Christ our Lord. (Rom 5:12–21)

> I permit no woman to teach or to have authority over men; she is to keep silent. For Adam was formed first, then Eve; and Adam was not deceived, but the woman was deceived and became a transgressor. (1 Tim 2:12–14)

This is doubtless an impressive array of texts, but they should not be treated indiscriminately, lest we be misled.

The Literary and the Historical Adam

Many scholars have attempted to distinguish between the *literary Adam* and the *historical Adam*.[4] Unfortunately, the distinction is not always clearly conceived.[5] The literary Adam is a character in a story, specifically the stories of Gen 2–3. The historical Adam is the person, if such there be, who actually

4. See Joseph A. Fitzmyer, *Romans*, AYB 33 (New Haven: Yale University Press, 1993), 408, 410, followed by Venema and McKnight, *Adam and the Genome*, 118, 190.

5. McKnight, for example, seems to think that the literary Adam is a person-relative figure rather than an objective literary figure, for he says, for instance, that the Adam of Paul was the result of both an engagement with prior Jewish literary Adams and the articulation of Paul's own literary Adam (Venema and McKnight, *Adam and the Genome*, 149). This is confused. One's *interpretation* of a piece of literature is person-relative, not the literary figures in that piece of literature. McKnight is evidently thinking of the various theological interpretations of the literary Adam (i.e., the Adam of the Genesis narratives) in extracanonical Jewish literature as well as Paul's own interpretation of that same literary Adam. McKnight agrees with Fitzmyer that the literary Adam of Genesis is a purely symbolic character, but that Paul interprets Adam to be a real historical individual. If that is accurate, then Paul has simply misinterpreted Genesis, like the freshman in a literature class who reads a piece of poetry literally.

existed, the actual individual that the stories are allegedly about.[6] By way of analogy, the Pompey of Plutarch's *Lives* is the literary Pompey, whereas the Roman general who actually lived was the historical Pompey. What we want to know is how closely the literary Pompey of the *Lives* descriptively resembles the historical Pompey. Pretty well, we think, for Plutarch was a good historian. Similarly, we want to know how closely the literary Adam of Gen 2–3 descriptively resembles the historical Adam, if such there be, or more precisely whether NT authors assert that the literary Adam of Gen 2–3 closely resembles the historical Adam.

This distinction implies a further distinction between *truth* and *truth-in-a-story*. A statement *S* is true iff *S* states what is the case. A statement *S* is true-in-a-story iff it is found in or implied by that story. So if I say, for example, that Gilgamesh slew the Bull of Heaven, my statement, though true-in-the-*Epic-of-Gilgamesh*, is false. Truth-in-a-story does not, however, preclude truth. In the *Epic of Gilgamesh* are, or are implied, statements, such as "Gilgamesh was an ancient Sumerian king," that are both true-in-the-epic as well as true. So the relevant question for us is whether the above NT passages are intended to assert truths or merely truths-in-the-stories-of-Genesis.

It is therefore pointless to say that Paul's Adam is the literary Adam. No one imagines that Paul had some secret, independent access to the historical Adam apart from the stories of Genesis. So of course the Adam Paul describes is the literary Adam. The relevant question is whether Paul, as well as other NT authors, teaches that the literary Adam accurately describes the historical Adam (and, if so, whether that belief was true).

With those distinctions in hand, we must further distinguish between a NT author's using a text *illustratively* and using a text *assertorically*. Using a text illustratively is using the text merely to provide an illustration, real or imagined, of the point that the author is trying to assert. Such an illustrative use of a text does not commit the user to the truth of the text itself, but merely to truth-in-a-text. For example, Greek mythology, so familiar to Western culture, is frequently the source of illustrations for us. We speak of some-

6. Again, McKnight does not so understand the expression "the historical Adam." As he uses the expression, "the so-called 'historical Adam' . . . is a theological construct in the history of the church but which was not believed by any single author in the entire Bible" (Jim Stump et al., "*Adam and the Genome*: Responses," *BioLogos* (blog), January 30, 2017, https://biologos.org/articles/adam-and-the-genome-responses). Such an understanding leads inevitably to confusion. I take "the historical Adam" to refer to that person, if any, who actually existed and "the literary Adam" to refer to that figure described in Gen 2–3.

thing's being a Trojan Horse, or of someone's having an Achilles' heel, or of someone's opening a Pandora's box, without thinking that we are thereby committing ourselves to the reality of the relevant mythical entities.

NT authors not infrequently appeal to pseudepigraphal and mythological stories to illustrate biblical truths. It is difficult to know when an author is using a story assertorically rather than merely illustratively. When an author goes beyond the bounds of the story in connecting some figure in the story with an indisputably historical person, then it seems plausible to infer that the story is being used assertorically, not merely illustratively. A paradigmatic example of this situation seems to be 1 Pet 3:19–20: following his death, Christ "went and preached to the spirits in prison, who formerly did not obey, when God's patience waited in the days of Noah, during the building of the ark." Who are these spirits in prison? On the basis of texts like 2 Pet 2:4 and Jude 6–7, one might plausibly take them to be the "sons of God" of Gen 6:1–4. In Jude and 2 Peter we find the sons of God equated with angels (a plausible inference from the story) along with information concerning the angels' fate, such as their being bound by God with chains in the underworld, that apparently derives from Jewish folklore such as we find in *1 Enoch*. The assertion that Christ went and preached to these fallen angels is, however, nowhere else to be found. This claim is not true-in-the-story in any form[7] but is alleged simply to be true. Since Christ, a real, historical person, cannot have gone and preached to fictional beings in a fictional realm, 1 Pet 3:19 on this interpretation commits us not only to the historicity of the Genesis story but also to the apocryphal details furnished by *1 Enoch*.

But are the spirits in prison in fact angels, or are they just as plausibly the wicked human contemporaries of Noah, now deceased? The modifying clause "who formerly did not obey, when God's patience waited in the days of Noah, during the building of the ark" is a much more suitable description for Noah's contemporaries than for the angels of Gen 6:1–4, who are not said to have disobeyed God, tried God's patience, or sinned during the building of the ark, as Noah's contemporaries are implied to have done. In *1 Enoch* the expression "spirits" is variously used to refer to human beings (10.15; 20.3, 6; 22.5–7), Nephilim (15.8–12), and angels (13.6, 19.1). Deceased persons, now disembodied and awaiting the eschatological resurrection and judgment, are very frequently referred to as spirits. For example,

7. However, for his assertion about Christ's preaching to the spirits in prison, the author of 1 Peter might have been inspired by *1 Enoch*'s prominent figure of the Son of Man (chaps. 46–48), to whom judgment has been entrusted.

> Then I went to another place, and he showed me on the west side a great and high mountain of hard rock and inside it four beautiful corners; it had [in it] a deep, wide, and smooth (thing) which was rolling over; and it (the place) was deep, and dark to look at. At that moment, Rafael, one of the holy angels, who was with me, responded to me; and he said to me, "These beautiful corners (are here) in order that the spirits of the souls . . . of the children of the people should gather here. They prepared these places in order to put them (that is, the souls of the people) there until the day of their judgment and the appointed time of the great judgment upon them." I saw the spirits of the children of the people who were dead, and their voices were reaching unto heaven until this very moment. (*1 Enoch* 22.1–5)

The "spirits of the righteous" are separated from the "spirits of men who were not righteous but sinners," as both await their fate (*1 Enoch* 22.8–13). Although wicked angels will be bound in chains in prison forever, sinners, too, when the Son of Man appears, "with chains shall . . . be bound and in their assemblage place of destruction shall they be imprisoned" (*1 Enoch* 69.28; cf. 10.13–15). Indeed, in the context of the intermediate state, the reference of "spirits" is to human beings, not angels. On this interpretation Christ visited, not the fallen angels of Gen 6:1–4, but disembodied spirits of people who once lived and were disobedient. The reality of such an intermediate state of the dead was common coin in Second Temple Judaism and so does not imply a commitment by the author of 1 Peter to a realm of angels in prison. In any case, this example serves to highlight the distinction between an assertoric and an illustrative use of a text.

The illustrative use of a text occasions a further distinction: the distinction between what a person citing a text *believes* and what that person is *asserting*. Perhaps someone using the illustration of the Trojan Horse believes that such an instrument actually existed and turned the tide of the Trojan War; but, right or wrong, his personal belief is irrelevant to the point he is trying to assert or teach. Thus, a text is used assertorically, as I am using the term, if and only if the user means to teach the truth of the text, not merely truth-in-a-text.

These distinctions are not drawn in order to weasel out of commitments on the part of NT authors to the truth of the Genesis stories and, hence, to the historical Adam. Rather, they are important in our treatment of many NT passages, which, if interpreted assertorically, would be unfounded in the OT and sometimes plausibly false. Intriguingly, as mentioned above, some of these passages involve the citation of pseudepigraphal and mythological texts to whose truth we should not wish to be committed. These texts seem to be used illustratively by NT authors, just as we use illustrations drawn from Greco-Roman mythology without thinking to commit ourselves thereby to their historicity.

New Testament Authors' Use of Extrabiblical Literary Figures

We find several examples of the illustrative use of extrabiblical literary traditions in the books of Jude and 2 Peter. There we are sometimes treated to expansions of canonical narratives that are apparently based on extrabiblical sources. In 2 Peter the author gives a list of illustrations of how God delivers the righteous while keeping the unrighteous under punishment:

> For if God did not spare the angels when they sinned, but cast them into hell and committed them to pits of nether gloom to be kept until the judgment; if he did not spare the ancient world, but preserved Noah, a herald of righteousness, with seven other persons, when he brought a flood upon the world of the ungodly; if by turning the cities of Sodom and Gomorrah to ashes he condemned them to extinction and made them an example to those who were to be ungodly; and if he rescued righteous Lot, greatly distressed by the licentiousness of the wicked (for by what that righteous man saw and heard as he lived among them, he was vexed in his righteous soul day after day with their lawless deeds), then the Lord knows how to rescue the godly from trial, and to keep the unrighteous under punishment until the day of judgment, and especially those who indulge in the lust of defiling passion and despise authority. (2 Pet 2:4–10)

These illustrations follow the sequence of events in Genesis. But the author is clearly not talking simply about the angels or Noah or Lot of Genesis, for he includes information that is not included in or implied by Genesis. Richard Bauckham identifies a rich tradition within Jewish literature of listing such examples of divine judgment on sinners that include judgment on the fallen angels (the so-called Watchers) or their offspring the giants, the generation of the flood, Sodom and Gomorrah, Israel in the desert, and so on.[8]

8. Richard J. Bauckham, *Jude, 2 Peter*, WBC 50 (Waco: Word, 1983), 46, 246–47. For

In the first of these illustrations we find a reference to the sons of God of Gen 6:1–4, interpreted now as angels, and their punishment. In Jude 6–7 we find a similar reference to the fallen angels' incarceration: "And the angels that did not keep their own position but left their proper dwelling have been kept by him in eternal chains in the nether gloom until the judgment of the great day; just as Sodom and Gomorrah and the surrounding cities, which likewise acted immorally and indulged in unnatural lust, serve as an example by undergoing a punishment of eternal fire." Although the identity of the sons of God as angels could be a reasonable inference from the text of Genesis alone, this identification was universal in Jewish tradition until the mid-second century after Christ,[9] and in Jude and 2 Peter we find information concerning the angels' fate that is not derivable from Genesis, such as their being bound by God with chains (*desmoi*) in the dark netherworld (*zophos*), a detail not found in Genesis.[10] *First Enoch,* however, later quoted explicitly by Jude, states that these angels, having "left the high, holy, and eternal heaven" (12.4; 15.3) that was "their dwelling" (15.7) in their lust for human women (chaps. 6–10), have now been bound "underneath the rocks of the ground until the day of their judgment and of their consummation, until the eternal judgment is concluded" (10.12).[11] They "shall remain inside

---

the traditional schema of examples of divine judgment Bauckham points to *Sirach* 16.7–10 (giants, Sodom and Gomorrah, Canaanites, Israel in the desert); *Damascus Document* 2.17–3.12 (Watchers, giants, generation of the flood, sons of Noah, sons of Jacob, Israel in Egypt, Israel at Kadesh); *3 Maccabees* 2.4–7 (giants, Sodom and Gomorrah, Pharaoh and Egyptians); *Testament of Naphtali* 3.4–5 (Sodom and Gomorrah, Watchers); *Jubilees* 20.2–7 (giants, Sodom and Gomorrah); Mishnah tractate *Sanhedrin* 10.3 (generation of the flood, generation of the dispersion, Sodom and Gomorrah, spies, Israel in the desert, company of Korah). This traditional schema of examples of divine judgment is found in Jude 5–7. In 2 Pet 2:4–10 we have the addition of instances of divine deliverance as well, as in *Wisdom* 10.

9. Bauckham lists *1 Enoch* 6–9; 21; 86–88; 106.13–15; *Jubilees* 4.15, 22; 5.1; *Damascus Document* 2.17–19; *Genesis Apocryphon* 2; *Targum Pseudo-Jonathan* Gen 6.1–4; *Testament of Reuben* 5.6–7; *Testament of Naphtali* 3.5; *2 Apocalypse of Baruch* 56.10–14 (Bauckham, *Jude, 2 Peter,* 54).

10. A variant of 2 Pet 2:4 reads *seirais* ("chains" in NRSV) rather than *seirois* ("pits" in RSV). If the preferred reading is "pits," this would connect with the abyss or valleys of *1 Enoch* 18.11; 21.7; 88.1, 3; 10.12, where the fallen angels were kept. According to 2 Pet 2:17, the false prophets menacing the church will share a similar fate: "These are waterless springs and mists driven by a storm; for them the nether gloom of darkness has been reserved." Cf. Jude 13: "wandering stars for whom the nether gloom of darkness has been reserved for ever."

11. Bauckham notes that the word "great," omitted in the Greek and Ethiopic versions

the earth, imprisoned all the days of eternity" (14.5). Enoch sees "their chains while they were making them into iron fetters of immense weight" and asks, "'For whom are these imprisonment chains being prepared?' And he said unto me, 'These are being prepared for the armies of Azaz'el, in order that they may take them and cast them into the abyss of complete condemnation, . . . and they shall cover their jaws with rocky stones'" (54.3–5; cf. 13.1; 14.5; 56.1–4).

Intriguingly, the word in 2 Pet 2:4 for "cast into hell" is *tartaroō*, referring to Tartarus, the realm in Greek mythology lower than even Hades.[12] According to Hesiod,

> Such is the distance from earth's surface
> to gloomy Tartarus
> [that] a brazen anvil dropping off the earth
> would take nine
> nights, and nine days, and land in Tartarus
> on the tenth day. (*Theogony* 720–25)

Tartarus is described as "gloomy," "misty," "an unpleasant, moldy place," where the Titans have been imprisoned by Zeus (*Theogony* 805–10). They, like Jude's angels, are bound in chains (*desmoi*) in nether gloom (*zophos*) (*Theogony* 718, 729). In the Greek *1 Enoch* the angel Uriel is said to be "over the world and Tartarus" (20.2), where "the spirits of the angels which have united themselves with women" are in prison (19.1; 18.14). We thus have in 2 Peter and Jude an expansion of the canonical narrative of the sons of God mating with women based on pseudepigraphal and mythological sources. Though not part of the canonical sons of God, these details are part of the angels of the pseudepigrapha and Greek myths, a rich source of illustrations.[13]

---

of *1 Enoch*, is found in the 4Q Aramaic fragment of the same, forming an unusual expression found in Jude designating the great day of judgment (*Jude, 2 Peter*, 52).

12. See BDAG, s.v. "ταρταρόω," for references. The verbal forms were almost always used with reference to the Greek myths. For the noun "Tartarus" in Hellenistic Jewish literature, see *Sibylline Oracles* 4.186; Philo, *On the Life of Moses* 2.433; Philo, *On Rewards and Punishments* 152.

13. Similarly, in Luke's story of the Gerasene demoniac we find the unique notice that the demons "begged him not to command them to depart into the abyss [*abyssos*]" (Luke 8:31), presumably to join the fallen angels there. This notice is not traditional but seems to be Luke's literary touch.

The second illustration in 2 Peter's list concerns Noah, who is said to have been "a herald of righteousness" (2:5). But in Gen 6–9 Noah is not presented as a proclaimer (*kēryx*) of righteousness.[14] Contrary, perhaps, to popular impression, Noah is not said to preach to the masses facing imminent destruction, vainly urging them to repent, but goes silently about his work. By contrast, in the *Sibylline Oracles* 1.150–99 Noah gives an impassioned plea:

> Men, sated with faithlessness, smitten with a great madness,
> what you did will not escape the notice of God, . . .
> who commanded me
> to announce to you, so that you may not be destroyed by
> your hearts.
> Be sober, cut off evils, and stop fighting violently
> with each other, having a bloodthirsty heart,
> drenching much earth with human blood.
> Mortals, stand in awe of the exceedingly great, fearless
> heavenly Creator, imperishable God, who inhabits the vault
> of heaven,
> and entreat him, all of you—for he is good—
> for life, cities, and the whole world,
> four-footed animals and birds, so that he will be gracious to all.
> For the time will come when the whole immense world of men
> perishing by waters will wail with the dread refrain. (*Sibylline*
> *Oracles* 1.150–63)

The author of 2 Peter seems to draw on a similar Jewish tradition in his characterization of Noah.[15] Being a herald of righteousness is not part of the literary Noah of Genesis but of the literary Noah of Jewish tradition, which 2 Peter exploits for illustrative purposes.

The third and fourth illustrations in 2 Peter's list refer to God's judgment on Sodom and Gomorrah in Gen 19 and, rather surprisingly, to the "righteous Lot, greatly distressed by the licentiousness of the wicked (for by what

14. As noted by Tremper Longman III and John H. Walton, *The Lost World of the Flood: Mythology, Theology, and the Deluge Debate* (Downers Grove, IL: IVP Academic, 2018), 72.

15. Bauckham, *Jude, 2 Peter*, 250–51, gives the following references for Noah's preaching of repentance to his contemporaries: Josephus, *Antiquities of the Jews* 1.74; *Midrash Rabbah* on Genesis 30:7; *Midrash Rabbah* on Ecclesiastes 9:15; *Pirqe Rabbi Eliezer* 22; Babylonian Talmud tractate *Sanhedrin* 108.

that righteous man saw and heard as he lived among them, he was vexed in his righteous soul day after day with their lawless deeds)" (2:7–8). Such a description of Lot's character hardly seems apt from the narrative of Gen 19. In Jewish tradition, however, Lot came to be portrayed as a righteous man. The author of *Wisdom*, in extolling the personified Wisdom's deliverance of the righteous from judgment, refers not only to Noah but also to Lot:

> Wisdom rescued a righteous man when the ungodly were
> perishing;
> he escaped the fire that descended on the Five Cities.
> Evidence of their wickedness still remains:
> a continually smoking wasteland,
> plants bearing fruit that does not ripen,
> and a pillar of salt standing as a monument to an
> unbelieving soul.
> For because they passed wisdom by,
> they not only were hindered from recognizing the good,
> but also left for mankind a reminder of their folly,
> so that their failures could never go unnoticed. (*Wisdom* 10.6–8)

Philo says, "But when the whole of that district was thus burnt, inhabitants and all, by the impetuous rush of the heavenly fire, one single man in the country, a sojourner, was preserved by the providence of God because he had never shared in the transgressions of the natives" (*On the Life of Moses* 2.58). As for the idea that Lot was distressed day after day by the people's lawlessness, that either reflects a tradition that has not survived or is purely the product of the author's imagination.

The conclusion to be drawn from these examples is not that the expansions of the canonical text are historical (or unhistorical) but rather that we are not committed to their historicity simply in virtue of an NT author's relating them. For the use of these incidents is illustrative, and the aptness of the illustration with respect to the point being made does not depend on the illustration's historicity. The only plausible exception to this conclusion is perhaps 1 Pet 3:19, which does seem to assert Christ's preaching to the spirits in prison, though even this passage is set forth by the author as an illustration of bearing suffering for doing right.

On other occasions we have, not merely expansions of canonical narratives, but wholesale importation of extrabiblical material for illustrative purposes. For example, in condemning the false teachers of his day, Jude contrasts them negatively to the archangel Michael in his dispute with the devil over Moses's body: "But when the archangel Michael, contending with the devil, disputed about the body of Moses, he did not presume to pronounce a reviling judgment upon him, but said, 'The Lord rebuke you.' But these men revile whatever they do not understand, and by those things that they know by instinct as irrational animals do, they are destroyed" (Jude 9–10). This tradition may have also been known to the author of 2 Peter, if he did not borrow it from Jude: "Bold and wilful, they are not afraid to revile the glorious ones, whereas angels, though greater in might and power, do not pronounce a reviling judgment upon them before the Lord" (2 Pet 2:10–11).

No such story is to be found in the OT Scriptures. According to the church father Origen, the story is to be found in the apocryphal book *The Assumption of Moses*: "In the book of Genesis, the serpent is described as having seduced Eve; regarding whom, in the work entitled *The Ascension of Moses* (a little treatise, of which the Apostle Jude makes mention in his Epistle), the archangel Michael, when disputing with the devil regarding the body of Moses, says that the serpent, being inspired by the devil, was the cause of Adam and Eve's transgression" (*On First Principles* 3.2.1). Unfortunately, the extant version of this treatise, known only from a single, incomplete, sixth-century manuscript, does not include the story. Bauckham believes, nonetheless, that "although the source of Jude's story of the dispute over the body of Moses is not extant, a wealth of material is available from early Christian sources from which it should be possible to reconstruct the story which Jude knew."[16]

Bauckham discerns two versions of the story in Christian tradition. In one version, Satan attempts to preclude Michael's burying Moses's body on the grounds that Moses had once murdered a man. But Michael vanquishes Satan and buries Moses.[17] In another version, Satan claims to have suzerainty over the material world and, hence, Moses's corpse. But Michael retorts that God is the Creator of all things.[18] Bauckham considers the latter version to be a later development reflecting the contest with Gnostic dualism. "It is

16. Bauckham, *Jude, 2 Peter*, 65.

17. Attested by the *Palaea historica* (a Byzantine collection of biblical legends); the Slavonic *Life of Moses* 16; Pseudo-Oecumenius, *Epistula Judae apostoli catholica* 9; and a Greek extract collected by J. A. Cramer, *Catanae Graecorum Patrum in Novum Testamentum* (Oxford: Oxford University Press, 1844), 8:163, lines 18–22—all conveniently cited in Bauckham, *Jude, 2 Peter*, 67–70.

18. *The Assumption of Moses* is known to Clement of Alexandria, Didymus the Blind,

hard to believe that a Palestinian work of the early first century AD would have included the kind of refutation of dualism which the texts quote from the [*Assumption of Moses*]."[19] This version of the dispute over Moses's body, Bauckham says, much more plausibly reflects Christian anti-Gnostic argument in the second century after Christ. Noting that ancient lists of apocryphal books mention both a *Testament of Moses* and *The Assumption of Moses*, Bauckham hypothesizes that the earlier, Palestinian *Testament of Moses* "was subsequently rewritten and entitled" *The Assumption of Moses*. The revision that transformed *The Testament of Moses* into *The Assumption of Moses* may have been almost entirely confined to the concluding part of the work. On the basis of Christian traditions, Bauckham reconstructs the version of the story that he thinks was known to Jude:

> God sent the archangel Michael to remove the body of Moses to another place and bury it there, but Samma'el, the devil, opposed him, disputing Moses' right to honorable burial. The devil brought against Moses a charge of murder, because he smote the Egyptian and hid his body in the sand. But this accusation was no better than slander against Moses, and Michael, not tolerating the slander, said to the devil, "May the Lord rebuke you, devil!" At that the devil took flight, and Michael removed the body to the place commanded by God, where he buried it with his own hands. Thus no one saw the burial of Moses.[20]

However we reconstruct the story and its evolution within Christian tradition, what is clear is that Jude is citing extrabiblical legends about the burial of Moses to illustrate his point about false teachers. We thus apparently have here illustrative reference to the literary Moses of *The Testament/Assumption of Moses*.

After providing various further examples to illustrate the danger and fate of false teachers, Jude then proceeds to actually quote *1 Enoch* as though it were authentic. Speaking of the false teachers, Jude declares, "It was of these also that Enoch in the seventh generation from Adam prophesied, saying, 'Behold, the Lord came with his holy myriads, to execute judgment on all, and to convict all the ungodly of all their deeds of ungodliness which they

and Origen; the anti-Gnostic version is attested by Gelasius Cyzicenus and later *scholia*; citations in Bauckham, *Jude, 2 Peter*, 73–74.

19. Bauckham, *Jude, 2 Peter*, 75.

20. Bauckham, *Jude, 2 Peter*, 76.

have committed in such an ungodly way, and of all the harsh things which ungodly sinners have spoken against him'" (Jude 14–15). The citation is a Greek version of *1 Enoch* 1.9: "Behold, he will arrive with ten million of the holy ones in order to execute judgment upon all. He will destroy the wicked ones and censure all flesh on account of everything that they have done, that which the sinners and wicked ones committed against him." Indeed, Jude is one of the textual witnesses used to establish the text of *1 Enoch* 1.9. Jude cites the author of *1 Enoch*, a pseudepigraphal book from 400–200 BC, as though he were identical to the Enoch of the antediluvian primaeval history.

This text is the *reductio ad absurdum* of facile arguments for OT authorship and historicity on the basis of NT citation. Jude's quoting a pseudepigraphal figure no more commits him to the authenticity and historicity of *1 Enoch* than our quoting a myth commits us to its authenticity and historicity. By failing to distinguish between an illustrative use of a text and an assertoric use of a text, those who offer such arguments are driven into a hopeless *Sackgasse*. For example, Guy Waters comments,

> Jude here identifies "Enoch" as descended from Adam, in the seventh generation from Adam. He treats Enoch as a historical personage, who utters the prophecies documented in verses 14–15. The fact that Enoch is identified as "the seventh from Adam" not only confirms Enoch's historicity but also assumes Adam's historicity.
>
> . . . Some have argued that Jude quotes from a book that his opponents regarded as authoritative, but that Jude did not. Others more plausibly have suggested that Jude regarded these words as a historically accurate, authentic utterance of the prophet Enoch, an utterance that, in the providence of God, was preserved in *1 Enoch*.[21]

There are two claims made in Waters's "more plausible" suggestion: first, that Jude personally believed that the words cited from *1 Enoch* were a historically accurate, authentic utterance of the antediluvian Enoch, and sec-

21. Guy Prentiss Waters, "Theistic Evolution Is Incompatible with the Teachings of the New Testament," in *Theistic Evolution: A Scientific, Philosophical, and Theological Critique*, ed. J. P. Moreland et al. (Wheaton: Crossway, 2017), 891. David McGee goes even further: "It would seem that Jude is supporting the chronogenealogical perspective, which states that no gaps exist between the genealogies of the patriarchs" ("Creation Date of Adam from the Perspective of Young-Earth Creationism," Answers in Genesis, November 28, 2012, https://answersingenesis.org/bible-characters/adam-and-eve/creation-date-of-adam-from-young-earth-creationism-perspective).

ond, that Enoch's words were, in God's providence, preserved in *1 Enoch*. The first claim is irrelevant and the second desperate. As we have seen, an author using a text illustratively may or may not believe in the factuality of the illustration, and the utility of the illustration is independent of the author's personal belief. So if Jude is using *1 Enoch* illustratively, as seems plausible, his personal beliefs about Enoch's historicity are irrelevant. The further suggestion that an oral tradition emanating from the antediluvian Enoch has been preserved over thousands of years to reach the ears of the author of *1 Enoch* can hardly be said to be plausible.

In response to John Walton's claim that Jude affirms "a literary truth, not a historical truth,"[22] Waters rejoins, "That Jude identifies Enoch with a precise genealogical marker and quotes him in the train of a host of historical Old Testament references (Jude 5–11) indicates Jude's understanding of Enoch in Jude 14–15 as a historical person. That Enoch is said to be 'the seventh from Adam' furthermore requires the conclusion that Jude understood Adam to be no less a historical person than Enoch."[23] This comment fails to engage Walton's point. Waters's two sentences may or may not be true but are in any case irrelevant, since Jude's personal beliefs about Enoch are not at issue. If Jude is using his various examples illustratively rather than assertorically, then overly easy historicity proofs of OT narratives must fail. That an assertoric interpretation of Jude 14 forces us to conclude that we hear in *1 Enoch* 1.9 the authentic voice of the antediluvian Enoch should give the NT theologian serious pause.

Another fascinating example comes from 2 Tim 3:8. Warning against religious hypocrites, the author (Paul?) says, "As Jannes and Jambres opposed Moses, so these men also oppose the truth, men of corrupt mind and counterfeit faith." These personages do not appear in the OT but are widely known in Jewish folklore as the unnamed magicians in Pharaoh's court who opposed Moses (Exod 7:11, 22). They became known even in Greek literature as famous sorcerers (Pliny, *Natural History* 30.2.11; Apuleius, *Apology* 90; Numenius, *On the Good*, cited by Eusebius, *Preparation of the Gospel* 9.8). The NT reference most closely resembles the account given in Targum Pseudo-Jonathan: "Then Pharaoh summoned the wise men and the sorcerers; and Yanis and Yambris, the sorcerers who were in Egypt, also did the same with the spells of their divinations" (on Exod 7:11;

22. John H. Walton, *The Lost World of Adam and Eve: Genesis 2–3 and the Human Origins Debate* (Downers Grove, IL: IVP Academic, 2015), 100.

23. Waters, "Theistic Evolution," 892.

cf. Exod 1:15). In his *Commentary on the Gospel of Matthew*, Origen says that "the statement 'as Jannes and Jambres withstood Moses' is not based on canonical books but on an apocryphal one entitled *Jannes and Jambre*" (27.8). Intriguingly, Origen reports that some of his contemporaries rejected 2 Timothy as a whole because it borrows from a *liber secretus*. Fragments of this book in Ethiopic, Coptic, and Greek exist.[24] The traditions behind this work may have been known in the Qumran community, for the *Damascus Document* among the Dead Sea Scrolls mentions the pair: "Moses and Aaron still continued in their charge . . . even though Belial in his cunning had set up Jannes [Yoḥanah] and his brother in opposition to them" (CD 5.17–19). Albert Pietersma argues that *the traditions* concerning Jannes and Jambres go back to at least 2 BC in Jewish internecine struggles under Hasmonean rule in Palestine, while *the book* was written during the darkest period of Egyptian Jewry under Roman rule around the turning of the era or shortly thereafter.[25] He thinks that the characters of the tradition named Yoḥanah (an indisputably Semitic name linguistically identical to Jannes) and his brother were actually portrayed as Israelites who led Israel astray but later evolved into the Egyptian magicians of the book.[26]

A bewildering variety of contradictory traditions concerning Jannes and Jambres grew up in Judaism. In the traditions employing the pair's Hebrew names, presumably more primitive, no magician's contest with Moses takes place; rather, they quarrel with Moses, accompany Pharaoh's army in pursuit of the Israelites, magically fly at the Red Sea, and are killed either by God or Moses. By contrast, in traditions featuring their Greek names retranscribed into Hebrew, we find that the pair serve at Pharaoh's court, lose to Moses in a magician's contest, convert as a result to Judaism, and go into the wilderness with the Israelites![27] Koji Osawa comments on the function of Jannes and Jambres in Jewish tradition: "They came to be seen as the exemplars of evil persons in

24. See Albert Pietersma, ed. and trans., *The Apocryphon of Jannes and Jambres the Magicians*, RGRW 119 (Leiden: Brill, 1994). In 2014 and 2015 fragments of the work in Ethiopian and Coptic were identified, supplying further details of the story. See Ted Erho, Frederic Krueger, and Matthias Hoffmann, "Neues von Pharaos Zauberern," *WUB* 2 (2016): 70–72. For discussion of the book and other traditions concerning Jannes and Jambres, see Koji Osawa, "Jannes and Jambres: The Role and Meaning of Their Traditions in Judaism," *FJB* 37 (2011–12): 55–73.

25. Pietersma, *Apocryphon of Jannes and Jambres*, 11, 59.

26. Pietersma, *Apocryphon of Jannes and Jambres*, 20–23. Pietersma thinks that Yoḥanah and his brother may have actually been the historical Maccabean brothers Jonathan and Simon.

27. Osawa, "Jannes and Jambres," 71–72.

Judaism, so that their names came to be used in a variety of scenes without restriction by time or place. That is to say, those who recorded the Judaic traditions included Jannes and Jambres in stories from whatever time to portray someone as an evil person in Judaism by comparing that someone with Jannes and Jambres and thus to emphasize the sinfulness of those who oppose God."[28] We should therefore be rash to assume that in appealing to these well-known figures to illustrate corrupt religion, the author of 2 Timothy means to assert the historicity of these two literary characters (whatever his personal belief).

Finally, we have Paul's allusion in 1 Cor 10:4 to the rock which accompanied the ancient Israelites through their wilderness wanderings: "All drank the same supernatural drink. For they drank from the supernatural Rock which followed them, and the Rock was Christ." Commentators commonly see a reference here to a Jewish legend based on Num 21:16–18 concerning a miraculous well, shaped like a rock, that continually supplied Israel with water in the desert. This legend, which flourished in later rabbinic Judaism,[29] is documented as early as the first-century *Biblical Antiquities* of Pseudo-Philo: "But as for his own people, he led them forth into the wilderness: forty years did he rain bread from heaven for them, and he brought them quails from the sea, and a well of water following them brought he forth for them. . . . The water of Mara was made sweet and followed them in the desert forty years" (10.7; 11.15). The tradition in some form doubtless goes back to the pre-Christian era. Paul picks up this extracanonical tradition in order to identify the Rock in the story as Christ, who sustained Israel throughout its sojourn in the wilderness, just as he can elsewhere say, "Hagar is Mt. Sinai in Arabia" (Gal 4:25).

On the basis of these examples, we can see how naive it is to argue that because some NT author refers to a literary figure, whether found in the OT

28. Osawa, "Jannes and Jambres," 72–73.

29. See references in Gordon D. Fee, *The First Epistle to the Corinthians*, NICNT (Grand Rapids: Eerdmans, 1987), 442. Ellis provides this convenient summary: "In full flower the legend went somewhat as follows: a movable well, rock-shaped and resembling a sieve, was given to the Israelites in the desert. As to origin, it was one of the ten things created on the evening of the Sixth Day. About the size of an oven or beehive, it rolled along after the wanderers through hills and valleys, and when they camped it settled at the tent of meeting. When the princes called, 'Rise up, O well' (Num. 21.17), water flowed from its many openings as from a flask" (E. Earle Ellis, *Paul's Use of the Old Testament* [1981; repr., Eugene: Wipf & Stock, 2003], 67). Ellis goes on to describe the many fantastic services that were thought to be provided by this well, which persisted with the Israelites until they reached the Sea of Tiberius. Ellis furnishes an abundance of references for these late legends.

or outside it, therefore that figure is asserted to be a historical person, much less is a historical person. We need to pay close attention to the context in order to determine whether the NT author does not merely believe in the historicity of the person referred to but is asserting his historicity, rather than referring to the figure illustratively. Again, use of a literary figure illustratively does not imply that the figure is unhistorical; it simply short-circuits overly easy proofs of historicity.

New Testament Authors' Use of the Literary Adam

Plausibly Illustrative Uses

As we turn to NT references to Adam and Eve, we need to keep firmly in mind what we learned in our discussion of various types of folklore—namely, that in contrast to fables and legends, myths are taken with utter seriousness by the culture that embraces them.[30] Myths are authoritative for such cultures, even if they are not regarded as literally true. So, for example, one might appeal to some feature of a creation myth—say, Adam's being assigned work in the garden—in order to prove that work is not a curse imposed by God on man but a noble and elevating feature of human life in a sinless paradise. This is the authoritative teaching of the creation story, and it would be inept to deny the point on grounds of historicity.

So returning to our list of texts concerning Adam in the NT, we find that some of them plausibly do not go beyond the literary figure of Adam in Genesis. The statements of our Lord concerning Adam in Matt 19:4–5 are plausibly illustrative. He begins by drawing attention to the literary Adam: "Have you not read . . . ?" He then cites Gen 1:27, "male and female he created them," and weds this statement with Gen 2:24, "Therefore a man leaves his father and his mother and cleaves to his wife, and they become one flesh." This forms the basis for his teaching on divorce. Jesus is exegeting the story of Adam and Eve to discern its implications for marriage and divorce, not asserting its historicity.[31]

30. Recall *supra*, pp. 38–39.

31. Recall our deep truth #4, p. 202. Davis and the young earth creationists he cites are almost certainly guilty of overreading the text when on the basis of Mark 10:6 they interpret it to imply that Jesus taught, or even believed, that the original human pair "were created at the beginning of the creation," thereby excluding a considerable time interval between the events of Gen 1:1 and 1:27 (Jud Davis, "Unresolved Major Questions: Evan-

Similarly, Jesus's statement that "the blood of all the prophets, shed from the foundation of the world, may be required of this generation, from the blood of Abel to the blood of Zechariah" (Luke 11:50–51) is a paradigmatic case of the use of literary figures. Commentators have often remarked that what is surveyed here is not the history of the world but the history of the OT canon.[32] Jesus is talking about the literary history of the OT and the literary bookends of it.

Another clear example of illustrative usage is 2 Cor 11:3: "I am afraid that as the serpent deceived Eve by his cunning, your thoughts will be led astray from a sincere and pure devotion to Christ." Here the use of "as" (*hōs*) shows that Paul is drawing a comparison. He uses the story of the fall as an illustrative analogy to the dangerous situation of the Christians in Corinth. The historicity of the story is neither germane nor asserted.

Other examples are less clear. First Timothy 2:13–14, "For Adam was formed first, then Eve; and Adam was not deceived, but the woman was deceived and became a transgressor," looks like an assertion of historical fact to ground his teaching on women's role in the church. But Paul's statement goes no further than the literary Adam and Eve. Paul is describing what the story says; he is basing his teaching about women's teaching authority (or lack thereof) in the church on his exegesis of the story of Eve's creation and transgression.[33] Similarly, his statement "For man was not made from

---

gelicals and Genesis 1–2," in *Reading Genesis 1–2: An Evangelical Conversation*, ed. J. Daryl Charles [Peabody, MA: Hendrickson, 2013], 210). NB that Jesus says *from* the beginning of creation (*apo archēs ktiseōs*), not *at* the beginning of creation. Not only is there no reason to think that Jesus was ruling out a time gap between the creation event and the creation of Adam and Eve, but pressing Jesus's words this hard falsifies his statement, since Adam and Eve were not created at the beginning of the creation (Gen 1:1). The meaning, rather, is that there was never a time when human beings were not differentiated as male and female. They have always been that way.

32. E.g., Marshall writes, "If the Books of Chronicles stood last in the OT canon of the time, then the reference is to the last murder of a prophet in the Scriptures. There is no doubt that Luke has rightly understood his source in this sense" (I. Howard Marshall, *The Gospel of Luke*, NIGTC [Grand Rapids: Eerdmans, 1978], 506).

33. Harlow opines, "This literary appeal to figures of tradition, though, cannot establish the historicity of Adam and Eve for us, even if the author probably regarded them as historical figures" (Daniel C. Harlow, "After Adam: Reading Genesis in an Age of Evolutionary Science," *PSCF* 62 [2010]: 195). Carson protests,

> What must be pointed out is that Paul's argument has no force if it is taken to be a mere illustration drawn from mythological sources. Even in the highest sense of "myth," in which the "myth" somehow pictures general truths, it is not obvious what general truths are being expounded. Is it an obvious general truth that males

woman, but woman from man. Neither was man created for woman, but woman for man" (1 Cor 11:8–9) can be plausibly taken as purely literary. Paul is here summarizing what the story says, how Eve was created as Adam's helper, and basing his teaching on his exegesis of that story.

Plausibly Assertoric Uses

By contrast the geneaology of Luke 3, whether accurate or inaccurate, is intended to be assertoric, just as the genealogies in the primaeval history evince a historical interest. Similarly, Paul's statement before the Areopagus, "[God] made from one every nation of men to live on all the face of

> were created before females? Or that females are intrinsically more susceptible to deception? Some might wish to argue along such lines, I suppose; but such argument is becoming increasingly difficult (to say the least) in the contemporary climate. In fact, Paul can be so unbending on the restrictions he lays down in this passage ("I do not permit," v. 12) precisely because his appeal is to history made known through revelation. If there were no Adam and Eve at the head of the race, no fall, no creation narratives as recorded in Gen. 1–3, Paul's argument would simply not hold up: its basis would have been destroyed. (D. A. Carson, "Adam in the Epistles of Paul," in *In the Beginning . . . : A Symposium on the Bible and Creation*, ed. N. M. de S. Cameron [Glasgow: Biblical Creation Society, 1980], 38)

Whether we think that Paul is speaking of the literary Adam or the historical Adam, the claim that Paul's *argument* depends crucially on the historicity of Adam and Eve is weak. What his argument depends crucially on is the authority of the Hebrew myths of Eve's creation and transgression. As we have seen, myths are sacred narratives for the societies that embrace them and are therefore determinative for them. By exegeting those stories Paul is able, in his mind, to extract some specific applications of those myths for the behavior of women in the churches. A good example of such authoritative use of a text in moral teaching is 1 Cor 6:16–18: "Do you not know that he who joins himself to a prostitute becomes one body with her? For, as it is written, 'The two shall become one flesh.' But he who is united to the Lord becomes one spirit with him. Shun immorality." One can envision, analogously, an ancient Mesopotamian saying, "We must labor in the fields, for when Mami created man, she said, 'I have imposed your toil on man.'" Carson is entirely off-point in thinking that there must be some "general truths" such as he suggests expressed by the Genesis stories. Similarly, Beall is off-point in defending a literal interpretation of the Pauline passages on the grounds that Paul "uses the specific details of the account" (Todd Beall, "Reading Genesis 1–2: A Literal Approach," in Charles, *Reading Genesis 1–2*, 53). See Longman's retort: "I am not sure why he thinks a figurative approach would only be making broad conceptual claims to make their points" (Tremper Longman III, "Responses to Chapter Two," in Charles, *Reading Genesis 1–2*, 67). Of course, NT authors refer to the details of the stories to make their theological and ethical points, whose validity is independent of the historicity of the stories.

the earth, having determined allotted periods and the boundaries of their habitation" (Acts 17:26), seems to be assertoric, for it describes the historical advance of peoples throughout the world from their common historical origin. Doubtless the reference to the "one" is to Adam, not Noah, as Paul's contrast between Adam and Christ in 1 Cor 15 and Rom 5 requires.[34] Paul's teaching thus seems to assert a historical Adam.

John Collins remarks that while it is not easy to insist that Paul's argument in 1 Cor 11:7–12, 2 Cor 11:3, and 1 Tim 2:13–14 depends on the assumption of Adam and Eve's historicity for its validity, the case is different with Acts 17:26; 1 Cor 15:20–23, 42–49; and Rom 5:12–19.[35] In these latter passages Paul lays out his Adam Christology. In treating these theologically rich passages, we shall not attempt in this brief compass to unpack them thoroughly but shall restrict our attention to their implications for the issue of the historical Adam.

1 Corinthians 15:21–22, 45–46

In dealing with Paul's two passages about Adam in 1 Cor 15, the question we face is whether Paul's meaning requires more than a merely literary Adam.[36] Paul's expression "Thus it is written," followed by his paraphrase of Gen 2:7 in vv. 45–46, directs our attention immediately to the Genesis narrative. There is little in the ensuing paragraph that takes us beyond the literary character who appears in Gen 2. Adam is said to be the first man, physical

34. Contra Walton, *Lost World of Adam and Eve*, 186. Moreover, Adam is here conceived to be the progenitor of the entire human race on the face of the earth, wherever and whenever people may have lived, not merely someone selected from a wider mass of humanity to fulfill God's calling. It would be *ad hoc* to try to escape this conclusion by saying that Paul is talking only about people alive at that time, all of whom have a common genealogical ancestor. Paul speaks of people living at all times and places in history and has no conception of modern notions of universal common ancestors discovered by recent science.

35. C. John Collins, *Did Adam and Eve Really Exist? Who They Were and Why You Should Care* (Wheaton: Crossway, 2011), 78.

36. Carson's treatment of Adam in 1 Cor 15 is directed against the interpreter who takes Paul's Adam to be a merely generic symbol of humanity ("Adam in the Epistles of Paul," 31–33). He thus fails to address the issue before us. We can agree that, for Paul, Adam is an individual person, not a symbolic figure; but if the stories are mythical, then the individuality of the person in the stories is no more relevant to historicity than the individuality of Odysseus or Gilgamesh in their respective stories. See further our discussion of Joseph Fitzmyer's interpretation of Paul's Adam *infra*, pp. 239–41.

or natural (*psychikos*), from the earth, made of dust. All that is true of the figure we meet in the Genesis account. He was, according to the story, the first human being that God made, formed by him out of the dust of the earth, and therefore having a natural body. In saying that we all bear the image of the one made of dust, Paul may not be saying anything more than that we are all like the man described in the story. Each of us has a natural body (*sōma psychikon*), made of dust, and therefore mortal.

There may, however, be a hint of the historical Adam in the expression "It is not the spiritual which is first but the physical, and then the spiritual." Paul might mean simply that in the story the physical or natural body is created first. But it is not the case that in the story after the physical "then the spiritual" is created. True, God breathes into the earthly man the divine breath so that the man becomes a living being (*psychēn zōsan*); but that belongs still to the natural (*to psychikon*), not to the spiritual (*to pneumatikon*). We shall have to wait until Christ's resurrection for the spiritual to appear (1 Cor 15:23). So Paul may be attributing a genuine chronological or historical priority of Adam to Christ, in which case we have moved outside the story to postulate a historical Adam.

Ultimately, whether Paul is using Adam more than just illustratively in 1 Cor 15:45–46 is apt to depend on what he meant by his earlier statement "As in Adam all die, so also in Christ shall all be made alive" (15:22). An illustrative reference to the literary Adam would suffice for the statement "As by a man came death, by a man has come also the resurrection of the dead" (15:21), for the protasis of this sentence does not clearly move outside the Genesis narrative, although the apodosis is external to the narrative. His statement "in Adam all die" may look like a truth asserted external to the narrative, since it does not seem to be part of the literary Adam of Genesis that in him all die. But if Paul is talking about physical death, not spiritual death, then mortality does seem to belong to the literary Adam. It is important to note that while Rom 5 contrasts spiritual death and condemnation in Adam with justification and righteousness in Christ, here in 1 Cor 15 the contrast is not forensic but physical: in Adam all persons die physically, but in Christ we shall someday enjoy resurrection life. The concern here is with immortality, not righteousness and salvation. In 1 Cor 15 Paul associates human mortality with the creation of Adam, not with his fall.[37] Adam is created with a *sōma*

37. Contra Carson, who writes, "The reference to death as the last enemy to be destroyed (v. 26) almost certainly casts a backward glance at the introduction of death into the race effected by the disobedience of our first parent (Gen. 3)" ("Adam in the Epistles of

psychikon; he does not obtain one by sinning. Paul implies that physical mortality is the natural human condition. In saying that in Adam all die, Paul may be saying that in virtue of sharing a common human nature with Adam we share in his natural mortality. If the creation of Adam from the dirt is a figurative way of recounting how mortal man came to be, then the claim that we, too, are mortal does not depend on the historicity of the narrative, just on our sharing a similar constitution to the man described in the story. Paul may draw the inference of human mortality on the basis of the literary Adam alone, though it is difficult to exclude that his argument may go beyond the boundaries of the literary Adam to touch the historical Adam.

Romans 5:12–21

Turn now to Rom 5:12–21. This passage has been called the second most important passage in Paul's letter to the Romans after 3:21–26, the summation of all that he had thus far said in his letter.[38] He here extends his typology of Christ as the eschatological Adam from 1 Cor 15. Our interest in interpreting this rich passage (perversely, perhaps) is not in the benefit won for mankind by Jesus Christ in his obedience unto death but in what Paul asserts concerning Adam. So in the series of contrasts drawn between Adam and Christ, our focus is in each case on the protasis or initial clause of each relevant sentence. There has, of course, been enormous theological controversy about how to understand such expressions as "many died through one man's trespass" (v. 15), "the judgment following one trespass brought condemnation" (v. 16), "because of one man's trespass, death reigned through that one man" (v. 17), "one man's trespass led to condemnation for all men" (v. 18), and "by one man's disobedience many were made sinners" (v. 19).

We may dismiss at the outset as irrelevant, not to say false, Rudolf Bultmann's suggestion that Paul's distinction between Adam and Christ is similar

Paul," 31). This is to conflate 1 Cor 15 with Rom 5. There is no mention of the fall in 1 Cor 15. Legarreta-Castillo is guilty of a similar conflation despite his statement "In 1 Corinthians 15 Paul addresses the question of the future and bodily resurrection of the believers who have died. In Rom 5:12–21 Paul emphasizes the greater effects of Christ's expiatory death" (*Figure of Adam*, 13). For he reads 1 Cor 15:20–23 differently than 15:45–49, interpreting the former against the backdrop of Jewish traditions concerning Adam's fall and the death that befell him and his descendants and the latter against the backdrop of a different set of Jewish traditions concerning Adam's natural mortality as a result of his creation from the dust of the earth. Thus, he imports the legal and moral concerns of Rom 5 into 1 Cor 15.

38. So Fitzmyer, *Romans*, 406.

to Philo's distinction between the heavenly man of Gen 1:27 and the earthly man of Gen 2:7, drawing on a prior Gnostic myth concerning the archetypal heavenly *Urmensch*.[39] Bultmann opines, "The Adam-Christ parallel, i.e., the thought of two mankinds (or two epochs of mankind) and their determination each by its originator, is a gnostic idea which is conceived cosmologically and not in terms of salvation history."[40] Fitzmyer rightly responds that "if there is a myth behind the discussion, it is not the gnostic myth of the *Urmensch*, but that of Genesis 2:4b–3:24, to which Paul alludes, viz., the Yahwist account of the creation of Adam and Eve and of their transgression of the command that Yahweh had laid on them."[41] Paul is contrasting two individuals, Adam and Jesus, and therefore a symbolic reading "does violence to the contrast Paul uses in this paragraph between Adam as 'one man' and Christ as 'one man.'"[42]

Fitzmyer remarks that Paul does not explain just how Adam's sin is transmitted to his posterity.[43] Paul may mean that in virtue of Adam's representative status or our corporate solidarity with Adam or some such notion, Adam's sin in the garden is imputed to each of us, his progeny. That is to say, we are guilty before God in virtue of Adam's wrongdoing and so under condemnation of death. Whether the notion of imputation of sin is palatable to modern sensibilities is irrelevant to the interpretive question before us.[44]

39. James D. G. Dunn, *Romans 1–8*, WBC 38A (Grand Rapids: Zondervan, 1988), 277–79, offers a three-pronged critique of Bultmann's analysis: (1) Philo's treatment of the heavenly man can be explained wholly on the basis of Platonistic and Wisdom motifs intrinsic to his own philosophical theology; (2) for Paul, Christ as the heavenly Adam is not the primal man, the model for the earthly Adam, but is, on the basis of his resurrection, subsequent to the earthly Adam, the model for resurrected believers; and (3) Paul's thought is at home in Judaism and is markedly distinct from later Gnostic systems, particularly in his treating sin and death as quasi-cosmic powers and in his emphasizing human responsibility in sinning. Dunn rightly says, "Jewish eschatology is everything here; of a primal Man mythology there is no trace" (278).

40. Rudolf Bultmann, "Adam and Christ according to Romans 5," in *Current Issues in New Testament Interpretation*, ed. William Klassen and Graydon F. Snyder (London: SCM, 1962), 154.

41. Fitzmyer, *Romans*, 407.

42. Fitzmyer, *Romans*, 408.

43. Fitzmyer, *Romans*, 409.

44. I suspect that many theologians would be surprised to discover that imputation of liability and guilt for wrongdoing to a blameless third party is a widely accepted and common practice in Western systems of justice. In both civil and criminal law, persons can be found vicariously liable for wrongs committed by another person. For discussion in connection with Christ's atonement, see my *Atonement and the Death of Christ:*

Douglas Moo has ably argued that such is indeed Paul's meaning.[45] Moo grants that in Rom 5:12–14 Paul's emphasis is not on the corporate significance of Adam's sin but on his role as the instrument through which sin is unleashed in the world. But Moo wants to know how we can logically relate the assertions "Each person dies because *each person* sins [in the course of history]" (v. 12cd) and "*One man*'s trespass led to condemnation for all people" (v. 18a). We cannot ascribe the universality of human sin and condemnation to utter coincidence, for Paul clearly takes Adam's sin to be in some sense the cause of universal condemnation. Moo finds it significant that Paul attributes the entrance of sin into the world to Adam, even though Paul knows from Genesis that it was Eve who sinned first. Adam is already being given a status that is not tied merely to temporal priority. Moo thinks that we should not posit a corrupted human nature as a sort of middle term between Adam's sin and ours, for that adds a middle step to Paul's argument that is not explicit in the context—namely, Adam's having and passing on a corrupt nature. Rather, Moo argues that if we read v. 12d in light of vv. 18–19, which seems to be a legitimate procedure in view of v. 18a's recapitulation of v. 12, then "'all sinned' must be given some kind of corporate meaning: sinning not as voluntary acts of sin in one's own person but sinning in and with Adam." The sin attributed to all "in some manner is identical to the sin committed by Adam. . . . The sin of Adam *is* the sin of all."[46] It is fair to speak of this as the imputation of Adam's sin.[47] One last point inclines Moo toward such a reading of Paul—namely, the conception of corporate solidarity popular in the Jewish world of Paul's day. The Jewish text that comes closest to Paul's teaching, he thinks, is *4 Ezra* 7:118: "O Adam, what have you done? For though it was you who sinned, the fall was not yours alone, but ours also who are your descendants." For Paul, Adam was both a historical figure and the corporate figure whose sin could be regarded as the sin of all his descendants.

An Exegetical, Historical, and Philosophical Exploration (Waco: Baylor University Press, 2020), chaps. 9–10.

45. Douglas J. Moo, *The Letter to the Romans*, 2nd ed., NICNT (Grand Rapids: Eerdmans, 2018), 347–56. It is troubling, however, that when it comes to the question of the fairness or justice of my being held liable for the act of another, Moo offers no robust defense but concludes that "no explanation ultimately removes the problem. 'Original sin' remains an 'offense to reason'" (356). It is one thing to confess mystery, but quite another to say that Paul's teaching is an offense to reason, for that is to declare that Christianity really is irrational.

46. Moo, *Romans*, 354.

47. Moo, *Romans*, 372.

Now it is evident that if the above interpretation of Paul's teaching is correct, then the historicity of Adam and his fall into sin follow. For the sin of a nonexistent person cannot be imputed to me such that I am held objectively guilty before God. The sin of a purely literary Adam can have no effect on the world outside the fiction. Moo correctly argues,

> The effects of Adam's act *in history* (universal sinfulness and death) would seem to demand an Adam who sinned *in history*. I might, for instance, compare or contrast Aslan (from *Chronicles of Narnia*) with Christ to make a general theological point (as Aslan died for Edmund on the stone table, Christ died for us on the cross), but my listeners would be quite confused if I claimed that the White Witch introduced into our world a condition that Christ has saved us from. And the confusion would be quite natural: I would be positing events in our history caused by, respectively, a fictional character and a real character. Adam, as Paul makes clear, functions on the same historical plane as Moses, the law, and Christ (of whom he is the "type").[48]

The imputation of Adam's sin to his posterity requires, then, a historical Adam. If Paul's doctrine involves such imputation, it follows that he is teaching the historicity of Adam and his sin.

But is that in fact Paul's doctrine? Perhaps; but there is plenty of room for doubt that it is. The question is, indeed, how to relate v. 12cd, "As sin

48. Moo, *Romans*, 355. Although it is often asserted that typology alone is sufficient to establish a purported historical connection between the type and the antitype (e.g., Ellis, *Paul's Use of the Old Testament*, 127), such a claim is both conceptually and biblically flawed. Conceptually, it is perfectly possible to draw a comparison between a literary figure and a historical person as pattern/model and instance (Dunn, *Romans 1–8*, 289: "An act of mythic history can be paralleled to an act in living history without the point of comparison being lost"). Biblically, Jude and 2 Peter present illustrations, not just from the OT but from Jewish folklore, that serve as types of the false teachers (Bauckham, *Jude, 2 Peter*, 47, 256). Carson argues that typological categories are meaningful "only if the first figure is a figure in history. One cannot fail to be reminded of the argument of 2 Peter 3:1–7. There we are told that those who scoff at the prospect of the second coming have two historical examples of God's cataclysmic intervention to stand as witnesses to what God can do—viz., the creation and the flood" ("Adam in the Epistles of Paul," 33). If we follow such an argument, we shall be led into affirming the historicity, not only of creation and the worldwide flood, but also of the Watchers (now imprisoned in Tartarus), Noah the herald, and the righteous Lot. Moo instead argues correctly that real-world effects cannot be caused by the actions of a character in a story.

came into the world through one man and death through sin, and so death spread to all men because all men sinned," to v. 18a, "One man's trespass led to condemnation for all men." Moo rightly insists that some explanation is needed for why "people so consistently turn from good to evil of all kinds."[49] No one thinks that every person sins by sheer coincidence. Moo says, "Paul affirms in this passage that human solidarity in the sin of Adam is the explanation—and whether we explain this solidarity in terms of sinning in and with Adam or because of a corrupt nature inherited from him does not matter at this point."[50]

Now it is crucial that we understand that the first proffered explanation of our solidarity with Adam (sinning in and with Adam) in fact does nothing to explain why people consistently sin, for imputation is purely a legal or forensic notion that has no effect whatever on a person's moral character. Moo later explains, "Paul is insisting that people were really 'made' sinners through Adam's act of disobedience just as they are really 'made righteous' through Christ's obedience. But this 'making righteous' . . . means not to become 'morally righteous' people but to become 'judicially righteous'—to be judged acquitted, cleared of all charges."[51] Similarly, "people can be 'made' sinners in the sense that God considers them to be such by regarding Adam's act as, at the same time, their act. . . . It seems fair, then, . . . to speak of imputation here." So "we are dealing with a real, though forensic, situation: people actually become sinners in solidarity with Adam—by God's decision; people actually become 'righteous' in solidarity with Christ—again, by God's decision."[52] Such forensic transactions cannot explain why people consistently turn from good to evil. Just as the pardon of a condemned criminal does not make him suddenly a virtuous person but simply no longer legally guilty, so also the imputation of legal guilt does not transform the moral character of an otherwise blameless person.

So what about the second proffered explanation of our solidarity with Adam (a corrupt nature inherited from him)? The traditional doctrine of original sin postulates minimally a corrupted or deprived nature inherited from

49. Moo, *Romans*, 356.

50. Moo, *Romans*, 356. Since Moo argues against the postulation of a corrupted human nature, I take it that "by this point" he must mean v. 12, for later in the passage that option will be disfavored.

51. Moo, *Romans*, 372. The proper legal notion here is not acquittal but rather pardon. God's guilty verdict is not overturned, as though there had been a miscarriage of justice; rather, we are graciously given a divine pardon for our crimes.

52. Moo, *Romans*, 372.

Adam, if not imputed guilt.[53] Thomas Aquinas offers this pithy summary: "Original sin spread in this way, that at first the person infected the nature, and afterwards the nature infected the person" (*Summa theologiae* III.69.3 *ad* 3). Now the postulation of an impaired human nature inherited from Adam requires a historical Adam just as certainly as does the doctrine of imputation. So if that is Paul's doctrine, then his teaching implies the existence of a historical Adam. But does Paul teach such a thing? As Moo observes, the doctrine is, perhaps surprisingly, nowhere to be found in Rom 5:12–21. That occasions the question: Is there no other alternative to either imputation or corrupted nature for explaining people's proclivity toward sin?

Of course there is: our inherent self-seeking animal nature in combination with the web of corruption in which we are born and raised. Christopher Hays and Stephen Herring rightly point out, "Even if one did not believe that Adam's fall was the source of human concupiscence, one could quite easily provide an alternative account of the doctrine, saying, for example, that humans have an evolutionary biological propensity to selfishness that is reinforced and quickened by our society, psychology and spiritual estate."[54] Daryl Domning expands on this view:

> The overt selfish acts that, in humans, demonstrate the reality of original sin by manifesting it as actual sin do indeed owe their universality among humans to natural descent from a common ancestor. However, this ancestor must be placed not at the origin of the human race but at the origin of life itself. Yet these overt acts did not acquire their sinful character until the evolution of human intelligence allowed them to be performed by morally responsible beings.
>
> We all sin because we have all inherited—from the very first living things on earth—a powerful tendency to act selfishly, no matter the cost to others. Free will enables us to override this tendency, but only sporadically and with great effort; we more readily opt for self. This tendency in all of us is what our tradition calls "the stain of original sin."[55]

53. Catholic doctrine affirms transmission of both guilt and corruption; Orthodoxy only the corrupted nature. For a sensitive discussion of Jonathan Edwards and Thomas Aquinas on original sin, see Matthew Levering, *Engaging the Doctrine of Creation: Cosmos, Creatures, and the Wise and Good Creator* (Grand Rapids: Baker Academic, 2017), 249–67.

54. Christopher M. Hays and Stephen Lane Herring, "Adam and the Fall," in *Evangelical Faith and the Challenge of Historical Criticism*, ed. Christopher M. Hays and Christopher B. Ansberry (Grand Rapids: Baker Academic, 2013), 53.

55. Daryl P. Domning, "Evolution, Evil and Original Sin," *America*, November 12, 2001, http://americamagazine.org/issue/350/article/evolution-evil-and-original-sin.

Such a natural biological tendency toward survival and hence selfishness, coupled with a morally corrupt environment, suffices to explain why all have sinned. Domning notwithstanding, this explanation of the universality of human sin is not incompatible with tracing the origin of our selfish behavior back to the first human ancestor; indeed, the view does not require even that Adam and Eve had biological ancestors, merely that they were created with a biological propensity to survival that is reinforced by society and upbringing. Biological ancestry is no more required (or excluded) than imputation of corrupted nature in order to explain the universality of human sin. It is worth noting in passing that when in Rom 1–3 Paul develops his doctrine of the universality of sin and condemnation, he makes no appeal at all to the doctrine of original sin in any form.[56]

However that may be, Moo's argument in favor of imputation depends on reading v. 12 in light of vv. 18–19. Moo acknowledges that his interpretation "rests almost entirely on the juxtaposition of v. 12 with vv. 18–19."[57] But that understates the situation; rather, his interpretation rests almost entirely, as he initially stated, on reading v. 12 "*in light of* vv. 18–19." But that seems to stand things on their head; vv. 18–19, which complete the original sentence interrupted after v. 12d, ought more naturally to be read in light of v. 12. In that way Paul does not need to take back, as it were, something he has already said; rather, he stands by it. Paul says that just as Adam's sin was followed by death, so "death spread to all men because all men sinned." Most commentators construe *eph' hō* as a causal conjunction, "because," and take "all men sinned" to refer to people's own individual acts of sin.[58] So Adam was the floodgate through which sin and death entered the world, and death then spread to all men because each one sinned in his own turn. (Paul does not here address the question why, though one recalls his remarks in 1:20–23.) When Paul affirms that "by one man's disobedience many were made sinners," that "one

56. This belies Enns's hypothesis that Paul's motivation for using Adam as he does is to explain how Christ's crucifixion and resurrection put all of humanity, Jew and gentile alike, on the same footing, subject to the same universal plight of sin and death and so both equally in need of the same savior (Peter Enns, *The Evolution of Adam: What the Bible Does and Doesn't Say about Human Origins* [Grand Rapids: Brazos, 2012], 81–82, 131).

57. Moo, *Romans*, 354.

58. See the list of eleven interpretations of *eph' hō* that have been offered in Fitzmyer, *Romans*, 413–16, most of which are quite implausible. Fitzmyer's own interpretation that *eph' hō* has a consecutive meaning, "so that, with the result that," seems to succumb to his critique of the fifth alternative, "on the grounds of which, because of which"—viz., that this interpretation fails because death is thought by Paul to be the result of sin, not its source. According to Dunn, the classic debate on the meaning of *eph' hō* has more or less been settled in favor of the meaning "for this reason that, because" (*Romans 1–8*, 273).

man's trespass led to condemnation for all men," that "because of one man's trespass, death reigned through that one man," and that "many died through one man's trespass," he may be understood to trace all sinning and, hence, condemnation and death back to Adam's initial transgression, through which sin entered the world. That Adam is singled out instead of Eve is as plausibly an expression of Jewish patriarchy (she was, after all, Adam's "helper") as an affirmation of Adam's federal headship of the human race.

Scholars who, like Moo, find in *4 Ezra* 7.118 an anticipation of the doctrine of the imputation of Adam's sin to all men typically fail to quote the verse in context:

> I answered and said, "This is my first and last word: It would have been better if the earth had not produced Adam, or else, when it had produced him, had restrained him from sinning. For what good is it to all that they live in sorrow now and expect punishment after death? O Adam, what have you done? For though it was you who sinned, the fall was not yours alone, but ours also who are your descendants. For what good is it to us, if an eternal age has been promised to us, but we have done deeds that bring death? And what good is it that an everlasting hope has been promised us, but we have miserably failed? Or that safe and healthful habitations have been reserved for us, but we have lived wickedly? Or that the glory of the Most High will defend those who have led a pure life, but we have walked in the most wicked ways? Or that a paradise shall be revealed, whose fruit remains unspoiled and in which are abundance and healing, but we shall not enter it, because we have lived in unseemly places? Or that the faces of those who practiced self-control shall shine more than the stars but our faces shall be blacker than darkness? For while we lived and committed iniquity we did not consider what we should suffer after death."
>
> He answered and said, "This is the meaning of the contest which every man who is born on earth shall wage, that if he is defeated he shall suffer what you have said, but if he is victorious he shall receive what I have said." (*4 Ezra* 7.116–29)

The text actually expresses beautifully the balance between Adam's failure and people's responsibility for their own acts of sin, just as we find in Rom 5:12: "as sin came into the world through one man and death through sin, and so death spread to all men because all men sinned."[59]

59. It is worth noting that despite espousing a view like Moo's, Fitzmyer denies that there is any clear reference in pre-Christian Jewish literature to such a notion as the incor-

It is generally agreed that in v. 13 Paul interrupts his train of thought with a possible objection—namely, even if people lied and stole and murdered and so on prior to the giving of the Mosaic law, how could such acts count as sin, since they had not been forbidden? Such an objection seems to arise from Paul's own theology, for he has just said, "Where there is no law there is no transgression" (Rom 4:15). The objection is a profound one, which still occupies Christian ethicists today.[60] On a typical divine command theory of ethics, moral values are rooted in God's nature and our moral duties in his commands. The question arises, then, concerning acts that are objectively evil, since they are incompatible with the divine nature, but which have not been forbidden to certain persons at various times and places in history and therefore are not wrong for them. Such acts are morally *bad* but not morally *wrong*. Someone engaged in such acts is therefore evil but blameless, since he contravenes no moral duty. Such persons therefore cannot be justly punished for their acts, since they have done nothing wrong, but nevertheless find themselves alienated from God by their evil character. Paul seems to envision just such persons living between the time of Adam and Moses.

Unfortunately, Paul's thinking about this problem is not as clear as we might wish. One should have expected Paul to answer the objection by repeating what he said earlier, "When Gentiles who have not the law do by nature what the law requires, they are a law to themselves, even though they do not have the law. They show that what the law requires is written on their hearts" (Rom 2:14–15). Hence, they are indeed accountable. Why Paul does not answer in this way is a puzzle. Dunn suggests that Paul is anticipating his later introduction of the law as something that exacerbates sin (Rom 7:7–25), and so he argues *ex concessis* that people without the Torah are not

---

poration of all human beings in Adam (*Romans*, 412). Similarly, Dunn thinks that the concept of corporate personality is more of a hindrance than a help here (*Romans 1–8*, 272).

60. The issue comes up in my debate with naturalistic ethicist Erik Wielenberg, *A Debate on God and Morality: What Is the Best Account of Objective Moral Values and Duties?*, ed. Adam Lloyd Johnson (Abingdon, UK: Routledge, 2020). Wielenberg objects to a divine command theory of ethics on the grounds that people who fail to discern God's commands have no moral duties to fulfill and so do nothing wrong in committing the most horrendous evils. Were God to issue commands to them, knowing that they would disobey them, God would actually be making the world morally worse because now their acts would become, not merely evil, but morally wrong. For my response, see *A Debate on God and Morality*, 82; cf. pp. 45–46, 49–50, 59–60, 63, 70.

responsible for meeting its demands.[61] Paul could maintain both positions by holding that the law introduces a degree of specificity (e.g., Sabbath observance) not available through general revelation. That would accord with his saying, "Law came in, to *increase* the trespass; but where sin increased, grace abounded all the more" (Rom 5:20).

Be that as it may, Paul seems willing to countenance the existence of people who lived between the times of Adam and Moses who were evildoers but not wrongdoers; that is to say, they were morally evil but not accountable. Commentators seem to agree that in saying that their sins (*hamartiai*) were not like Adam's transgression (*parabasis*), Paul makes this very differentiation: since they do not have the law, the morally evil things they do are not, properly speaking, transgressions—that is, the breaking of a law.[62]

Paul asserts that death nevertheless reigned over such people. So saying seems to require an implicit differentiation between death as a *consequence* of sin and death as a *penalty* for sin. Since the relevant persons are not accountable, death cannot be their just desert—that is, the punishment that justice requires. Rather, death would have to be a consequence of their sin. This fact shows that Paul is talking here about spiritual death.[63] It would be outlandish to think that each person is born physically immortal and then by sinning brings physical mortality on himself. But each person might be reasonably said to bring spiritual death on himself in virtue of his sinning. Evildoing is spiritually deadly and alienates us from God, so that spiritual death can be a consequence of sin even if not a punishment for sin for those who have no law.

What about the relation between sin and physical death? Think again about 1 Cor 15. In contrast to Rom 5, Paul's employment of the Adam/Christ typology in 1 Cor 15 is focused on physical death and resurrection. Although we might think that physical death is the result of Adam's sin, Paul does not affirm this. Gordon Fee comments on 1 Cor 15:45, "The first Adam, who became a living *psychē* was thereby given a *psychikos* body at creation, a body subject to decay and death. . . . The last Adam, on the other hand, whose

61. Dunn, *Romans 1–8*, 275.

62. Commentators also agree, contra Carson, "Adam in the Epistles of Paul," 42, that the status of those who die in infancy does not come into view here. The reason infants may die physically is not due to sin but to natural human mortality.

63. Moo comments that the fact that Paul uses condemnation in the same way as death and that he contrasts death with the eternal life suggests that Paul may refer to spiritual death (*Romans*, 348).

'spiritual (glorified) body' was given at his resurrection, . . . is himself the source of the *pneumatikos* life as well as the *pneumatikos* body."[64] On this view Adam was created with a mortal natural body.[65]

As Walton emphasizes, Gen 3:19 supports the natural mortality of Adam and Eve due to their physical constitution.[66] If Adam and Eve were naturally immortal, moreover, then why have a tree of life in the garden at all? It would serve no physical purpose in paradise. The tree serves to rejuvenate its eater physically, not spiritually, hence the concern in Gen 3:22 about fallen man's eating from the tree and living forever (NB not his being spiritually regenerated). John Day thus reports that among OT scholars "the majority scholarly view nowadays" is that Adam and Eve were mortal in the garden, as implied by Gen 3:22.[67]

John Collins further points out that "the 'death' that Gen. 2:17 threatens is human 'spiritual death,' namely, alienation from God. This becomes clear once we see what happens to the human pair when they disobey in Genesis 3."[68] The only sense in which physical death might be seen as a con-

64. Fee, *First Epistle to the Corinthians*, 789. Moreover, Jesus Christ, though sinless, also had a body that was nonetheless *psychikos* and therefore mortal. It is only with his resurrection that his *sōma psychikon* was transformed to a *sōma pneumatikon*. It cannot be said therefore that physical death is solely a consequence of personal sin, or Christ could not die.

65. Levering's protest against Adam's natural mortality—"I think that this position inevitably undermines the goodness and justice of the creator, by implicating the creator in our sinfulness and by having no answer (other than our created condition) for why our alienation and death are so terrible" (*Engaging the Doctrine of Creation*, 235; cf. 269)—is predicated on his failure to distinguish between physical death and spiritual death (cf. 269n22). Only the latter is directly connected to sin and alienation. Collins cites Gen 3:19 in an effort to show that Adam and Eve's physical death results from their spiritual death, which forces him into *ad hoc* conjectures about Adam and Eve's having "a fresh start" in comparison with their mortal ancestors (C. John Collins, "Adam and Eve as Historical People, and Why It Matters," *PSCF* 62, no. 3 [September 2010]: 158).

66. Walton, *Lost World of Adam and Eve*, 73. Walton's mistake lies in thinking that their mortality is not consistent with, and even an implication of, their material creation.

67. John Day, *From Creation to Babel: Studies in Genesis 1–11*, LHBOTS 592 (London: Bloomsbury, 2013), 45–46.

68. Collins, "Adam and Eve as Historical People," 158. By contrast, Day argues "by process of elimination" that the most likely view of the prediction of death is that the couple did not die immediately because of God's grace and mercy. But this alternative is not eliminated by Day only because Day considers it last! He admits that there is nothing in the narrative drawing attention to an act of grace. Day characterizes the alternative favored by Collins as interpreting "death as metaphorical, referring to the alienation from God implied by the expulsion from the garden" (Day, *From Creation to Babel*, 39). Day

sequence of sin is indirect: it is a consequence of Adam and Eve's expulsion from the garden, cutting off any hope of immortality, symbolized by the tree of life. As Day nicely phrases it, "What has happened is that they have missed out on a chance of immortality."[69]

This is the same paradoxical conclusion found in Jewish pseudepigraphal and apocryphal writings touching on Adam. Legarreta-Castillo observes that Jewish texts affirm that death is natural to humankind as a result of creation (*Sirach* 16.30b; 17.30; 18.9; 33.10; 37.25; 40.1–11; 41.3–4; *Wisdom* 7.1–6; 15.8b; Philo, *On the Creation of the World* 134). On the other hand they strongly emphasize that Adam's disobedience brought death on him and his descendants (*Wisdom* 2.23–24; Philo, *On the Creation of the World* 167–70; Pseudo-Philo, *Biblical Antiquities* 13.8–9; 37.3; *Life of Adam and Eve* 7.1; 8.2; 14.1; *Sibylline Oracles* 1.38–58, 80–82; *4 Ezra* 3.4–11; 7.48, 116–18; *2 Baruch* 17.2–4; 19.8; 23.4–5). The paradox is resolved by realizing that although man was created naturally mortal, he had the opportunity to live forever, an opportunity forfeited forever by Adam. Legarreta-Castillo summarizes,

> Jewish authors interpret variously the story of the creation and fall of humankind according to their historical and cultural context. . . . Thus, on the one hand, made after God's image (Gen 1:26–27), humankind has its origins in God; on the other hand, made out of the *adamah* (Gen 2:7), Adam and his descendants are bound back to the earth and mortal by nature. The second creation account is closely related to the tale of paradise, the fall, and expulsion from the garden. Jewish interpreters see in this story the paradigm of the loss of their land, the fall of Jerusalem and the temple, and their sufferings as due to their disobedience and failure to keep the covenant and God's commands. Thus, Adam's disobedience stands as the first—and, in some instances, as the origin of—sin and death for all humankind.[70]

---

thinks that this is not the most natural way of taking what is said, for there are about forty other instances in the Hebrew Bible where we read that someone will surely die, and these all imply imminent literal death. But this characterization of the alternative is a straw man. On the view favored by Collins, spiritual death is literal, not metaphorical, and so examples where literal physical death is at issue do not compromise this case. Indeed, one can admit that the most natural way of reading the prediction of 2:17 is as a threat of physical death; but in light of the consequences one comes to see that literal spiritual death is at issue.

69. Day, *From Creation to Babel*, 46.

70. Legarreta-Castillo, *Figure of Adam*, 111; cf. 116.

So, for example, in *Biblical Antiquities* 13.8–9 and 26.6, Pseudo-Philo affirms that by their disobedience Adam and Eve "lost the ways of paradise" and so "death was ordained for the generations of men." Similarly, in *Life of Adam and Eve* 7.1, the author explains that their expulsion from the garden and their death were the result of their disobedience. Adam lost his dominion and died (39.1–3), and now man returns to the earth because we are dust and to dust we shall return (41.1–2). In *Sibylline Oracles* 1.51, Adam and Eve are said to have been expelled from "the place of the immortals." Being naturally mortal, man is doomed to death by Adam's forfeiture of the goods of paradise.

In the remainder of Rom 5:12–21, then, Paul is, on this view, describing how the sin of Adam unleashes the power that results in all persons' sinning, with the result that they are condemned to spiritual death. When Paul says, "The judgment following one trespass brought condemnation," we may take that to refer to God's swift judgment on Adam's sin; but when he thinks of the result of Adam's sin, he says, "One man's trespass led to condemnation for all men," since all men sinned. Paul would be confused if he thought that the judgment following Adam's one trespass involved the condemnation of all people, since nonexistent persons cannot be condemned.

Perhaps the greatest objection to this diachronic view of the effect of Adam's sin is that the parallelism with Christ's atoning death seems to become rather loose. For in Christ's case, we do not seem to have his act of obedience leading over time to justification and life for all. Rather, all are made righteous and alive in his act of obedience. But, in fact, the doctrine of the imputation of our sins to Christ and of his righteousness to us (found elsewhere in Paul) does not appear in this passage any more than does the imputation of Adam's sin to us. Rather, Paul does here seem to be speaking diachronically of the benefits won by Christ's death. For he says, "Those who receive the abundance of grace and the free gift of righteousness will reign in life through the one man Jesus Christ," a process that is ongoing throughout history as people are born, come to hear the gospel, and embrace it. So "by one man's obedience many will be made righteous," and "one man's act of righteousness leads to acquittal and life for all men." We seem to have here the same sort of diachronic impact of Christ's atoning death as we have in the case of Adam's sin, making them surprisingly parallel.

Returning to the question of the connection of Adam's sin and our condemnation, Moo rejects what he calls a "mediate" connection (namely, Adam's "trespass" → human sinning → "condemnation" of all) in favor of an "immediate" connection (namely, Adam's "trespass" → "condemnation" of all). He says, "While the text does not rule out the former, we think the latter, in light of the parallel with Christ and the lack of explicit mention of an intermediate stage, to be more likely."[71] With respect to the parallel with Christ, to add a middle term, "believing," between Christ's "obedience" and our being "made righteous" "destroys the analogy. To maintain strict parallelism, we would have to argue rather that, as people are made sinners by sinning, they are made righteous by being righteous, or doing righteous things. Yet this interpretation is obviously impossible."[72] This reasoning overlooks what Paul actually says. Paul explicitly adds the middle term between Christ's obedience and our being made righteous: "Those who *receive* the abundance of grace and the free gift of righteousness will reign in life through the one man Jesus Christ." It is the addition of this mediating term that obviates the inference to either the doctrine of universalism on the one hand or the doctrine of limited atonement on the other. For while Christ has truly died for all, making salvation available to all, his death does not result in life for all, since some fail to receive the gift of righteousness. This process does not imply an impossible justification by works, for receiving the free gift of righteousness is not a work in Paul's understanding. We thus see that Paul has explicitly connected sin and condemnation on the one hand and Christ's death and our salvation on the other by an intermediate step in each case—namely, sinning (v. 12d) and receiving (v. 17), respectively. Thus, the cases of Adam and Christ are actually quite parallel.

A moment's reflection reveals that this interpretation of Paul's Adam Christology also requires that Adam be a historical person. For sin and spiritual death are said to enter the world through him and to affect in turn all his descendants, including us. Paul's expressions "before the law was given" and "from Adam to Moses" show that he is denominating real epochs of human history as affected by Adam's act.[73] An action that is wholly internal to a fiction cannot have effects outside the fiction; only an action that is external to the fiction can have real-world effects. It follows that Paul not only believes but also asserts that Adam and his sin are historical.

At first blush, Fitzmyer might seem to agree with this conclusion. He says, "Paul treats Adam as a historical human being, humanity's first parent, and

71. Moo, *Romans*, 368–69.

72. Moo, *Romans*, 372.

73. Carson's recognition that "Paul's reference to the time period from Adam to Moses (5:13–14) certainly presupposes a historical figure (i.e. Adam) at the beginning of the period" is thus at odds with his claim that the Pelagian view of sin's entering human history through Adam is "little affected if Adam is not a figure of history" ("Adam in the Epistles of Paul," 36).

contrasts him with the historical Jesus Christ. But in Genesis itself *ʾAdām* is a symbolic figure, denoting humanity. . . . Some commentators on Romans have tried to interpret *Adam* in this symbolic sense here . . . ; but that reading does violence to the contrast that Paul uses in this paragraph between Adam as 'one man' and Christ as 'one man,' which implies that Adam was a historical individual as much as was Jesus Christ. So Paul has historicized the symbolic Adam of Genesis."[74] It appears that Fitzmyer is affirming that, for Paul, Adam was a real person of history. In fact, however, Fitzmyer is still talking solely of the literary Adam and never exits the story world of Genesis. His claim is that in Genesis Adam is a symbolic figure; that is to say, Genesis is some sort of allegory. But, he says, Paul does not treat Genesis allegorically but as a story simply about an individual man. Fitzmyer confuses the issue by saying that Paul treats Adam as a historical human being. That sounds as if Paul is talking about someone who actually lived. But on Fitzmyer's view, Paul is still talking about truth-in-the-story, not truth. *In the story* Adam is on Paul's view a historical figure, not a symbolic figure. Paul has thus misinterpreted the literary Adam. Just as some commentators do violence to Rom 5:12–21 by interpreting Adam symbolically, so Paul does violence to Gen 2–3 by interpreting Adam literally.

That this understanding of Fitzmyer is correct is confirmed by his later, otherwise puzzling comments: "Above I distinguished 'Adam' in Genesis 2–3 as a symbolic figure from 'Adam' in 5:12–21 as a historical individual, or as a historicized individual, as he had already become in contemporary Jewish literature. Paul, however, knew nothing about the Adam of history. What he knows about Adam, he has derived from Genesis and the Jewish tradition that developed from Genesis. 'Adam' for Paul is *Adam in the Book of Genesis*; he is a literary individual, like Hamlet, but not symbolic, like Everyman."[75] Notice that Fitzmyer equates *a historical individual* with *a historicized individual*, an equation impossible for a real person. In Jewish literature Adam is said to have been already historicized; that is to say, the symbolic figure of Genesis had come to be taken literally. Similarly, for Paul, Adam is said to be *Adam in the Book of Genesis*, a literary figure like Hamlet. Hamlet, though an individual in the Shakespearean play, was not a real person. There was no Hamlet of history. But the literary figure of Hamlet is not a symbol, as is the figure of Everyman, but an individual. So also, in Fitzmyer's view, Adam in Paul's (mis)interpretation of the story of Genesis is an individual, not a symbol.

74. Fitzmyer, *Romans*, 407–8.
75. Fitzmyer, *Romans*, 410.

The reason that Fitzmyer says that Paul knew nothing of the Adam of history (the Adam, if any, outside the story) is that the story, *pace* Paul, is symbolic, not historical. Otherwise knowledge of the literary Adam could yield some knowledge of the Adam of history. No one reading Plutarch's *Lives*, for example, could be said to know nothing about the Pompey of history simply because his only source of knowledge of Pompey is the *Lives*. That is because the *Lives* belongs to a historical genre and the literary figure of Plutarch's Pompey corresponds well to the Pompey of history. The reason Paul's knowledge of the Adam of Genesis yields no knowledge of the Adam of history is that, in Fitzmyer's view, the stories in Genesis are about a purely symbolic figure and so are not of a historical genre.

It should be evident that the argument presented above for taking Paul to assert, not merely that the Adam-of-Genesis is an individual rather than a symbol, but that Adam was a real person of history is not defeated by Fitzmyer's claims. For our argument is not based on Paul's contrasting Adam with Christ, a literary figure with a person of history, but rather on the real-world causal effects of Adam's sin. It is impossible for Hamlet, though an individual in the play, to have real-world effects because he does not exist in the real world but exists only in the play (that is to say, in the play he—unlike, for instance, Macbeth's dagger—exists). Paul thus teaches that Adam was a real person of history.[76] Fitzmyer's further claim that Paul has no knowledge of the Adam of history on the basis of his knowledge of Genesis will depend on Fitzmyer's view that Genesis is purely symbolic, a view that sits ill with the genealogies that order the primaeval narratives, as we have seen, for the genealogies treat Adam and his descendants as real people. In that case one cannot rule out *a priori* the possibility of Paul's having some knowledge of the Adam of history on the basis of his knowledge of Genesis.

Conclusion

The several references by NT authors to mythological or pseudepigraphal figures caution us to avoid overly easy proofs of OT historicity on the basis of NT citations. Such figures may be merely literary and illustratively em-

76. Cf. Collins's pinpointing "the fatal flaw" in Dunn's view, which is similar to Fitzmyer's: "Someone did something, and as a result something happened, and then Jesus came to deal with the consequences of it all" (C. John Collins, "Responses to Chapter Four," in Charles, *Reading Genesis 1–2*, 137).

ployed. Similarly, some NT references to Adam and other figures and events of the primaeval history may describe merely the story world of Genesis, requiring at most truth-in-the-story. But in 1 Cor 15:21–22 and especially Rom 5:12–21 we do have clear assertions of the historicity of Adam. What is asserted of the historical Adam in these key passages does not, however, really go beyond what we have already affirmed on the basis of our genre analysis of the primaeval history of Gen 1–11—namely, that there was a progenitor of the entire human race through whose disobedience moral evil entered the world.

Whether we understand Paul to teach that Adam's sin was imputed to every one of his descendants, or that Adam's sin corrupted human nature and thus affected all of his progeny, or that Adam's sin opened the floodgates to sin, which then infected all who came after him, Adam is regarded by Paul as a historical person whose actions affected the course of history. We might prefer not to settle the question of how Adam's sin affects all mankind. Since Paul did not seek to explain this relationship, Dunn thinks that we should refrain as well. "The relationship between the one man's initial failure and all men's sin is not an issue to which Paul addresses himself, and the imprecision of the syntax forbids us to press for a clear-cut decision on the point."[77] This cautious advice is sensible for the biblical exegete, if not the systematic theologian; still it remains the case that Adam's sin is, in Paul's thinking, in some sense the fount of the sin and spiritual death that beset our world, which suffices for the affirmation of a historical Adam.

77. Dunn, *Romans 1–8,* 290; cf. Moo, *Romans,* 352, who sees a similar unresolved tension in other Jewish texts like *Apocalypse of Baruch* 23.4; 48.42; 54.19; 54.15; Pseudo-Philo, *Biblical Antiquities* 13.8, 9.

PART 3

Scientific Evidence and the Historical Adam

Chapter 8

SCIENTIFIC AND PHILOSOPHICAL PRELIMINARIES

If the biblical Adam is, or was, a historical person who actually lived, then the obvious question arises: *When* did he live? Given the mythical nature of the primaeval history of Gen 1–11, it is to modern science that we must turn in the attempt to answer this question. Now in one sense science has nothing to contribute positively with regard to this question, since it does not contemplate the existence of such a person. Nevertheless, contemporary scientists are vitally interested in a question that is empirically equivalent to our question—namely, when did human beings first appear in the evolutionary process?[1] In this part of the book we seek to summarize briefly the scientific evidence concerning human origins with a view toward determining approximately when human beings first began to exist. The historical Adam may then be located around that time.

The quest of the historical Adam brings together a surprising number of scientific fields united in a common quest of human origins, such as palaeontology, palaeoanthropology, palaeogenetics, palaeoneurology, palaeoproteomics, and, one is tempted to say, palaeoarchaeology (*really, really* old archaeology!). In order to discuss the question of human origins, we must first set the framework for modern science's treatment of the subject.

1. Francesco d'Errico and Chris B. Stringer report, "The question of the origin of the attributes that define us as humans is the subject of a lively debate among scholars from disciplines such as primatology, archaeology, paleoanthropology, genetics, evolutionary psychology and linguistics" ("Evolution, Revolution or Saltation Scenario for the Emergence of Modern Cultures?," *PTRSB* 366, no. 1567 [April 12, 2011]: 1060).

Timescales

We begin by looking at the various timescales involved.

Geological Timescale

In terms of the geological timescale (fig. 8.1), our discussion focuses on the third period of the Cenozoic era known as the Quaternary period, which began around 2.5 mya (million years ago) and continues through the present.

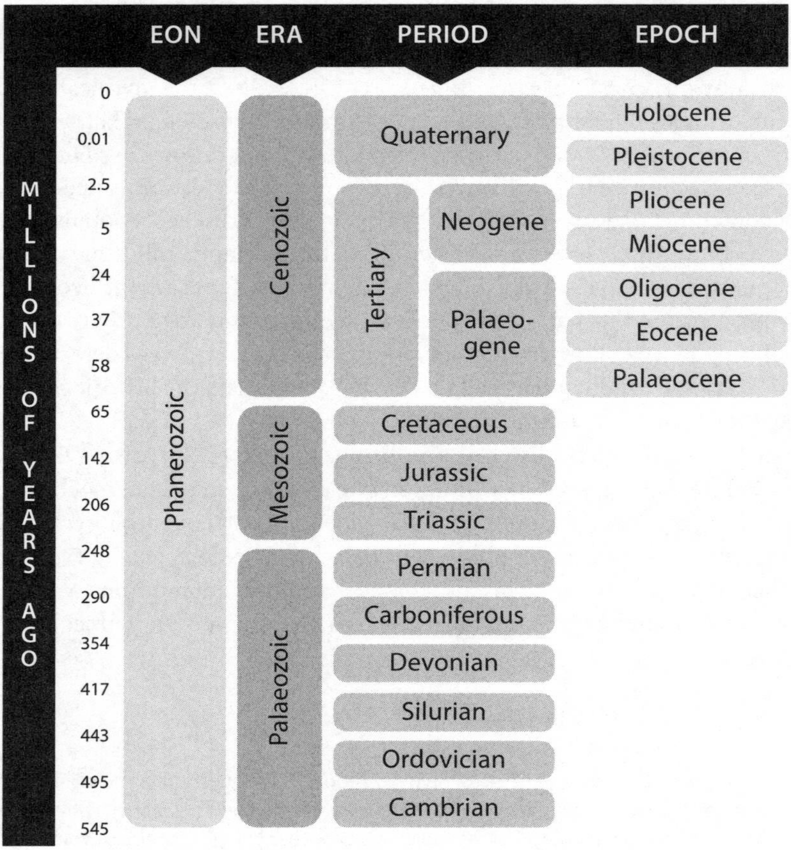

Figure 8.1. Geological ages relevant to our investigation. Based on Stringer and Andrews, *The Complete World of Human Evolution*, 27.

The Quaternary period is divided into two subintervals, the Pleistocene epoch, dating from around 2.5 mya until around 12 kya (thousand years ago), and the Holocene epoch, dating from the close of the last major glaciation around 12 kya until today. It will be during the Pleistocene epoch that the origins of the human race are to be sought.

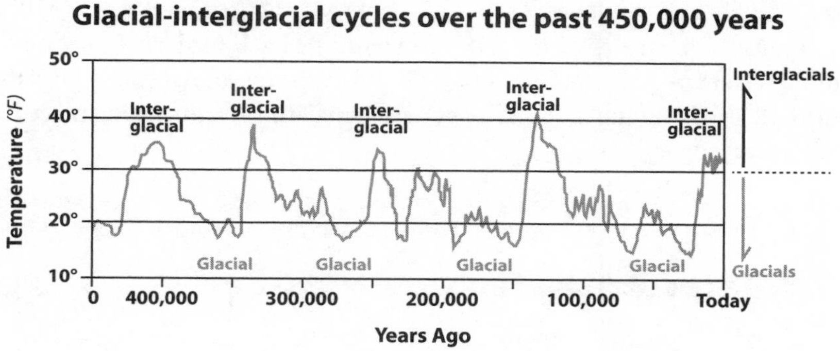

Figure 8.2. Glacial and interglacial cycles over the past 450,000 years. Based on Sandy Eldredge and Bob Biek, "Glad You Asked: Ice Ages—What Are They and What Causes Them?," *Survey Notes* 42 (2010), https://geology.utah.gov/map-pub/survey-notes/glad-you-asked/ice-ages-what-are-they-and-what-causes-them/.

The Pleistocene is the epoch popularly known as the Ice Age, during which a series of glacial expansions (called glacials) and recursions (called interglacials) occurred, each lasting several thousand years (fig. 8.2).[2] We are ourselves living in an interglacial within the ongoing ice age, which is actually the most recent of a series of at least five such ice ages in Earth's history.

The ice age of the Pleistocene epoch periodically covered much of northern Europe and Asia in mile-thick ice, forcing human beings in those regions to adapt to and endure the bitterly cold and harsh climate. The glacial and interglacial periods have been assigned many different names in different

2. These are thought to follow so-called Milankovitch cycles, which are determined by the coincidence of changes in the shape of the earth's orbit, the tilt of the earth's axis, and the earth's distance from the sun. These cycles correlate with the Marine Isotope Stages mentioned in the text.

geographic locales. Particularly important for our purposes will be the Riss (180 kya–130 kya) and Würm (70 kya–10 kya) glaciations in the Alpine region of Europe.

The timeline of the glacial and interglacial stages is calculated by oxygen isotope samples extracted from the seabed. By comparing the ratio between ^{16}O and ^{18}O (oxygen with an atomic mass of 16 or 18, respectively), palaeoclimatologists are able to chronicle the glacials and interglacials, high levels of ^{18}O corresponding to glacial stages and high levels of ^{16}O to interglacials. One can thus enumerate successive Marine Isotope Stages (MIS) beginning in the present with MIS 1 and working backward, such that odd-numbered stages represent interglacials and even-numbered stages glacials (fig. 8.3). The MIS timescales are often used in dating events taking place in the Pleistocene epoch.

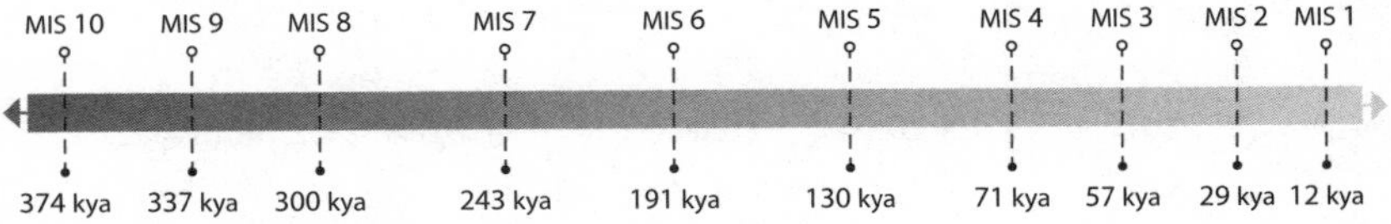

Figure 8.3. Start dates of the most recent Marine Isotope Stages.

Thus, if archaeologists say that an artifact dates from MIS 6, we understand that they mean between 191 kya and 130 kya.

Archaeological Timescales

To complicate matters further, archaeologists have developed a different framework for prehistory on the basis of the manufacture of various stone tools. These so-called lithic industries record the progression in the sophistication of stone tools over millions of years. Unfortunately, archaeologists have not used uniform terminology to describe the timelines in Eurasia and Africa. In Eurasia and North Africa, the earliest period is called the Palaeolithic, the intermediate period the Mesolithic, and the most recent period the Neolithic. Within this chronological framework the adjective *lower* is further used to indicate an earlier subinterval, while *upper* indicates a more recent subinterval—for example, the Upper Palaeolithic. In sub-Saharan Africa, the Palaeolithic is called the Stone Age, which is subdivided into the

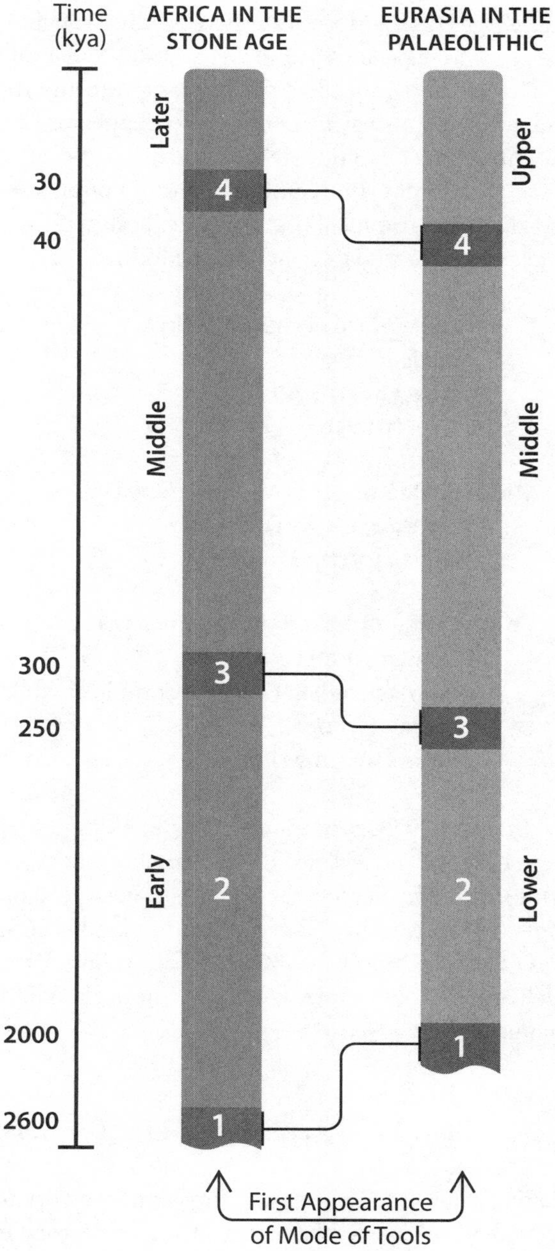

Figure 8.4. Comparison of archaeological ages in Africa and Eurasia. Numbers indicate successive modes of toolmaking.

Early Stone Age (ESA), the Middle Stone Age (MSA), and finally the Later Stone Age (LSA). Moreover, there is only a rough correspondence between the respective periods in Eurasia and sub-Saharan Africa (see fig. 8.4).

Our interest is in the African Stone Age and the Eurasian Palaeolithic, which run all the way from the earliest appearance of stone tools around 2.5 mya until the end of the Pleistocene epoch. Because invention of tools took place at different times among scattered populations, local tool industries are given geographical place-names. Some of the more well-known, with approximate start dates, include the following:

Upper Palaeolithic (50 kya–10 kya)
Gravettian (33 kya)
Aurignacian (37 kya)
Châtelperronian (43 kya)

Middle Palaeolithic (300 kya–50 kya)
Mousterian (160 kya)
Levallois (300 kya)

Lower Palaeolithic (2.5 mya–300 kya)
Clactonian (300 kya)
Acheulo-Yabrudian Cultural Complex (350 kya)
Acheulean (1.7 mya)
Oldowan (>2.5 mya)

There are five broad modes of toolmaking associated with these periods from earliest to latest: (1) Oldowan: chopping tools (ESA, Lower Palaeolithic); (2) Acheulean: bifaces (ESA, Lower Palaeolithic); (3) prepared core tools (MSA, Middle Palaeolithic); (4) blades (LSA, Upper Palaeolithic); and (5) microliths (LSA, Mesolithic). An important question will be what such stone tools enable us to infer about the cognitive capacities of their manufacturers and users.

Palaeoanthropological Classifications

Having established the chronological framework for our investigation, we now need to say a word about the classificatory framework of palaeoanthropology. Roger Lewin and Robert Foley explain that the new genetics

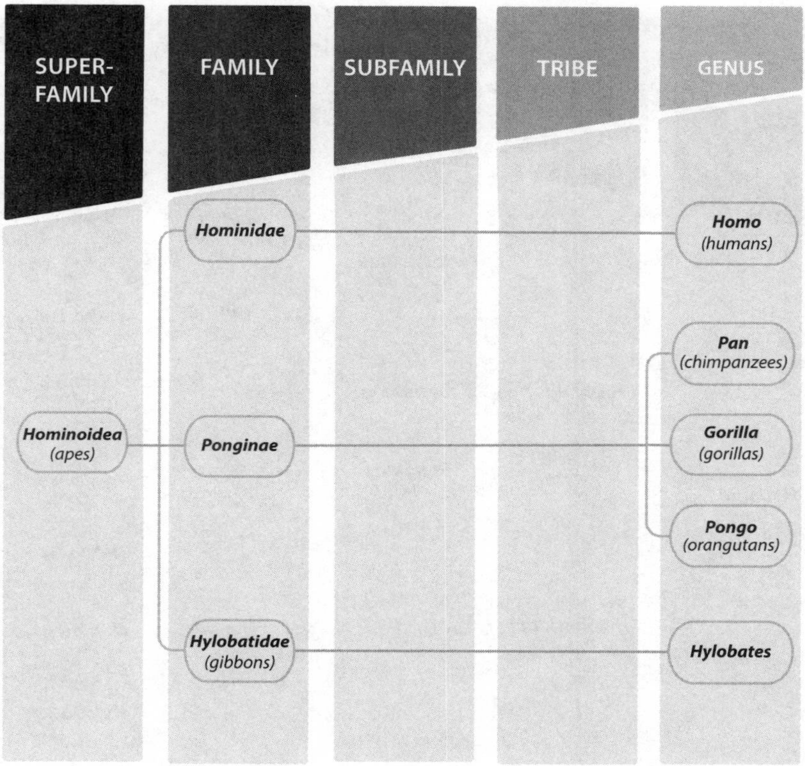

Figure 8.5. Traditional classification of apes and humans.

has overthrown the traditional classificatory scheme that subdivided the superfamily Hominoidea into three families: Hylobatidae (gibbons and siamangs), Pongidae (orangutans, gorillas, and chimpanzees), and Hominidae (humans) (fig. 8.5).[3]

This classification, claim Lewin and Foley, links together too closely the modern great apes, when in fact chimpanzees are more closely related to humans than to orangutans and gorillas. So the better classification, while leaving the Hylobatidae intact, would subdivide the family Hominidae into

3. Roger Lewin and Robert A. Foley, *Principles of Human Evolution*, 2nd ed. (Oxford: Blackwell, 2004), 211.

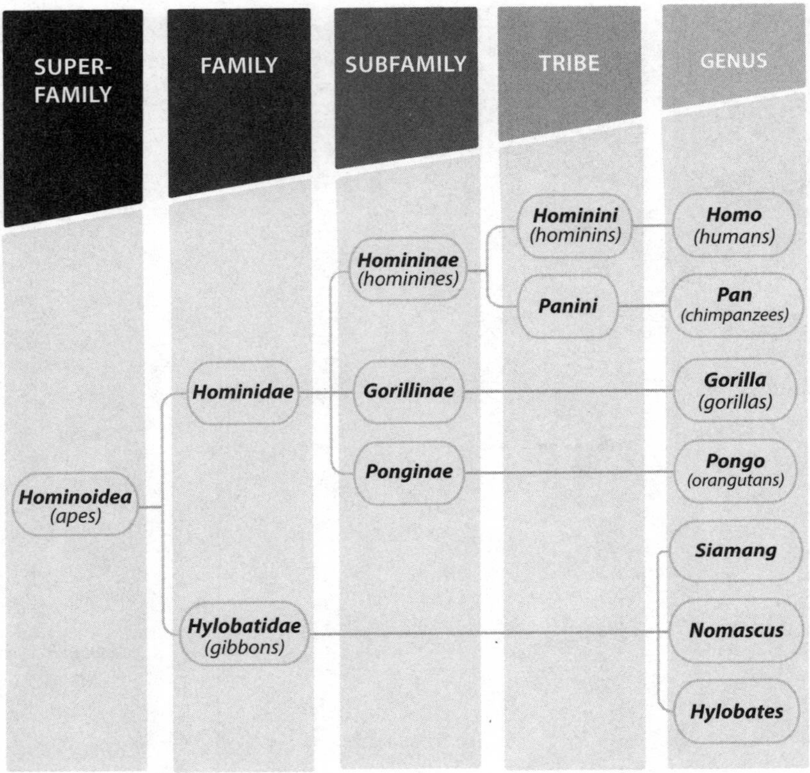

Figure 8.6. Revised classification of apes and humans.

the Ponginae (orangutans), Gorillinae (gorillas), and Homininae, which comprises both Panini (chimpanzees) and Hominini (humans) (fig. 8.6).[4]

It would be nice to have English equivalents of these Latin terms. Lewin and Foley refer to the Hominoidea as hominoids, the Hominidae as hominids, the Homininae as hominines, and the Hominini as hominins. We shall adopt this vocabulary.[5]

4. A somewhat different classification distinguishes between Hominini (chimpanzees and humans) and Hominina (humans).

5. But it deserves to be emphasized just how biologically uninformative such a classificatory schema is. On this schema, to be a hominin is to be on the lineage eventually leading to modern man, whereas to be a paninin is to be on the lineage eventually leading

But an important point of clarification remains. While the genus *Homo* may include today the only representative of the hominins, in the past there were members of another genus, *Australopithecus*, bipedal apes that most palaeoanthropologists assume to be hominins, part of the lineage leading to modern humans (*Homo sapiens*) after its divergence about 5–6 mya from the lineage leading to modern chimpanzees.[6] Moreover, there were other

---

to modern chimpanzees. The two lineages are thought to have diverged from a last common ancestor about 5–6 mya.

> If the divergence is just the separation of two populations (divided by the Rift Valley, for example), and it was only much later that there was any actual change in the morphology, then a hominin would be indistinguishable in the fossil record from the last common ancestor. In other words, if the divergence did not involve a substantial evolutionary change, then a hominin would remain invisible in the fossil record for as long as it takes for drift or selection to produce novelties that we now associate with humans—and there is no reason why this might not have occurred only several million years later. (Lewin and Foley, *Principles of Human Evolution*, 253)

Worse, on this scenario a hominin may be literally the same sort of organism as one living on the other side of the valley that is not a hominin, which seems perverse. The two organisms are perfectly similar, and all that distinguishes them is the future destiny of their lineages.

So Lewin and Foley muse that "a more practical approach" is to say that a hominin can be recognized from its having present-day (or derived) hominin features such as bipedalism, large brains, small faces, reduced canine teeth, and so on. Now all of these derived features or characters are unlikely to have evolved simultaneously. So bipedalism, as a very complex adaption, is currently thought to be the most diagnostic and significant evidence for the presence of the hominin lineage. On this view bipedalism or other derived characters serve merely as *evidence* of an organism's being a hominin but do not constitute it a hominin. But Lewin and Foley report, "The current position is therefore that hominins are defined by bipedalism, and this is the feature to seek traces of in the fossil material. But if it is not present, that would not . . . necessarily mean that the fossil is not a hominin, merely that we have yet to define what the earliest changes were" (*Principles of Human Evolution*, 253). This position is unfortunately self-contradictory. If hominins are *defined* by bipedalism, rather than merely *identified* by it, then it is impossible that a nonbipedal organism was a hominin. Thus, we seem stuck with the perverse consequences of the current classificatory schema and must accept that early paninins and hominins may actually be the same organisms and so accept the invisibility of early hominins in the fossil record. Lewin and Foley note that the problem becomes even more intractable because there is evidence that bipedalism may not be unique to hominins but may have evolved independently more than once, which undermines even its diagnostic value.

6. The expression "human ancestors" is thus ambiguous and may be misleading. Aus-

species of *Homo* about at various times, such as *Homo habilis*, *Homo erectus*, and, perhaps the most well known, *Homo neanderthalensis*, or Neanderthals. So hominins would include both Australopithecines of various species and various species of *Homo*.

None of these classificatory categories should be equated *tout court* with the natural kind *human being*.[7] We have therefore avoided translating "*Homo*" as "human" or "man." In figure 8.7 we see illustrated various members of the hominin lineage going all the way back to *Sahelanthropus tchadensis*, an apelike creature near the beginning of our lineage.[8] The last common ancestor of chimps and humans has not yet been identified.

Notice that the species classed as *Homo* in figure 8.7 should not be automatically regarded as "humans," in contrast to early hominins and Australopithecines. Such a designation is simplistic and misleading. Ian Tattersall of the American Museum of Natural History explains that the lumping of fossil forms into either *Australopithecus* or *Homo* is the result of historical accident. When Carl Linnaeus formulated the traditional classification, there were no hominids other than *Homo*, and so when other primitive fossil forms began to be discovered they were classed as primitive species of *Homo*. The Australopithecines were classed as *Homo transvaalensis* and thought to have evolved into *Homo erectus* and finally into *Homo sapiens*. Tattersall complains, "Lumping this huge variety of hominids into the single genus *Homo* was an act of systematic extremism that in practice made it impossible to characterize the human genus in either anatomical or behavioral terms. Yet the paleoanthropologists capitulated instantly." Although palaeo-

tralopithecines may be said to be human ancestors in the sense that they are (nonhuman) ancestors of humans, but they are not human ancestors in the sense that they are among our ancestors that were human.

7. Ian Tattersall notes that "human" can be taken in either an exclusive or inclusive sense. The inclusive sense (used by Lewin and Foley) means "being related to us by descent"; the exclusive sense applies only to creatures with all the qualities that distinguish us from the rest of the living world. Tattersall muses that these two senses of the word are clearly in conflict. An early member of our lineage need not have possessed any of the qualities of the mind that we see as unique to ourselves (Ian Tattersall, *The Fossil Trail: How We Know What We Think We Know about Human Evolution*, 2nd ed. [Oxford: Oxford University Press, 2009], 70). Although Tattersall says that the inclusive sense of "human" requires that an organism possess only one or two of the anatomical novelties that *Homo sapiens* has acquired, Lewin and Foley's scenario in the earlier note (see note 5) reveals that even that much is not required.

8. Cf. Louise Humphrey and Chris Stringer, *Our Human Story* (London: Natural History Museum, 2018), 18–19, for a similar chart.

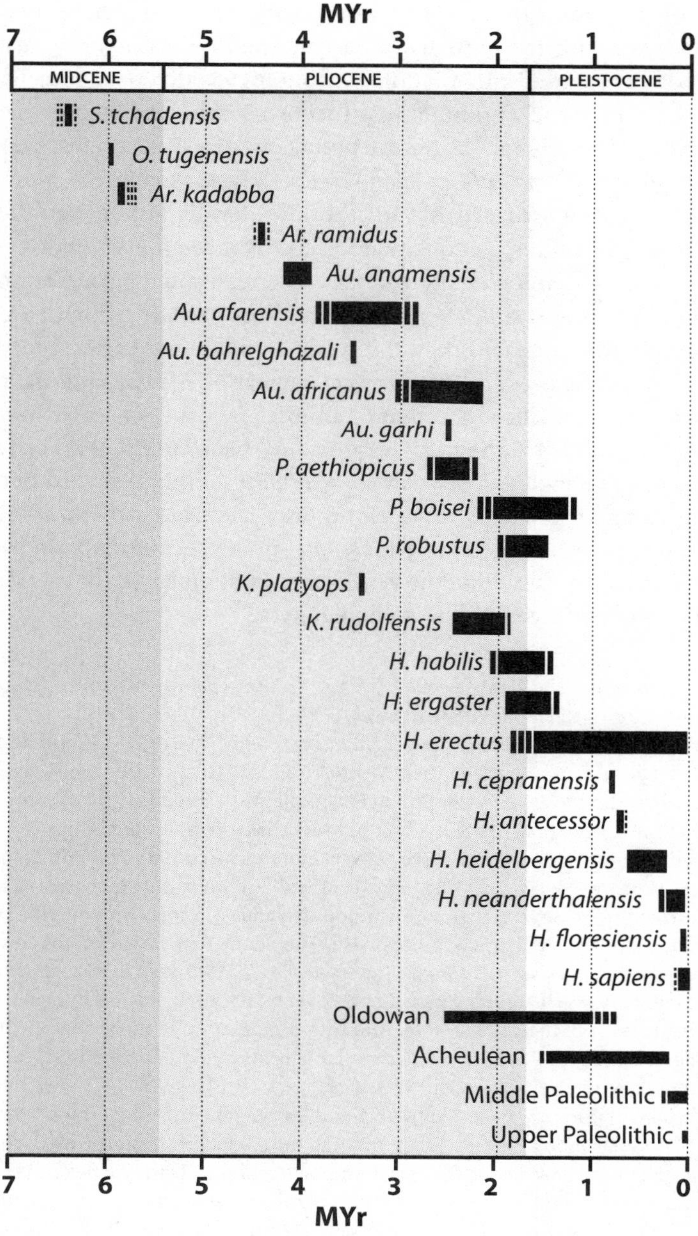

Figure 8.7. Hominin lineages back to *Sahelanthropus tchadensis*. Based on Ian Tattersall, *The Fossil Trail*.

anthropologists came to recognize *Australopithecus* as a distinct genus, "the problem lay in the attempt to divide early hominids into *Homo* vs australopiths, rather than admitting that the morphological diversity actually seen way back into the early hominid fossil record would best be organized by recognizing more genera."[9] Tattersall points out that the early forms classed as *Homo*, such as *Homo habilis*, *Homo erectus*, *Homo rudolfensis*, and so on, all have in common remarkably small brains, hardly larger than those of the Australopithecines, in conspicuous contrast to *Homo sapiens*, which has a brain more than twice the volume. Although some palaeoanthropologists have proposed that *Homo* be limited only to forms that resemble more closely *Homo sapiens* than the Australopithecines, this "sage advice has been widely ignored."[10] The recent classification of *Homo naledi*, a creature with a brain smaller than that of almost any other claimed *Homo*, illustrates the problem. "The main lesson *naledi* has to teach us is the futility of trying to divide what is now a very extensive hominid record between australopiths and *Homo*. There is a lot more systematic structure—a more complex geometry of species relationships—in this record than can usefully be characterized by bundling the very diverse assemblage of hominids now known into one of two predetermined genera."[11]

9. Ian Tattersall, "The Genus *Homo*," *Inference* 2, no. 1 (February 2016), https://inference-review.com/article/the-genus-homo.

10. Tattersall, "Genus *Homo*." Tattersall has reference to Bernard Wood and Mark Collard's proposal that membership in *Homo* requires that any candidate species (1) is more closely related to *Homo sapiens* than it is to the Australopiths; (2) has a body mass closer to *Homo sapiens* than to the Australopiths; (3) has reconstructed body proportions that match those of *Homo sapiens* more closely than those of the Australopiths; (4) has a postcranial skeleton consistent with modern humanlike bipedality; (5) has teeth and jaws closer in size to *Homo sapiens* than to Australopiths; and (6) shows a modern humanlike extended growth and development life phase. They deny that *Homo habilis* and *Homo rudolfensis* should be classed as *Homo* (Tattersall, *Fossil Trail*, 271). Having rejected this advice, "scientists are still arguing vehemently over which ancient fossil human relatives should be included in the genus *Homo*. And they are doing so in the absence of any coherent idea of what the genus that includes our species *Homo sapiens* might reasonably be presumed to contain" (Tattersall, "Genus *Homo*").

11. Tattersall, "Genus *Homo*." Schwartz and Tattersall conclude, "If we want to be objective, we shall almost certainly have to scrap the iconic list of names in which hominin fossil specimens have historically been trapped, and start from the beginning by hypothesizing morphs, building testable theories of relatedness, and rethinking genera and species" (Jeffrey H. Schwartz and Ian Tattersall, "Defining the Genus *Homo*," *Science* 349, no. 6251 [August 28, 2015]: 932).

What Is It to Be Human?

With the above frameworks in mind, we propose to survey some of the scientific evidence from a variety of fields concerning the most likely date of human origins. But first we must figure out exactly what we are looking for.

We have seen that it would be rash to assume that organisms classified as *Homo* are *ipso facto* human beings. Rather, we need to specify certain conditions that are jointly sufficient for humanity. There is, in fact, a noteworthy consensus among scientists as to what these conditions are. We are, after all, familiar with ourselves as human beings and therefore know what a paradigmatic human being is like.

Sufficient Conditions for Humanness

We know, for example, that any putative human being must be anatomically similar to ourselves. While a self-conscious, rational extraterrestrial (or even chimpanzee) would be a person, he would not be a *human* person. This necessary condition of humanness need not involve an exact anatomical match. There is a range of anatomical differences even between modern and archaic *Homo sapiens*, as we shall see, that do not count against the humanity of the latter. By contrast, no one thinks that given their significant anatomical differences to modern man, Australopithecines, for example, were human beings, despite their having some shared features with humans.[12] They were bipedal

12. The presence of shared physical features (so-called characters) cannot in any case be assumed to indicate even an evolutionary connection between hominin forms, much less their humanity, for environmental factors could drive the independent evolution of certain features—for example, of reduced dentition or gracile skeletal structure—so that the similarities are homoplasies (similar features resulting from convergent evolution). According to Robert Foley, among hominids "very large numbers of characters evolved convergently in different lineages, both closely and distantly related," so that convergence is "a common and normal part of the evolutionary process for hominids" ("Striking Parallels in Early Hominid Evolution," *TEE* 8, no. 6 [June 1993]: 197; cf. Randall R. Skelton and Henry M. McHenry, "Evolutionary Relationships among Early Hominids," *JHE* 23, no. 4 [October 1992]: 309–49, who construct a phylogenetic tree of hominin evolution on the basis of seventy-seven traits that are frequently homoplastic; John G. Fleagle, "Beyond Parsimony," *EA* 6, no. 1 [1997]: 1, who complains that Ockham's razor is pretty dull when the most parsimonious tree has 45 percent homoplasy). For example, *Australopithecus sediba* shares humanlike features in its lower body and hands that "are likely to have developed independently of the processes that produced early *Homo* in East Africa, showing

apes of various sorts with tiny brains (around 460 cubic centimeters [cm^3]) that could not have supported modern human behavior. The question remains as to the degree of anatomical variation that would be permissible for a human being. For example, brow ridges would hardly seem sufficient to disqualify a species of *Homo* from being reckoned human,[13] but a small braincase plausibly would, given the correlation between brain size and cognitive capacity.

On the basis of our paradigmatic examples of humans, we can delineate certain features that, given sufficient anatomical similarity, are sufficient (if not necessary) for human personhood. What are some of these features? Anthropologists Sally McBrearty and Alison Brooks list four characteristics of modern human behavior:

- abstract thinking, the ability to act with reference to abstract concepts not limited in time or space
- planning depth, the ability to formulate strategies on the basis of past experience and to act on them in a group context
- behavioral, economic, and technological innovativeness
- symbolic behavior, the ability to represent objects, people, and abstract concepts with arbitrary symbols, vocal or visual, and to reify such symbols in cultural practice[14]

McBrearty and Brooks observe that the standards for behavioral modernity that they apply "are universally recognized and are frequently repeated in the literature."[15]

---

that selection may have been driving the evolution of 'human' traits in different species at this time" (Humphrey and Stringer, *Our Human Story*, 94; cf. Andrew Du and Zeresenay Alemseged, "Temporal Evidence Shows *Australopithecus sediba* Is Unlikely to Be the Ancestor of *Homo*," *SA* 5 [May 2019], eaav9038, https://doi.org/10.1126/sciadv.aav9038). What is important with respect to determining humanity is that a certain minimum brain size is a necessary condition for a hominin to be counted as human.

13. The fossil skulls discovered at Muhharet es-Skhūl, Israel, are regarded by most experts as essentially modern, despite their having distinct brow ridges (Tattersall, *Fossil Trail*, 82). Even contemporary humans may have brow ridges, and they differ from archaic *Homo sapiens* in this respect only by having a tiny notch in those ridges called the superorbital foramen—hardly grounds for disqualification from the human race!

14. Sally McBrearty and Alison S. Brooks, "The Revolution That Wasn't: A New Interpretation of the Origin of Modern Human Behavior," *JHE* 39, no. 5 (November 2000): 492.

15. McBrearty and Brooks, "Revolution That Wasn't," 534. Francesco d'Errico questions the criteria Brooks and McBrearty used to find these criteria. He expresses concern

It is worth pausing to underline the fact that McBrearty and Brooks are not offering anatomical conditions for biological humanness but philosophical conditions for human personhood. To see the sufficiency of these characteristics for human personhood, one has only to ask oneself whether a mere beast could exhibit all these sorts of behavior. Although some glimmerings of some of these behaviors, such as behavioral and technological innovativeness, might appear among nonhuman animals, they will pale next to the degree to which they are found among modern humans, and the combination of all four behaviors would remain unprecedented. To deny the humanity of past individuals anatomically similar to modern humans who exhibited such behaviors would be problematic because (1) it is implausible to think that such behaviors did not require the cognitive capacities of human beings and (2) to deny the humanity of past individuals exhibiting such behavior would permit one similarly to deny the humanity of people living today who share such behavior, which is not only implausible but morally unconscionable.

The more difficult question is whether we can discern when such behaviors first appear in the prehistorical record. Even if we can, it is useful to remember that signs of such behavior give us only the *latest* date at which humanity came on the scene, not the earliest, and provide an indication of only the *minimum* level of cognitive capacity of persons exhibiting that behavior, not the maximum level of their cognitive ability.[16]

---

that the criteria are inspired by African MSA and European Upper Palaeolithic material culture, thus courting "the danger of creating a theory that fits one's expectation" ("The Invisible Frontier: A Multiple Species Model for the Origin of Behavioral Modernity," *EA* 12, no. 4 [August 5, 2003]: 188–202, https://doi.org/10.1002/evan.10113. But d'Errico conflates McBrearty and Brooks's sufficient conditions of humanness with the archaeological signatures of such behaviors (to be discussed below). Only the latter are based on Upper Palaeolithic and LSA features; the modern behaviors they identify are surely not culture-specific but universal. In any case, d'Errico uses these same criteria to show that the African MSA material culture and the contemporary material culture left by Neanderthals in Europe and the Near East exhibit "no dramatic differences . . . between the two records," thereby rendering his expressed hesitations academic.

16. Thus, we should not interpret McBrearty and Brooks to be endorsing what Kim Sterelny calls a "simple reflection model," according to which modern human cognitive capacity is immediately reflected in the archaeological record; rather, their results are consistent with a "niche construction model," according to which the archaeological signatures of modern human behaviors do not emerge until humans have so shaped their environment that such signatures become selectively advantageous (Kim Sterelny, "From Hominins to Humans: How *sapiens* Became Behaviourally Modern," *PTRSB* 366, no. 1566 [March 27, 2011]: 809–22, https://doi.org/10.1098/rstb.2010.0301). According to Lewin and Foley, for an increasing number of archaeologists, the evidence reveals a gradual

Terminus a Quo *and* Terminus ad Quem *for Humanity*

We can set boundaries of our quest for human origins by establishing a *terminus a quo* and a *terminus ad quem* for the first appearance of human beings. How far back can the first appearance of humans be extended? Palaeontological evidence continues to push *Homo sapiens* further and further into the past. The hominin fossils of Jebel Irhoud in Morocco are the earliest fossils of *Homo sapiens* discovered to date.[17] Layer 7 of the excavation contained the remains of at least five individuals (three adults, one adolescent, and one child). The brain volume of these individuals was large, between 1,300 and 1,400 cm^3, comparable to that of modern man (1,100–1,500 cm^3). With an age of 315 ± 34 thousand years (as determined by thermoluminescence dating), Jebel Irhoud is the oldest and richest MSA hominin site to document early stages of the *Homo sapiens* lineage in which key features of modern morphology were established. Although there are differences in the cranial shape of these archaic humans compared to modern humans, specifically their elongated braincase and heavy brow ridges, the excavating archaeologists emphasize that already 300 kya "their facial morphology is almost indistinguishable from that of R[ecent] M[odern] H[umans], corroborating the interpretation of the fragmentary specimen from Florisbad (South Africa) as a primitive *H. sapiens* tentatively dated to 260 ka."[18] Moreover, mandibular and dental morphology, as well as the slow pattern of dental development, also align the fossils of Jebel Irhoud with anatomically modern humans. The

---

emergence of modern human behavior. Once it passed a certain threshold, that behavior appears to have exploded, producing the rich fabric of social complexity associated with the Upper Palaeolithic and LSA. "That explosion was a cultural change, however, not a biological one" (Lewin and Foley, *Principles of Human Evolution*, 439). For more on niche construction, see Kevin N. Laland, *Darwin's Unfinished Symphony: How Culture Made the Human Mind* (Princeton: Princeton University Press, 2017), chap. 9: "Gene-Culture Coevolution"; Agustín Fuentes, *The Creative Spark: How Imagination Made Humans Exceptional* (New York: Dutton, 2017).

17. J. J. Hublin et al., "New Fossils from Jebel Irhoud, Morocco and the Pan-African Origin of *Homo sapiens*," *Nature* 546, no. 7657 (June 8, 2017): 289–92, https://doi.org/10.1038/nature22336. See also Daniel Richter et al., who call the remains associated with Jebel Irhoud "the oldest reported for *H. sapiens*" ("The Age of the Hominin Fossils from Jebel Irhoud, Morocco, and the Origins of the Middle Stone Age," *Nature* 546, no. 7657 [June 8, 2017]: 293–96, https://doi.org/10.1038/nature22335).

18. Hublin et al., "New Fossils from Jebel Irhoud." For a striking photo array of *Homo sapiens* skulls dating from 300 kya to 100 kya and exhibiting a marked variety of shapes and sizes, see Humphrey and Stringer, *Our Human Story*, 137.

contemporaneous presence of similar individuals at two ends of the African continent implies that *Homo sapiens* had become widespread by that time and so may have originated a hundred thousand years earlier. While such skeletal remains alone may not prove the humanity of such individuals, they make it at least possible that human beings date back to over 300 kya.

But what shall we say about earlier forms of *Homo*? Despite being classified as *Homo*, so-called *Homo habilis* was, as mentioned, almost certainly not human, given its brain size of 550–687 cm^3.[19] Many palaeoanthropologists would have it renamed *Australopithecus habilis*. Since it is the earliest species of *Homo*, dating to around 2 mya, we already have a *terminus a quo* for the origin of humanity. Human beings, according to the evidence, do not date as far back as *Homo habilis*. The same can probably be said with respect to the poorly attested *Homo rudolfensis*, a contemporary of *Homo habilis* that had a brain size estimated at 526–700 cm^3 and that may not even be a distinct species.

Louise Humphrey and Chris Stringer caution that the diversity of hominin fossil remains dating around 2 mya complicates the question of human origins. "Are we defined by our small jaws and teeth, our large brain, our long legs, habitual tool-making and meat-eating, or some combination of these or other traits?" they ask. "If we require the combined presence of several traits to recognize a fossil as human, many of these early *Homo* specimens are simply too incomplete to make a confident diagnosis, and that is true overall until we arrive at the more complete remains and behavioral evidence of *Homo erectus*."[20] So long as we have fossil skulls of specimens of early *Homo* (and *Australopithecus*), however, the incompleteness of the skeletal remains does not prevent a negative diagnostic judgment excluding a specimen as human on the basis of inadequate brain size.

When we come to *Homo erectus*, the picture becomes less clear, especially given the lengthy history and geographical spread of this particular homi-

19. Its classification as *Homo* was due to the historical accident that its discoverer, Louis Leakey, was enamored with Kenneth Oakley's notion of "Man the Toolmaker," a notion now abandoned by palaeoanthropologists in view of Australopithecine (not to mention modern apes') manufacture and use of tools. *Homo habilis* is associated with Oldowan tools.

20. Humphrey and Stringer, *Our Human Story*, 94. They note the further complication that the different supposed "*Homo*" lineages "could . . . have evolved in parallel from separate australopith-like ancestors," in which case the members of these lineages "cannot all justifiably be assigned to the one genus *Homo*" (94). Humphrey and Stringer implicitly reject polygenesis of the human race, as do most scientists today, given the enormous improbability of multiple origins of the same interbreeding species.

nin. Specimens have been found throughout Asia and Africa over a span of nearly one and a half million years from around 2 mya, thus permitting a plethora of identifiable subspecies. It is possible that some late-developing member of the species might be arguably human, even if more primitive members are not. For example, the very early fossils of *Homo erectus* from Dmanisi, Georgia, have a brain volume of only about 600 cm^3, whereas later specimens from Java reach 1,100 cm^3, touching the lower bound of modern *Homo sapiens* (1,100–1,500 cm^3). By the time we get to *Homo heidelbergensis* and *Homo neanderthalensis*, brain sizes are large enough (1,100–1,400 cm^3 and 1,200–1,750 cm^3, respectively) to support human personhood, the brain volume of Neanderthals in fact exceeding that of *Homo sapiens*, whose brain size has actually been shrinking over the last ten thousand years. So *Homo erectus* provides a *terminus a quo* for the origin of human beings.

As for a *terminus ad quem*, the beautiful cave art from the Upper Palaeolithic found, for example, at Lascaux (17 kya) (fig. 8.8) and Chauvet (30 kya) (fig. 8.9) in France was undoubtedly created by human beings.

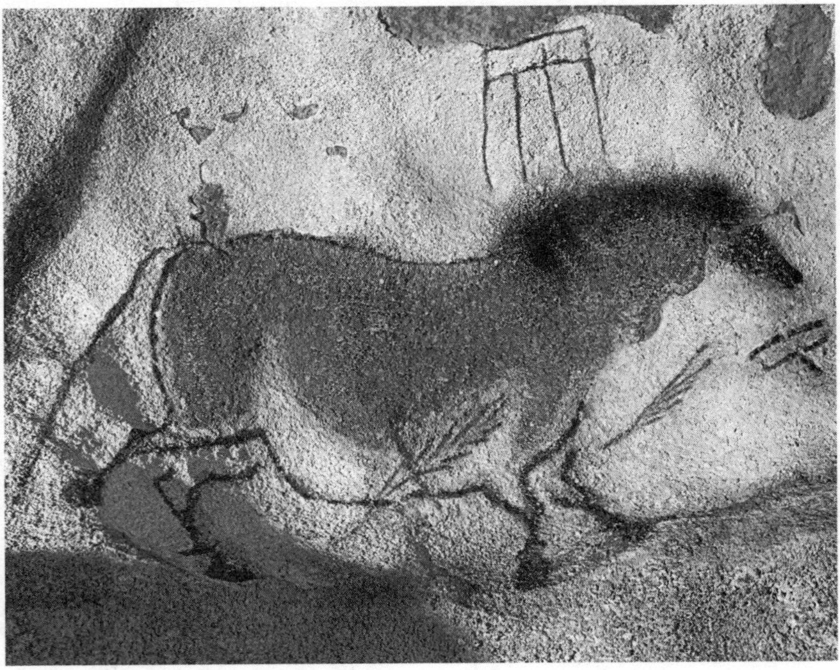

Figure 8.8. Cave painting of a horse from Lascaux, France. Photo courtesy of N. Aujoulat, Ministère de la Culture et de la Communication, France.

Figure 8.9. Cave drawing of a pride of lions from Chauvet, France. Photo courtesy of N. Aujoulat, Ministère de la Culture et de la Communication, France.

Indeed, there is a numinous quality about these paintings that takes one's breath away. Viewing these paintings, we sense ourselves standing in the presence of a "thou," someone who is one of us. The hand stencils, which are among the oldest forms of cave art yet discovered (fig. 8.10), seem almost to be reaching out across the millennia to touch us.

It is universally recognized that the persons who produced such art possessed symbolic thought so as to be able to represent real animals and scenes via painted images. Any attempt therefore to date the origin of human persons later than the earliest time of such cave art is excluded, thus giving us a *terminus ad quem* for the origin of humanity.[21]

21. To see these and other stunning cave paintings in color, go to https://images.google.com and search for "Lascaux cave paintings," "Chauvet cave paintings," or "cave art from Sulawesi."

Figure 8.10. Hand stencils from Sulawesi, Indonesia, dated 35–40 kya. Photograph by Cahyo Ramadhani. Representations of animals are also found nearby.

Summary and Prospect

Human beings, in the full sense of organisms anatomically similar to ourselves and capable of abstract thought; deep planning; behavioral, economic, and technological innovativeness; and symbolic behavior, therefore originated on this planet sometime between the Lower and Middle Palaeolithic (or ESA and MSA). By pushing these boundaries inward, if we can, we now want to try to determine the point of this origin more closely. We shall begin with the evidence of palaeoneurology concerning brain size and development among ancient hominins and then turn to an examination of some of the most noteworthy archaeological discoveries bearing on the origin of modern cognitive capacities.

Chapter 9

THE EVIDENCE OF PALAEONEUROLOGY

We open our review of the scientific evidence for the date of human origins by examining the evidence from the budding field of palaeoneurology, which is the study of the evolution of the human brain.

Palaeontology

Especially relevant to palaeoneurology is palaeontology, which studies the fossil remains of ancient hominins. The major part of palaeoneurology involves the analysis of endocasts or molds of the inside surface of fossil skulls.

Cranial Endocasts

"Brain endocasts from fossil hominin crania can yield important information regarding brain size, possible brain to body relationships, and brain structure and organization"—"despite the paucity of that information."[1] There is a general appreciation that in primate evolution larger brains and larger ratios of brain to body size (encephalization quotient, or EQ) are correlated with higher cognitive skills.[2] Increasing brain size is correlated with an in-

1. Nicholas Toth and Kathy Schick, "Hominin Brain Reorganization, Technological Change, and Cognitive Complexity," in *The Human Brain Evolving: Paleoneurological Studies in Honor of Ralph L. Holloway*, ed. Douglas Broadfield et al., SAIPS 4 (Gosport, IN: Stone Age Institute Press, 2010), 294, with the caveat from Ralph L. Holloway, "The Human Brain Evolving: A Personal Retrospective," in Broadfield et al., *Human Brain Evolving*, 8.

2. Toth and Schick, "Hominin Brain Reorganization," 295. The encephalization quotient is the ratio of a species' brain size divided by the average brain size of a mammal with

creasingly complex behavioral repertoire that includes complex tool use, symbolic thought and language, and artistic expression.[3]

"The increase in size of the human brain over human evolution," notes P. T. Schoenemann, "is one of the most extensively and clearly documented changes of any species so far documented in the fossil record."[4] During the three million years of hominin evolution, brain volume has undergone around a threefold increase. Given the tremendous costs associated with an increase in hominin brain tissue,[5] there must have been considerable advantages in terms of cognitive capacity attending this increase. As brains increase in size, areas of the brain are increasingly able to carry out processing independent of other regions. This leads in turn to functional specialization, different areas processing different kinds of information in different ways. It has been pointed out that the expansion of the human brain has not been proportional; rather, certain regions, including the cerebral cortex, have seen size and complexity increases even relative to other human brain regions. In particular, the prefrontal cortex, which may play an important and unique role in social behavior, has seen significant enlargement.[6] This increase in functional specialization leads in turn to behavioral consequences that we generally associate with intelligence: "an increase in the complexity, subtlety, and sophistication of . . . the totality of all our conceptual understanding."[7]

Following Ralph Holloway, one of the pioneers in palaeoneurology, Nicholas Toth and Kathy Schick distinguish four stages in hominin brain evolution:[8]

---

the same body size. Thus, while elephants, for example, have larger brains than humans, their EQ is only 1.75–2.36 compared to a human EQ of 7.4–7.8. Unfortunately, however, brain size does not tightly parallel body size: in mammals of the same size there can be a tenfold difference in brain size, which reduces the usefulness of EQ. Both absolute size and EQ should be taken into account in assessing cognitive capacity.

3. Eric J. Vallender and Bruce T. Lahn, "Study of Human Brain Evolution at the Genetic Level," in Broadfield et al., *Human Brain Evolving*, 107.

4. P. Tom Schoenemann, "The Meaning of Brain Size: The Evolution of Conceptual Complexity," in Broadfield et al., *Human Brain Evolving*, 37.

5. Schoenemann mentions three such costs: (1) brain tissue is one of the most metabolically expensive tissues in the human body, sucking up 20 percent of the body's energy intake; (2) larger brains take longer to mature, requiring prolonged care of offspring; and (3) there is a conflict between the need for a large birth canal for increasingly larger-brained infants and the biomechanical efficiencies of narrow hips in bipeds.

6. Vallender and Lahn, "Study of Human Brain Evolution," 107.

7. Schoenemann, "Meaning of Brain Size," 44.

8. Toth and Schick, "Hominin Brain Reorganization," 295 (with minor stylistic alterations).

STAGE 0: Last common ancestor of African chimpanzees/bonobos and hominins (ca. 7–8 mya). Apelike features of hypothetical brain organization might include:

a. An apelike, [more] anterior position of the lunate sulcus, indicating more primary visual cortex than found in hominins[9]
b. Less posterior association cortex than seen in hominins[10]
c. An overall African apelike (gorilla-, chimpanzee-, bonobo-like) size (ca. 350–450 cm^3) and apelike organization of the brain

STAGE 1: Earlier Australopithecine grade (e.g., *Australopithecus afarensis* and *africanus*, by ca. 3.5 mya). Neurological and cognitive changes at this stage include:

a. Reduction of primary visual cortex (as seen in a more posterior position of the lunate sulcus)
b. Relative increase in posterior association cortex (a humanlike pattern)
c. A reorganization of the brain before any major expansion in overall brain size
d. The beginnings of a development in cerebral asymmetries (beyond that seen in modern apes?)
e. By inference, the possibility of more foresight and memory as compared to modern apes

STAGE 2: Early *Homo* grade (e.g. *Homo rudolfensis*, *Homo habilis*, early *Homo ergaster/erectus*, by ca. 1.9 mya). Neurological and cognitive changes at this stage include:

a. An overall increase in brain volume and encephalization quotient
b. Clear-cut and modern humanlike brain asymmetries
c. A prominent Broca's cap region[11]

9. The lunate sulcus is a fissure in the occipital lobe of the brain, which is the most posterior lobe of the four main lobes (viz., frontal, parietal, temporal, and occipital) of the cerebral cortex and the seat of the visual cortex responsible for visual processing.

10. The association cortex comprises parts of the cerebral cortex that are not part of the four main lobes and that contribute to learning and reasoning.

11. Broca's area in the frontal lobe is associated with linguistic ability.

d. By inference, more strongly developed language capabilities and language behavior
e. By inference, increased postnatal development and learning
f. By inference, social learning in toolmaking, hunting, collecting, scavenging, and reproductive strategies.

STAGE 3: *Homo heidelbergensis/neanderthalensis/sapiens* grade (by ca. 500 kya to present). Neurological and cognitive changes at this stage include:

a. An overall increase in brain size and encephalization quotient
b. Refinement in hemispherical asymmetries and specializations for visuospatial, verbal, and sociality skills
c. By inference, growing elaboration of cultural skills based on language
d. By inference, arbitrary symbol systems
e. By inference, feedback between behavioral complexity (including stone technology) and brain enlargement

Significantly, on the basis of endocasts we know that there is little structural or brain-size difference evident between *Homo heidelbergensis, Homo neanderthalensis*, and *Homo sapiens*. Beyond that conclusion, unfortunately, most of the above reconstruction is explicitly based on inference from assumptions that cannot be established from analysis of endocasts. Toth and Schick rightly turn to archaeological evidence in order to chart the course of the evolution of human cognitive capacity, an issue to which we shall return in chapters 10 and 11.

Arterial Foramina

Roger Seymour et al. point to another measure of cognitive capacity different from brain size based on endocasts—namely, the brain's metabolic rate as determined by the size of the arterial foramina, or openings in the skull through which arteries supplying the brain pass, a measure that confirms what we have already seen concerning the cognitive capacities of ancient hominins. According to Seymour et al., "although absolute brain size appears to correlate better with cognitive ability than encephalization quotient, . . . an even better correlate might be brain metabolic rate (MR), because it represents the energy cost of neurological function."[12] The sizes of arterial

12. R. S. Seymour et al., "Cerebral Blood Flow Rates in Recent Great Apes Are Greater

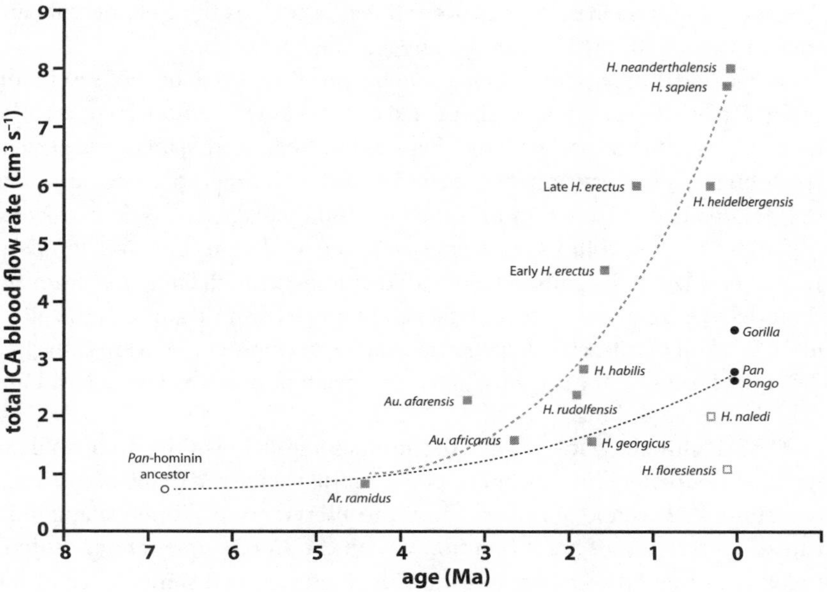

Figure 9.1. Total blood-flow rate of both internal carotid arteries for hominins and recent great apes. Based on Seymour et al., "Cerebral Blood Flow Rates," fig. 4.

foramina in recent and fossil primate skulls can be used to evaluate brain blood-flow rate, which is proportional to brain MR. Figure 9.1 charts the blood-flow rate of both internal carotid arteries that supply most of the primate cerebrum.

Significantly, early members of *Homo*, including early *Homo erectus*, are comparable to modern apes, whereas later *Homo erectus* and *Homo heidelbergensis* score much closer to *Homo sapiens*, while the blood-flow rate of *Homo neanderthalensis* actually exceeds that of *Homo sapiens*.

Cranial Globularization

It has been argued on palaeoneurological grounds, however, that "modern humanization . . . developed gradually in scattered locations across Africa

Than in *Australopithecus* Species That Had Equal or Larger Brains," *PTRSB* 286, no. 1915 (November 13, 2019): 20192208, https://doi.org/10.1098/rspb.2019.2208.

within species *Homo sapiens*."[13] The implication is that humanity, therefore, does not comprise members of other lineages such as the Neanderthal lineage but arises somewhere on the lineage of *Homo sapiens*.

What evidence supports such a conclusion? David Wilcox focuses not on brain size or EQ but on brain shape. He notes that while modern newborns have an elongated brain, the same shape as did Neanderthal infants, a perinatal globularizing expansion takes place in modern humans that did not occur in Neanderthals. Citing Simon Neubauer and colleagues,[14] Wilcox traces a trajectory in the evolution of *Homo sapiens* from the archaic specimens at Jebel Irhoud, which exhibited elongated crania, through later *Homo sapiens* skulls like Qafzeh 6 and 9 from Israel and Omo 2 from Ethiopia to the globularized skull of modern *Homo sapiens*. African populations were thus on a different evolutionary trajectory than Eurasian populations, which did not exhibit similar globularization.

Cranial globularization is due to the changing shape of the brain. Wilcox writes, "Neubauer and colleagues point out that since the shape of the brain determines the shape of the cranium, the altered cranial/brain shape indicates an alteration of brain function within the *Homo sapiens* line." Wilcox recognizes that "the critical question" is the functional significance of the brain changes that shaped the cranium. He claims that "the areas which are enlarged in the modern human brain are crucial for what it means to be human."[15] Specifically, cranial globularization is due to the rapid enlargement of the parietal area of the brain, notably the precuneus, and of the cerebellum—"areas central to theory of mind, self-consciousness, language, the default system, and others." The selective pressure responsible for the changes is taken to be the demand for "increasingly complex cognitive work, which requires structured learning/teaching."[16] "Logically, therefore, the force driving selection for these neural/genetic alterations would be natural selection for socially enhanced learning."[17] This analysis seems to imply that Neanderthals did not experience similar selective pressures. Wilcox asks,

> If the *Homo sapiens* lineage was being driven by the need to teach by instruction, and by the need to process increasingly larger and complex

13. David L. Wilcox, "Updating Human Origins," *PSCF* 71, no. 1 (2019): 46.

14. S. Neubauer, J. J. Hublin, and P. Gunz, "The Evolution of Modern Human Brain Shape," *SA* 4, no. 1 (January 24, 2018): 1–8.

15. Wilcox, "Updating Human Origins," 41.

16. Wilcox, "Updating Human Origins," 42.

17. Wilcox, "Updating Human Origins," 43.

> social interactions (both leading to parietal enlargement), what was driving selection in the Neanderthal lineage? Of course, we cannot really be sure, but we can speculate based on which areas were enlarged in the Neanderthal brain. Neubauer's analysis of cranial change in the Neanderthals indicates enlargement of both primary and secondary visual cortexes, and motor cortexes, resulting in visual pattern recognition and the learned selection of appropriate motions for various situations. Verbal instruction, the evaluation and correction of student efforts, and the coordination of groups—which are so typical of modern human socialization—would be greatly handicapped if language and theory of mind were significantly less effective.[18]

There can be no doubt that Wilcox's analysis significantly depreciates the humanity of Neanderthals. But is it justified?

There is a good deal of conjecture in his analysis concerning both the causes and the consequences of differential cranial globularization in the two lineages.[19] But leave that to the side. The most important point is that Wilcox

18. Wilcox, "Updating Human Origins," 43.

19. As to causes, are we to imagine that the same sort of demands for increasingly complex cognitive work, which required structured learning/teaching, did not also face Neanderthals? Given their communal living and group hunting in a very challenging climate demanding clothing and shelter, they surely experienced urgently the need for socially enhanced learning. Moreover, that globularization is due in part to enlargement of the precuneus is conjectural. Neubauer, Hublin, and Gunz explain, "Because parietal bulging is not associated with an increase of outer parietal surface area, it is likely that a size increase of regions that are not visible on the external surface of the brain is responsible for parietal bulging" (Neubauer, Hublin, and Gunz, "Evolution of Modern Human Brain Shape," 5). That implies that the regions responsible cannot therefore be detected through endocasts of specimen skulls.

As to consequences, Neubauer, Hublin, and Gunz's claim that "the evolutionary brain globularization in *H. sapiens* parallels the emergence of behavioral modernity documented by the archeological record" not only courts a sort of *post hoc, ergo propter hoc* fallacy, but seems to be simply false. Consider their three points offered in support: (1) *The emergence of the MSA is close in time to the currently earliest known fossils of early* H. sapiens *that had large brains but did not exhibit any major changes to (outer) brain morphology* (e.g., at Jebel Irhoud). How does this display parallelism? A change in the toolmaking industry is said to have occurred *without* a change in brain morphology. (2) *As the* H. sapiens *brain gradually became more globular, features of behavioral modernity accumulated gradually with time*. The very article they cite from McBrearty and Brooks tends to show the opposite, as we shall see in the sequel. See also the examples mentioned in the text of Bruniquel Cave and Neanderthal art. (3) *At the time when brain globularity of our ancestors fell within the range of variation of present-day humans, the full set of features of behavioral modernity*

has overinterpreted Neubauer, Hublin, and Gunz's findings. Even if cranial globularization is correlated with the development of modern behaviors in *Homo sapiens*, that implies neither a causal connection nor an incapacity for or absence of modern behaviors in Neanderthals, who do not exhibit similar globularization. (So to infer confuses sufficient with necessary conditions.)[20] Neubauer, Hublin, and Gunz nowhere treat globularization changes as "crucial for what it means to be human." Indeed, when asked what his findings imply for the cognitive capacities of Neanderthals, Neubauer responded,

> There is no reason to expect any straightforward correlation between overall brain shape and behaviour, and it is unlikely that brain shape has itself been directly subject to evolutionary selection. Braincase shape depends on a complex interplay between cranial bone growth, facial size, and the tempo and mode of neurodevelopment. In our earlier work we have shown that the difference in endocranial shape between Neanderthals and modern humans arises pre- and early postnatally: only modern humans develop a more globular shape. This suggests potential developmental differences in early brain development, which is a critical phase for establishing the wiring network of the brain. Note that potential differences do not necessarily imply that one group's cognitive abilities are superior. We do not argue that Neanderthals are less intelligent than modern humans, but that they may have seen and interacted with the world differently than us.[21]

---

had accumulated at the transition from the MSA to the LSA in Africa and from the Middle to the Upper Palaeolithic in Europe around 50–40,000 kya. Precisely! Brain globularity came into the modern range about 35 kya according to their estimates, and by that time the full set of modern behaviors had already accumulated.

20. André Sousa et al. remind us that humans affected by either congenital or acquired conditions causing portions of the brain to be severely underdeveloped or missing can nonetheless have normal or near-normal intelligence and cognitive skills, with examples including some severe forms of microcephaly, a case of severe hydrocephaly, childhood hemispherectomy (i.e., disconnection or removal of an entire cerebral hemisphere), a patient born with only one hemisphere, craniopagus malformation, and, significantly, individuals with an almost complete absence of the cerebellum (A. M. M. Sousa et al., "Evolution of the Human Nervous System Function, Structure, and Development," *Cell* 170, no. 2 [July 13, 2017]: 229). They go on to say, "The key to our brain's unique capacities may not be simply its absolute or relative size, or even its number of neurons and glia, but instead more nuanced components such as increased diversity of neural cell types, molecular changes, and expanded or more complex patterns of neuronal connectivity" (229)—features that are not readable off cranial endocasts.

21. Neubauer to William Lane Craig, February 8, 2020.

There is thus nothing in Neubauer, Hublin, and Gunz's results that imply a diminished cognitive capacity for Neanderthals.

The brain of extinct hominins is something of a black box, since little can be inferred about brain structure and functioning based on endocasts taken from empty skulls. Holloway comments, "Some knowledge of . . . paleoneurology, or the study of the only truly direct evidence, the endocasts of our fossil ancestors, is necessary. Endocasts, i.e., the casts made of the internal table of bone of the cranium, are rather impoverished objects (the cerebrum is covered by three meningeal tissues) to achieve such an understanding, but these are all we have of the direct evolutionary history of our brains and should not be ignored."[22] Differences in the brain shape of Neanderthals and *Homo sapiens* thus do not tell us about their comparative cognitive capacities. Chris Stringer and Peter Andrews comment, "Judging from the inside of the braincase, the large Neanderthal brain was somewhat differently shaped from our own—somewhat smaller in the frontal region, and larger at the back (the occipital lobes)—but it is impossible to judge the quality of their brains from such limited data."[23] Indeed, as we shall see in the sequel, we have archaeological evidence of modern human behaviors among Neanderthals, as noted by Neubauer: "Recent archaeological evidence has provided new insights into Neanderthal cognition by documenting a suite of sophisticated symbolic behaviors in Neanderthals that had previously been attributed exclusively to modern humans, such as the enigmatic structure built deep inside Bruniquel cave, and the Neanderthal cave-art from Iberia."[24]

Dentition

It will be recalled that the fossils at Jebel Irhoud give evidence of a prolonged period of dental development. This slow growth has surprising implications

22. Holloway, "Human Brain Evolving," 1.

23. Chris Stringer and Peter Andrews, *The Complete World of Human Evolution*, 2nd ed. (New York: Thames & Hudson, 2012), 155. Consider, for example, the capacity for language. "The outside surface of the human brain does show some structural features that are important in the production of speech, and if these are damaged, speech may be deficient or lost completely. However, trying to recognize equivalent surface features on endocasts (replicas taken from the brain cavities of fossil skulls) is difficult, and of debatable value. It is probably more realistic to try to assess the presence of language from the degree of behavioral complexity which we can infer from the archaeological record" (130–31).

24. Neubauer to Craig, February 8, 2020.

for the brain development of such archaic humans, in marked contrast to apes, Australopithecines, and early *Homo*. What we cannot learn from endocasts may be illuminated by the study of teeth.

Christopher Dean of the Department of Anatomy and Developmental Biology at University College, London, explains that such "life-history traits" in human beings as brain size, age of reproductive ability, life span, and so on parallel tightly dental development. What is important here is not just the size of the brain but its slow development. "The size of key brain components associated with learning and cognition correlates with the timing of dental development in primates, as the cost in time needed to grow and learn to use a larger brain increases. In this context a slower trajectory of enamel growth in permanent teeth . . . can be regarded as a life-history attribute associated with the extended, or prolonged, growth period of modern humans."[25]

Dean and his colleagues compared enamel growth in human beings to enamel growth in the teeth of great apes, ancient Australopithecines, and ancient *Homo*. They identified regions in enamel that showed a well-preserved record of daily enamel cross-striations in thirteen teeth or tooth fragments of specimens firmly attributed to three species of early *Homo*, to four species of Australopithecine, and to one Neanderthal. They then compared enamel growth rates in fossil hominins with those in modern humans and modern African great apes and with two teeth attributed to the African Miocene stem hominoid, *Proconsul nyanzae*. They found that neither the Australopithecines nor fossils currently attributed to early *Homo* (specifically *Homo habilis*, *Homo rudolfensis*, and *Homo erectus*) shared the slow trajectory of enamel growth typical of modern humans; rather, they all resembled modern and fossil African apes. On this basis, Dean and his colleagues go so far as to suggest that these putative specimens of early *Homo* be reclassified as members of the genus *Australopithecus*, not *Homo*.

When Dean and his colleagues examined the fossil teeth of the Neanderthal from Tabūn Cave, Israel, however, they found the same slow development of enamel that is characteristic of modern humans. This finding has been confirmed by Antonio Rosas et al. on the basis of their examination of

25. Christopher Dean et al., "Growth Processes in Teeth Distinguish Modern Humans from *Homo erectus* and Earlier Hominins," *Nature* 414, no. 6864 (December 6, 2001): 628. See also Timothy G. Bromage and M. Christopher Dean, "Re-evaluation of the Age at Death of Immature Fossil Hominids," *Nature* 317, no. 6037 (October 10, 1985): 525–27, where they show that *Australopithecus*, *Paranthropus*, and early *Homo* have biological equivalence to modern humans at roughly two-thirds the chronological age, demonstrating that they had growth periods similar to the modern great apes.

the skeleton of a Neanderthal child found at El Sidrón, Spain. They found that "growth and development in this juvenile Neandertal fit the typical features of human ontogeny, where there is slow somatic growth between weaning and puberty that may offset the cost of growing a large brain."[26] Intriguingly, they report that "compared with early *Homo* specimens at a comparable stage of dental development, El Sidrón J1 is . . . almost identical in age (7.78 years) to a 315-thousand-year-old *Homo sapiens* specimen from Jebel Irhoud, Morocco, that shows a prolonged modern humanlike period of dental developmental [growth]."[27] They note that divergent morphogenetic trajectories underlying brain shape differences can exist within this broadly human growth pattern. Dean and his colleagues conclude that it is increasingly likely that a period of development truly like that of modern humans arose only after the appearance of *Homo erectus*, when both brain

26. A. Rosas et al., "The Growth Pattern of Neandertals, Reconstructed from a Juvenile Skeleton from El Sidrón (Spain)," *Science* 357, no. 6357 (September 22, 2017): 1285. This slow growth pattern connects closely with the hypothesis of Michael Tomasello that "uniquely human forms of cognition and sociality emerge in human ontogeny through, and only through, species-unique forms of sociocultural activity" (*Becoming Human: A Theory of Ontogeny* [Cambridge, MA: Belknap Press of Harvard University Press, 2019], 6). On this view not prenatal but postnatal ontogenetic processes are the source of uniquely human traits. What is crucial is the emergence of the joint intentionality in newborns and of collective intentionality in children. Humans have evolved a suite of unique cognitive and social skills for coordinating with others in two steps. The first step comprised adaptations enabling human individuals to cooperate in foraging. These are the skills of joint intentionality. The second step comprised adaptations enabling modern individuals to cooperate in the larger collaborative enterprise known as culture. These are the skills of collective intentionality. Tomasello thinks that around 400 kya some early humans (the best guess is *Homo heidelbergensis*) began obtaining the majority of their food through more active collaboration, which became obligate. This meant that they were interdependent with strong social selection for cooperative individuals, resulting in new forms of cognition and sociality. Tomasello reports that it is "virtually universally accepted" that our slow ontogeny, including slow brain growth, is partly an adaptation to human culture (*Becoming Human*, 27). If that is true, then there is no reason to delay the emergence of collective intentionality and culture until *Homo sapiens*, since *Homo heidelbergensis* and *Homo neanderthalensis* already exhibit our slow ontogeny. Kevin Laland traces the dawn of cumulative culture to "when our ancestors first began manufacturing stone tools, using the flakes to butcher carcasses and in a variety of other ways" (*Darwin's Unfinished Symphony: How Culture Made the Human Mind* [Princeton: Princeton University Press, 2017], 185). "Acheulian technologies, together with . . . evidence for systematic hunting and the use of fire, leave no doubt that by at least this juncture in our history, our ancestors benefitted from cumulative cultural knowledge" (10).

27. Rosas et al., "Growth Pattern of Neandertals," 1283.

size and body size were well within the range known for modern humans. Thus, evidence from the slow growth of tooth enamel not only is consistent with the humanity of Neanderthals but counts against the humanity of *Homo erectus*, a conclusion not inferable from brain size alone.[28]

Genetics

The revolution in human genetics has now opened up new avenues of study in palaeoneurology beyond reliance on endocasts and fossil evidence. The amazing achievement of the successful sequencing of the Neanderthal genome in 2010 and the subsequent discovery of Denisovan DNA enable scientists to compare the DNA of these ancient individuals with that of modern persons with a view toward discerning what impact genetic differences might have in brain structure and growth and, hence, cognitive capacity. Still in its nascence, this field of study is fraught with uncertainty, but it is nonetheless worthwhile examining some of the recent developments.[29]

Perhaps the most significant of these developments is the discovery that the expansion of the human neocortex (the principal part of the cerebral cortex overlaying the cerebrum) is due in part to a genetic mutation that occurred in the gene *ARHGAP11B*, a protein-coding gene that affects the generation and division of neocortical brain cells.[30] The mutation involves the substitution of a single nucleotide letter C for a G, which transforms the protein into a very different form unique to the human lineage. As a result of the mutation, certain brain cells in the neocortex, so-called basal progenitor

28. Note that Dean's argument is not guilty of *post hoc, propter hoc* reasoning, since it is no part of his claim that slow enamel growth causes slow brain development.

29. I leave to the side as tangential to our interest the recent identification of *BOLA2* as a gene duplicated exclusively in *Homo sapiens* around 282 kya (X. Nuttle et al., "Emergence of a *Homo sapiens*–Specific Gene Family and Chromosome 16p11.2 CNV Susceptibility," *Nature* 536, no. 7615 [August 3, 2016]: 205–9). For it is not related to brain evolution. Rather, "the duplicative transposition of *BOLA2* at the root of the *Homo sapiens* lineage about 282 ka simultaneously increased copy number of a gene associated with iron homeostasis and predisposed our species to recurrent rearrangements associated with disease."

30. M. Florio et al., "A Single Splice Site Mutation in Human-Specific *ARHGAP11B* Causes Basal Progenitor Amplification," *SA* 2, no. 12 (December 7, 2016), https://doi.org/10.1126/sciadv.1601941. For a popular account, see Reinier Prosee, "The Mutation That Allowed Our Brain to Grow," *Science Breaker*, August 24, 2017, https://thescience-breaker.org/breaks/evolution-behaviour/the-mutation-that-allowed-our-brain-to-grow.

cells, grow and divide at an unprecedented rate.[31] When the human-specific gene was inserted into mice, their brain cells underwent significant growth. Subsequent experiments introducing human-specific *ARHGAP11B* into embryonic ferrets, which were considered more apt subjects than mice because of their more numerous basal progenitors, resulted in an expansion of the ferret neocortex. "This suggests that this gene may have a similar role in human brain development."[32] Even more recently, scientists have inserted *ARHGAP11B* into fetal members of a primate species, with dramatic results.[33] The gene increased the number of basal progenitor cells in the subventricular zone, increased the number of upper-layer neurons, enlarged the neocortex, and induced folding in the surface of the brain. Michael Heide et al. conclude that their results suggest that *ARHGAP11B* may indeed have caused an expansion of the human neocortex in the course of human evolution.

When did this crucial mutation occur? *ARHGAP11B* is actually a duplicate of another gene, *ARHGAP11A*, the result of a gene-duplication event in the human lineage since our last common ancestor with chimpanzees. The ancestral *ARHGAP11B*, lacking the C→G base substitution, did not amplify basal progenitors.[34] Therefore Floria et al. state,

31. Neocortical neurogenesis involves two main classes of neural progenitor cells that reside in two distinct zones of the brain: apical progenitors and basal progenitors. Basal progenitors are better suited for maximizing neuron production than apical progenitors because they are not subject to the constraint imposed on the proliferation of apical progenitors by limited ventricular space but rather can make use of the much larger space available in the subventricular zone. Accordingly, the evolutionary expansion of the neocortex is associated with an increase in the generation of basal progenitors and their proliferation before generating neurons.

32. N. Kalebic et al., "Human-Specific *ARHGAP11B* Induces Hallmarks of Neocortical Expansion in Developing Ferret Neocortex," *eLife* 7 (November 28, 2018): e41241, https://doi.org/10.7554/eLife.41241.

33. M. Heide et al., "Human-Specific *ARHGAP11B* Increases Size and Folding of Primate Neocortex in the Fetal Marmoset," *Science* 369, no. 6503 (July 31, 2020): eabb2401, https://doi.org/10.1126/science.abb2401. This experiment initiates a disturbing direction in research. The team reports, "In light of potential unforeseeable consequences with regard to postnatal brain function, we considered it a prerequisite—and mandatory from an ethical point of view—to first determine the effects of *ARHGAP11B* expression on the development of fetal marmoset neocortex. To this end, we collected fetuses after Caesarean section at day 101 of the ≈150 day gestation, a stage . . . which corresponds to fetal human neocortical development at ≈16 weeks post conception" (1).

34. Florio et al. explain, "It is not the *ARHGAP11* partial gene duplication event ~5 million years ago, as such, that impacted human neocortex evolution. Presumably, *ARHGAP11A* and ancestral *ARHGAP11B* coexisted as functionally similar proteins

> It was important to determine whether the single C→G base substitution in the *ARHGAP11B* gene that ultimately causes its human-specific C-terminal sequence occurs not only in modern humans but if it was also present in Neanderthals, whose brains were as large as those of modern humans, and Denisovans. The crucial C→G base substitution was also found in Neanderthal and Denisova *ARHGAP11B*. Moreover, all present-day humans analyzed carry the C→G substitution. Together, these observations indicate that the C→G base substitution, which presumably occurred in the ~5 million years since the *ARHGAP11* gene duplication event, took place before the archaic hominins diverged from the modern human lineage >500,000 years ago.[35]

The evidence is thus consistent with the humanity of Neanderthals and Denisovans, since they share in this crucial genetic mutation that helps to explain the extraordinary expansion of the brain unique to human beings. Indeed, since the mutation occurred in the species ancestral to Neanderthals, Denisovans, and *Homo sapiens*, these findings are consistent with the humanity of someone belonging to a large-brained ancestral species like *Homo heidelbergensis*, in which the mutation occurred.

More recently, a second genetic factor promoting neuronal growth and, hence, neocortical brain expansion has been identified—namely, *NOTCH2NL* genes, which are, again, human-specific.[36] *NOTCH2NL* comes in three versions that amplify neuron progenitors. None of these three genes is to be found in the genomes of the extant great apes. But when the genomes of Neanderthals and Denisovans were examined, the same *NOTCH2NL* genes were discovered. Fiddes et al. comment, "The peculiar evolutionary

---

for some time after the gene duplication event. The ability of *ARHGAP11B* to amplify B[asal] P[rogenitor]s likely arose more recently from a change that is tiny on a genomic scale but substantial in its functional and evolutionary consequences" ("Single Splice Site Mutation").

35. Florio et al., "Single Splice Site Mutation." When Florio et al. refer to the relevant mutation as "human-specific," they presumably mean that among currently existing organisms the mutation is unique to human beings. Whether it is also found in Neanderthals and Denisovans is a question to be settled empirically, not *a priori* by definition.

36. I. T. Fiddes et al., "Human-Specific *NOTCH2NL* Genes Affect Notch Signaling and Cortical Neurogenesis," *Cell* 173, no. 6 (May 31, 2018): 1356–69. For the meaning of "human-specific," see previous note. For a popular account, see "Humans' Big Brains May Be Partly Due to Three Newly Found Genes," *Genetic Engineering and Biotechnology News*, June 1, 2018, https://www.genengnews.com/topics/omics/humans-big-brains-may-be-partly-due-to-three-newly-found-genes/.

history of *NOTCH2NL* includes a series of genomic reorganization events resulting in three functional *NOTCH*-related genes only in humans. The most plausible scenario is that in a common ancestor of humans, Neanderthals, and Denisovans, the ancestral *PDE4DIP-NOTCH2NL* pseudogene was repaired by ectopic gene conversion from *NOTCH2*. This event may have been crucial to human evolution, marking the birth of a novel human-specific *NOTCH*-related gene involved in differentiation of neuronal progenitor cells."[37] Our attention is thus directed once again to a large-brained ancestral species like *Homo heidelbergensis* as the locus of these genetic reorganization events where the human species may have originated.

Summary and Prospect

The palaeontological evidence concerning ancient crania and the recent evidence drawn from the genetic study of ancient *Homo* are thus consistent with pushing the boundary for the origin of humanity back before the origin of *Homo sapiens* so as to include Neanderthals and Denisovans as members of the human family. While this evidence is powerfully suggestive, the decisive question is whether these ancient hominins actually engaged in activities indicative of human cognitive capacity. We shall turn to that question in the next two chapters.

37. Fiddes et al., "Human-Specific *NOTCH2NL* Genes," 1366.

Chapter 10

THE EVIDENCE OF ARCHAEOLOGY (PART 1)

While palaeoneurological evidence provides significant support for humanity's origin prior to the divergence of *Homo sapiens* and Neanderthals, the most important positive evidence for the historical presence of human beings at any time will be the archaeological evidence for modern human behaviors.[1] If ancient humans engaged in behaviors essentially like our own, then to be skeptical of their humanity is to risk skepticism about the humanity of our contemporaries.[2]

Archaeological Signatures of Modern Behavior

Recall that anthropologists Sally McBrearty and Alison Brooks identified four widely recognized conditions that are sufficient for modern human behavior:

- abstract thinking
- planning depth

1. Francesco d'Errico, "The Invisible Frontier: A Multiple Species Model for the Origin of Behavioral Modernity," *EA* 12, no. 4 (August 5, 2003): 188–202, https://doi.org/10.1002/evan.10113. D'Errico rightly cautions against equating biological modernity with cultural modernity. He supports a scenario according to which the traits that define cultural modernity are not peculiar to our species and arose over a long period of time among different human species or kinds, including Neanderthals (189).

2. One thinks of skeptical arguments in the philosophy of mind concerning the existence of other minds than one's own. We must not allow ourselves to be backed into a position whereby skepticism about other minds is justified by skepticism about the cognitive capacities of ancient humans. Even in such a case, however, we could still affirm that we have the same sort of reasons to accept the humanity of our prehistoric ancestors as we do that of our contemporaries.

- behavioral, economic, and technological innovativeness
- symbolic behavior

The obvious difficulty is how to establish the presence of such behaviors on the basis of artifactual evidence. To illustrate the difficulty, while the use of language among ancient human beings would be decisive evidence of symbolic behavior (defined as including the ability to represent objects, people, and abstract concepts with arbitrary symbols, vocal or visual), language use will not be directly detectable until the invention of writing. So language use will have to be indirectly inferred, if at all. McBrearty and Brooks claim that there are a number of "archaeological signatures of modern human behavior" that provide "tangible traces" of the four behaviors listed above:

- *Ecological aspects* of the record reflect human abilities to colonize new environments, which require both innovation and planning depth.
- *Technological features* reveal human inventiveness and capacity for logical thinking.
- *Economic and social features* show human abilities to draw models from individual and group experience, to develop and apply systematic plans, to conceptualize and predict the future, and to construct formalized relationships among individuals and groups.
- *Symbolic features* demonstrate a capacity to imbue aspects of experience with meaning, to communicate abstract concepts, and to manipulate symbols as a part of everyday life.[3]

These "signatures" are not correlated one-to-one with the four types of modern behavior listed above. For example, ecological aspects seem to manifest both planning depth and behavioral, economic, and technological innovativeness; and technological features as well as symbolic features seem to require abstract thinking. It is hardly surprising that a given archaeological signature would manifest a number of modern behaviors; indeed, this is to be expected, since a modern mentality will permeate everything one does.

McBrearty and Brooks then tabulate examples of the archaeological signatures manifesting modern human behaviors:

3. Sally McBrearty and Alison S. Brooks, "The Revolution That Wasn't: A New Interpretation of the Origin of Modern Human Behavior," *JHE* 39, no. 5 (November 2000): 492–93, https://doi.org/10.1006/jhev.2000.0435.

Archaeological signatures of modern human behavior

Ecology
Range extension to previously unoccupied regions (tropical lowland forest, islands, the far north in Europe and Asia)
Increased diet breadth

Technology
New lithic technologies: blades, microblades, backing
Standardization within formal tool categories
Hafting and composite tools
Tools in novel materials (e.g., bone, antler)
Special-purpose tools (e.g., projectiles, geometrics)
Increased numbers of tool categories
Geographic variation in formal categories
Temporal variation in formal categories
Greater control of fire

Economy and social organization
Long-distance procurement and exchange of raw materials
Curation of exotic raw materials
Specialized hunting of large, dangerous animals
Scheduling and seasonality in resource exploitation
Site reoccupation
Intensification of resource extraction, especially aquatic and vegetable resources
Long-distance exchange networks
Group and individual self-identification through artifact style
Structured use of domestic space

Symbolic behavior
Regional artifact styles
Self-adornment (e.g., beads and ornaments)
Use of pigment
Notched and incised objects (bone, egg shell, ocher, stone)
Image and representation
Burials with grave goods, ocher, ritual objects

In order to illustrate the antiquity of many of these archaeological signatures, McBrearty and Brooks provide a helpful chronological chart of the varying depth of these signatures in the African MSA back to the ESA-MSA transition.[4] Francesco d'Errico has expanded the scope of their chart to include European and Near Eastern, as well as African, archaeological signatures of modern human behavior (fig. 10.1).[5]

Francesco d'Errico and Chris Stringer use these signatures to evaluate three competing accounts of the origin of cultural modernity:

1. Modern cognition is unique to our species and is the consequence of a genetic mutation that took place approximately 50 kya in Africa among already evolved anatomically modern humans.
2. Cultural modernity emerged gradually in Africa starting at least 200 kya in concert with the origin of our species on that continent.
3. Innovations indicative of modern cognition are not restricted to our species and appear (and disappear) in Africa and Eurasia between 200 and 40 kya before becoming fully consolidated.[6]

As the chart reveals, the evidence supports the third, multispecies model, implying that "the cognitive prerequisites of modern human behaviour were already largely in place among the ancestors of Neanderthals and modern humans" and that "'modernity' and its corollary 'cumulative culture' is the end product of a saltational cultural evolution within human populations that were to a large extent, and irrespectively of their taxonomic affiliation, cognitively modern."[7]

4. McBrearty and Brooks, "Revolution That Wasn't," 530, fig. 13.

5. D'Errico, "Invisible Frontier," 200.

6. Francesco d'Errico and Chris B. Stringer, "Evolution, Revolution or Saltation Scenario for the Emergence of Modern Cultures?," *PTRSB* 366, no. 1567 (April 12, 2011): 1060, https://doi.org/10.1098/rstb.2010.0340.

7. D'Errico and Stringer, "Evolution, Revolution or Saltation," 1061. Noting that by around 300 kya men were combining wooden spears with flint flakes, building dwellings with fire hearths, and producing fire-hardened spears for hunting, Kevin Laland agrees: "Acheulian technologies along with evidence for systematic hunting and the use of fire leave no doubt by this time our ancestors benefited from cumulative cultural knowledge" (*Darwin's Unfinished Symphony: How Culture Made the Human Mind* [Princeton: Princeton University Press, 2017], 10).

For an odd, Pyrrhic argument that is the mirror image of d'Errico and Stringer's, see J. M. Lindly et al., "Symbolism and Modern Human Origins," *CA* 31, no. 3 (June 1990): 233–61, who argue for a multiregional model on the grounds that symbolic behavior is no more exhibited by anatomically modern *Homo sapiens* during the Middle Palaeolithic than by archaic *Homo sapiens* and Neanderthals during that time. Unfortunately, their case is undermined, not only by more recent discoveries of such behavior in the Middle Palaeolithic, but also by their handling of known cases (e.g., the wooden

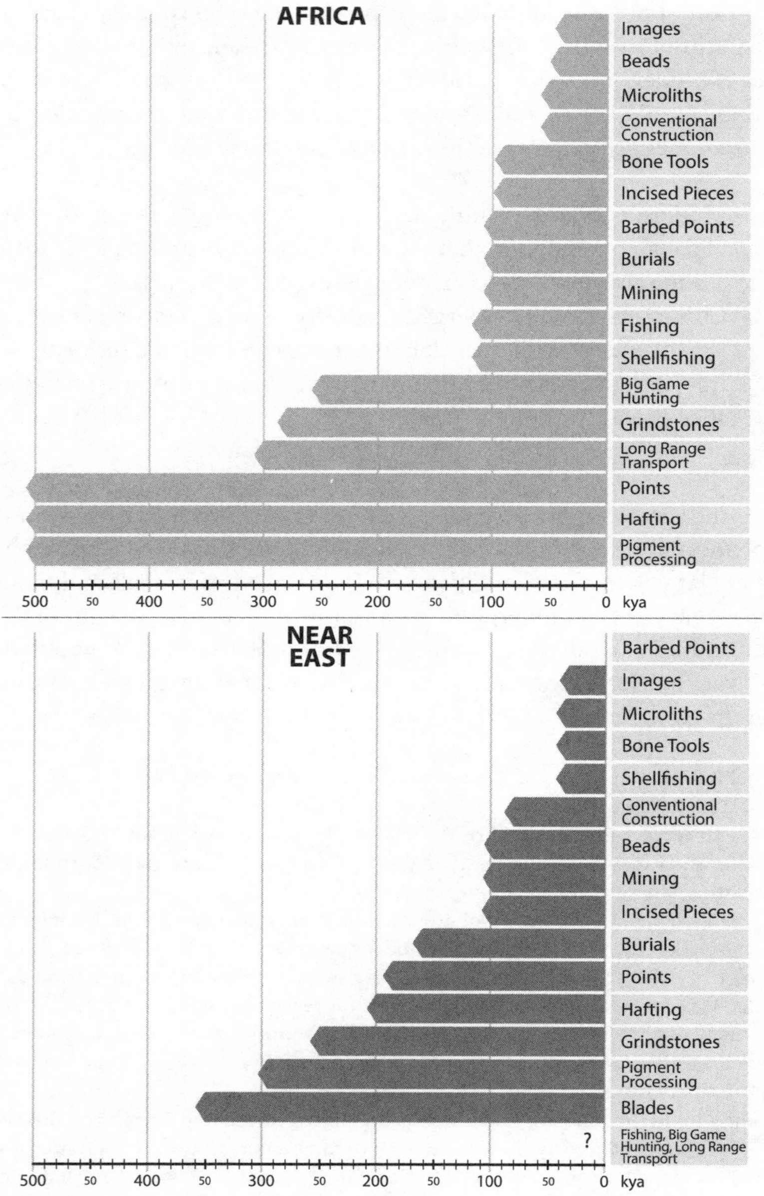
AFRICA
Images
Beads
Microliths
Conventional Construction
Bone Tools
Incised Pieces
Barbed Points
Burials
Mining
Fishing
Shellfishing
Big Game Hunting
Grindstones
Long Range Transport
Points
Hafting
Pigment Processing
500 50 400 50 300 50 200 50 100 50 0 kya
NEAR EAST
Barbed Points
Images
Microliths
Bone Tools
Shellfishing
Conventional Construction
Beads
Mining
Incised Pieces
Burials
Points
Hafting
Grindstones
Pigment Processing
Blades
?
Fishing, Big Game Hunting, Long Range Transport
500 50 400 50 300 50 200 50 100 50 0 kya

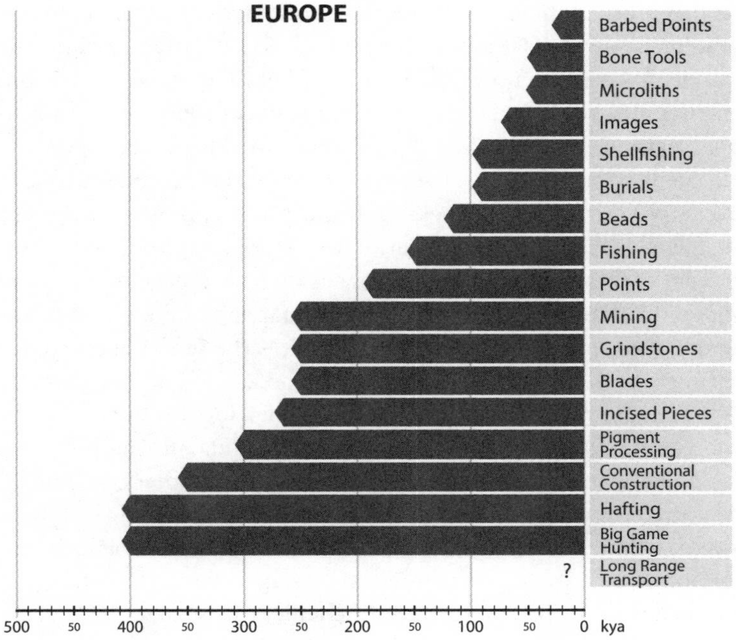

Figure 10.1. Appearance of archaeological signatures of modern cognitive capacity in Africa, the Near East, and Europe. Based on d'Errico, "Invisible Frontier," fig. 8.

Technology

Let us selectively review a few of the most revealing and ancient signatures. Changes in technology will obviously be one of the most abundantly attested and easily observable archaeological signatures.

implements at Florisbad) that show symbolic behavior among nonmodern humans. On the burials at Qafzeh and Skhūl, they reply to Bar-Yosef et al., Mellars, and Stringer that these commentators are unable to explain why the relevant grave goods are any more significant than similar objects associated with archaic *Homo sapiens* that are dismissed as nonsymbolic. Lindly and colleagues would be better advised to argue straightforwardly that there is symbolic behavior widely manifested during the Middle Palaeolithic.

The manufacture and use of even the most primitive stone tools might appear at first blush to indicate considerable cognitive capacity. But in fact the manufacture and use of Oldowan stone tools has been taught to chimpanzees in captivity.[8] While chimpanzees in the wild have mastered the technique of cracking nuts with rocks, certain chimps in captivity have, after much training, learned the skill of knapping—that is, striking rocks together at an oblique angle so as to produce flakes that can be used as crude cutting tools. Significantly, young chimpanzees, observing the knapping activities of their elders, have learned through imitation the art of knapping. Whether one infers from such activity that chimpanzees do have considerable cognitive capacity after all or that Oldowan tool manufacture and use does not after all require great cognitive capacity, the result is the same: because nonhuman primates can master the manufacture and use of Oldowan tools, such artifacts are not evidence of modern human behavior. The ancient Oldowan tool industry is associated with the remains of various Australopithecines or *Homo habilis*, whose brain size in both cases exceeded that of chimpanzees and who therefore could have acquired the requisite skills. The fact that such tools persisted in the archaeological record without change for an incredible one million years is indicative of intellectual stagnation and less than human cognitive capacity.[9] The emergence of Acheulean bifacial tools is correlated with the emergence of *Homo erectus*, who was "almost certainly the maker of the earliest Acheulean tools," despite the lingering presence of Australo-

8. See the entertaining account by Sue Savage-Rumbaugh and William Mintz Fields, "Rules and Tools: Beyond Anthropomorphism," in *The Oldowan: Case Studies into the Earliest Stone Age*, ed. Nicholas Toth and Kathy Schick, SAIPS 1 (Gosport, IN: Stone Age Institute Press, 2006), 223–41. Both of these authors have unfortunately succumbed to anthropopathism. For a more objective, scientific treatment, see Nicholas Toth, Kathy Schick, and Sileshi Semaw, "A Comparative Study of the Stone Tool-Making Skills of *Pan*, *Australopithecus*, and *Homo sapiens*," in Toth and Schick, *The Oldowan*, 155–222.

9. Lewin and Foley deem the lack of innovation in stone tools over one million years to be "unthinkable" to the modern human mind (Roger Lewin and Robert A. Foley, *Principles of Human Evolution*, 2nd ed. [Oxford: Blackwell, 2004], 319). Richard Fortey remarks, "Such conservatism is staggeringly uninventive by modern human standards, and has led to claims that these early 'men' gave no thought to the construction of tools. Rather, it was as automatic as the nest building of a weaver bird" (*Life: An Unauthorized Biography* [London: Folio Society, 2008], 324). Laland thinks that "the simplicity and stasis of Oldowan technology are indicative of a restricted form of information transmission, such as observational learning, that only allowed the communication of the broadest concepts of stone-knapping technology" (*Darwin's Unfinished Symphony*, 265). Oldowan tools are adventitious and do not conform to tightly restricted categories that would require distinct mental templates in the mind of a stone knapper.

Figure 10.2. A beautifully crafted Acheulean hand axe displaying the aesthetic sensitivity of its maker. It was found at Kathu Pan, in the Northern Cape, and is thought to be 750,000–800,000 years old. Housed at the McGregor Museum in Kimberley, South Africa. Photograph courtesy of Michael Cope. Used with permission.

pithecines.[10] Lewin and Foley, however, note that the precise path through which the Acheulean innovation emerged remains unclear.[11] They observe that no early hand axes were the product of long, careful flaking to yield an aesthetically pleasing, perfectly symmetrical teardrop shape.

Later hand axes are associated with *Homo heidelbergensis*—for example, at Boxgrove, England, where hundreds of examples were discovered. Because some design aspects of these tools appear to lack utility but manifest aesthetic design elements, such as a convincingly symmetrical shape (fig. 10.2), they manifest a grasp of artistic symmetry, which has been taken as evidence of an understanding of the geometrical ideal as a good to realize concretely, thereby reflecting true, human intellective activity.[12]

Blades

But the sort of tools to which McBrearty and Brooks are appealing as evidence of truly human behavior requires greater cognitive capacity. Consider, for example, blades, which are, at the simplest, flakes with a ratio of breadth to length of ≤0.5. Although there are different methods of blade production,[13] the repeated, consistent production of blades is said to require a de-

10. Richard G. Klein, "The Stone Age Prehistory of Southern Africa," *ARA* 12 (1983): 25–48.

11. Lewin and Foley, *Principles of Human Evolution*, 348.

12. Dennis Bonnette, *Origin of the Human Species*, VIBS 106 (Amsterdam: Rodopi, 2001), 108–9.

13. D'Errico, "Invisible Frontier," 192.

liberate series of technological steps. "Blade production, whether by direct or indirect percussion, requires the cognitive skills to perceive artefact forms not preordained by the raw material and to visualize the manufacturing process in three dimensions, in addition to the dexterity to carry out a complex series of operations and corrections as the process advances."[14] Blade production, a feature of the Mode 4 toolmaking industry, is both very old and characteristic of both *Homo sapiens* and Neanderthals. Blades from Middle Palaeolithic European sites like Coquelles, France; Crayford, England; and Le Rissori, Belgium, may be as old as 250 kya, prior to the arrival of *Homo sapiens*, while blades belonging to the Acheuleo-Yabrudian industry shared by Neanderthals and *Homo sapiens* in the Levant may predate 350 kya. In Africa, the Kapthurin Formation, Kenya, provides unequivocal evidence for early blades in a late Acheulean industry, thus demonstrating the presence of "a fully conceptualized, well executed method of blade production, and high level of technical competence in East Africa before 280 ka."[15] Blades in the form of backed pieces—tools modified by retouch on one side—have been found at sites like Twin Rivers and Kalambo Falls, Zambia, dated to approximately 300 kya. There is evidence of blade making at Kathu Pan in South Africa dated to 500 kya.[16]

Points

More sophisticated than blades are stone points, which were doubtless used to arm the tips of spears or perhaps even arrows. Retouched MSA stone points come from sites all around the African continent and exhibit a range of regional stylistic variations. They were carefully crafted to be used on projectiles, being thin, symmetrical, and aerodynamic. MSA points have often been deliberately modified either by thinning at the base or by fabricating a tang to facilitate hafting onto a wooden shaft. In Africa, retouched points are among the earliest MSA artifacts, going back to at least 235 kya. At Kathu Pan 1 in South Africa, archaeologists claim to have found the oldest evidence yet of stone-tipped spears dating to an incredible 500 kya.[17] "The find does

14. McBrearty and Brooks, "Revolution That Wasn't," 495.

15. McBrearty and Brooks, "Revolution That Wasn't," 496.

16. Jayne Wilkins and Michael Chazan, "Blade Production ~500 Thousand Years Ago at Kathu Pan 1, South Africa: Support for a Multiple Origins Hypothesis for Early Middle Pleistocene Blade Technologies," *JAS* 39, no. 6 (2012): 1883–1900.

17. J. Wilkins et al., "Evidence for Early Hafted Hunting Technology," *Science* 338, no. 6109 (November 16, 2012): 942–46, https://doi.org/10.1126/science.1227608.

more than simply extend the prehistory of stone-tipped spears—it puts those first spears firmly in the hands of *Homo heidelbergensis*," says Wilkins.[18]

Similarly, at a number of Neanderthal sites in Europe and the Levant, dating at least to early MIS 6 (186 kya), Levallois and retouched Mousterian stone points were used to arm weapons employed in hunting. In contrast to the lighter points of the MSA and Upper Palaeolithic, Middle Palaeolithic spear tips have a large, thick base, implying a large, heavy shaft. This sort of spear may have been used in close-range hunting for thrusting at prey rather than throwing.

Hafting and Composite Tools

The construction of composite tools and the hafting of stone points onto wooden shafts seems a clear earmark of human cognitive capacity, evincing not merely forethought but design. While the materials used to attach the points to handles or shafts have largely perished, the points themselves, as we have noted, bear evidence of having been designed with such an end in view. McBrearty and Brooks note that "point design is tightly constrained by aerodynamic and hafting requirements."[19] Traces of adhesive have been found on an MSA blade at the Apollo 11 Cave in southwestern Namibia and on small, backed pieces from the Howiesons Poort layers (65–59 kya) of Sibudu Cave in KwaZulu Natal, South Africa, indicating that the latter were used as barbed spear or arrow points. In Mousterian levels dated to about 60 kya at Umm El Tlel, Syria, a stone scraper and flakes with traces of bitumen adhesive used for hafting have been found. A blade from the Middle Palaeolithic levels at nearby Hummal bears similar traces. At the Italian site of Campitello (MIS 6), Neanderthals heated birch bark to around 350°F in order to obtain pitch for hafting flint flakes.

Now a 6.2-millimeter fragment of three-ply fiber cord, perhaps used in hafting, has been recovered from the Neanderthal site of Abri du Maras in France.[20] Found with implements dating to 40–50 kya (MIS 3), the cord has

18. As reported by Colin Barras, "First Stone-Tipped Spear Thrown Earlier Than Thought," *New Scientist*, November 15, 2012, https://www.newscientist.com/article/dn22508-first-stone-tipped-spear-thrown-earlier-than-thought.

19. McBrearty and Brooks, "Revolution That Wasn't," 498. See further Alison S. Brooks et al., "Long-Distance Stone Transport and Pigment Use in the Earliest Middle Stone," *Science* 360, no. 6384 (April 6, 2018): 90–94. The authors report on a series of MSA sites from the Olorgesailie basin, Kenya, dating from 295 kya to 320 kya. Hominins at these sites made prepared cores and points, manufactured red pigment, and procured stone tool materials from distances of twenty-five to fifty kilometers.

20. B. L. Hardy et al., "Direct Evidence of Neanderthal Fibre Technology and Its

three strings of fibers obtained from the inner bark of a gymnosperm (conifer tree) and each twisted clockwise (S-twist) and then as a group twisted counterclockwise (Z-twist). The excavators emphasize that cordage manufacture involves a complex *chaîne opératoire* (sequence of operations), including processing of the bark fibers and keeping track of multiple, sequential operations simultaneously to weave a cord. "Indeed, the production of cordage requires an understanding of mathematical concepts and general numeracy in the creation of sets of elements and pairs of numbers to create a structure," say B. L. Hardy et al. As the structure becomes more complex (multiple cords twisted to form a rope, ropes interlaced to form knots), it "requires a cognitive complexity similar to that required by human language." Hardy et al. believe that such cordage could imply a much vaster fiber-based technology: "While it is clear that the cord from Abri du Maras demonstrates Neanderthals' ability to manufacture cordage, it hints at a much larger fibre technology. Once the production of a twisted, plied cord has been accomplished it is possible to manufacture bags, mats, nets, fabric, baskets, structures, snares, and even watercraft." They opine that in view of the ongoing revelations of Neanderthal art and technology (to be surveyed below), "it is difficult to see how we can regard Neanderthals as anything other than the cognitive equals of modern humans."[21]

In Germany the excavations at Schöningen (to be discussed below) revealed four wooden shafts, showing that halfway through the Middle Pleistocene (MIS 11), 400 kya, composite tools were already in use. Accordingly, if we take "hafting" to comprise composite tools, then this item on d'Errico's chart ought to extend in Europe all the way back to 400 kya. Indeed, d'Errico thinks that the evidence for hafting and composite tools from Mousterian and Near Eastern sites is better than from African MSA sites, thus displaying the cognitive capacity of Neanderthals.[22]

Grindstones

The significance of grindstones as evidence of human cognition lies not in the stones themselves but in the activity of grinding, which involves the

---

Cognitive and Behavioral Implications," *SR* 10, no. 4889 (2020), https://doi.org/10.1038/s41598-020-61839-w.

21. Hardy et al., "Neanderthal Fibre Technology."

22. D'Errico, "Invisible Frontier," 194. D'Errico was writing prior to Wilkins et al.'s discovery of 500,000-year-old points at Kathu Pan. D'Errico and Stringer think that so far as hafting and composite tools are concerned, the level of technical development of Neanderthals seems comparable to that identified at Howiesons Poort sites of approximately 65–59 kya in South Africa ("Evolution, Revolution or Saltation," 1064).

processing of plant material and, most significantly, of pigment, one of the signatures of symbolic behavior. We shall say more about the significance of pigment later. The general presence of grindstones at so many MSA sites, including Bir Tarfawi, Egypt; Katanda, Democratic Republic of the Congo; ≠Gi, Botswana; and Mumbwa, Zambia, shows that processing of plant food was routine during the MSA. At other MSA sites, grindstones were apparently used to process pigment. Grindstones stained with traces of ocher, numerous in the LSA, have also been discovered in MSA levels at sites like Pomongwe, Zimbabwe; Die Kelders, South Africa; and ≠Gi, Botswana. Large grinding slabs were also recovered from MSA layers dating to 121 ± 6 kya at Florisbad, South Africa. Red ocher and ocher stained grindstones dating to well over 200 kya have been recovered from GnJh-15 in the Kapthurin Formation, Baringo, Kenya, and from Twin Rivers, Zambia.

In Europe, evidence of pigment use extends back to the Acheulean. Fragments of pigment along with grindstones perhaps used for ocher preparation have been found in Mousterian levels at Cueva de Castillo and Cueva Morín in Spain. The richest collection, comprising 451 colorant fragments and grinding stones, comes from Mousterian levels, dated to around 60–50 kya, of Pech-de-l'Azé I in France. These artifacts imply that Neanderthals were also involved in the processing and use of pigment or plant foods.

Economy and Social Organization

Specialized Hunting

One of the archaeological signatures of modern human behavior is said to be specialized hunting of large, dangerous animals. MSA people did not merely scavenge for food, feasting on the prey killed by predators like lions, but rather were themselves engaged in hunting large and dangerous game.[23] At ≠Gi the more than six hundred stone points recovered from MSA levels along with faunal remains are indicative of deliberate hunting. The fauna associated with these levels includes zebra (*Equus burchelli* and *E. capensis*), cape warthog (*Phacochoeorus aethiopicus*), and large bovids, including at least one *Pelorovis*, a huge (>900 kg), extinct relative of the smaller cape buffalo,

23. According to d'Errico and Stringer, "data now show that MSA people were competent hunters with a focus on large ungulate prey, but who also opportunistically exploited smaller ungulates, tortoises and small mammals, probably using traps and snares" ("Evolution, Revolution or Saltation," 1062).

widely regarded as the most dangerous big-game animal in Africa today. The taking of such large and aggressive animals as warthogs and *Pelorovis* as well as of such elusive herd animals as zebras is testimony to proficiency in hunting. Also, the location of the site and the presence of remains of water-dependent fauna support an interpretation of tactical hunting. In MSA levels at Klasies River, a cervical vertebra of an adult *Pelorovis* was found with the remnants of a stone point embedded in it, indicative of big-game hunting, along with the thoracic vertebra of an eland, a large antelope, showing a similar puncture wound.

In Europe "it has also become increasingly clear that Neandertals were expert hunters who could hunt a wide range of large mammals, including dangerous animals such as bison, rhinos, and bear, and could concentrate, if necessary, on selected species."[24] A growing body of evidence from sites dating 125–55 kya shows that Neanderthal subsistence strategies were based on hunting. At Mauran, France, Neanderthals slew hundreds of bisons and processed the carcasses on site; similar activity occurred at French sites such as La Borde, Champlost, and Coudoulous, and at Wallertheim, Germany. Neanderthals systematically hunted reindeer at Salzgitter-Lebenstedt, Germany, 58–54 kya. Around 200 kya at Biache-Saint-Vaast, France, Neanderthal hunters took mainly adult bovids but also hunted large bears. Moreover, the hunting equipment of Neanderthals was not limited to wooden spears. As we have seen, the evidence of hafting, not to mention the presence of impact scars on fossil remains, indicates that Neanderthals in Europe and the Levant, going back to at least 186 kya, were arming their weapons with stone points.

As a result of such finds, "very few scholars would argue now, as was routine in the early 1980s and 1990s, that . . . Neanderthal subsistence strategies were based on scavenging large mammal carcasses, that these populations had limited planning capacities, and were only able to develop expedient technologies involving a low degree of conceptualization. Now we know from prey hunted that Neanderthals were effective, flexible hunters, at a number of sites they were able to live in cold inhospitable environments, and at times they also exploited a broad range of terrestrial and marine resources."[25] Interesting in this connection is the fact, noted by palaeoanthropologists, that Neanderthal remains exhibit an unusually high frequency of fractures. According to Chris Stringer and Peter Andrews, when medical experts compared the distribution of Neanderthal skeletal injuries with those of different athletes and sportsmen, they found that the closest match was with rodeo riders, who regularly get

24. D'Errico, "Invisible Frontier," 190.
25. D'Errico and Stringer, "Evolution, Revolution or Saltation," 1062.

into close proximity to large, dangerous animals, suggesting that many Neanderthal injuries could have been sustained during big-game hunting.[26]

Undoubtedly the most amazing evidence of prehistoric hunting indicative of modern cognitive capacity comes from the discovery during the mid-1990s of eight wooden spears at the Lower Palaeolithic site of Schöningen, Germany.[27] The open-pit coal mine from which the spears were excavated has six sequences of multiple layers of sedimentary deposits. The spears were found in the fourth layer of the second sequence (13. II-4), dated to the third interglacial period 400–300 kya. These spears are nothing like the sticks that chimpanzees sharpen with their teeth and use to stab things. They are over six or seven feet long and are sculpted carefully from shafts of spruce or pine and designed for throwing (fig. 10.3).

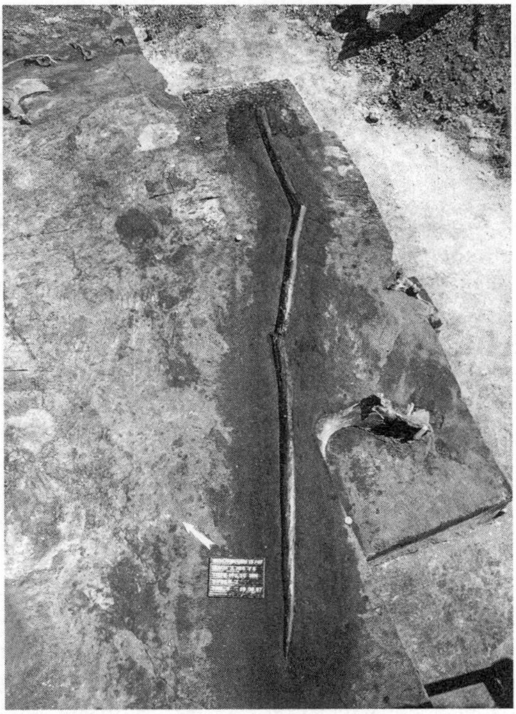

Figure 10.3. Wooden spear discovered at Schöningen, now distorted in shape as a result of lying under crushing sediments for hundreds of thousands of years.

The circumference of the first third of each spear is greater, so that it tapers off toward the butt. As a result, most of the weight is forward, to assist in throwing like a javelin. In fact, reproductions of the Schöningen spears have been made, and they turn out to be on a par with Olympic javelins![28] Hart-

26. Chris Stringer and Peter Andrews, *The Complete World of Human Evolution*, 2nd ed. (New York: Thames & Hudson, 2012), 223.

27. For a thorough account, see Hartmut Thieme, ed., *Die Schöninger Speere: Mensch und Jagd vor 400 000 Jahren* (Stuttgart: Theiss, 2007).

28. See the entertaining account by Hermann Rieder, "Zur Qualität der Schöninger Speere als Jagdwaffen—aus der Sicht der Sportwissenschaften," in Thieme, *Die Schöninger*

mut Thieme, the chief excavator at Schöningen, contends that the manufacture alone of the spears, not to mention the cooperation involved in hunting wild herd animals, is sufficient for abstract, conceptual thinking.[29]

The spears are found in association with remains of a herd of wild horses, the prey of the hunters. While other faunal remains are found at the site, 96 percent of the remains were from horses, indicating that they were targeted by the hunters.[30] The hunters apparently pinned the herd of horses against the shore of a lake and may have driven them into the water, where their escape could be slowed, thus evincing a hunting strategy. Thieme believes that in order for such a venture to succeed, "extremely careful planning, coordination, and discussion among the hunters" must have taken place, right down to the many details.[31] "Found in association with stone tools and the butchered remains of more than ten horses, the spears strongly suggest that systematic hunting, involving foresight, planning and the use of appropriate technology, was part of the behavioral repertoire of pre-modern hominids."[32] Thieme even believes that there must have already existed among the hunters at this early time "highly evolved, richly diverse, verbal communication."[33]

Big-game hunting is a risky business that would have required cooperation and perhaps even language ability, which is, of course, uniquely human. Possible big-game hunting has also been suggested at sites such as Boxgrove, England (ca. 500 kya), where the shoulder blade of a horse bears a puncture mark; Clacton, England (ca. 300 kya), where a fragment of a wooden spear was found;

Speere, 159–62. The Schöningen spears average about 2.2 meters in length and 500 grams in weight, making them only slightly heavier (100 grams) than javelins thrown by female athletes. Three wooden replicas of the spears were tested for distance, accuracy, and penetration. Without training with the spears, athletes were able to achieve comparable results to modern javelins. For example, an athlete with a modern range of 80 meters threw the replica 77 meters. So far as accuracy is concerned, the spears were found to have good accuracy within 25 meters and very good accuracy within 15 meters. As to penetration, the wooden spears penetrated the target up to 23 centimeters, while the modern, metal-tipped javelins penetrated to a depth of 29 centimeters. The Schöningen spears appear to have been adapted to their respective users, with the lighter spear III of 1.82 meters used perhaps by a woman or youngster and the heaviest spear VI of 2.5 meters by a very big man.

29. Hartmut Thieme, "Der grosse Wurf von Schöningen: Das neue Bild zur Kultur des frühen Menschen," in Thieme, *Die Schöninger Speere*, 227.

30. Rudolf Musil, "Die Pferde von Schöningen: Skelettreste einer ganzen Wildpferdherde," in Thieme, *Die Schöninger Speere*, 136–40.

31. Hartmut Thieme, "Überlegungen zum Gesamtbefund des Wild-Pferd-Jagdlagers," in Thieme, *Die Schöninger Speere*, 178.

32. Hartmut Thieme, "Lower Paleolithic Hunting Spears from Germany," *Nature* 385, no. 6619 (February 27, 1997): 807.

33. Thieme, "Der grosse Wurf von Schöningen," 227.

and Lehringen, Germany (ca. 125 kya), where a seven-foot yew spear was discovered between the ribs of an extinct elephant.[34] The remains at Boxgrove of several rhinoceros and horse skeletons bear butchery marks from stone tools, indicating that the butchery was "skillful, following a logical progression from skinning, through disarticulation to filleting and bone smashing."[35] Microscopic analysis of the wear on retouched stone-flake scrapers from sites such as Clacton indicates that a number of these tools were used for hide scraping. Hides could have been used for blankets, simple clothing, cords for stitching or tying things together, or carrying items. At Schöningen some two tons of meat would have been taken in the hunt, which could indicate preservation of meat by roasting or curing and the use of hides for clothing and similar purposes.[36]

As mentioned, also found with the spears at Schöningen were wooden tools incised with diagonal grooves at one end where stone points or flakes could have been attached. If this interpretation is correct, they represent the oldest composite tools yet discovered and are further evidence of the cognitive capacity of their manufacturers.

Unfortunately, no human remains were found in connection with the Schöningen spears, leaving us to guess at the identity of the hunters. The incredible antiquity of these artifacts and their similarity to the finds at Clacton and Boxgrove, where human remains have been found, suggest that they are the design and manufacture of *Homo heidelbergensis*, the ostensible progenitor of *Homo neanderthalensis* and *Homo sapiens*. Dietrich Mania insists that the hunters at Schöningen belong to late *Homo erectus*.[37] This may be correct, but *Homo erectus* is not associated anywhere with such artifacts as the spears or composite tools or advanced cognition. Mania tends to lump diverse *Urmenschen* into *Homo erectus*, even the fossils at Gran Dolina, which have since been shown to belong to a sister species of Neanderthals and

34. Hallam L. Movius Jr., "A Wooden Spear of Third Interglacial Age from Lower Saxony," *SJA* 6, no. 2 (1950): 139–42. This article contains an intriguing account of how such a large beast could have been hunted and killed.

35. Stringer and Andrews, *Complete World of Human Evolution*, 222. Moreover, they point out, the cut marks from stone tools always underlie any gnaw marks from other carnivores, who must therefore have scavenged the carcasses after the people had finished with them. Also, the people must have killed the prey, since animals like rhinoceroses have no natural predators.

36. Thieme, "Überlegungen," 182–83. Many questions remain unanswered. Thieme raises the intriguing question, *Why were the spears left behind?* He speculates that some sort of hunting ritual, perhaps involving a proto-religious belief, may have required their being abandoned (188).

37. Dietrich Mania, "Wer waren die Jäger von Schöningen?," in Thieme, *Die Schöninger Speere*, 222–24.

Homo sapiens, as well as fossils from Bilzingsleben, Germany; Ceprano, Italy; Arago, France; and Vertesszöllös, Hungary, which are usually regarded as belonging to *Homo heidelbergensis.* Mania rigidly restricts the designation *Homo heidelbergensis* to the Mauer mandible[38] alone, which he takes to be erectoid. Stringer and Andrews comment,

> One view was that all these fossils represented late forms of *Homo erectus,* like the Mauer jaw, but gradually it was realized that there were enough distinctive features in these fossils to distinguish them from *erectus.* In particular the braincase was higher and more filled out, especially at the sides, and this is a reflection of a larger average brain size, closer to that of living humans. In addition, the bony reinforcements of the skull, which are such a feature of *Homo erectus,* were reduced in this group of fossils. The face also retracted under the braincase compared to the jutting face of *erectus.*[39]

As a result, many have recognized the classification of these fossils as belonging to *Homo heidelbergensis,* which is regarded as the last common ancestor of *Homo sapiens* and Neanderthals.

Structured Use of Domestic Space

Many consider the designation of different areas of a habitation site for different activities to manifest a formalized conceptualization of the living space that is indicative of sophisticated cognitive functions.[40] Despite the difficulties posed by disturbance of the original site, there are a number of unambiguous examples of structured use of domestic space in MSA contexts. Some of the most intriguing concern deliberate arrangements of large piles of stones, whose purposes remain as yet unknown. For example, at Dar-es-Soltane 2, Morocco, an enigmatic heap of sandstone slabs about 1 meter in diameter and 30 centimeters high has been found. A larger pile of approximately sixty limestone balls was discovered in a fossil spring at El-Guettar, Tunisia. Similarly, a 1.3-meter-by-75-centimeter pile of thirty-six stone spheroids, each weighing between 600 and 1,200 grams, was found in an ancient spring near Windhoek, Namibia. Mumbwa Cave, Zambia, provides a striking example of MSA structures from sub-Saharan Africa. This cave contains three arch-

38. See *infra,* p. 330.
39. Stringer and Andrews, *Complete World of Human Evolution,* 150.
40. McBrearty and Brooks, "Revolution That Wasn't," 517.

shaped features built atop one another and made of stone blocks, ash, baked sediment, and lithic and bone debris that may have served as windbreaks, along with a number of hearths and post holes. There are six deliberately constructed stone-lined hearths in the cave built of large limestone blocks as well as of transported stone. These hearths contain quantities of indurated ash, burned bone, and burned limestone and sediment. Five of them superposed, the hearths display a clear conception of the space and the deliberate, repeated use of the space for the same function.

Bruniquel Cave

The most striking structured use of domestic space, however, comes from the strange, annular structures discovered deep inside Bruniquel Cave, France, and reported in 2016. No humans had entered the cave since its natural closing in the Pleistocene and its reopening in 1990, guaranteeing that the structures inside are undisturbed. The cave itself is a long, snaking corridor 10–15 meters wide, 4–7 meters high, and 482 meters long. The structures are found in a room at an astonishing depth of 336 meters, which places them in complete darkness. They consist of about four hundred whole or partial calcite stalagmites

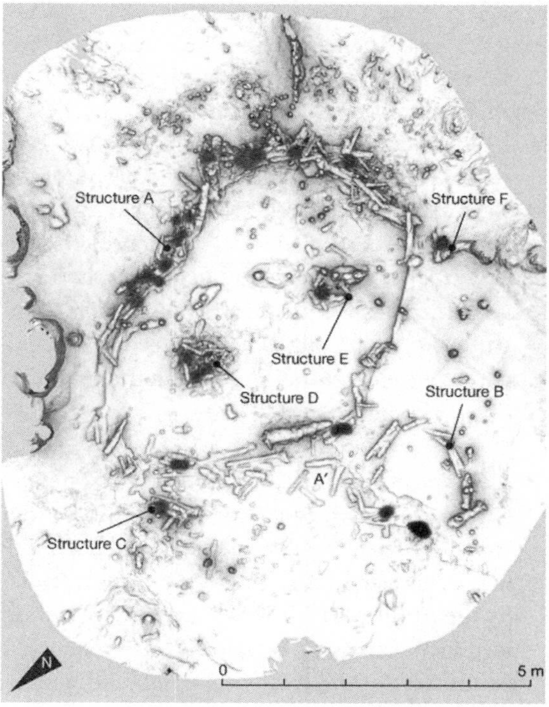

Figure 10.4. Layout of the Bruniquel Cave constructions, particularly the two larger rings. Blacked-out spots indicate burned areas. Jaubert et al., "Early Neanderthal Constructions Deep in Bruniquel Cave in Southwestern France," fig. 1. Used with permission.

weighing 2.2 tons and well calibrated to mean lengths of 34.4 centimeters for the long ones and 29.3 centimeters for the small ones. The pieces are arranged in two annular structures, one measuring 6.7 meters by 4.5 meters and the other 2.2 meters by 2.1 meters, and four smaller heaps. The two annular structures are composed of one to four stacked layers of aligned stalagmites. Short pieces were placed inside the superposed layers as supports, while others were placed vertically against the main structure perhaps as stays to reinforce the constructions. Traces of fire are to be found on all six structures (fig. 10.4).

Uranium-series dating of stalagmite regrowths on the structures and on burnt bone, combined with the dating of stalagmite tips in the structures, "give a reliable and replicated age of 176.5 thousand years (±2.1 thousand years), making these edifices among the oldest known well-dated constructions made by humans."[41] Neanderthals were the only humans living in Europe at that time. The attribution of the constructions to early Neanderthals is unprecedented in two ways, according to Jacques Jaubert, the lead archaeologist at the site.[42] First, it reveals the appropriation of a deep karst space (including lighting) by a premodern human species. Second, it involves elaborate constructions that have never been reported before, made with hundreds of partially calibrated, broken stalagmites that appear to have been deliberately moved and placed in their current locations, along with the presence of several intentionally heated zones.

Jaubert et al. include a figure (see fig. 10.5) to illustrate the sequence of tasks (*chaîne opératoire*) involved in these constructions.

They comment,

> This type of construction implies the beginnings of a social organization: This organization could consist of a project that was designed and discussed by one or several individuals, a distribution of the tasks of choosing, collecting and calibrating the speleofacts [stalagmites], followed by their transport (or vice versa) and placement according to a predetermined plan. This work would also require adequate lighting. . . . The complexity of the structure, combined with its difficult access (335 m from the cave entrance), are signs of a collective project and therefore suggest the existence of an organized society that was already on the path to "modernity."[43]

41. J. Jaubert et al., "Early Neanderthal Constructions Deep in Bruniquel Cave in Southwestern France," *Nature* 534, no. 7605 (May 25, 2016): 111.

42. Jaubert et al., "Early Neanderthal Constructions," 114.

43. Jaubert et al., "Early Neanderthal Constructions," Extended Data, fig. 8. Cf. the remarks of Paul Mellars on the design evident in the circular living structures in the Châtelp-

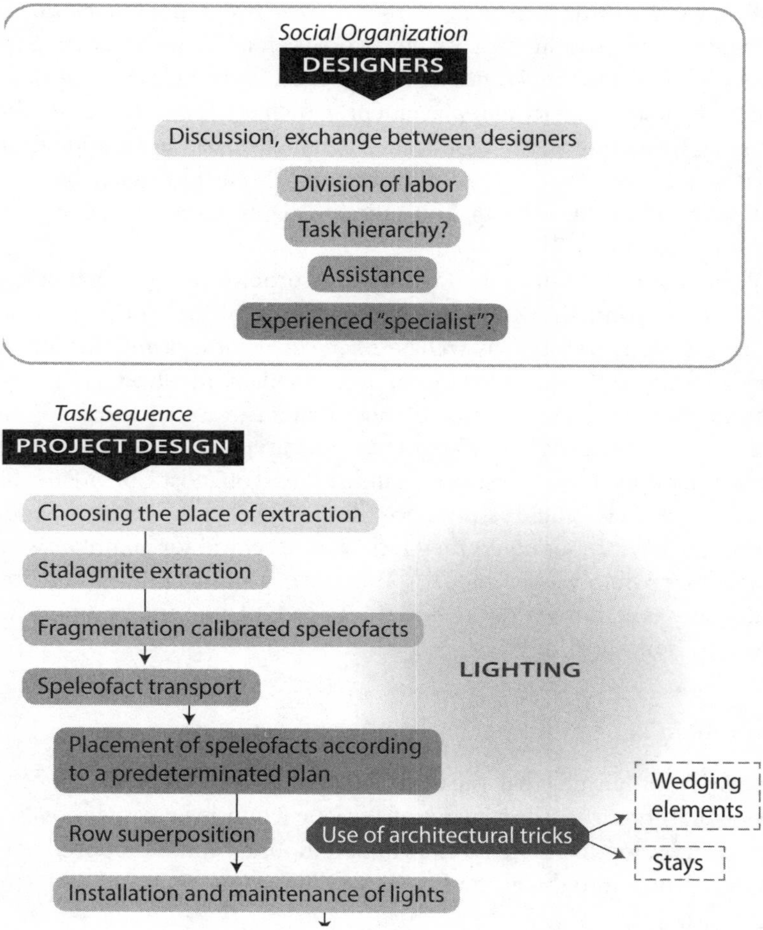

Figure 10.5. The sequence of tasks involved in the Bruniquel Cave constructions, illustrating the cognitive capacity of the builders. Based on Jaubert et al., "Early Neanderthal Constructions Deep in Bruniquel Cave in Southwestern France," Extended Data Figure 8.

It is not just the complexity of the structure, however, that is indicative of design. Beavers' dams and huts are probably just as complex but, like the

erronian levels at Arcy-sur-Cure in France, which appear quite similar to the remains of the constructions in Bruniquel Cave ("Cognitive Changes and the Emergence of Modern Humans in Europe," *CAJ* 1, no. 1 [1991]: 69).

nests of weaver birds mentioned earlier, are the result of blind instinct, not conception and planning, as is evident from their uniformity and frequency. What distinguishes the Neanderthal constructions is their conventionality, evident from their rarity and placement, which is the essence of symbolic thinking. Reflecting on the significance of the discovery at Bruniquel Cave, Chris Stringer remarks, "This discovery provides clear evidence that Neanderthals had fully human capabilities in the planning and the construction of 'stone' structures."[44]

It remains to be determined what would prompt these early humans to penetrate deep into the dark interior of a cave, torches in hand, to build such structures. Such activity may well betoken ritualistic or symbolic behavior, thus underlining the human status of the individuals involved. Jaubert et al. wonder, "What was the function of these structures at such a great distance from the cave entrance? Why are most of the fireplaces found on the structures rather than directly on the cave floor? Based on most Upper Paleolithic cave incursions, we could assume that they represent some kind of symbolic or ritual behavior, but could they rather have served for an unknown domestic use or simply as a refuge?"[45] The idea of a simple refuge is obviously inadequate as an answer to the questions posed above, and one can always appeal to "unknown" uses.

Terra Amata

Even more astonishing than the constructions in Bruniquel Cave, though not as well preserved, are the remains of a seasonal hunting camp discovered at Terra Amata, France. Here hunters built temporary huts composed of bent saplings driven into the ground in an oval shape and encircled with stones (fig. 10.6).

Inside the huts, remains of campfires were found, showing the domestication of fire by this time. Given the huts' evident design and complexity, there can be no doubt that the makers of such huts were human in the fullest sense of the word.

The campsite has been dated to an amazing 350 kya, roughly twice the age of the constructions in Bruniquel Cave. Again, the hunters could not have

44. Chris Stringer, "A Comment on the 'Early Neanderthal Constructions Deep in Bruniquel Cave in Southwestern France' Paper Published in *Nature*," press release, Natural History Museum, London, May 25, 2016, https://www.nhm.ac.uk/press-office/press-releases/comment-on-early-neanderthal-constructions-in-brunique-cave.html. "Stone" is in scare quotes because the speleofacts were stalagmites.

45. Jaubert et al., "Early Neanderthal Constructions," 114.

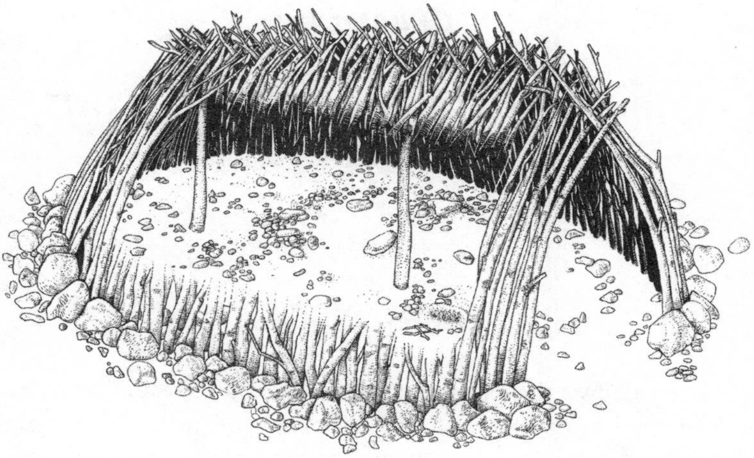

Figure 10.6. Artist's rendering of a hunter's hut at Terra Amata dating to 350 kya. Tattersall, *The Fossil Trail*, 169. Used with permission.

been *Homo sapiens* but must have been representatives of *Homo heidelbergensis*. The finds thus reinforce the great antiquity of the origin of humanity.

Summary and Prospect

We have highlighted examples of archaeological signatures from the domains of technology, including production and use of blades, stone points, hafting and composite tools, and grindstones, and of economy and social organization, including specialized hunting and the structured use of domestic space. Some of these signatures are equally manifest among Neanderthals as well as *Homo sapiens*, and some push us all the way back to *Homo heidelbergensis* as the bearer of modern human cognitive capacity. In the next chapter we shall turn to the most decisive domain, symbolic behavior.

Chapter 11

THE EVIDENCE OF ARCHAEOLOGY (PART 2)

Symbolic Behavior

Symbolic thinking is the quintessential human cognitive ability. We earlier appealed to prehistoric art to establish a firm *terminus ad quem* for the origin of humanity. Now we want to examine various archaeological signatures of such symbolic behavior.

Figure 11.1. Cave painting from Lubang Jeriji Saléh Cave on Borneo.

Figure 11.2. Cave painting from Leang Bulu'Sipong 4 Cave on Sulawesi.

Image and Representation

In recent years, discoveries have pushed the date of prehistoric art into the ever more distant past. On the island of Borneo, Indonesia, a cave painting of a bull has been dated by uranium-thorium testing of calcium carbonate deposits overlying the figure to greater than 40 kya (fig. 11.1).[1]

In Sulawesi, Indonesia, the oldest-known instance of figurative art, depicting a scene with a buffalo and pigs, and perhaps human hunters, has been dated by uranium-thorium testing of calcite deposits overlying the figures to a minimum age of 44 kya (fig. 11.2).[2] These caves also contain, as we have seen, hand stencils of comparable age.

Now even older hand stencils have been identified in Maltravieso Cave in Spain, along with other instances of nonfigurative paintings in La Pasiega Cave and Ardales Cave. Uranium-thorium testing of carbonate crusts overlying the stencil dated it to at least 66.7 kya and dated the paintings collectively at a minimum of 64.8 kya, predating the arrival of *Homo sapiens*

1. M. Aubert et al., "Paleolithic Cave Art in Borneo," *Nature* 564, no. 7735 (November 7, 2018): 254–57, https://doi.org/10.1038/s41586-018-0679-9. The date of the deposit over the painting yields a minimum age for the painting, whereas the date of a deposit that has itself been painted over would give a maximum age of that painting. The former is obviously more significant.

2. Ewen Callaway, "Is This Cave Painting Humanity's Oldest Story?," *Nature*, December 11, 2019, https://doi.org/10.1038/d41586-019-03826-4.

in Europe by some twenty thousand years. "The implication is, therefore, that the artists were Neandertals."[3]

Reflecting on the significance of this finding, Hoffmann et al. state,

> This cave painting activity constitutes a symbolic behavior by definition, and one that is deeply rooted. At Ardales, distinct episodes over a period of more than 25 ka corroborate that we are not dealing with a one-off burst but with a long tradition that may well stretch back to the time of the annular construction found in Bruniquel cave, France, dated to 176.5 ± 2.1 ka ago. Dating results for the excavation site at Cueva de los Aviones, Spain, which place symbolic use of marine shells and mineral pigments by Neandertals at >115 ka ago, further support the antiquity of Neandertal symbolism.[4]

Given that the use of imagery and representation in art is a signature of modern human behavior among *Homo sapiens*, it would be prejudicial to deny the humanity of the Neanderthal artists. The contemporaneous presence of similar cave art in both Spain and Indonesia half the world away and the age of ornamental use of shells by Neanderthals imply an origin of symbolic behavior and hence humanity that is vastly older still. Hoffmann et al. conclude, "The corollary of these findings is that the capacity for symbolism must have been inherited from a common ancestor. As a working hypothesis, we suggest that the origins of language and the advanced cognition characteristic of extant humans may precede the period before the divergence of the Neandertal lineage, more than half-a-million years ago."[5]

3. D. L. Hoffmann et al., "U-Th Dating of Carbonate Crusts Reveals Neandertal Origin of Iberian Cave Art," *Science* 359, no. 6378 (February 23, 2018): 912–15, https://doi.org/10.1126/science.aap7778.

4. Hoffmann et al., "U-Th Dating," 915. See Dirk L. Hoffmann et al., "Symbolic Use of Marine Shells and Mineral Pigments by Iberian Neandertals 115,000 Years Ago," *SA* 4, no. 2 (February 2018): eaar5255, https://doi.org/10.1126/sciadv.aar5255. Of this evidence, they conclude, "In conjunction with the evidence that cave painting in Europe dates back to at least 64.8 ka ago, it leaves no doubt that Neandertals shared symbolic thinking with early modern humans and that, as far as we can infer from material culture, Neandertals and early modern humans were cognitively indistinguishable." NB that the discovery of such ancient beads suggests even greater antiquity of the Neanderthal manufacture and use of fiber strings examined in the previous chapter under "Hafting and Composite Tools," pp. 289–90.

5. Hoffmann et al., "Symbolic Use."

Pigment

Closely related to prehistoric art is the processing and use of pigment. The traces of pigment use in the archaeological record most frequently involve iron oxides, which are found in the form of red hematite or yellow limonite. Whether pigment was used for artistic or decorative purposes or for merely functional purposes such as tanning hides, sunscreen, or medicine can be ambiguous in isolated cases, but as Sally McBrearty and Alison Brooks remind us, "If metallic oxides are recovered in association with undoubted art objects, or at sites whose inhabitants are known to have functioned within a well articulated symbolic system, the materials are usually assumed to have been used as a coloring medium."[6] Such an aesthetic interest is symptomatic of modern humanity.

In the MSA levels of Blombos Cave, South Africa, two ocher pieces bearing similar engraved geometric patterns have been found, dating to 77 kya. Francesco d'Errico comments, "The presence of symbolic engravings on artifactual pigment makes it unlikely that the thousands of pigment fragments found at Middle Stone Age sites were strictly functional and suggests instead that they were used for symbolic purposes."[7] Evidence for "nonfunctional" use of pigment includes the deliberate preference for intense red hues, preference for pigment from faraway sources, deliberate heating to change pigment color, presence of pigment on just one side of an object, coloration of shell beads, and so on.[8] Moreover, what we have seen above concerning the antiquity of cave art should settle the question.

Evidence indicates an ancient and widespread use of pigment in Africa during the MSA. Excavations at the site of GnJh-15 in the Kapthurin Formation uncovered more than seventy pieces of red pigment as part of an assemblage of stone artifacts, fragmentary bone, and ostrich eggshell fragments, covered by many meters of volcanic debris dating from 285 kya. Similarly, excavations at Twin Rivers yielded 176 fragments of pigment in layers

6. Sally McBrearty and Alison S. Brooks, "The Revolution That Wasn't: A New Interpretation of the Origin of Modern Human Behavior," *JHE* 39, no. 5 (November 2000): 524, https://doi.org/10.1006/jhev.2000.0435.

7. Francesco d'Errico, "The Invisible Frontier: A Multiple Species Model for the Origin of Behavioral Modernity," *EA* 12, no. 4 (August 5, 2003): 188, https://doi.org/10.1002/evan.10113; cf. Francesco d'Errico and Chris B. Stringer, "Evolution, Revolution or Saltation Scenario for the Emergence of Modern Cultures?," *PTRSB* 366, no. 1567 (April 12, 2011): 1066, https://doi.org/10.1098/rstb.2010.0340.

8. D'Errico and Stringer, "Evolution, Revolution or Saltation," 1065.

dated 400–260 kya at the transition from the Acheulean to the MSA.[9] "The chronological attribution of the older pigments from Africa (Kapthurin, Twin Rivers) and their association with Lupemban stone tools [dating to around 300 kya] seem to indicate that the use of pigments originated with *Homo heidelbergensis* or archaic *Homo sapiens*," d'Errico explains. "If colorant use is taken as an archeological indication of symbolic behavior, then the origin of these abilities, traditionally attributed to anatomically modern humans, has to be considered more ancient."[10] That conclusion is confirmed by evidence for extremely early use of specularite—a glittery form of hematite useful only for visual display—at Fauresmith, South Africa, from >500 kya.[11]

Pigment use is not limited to the African MSA. Neanderthals in Europe were using pigment, mostly black but also red, since approximately 300 kya, though systematic use occurs only after 60 kya. Fragments of pigment come from some forty Middle and Upper Palaeolithic sites in Europe, the richest collection being Pech-de-l'Azé I, dated 60–50 kya. Marie Soressi and Francesco d'Errico reject the idea of an *exclusively* functional use of pigment on ethnographic grounds: "In traditional societies studied by ethnography pigments are always used for symbolic activities. . . . If the current model is applicable to Neanderthal society, the systematic use of pigments by these societies is a strong argument in favor of their capacity to produce symbolic cultures."[12] Whatever we make of this argument, the cave paintings at Maltravieso, La Pasiega, and Ardales bear witness, as we have seen, to Neanderthal artistic use of pigment >64 kya. Such use supports the multispecies model of human cognitive capacity.

9. Lawrence S. Barham, "Possible Early Pigment Use in South-Central Africa," *CA* 39, no. 5 (1998): 703–10.

10. D'Errico, "Invisible Frontier," 198.

11. Ian Watts, Michael Chazan, and Jayne Wilkins, "Early Evidence for Brilliant Ritualized Display: Specularite Use in the Northern Cape (South Africa) between ~500 and ~300 Ka," *CA* 57, no. 3 (June 2, 2016): 287–301, https://doi.org/10.1086/686484. "Specularite circumvents the objections most frequently raised about assigning a pigment status to ferruginous materials: its only use seems to have been for visual display, and it is unlikely to be a natural component of archaeological deposits" (298).

12. Marie Soressi and Francesco d'Errico, "Pigments, gravures, parures: Les comportements symboliques controversés des Néandertaliens," in *Les Néandertaliens: Biologie et cultures*, ed. Bernard Vandermeersch and Bruno Maureille (Paris: Éditions du CTHS, 2007), 306.

Burials

Burial of the dead is actually better attested in the archaeological record among Neanderthals than among *Homo sapiens*. There are only three MSA sites where evidence of burial has been found: Nazlet Khater and Taramsa in Egypt, dated respectively to 40 kya and 68 kya, and Border Cave, which appears to be the oldest MSA burial. Sediments overlying the grave are dated to 105 kya. Interestingly, hematite pencils are found throughout the entire MSA sequence, and the human infant (BC 3) burial site is stained through the application of hematite and associated with a perforated *Conus* shell, which may have been ornamental.

The earliest evidence for burial among *Homo sapiens* comes not from Africa but from the Levant at the site of Qafzeh. Of the fifteen individuals represented in the cave, at least four appear to have been deliberately buried. Dated to 120–90 kya, these remains are associated with perforated and ocher-stained *Glycymeris* shells. Deer antlers were buried with the body of one child. Cultural iconic objects seem also associated with the burials at Skhūl, where a man was buried holding the lower jaw of a massive wild boar, and shells similar to those at Qafzeh are found in the Mousterian layers.

Of the fifty-eight known Middle Palaeolithic burial sites in Europe and the Near East, however, thirty-five belong to Neanderthals. D'Errico reports that there is a growing consensus among palaeoanthropologists that Neanderthals buried their dead.[13] We have about twenty reasonably complete Neanderthal skeletons out of over five hundred individuals represented. Complete skeletons are so rare that it is likely that these dead were deliberately buried. Apart from intentional burial of these individuals, it is difficult to explain why articulated skeletons are completely lacking in earlier occupation of caves at numerous sites with good preservation of faunal remains in Middle Pleistocene Europe, in the Near East, and in Africa. So there is "general agreement that most if not all relatively complete Neanderthal skeletons were deliberately interred."[14]

Neanderthal burial sites in the Levant are at least as old as those of *Homo sapiens*. The C layer at Tabūn has been dated by thermoluminescence to 160 kya, making the burial of the Neanderthal specimen C1 the oldest in the world. McBrearty and Brooks observe that burial and other

13. D'Errico, "Invisible Frontier," 72–73.

14. McBrearty and Brooks, "Revolution That Wasn't," 519. Stringer and Andrews confirm, "Although some scientists dispute it, it is generally agreed that Neanderthals buried their dead" (Chris Stringer and Peter Andrews, *The Complete World of Human Evolution*, 2nd ed. [New York: Thames & Hudson, 2012], 154).

special treatments of the dead are a consistent feature of the symbolic life of modern human societies, so the belief that the Neanderthals deliberately buried their dead has been a major factor contributing to an impression of their humanity.[15] This impression does not depend, however, on investing the burial procedure with a ritual significance, though it does not exclude such significance. That the corpses of their fellows were treated differently from dead animals suggests that something more was going on than mere housecleaning.[16]

Language

The nineteenth-century philologist Max Müller declared, "The one great barrier between the brute and man is *Language*. Man speaks, and no brute has ever uttered a word. Language is the Rubicon, and no brute will dare to cross it."[17] Language may be thought of as a symbolic and freely extensible communication system, and speech as the externalization of language in

15. McBrearty and Brooks, "Revolution That Wasn't," 518–19. For example, Stringer and Andrews state, "The burials . . . hint at complexity in Neanderthal minds and lives, since some appear to show particular care and treatment to the body" (*Complete World of Human Evolution*, 154).

16. Contrast careful Neanderthal interment of the dead with the apparent tossing of corpses down a thirteen-meter shaft at Sima de los Huesos, Atapuerca, Spain.

17. Cited in Derek Bickerton, *Adam's Tongue: How Humans Made Language, How Language Made Humans* (New York: Hill & Wang, 2009), 74. But do not parrots utter words? Not in the linguistic sense, since their vocalizations, though homophonous with genuine words, lack reference. Tomasello thus emphasizes that in language acquisition simple association of words is not enough; a child must understand reference:

> If simple association were sufficient, then we would have to say that many domestic dogs—as well as some apes, parrots, and dolphins—are linguistic creatures. For the child to understand a word as a piece of language she must understand it as something the adult is using to direct her attention to some referent in the environment—he is inviting her to jointly attend with him to that referent—in a way that she, the child, could do in reverse toward the adult if she so wished. Then we can say that the child is comprehending language qua language. (Michael Tomasello, *Becoming Human: A Theory of Ontogeny* [Cambridge, MA: Belknap Press of Harvard University Press, 2019], 113)

Chimpanzees that have been taught to use signs, like the celebrated Kanzi, lack the ability to read intentions (Tomasello, *Becoming Human*, 123–24). Laland observes that one can train a rat or a pigeon to form an association between a cue and an action, and likewise there is little in the ape sign-language literature that cannot be explained by simple rules of associative learning and perhaps a little imitation (Kevin N. Laland, *Dar-*

sound.[18] Extensive studies of so-called animal communication systems bear out Müller's judgment.[19] Language involves symbolism, the use of conven-

---

win's Unfinished Symphony: How Culture Made the Human Mind [Princeton: Princeton University Press, 2017], 178).

For a dramatic illustration of how essential intentionality is to reference and, hence, to genuine language, see the film *The Miracle Worker* (Beverly Hills, CA: United Artists, 1962), which tells the story of how Helen Keller, who was blind and deaf from nineteen months of age, achieved breakthrough to language by suddenly coming to grasp that one can use words to refer to things. The climactic scene may be found online at "Helen Keller—Water Scene from 'The Miracle Worker,'" YouTube video, 6:11, posted by Helen Keller Channel, March 26, 2010, https://www.youtube.com/watch?v=lUV65sV8nuo. For a brilliant philosophical account of reference, appealing to the intentionality of agents, see Arvid Båve, "A Deflationary Theory of Reference," *Synthèse* 169 (2009): 51–73.

18. Sverker Johansson, "Language Abilities in Neanderthals," *ARL* 1 (2015): 313, https://doi.org/10.1146/annurev-linguist-030514-124945. Johansson points out that much of the debate over ancient hominins' capacity for language is really about their capacity for speech. Fortunately, the presence of speech entails the presence of language, since the term *speech* is usually reserved for the externalization of language in sound and is not used for other vocalizations. With most writers, therefore, I shall not be concerned always to distinguish one from the other.

19. See Marc D. Hauser, *The Evolution of Communication* (Cambridge, MA: MIT Press, 1996). Just how diluted an understanding of communication is at stake is evident in Hauser's assertions that flowers must communicate with bees in order for pollination to be successful and computer programmers must design software to communicate with their hardware (1). On "comparative animal behavior," see further M. D. Hauser et al., "The Mystery of Language Evolution," *FP* 5 (May 7, 2014): 2–5, who contend that animal communication systems are of no help in understanding the origin of human language:

> The question of interest is whether these seemingly modest claims about animal signals help us understand the evolution of our capacity to represent words, including not only their referentiality but their abstractness, their composition via phonology and morphology, and their syntactic roles. Our simple answer is No, for five specific reasons: for animals, (i) acquisition of the entire lexicon is complete by the end of the early juvenile period, and for most species, the sounds or gestures are innately specified; (ii) those sounds and gestures refer, at best, to directly observable objects or events, with great uncertainty about the precise meaning, and no evidence for signals that map to abstract concepts that are detached from sensory experiences; (iii) with a few rare exceptions, individuals only produce single utterances or gestures, never combining signals to create new meaning based on new structures; (iv) utterances are holistic, with no evidence of complex syntactic composition derived from an inventory of discrete morphological elements; (v) the utterances or gestures are not marked by anything remotely resembling grammatical classes, agreement, etc. Given these differences, it is not possible to empirically support a continuity thesis whereby a nonhuman animal form served as a precursor to the modern human form. (4)

tional signs to refer to something other than the animals themselves. Animal vocalizations do not exhibit genuine referentiality but at most so-called "functional reference." Vervet monkey calls, for example, differ depending on whether the perceived predator is a leopard, a snake, or an eagle, but the calls are not words having leopards, snakes, or eagles as referents. Such calls are not conventional but are hardwired by evolutionary conditioning in vervet brains, and the response to the call by other monkeys can be similarly explained as the result of Pavlovian conditioning. Like a fire alarm, the monkey vocalizing the call lacks any intention of referring, for example, to a leopard, and "specific responses to signals can develop with experience based on simple classical conditioning and without drawing on the concept of information, the meaning of calls, or mental representations of a signal's purported referent in listeners."[20] Since animal signals lack symbolic meaning, questions like "What did that monkey mean by that signal?" or "What was that monkey referring to?" are ill-posed.[21] Such calls are at best functionally referential; that is to say, although context-specific calls may function much in the same way as human words like "Fire!" do, that implies nothing about the underlying mental processes involved. Thus, "the vervet leopard alarm does not refer to leopards in the way the English word 'leopard' does. Rather, to a listener the call means that a leopard is present in the same way that the leopard's growl does, or even the way that the sound of dry leaves crunching under a leopard's foot might."[22] Functional reference is thus wholly different from linguistic reference. Brandon Wheeler and Julia Fischer conclude: "The concept of functional reference, while historically important for the field,

20. Brandon C. Wheeler and Julia Fischer, "Functionally Referential Signals: A Promising Paradigm Whose Time Has Passed," *EA* 21, no. 5 (September 2012): 199, https://doi.org/10.1002/evan.21319. Tomasello thinks that the reason apes do not naturally communicate referentially is that they do not possess the shared intentionality infrastructure on which human communication is built (*Becoming Human*, 92–93).

21. Brandon C. Wheeler and Julia Fischer, "The Blurred Boundaries of Functional Reference: A Response to Scarantino & Clay," *AnBehav* 100 (2015): e9–e13, https://doi.org/10.1016/j.anbehav.2014.11.007.

22. Wheeler and Fischer, "Functionally Referential Signals," 203. They conclude: "It follows that neither the production nor the perception of functionally referential signals is anywhere closer to human communication than is that of nonfunctionally referential signals" (203). Wheeler and Fischer recommend that, rather than pursue vainly further attempts to find true referentiality in animal signals, we drop the term "functionally referential signals" from the animal communication literature in favor of more accurate and linguistically neutral descriptions such as "context-specific signals," "predator-specific alarm calls," or "food-specific calls."

has outlived its usefulness and become a red herring in the pursuit of the links between primate communication and human language."[23]

Similarly, while chimpanzees in captivity have been trained to punch certain buttons or make a gesture in order to obtain various specific foods, there is no reason to think that when the chimpanzees press a button or select a picture depicting a banana, they are referring to a banana.[24] They are conditioned by training to participate in response-reward activity that is at best functionally referential in obtaining the desired benefits. Trained chimpanzees are thus no nearer to genuine language acquisition.

As fascinating as the question of *how* language and its externalization in speech originated may be, it is only indirectly related to the question that interests us—namely, *when* they originated. Language's distinctness from animal communication systems at best suggests that language is something that does not originate early in the *Homo* lineage close to animality. To gain some insight as to the time of its origin, we may look to anatomical, genetic, and archaeological clues.

Anatomical Clues

Anatomically, a large brain size in a hominin is a prerequisite for language capacity, and the presence of a large brain increases the probability of linguistic ability. So Roger Lewin and Robert Foley think that once hominins attained a brain size in excess of one thousand cubic centimeters, there seems to be little doubt that linguistic capabilities existed and that therefore language may have been present at least in Neanderthals.[25] "Given their large brains, there is little doubt that Neanderthals are intelligent flexible hominins, even if there may have been some differences between them and modern humans."[26]

23. Wheeler and Fischer, "Functionally Referential Signals," 195.

24. Noting that "the main question is whether animals, limited to sense faculties alone, can ever understand the nature of referencing at all," Dennis Bonnette aptly remarks, "A chimpanzee's correct identification of, communication about, and employment of an appropriate tool to obtain food is no assurance of true intellective understanding. A spider weaving its web to catch insects repeatedly creates the same type of tool designed exquisitely to catch the same type of victim. . . . Nature programs the spider, human beings the chimpanzee" (*Origin of the Human Species*, VIBS 106 [Amsterdam: Rodopi, 2001], 59, 56).

25. Roger Lewin and Robert A. Foley, *Principles of Human Evolution*, 2nd ed. (Oxford: Blackwell, 2004), 474.

26. Lewin and Foley, *Principles of Human Evolution*, 397.

In addition to brain size, brain organization is vital. Linguistic ability is associated with both Wernicke's area and Broca's area, among others, in the brain. Studies of hominin endocasts reveal signs of Broca's area in *Homo rudolfensis* and later species but not in Australopithecines.[27] Therefore doubt has been cast on linguistic ability among Australopithecines. Unfortunately, as previously mentioned, palaeoneurologists can learn precious little about hominin language ability from fossil endocasts.

Given the paucity of information to be gained from endocasts, investigators have turned to the study of other anatomical features requisite for speech. Hearing will obviously be important for human speech. Bones of the human ear can be compared with those of both living apes and fossil hominins. Although the aural capability of chimpanzees is basically identical to our own, human ears do have a higher sensitivity in the 2–4 kilohertz range, reflecting differences in the ossicles of the middle ear. Key features of certain speech sounds lie within this range.[28] Fossil remains from both Neanderthals and *Homo heidelbergensis* exhibit middle ear ossicles that lie within the range of modern human ears.[29]

What about the capability of speech? Hauser et al. are skeptical about the presence of language outside *Homo sapiens.* With respect to the palaeontological evidence, they state, "Recent studies suggest that approximately equal proportions of the horizontal and vertical sectors of the vocal tract are necessary for speech production (Lieberman, 2011). This conformation is present in *Homo sapiens* alone, as a result of the autapomorphic retraction of its face below the neurocranium. This points to a critical change *after* divergence from the Neanderthals."[30] With respect to the archaeological evidence, they observe that Neanderthals "failed to leave any unequivocal evidence for the symbolic behavior patterns . . . that characterize modern, linguistic, human beings." By way of comparison, "the artifactual record of

27. Lewin and Foley, *Principles of Human Evolution*, 465–66.

28. Sound waves have a frequency measured as the number of oscillations, or cycles, per second, called hertz. The sounds that constitute human speech are distributed across a range of frequencies, mostly between 100 and 5,000 hertz. The full range of human hearing extends approximately from 20 to 20,000 hertz.

29. As reported by Johansson, "Language Abilities in Neanderthals," 317; Stringer and Andrews, *Complete World of Human Evolution*, 44.

30. Hauser et al., "Mystery of Language Evolution," 5 (my emphasis). The reference is to Daniel E. Lieberman, *The Evolution of the Human Head* (Cambridge, MA: Harvard University Press, 2011). NB that this is a different Lieberman than Philip Lieberman, cited below.

contemporaneous Middle Stone Age sapiens in Africa after about 100k year ago tells a very different story, a qualitative transformation in behavior that was reflected in the earliest symbolic objects, complex planning, multi-stage technologies, and other anticipations of Cro-Magnon cognitive prowess." Thus, "archaeological evidence . . . points to the emergence of a language of thought in early *Homo sapiens*, replete with symbolic representations that were externalized in iconic form. . . . Whenever this occurred, present evidence suggests it was *after* [my emphasis] our divergence with Neanderthals, and thus, a very recent event."[31]

Let us look more closely at each of these considerations. Consider first the anatomical features evidenced by palaeontology. Philip Lieberman explains that the position of the larynx is the key to the difference between the supralaryngeal vocal tract (SVT) of all other mammals and the adult modern human SVT.[32] The SVT of chimpanzees is significantly different from that of humans, so that although they can hear what we hear, they cannot produce articulate speech.[33]

In early *Homo sapiens* there occurred a restructuring of the skull that brought the human face into line with the braincase, thus reducing prognathism. In the process the oral cavity was shortened, forcing the tongue up and back into the throat. The larynx is pushed lower in the throat to a position opposite the fourth, fifth, and sixth cervical vertebrae. The hyoid bone, a U-shaped bone positioned above the larynx and connected to it by ligaments and muscle, also descends with the larynx. The adult human SVT thus features a curved tongue partly occupying the "horizontal" oral cavity and, at a right angle to it, the vertical pharyngeal cavity.

Remarkably, in human ontogeny, from embryogenesis to childhood, this process is recapitulated. The tongue moves back into the pharynx, pushing

31. Hauser et al., "Mystery of Language Evolution," 6. Cf. Tattersall's slightly more nuanced claim that when we put the cranial evidence together with what the archaeological record suggests, it is hard to avoid the conclusion that *articulate* [my emphasis] language is the sole province of fully modern humans (Ian Tattersall, *The Fossil Trail: How We Know What We Think We Know about Human Evolution*, 2nd ed. [Oxford: Oxford University Press, 2009], 212). As we shall see, the adjective *articulate* has to bear enormous weight if this claim is not to be plainly false.

32. Philip Lieberman, "Current Views on Neanderthal Speech Capabilities: A Reply to Boe et al. (2002)," *JP* 35, no. 4 (2007): 552–63. The supralaryngeal vocal tract is the airway above the larynx.

33. Hauser et al., "Mystery of Language Evolution," 5. See fig. 8.3 in D. Liebermann, *Evolution of the Human Head*, 287. But see *infra* on the overriding importance of neural circuitry.

the larynx down, until the "horizontal" oral cavity and vertical pharyngeal cavity of the SVT have equal 1:1 proportions. In the first two years of life the face retracts and the base of the skull flexes from the relatively flat contour that it had at birth. This cranial base flexion ceases by two to three years of age, but the tongue and larynx continue to descend until ages six to eight, when the proportions of the oral and pharyngeal cavities become equal.

The descent of the larynx in adult humans enlarges the space above the larynx, so that sounds emitted from the larynx can be modified to a greater degree than is possible for any other mammal. Movements of the tongue in the right-angle space defined by the mouth and pharynx are able to produce the changes necessary for utterance of the so-called quantal vowels (phonetically discrete vowels) [i], [u] and [a] (fig. 11.3).[34] By contrast, the tongues of apes, like the tongues of human newborns, are located almost entirely within their mouths, making the production of these vowel sounds impossible.

Fossil remains at Skhūl and Qafzeh revealed a fully human SVT in archaic humans 100 kya. Philip Lieberman points out that the biological disadvantages of the human SVT (such as choking on food, impacted molars, reduced chewing efficiency) would reduce fitness unless it was being used to enhance the intelligibility of speech communication.[35] The presence of "such an odd, seemingly maladaptive configuration" is thus indicative of articulate speech.[36]

What about other ancient hominins? The discovery in 1989 at Kebara, Israel, of a Neanderthal hyoid bone virtually identical to the modern bone has been taken by some as evidence for their language ability. Two similar hyoid bones have been found for *Homo heidelbergensis*. By contrast, a hyoid

34. Lieberman maintains that in order to produce stable, quantal vowels, an SVT must consist of an oral cavity and a pharyngeal cavity of 1:1 proportions and have a tongue that is able to modify each cavity to a ratio of about 10:1. For example, when we say the vowel [i], we raise and extend the tongue, making the cross-sectional area of the oral cavity about ten times smaller than the pharyngeal cavity. But when we say the vowel [a], we depress and retract the tongue, making the cross-sectional area of the pharyngeal cavity about ten times smaller than the oral cavity. See figure 11.3, which shows tongue positions and formant frequencies differentiating speech sounds. Lieberman explains that formant frequencies are the frequencies at which maximum acoustic energy can pass through the SVT, denoted F1, F2, and so on. The relative positioning of F1 and F2 is usually sufficient to distinguish a sound from all others. The formant frequency patterns that differentiate vowels are produced by changes in the shape of the SVT, allowing maximum energy through at particular formant frequencies (Lieberman, *Evolution of the Human Head*, 318).

35. Philip Lieberman, "On Neanderthal Speech and Human Evolution," *BBS* 19, no. 1 (1996): 157.

36. D. Lieberman, *Evolution of the Human Head*, 299; cf. 327.

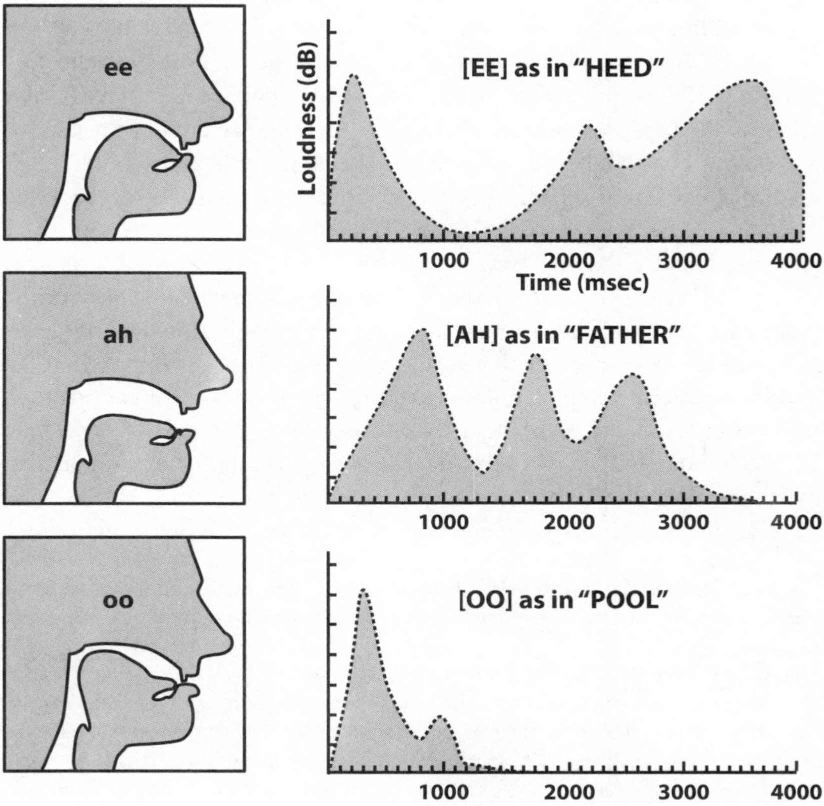

Figure 11.3. Changes in the shape of the tongue modify the harmonic peaks (formant frequencies) that differentiate speech sounds. Tongue position and formant frequencies are shown for the sounds [i], [a], and [u].

bone from *Australopithecus afarensis* is basically apelike. Philip Lieberman protests that it is impossible to determine larynx position and SVT morphology from an isolated hyoid bone.[37] Rather, what is critical is the proportion-

37. But see the paper by Ruggero D'Anastasio et al., "Micro-Biomechanics of the Kebara 2 Hyoid and Its Implications for Speech in Neanderthals," *PLoS ONE* 8, no. 12 (2013), e82261, https://doi.org/10.1371/journal.pone.0082261. On the basis of a microscopic biomechanical analysis of the Kebara Neanderthal hyoid bone, they show "that this bone not only resembled that of a modern human, but that it was used in very similar ways. This is because the internal microarchitecture is a response to the vectors and magnitudes

ality of the sections of the SVT. The oral cavity in modern humans measures 57 ± 5.1 millimeters. This is shorter than in *Homo heidelbergensis* (68.3 ± 5.1 mm) and *Homo neanderthalensis* (62.3 ± 6.5 mm).[38] Moreover, the cranial base of *Homo sapiens* is approximately 10–15 degrees more flexed, thus retracting the face and shortening the pharyngeal space behind the palette by about one centimeter.[39] As a result, the skeletal length of the "horizontal" SVT in ancient *Homo sapiens* (10.5 cm) is about 10 percent shorter than that of *Homo neanderthalensis* (11.7 cm) and *Homo heidelbergensis* (11.8 cm). To have a modern SVT with a ratio of 1:1, they would have needed a vertical SVT two to three centimeters longer than that of the average adult modern human. A modern SVT configuration in an archaic *Homo* would have positioned the larynx so low that swallowing might become impossible. So Neanderthal vocal tracts could not produce the full range of sounds that characterize human speech, in particular so-called quantal vowels such as [i] in "tea" and [u] in "to."[40] Therefore, the Neanderthal phonetic repertoire was inherently limited.

Lieberman's claims have been challenged.[41] But the more fundamental

---

of the forces to which it is routinely subjected. These findings are consistent with the suggestion that the Kebara 2 Neanderthal practiced speech although they do not prove that this was so."

38. D'Anastasio et al., "Micro-Biomechanics," 588–89.

39. Lewin and Foley muse that because less basicranial flexion appears to characterize Neanderthals than that observed in even earlier archaic *Homo sapiens*, it seems as if the direction of evolution had been reversed, depriving Neanderthals of fully articulate speech (*Principles of Human Evolution*, 467). On this account, any attendant speech defect is not due to diminished cognitive capacity but is a physical impairment akin to diminished hearing that had evolved in a certain species. Lewin and Foley also note that the degree of basicranial flexion differs geographically and that the reduction may be related to Neanderthals' unusual upper respiratory tract anatomy, a possible adaptation to cold climes.

40. Philip Lieberman and Edmund S. Crelin, "On the Speech of Neanderthal Man," *LI* 11, no. 2 (1971): 213.

41. Phoneticists Louis-Jean Boë et al. have argued that the height of the larynx has only a minor influence on the realization of maximal vowel contrasts such as [i a u]; indeed, they claim, articulatory gestures of the tongue and lips allow compensation for differences in the ratio between the dimensions of the oral cavity and pharynx. "The brain is entirely capable of controlling a vocal instrument with a somewhat longer or shorter pharynx: these differences do not actually change the capacity for maximally contrasting vowels" (Louis-Jean Boë et al., "The Potential Neandertal Vowel Space Was as Large as That of Modern Humans," *JP* 30, no. 3 [2002]: 481–82, https://doi.org/10.1006/jpho.2002.0170). In his reply Lieberman challenges the quite different claim that a Neanderthal skull could support a modern adult human SVT of 1:1 proportions, but so far as I can tell, he does not address their claim about compensatory mechanisms for a differently proportioned SVT

point is that having an inherently limited phonetic repertoire obviously does not imply a lack of language, for all of us are limited in our phonetic repertoire, even if not inherently so. We may all have the capacity to produce the full range of sounds that characterize human speech in the sense that if we were born and raised in any given culture, we should learn its language without difficulty; but as any American who has struggled to speak a foreign language can testify, there are sounds that native English speakers do not normally use and have difficulty learning, such as the French *soeur* or the German *Mönch*. There are living languages that do not, in fact, include any of the quantal vowel sounds.

So Lieberman does not draw the inference that Neanderthals therefore lacked speech. He asks, "Does this mean that Neanderthals lacked speech and language? Probably not. . . . The archaeological record indicates that they had some form of language and speech."[42] "The general level of Neanderthal culture is such that this limited phonetic ability was probably utilized and that some form of language existed."[43] Indeed, "speech must have been in place in archaic hominids ancestral to humans and Neanderthals. There would have been no selective advantage for retaining mutations that yielded the species-specific human speech producing anatomy at the cost of increased morbidity from choking, unless speech was already present."[44]

But he cautions, "Their speech was different, however, being less intelligible than ours."[45] But then we must ask, Less intelligible to whom? Surely

(P. Lieberman, "Current Views," 608–22). Lieberman sharply criticizes the claim of Boë et al. on the grounds that their Variable Linear Articulatory Model (VLAM) computer modeling technique produces anatomically impossible SVTs in newborns in order to enable them to produce the formant frequency patterns of the quantal vowels. NB that Lieberman is talking about newborns, not small children, which are more relevant to Neanderthal speech. In a subsequent response to Lieberman, Boë et al. compare acoustic data on infant and child vocalizations from the literature with age-appropriate VLAM simulations and show that the agreement is globally quite good, with no overestimation of the vowel range above the age of six months for formant F1 and fifteen months for F2 (Louis-Jean Boë et al., "Anatomy and Control of the Developing Human Vocal Tract: A Response to Lieberman," *JP* 41, no. 5 [2013]: 379–92). They conclude that "more than 40 years after his first paper on the 'larynx assumption,' it is now entirely clear that Lieberman's laryngeal descent hypothesis is incorrect. It is neither anatomically valid nor acoustically accurate" (390). They claim that the main articulatory question is constriction location and control rather than larynx position.

42. P. Lieberman, "Neanderthal Speech and Human Evolution," 157.

43. Lieberman and Crelin, "Speech of Neanderthal Man," 221.

44. P. Lieberman, "Current Views," 559.

45. P. Lieberman, "Neanderthal Speech and Human Evolution," 157.

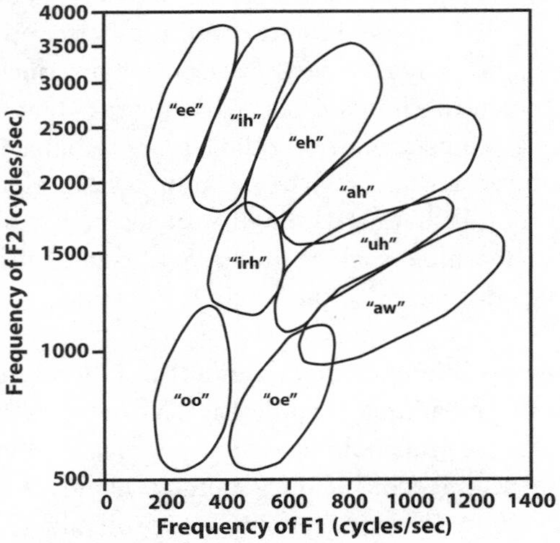

Figure 11.4. Quantal vowels from a large sample of speakers. The vowels are quantal (distinct) in the sense that they occupy almost completely nonoverlapping positions on the graph.

Lieberman has chosen the wrong word. *Intelligible* means "comprehensible." Are we seriously to think that Neanderthals had difficulty understanding one another? Such a claim not only goes far beyond the evidence but seems quite implausible from what we know of Neanderthal culture. I suspect that Lieberman meant something more like "articulate," in view of Neanderthals' limited phonetic range. For he also asserts that "the chimpanzee SVT could produce nasalized, vowel-reduced speech that, though it wouldn't be as intelligible as normal human speech, would suffice for communication."[46] If such vowel-reduced speech is sufficient for communication, it is necessarily intelligible, even if it is relatively inarticulate. The reason "chimpanzees cannot produce *any* speech" is that they lack the "specialized brain mechanisms that are necessary to regulate the complex, involuntary, *articulatory* gestures that underlie speech."[47]

Daniel Lieberman explains that what makes the quantal vowels so useful for oral communication is that, being discrete sounds, they are not so easily

46. P. Lieberman, "Neanderthal Speech and Human Evolution," 157. Johansson similarly remarks that with a human brain in control, virtually any mammalian vocal tract could produce useful speech ("Language Abilities in Neanderthals," 316). Cf. Philip Lieberman, "Vocal Tract Anatomy and the Neural Bases of Talking," *JP* 40, no. 4 (July 2012): 613, on the vocal capability of monkeys and apes to talk, despite their inability to produce the quantal vowels.

47. P. Lieberman, "Neanderthal Speech and Human Evolution," 157 (my emphasis). Daniel Lieberman explains, "Chimpanzees and other mammals apparently lack much of the neural circuitry necessary to move the lips and tongue with enough speed, precision, and coordination to make the kind of rapid, endlessly recombinatorial sequences of distinct formant frequencies that make up speech" (*Evolution of the Human Head*, 323).

confused with other vowels. When different speakers utter words in random order, listeners occasionally make identification errors for most vowels—for example, the [ɛ] in "beg" with the [I] in "big." But [i] and [u] are not so frequently confused. Since they have almost no overlap among different speakers (see fig. 11.4), they are especially useful sounds for vocal communication.

Thus, a speaker can be less precise in articulation and yet still produce sounds such as [i], [a], and [u] with a high degree of perceptibility. "Put differently," says Daniel Lieberman, "they permit sloppy articulation."[48] Indeed, "one can approximate the vowels with a nonhuman vocal tract of a different configuration, but the formant frequencies are less distinct."[49] Without quantal vowels to set the standard, random vowel sounds would indeed be less intelligible; but then, of course, we are not dealing with random vowel sounds in speech. If we let our imaginations run, we can imagine one Neanderthal saying to another, "That is a beg rhinoceros!" or "I big you to come on the hunt," and the context of utterance makes the meaning quite plain, despite any problems with articulation. Phonetic differences in articulation need not impinge seriously on the intelligibility of Neanderthal speech to one another.

The speech of little children furnishes a wonderful illustration here. Recall that children do not arrive at an adult configuration of their SVT until ages six to eight, and yet younger children can talk and be understood. Daniel Lieberman observes that children whose SVTs have not yet reached 1:1 proportion "do speak, often well," but because "their formant frequencies are not as quantal, . . . perception errors by listeners are higher."[50] But he immediately adds, "Some of these problems, however, may be due to less motor control of the tongue."[51] Of course; and it would be very unfair to expect little children, who are just learning to speak, to exemplify the same degree of articulate speech as an adult Neanderthal, even if the latter also lacked the SVT of a modern adult. Parents of youngsters learning to talk are especially good at interpreting their speech, and we can surmise that Neanderthals would be similarly accustomed to hearing and understanding one another correctly. Noting studies that purport to show that a Neanderthal equipped with a modern SVT would have a larynx impossibly low in the chest, Daniel Lieberman asks, "If true, does this result mean that Neander-

48. D. Lieberman, *Evolution of the Human Head*, 324.

49. D. Lieberman, *Evolution of the Human Head*, 325. Lieberman explains that [i] and to a lesser extent [u] serve as supervowels which are the standards for hearing correctly other vowel sounds.

50. D. Lieberman, *Evolution of the Human Head*, 327.

51. D. Lieberman, *Evolution of the Human Head*, 327.

thals, other species of archaic *Homo*, and possibly even some early modern humans couldn't speak? Of course not. It is hard to imagine that they lacked the capacity for speech, particularly given the large size of their brains. But it may be possible that their articulation was less precise than an adult modern human's, perhaps more like that of a 4–6 year-old, lacking fully quantal *eehs* and *oohs*."[52]

As for Hauser et al.'s second point—namely, the lack of archaeological evidence of Neanderthal cognitive capacity—our survey of the archaeological evidence leads to a quite different conclusion, that Neanderthals compared very favorably with MSA *Homo sapiens* in anticipating Cro-Magnon cognitive ability. I must agree with Dan Dediu and Stephen Levinson that

> language affords culture-carrying capacity (e.g. there are no advanced technologies without language), and this linkage allows reasonable inferences from the archeological record. Therefore, we think it is overwhelmingly likely that Neanderthals were as much articulate beings as we ourselves are, that is, with large vocabularies and combinatorial structures that allowed propositional content and illocutionary force to be conveyed. Only such an advanced communication system could have carried the advanced cultural adaptations that Neanderthals exhibited. . . .
>
> If one considers all of the cultural skills needed to survive in ecologies from the Arctic to game-poor Mediterranean littorals, it is difficult to argue that Neanderthals lacked complex linguistic codes, capable of communicating about spatial locations, hunting and gathering, fauna and flora, social relations, technologies, and so on. This would imply a large lexicon, and propositional encoding. Granting Neanderthals advanced language capacities seems to us inevitable.[53]

We have seen that the evidence supports a multispecies development of modern cognitive capacity rather than the single species African model

52. D. Lieberman, *Evolution of the Human Head*, 330–31. He says a longer oral cavity "does not rule out the possibility that archaic *Homo* could speak or had sophisticated language, but it does suggest slightly less articulate (quantal) speech, perhaps comparable to a 4–6-year-old modern human's" (589). Perhaps in a popular-level book like this one, I might be permitted to report anecdotally that when my two-and-a-half-year-old grandson Oliver says his ABCs, his [i] and [u] sounds are perfectly clear. It is the consonants like "j" that challenge him.

53. Dan Dediu and Stephen C. Levinson, "Neanderthal Language Revisited: Not Only Us," *COBS* 21 (2018): 52–53.

espoused by Hauser et al. At the end of the day, Hauser et al. admit, "In terms of the archaeological record, we can certainly imagine the discovery of richer symbolic artifacts . . . dating before the emergence of *Homo sapiens*. Such findings would push back the origins of symbolic capacities, and provide greater traction into questions of both origin and subsequent evolution."[54] The artistic representations subsequently discovered at Neanderthal sites in Spain seem to have supplied evidence of just the symbolic artifacts that, if not themselves dating before the emergence of *Homo sapiens*, disclose a cognitive capacity independent of *Homo sapiens*, which is therefore just as significant for questions of the origin and subsequent evolution of language.

Are there other anatomical clues to language capacity in Neanderthals? Recall our discussion of the arterial foramina, which are indicative of increased brain metabolism in Neanderthals consistent with the capacity for speech.[55] R. F. Kay, M. Cartmill, and M. Balow have also pointed to the hypoglossal canal through which the nerves controlling the tongue pass as indicative of a capacity for speech not only in early *Homo sapiens* but also in *Homo heidelbergensis* and *Homo neanderthalensis*. They found that, by contrast, the hypoglossal canals of Australopithecines, and perhaps also *Homo habilis*, not only are significantly smaller than those of modern humans but fall within the range of modern chimpanzees, who, it will be recalled, lack the motor control of the tongue and lips requisite for speech. Kay, Cartmill, and Balow conclude, "The vocal abilities of *Australopithecus* were not advanced significantly over those of chimpanzees whereas those of *Homo* may have been essentially modern by at least 400,000 years ago."[56]

Subsequent studies, however, have challenged their conclusions, finding no correlation between the size of the hypoglossal canal and language ability.[57] Monkeys, for example, have no capacity for speech, yet more than

54. Hauser et al., "Mystery of Language Evolution," 10.

55. See *supra*, pp. 268–69.

56. R. F. Kay, M. Cartmill, and M. Balow, "The Hypoglossal Canal and the Origin of Human Vocal Behavior," *PNAS* 95, no. 9 (April 28, 1998): 5417–19, https://doi.org/10.1073/pnas.95.9.5417, quotation from 5417. They studied three specimens from the Sterkfontein deposits in South Africa, representing gracile *Australopithecus africanus* (and/or *Homo habilis*), two middle Pleistocene *Homo* from Kabwe and Swanscombe, two Neanderthals from La Chapelle-aux-Saints and La Ferrassie, and one early *Homo sapiens* from Skhūl.

57. David DeGusta, W. Henry Gilbert, and Scott P. Turner, "Hypoglossal Canal Size and Hominid Speech," *PNAS* 96, no. 4 (February 16, 1999): 1800–804, https://doi.org/10.1073/pnas.96.4.1800. They conclude, "Many nonhuman primate specimens have hypoglossal canals that are absolutely and relatively within the size range of modern

half the monkeys measured have hypoglossal canals that are in the modern human size range, both absolutely and relative to mouth size. These results show that a large hypoglossal canal is no guarantee of linguistic ability. But that was surely not Kay, Cartmill, and Balow's claim. In addition to motor control of the tongue, a large brain is a prerequisite for language. Their claim is better understood to be that a large hominid brain and a large hypoglossal canal are jointly sufficient for, or at least evidence of, language ability.[58] To refute this claim one would need to point to language users who have a large brain but a narrow hypoglossal canal, which has not been done. At the least, the large hypoglossal canal in various *Homo* species is consistent with their being capable of speech.

Additional anatomical evidence comes from the enlarged thoracic vertebral canal in human beings, through which pass the nerves that control the muscles used to regulate breathing. Such fine respiratory control is crucial for human speech. Ann MacLarnon and Gwen Hewitt explain that "full human language requires extended exhalations for vocalizations and increased control of volume, emphasis, and intonation compared with nonhuman primates and therefore presumably compared with early hominids. Such features require fast, intricate, flexible, and integrated neural control of intercostal and abdominal muscles."[59] The muscles enabling such fine respiratory control are all thoracically innervated.

So MacLarnon and Hewitt measured the thoracic vertebral canal for a variety of fossil hominins: *Australopithecus afarensis*, *Australopithecus africanus*, *Homo ergaster* (or early *Homo erectus*), four Neanderthals, and one early *Homo sapiens*, in addition to three modern human samples. They found that both the Neanderthals and the early and contemporary modern humans have larger relative thoracic canal cross-sectional areas than any of the non-

humans. The hypoglossal canals of *Australopithecus afarensis*, *A. boisei*, and *A. africanus* are also within the modern human size range. The size of the hypoglossal nerve and the number of axons it contains do not appear to be significantly correlated with the size of the hypoglossal canal. We conclude that the size of the hypoglossal canal is not a reliable indicator of speech" (1804).

58. Daniel Lieberman points out that movements of the human tongue during oral transport and swallowing can actually be more complex than during speaking, so that a large hypoglossal canal may be the result of tongue innervation, not for speech, but for feeding (*Evolution of the Human Head*, 331–32). But, as we have seen, the exquisite motor control of the tongue for the purpose of swallowing is in human beings likely an adaptation for speech to prevent choking.

59. A. M. MacLarnon and G. P. Hewitt, "The Evolution of Human Speech: The Role of Enhanced Breathing Control," *AJPA* 109, no. 3 (1999): 358.

human primates. "This evidence indicates that thoracic innervation in earlier fossil hominids, australopithecines and *Homo ergaster*, was similar to that of extant nonhuman primates, but that Neanderthals and early modern humans had expanded thoracic innervation similar to that in extant humans."[60]

Examining the possible explanations for this increased thoracic innervation—such as postural control for bipedalism, increased difficulty of parturition, respiration for endurance running, an aquatic phase, choking avoidance, and increased control of breathing for speech—MacLarnon and Hewitt argue that all but the last can be ruled out, either because of their evolutionary timing or because they are insufficiently demanding neurologically. By way of positive evidence for this explanation, they appeal to studies of human speech production, which show that human speech "requires very fast, fine control of subglottal pressure which responds to cognitive factors and is integrated with control of the upper respiratory tract and other body changes,"[61] and to comparisons of human speech production and the vocalizations of nonhuman primates, which show that human speech is unique in the respiratory control required for its production. MacLarnon and Hewitt conclude, "Neanderthals and early modern humans had expanded thoracic innervation, like extant humans. It seems most probable that this increased innervation evolved to enable enhanced breath control, and the most likely functional reason for this was the evolution of human speech, i.e., the physical production of language."[62]

Even if one does not accept that the explanation for increased thoracic innervation is the need of respiratory control for speech, minimally what MacLarnon and Hewitt's results imply is that one of the singly necessary and jointly sufficient conditions for human speech is already present, along with other similar conditions, in Neanderthals. Neanderthal speech is thus more probable given the presence of this condition than otherwise, so that it constitutes evidence for Neanderthal speech.

Genetic Clues

The sequencing of a complete Neanderthal genome in 2010 revolutionized palaeoanthropological studies. We now have nearly twenty partial or complete specimens of the Neanderthal genome, which can be compared to the

60. MacLarnon and Hewitt, "Evolution of Human Speech," 347.
61. MacLarnon and Hewitt, "Evolution of Human Speech," 351.
62. MacLarnon and Hewitt, "Evolution of Human Speech," 358.

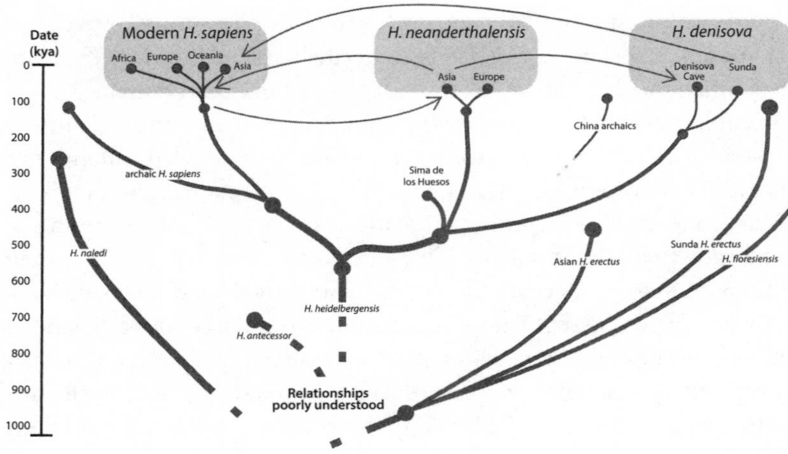

Figure 11.5. Interbreeding between lines of ancient humans.

genome of modern humans. As a result, the debate as to whether Neanderthals and *Homo sapiens* interbred has now been decisively answered in the affirmative on the basis of evidence of mutual introgression of genetic materials (fig. 11.5). Approximately 2 percent of the DNA of all living non-Africans is derived from Neanderthals, and Oceanic populations have an additional 2–4 percent of their DNA from Denisovans.

The simple fact alone of interbreeding carries implications for the capacity of Neanderthals and Denisovans for speech. They interacted repeatedly with anatomically modern human beings over tens of thousands of years, in Dediu and Levinson's memorable words, "exchanging genes, parasites and culture."[63] Such social and sexual intercourse plausibly requires communication and hence language. Kai Whiting et al. comment, "It seems quite unreasonable to assume that all sexual encounters between the different *Homo* species were of the non-consensual variety. It is much more likely that at least some of the instances of interbreeding between co-existing *Homo* species, including anatomically modern humans, were the result of communication and a degree of affection or appreciation. Regardless of the exact dynamics of sexual relations, we know for certain that some resulted in

63. Dediu and Levinson, "Neanderthal Language Revisited," 52.

offspring that could claim kinship to more than one set of human species."[64] Thus, interbreeding and the production of hybrid offspring who could, like the *Homo sapiens* parent, speak are themselves suggestive of language ability in the partners.

We have already mentioned crucial mutations in the gene *ARHGAP11B* and the *NOTCH2NL* genes in the human lineage prior to the divergence of *Homo sapiens*, Neanderthals, and Denisovans, and hence shared by all, that contributed significantly to brain growth.[65] We do not know if there was any direct effect on language ability as a result.

The significance of the differences between the genome of *Homo sapiens* and those of Neanderthals and Denisovans remains poorly understood. André Sousa et al. examined so-called human accelerated regions (HARs) of the modern human genome to compare them with genomic material from these ancient hominins.[66] HARs are DNA sequences that changed very little throughout mammalian evolution but then experienced a burst of changes in hominins since divergence from chimpanzees. Sousa et al. determined that 8 percent of HAR substitutions are not found in Neanderthals and Denisovans and are thus recent in the sense that the derived allele had not come to fixation in the common ancestor of modern humans and archaic hominins. Some of these substitutions are found in an HAR of *AUTS2*, a gene associated with several neurological features, in a region also showing strong evidence of a selective sweep that occurred in modern humans after the split with Neanderthals. *AUTS2* contains the most significantly accelerated genomic region differentiating humans from Neanderthals, but unfortunately the function and regulation of this gene remain largely unknown.

The celebrated *FOXP2* gene is, however, more directly related to a capacity for speech.[67] Mutations of this gene have been linked to verbal dyspraxia. So *FOXP2* seems to be necessary for human speech. Significantly, human *FOXP2*, while differing from that of chimpanzees and gorillas in two amino acid coding positions, was found to be identical in *Homo sapiens* and Nean-

64. Kai Whiting et al., "Were Neanderthals Rational? A Stoic Approach," *Humanities* 7, no. 2 (2018): 39, https://doi.org/10.3390/h7020039.

65. See *supra*, pp. 276–79.

66. A. M. M. Sousa et al., "Evolution of the Human Nervous System Function, Structure, and Development," *Cell* 170, no. 2 (July 13, 2017): 226–40, https://doi.org/10.1016/j.cell.2017.06.036.

67. For a brief overview, see Simon E. Fisher, "Evolution of Language: Lessons from the Genome," *PBR* 24, no. 1 (2017): 34–40, https://doi.org/10.3758/s13423-016-1112-8.

derthals.[68] Neanderthal and *Homo sapiens FOXP2* is identical in the very two positions (911 and 977 in exon 7) that differ from ape *FOXP2*. In this respect, at least, Neanderthals and *Homo sapiens* would share whatever linguistic benefit these changes confer. Johannes Krause et al. deem the most probable explanation for these shared genetic changes to be that these changes took place in the common ancestor of modern humans and Neanderthals before their divergence.[69]

Summary

In the last two chapters we have briefly surveyed evidence from palaeoneurology, archaeology, and genetics for the time of human origins.

With respect to the evidence of palaeoneurology, we saw that on the basis of analysis of cranial endocasts there has been in the course of hominin evolution a striking increase in both brain size and encephalization quotient, as well as brain reorganization, that brings hominin brains well into the modern range by 500 kya with *Homo heidelbergensis*. These features are correlated securely with greater cognitive capacity in humans. Moreover, measurements of the arterial foramina, through which the carotid arteries supplying the brain pass, show that only with later *Homo erectus* and *Homo heidelbergensis* do we arrive at the range of modern humans. Larger arterial openings in the skull indicate a higher metabolic rate of the brain, which is suggestive of increased cognitive capacity. Studies of fossil hominin teeth show slow enamel growth in both Neanderthals and archaic *Homo sapiens*, an index of slow maturation of the brain past birth and well into childhood. The slow trajectory of enamel growth typical of modern humans is not found in Australopithecines or early *Homo*, which are more apelike in

68. Johannes Krause et al., "The Derived *FOXP2* Variant of Modern Humans Was Shared with Neandertals," *CB* 17, no. 21 (November 6, 2007): 1908–12. Fisher reports that when the two amino acid coding changes were inserted into genetically modified mice, the mice showed higher levels of plasticity of synapses in cortico-basal ganglia circuits, but when mice were genetically modified to carry a *FOXP2* mutation known to cause dyspraxia, such mice showed lower levels of synaptic plasticity in cortico-basal ganglia circuits, consistent with a loss of function (Fisher, "Evolution of Language"). Fisher notes that further comparisons of modern human and Neanderthal versions of *FOXP2*, examining the parts of the genetic locus that do not code for protein, identified human-specific changes that might potentially affect the way that the gene is regulated.

69. Krause et al., "Derived *FOXP2* Variant."

development. Thus, slow brain development is positively correlated with the increased cognitive capacity of modern humans. Genetic comparisons of hominin DNA reveal that a mutation in the gene *ARHGAP11B* that contributed to the expansion of the human neocortex is shared by both Neanderthals and Denisovans. Since the identical mutation is unlikely to have occurred thrice, it is doubtless a derived feature that was inherited from their last common ancestor, *Homo heidelbergensis*. Again, the presence of the identical *NOTCH2NL* genes in Neanderthals, Denisovans, and *Homo sapiens* points to genomic reorganization events in the brain of their last common ancestor, which resulted in amplification of neuron progenitors and, hence, increased cognitive capacity.

With respect to the evidence of archaeology, the most important evidence for the cognitive capacity of ancient hominins, we saw that generally accepted sufficient conditions of modern humanity may be discerned by the presence of a wide variety of archaeological signatures. These mutually reinforce one another and provide a powerful cumulative case for modern human consciousness that is stronger than its weakest link. We surveyed briefly some of the most important evidence from archaeological signatures in the areas of technology, economy and social organization, and symbolic behavior.

With respect to technology, the production of stone blades, a feature of the Mode 4 toolmaking industry, was practiced by both Neanderthals and *Homo sapiens* well before 300 kya, marking a technological advance that required significant cognitive capacity to execute. Even more sophisticated was the production of stone points, which both Neanderthals and *Homo sapiens* crafted at least 186 kya, and which may have been manufactured and employed by *Homo heidelbergensis* 500 kya. The production of composite tools and hafting required not merely forethought but design and characterized the tool industries of both Neanderthals and *Homo sapiens*. The extraordinary finds at Schöningen show that 400 kya composite tools were already in use, pointing once more to *Homo heidelbergensis*. Grindstones are important signatures of cognitive capacity, since their use indicates the processing of plant material and, most significantly, of pigment, one of the signatures of symbolic behavior. They have been found both at MSA sites and at Mousterian sites, indicating use by both *Homo sapiens* in Africa and Neanderthals in Europe.

With respect to economy and social organization, we saw that big-game hunting involves cooperative behavior indicative of human consciousness and plausibly even language ability. Such behavior evinces a collective intentionality that many psychologists take to be a cognitive skill unique to, even definitive for, human beings.[70] Both MSA *Homo sapiens* and Neanderthals engaged in such hunting activities. Again, the stunning Schöningen spears, whose manufacture alone requires extraordinary cognitive capacity, together with the evidence from Boxgrove and Clacton, show that such behavior goes back to *Homo heidelbergensis* 500 kya. Equally amazing are the Neanderthal constructions in Bruniquel Cave dating to 176 kya. Nothing like these, involving a *chaîne opératoire* of astounding complexity and depth, has ever been found before. These constructions exhibit even more clearly than big-game hunting the collective intentionality of their Neanderthal builders. To add to our astonishment, we find the hunters' huts at Terra Amata, which evince so patently the planning and design of their fabricators. Dating to 350 kya, *Homo heidelbergensis* was likely responsible for them.

Finally, with respect to the evidence of symbolic behavior, the date of imagistic and representational art among *Homo sapiens* has now been driven back to >40 kya by the discovery of the Indonesian cave art, and among Neanderthals >66 kya by the Iberian cave art. The contemporaneous presence of similar cave art in Spain and in Indonesia, half the world away, implies an origin of symbolic behavior and hence humanity that is vastly older still. We also saw that the use of pigment, which may be used for art or body decoration, has been attested in Africa to >300 kya and among Neanderthals in Europe to >60 kya. Burials of the dead, whether invested with spiritual significance or not, exhibit a care for the remains of one's fellows that shows an estimate of their worth. At Qafzeh 120 kya we have the earliest evidence for burial of the dead among *Homo sapiens*, replete with items interred with the deceased, and at Tabūn 160 kya the earliest evidence for Neanderthal burials. Finally, language use, the paradigmatic symbolic behavior, though difficult to detect, is supported among both *Homo sapiens* and Neanderthals by anatomical clues like a large and complex brain, aural structures suited to human speech, an SVT suitable to the production of speech despite the

70. See, e.g., Michael Tomasello, *A Natural History of Human Thinking* (Cambridge, MA: Harvard University Press, 2014), chap. 1; Tomasello, *Becoming Human*, chap. 1. Tomasello emphasizes that group hunting by chimpanzees does not involve even joint intentionality (it's every chimp for himself!), much less collective intentionality. He thinks that chimpanzees' group hunting of monkeys is not so different cognitively from the group hunting of other social mammals, such as lions and wolves. But early humans—perhaps *Homo heidelbergensis*—evolved skills and motivations for joint intentionality that transformed great apes' parallel group activities into truly joint collaborative activities (Tomasello, *Becoming Human*, 48).

dangers posed thereby, enlarged arterial foramina, a large hypoglossal canal, and an enlarged thoracic vertebral canal, as well as genetic clues pointing to interbreeding among Neanderthals, Denisovans, and *Homo sapiens* and to their sharing the mutated *FOXP2* gene crucial to speech that they probably derived from their common ancestor, *Homo heidelbergensis*.

Accordingly, we have very powerful evidence that human behaviors that exhibit modern cognitive capacity did not originate recently, or even very early, among *Homo sapiens* alone but were already in place in our last common ancestor with Neanderthals and Denisovans.

Chapter 12

LOCATING THE HISTORICAL ADAM

As we have probed human origins, the evidence has pointed us again and again to the progenitor of *Homo sapiens* and *Homo neanderthalensis* as the fount of humanity, "the ever mysterious *Homo heidelbergensis*."[1] What do we know of him?

ADAM AS *HOMO HEIDELBERGENSIS*

In 1907 the lower jaw of a hominin was discovered at the Grafenrain sand and gravel quarry in Mauer, Germany, in the vicinity of Heidelberg. Dating from about 600 kya, the jaw appeared to belong to a previously unknown species of early hominin. The following year the name *Homo heidelbergensis* was bestowed on this species by Otto Schoetensack. In 1921 a nearly complete skull appropriate to the Mauer mandible, along with a shin bone, was unearthed in a metal ore mine at Broken Hill, Rhodesia. Initially classed as belonging to a new species, *Homo rhodesiensis*, the new find eventually came to be regarded an instance of *Homo heidelbergensis*. Although the braincase was relatively long and low compared to that of modern humans, it was higher and more expansive than that of *Homo erectus* and had a capacity between 800 and 1,300 cubic centimeters, thus overlapping the modern range. The man at Broken Hill is estimated to have stood six feet tall and to have weighed about 159 pounds. Since the discovery at Broken Hill, a number of finds have been identified as belonging to *Homo heidelbergensis*, including remains from Boxgrove, England; Arago, France; Bilzingsleben, Germany;

1. Michael Tomasello, *A Natural History of Human Thinking* (Cambridge, MA: Harvard University Press, 2014), 36.

Petralona, Greece; Bodo, Ethiopia; Kapthurin, Kenya; and Elandsfontein, South Africa.[2]

The Schöningen spears, dating back to 400–300 kya, were probably manufactured and used by *Homo heidelbergensis,* as were the spearpoints dating from 500 kya unearthed at Kathu Pan 1. Their extreme age and complexity point in that direction, as does the cooperative activity of big-game hunting, which is also attested at Bilzingsleben. The evidence of systematic butchery of large animals like rhinoceroses at Boxgrove, dating from about 500 kya, mirrors the hunting activity at Schöningen and Bilzingsleben. Moreover, direct evidence of hunting comes from an apparent spearpoint hole on a horse shoulder blade.

Ian Tattersall calls *Homo heidelbergensis* "a truly cosmopolitan hominid species," which may lie at the origin of the European and African lineages that led to Neanderthals and *Homo sapiens.*[3] The origin of *Homo heidelbergensis* is shrouded in antiquity. He may have originated in either Asia or Europe or Africa and migrated to the other regions.[4]

The date range for the last common ancestor of Neanderthals and *Homo sapiens* has been pushed back by analysis of the Neanderthal genome. Svante Pääbo initially estimated the range to be 690–550 kya, then in 1999 broadened the range to 741–317 kya. This lower bound is far too recent. On the basis of a complete genome analysis of the Altai Neanderthal, the best estimate for the divergence of *Homo sapiens* and Neanderthals is now 765–550 kya (fig. 12.1).[5]

The extreme antiquity of the last common ancestor of *Homo sapiens* and Neanderthals has put pressure on its identification with *Homo heidelbergensis.* Such an ancient divergence is difficult to reconcile with the suggestion that younger specimens often classified as *Homo heidelbergensis,* such as the Arago or Petralona fossils, belong to an ancestral population of both *Homo*

2. For a list of fossils that may represent *Homo heidelbergensis,* see Chris Stringer, "The Status of *Homo heidelbergensis* (Schoetensack 1908)," *EA* 21, no. 3 (May 2012): 103, table 2; for a list of traits characteristic of this assemblage, see 102, table 1.

3. Ian Tattersall, *The Fossil Trail: How We Know What We Think We Know about Human Evolution,* 2nd ed. (Oxford: Oxford University Press, 2009), 281.

4. Stringer states that we cannot exclude an Asian origin for *Homo heidelbergensis* given the similar ages (~600 kya) assigned to the earliest potential examples in Germany (Mauer), China (Yunxian), and Ethiopia (Bodo) ("Status of *Homo heidelbergensis,*" 105).

5. K. Prüfer et al., "The Complete Genome Sequence of a Neanderthal from the Altai Mountains," *Nature* 505, no. 7481 (January 2014): 44, https://doi.org/10.1038/nature12886.

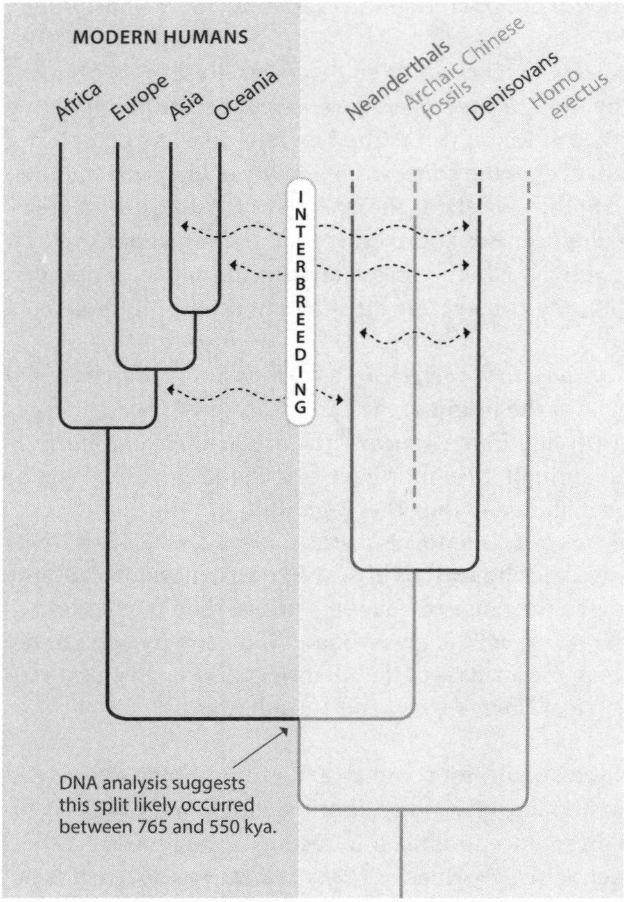

Figure 12.1. Time of the divergence of Neanderthals and *Homo sapiens*. The divergence of Denisovans from Neanderthals is estimated 473–381 kya.

sapiens and Neanderthals.[6] But even if these fossils need to be reassigned to either early *Homo sapiens* or early *Homo neanderthalensis*,[7] we need to keep in mind Lewin and Foley's caution that organisms on separate lineages may

6. M. Meyer et al., "Nuclear DNA Sequences from the Middle Pleistocene Sima de Los Huesos Hominins," *Nature* 531, no. 7595 (March 2016): 506, https://doi.org/10.1038/nature17405.

7. The fossils discovered at Sima de los Huesos in Spain, for example, once assigned to *Homo heidelbergensis*, have recently been established by analysis of their nuclear DNA, in conjunction with their mitochondrial DNA, to belong to the Neanderthal lineage after its divergence from the Denisovan lineage. See J. L. Arsuaga et al., "Neandertal Roots: Cranial and Chronological Evidence from Sima de Los Huesos," *Science* 344, no. 6190

not differ morphologically from their last common ancestor (or each other) for hundreds of thousands (indeed, millions) of years.[8] Moreover, *Homo heidelbergensis* did not simply vanish after the divergence of the lines leading to Neanderthals/Denisovans and *Homo sapiens* but continued for an indeterminate time, as did *Homo erectus* after the emergence of other *Homo* species. Specimens that have been identified as *Homo heidelbergensis* from Bodo, Ethiopia (600 kya), and Gran Dolina, Spain (780 kya), are well within the range of a Eurafrican stem species for Neanderthals and *Homo sapiens*.[9]

(June 20, 2014): 1358–63, https://doi.org/10.1126/science.1253958; Meyer et al., "Nuclear DNA Sequences," 504–6.

8. See *supra*, pp. 252–53.

9. G. Philip Rightmire, "Human Evolution in the Middle Pleistocene: The Role of *Homo heidelbergensis*," *EA* 6, no. 6 (December 7, 1998): 218–27, https://doi.org/10.1002/(sici)1520-6505(1998)6:6<218::aid-evan4>3.0.co;2-6. The Spanish palaeoanthropologists preferred to give the Gran Dolina fossils a new classification, nowhere else attested, *Homo antecessor*. Whatever its name, this species is deemed by Rightmire to be a good candidate for the stem from which both Neanderthals and *Homo sapiens* are descended. In fact, Rightmire thinks that a good case can be made for attributing the Spanish fossils to *Homo heidelbergensis*, broadly defined so as to include European and African remains. "One possibility is that fossils from Africa and Europe can be sorted together to a single taxon, appropriately called *Homo heidelbergensis*. If the Gran Dolina fossils are also *Homo heidelbergensis*, then these people apparently reached Europe at an early date. In this region, populations isolated by glacial conditions perhaps were eventually ancestral to the Neanderthals. In other parts of the species range, including Africa, there are indications that later Middle Pleistocene groups were evolving in the direction of *Homo sapiens*. *Homo heidelbergensis* is thus the stem from which both Neanderthals and modern humans are derived" (226).

Humphrey and Stringer seem more sympathetic to the identification of a new species *Homo antecessor* for the Gran Dolina fossils and, hence, of the stem species for Neanderthals and *Homo sapiens* (Louise Humphrey and Chris Stringer, *Our Human Story* [London: Natural History Museum, 2018], 109, 113). Remarkably, the Gran Dolina fossils have a facial morphology resembling modern humans even more closely than typical specimens of *Homo heidelbergensis*.

Now the new field of palaeoproteomics (analysis of ancient proteins using mass spectrometry) promises to clarify relationships among ancient hominins. Analysis of an ancient protein sequence from a tooth from Gran Dolina, when compared with analysis of protein sequences from three Neanderthals, a Denisovan, and a panel of present-day humans, reveals that the divergence of the amino acid sequences between *Homo antecessor* and the clade containing *Homo sapiens*, Neanderthals, and Denisovans is larger than the divergence between the members of this clade itself. Welker et al. infer that *Homo antecessor* does not represent the last common ancestor of *Homo sapiens*, Neanderthals, and Denisovans but is rather a closely related *sister taxon* of their last common ancestor (F. Welker et al., "The Dental Proteome of *Homo antecessor*," *Nature* 580, no. 7802 [April 1, 2020], https://doi.org/10.1038/s41586-020-2153-8). They note that such a phylogenetic positioning of *Homo antecessor* agrees with the accepted date of the divergence of the

As we have seen, *Homo heidelbergensis* is associated with a number of archaeological signatures of modern behavior. Nicholas Toth and Kathy Schick chart the parallel development of the hominin brain and technological development. Concerning the most advanced stage (Stage 3) of brain development (750–250 kya), they write,

> This time interval documents the emergence of the larger-brained *Homo heidelbergensis* (sometimes called "archaic *Homo sapiens*"). It also documents the development of finely made Acheulean handaxes and cleavers and a gradual shift to flake tool industries, some with prepared core technologies, of the Middle Stone Age/Middle Palaeolithic. The earliest wooden spears are known from this time as well as the first possible evidence of ritualistic behavior. . . .
>
> A number of technological advances are observed in the archaeological record during this time interval. These include much more refined forms of artifacts, more formal tool forms, new and more elaborate techniques for tool production, new categories of tools in evidence at some sites, indirect evidence of improved hunting technology, and possible evidence of symbolic behavior, including the use of ocher pigments.
>
> - Refined handaxes and cleavers. . . . Microwear analysis of later Acheulean handaxes from some well-preserved sites, e.g. Hoxne and Boxgrove, indicate wear-patterns consistent with animal butchery.
> - Soft hammers of antler, bone, or ivory or softer stone were evidently used at many localities to produce finely flaked stone artifacts beginning around 500,000 years ago . . . e.g., antler and bone percussors from Boxgrove. . . .
> - Platform preparation on the edges of cores and bifaces. . . . Such striking platform preparation . . . begins around 500,000 years ago.

Homo sapiens and Neanderthal/Denisovan lineages between 765 and 550 kya. They also comment that their phylogenetic placement of *Homo antecessor* implies that a modern-like face must have a considerably deep ancestry in the genus *Homo*. Welker et al. do not address the identity of the last common ancestor, but if it is *Homo heidelbergensis*, as usually thought, then *Homo heidelbergensis* could be regarded as the last common ancestor of all these species. In both personal correspondence and public interviews, Welker et al. state that *Homo antecessor* "was a sister group to the group containing *Homo sapiens*, Neanderthals, and Denisovans," thus implying that they all share a common ancestor (University of Copenhagen, Faculty of Health and Medical Sciences, "Oldest Ever Human Genetic Evidence Clarifies Dispute over Our Ancestors," *Science Daily*, April 1, 2020, https://www.sciencedaily.com/releases/2020/04/200401111657.htm; Welker to William Lane Craig, April 3, 2020; also José-Maria Bermúdez de Castro to Craig, April 3, 2020).

- . . . Stylistic norms become more prevalent and more clearly defined in later Acheulean times. . . .
- Prepared cores appear . . . in the latter part of this time interval. . . .
- Wooden spears are seen at such well-preserved sites as Schöningen in Germany (ca. 400,000 years old) and the broken spear tip from Clacton in England (ca. 300,000). Carefully sharpened and shaped wooden spears suggest that they were part of hunting paraphernalia, either as hand-held stabbing weapons or as thrown projectiles.
- Possible big-game hunting has also been suggested at some sites such as the Acheulean site of Boxgrove in England (ca. 500,000 years ago). The remains from several rhinoceros and horse skeletons bear butchery marks from stone tools.
- Micro-wear analysis on retouched flake scrapers from sites of this period (e.g. Clacton, Hoxne) indicate that a number of these tools were used for hide-scraping, suggesting that cured hides could have been used for such items as blankets, simple garments, thongs for stitching or tying things together, or containers.
- Ground pigment pieces from sites such as Twin Rivers, Zambia, are believed to be about 300,000 years old. . . .
- Possible ritualistic or funerary behavior may be seen at the Atapuerca locality, Sima de Los Huesos (ca. 400,000 years ago), where the remains of approximately thirty individuals appear to have been disposed of down a forty-foot shaft in a cave. . . .
- Abstract decoration may be seen in a geometric, evenly-spaced fan-shaped set of cut-marks on a fragment of elephant tibia from the site of Bilzingsleben in eastern Germany, estimated to be between 280,000 and 400,000 years ago. This is an unusual and anomalous occurrence, and such design will not be seen again until the last 100,000 years.[10]

Many of these signatures may be already attributable to *Homo heidelbergensis*, who, with a cranial capacity of 1,260 cubic centimeters, is appropriate as an author of cognitively modern behaviors. We have also seen evidence of derived mutations promoting neuronal proliferation in Neanderthals and *Homo sapiens*, stemming from their last common ancestor. Since language is highly unlikely to have evolved twice, the probable presence of language

10. Nicholas Toth and Kathy Schick, "Hominin Brain Reorganization, Technological Change, and Cognitive Complexity," in *The Human Brain Evolving: Paleoneurological Studies in Honor of Ralph L. Holloway*, ed. Douglas Broadfield et al., SAIPS 4 (Gosport, IN: Stone Age Institute Press, 2010), 300–301 (citations and boldface removed).

among Neanderthals and *Homo sapiens* is likely also derived from *Homo heidelbergensis*.

Richard Fortey nicely sums it up: "The tendencies towards large brain size were carried further, while the social habits, tool-making, and all the paraphernalia attached to hunting and gathering tribes were added piece by piece until you could say of the creature standing before you: *ecce homo*."[11]

Adam, then, may be plausibly identified as a member of *Homo heidelbergensis*, living perhaps >750 kya. He could even have lived in the Near East in the biblical site of the Garden of Eden—though vastly earlier than usually thought, of course. His descendants migrated southward into Africa, where they gave rise to *Homo sapiens*, and westward into Europe, where they evolved into Neanderthals/Denisovans. Once *Homo sapiens* began to migrate out of Africa >130 kya, these separate lines of his descendants began to interbreed.

Palaeoanthropologists debate whether modern humans emerged through a gradual, multispecies development or by a sudden, mutational event occurring within a single species. Francesco d'Errico and Chris Stringer explain that "some authors consider that a genetic mutation in the functioning of the brain is the most probable prime mover and have argued that such a mutation, leading to a sudden diffusion of modern traits, must have occurred approximately 50 000 years ago (50 ka) among African anatomically modern humans. Others situate this neurological switch between 60 and 80 ka and associate it with cultural innovations recorded at this time in southern Africa."[12]

Tattersall appears to defend such a view. He says, "*Homo sapiens*, certainly in the inclusive sense, originated in a major developmental reorganization of systems throughout the body, as a result of what was probably a relatively simple modification in DNA terms."[13] He thinks that such a claim is defensible without sounding like a nineteenth-century saltationist because of the major advance wrought by the emergence of so-called evo-devo (evolutionary developmental biology), which studies the constraints that developmental (ontogenetic) processes place on evolutionary changes and how

11. Richard Fortey, *Life: An Unauthorized Biography* (London: Folio Society, 2008), 349.

12. Francesco d'Errico and Chris B. Stringer, "Evolution, Revolution or Saltation Scenario for the Emergence of Modern Cultures?," *PTRSB* 366, no. 1567 (April 12, 2011): 1060–61, https://doi.org/10.1098/rstb.2010.0340.

13. Tattersall, *Fossil Trail*, 243. Recall that the inclusive sense comprises any organism on the lineage leading to *Homo sapiens* since its divergence from the lineage leading to chimpanzees. Neanderthals would not be included, since they are not on the lineage leading to *Homo sapiens*.

changes in those processes promote evolutionary change. It has been proved that integrated structural complexes may be radically modified by relatively simple changes in gene structure. In contrast to the old gradualism, Tattersall explains, we now know that relatively small changes in the structure of genes can have cascading consequences throughout an individual's growth and form. "Such a change, minor at the structural genetic level, may well have been involved in the origin of *Homo sapiens* as the anatomical entity we know today."[14] For Tattersall such a scenario does not imply that cognitive innovation followed immediately upon this physical innovation. Behavioral change is detected in the archaeological record well after *Homo sapiens* had been established as an anatomical entity.

In contrast to this view, d'Errico and Stringer explain, partisans of what could be called the "cultural" model argue that "the cognitive prerequisites of modern human behaviour were already largely in place among the ancestors of Neanderthals and modern humans and cite social and demographic factors . . . to explain the asynchronous emergence, disappearance and re-emergence of modern cultural traits among both African 'modern' and Eurasian 'archaic' populations." According to this scenario, "'modernity' and its corollary 'cumulative culture' is the end product of a saltational cultural evolution within human populations that were to a large extent, and irrespectively of their taxonomic affiliation, cognitively modern."[15]

It should be evident that these two views are not mutually exclusive. One can imagine a scenario in which a regulatory mutation, perhaps divinely caused, occurs in a member or members of a population belonging to *Homo heidelbergensis*, effecting a change in the functioning of the brain that results in a significantly greater cognitive capacity. Some behavioral outworkings of this increased cognitive capacity would be immediate, but others would emerge slowly over time among this person's descendants though niche construction and gene-cultural coevolution. Thus, we are to imagine, in line with the cultural model, that both Neanderthals and *Homo sapiens* are heirs to the cognitive capacity for modern behaviors already present in *Homo heidelbergensis* and, in line with the first model, that this increased cognitive capacity is itself the result of a crucial mutation in some ancestral individual (or individuals) belonging to *Homo heidelbergensis*.

Though he underestimates the degree to which the cooperative activities of *Homo heidelbergensis* evinced collective intentionality, Michael Tomasello does point to this species as "the first hominin to engage systematically in

14. Tattersall, *Fossil Trail*, 244.
15. D'Errico and Stringer, "Evolution, Revolution or Saltation," 1061.

the collaborative hunting of large game, using weapons that almost certainly would not enable a single individual to be successful on its own and sometimes bringing prey back to home base. This is also a time when brain size and population size were both expanding rapidly. We may hypothesize that these collaborative foragers lived as more or less loose bands comprising a kind of pool of potential collaborators."[16] He imagines that such collaboration among *Homo heidelbergensis* would become obligate: they would become interdependent in much more urgent ways with strong social selection for cooperative individuals.[17] It is precisely this sort of cooperative activity that characterizes modern human cognition and forms the basis for gene-cultural coevolution.[18] Thus, a blended scenario is certainly possible and, moreover, consistent with the evidence we have reviewed.

Challenges to a Founding Pair

What scientific objections might arise to our suggested identification of Adam and Eve as a founding pair of the human race belonging to the species *Homo heidelbergensis*? Genetic studies may pose both temporal and geographical challenges to our proposal.

Temporal Challenge

The temporal challenge arises from the field of population genetics. Some students of population genetics have argued that it is impossible that the human population was ever reduced to but two persons, regardless of their his-

16. Tomasello, *Natural History*, 36–37.

17. Michael Tomasello, *Becoming Human: A Theory of Ontogeny* (Cambridge, MA: Belknap Press of Harvard University Press, 2019), 15. I see no reason to delay the emergence of collective intentionality until the divergence of Neanderthals and *Homo sapiens*, as Tomasello suggests.

18. See Kevin N. Laland, *Darwin's Unfinished Symphony: How Culture Made the Human Mind* (Princeton: Princeton University Press, 2017), 10, 174, 204, where he asserts that Acheulean technologies along with evidence for systematic hunting and the use of fire "leave no doubt that by at least this juncture in our history, our ancestors benefitted from cumulative cultural knowledge." The key to cumulative culture is "sufficiently high-fidelity information transmission mechanisms, including an unusually accurate capacity for imitation, teaching, and language." Laland surmises that the transmission of Acheulean technology relied on gestural or verbal protolanguage.

torical location. Thus Adam and Eve, in the traditional sense of the universal common ancestors of every other human being, could never have existed.

Although the discussion can rapidly become very technical, the basic idea behind this challenge is quite simple—namely, that certain genetic features of the contemporary human population are such that the human race could not have stemmed from an original human pair. Unfortunately, just what those features are is often ill-defined in the popular literature, resulting in confusion and conflation of arguments of varying worth.

Arguments against a Founding Pair

Computational biologist Joshua Swamidass distinguishes six genetic features that have been put forward as allegedly incompatible with an original human couple:[19]

1. Multiplicity of alleles
2. Effective population size (*Ne*) estimates
3. Trans-species variation
4. Allele variation distribution
5. Divergence of allele variation
6. Introgression data

Arguments based on these features are of varying worth. Let us look briefly at each.

Dennis Venema has recourse to some of these features in order to dispute a single-couple origin of humanity.[20] He seems to be appealing to (1), the *multiplicity of alleles*, when he says that "there is a connection between the number of variants [alleles] present in a population and the size of the population—a connection that scientists can use to estimate one from the other."[21]

19. S. Joshua Swamidass to William Lane Craig, June 19, 2018.

20. Dennis R. Venema and Scot McKnight, *Adam and the Genome: Reading Scripture after Genetic Science* (Grand Rapids: Brazos, 2017), chap. 3: "Adams Last Stand?"; BioLogos Editorial Team, "Adam, Eve, and Human Population Genetics," *BioLogos* (blog), November 12, 2014, https://biologos.org/articles/series/genetics-and-the-historical-adam-responses-to-popular-arguments/adam-eve-and-human-population-genetics (part 7: "Coalescence, Incomplete Lineage Sorting, and Great Ape Ancestral Population Sizes"); Dennis R. Venema, "Genesis and the Genome: Genomics Evidence for Human-Ape Common Ancestry and Ancestral Hominid Population Sizes," *PSCF* 62, no. 3 (2010): 166–78.

21. Venema and McKnight, *Adam and the Genome*, 46. An allele is a variant in a stretch

He notes that species with a large population size can support a large number of alleles, since each member of the species can have two distinct alleles of any given DNA sequence in its genome.[22] So one simple way to measure how large our population has been in the past "is to select a few genes and measure how many alleles of that gene are present in present-day humans."[23] Using this method, we find that the human population has never fallen below ten thousand individuals. In fact, says Venema, "to generate the number of alleles we see in the present day from a starting point of just two individuals, one would have to postulate mutation rates far in excess of what we observe for any animal."[24] In short, there are just too many alleles in the present human population for that population to have arisen from an original human couple.

Venema also appeals to (2), *effective population size (*Ne*) estimates*, using so-called linkage disequilibrium to estimate ancient population sizes.[25] The basic idea, he explains, is that if two genes are located close to each other on the same chromosome, then their alleles tend to be inherited together.[26] The closer two loci are on a chromosome, the less likely it is that the alleles will be broken up, while the further apart they are, the more likely it is that their alleles will undergo recombination. Observations show that many alleles in the human genome are in linkage disequilibrium—that is, are recombined to a greater extent than would be expected. Knowing the rate at which recombi-

(a locus) of DNA, a different sequence of nucleotide base pairs of the DNA. A population typically exhibits different alleles at each locus in different individuals.

22. Since multicellular organisms like humans are typically diploid (i.e., have two sets of similar chromosomes made up of DNA in each cell), such an organism can have two different alleles at each locus of the pair. Thus, a gene in such an organism may have two alleles or variants. We speak here of autosomal chromosomes, of which we each have twenty-two pairs, not the X and Y chromosomes that determine male or female sex in humans.

23. Venema and McKnight, *Adam and the Genome*, 48.

24. Venema and McKnight, *Adam and the Genome*, 48.

25. The effective population size *Ne* is not the total population but the breeding subset of that population.

26. In his "Genesis and the Genome," 174–75, Venema frames the argument in terms of single nucleotide polymorphisms (SNPs)—i.e., alleles involving the substitution of a single nucleotide at a given locus of the DNA molecule. SNPs that are far apart recombine easily during cell meiosis, while closely linked SNPs do not. Examination of the human genome reveals that many SNP pairs are in linkage disequilibrium; i.e., they are linked to other SNP alleles more frequently than a random distribution would lead one to expect. Venema claims that by knowing the rate at which recombination occurs, along with the distribution and proportions of SNP pairs in a population, we can estimate population sizes over time, thereby proving that humans are descended from an ancestral population no fewer than several thousand individuals.

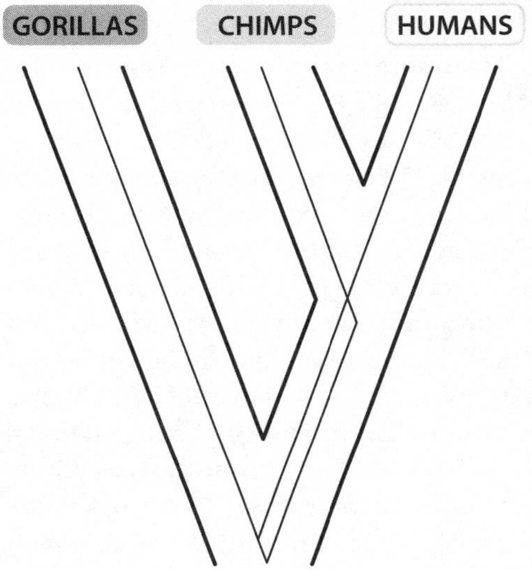

Figure 12.2. Incomplete lineage sorting. Broad channels represent evolving populations of gorillas, chimps, and humans. Single lines represent certain alleles carried by those populations. Because the populations were sufficiently large, some alleles shared with gorillas passed into the human population but not into the chimpanzee population, while others passed into the chimpanzee population but not into the human population.

nation occurs, we can calculate the number of ancestors required for the observed linkage disequilibrium to result (presumably, in the time available). "The results indicate that we come from an ancestral population of about 10,000 individuals—the same results we obtained when using allele diversity alone."[27]

Venema also presents a different version of (2), appealing to Li and Durbin's oft-cited estimate of past population sizes based, not on linkage disequilibrium, but on the so-called pairwise sequentially Markovian coalescent (PSMC) model applied to various individuals.[28] Although they found recent population bottlenecks, Li and Durbin determined that the human population between 1 mya and 10 kya never sank below several thousand.

Venema also offers a third version of (2) appealing to so-called *incomplete lineage sorting*. He explains that alleles present within an ancestral population may not sort completely down to every descendant species because of losses along the way (fig. 12.2). So, for example, there are regions of the human genome that are more similar to the gorilla genome than to the chimpanzee

27. Venema and McKnight, *Adam and the Genome*, 51.

28. Heng Li and Richard Durbin, "Inference of Human Population History from Individual Whole-Genome Sequences," *Nature* 475, no. 7357 (2011): 493–96. They applied the model to the genomes of a Chinese man, a Korean man, three Europeans, and two Yoruban men. PSMC is a specialization to the case of two chromosomes of the sequentially Markovian coalescent model (SMCM), also used to estimate population sizes.

genome, despite the fact that chimpanzees are more closely related to humans than are gorillas.

How is it that human DNA could be more similar in some respects to gorilla DNA than to chimpanzee DNA, even though chimpanzees and humans evolved from a more recent common ancestor? Incomplete lineage sorting explains how this could have happened. The claim is that the ancestral population for gorillas, chimps, and humans must have been sufficiently large that it could carry a wide variety of genetic traits. Certain of those traits passed into the gorilla lineage and human lineage but skipped the chimpanzee lineage. Other traits skipped the gorilla lineage and passed into both the chimpanzee and human lineages. So, as a result, human beings resemble gorillas in some of their genetic traits more than they resemble chimps. Such incomplete lineage sorting requires a large enough population of the last common ancestor in order for different genetic traits to pass selectively into different diverging lineages. In order to carry this diversity of genetic material, that ancestral population had to be in the range of ten thousand individuals. Venema claims that this value "is a measure of the effective population size of our lineage since speciation with chimpanzees (~4–6 million years ago) or gorillas (~6–9 million years ago)."[29] We can thus "infer the effective population size of the lineage leading to humans from the present to the point of divergence with gorilla"[30]—that is to say, the population of the human lineage from the time of its divergence from the gorilla lineage up until the present day, or during roughly the past nine million years. On this same basis Venema later expanded the time frame: "It seems that our smallest effective population size over the last 18 million years was when we were already human, at around the time some of our ancestors left Africa."[31]

The eminent evolutionary biologist Francisco Ayala argued on the basis of (3), *trans-species variation*, that the mean population size of the human lineage over the past thirty million years is 100,000 individuals.[32] Although this mean figure does not imply that population bottlenecks could not have

29. Venema, "Genesis and the Genome," 174.

30. Venema, "Genesis and the Genome," 174, caption to fig. 2. Again, he says, "Taken individually and collectively, population genomics studies strongly suggest that our lineage has not experienced an extreme population bottleneck in the last nine million years or more (and thus not in any hominid, nor even an australopithecine species), and that any bottlenecks our lineage did experience were a reduction only to a population of several thousand breeding individuals" (175).

31. Venema and McKnight, *Adam and the Genome*, 55.

32. Francisco J. Ayala et al., "Molecular Genetics of Speciation and Human Origins," *PNAS* 91, no. 15 (July 1994): 6787–94, https://doi.org/10.1073/pnas.91.15.6787.

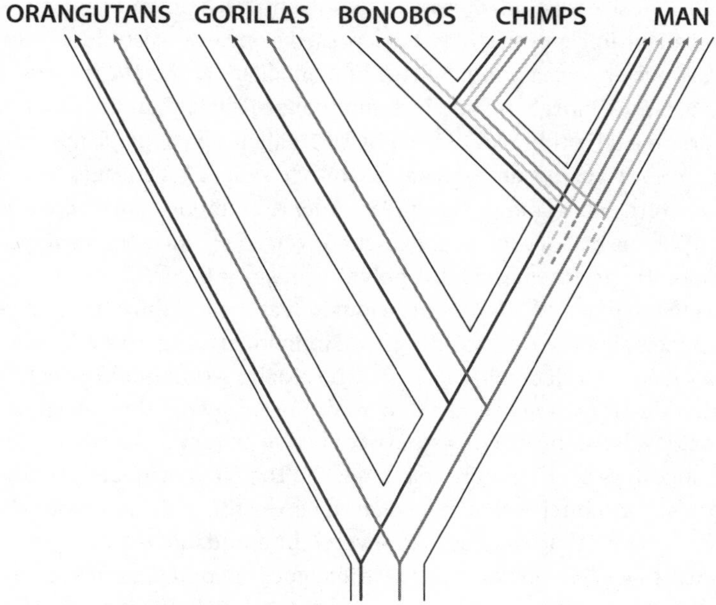

Figure 12.3. Trans-species variation. In order to transmit a sizable number of alleles into a daughter population, both the ancestral population and the daughter population must be large enough to carry the trans-species variations.

occurred along the way, still Ayala estimates that "human ancestral populations could never have been smaller than two or three thousand individuals at any time over the last several million years."[33] We saw that incomplete lineage sorting requires that the ancestral population of divergent species must be large enough to support the alleles that are differentially transmitted to the multiple daughter species. Ayala pushes the argument a notch further by drawing attention to the fact that in order to transfer a sizeable number of alleles to a daughter species, the respective populations of both the ancestral species and the daughter species must be relatively large (fig. 12.3).

Ayala focuses on allelic diversity in the human leukocyte antigen (HLA) complex, an array of genetic loci consisting of about one hundred genes located on chromosome 6, and specifically one particular HLA class II locus,

33. Ayala et al., "Molecular Genetics," 6791. Whatever bottlenecks there are have to be large enough to carry all the trans-specific lineage.

the *DRB1* gene. He seeks to identify trans-specific DNA polymorphisms—that is, sets of allelic lineages that have been passed from an ancestral species to its daughter species. Ayala points to two human alleles at the *DRB1* locus, each of which is more closely related to a chimpanzee allele than the two human alleles are to each other. All fifty-eight *DRB1* alleles have persisted through the last 500,000 years, but they coalesce into ten ancestral lineages by 13 mya. Ayala then turns the argument around in order to extrapolate from the existing polymorphisms back to the events that converted an ancestral gene pool to a new pool. He finds that the HLA polymorphism at the *DRB1* locus requires a mean effective size of 100,000 individuals over the last thirty million years, never falling below two or three thousand individuals at any time. These findings lead Ayala to reject what he calls "the Noah's Ark model," which "proposes that the transition of archaic to modern *H. sapiens* was associated with a very narrow bottleneck, consisting of only two or very few individuals who are the ancestors of all modern mankind."[34] "The *HLA* evidence contradicts the Noah's Ark model and evinces that the ancestral population of modern humans was at no time smaller than several thousand individuals."[35]

Feature (4), *allele variation distribution*, goes beyond the mere multiplicity of alleles in a given population to consider the allele frequency in that population—that is to say, how often a particular allele appears at a certain locus in that population. What is the percentage of chromosomes in a population that have that allele at that locus? Compiling the allele frequencies for various loci yields an allele frequency spectrum (AFS), which is the distribution of the allele frequencies across a set of loci in a population. The AFS of a given population is sensitive to changes in population size. The claim is that the observed AFS for the human population does not fit well the expected AFS, had the population experienced severe bottlenecks in the past. For a great deal of time would be necessary for any new alleles produced through mutations to become as frequent in the population as even 5 percent, yet there are hundreds of thousands of such alleles.

Feature (5), *divergence of allele variation*, is in Swamidass's thinking the key consideration in population genetics' challenge to a single-couple origin of humanity. It is vital in this regard to differentiate genetic *divergence* from genetic *diversity*. Terms like "genetic diversity" and "genetic variation/variability" are ambiguous, leading to confusion and conflation of arguments.[36] I shall take

34. Ayala et al., "Molecular Genetics," 6792.

35. Ayala et al., "Molecular Genetics," 6793.

36. Venema uses all these words without clear definitions and, it seems, equivocally; e.g., Venema, "Genesis and the Genome," 173, 174, 175; Venema and McKnight, *Adam and the Genome*, 44, 45, 46, 47, 48, 51, 53, 55, 60.

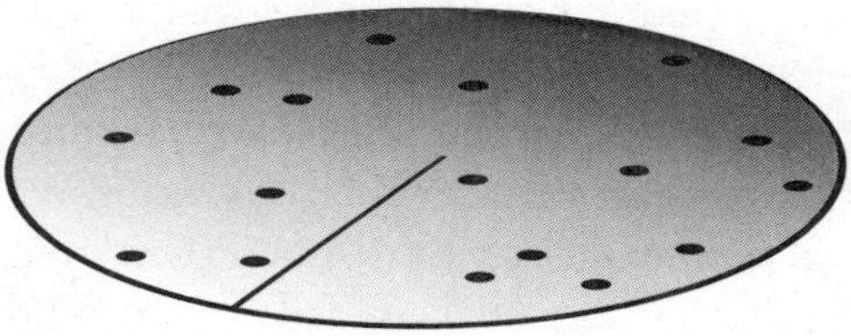

Figure 12.4. Genetic divergence. Dots represent different alleles in a population. Distances between the dots represent genetic divergence due to mutations. The radius of a circle encompassing the dots provides a measure of their genetic divergence.

"genetic diversity" or "variation" to refer to the multiplicity of alleles in a population. Genetic divergence, on the other hand, has to do with the mutational distances between alleles in a population. We can visualize divergence by representing alleles as dots plotted on a plane (fig. 12.4).[37]

The more mutations separating two alleles, the greater the distance between them on the plot. One way to measure divergence would be to measure the distances of the farthest alleles from the most central allele. One draws a circle, as it were, around all the dots, and the radius of that circle provides a measure of their genetic divergence. Notice that the multiplicity of alleles (genetic diversity) is irrelevant; what matters is the spread of the alleles (genetic divergence). We want to compute genetic divergence across the whole human genome, or at least that part of it that has been sequenced, which is about 90 percent.[38] We can then ask how long and how rapidly mutations must have been occurring for the distances separating alleles in the present population to arise from a pair of sole genetic progenitors.[39] Given the known mutation rate, we can use genetic divergence to calculate the *time of the most recent common ancestor* (TMRCA), which will be the median time of all estimates for various loci.[40] The argument is that

37. I am indebted to Swamidass for personally providing this illustration to me.

38. Swamidass reports that as a result of a recent advance involving the computer program ArgWeaver, geneticists are able to determine more accurately the boundary points of loci and to draw more accurately the "circles" genome-wide than ever before. ArgWeaver uses a generation time of twenty-five years with a mutation rate of 1.26^{-8} mutations per generation. Swamidass cautions that one is not really drawing circles around points, though this is a good analogy, but computing phylogenetic trees depicting ancestral lines. In fact, he advises, the actual model is a bit more complex than even a tree. It is something called an ancestral recombination graph (ARG), which makes neighboring trees (along the genome) more similar and also pools data from multiple loci to estimate times.

39. Mutational distance is the product of mutational rate and time ($D = R \times T$). So $T = (D/R)$.

40. One takes the median in order to cancel out errors in calculating the TMRCA for individual loci, some estimates of which may be too high and others too low.

a single pair of sole genetic progenitors cannot be obtained within the time during which hominins have existed on the earth.[41]

The last argument on our list appeals to (6), *introgression data*, concerning the interbreeding between *Homo sapiens* and other ancient species. We have seen that the genomes of modern humans carry DNA inherited from Neanderthals and Denisovans. These data are a challenge to anyone who wants to postulate two sole genetic human progenitors belonging to *Homo sapiens*. The introgression data make clear that our ancestral lines were not hermetically sealed to outside input but absorbed genetic material from individuals who were not *Homo sapiens* and therefore not descended from the original pair. The challenge becomes acute if one admits the humanity of Neanderthals and Denisovans, since in that case one would have human beings not descended from the primordial couple. One must therefore deny the humanity of members of those species.

On the basis of evidence such as the above, Venema expresses supreme confidence that humanity did not descend from a single human couple: "Some ideas in science are so well supported that it is highly unlikely new evidence will substantially modify them, and these are among them. The sun is at the center of our solar system, humans evolved, and we evolved as a population."[42]

41. As one writer put it, this would make Adam literally a "monkey's uncle"! (David Wilcox, "Finding Adam: The Genetics of Human Origins," in *Perspectives on an Evolving Creation*, ed. Keith B. Miller [Grand Rapids: Eerdmans, 2003], 252).

42. Venema and McKnight, *Adam and the Genome*, 55. Venema takes *evolving as a population* to be incompatible with the view that humans, while sharing ancestry with apes, "got their start when a founding couple 'mutated away' in tandem from their ape-like ancestors" (Venema and McKnight, *Adam and the Genome*, 44–45). He subsequently sought to soften his claim, explaining, "The heliocentric quote . . . is about humans (*Homo sapiens*). When I'm speaking about our lineage leading up to humans at 200KYA I use 'lineage' or similar" (Dennis Venema, comment #308 on Dennis Venema, "Adam, Eve and Population Genetics: A Reply to Dr. Richard Buggs (Part 1)," BioLogos Forum, December 21, 2017, https://discourse.biologos.org/t/adam-eve-and-population-genetics-a-reply-to-dr-richard-buggs-part-1/37039/308). According to this clarification, it is with heliocentric certainty that we know that *Homo sapiens* evolved as a population rather than from a founding couple. Though less outrageous, this statement still requires us to know with heliocentric certainty that human = *Homo sapiens*, if we are to know that humans evolved as a population rather than from a founding couple.

As for the possibility that there was such a founding pair prior to *Homo sapiens* (and Neanderthals and Denisovans), Venema had written earlier, "It seems that our smallest effective population size over the last 18 million years was when we were already human, at around the time some of our ancestors left Africa" (Venema and McKnight, *Adam and the Genome*, 55). Later he comments on that statement, "Does 'it seems' sound like I'm saying this is as certain as heliocentrism? That would be quite the understatement.

He here expresses what has been called "heliocentric certainty" against an original human pair.[43]

Critique of Arguments against a Founding Pair

Swamidass has subjected the above arguments to searching criticism.[44] He dismisses arguments based on (1) and (2) as "just wrongheaded. These arguments are total misdirections that have nothing to do with the key question. They are category errors."[45] There is no known way of estimating human population sizes in the deep past merely on the basis of the number or variety of alleles in the human population today. What matters, rather, is the divergence of alleles in the population. The argument from genetic diversity, as we have defined the term, is a red herring.[46]

Arguments based on past population size are misleading because such estimates are averages over a window of time and so are consistent with peaks and valleys within the intervals. Venema consistently errs in taking these estimates to concern *minimum* population size rather than *average*

That is a summary statement of all the lines of evidence in the literature to date that do not provide support for a bottleneck below ~10,000 at any time in the last 18MY (which remains the case)" (Venema, comment #308). This comment does not make clear sense. Is Venema walking back his statement or doubling down? I think Venema expects a negative answer to his question and meant to say that it would be quite the *overstatement* to claim heliocentric certainty. For later he summarizes: "So: 'heliocentric certain': humans. Pretty darn certain: lineage leading to humans over the last several hundred thousand years (say back to ~500,000 years ago). Confident but not as definitive: lineage over the last few million years" (Venema, comment #308).

43. S. Joshua Swamidass, "Heliocentric Certainty against a Bottleneck of Two?," *Peaceful Science* (blog), December 31, 2017, https://discourse.peacefulscience.org/t/heliocentric-certainty-against-a-bottleneck-of-two/61.

44. Swamidass, "Heliocentric Certainty."

45. Swamidass to Craig, June 6, 2018.

46. In response to Venema's claim that a bottleneck of two would be disastrous for the population's health, Buggs points out that studies show that "even a bottleneck of a single pair would not lead to massive decreases in genetic diversity, if followed by rapid population growth. . . . From a bottleneck of a single fertilised female, if population size doubles every generation, after many generations the population will have over half of the heterozygosity of the population before the bottleneck. If population growth is faster than this, the proportion of heterozygosity maintained will be higher" (Richard Buggs, "Adam and Eve: A Tested Hypothesis?," *Ecology & Evolution* (blog), October 28, 2017, https://natureecoevocommunity.nature.com/channels/522-journal-club/posts/22075-adam-and-eve-a-tested-hypothesis). NB Buggs's taking genetic diversity to be about the multiplicity of alleles and heterozygosity, thus pursuing Venema's red herring.

population size.[47] In 2017 Richard Buggs pointed out that the hypothesis of a bottleneck of two had in fact never been tested scientifically.[48]

Indeed, as Swamidass observes, we know—one is tempted to add "with heliocentric certainty"—that at some point in the past the number of human beings goes to zero and therefore to fewer than ten thousand individuals. In thinking otherwise, Venema is guilty of a crucial equivocation between "ancestors" and "humans."[49] Even if the ancestral population of hominins leading to humans remains constantly above several thousand, it does not follow that there were not at some time exactly two humans who emerged within that population. This fact highlights the evident fallacy of Venema's argument from incomplete lineage sorting: it does not follow from the large size of the ancestral population of chimps and humans, or of gorillas, chimps, and humans, that therefore the human population was more than two. (To show that, one would need to appeal instead to the problem of trans-species variation, to which we shall return.)

All population size estimates include both human and nonhuman hominins that existed during a period of time. "No one," Swamidass muses, "has found a way to figure out what the ratio . . . between the two population [*sic*] is; nor has anyone asked the question in a research study."[50] It is entirely possible that at some time in the past the total number of breeding humans was exactly two, even though the total population at the time was much greater. These early humans might or might not have interbred with their contemporaries. If they did, then the founding couple would not be our sole genetic progenitors, for their partners would have had genetic input into the human race. If such interbreeding never occurred, the founding couple would be the sole genetic progenitors of the human race, there being no outside input.

What, then, of the argument from *trans-species variation*? While initially plausible, the argument dissolves upon examination. Since every human being has two sets of similar chromosomes (not counting the X and Y chromosomes determining sex), a founding human pair can carry at most four alleles at any locus into the descendant population. So if it can be shown that there are more than four allele lineages exhibiting trans-species variation, then we should have strong evidence against an originating human

47. Venema and McKnight, *Adam and the Genome*, 44, 52, 53, 60.

48. Buggs, "Adam and Eve."

49. Swamidass, "Heliocentric Certainty." For some reason Swamidass calls this equivocation "the ecological fallacy."

50. Swamidass, "Heliocentric Certainty."

pair. Ayala, it will be remembered, claimed that this is exactly what we find for the HLA gene *DBQ1*.

Swamidass, however, sees reason to question Ayala's conclusion. The salient question here concerns the number of trans-species lineages that, if we accept Ayala's analysis, might require a minimum human population size of more than two at any time in the past. Although the issue is still under debate, most studies have failed to uncover evidence of trans-species variation between humans and nonhuman ancestors involving more than four allele lineages.[51] A survey of trans-species variation across the genome showed that, other than the possible exception of HLA genes, human trans-species variation never seems to involve more than four allele lineages.[52] A single-couple bottleneck is thus consistent with established instances of trans-species variation. Thus, Ayala's paper fails to demonstrate that our ancestral population could at no point have been as low as two.

More significantly, perhaps, there is a plausible alternative explanation of trans-species variation among hominins—namely, convergent evolution. We saw earlier that convergent evolution is likely common among hominin species, producing homoplasies that may be misleading in determining lines of descent.[53] In such a case, similar alleles evolved through independent mutations in different species. Swamidass explains that if convergent evolution is at play, then we should see a large number of mutations that cannot fit into a treelike structure, but we shall instead see two independent paths taken by alleles, forming a square or diamond. A large number of such squares for a particular part of the genome is a tip-off that the observed similarity between sequences is due not to common descent but to convergent evolution. As it turns out, scientists studying the HLA portion of the genome find that "*HLA* genes have a massive excess of squares, a clear sign of pervasive convergent evolution."[54] The most variable HLA gene is *DRB1*, which exhibits over five hundred squares in the DNA of about merely one thousand individuals. Swamidass reflects, "That means if we had tried to put the DNA into

51. Swamidass, "Heliocentric Certainty." Even if such variation should be discovered, it could indicate no more than the fact that Adam and Eve were not our sole genetic progenitors, but that there was interbreeding with outsiders, who introduced more alleles into the human population.

52. E. M. Leffler et al., "Multiple Instances of Ancient Balancing Selection Shared between Humans and Chimpanzees," *Science* 339, no. 6127 (March 29, 2013): 1578–82, https://doi.org/10.1126/science.1234070.

53. See *supra*, p. 257.

54. Swamidass, "Heliocentric Certainty."

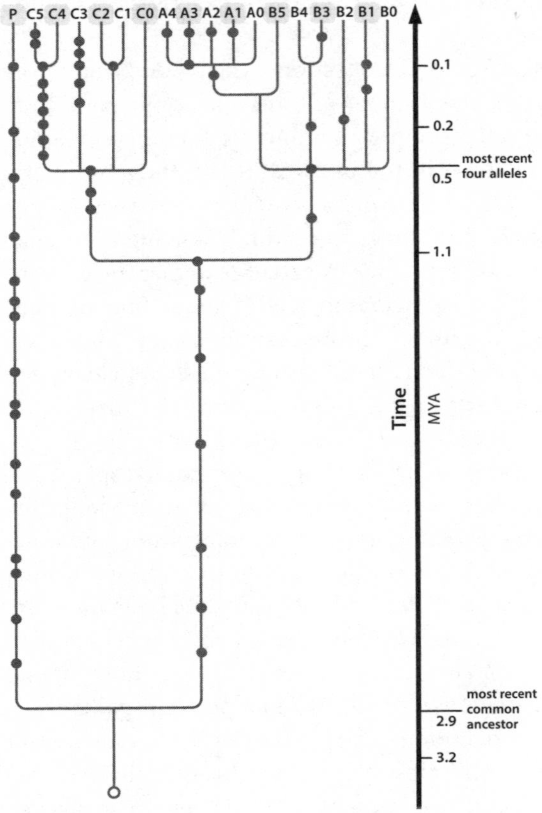

Figure 12.5. A phylogenetic tree constructed from human variation data at a particular place in the genome. The tree is the inferred history of a gene, tracing back to a common genetic ancestor about 2.9 mya. If Adam and Eve were heterozygous, then we should instead look for the most recent time at which there were four alleles (TMR4A). This tree shows the TMR3A to be about 500 kya.

a tree, we would see *at least* 500 mutations discordant with a phylogenetic tree. This is just a *stunning* result, because it means that *HLA-DRB1* alleles are just not well described as a tree. The variation we see is evolving and re-evolving over and over again. Amazing."[55] Swamidass notes that "Ayala's gene *HLA-DBQ1* is not mentioned in the text [of the cited study], but we find it in the supplementary data as one of the genes with clear evidence of convergent evolution."[56] This finding robs the argument from trans-species variation of its probative force.

That brings us to (4), the *allele frequency spectrum*. The problem here, says

55. Swamidass, "Heliocentric Certainty." Moreover, the homoplasies created by convergent evolution will artificially increase the estimated TMRCA because of the impossibility of constructing a parsimonious phylogenetic tree.

56. Swamidass, "Heliocentric Certainty."

Swamidass, is that this analysis considers only a limited summary of the genetic data and rules out a bottleneck only more recently than 500 kya.[57] This leaves it an open question what a more complete analysis of the data would tell us.

The decisive question, rather, concerns (5), *the divergence of alleles in the human population.* Venema had drawn attention to a phylogenetic tree for a segment of DNA showing that the TMRCA had to be about 2.9 mya in order for the observed mutational divergence to be produced in the present population (fig. 12.5).

Swamidass notes, however, that the bottleneck couple (or a founding couple) could have been heterozygous, each carrying two different alleles at any locus of their chromosome pairs, for a total of four alleles for any locus to be passed on to their descendants.[58] In that case the relevant time is not the TMRCA but the *time to the most recent four alleles* (TMR4A).

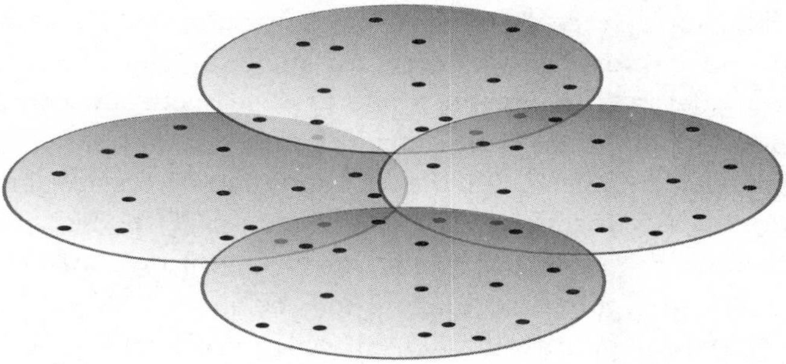

Figure 12.6. Computing the time required to arrive at the genetic divergence of the present human population from a heterozygous founding pair. To make this calculation, we must draw four circles encompassing the alleles plotted on the diagram.

Returning to the illustration of the dots and circles, in order to take into account four founding alleles per locus rather than one, we should draw, not one, but four circles around different subsets of the dots, calculate the TMRCA for each circle, and then take the median value of the four together (fig. 12.6).

Assuming a constant population, we should expect the time to be cut to 25 percent of the TMRCA, so that the TMR4A could be reached by 500 kya. Population genetics has been concerned only with the TMRCA, so that no studies of the TMR4A had been published prior to Swamidass's work, requiring him to do his own original modeling in order to obtain a date.

57. Swamidass to Craig, July 13, 2020.
58. Swamidass, "Heliocentric Certainty."

Using the ArgWeaver dataset, Swamidass found that the actual relationship between the relevant times is TMR4A = 0.38 × TMRCA. This yields a rough estimate for only a segment of DNA; what we need is a genome-wide estimate of the TMR4A, to be obtained by computing the TMR4A for every locus and then finding their median value. Using genome-wide data for ancestral recombination graphs from Matthew Rasmussen et al.,[59] Swamidass was able to estimate, independently of the TMRCA, a date for the TMR4A of 431 kya. Computing the TMR4A another way, Swamidass obtained a date of 437 kya, thereby increasing confidence in his estimate. Finally, he refined his estimate by differentially weighting coalescents to arrive at a date of 495 kya for the TMR4A. Given all the uncertainties involved, Swamidass assigns an error bar of ± 100 kya to that estimate.

More recently the above findings have been confirmed by Ola Hössjer and Ann Gauger, who explore what they call a Single-Couple Origin (SCO) model of the human race.[60] Using a previously published backward simulation method and some newly developed and faster algorithms, they run their SCO model and compare the results to allele frequency spectra (AFS) and linkage disequilibrium (LD) statistics from current genetic data. They find that the data summarized in the AFS and simple LD statistics are consistent with at least two different but parsimonious SCO models: (1) a model featuring a homozygous first couple dating to about 2 mya and (2) a model featuring a heterozygous first couple who lived about 500 kya. Thus, they conclude, given common assumptions shared by evolutionary geneticists, a single-couple origin is possible, despite claims to the contrary.

So while a recent bottleneck is ruled out by the genetic divergence exhibited by today's human population, a bottleneck before 500 kya is possible, in which case the founding pair would be the common ancestors of *Homo sapiens*, Denisovans, and Neanderthals. "The dust has yet to settle on the scientific details," says Swamidass. "But it looks likely at this point that a bottleneck anytime before 700 kya is undetectable in genetic data,"[61] a date well within the range of our proposed classification of Adam as *Homo heidelbergensis*.

Finally, the argument based on (6), *introgression data*, may be quickly dismissed. It assumes without justification the identity relation human =

59. M. D. Rasmussen et al., "Genome-Wide Inference of Ancestral Recombination Graphs," *PLOS Genetics* 10, no. 5 (May 15, 2014): e1004342, https://doi.org/10.1371/journal.pgen.1004342.

60. Ola Hössjer and Ann Gauger, "A Single-Couple Human Origin Is Possible," *BIO-Complexity* 2019, no. 1 (October 2019): 1–20.

61. S. Joshua Swamidass, "Reworking the Science of Adam," *Peaceful Science* (blog), March 22, 2018, http://peacefulscience.org/reworking-Adam/.

Homo sapiens, an assumption that is not only unjustified but against which the evidence strongly inclines, as we have seen. Still, this sixth feature serves to raise an important point: Swamidass's and Hössjer and Gauger's modeling assumed that the most recent four alleles (or, alternatively, the most recent common ancestors) were our sole genetic progenitors—that is to say, that interbreeding between their descendants and outsiders never took place. If the TMR4A is >500 kya, then that single couple could indeed be our sole genetic progenitors, since Neanderthals, Denisovans, and *Homo antecessor* are among their descendants. But if, as Venema assumed, only members of *Homo sapiens* are human, then the estimates of the TMR4A are subverted, for the genetic divergence observed in the present human population derives, not just from human ancestors, but from outsiders as well. One will need to recalculate the TMR4A, taking account of introgression of genetic material into the "human" genome. No one knows how to do this, since genetic material has also passed from archaic *Homo sapiens* to Neanderthals, been reprocessed, and then passed back to us again at a later date. It is of no avail to consider the genomes of modern sub-Saharan populations alone on the grounds that they have not suffered introgression, for recent discoveries show interbreeding between archaic African populations and Neanderthals as well.[62] For all we know, given interbreeding, a bottleneck of two could have occurred among *Homo sapiens* as recently as 200 kya.[63]

After extended discussion with Buggs, Swamidass, and others,[64] Venema came to acknowledge the failure of his arguments against a single-couple origin. "Based on some new simulations and some other published studies that we

62. L. Chen et al., "Identifying and Interpreting Apparent Neanderthal Ancestry in African Individuals," *Cell* 180, no. 4 (January 2020): 677–87. They conclude that "remnants of Neanderthal genomes survive in every modern human population studied to date." See also Arun Durvasula and Sriram Sankararaman, "Recovering Signals of Ghost Archaic Introgression in African Populations," *SA* 6, no. 7 (February 12, 2020), https://doi.org/10.1126/sciadv.aax5097, who claim to show that four West African populations derive 2–19 percent of their genetic ancestry from an archaic population that diverged from the *ancestors* of modern humans and Neanderthals before that ancestral population split into Neanderthals and modern humans; and B. Lorente-Galdos et al., "Whole-Genome Sequence Analysis of a Pan African Set of Samples Reveals Archaic Gene Flow from an Extinct Basal Population of Modern Humans into Sub-Saharan Populations," *GB* 20, no. 1 (April 26, 2019), https://doi.org/10.1186/s13059-019-1684-5, who find evidence of "the presence of a deep archaic population substructure . . . in the African continent," not just in West Africa.

63. S. Joshua Swamidass, "Three Stories on Adam," *Peaceful Science* (blog), August 5, 2018, https://peacefulscience.org/three-stories-on-adam/.

64. For a fascinating personal retrospective on the dialogue, see Swamidass, "Three Stories on Adam."

drew on, our group came to an agreement—that if an event like this had happened, we would be able to detect it if it happened more recently than 500,000 years ago. That was surprising to me, to be sure—I thought beforehand that an event like that would show up even further back in time."[65] Though he doubles down on the claim that "there is no positive evidence at all that such an event occurred,"[66] that is a red herring, since no one has asserted that there is.

Buggs offered this consensus statement:

> The hypothesis of a bottleneck of two in the human lineage has not been directly addressed in the scientific literature using genome-wide human diversity data. Nonetheless, from those published studies of human diversity that we have reviewed, and based on our understanding of current theory, we have drawn tentative conclusions. We conclude that current human genetic diversity data does not rule out a bottleneck of two individuals in the human lineage between approximately 400,000 and 7,000,000 years ago, but neither do they show that such a bottleneck has happened. Current analyses and models suggest that a two-person bottleneck has not occurred below a threshold of approximately 400,000 years before present. More research is needed in this area, and we are open to new analyses moving this threshold up or down.[67]

While concurring with these sentiments, Venema nonetheless insists that, despite the possibility of a founding pair before 500 kya, the existence of such a couple is highly improbable. "In order for this to work, one would have to propose that in one generation all of them were obliterated, save two."[68] This bold claim is obviously false, since a founding pair could have existed as part of a wider population with whom the founding pair's descendants may or may not have interbred. Venema is oddly fixated on sole genetic

65. Dennis Venema, "Adam—Once More, with Feeling," *Jesus Creed* (blog), November 24, 2019, https://www.patheos.com/blogs/jesuscreed/2019/11/04/adam-once-more-with-feeling/. NB that his statement confuses necessary and sufficient conditions. Venema should say "only if it happened."

66. Venema, "Adam—Once More, with Feeling."

67. Richard Buggs, comment #592 on Venema, "Adam, Eve, and Population Genetics," BioLogos Forum, February 11, 2018, https://discourse.biologos.org/t/adam-eve-and-population-genetics-a-reply-to-dr-richard-buggs-part-1/37039/592. NB that Buggs takes "diversity" to be synonymous with "divergence," thereby highlighting the ambiguity of these terms, of which I complained earlier.

68. Venema, "Adam—Once More, with Feeling."

progenitorship rather than genealogical ancestry: "In order to have sole genetic progenitors, all other hominins that could interbreed with Adam and Eve's offspring must be eliminated in some way, or Adam and Eve must be reproductively isolated. . . . Geographic isolation isn't going to cut it—after all, eventually this pair will populate the whole globe, which requires *not* being isolated."[69] But the existence of a historical Adam and Eve need not imply their sole genetic progenitorship, especially over tens of thousands of years; and even if their descendants were for a time reproductively isolated, such isolation could result from social distancing due to a myriad of factors, including geographic isolation, tribalism, language barriers, xenophobia, cognitive capacity differences, racism, just plain revulsion, and so on, as well as any population reduction we might imagine. Perhaps these barriers were sometimes breached, but then we do not have any idea whether there were offspring of such unions that had genetic input into the human line. Of course, once Adam and Eve's descendants replaced *Homo heidelbergensis*, we know that there was interbreeding among the extended human family, but we can only conjecture as to what happened in the interim.

69. Venema, "Adam—Once More, with Feeling." Cf. Denis Alexander's similar preoccupation. He claims that a model featuring an ancient founding pair does not work scientifically because individuals alive today would contain few, if any, copies of that particular couple's genes.

> It is not therefore clear what might be gained theologically by envisaging the putative Adam and Eve as being embedded somewhere within one of these early populations. They could not have been the physical ancestors of the whole of humanity, so the idea of a single couple who somehow transmitted their sin by inheritance to the whole of humanity cannot be sustained by such a scenario. True, their genes would have contributed to the subsequent human population in succeeding generations, but so would the genes of all the others in their community in that generation and in the generations before and after. (Denis R. Alexander, *Creation or Evolution: Do We Have to Choose?*, 2nd ed. [Oxford: Monarch Books, 2014], 298–99)

In the space of this one paragraph, Alexander (1) falsely claims that in order to be the physical ancestors of the whole of humanity, Adam and Eve had to be the sole genetic progenitors of all humanity; (2) falsely claims that Adam and Eve could not have been the sole genetic progenitors of all humanity; (3) falsely claims that Adam and Eve's being our sole genetic progenitors necessitates their genes' being transmitted down to us today; (4) falsely ties the doctrine of original sin to the genetic transmission of sin from parents to offspring; and (5) falsely assumes that the theological gain to be had from a single-couple origin of humanity is exhausted by the doctrine of original sin, thus ignoring the universality of God's dealings with humanity, a central emphasis of the primaeval history of Genesis.

Geographical Challenge

We have seen that, contrary to the single species model of the origin of modern cognitive capacity with respect to human beings, the evidence supports a multispecies, cultural model of the development of modern cognitive capacity in Asia, Africa, and Europe. We have surveyed remarkable archaeological signatures of modern behavior going back hundreds of thousands of years in Africa and Europe, some quite stunning, such as the constructions at Bruniquel Cave and the Schöningen spears. Reflecting on such evidence, d'Errico and Stringer assert, "Exactly as with our present genetic diversity, 'modernity' was not a package that had a unique African origin in one time, place and population, but was a composite whose elements appeared at different times and places, including some outside the African continent, either shared or developed in parallel. These were then gradually assembled through a variety of paths and processes to assume the form that we recognize as behavioural modernity today."[70]

The geographic challenge, then, is to find a single human pair early enough to have been the fount of this widespread cultural evolution. We have seen that *Homo sapiens* and Neanderthals were thought to have diverged from a common ancestor 750–550 kya, one population remaining in, or migrating to, Africa to eventually become modern man and another migrating into Eurasia to become Neanderthals and Denisovans. Perhaps even earlier another population diverged to become *Homo antecessor*. Modern behaviors emerged broadly within these populations in tandem and perhaps on occasion in concert with one another. The currently fashionable "pan-Africanism," which holds that modern behavior did not originate merely in one locale within Africa but across the entire continent,[71] is not inconsistent with this scenario, since it concerns the emergence of modern behavior among *Homo sapiens* only; for the entire human race we need an even wider perspective that encompasses Europe and Asia as well.

Unless we are to postulate improbable coincidences, the emergence of modern cognitive capacity must have already characterized the common ancestor of all these species and been carried forward by them all. We have found our attention repeatedly directed toward *Homo heidelbergensis* as the

70. D'Errico and Stringer, "Evolution, Revolution or Saltation," 1067.

71. Robin McKie, "The Search for Eden: In Pursuit of Humanity's Origins," *Guardian*, January 5, 2020, https://www.theguardian.com/world/2020/jan/05/the-search-for-eden-in-pursuit-of-humanitys-origins.

most likely candidate for the office of common ancestor, though it does not really matter here what we call that ancestral species. "*Homo heidelbergensis*" can be regarded simply as a placeholder for that large-brained species from which we all evolved and which was the fount of modern cognitive capacities, until palaeoproteomic analysis of teeth from Boxgrove or Mauer confirms this identification.

In time, those primaeval cognitive capacities of *Homo heidelbergensis* would express themselves and eventually leave traces discoverable by us. Marc Kissel and Agustín Fuentes provide a nice summary:

> By 200,000–400,000 years ago, *Homo* brain size was the same as in modern humans, and its functional capacity close to ours if not nearly identical. At this same time, the inner ear and vocal apparatus for language had developed, and the neurobiology for speech was likely in place. In this time period we see evidence for a substantial uptick in the complexity of tools and lifeways in *Homo* populations across Africa and Eurasia. Fire use become [*sic*] ubiquitous, and there is evidence for at least a few "symbolic" materials being produced/used, the manufacture and use of more and more complex tools, and even the first possible burials of the dead. The human niche was changing. More complex information was being exchanged, more types of tools and uses for them were being created, more learning and teaching were needed to successfully be a member of the genus *Homo*. The ways in which populations of the genus *Homo* interacted with the world and each other was deepening in complexity and the capacity for meaning-making likely played a role in opening up the possibilities for these groups.[72]

At some time and place in the gray mists of antiquity, we hypothesize an original human pair uniquely endowed with the cognitive capacities that would come to be associated with *Homo heidelbergensis*. Exactly when and where the hypothetical founding couple lived cannot as yet be determined more closely.

As mentioned, one might ask why it took the descendants of Adam and Eve so long to become behaviorally modern. But we must keep in mind that the manifestation of ancient cognitive capacity proceeds in fits and starts,

72. Marc Kissel and Agustín Fuentes, "'Behavioral Modernity' as a Process, Not an Event, in the Human Niche," *TM* 11, no. 2 (April 3, 2018): 176, https://doi.org/10.1080/1751696x.2018.1469230.

appearing and disappearing and then, sometimes after enormous stretches of time, reappearing. This uneven palaeoanthropological record of human cognitive achievement is not entirely ascribable to the incompleteness of the archaeological record. Rather, it plausibly indicates that changing environmental conditions serve to call forth behaviors latent in human cognitive capacity. The slow climb of behavioral modernity is a problem only if one assumes what Kim Sterelny calls "the simple reflection model," which holds that behavioral modernity is a simple reflection of increased cognitive capacity.[73] Sterelny's preferred model, the niche construction model, does not predict an inevitable, constant, unidirectional mobilization of cognitive resources, even after the fundamental capacities essential to that mobilization have evolved. "For the developmental environment is critical, and subject to multiple routes of disturbance."[74] Even cognitive adaptations for learning and teaching were not in themselves sufficient for expressions of behavioral modernity. "An adapted learning environment—best understood as apprentice transmission—and a favourable demographic profile were also necessary." In short, "the specific component signatures of modernity (symbol use, composite tool making, ecological breadth and the like) are just fallible indicators of this basic cognitive-cum-cultural capacity."[75]

Summary and Conclusion

Our study of the scientific evidence for human origins has yielded rich rewards. We have seen that on the basis of paradigmatic examples of human beings we can delineate certain features that, given sufficient anatomical similarity of those having such features to human beings, are sufficient for human personhood, including abstract thinking, planning depth, various sorts of innovativeness, and especially symbolic behavior. The evidence of palaeoneurology concerning brain size and development inclines us to regard such ancient species as *Homo heidelbergensis* and *Homo neanderthalensis* as, like us, human. The manifold evidence of archaeology discloses archaeological signatures associated with the sufficient conditions for human cognitive capacity, especially art and language indicative of symbolic behavior,

73. Kim Sterelny, "From Hominins to Humans: How *sapiens* Became Behaviourally Modern," *PTRSB* 366, no. 1566 (March 27, 2011): 813, https://doi.org/10.1098/rstb.2010.0301.

74. Sterelny, "From Hominins to Humans," 813.

75. Sterelny, "From Hominins to Humans," 814.

that together provide a powerful cumulative case for the humanity of these same ancient species. Since these modern cognitive capacities did not in all probability evolve independently among ancient species of *Homo*, they are best regarded as inherited from a common ancestor, who is typically identified as *Homo heidelbergensis*, a large-brained, cosmopolitan species that may have originated anywhere in Eurasia or Africa prior to 750 kya. Members of this species migrated to diverse regions, where their regional populations evolved into *Homo sapiens*, Neanderthals, and other human species.

Adam and Eve may therefore be plausibly identified as members of *Homo heidelbergensis* and as the founding pair at the root of all human species. Challenges to this hypothesis from population genetics fail principally because we cannot rule out on the basis of the genetic divergence exhibited by contemporary humans that our most recent common ancestors, situated more than 500 kya, are the sole genetic progenitors of the entire human race, whether past or present. The challenge of the wide geographic distribution of humanity is similarly met by situating Adam and Eve far in the past, prior to the divergence of *Homo sapiens*, Neanderthals, and other species, and allowing multispecies cultural evolution to proceed thereafter in response to environmental changes to produce modern human behaviors wherever their descendants are to be found.

PART 4

Reflections on the Historical Adam

Chapter 13

PUTTING IT ALL TOGETHER

On the basis of a detailed genre analysis of the primaeval history of Gen 1–11, we concluded that it is plausible to regard these chapters as a Hebrew mytho-history that serves as a universal foundational charter for the election and identity of Israel over against its neighbors. While these narratives need not be read as literal history, the ordering presence of genealogies terminating in persons who were indisputably taken to be historical and the teaching of Paul in the NT about Adam's impact on the world, which bursts the bounds of a purely literary figure, oblige the biblically faithful Christian to affirm the historicity of Adam and Eve. Adam and Eve are asserted to be the fount of all humanity, the genealogical ancestors of every human being who has ever lived on the face of this planet.

A review of the scientific evidence concerning the time of human origins reveals that, on the basis of widely accepted criteria for human cognitive capacity, human beings ought not to be identified with *Homo sapiens* alone but ought to be taken to include Neanderthals as well. Given that all human beings are descendants of a founding couple—a theological, not a scientific, commitment—Adam and Eve may be plausibly identified as belonging to the last common ancestor of *Homo sapiens* and Neanderthals, usually denominated *Homo heidelbergensis*. Such an identification is fully consonant, both temporally and geographically, with the data of population genetics, which does not rule out the existence of two heterozygous, sole genetic progenitors of the human race earlier than 500 kya. In this final chapter we want to reflect on the ramifications of such an identification.

Eschatological Reflections

Given the Judaeo-Christian doctrine of physical, bodily, eschatological resurrection, it would be disconcerting if Adam and Eve were so different from us in their morphology that they and their immediate descendants would be physically repugnant to the vast majority of the risen saints. Fortunately, *Homo heidelbergensis* was not some hybrid ape-man but was recognizably human (fig. 13.1).

Indeed, as we have seen, *Homo antecessor*, a sister species of *Homo sapiens* and Neanderthals, had a remarkably modern facial morphology, suggesting that the modern face is deeply rooted in human evolutionary history. The morphological differences between Neanderthals and modern humans, including the large Neanderthal nose, may well be, in the opinion of many palaeoanthropologists, the result of adaptation to ice-age climates and so derived, not ancestral, characters.[1] When one thinks of the diversity within our contemporary human population, from Australian Aborigines to Nordic Laplanders to Inuits in Canada and Greenland, then including archaic humans within the human family is not so radical a step. Many of us in the West have a deeply inherited tendency to think of Adam and Eve as European Caucasians, which is nothing more than a cultural and racial prejudice. If we can get used to the thought that Adam and

Figure 13.1. Artist's reproduction of *Homo heidelbergensis* (also called *Homo rhodesiensis*) based on skeletal remains.

1. James Hurd reports that palaeoanthropologists have opined that "if a Neanderthal were seen today dressed in a three-piece suit and boarding a subway train in New York, he would not have attracted undue attention" (James P. Hurd, "Hominids in the Garden?," in *Perspectives on an Evolving Creation*, ed. Keith B. Miller [Grand Rapids: Eerdmans, 2003], 217). Presumably this is not a comment on the insouciance of New Yorkers!

Eve may have resembled African San more than white people, then surely we can get used to the idea that Adam and Eve looked like *Homo heidelbergensis* rather than us. Indeed, I can imagine that in the eschaton Neanderthals and other archaic humans might be subjects of special regard: "You were there near the beginning, weren't you? Tell me what it was like!"

The thought that Neanderthals and other archaic humans might share with us Christians the eschatological state of "a new heaven and a new earth" (Rev 21:1) brings the startling realization that, as members of the human family, Neanderthals, Denisovans, and others were, like us, people whom God loves and for whom Christ died. Paul describes how God "overlooked the times of human ignorance" (Acts 17:30 NRSV) and "passed over former sins" committed prior to Christ's advent (Rom 3:25). Christ's death atoned for the sins of past humanity all the way back to Adam's sin. Unless one embraces the strange teaching of limited atonement, Christ's atoning death must have therefore encompassed the sins of these archaic humans. This realization raises the difficult question of the accessibility of salvation for those who, like Job, lived outside the orbit of the OT covenant with Israel; but any solution to that problem, such as appeal to God's general revelation in nature and conscience, can be applied *mutatis mutandis* to Neanderthals and other archaic humans.[2] We may well see some of them, therefore, in the eschaton, and I think that we shall be delighted to do so.

The Image of God

If Adam and Eve were the ancestors of Neanderthals and other archaic humans, then it follows that members of these species are, like Adam and Eve, made in the image of God, for they are included in the generic statements of Gen 1:26–27. How should we understand this? In his highly acclaimed book *The Liberating Image: The* Imago Dei *in Genesis 1*, Richard Middleton distinguishes between what he calls a substantialistic, a relational, and a functional interpretation of the image of God. Rather than find the image of God in some ontological similarity between God and man or in man's capacity to

2. For a discussion of the doctrine of salvation through Christ alone and challenges thereto, see my "'No Other Name': A Middle Knowledge Perspective on the Exclusivity of Salvation through Christ," in *The Philosophical Challenge of Religious Diversity*, ed. Philip L. Quinn and Kevin Meeker (Oxford: Oxford University Press, 2000), 38–53.

stand in "I-Thou" relations with God and other persons, Middleton plumps for a functional interpretation of the *imago Dei.* "On this reading the *imago Dei* designates the royal office or calling of human beings as God's representatives and agents in the world, granted authorized power to share in God's rule or administration of the earth's resources and creatures."[3] Middleton reports that today there is virtual unanimity among OT scholars in favor of the functional interpretation.

In support of the functional interpretation, Middleton first points out that the context in Gen 1 has a predominantly royal flavor, beginning with the close linkage of the image of God with the mandate to rule and subdue the earth in Gen 1:26 and 28, where God commands man to have dominion over the earth and its creatures. Moreover, the God in whose image and likeness human beings are created is depicted as the king or the sovereign over the cosmos. He rules by royal decree—"Let there be . . . !"—and addresses the divine council of the heavenly court of angelic beings, saying, "Let us make man in our image." So the writer portrays God as a king presiding over heaven and earth. Humanity is created like this God in having the special role of representing or imaging God's rule in the world.

Now certainly OT scholars are correct in seeing man as having this royal duty and role on the earth, for it is clearly assigned in Gen 1:26–27. But that fact in itself does not imply that the image of God just *is* that function. Man's royal duty may be, rather, *the role* that God has given to him to fulfill. Middleton, however, insists that the royal function or purpose of humanity in 1:26 is not a mere add-on, separable in some way from man's essence or nature. Middleton says that while rule may be grammatically only the purpose, and not the definition, of the image in 1:26, the overall rhetorical world of the text suggests that it is a necessary and inseparable purpose, and therefore virtually constitutive of the image.

But Middleton's conclusion is overdrawn. In the first place, it is far from evident that the royal assignment given by God to man is not a contingent, freely given bequest of God. God could have created a human being without giving him that function, just as he could have created the firmament or the heavenly luminaries without giving them the functions that he has assigned to them.[4] Second, and more important, a thing's having a necessary and

3. J. Richard Middleton, *The Liberating Image: The* Imago Dei *in Genesis 1* (Grand Rapids: Brazos, 2005), 27.

4. Middleton argues by analogy that Gen 1:6 shows that the function of separation is not extrinsic to the firmament but defines its nature and that 1:14–18 describes the intrinsic purpose of the two luminaries, which cannot be separated from their existence. These

inseparable purpose is just not the same thing as a thing's definition. An essential function of an automobile, for example, is to transport people, but that is not the definition of an automobile. The stubborn fact is that Genesis leaves *the image and likeness of God* undefined.

Rather, what is key to Middleton's case for the functional interpretation is his second reason for the consensus among OT scholars—namely, the ANE ideology of kings in Mesopotamia and Egypt that describes their function as the images of the gods. Although many scholars would draw our attention to the fact that these ancient kings would often set up statues or images of themselves in distant lands under their control, Middleton contends that the meaning of this practice is contested. The images could just be monuments to the kings and their accomplishments. Many of these images are votive objects that are dedicated to the gods. More significant in Middleton's judgment is the practice of Egyptian pharaohs of setting up images of themselves in distant lands as representing the absent king in some way. Middleton thinks that since this representative notion is intrinsic to the understanding of images in the ANE, it seems quite plausible to regard the kings' practice of setting up images of themselves in distant lands as a legitimate parallel to the creation of humans in the image of God. Man is God's image and represents God and his authority on the earth.

While this kingly practice is interesting, it is not clear that it is, in fact, a legitimate parallel to man's being created in God's image and likeness. Genesis does not portray the earth as being like a distant land from which God is absent. Quite the contrary, God is himself active in the world. He does not need some surrogate to stand in his place. Moreover, notice that the king's statue in a distant land does not really function in the king's place. It does not, in fact, do anything. It just represents the king's authority over the land. The king's statue is rather like the pictures of the president on the walls of our police stations and post offices. They represent his authority. But humans are living images of God. They are not images of God in the ANE sense of a statue.

Middleton contends, however, that the best ANE parallels to the *imago Dei* are texts that describe the various kings and priests as themselves images

two examples of creatures whose existence is explicitly defined by their function or purpose allegedly set up the presumption that the royal function or purpose of humanity in 1:26 is inseparable from man's essence or nature. This argument is very weak. God could have assigned to the firmament other purposes—e.g., a place to fix the heavenly luminaries. Nor do the luminaries themselves have to serve the function of marking times and seasons and years, rather than, say, illumination and warmth.

of a god. This is the most widely cited set of parallels for Gen 1:26–27. To give just a few examples: Pharaoh Ahmose I is described as "a prince like Re, the child of Qeb, his heir, the image of Re, whom he created, the avenger (or the representative), for whom he has set himself on earth." Queen Hatshepsut is described as "superb image of Amon; the image of Amon on earth; the image of Amon-Re to eternity, his living monument on earth." Amenhotep II is described variously as "image of Re," "image of Horus," "image of Atum," "holy image of the lord of the gods," "foremost image of Re," "holy image of Re," "holy image of Amon," "image of Amon like Re," and so on.[5]

Middleton comments on these texts,

> To understand the meaning and function of this idea, we need to grasp something of the wider ideology of kingship in Egypt. Central to this ideology was the divinity of the pharaoh, by which he was set apart from all other human beings. . . . The notion of the pharaoh as an image of a god must be understood in this context. In one sense, the notion of image is but one among many other ways of expressing the pharaoh's divine origin and kinship to the gods. . . . The pharaoh was thought, in a fairly strong sense, to be a physical, local incarnation of deity, analogous to that of a cult statue or image of a god, which is also such an incarnation. . . . "The king as the living image of god was," Curtis explains, "like the cult statue, a place where the god manifested himself and was a primary means by which the deity worked on earth."[6]

These texts are said to support a functional interpretation of the image of God in Genesis.

There are, however, two major flaws that undermine Middleton's case. First, Middleton admits that a functional interpretation does not preclude, and even presupposes, a substantial interpretation. He writes, "Both functional and . . . relational interpretations of the image are, like substantialistic interpretations, strictly speaking metaphysical, in that they also make ontological assumptions about human nature. . . . A functional interpretation might be seen as consonant with some version of action theory. . . . [The] focus is on persons as agents who act responsibly (or irresponsibly). Action, on this model, includes all that an agent does, including thinking,

5. Cited in Middleton, *Liberating Image*, 109.

6. Middleton, *Liberating Image*, 109–10. The embedded citation is from Edward Curtis, "Man as the Image of God in Light of Ancient Near Eastern Parallels" (PhD diss., University of Pennsylvania, 1984), on which Middleton depends.

as an integral unity."[7] This admission undermines Middleton's case for a purely functional interpretation, for he recognizes that humanity's function is rooted in ontology. More than that, it is rooted in personal agency, and personal agency is not a function. It is a property of personal agents—that is to say, personal, causally effective beings. Notice as well that the relation between ontology and function is asymmetrical. Functions are grounded in ontology, not vice versa. The substantialist is quite happy to recognize that human persons have been created by God to carry out a function. They can carry out that function, however, because of what they *are*—namely, personal agents. So the functional interpretation actually presupposes the substantial interpretation in grounding function in the ontology of human beings as personal agents.[8]

The second flaw in the argument is that the Mesopotamian and Egyptian texts cited do not in fact support a functional interpretation but rather a different, fourth interpretation. As Middleton convincingly shows, when the ANE texts speak of an idol or of the pharaoh as a god's image, what they mean is that the idol or the pharaoh embodies or incarnates the god. The deity is present in and lives through the idol or the king. The problem is, this is not a functional interpretation. It is a metaphysical view of the relation between the idol or king and the god. It is more accurate, therefore, to call it an *incarnational interpretation*. The king is the incarnation of the god; the idol is the embodiment of the god. But then this interpretation is irrelevant for the interpretation of the Genesis texts, for those texts do not think of human beings as incarnations of God, through which he lives and acts in the world. An anti-iconic religion like Judaism would have recoiled at the idea that human beings are embodiments of God.[9]

So it seems that a substantialist interpretation is practically unavoidable.[10] In order to function as God's co-regent on this planet, man must have cer-

7. Middleton, *Liberating Image*, 27n39.

8. NB that my point here is not merely *ad hominem*; rather, Middleton is plausibly correct in seeing function as grounded in ontology.

9. Perhaps that is the reason for the Hebrew prepositions in Gen 1:26–27, "in" (*b*^{e}) God's image and "according to" (*k*^{e}) his likeness. Man is not said to *be* God's image or likeness.

10. In Gen 5:1–3 Seth is said to be born in *Adam's* image and likeness. That seems decisive for a substantialist interpretation. For Seth was not Adam's representative or co-regent. That effectively rules out a functionalist interpretation of "image." The functionalist might retort that *being in the image of* is a transitive relation (like *less than*), so that Seth is in God's image, not just in Adam's image. The problem is that the resemblance relation is not transitive. A daughter may resemble her mother, and the mother may resemble her mother, but the granddaughter may not resemble the grandmother. Seth is said to be

tain faculties like rationality, self-consciousness, freedom of the will, and so forth. So we should not play off functional versus substantial understandings of God's image. The reason we can function as God has commanded us to is that we are created in God's image; that is to say, we have some ontological similarity to God that enables us to serve as his representative and co-regent. On this view, the reason that we can serve as God's co-regents and representatives on this planet is that we are in the image of God; that is to say, we are persons in the same way that God is personal and thus have the attributes of personhood. It is precisely the properties of personhood that are manifested by the cognitive behaviors to which we have appealed as evidence of humanity.

Body-Soul Dualism/Interactionism

Genesis 1:26–27 treats man holistically as created in God's image. While that precludes identifying God's image as the rational soul alone, it is consistent with maintaining that the reason a human being as a whole is in God's image is that he incorporates a rational soul, which makes him a person. In the OT we do not find clear terminological distinctions drawn between the soul and the body, which has led some theologians to affirm anthropological monism (physicalism). Nevertheless, the Hebrew idea of a shade in Sheol seems to be the equivalent of the Greek idea of a disembodied soul. The people who go down to Sheol are regarded as wraiths, as having a kind of shadowy existence in the nether realms of the dead. They are not extinguished at death; rather, they seem to exist in a state that is not fully human. In any case, in Second Temple Judaism anthropological dualism came to be the standard Jewish belief, being abundantly attested in the Jewish intertestamental literature (e.g., *2 Baruch* 30.1–5; *4 Ezra* 7.26–44; *1 Enoch* 22.1–5). The standard view was that when a person dies, his body (in particular his bones) rests in the ground until the day of judgment, while his soul goes to be with God, where it is securely kept until judgment day.[11] At that time, soul and body will be reunited and the person will be judged.

born not in God's image and likeness (as Adam was created) but rather in Adam's image and likeness. In other words, Adam brought forth another human being like himself.

11. See Robert H. Gundry, Sōma *in Biblical Theology: With Emphasis on Pauline Anthropology* (Cambridge: Cambridge University Press, 1976), 87–93; Paul Hoffmann, *Die Toten in Christus: Eine religionsgeschichtliche und exegetische Untersuchung zur paulinischen Eschatologie*, 3rd ed., NTA 2 (Münster: Aschendorff, 1978), 26–174.

The language of the NT is indisputably dualistic throughout. It consistently differentiates the soul and the body. That this distinction is meant to be literal rather than just figurative or functional is clearest when we consider the intermediate state between bodily death and resurrection (2 Cor 5:1–10; cf. Phil 1:21–23). Paul embraces the typical Jewish belief about the intermediate state in anticipation of the resurrection. In Paul's view, when a Christian dies, the soul goes to be with Christ until his return for judgment. Those who are still alive at the return of Christ will be immediately transformed into their resurrection bodies without the need of passing through the intermediate state of disembodied existence, which Paul describes as a state of nakedness. Paul's desire, if he had his way, is to live until the return of Christ and not have to go through that intermediate state. Nevertheless, he is comforted by the fact that such a state brings one into closer fellowship with Christ. When Christ returns, the remains of the body, if any, will be transformed into a resurrection body that will be incorruptible, immortal, powerful, and Spirit-filled, and the soul will be simultaneously united with that body. Then those who are alive will be similarly transformed into their resurrection bodies (1 Cor 15:42–52; cf. 1 Thess 4:14–17).

We therefore have ample biblical grounds in the teaching about the intermediate state of the soul for believing that the dualistic language in the Scriptures is to be taken seriously and that humans are composite entities made up of a soul and a body that, though united, are capable of existing independently of each other and therefore are ontologically distinct.[12]

At the same time, the implausibility of reductive and nonreductive physicalism with regard to the mind-body problem supports the notion that the soul is a spiritual substance distinct from the brain.[13] As the Nobel Prize–

12. Moreover, the denial of the reality of the soul has theological ramifications that threaten to undermine all of Christian theology. For as an unembodied mind, God just is an unembodied soul, analogous to us when we become disembodied souls at bodily death. So if one denies that unembodied souls are possible, it is very difficult to see how one can consistently believe in the existence of God, since that is exactly what God is.

13. For representative defenses of dualism/interactionism with respect to mind and body, see Jonathan J. Loose, Angus J. L. Menuge, and J. P. Moreland, eds., *The Blackwell Companion to Substance Dualism* (Oxford: Wiley-Blackwell, 2018); Richard Swinburne, *Mind, Brain, and Free Will* (Oxford: Oxford University Press, 2013); Mark C. Baker and Stewart Goetz, eds., *The Soul Hypothesis: Investigations into the Existence of the Soul* (London: Continuum, 2011); Alvin Plantinga, "Materialism and Christian Belief," in *Persons: Human and Divine*, ed. Peter van Inwagen and Dean W. Zimmerman (Oxford: Oxford University Press, 2007), 99–141; E. J. Lowe, *Personal Agency: The Metaphysics of Mind and Action* (Oxford: Oxford University Press, 2008); William Hasker, *The Emergent Self*

winning neurologist Sir John Eccles explains, on a dualist/interactionist view the soul, though not identical with the brain, uses the brain as an instrument for thought, just as a pianist uses a piano as an instrument to produce music.[14] Just as an out-of-tune piano impairs the pianist's ability to produce music, so a damaged brain impairs the soul's ability to think.

While we do not want to become overly distracted by pursuing the debate over mind-body dualism, it is worth saying a brief word in defense of a dualist/interactionist view of the human mind and body. Philosopher of mind Angus Menuge mentions several problems confronting a materialist or physicalist philosophy of mind:

> *Reductive* and eliminative forms of physicalism fail to account for our mental lives. But . . . the varieties of *non-reductive* physicalism also fail to account for mental causation. If these [non-reductive] theories are faithful to physicalism, then supervening or emergent mental properties cannot add anything new that was not going to happen anyway, as a result of their physical base properties. If we want to account for consciousness, mental causation, and reasoning, we need some entity over and above the body. This entity must be simple, have thoughts as inseparable parts, persist as a unity over time, and have active power. That sounds like a soul.[15]

Here Menuge distinguishes between two types of physicalism. First is the reductive or eliminative type of physicalism. Reductive or eliminative forms of materialism are increasingly unpopular. They do not seem to account, as Menuge says, for our mental lives because the brain, as a physical substance, has only physical properties, such as a certain volume, a certain mass, a certain density, a certain location, a certain shape. But the brain on this view does not have mental properties. The brain is not jubilant, the brain is not sad, the brain is not in pain, even though the brain is involved in the neural circuitry that gives us such experiences.

Reductive physicalism therefore cannot account for our mental lives.

(Ithaca, NY: Cornell University Press, 1999). I am grateful to Angus Menuge for these recommendations.

14. Karl R. Popper and John C. Eccles, *The Self and Its Brain: An Argument for Interactionism* (New York: Springer, 1977). I heard Sir John make the provocative comparison at the Sixteenth World Congress of Philosophy in Düsseldorf in 1978.

15. Angus Menuge, "Why Not Physicalism?" (paper presented at the Evangelical Philosophical Society panel for the Society of Biblical Literature, San Francisco, CA, November 19, 2011); my emphasis.

Take the phenomenon of fear. When we experience fear, there is brain activity that is correlated with the experience of fear. The dualist/interactionist agrees—it is not as though the soul operates independently of the brain. Rather, there is an interaction with the brain in the experience of fear. But the brain itself is not afraid. One cannot reduce fear to a physical brain state even if it is correlated with such a brain state. So reductive physicalism seems obviously untenable. It cannot be reconciled with our mental experience.

This fact has led many thinkers to affirm some sort of nonreductive physicalism—the brain gives rise to supervenient or epiphenomenal states of awareness like jubilance or sadness or pain. But there is not in such cases any *thing*—any soul or mind—that has these experiences. Rather, the brain is the only thing that really exists, and these mental states are just states of the brain. Menuge identifies a number of problems with this view.

First of all, he points out that it is incompatible with self-identity over time. If the brain endures from one moment to another, then the brain has identity through time, but its states of awareness do not endure from one moment to the next. There is no enduring self—no "I"—that endures from one moment to the next. This view of the self—the "I"—is rather like the Buddhist view of the self, which says that the soul or the self is something like the flame of a candle. The candle and the wick endure from one moment to the next, but the flame does not endure. There is a different flame at each moment of the candle's burning. The flame exhibits a sort of continuity in that the candle does not go out while it is burning, but there really is no identity of the flame over time. The situation is similar with states of awareness. Every state of the brain at different times has a state of awareness associated with it, but there is no enduring self or "I" from one moment to the next.

This leads a naturalist philosopher like Alex Rosenberg to boldly affirm that there is no enduring self. The existence of the self is an illusion.[16] In his book *The Atheist's Guide to Reality*, Rosenberg thus affirms, "I do not exist." Similarly, it is an illusion that we are the same persons who existed five minutes ago. In fact, we are not the same persons because there is no personal identity over time. So if we *do* believe that we exist and have endured for five minutes, then we ought to reject a nonreductive physicalist view of the self.

Second, intentional states of consciousness do not seem to make sense on nonreductive physicalism. The property of intentionality is the property

16. Alex Rosenberg, *The Atheist's Guide to Reality: Enjoying Life without Illusions* (New York: Norton, 2011), 147, 223–24, 315.

of being about something or being of something. For example, I can think about my summer vacation or I can think of my wife. Physical objects do not have these sorts of properties. The brain is not about something any more than a chair or a table is about something or of something. It is only thoughts that are of something and so have aboutness or intentionality. But on nonreductive physicalism there is no self that has states of intentionality; so intentionality is in effect an illusion.

So, again, Rosenberg says that we never really think about anything. It is just an illusion that we have intentional states.[17] He acknowledges that without intentionality sentences are not about anything because a sentence is just ink marks on paper and therefore not about anything—sentences are meaningless. So he affirms that every sentence in his book is meaningless—including that sentence! The denial of intentional states is not only contrary to experience—we are, after all, thinking *about* Rosenberg's claims—but it is actually self-refuting. For what is an illusion? An illusion is always an illusion *of* something. So an illusion is itself an intentional state. An illusion of intentionality is an intentional state—one is having an illusion *of* something. So the view that intentionality is merely an illusion is self-referentially incoherent.

Third, free will seems impossible to reconcile with either reductive or nonreductive physicalism because on these views there is no causal connection between the sequential states of awareness. The only causality is on the purely physical level, and that is totally determined by the laws of nature and the initial material conditions. So there just is no room for free will. That flies in the face of our experience of ourselves as free agents. I can freely choose to think about certain things or to freely do certain things or not. So if we believe that we ever do anything freely, we have reason to believe in the reality of the soul and to reject reductive and nonreductive physicalist views.

Fourth, Menuge points out that if we want to provide an account of reasoning, we need a soul. If there is no self who reasons from premises to conclusions, then we are just like a pocket calculator which is such that when one presses the buttons "2," "+," and "2" and then hits the button "=," the calculator reads "4." But the calculator does not reason to arrive at that conclusion. In such a device there is no reasoning going on at all. So, again, if we think that we ever reason to arrive at conclusions, we ought to think that we are more than just moist robots, that in fact we are selves who carry out such reasoning.

Finally, fifth, the last phenomenon that Menuge points to is mental causation. Notice that on nonreductive physicalist views the only arrow of

17. Rosenberg, *Atheist's Guide to Reality*, 170–93.

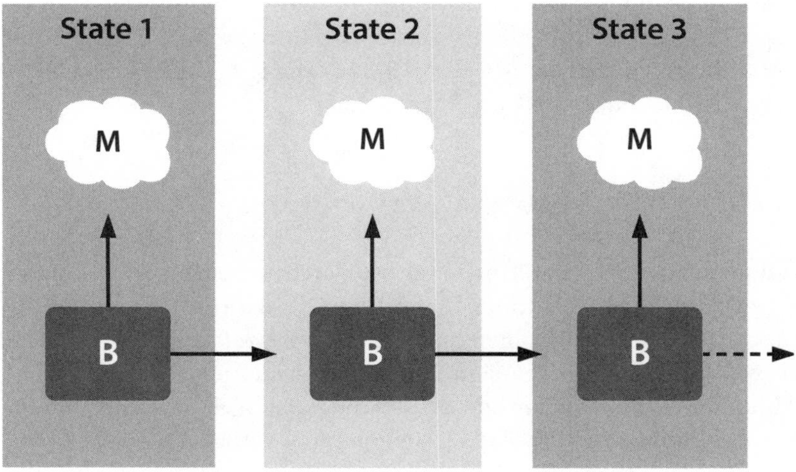

Figure 13.2. Mental and brain states. "M" represents mental states and "B" brain states. The arrows represent the causal connections between such states.

causation is from the physical brain states (B) to other brain states or to epiphenomenal mental states (M) (fig. 13.2).

The epiphenomenal mental states themselves do not cause anything. They are utterly causally impotent. So there is no return causality from states of awareness to the brain. Why? Because there is nothing there—there is no soul, no mind, that can exert a causal influence on the brain. So on this view the arrow of causality goes in only one direction—it is from the brain to these epiphenomenal states.

That is incompatible with our introspective grasp of our ability to cause things. I can cause my arm to go up by willing it. Menuge also discusses the fact of neuroplasticity, according to which thinking can actually affect the brain.[18] If one thinks in certain ways, it produces brain effects. There is even cognitive therapy that is more useful in some cases than drugs in changing patients' behavior. If one alters the way in which one thinks about something, this will affect one physiologically.[19]

18. See further Angus Menuge, "Is Downward Causation Possible? How the Mind Can Make a Physical Difference," *Philos. Christi* 11, no. 1 (2009): 93–110, https://doi.org/10.5840/pc20091117.

19. This is significant because in his book Rosenberg says that if you find all of this depressing—that there is no self, no identity over time, no free will, no intentionality—"there's always Prozac!" (*Atheist's Guide to Reality*, 315). He is serious! What else would a materialist say? He advises his readers to take brain-altering drugs, so that they will

So, for all of these reasons, we ought to reject physicalist views in favor of some sort of dualism/interactionism. That is to say, we are composites of soul and body, just as the Scriptures affirm, and the soul and the body—in particular the brain—work together to think.

Adam's Contemporaries

As human beings, Neanderthals and other archaic humans are in God's image and therefore have intrinsic moral value and share in man's vocation. But what of Adam and Eve's contemporaries that were not their descendants? On an evolutionary scenario, Adam and Eve emerged from a wider population of hominins.[20] Since Adam and Eve are the fount of all humanity, it follows necessarily that Adam and Eve's contemporaries were not human and therefore not in the image of God, since to be human is to be in God's image. No other earthly creature than man, according to the account in Gen 1, has been created in God's image and likeness.

The radical transition effected in the founding pair that lifted them to the human level plausibly involved both biological and spiritual renovation, perhaps divinely caused.[21] Biologically, as we have seen, we may envision a reg-

---

feel better. Just how sinister that advice is, I think, is shown by Menuge's point that we do not always need to resort to drugs. Sometimes there are cognitive therapies whereby changing one's thinking can actually alter the brain and improve mental health.

20. One can, with Swamidass and Hössjer and Gauger, postulate instead a *de novo* creation of Adam and Eve. But then one faces a difficult dilemma. One must explain our genetic similarity to chimps either on the basis of repetitive divine use of a similar design plan or on the basis of considerable interbreeding with nonhumans. The first has difficulty explaining broken pseudogenes that we share with chimps (Dennis R. Venema, "Genesis and the Genome: Genomics Evidence for Human-Ape Common Ancestry and Ancestral Hominid Population Sizes," *PSCF* 62, no. 3 [2010]: 167–73). The second looks as if God condones bestiality for our forebears.

21. Kemp objects to Andrew Alexander's view that there was a crucial mutation converting Adam and Eve to biologically apt beings for a rational soul: "It creates for him the necessity to posit a not impossible but extremely unlikely co-occurrence of exactly two instances of the same mutation (one in a man and one in a woman) at roughly the same time" (Kenneth W. Kemp, "Science, Theology, and Monogenesis," *ACPQ* 85, no. 2 [2011]: 231, https://doi.org/10.5840/acpq201185213). But if we envision a miraculously wrought event, which the infusion of a rational soul may require anyway, there is obviously no problem here. NB that on this view there is no ontological distinction between biological and theological humans, for they are coextensive. Similarly, there is no need or room for distinguishing a class of philosophical humans. There are just humans, viewed under

ulatory mutation that radically increases the cognitive capacity of the brain beyond what other hominins enjoy.[22] Such a transformation could equip the organism with the neurological structure to support a rational soul.[23] In that case Adam would be a case of what genetic engineers call a genetically modified organism (GMO). What is crucial here is that any changes introduced into Adam and Eve be heritable, so that they beget another human being (Gen 5:3). In somatic cell gene therapy, genetic modifications affect only the GMO, not its offspring, whereas in germline gene therapy the modifications to sperm or egg cells are heritable by subsequent generations. In order to produce heritable changes in Adam and Eve's genome, God may have induced mutations, not in them, even at an embryonic stage, but in the gametes of their parents, so that Adam and Eve were human from the moment of conception. On the other hand, some gene therapies breach the so-called Weissman barrier separating somatic from germline cells, so that the latter are affected by genetic engineering of the former, with the result that the somatic cell mutations are heritable.

---

different aspects. By way of analogy, consider a horse: a horse can be viewed biologically or financially or recreationally. But there are not three horses, but one.

22. Bonnette notes that the divinely caused biological transformation of their animal bodies into true, human bodies could have occurred the moment God infused a human soul into the material body of a mature human. Alternatively, the change could have been effected in the zygotic stage, so that highly evolved nonhuman primates raised and protected such human children as their own (Dennis Bonnette, *Origin of the Human Species*, VIBS 106 [Amsterdam: Rodopi, 2001], 114–15). This latter scenario seems to be the sort of transformation Tattersall has in mind (see *supra*, pp. 336–37).

23. Such a view is superior to Andrew Loke's view, which distinguishes human, "anatomical" *Homo sapiens* (those who bear God's image) and nonhuman, "anatomical" *Homo sapiens* (those who do not bear God's image) (*The Origin of Humanity: Science and Scripture in Conversation* [forthcoming], chap. 5). The use of "*Homo sapiens*" here is conventional; any species name under which one wished to classify Adam may be substituted. "Anatomical" is in scare quotes because in Loke's view the crucial issue concerns genetic structure, not body plan or morphology. "God's image" is understood structurally in terms of certain capacities—viz., the capacity for a unique kind of dominion that could extend to the whole world and over all kinds of plants and animals, the capacity for a sense of responsibility toward God the Creator for this kind of dominion, and the capacity to become conformed to Christ. So the claim is that hominins that share the same genetic structure may or may not be human, depending on whether they have these capacities. I seriously doubt that any hominin lacking these capacities, which are all reflections of personal agency, can be genetically identical to someone who has them. If they can, Loke's view leads to the horrific conclusion that there could be people today who look just like us but who are not in God's image and therefore subhuman. Better, therefore, to say that Adam and Eve's nonhuman contemporaries differed from them both biologically and spiritually.

In that case the enhancement of function due to God's neural engineering of Adam and Eve would be passed on to their children.

Thus, God's creation of Adam and Eve plausibly required both biological and spiritual renovations, biological to equip their brains with the capacity to serve as the instruments of rational thought and spiritual to furnish them with rational souls different from any sort of soul that nonhuman animals might be thought to possess. Thus, Adam and Eve were something radically new.

How would Adam and Eve consort, then, with their nonhuman contemporaries? We can plausibly conjecture that as bearers of a modern human consciousness and linguistic capacity, Adam and Eve would increasingly feel themselves at a distance from their nonhuman contemporaries and, as their descendants multiplied, their tribe would be naturally inclined to increasingly self-isolate. If there were sexual encounters with nonhuman hominins, these would be cases of bestiality, contrary to God's will for humanity, though not entirely surprising for a fallen race.[24] Eventually, as Adam and Eve's descendants superseded the other hominin species, the possibility of such liaisons disappears.

So we may envision, with Kenneth Kemp, an initial population of, say, five thousand hominins, animals that are in many respects like human beings but that lack the capacity for rational thought.[25] Out of this population, God selects two and furnishes them with intellects by renovating their brains and endowing them with rational souls. Only they are therefore truly human. At some point they become aware of God's moral requirements, which renders them responsible moral agents.[26] Unfortunately, they misuse their free

24. Some have appealed to interbreeding with other evolved hominin species in order to explain how Adam and Eve could have been *de novo* creations from inanimate material and yet their descendants bear such striking genetic similarity to chimpanzees, including broken pseudogenes that have ceased their original function (S. Joshua Swamidass, *The Genealogical Adam and Eve: The Surprising Science of Universal Ancestry* [Downers Grove, IL: IVP Academic, 2019]). Cf. Dennis Venema's critique of Hössjer and Gauger's *de novo* creationism on the grounds that the human genome is replete with evidence that we share common ancestors with other species, such as chimpanzees and gorillas (Dennis Venema, "Adam—Once More, with Feeling," *Jesus Creed* (blog), November 4, 2019, http://www.patheos.com/blogs/jesuscreed/2019/11/04/adam-once-more-with-feeling). No such appeal to interbreeding is necessary if we envision Adam and Eve as emerging from a hominin population that shared common ancestry with chimpanzees and other great apes. Indeed, on the view proposed here, Adam and Eve could be our sole genetic progenitors, whose descendants never fell into bestial relations with nonhuman hominins or at least produced no descendants from such liaisons.

25. Kemp, "Science, Theology, and Monogenesis," 231–32.

26. Recall the statement mentioned earlier (p. 231) by Daryl Domning: "There is virtually no known human behaviour that we call 'sin' that is not also found among non-

will by choosing to commit a (the original) sin or transgression, thereby becoming morally guilty before God and alienating themselves from God, though not from the offer of God's love and forgiveness. As we have seen from our study of Gen 3, 1 Cor 15, and Rom 5, Adam was thus responsible for introducing spiritual, but not physical, death into the human race, since as biological organisms Adam and Eve were naturally mortal.

We might think it unfair of God not to extend to Adam and Eve's contemporaries the same opportunity of a relationship with God that he bestowed on Adam and Eve. But Kemp effectively exposes the flaw in such thinking, asking,

> Would it not have been unjust of God to give to Adam and Eve the gift of a rational soul, a gift which would make them fully human (and immortal), with the additional prospect of eternal happiness with God in Heaven, while leaving in an animal state their siblings and cousins, who also (on my account, though not on Alexander's[27]) had a bodily constitution sufficient to sustain rational activity? I think not. . . . God did not owe Adam and Eve's cousins a rational and therefore immortal soul. Indeed the very idea that God owes an intellectual soul to those cousins risks incoherence—how could God owe it to some being to make it not exist and to make another being exist in its place?[28]

---

human animals. . . . Yet these overt acts did not acquire their sinful character until the evolution of human intelligence allowed them to be performed by morally responsible beings" (Daryl P. Domning, "Evolution, Evil and Original Sin," *America*, November 12, 2001, http://americamagazine.org/issue/350/article/evolution-evil-and-original-sin). For a somewhat analogous view, see Robin Collins, "Evolution and Original Sin," in *Perspectives on an Evolving Creation*, ed. Keith B. Miller (Grand Rapids: Eerdmans, 2003), 469–501, though I see no reason at all to think that Adam was not an individual but merely an ideal figure for "the first group of evolving hominids who gained moral and spiritual awareness" (486).

27. The reference is to Andrew Alexander, "Human Origins and Genetics," *CR* 49 (1964): 344–53.

28. Kemp, "Science, Theology, and Monogenesis," 233. We need not agree with Kemp's assumption that the bestowal of a rational soul makes Adam and Eve immortal, at least physically (see *supra*, pp. 235–36). I have elided Kemp's remark, "A theology in which the existence of a Chosen People is a central theme in salvation history can surely accommodate the existence of a Chosen Couple." For on the proposed scenario, God is not electing one human couple out of many; there are no other humans. As we saw in our discussion of the primaeval history of Genesis, we must resist attempts to collapse the primaeval history to salvation history by interpreting it in terms of election. God is not electing Adam and Eve in order to save their progenitors or contemporaries, as he did Abraham.

Moreover, I disagree with Kemp's emphasis on moral obligation, or what is owed. On

Kemp's retort is doubly correct if with Alexander we recognize a biological difference between Adam and his progenitors, as it seems we should, for there is nothing unjust about treating animals as animals.

Conclusion

Given the incompleteness of the data and the provisionality of science, the quest of the historical Adam will doubtless never be concluded in our lifetime—or in anyone's lifetime, for that matter. Fortunately, because of the relatively low theoretical level of the science of archaeology, our tentative conclusions are not highly susceptible to sweeping changes. The Bruniquel Cave constructions and the Schöningen spears are not going to disappear. At most they are subject to redating, but while dates can be revised to more recent times, that is unlikely in these and most cases. If anything, dates are usually revised to more distant times.

Despite the inconclusiveness of the quest, we have managed to narrow the window of opportunity considerably as to Adam's place in history. Adam plausibly lived sometime between around 1 mya to 750 kya, a conclusion consistent with the evidence of population genetics. The *terminus ad quem* will probably be pushed back with further palaeontological and archaeological discoveries. We may also expect clarification of the place of *Homo heidelbergensis* through palaeoproteomic analysis of the remains of this species. The name serves at least as a useful placeholder for that large-brained human species that was ancestral to *Homo sapiens* and our various sister species of the human family. We can live with uncertainty. For though we now see through a glass darkly, we shall one day see face to face (1 Cor 13:12). In the meantime, we await new discoveries with excitement and anticipation.

---

a divine command theory of ethics, according to which God's commands constitute one's moral duties, God plausibly has no obligations to anyone, since he does not issue commands to himself. Thus, language of "owing" hominins anything is a category mistake. Rather, the question is whether, in not giving Adam and Eve's progenitors human status, God does something inconsistent with his own nature. It is no more inconsistent with God's nature to treat *Homo erectus* as *Homo erectus* than to treat a pelican as a pelican or an elephant as an elephant or a chimpanzee as a chimpanzee.

BIBLIOGRAPHY

Alexander, Andrew. "Human Origins and Genetics." *Clergy Review* 49 (1964): 344–53.

Alexander, Denis R. *Creation or Evolution: Do We Have to Choose?* 2nd ed. Oxford: Monarch Books, 2014.

———. "The Various Meanings of Concordism." *BioLogos* (blog), March 23, 2017. http://biologos.org/blogs/guest/the-various-meanings-of-concordism.

Alexander, Hartley Burr. *Latin-American*. Vol. 11 of *The Mythology of All Races*, edited by Louis Herbert Gray and John Arnott MacCulloch. New York: Cooper Square, 1964.

Alexander, T. Desmond, and David W. Baker, eds. *Dictionary of the Old Testament: Pentateuch*. Downers Grove, IL: InterVarsity Press, 2003.

Allen, James P. *Genesis in Egypt: The Philosophy of Ancient Egyptian Creation Accounts*. Yale Egyptological Studies. San Antonio, TX: Van Siclen Books, 1988.

Ananikian, Mardiros H., and Alice Werner. *Armenian and African*. Vol. 7 of *The Mythology of All Races*, edited by Louis Herbert Gray and John Arnott MacCulloch. Boston: Marshall Jones, 1925.

Arnaud, Daniel. *Corpus des textes de bibliothèque de Ras Shamra-Ougarit (1936–2000) en sumérien, babylonien et assyrien*. Barcelona: Editorial AUSA, 2007.

Arnold, Bill T. *Genesis*. New Cambridge Bible Commentary. Cambridge: Cambridge University Press, 2009.

———. "The Genesis Narratives." In *Ancient Israel's History: An Introduction to Issues and Sources*, edited by Bill T. Arnold and Richard S. Hess, 23–45. Grand Rapids: Baker Academic, 2014.

———. "Pentateuchal Criticism, History of." In Alexander and Baker, *Dictionary of the Old Testament*, 622–31.

Arnold, Bill T., and David B. Weisberg. "A Centennial Review of Friedrich Delitzsch's 'Babel und Bibel' Lectures." *Journal of Biblical Literature* 121, no. 3 (2002): 441–57.

Arsuaga, J. L., I. Martínez, L. J. Arnold, A. Aranburu, A. Gracia-Téllez, W. D. Sharp, R. M. Quam, et al. "Neandertal Roots: Cranial and Chronological Evidence from Sima de los Huesos." *Science* 344, no. 6190 (June 20, 2014): 1358–63. https://doi.org/10.1126/science.1253958.

Aubert, M., P. Setiawan, A. A. Oktaviana, A. Brumm, P. H. Sulistyarto, E. W. Saptomo, B. Istiawan, et al. "Palaeolithic Cave Art in Borneo." *Nature* 564, no. 7735 (November 7, 2018): 254–57. http://doi.org/10.1038/s41586-018-0679-9.

Averbeck, Richard E. "A Literary Day, Intertextual, and Contextual Reading of Genesis 1–2." In Charles, *Reading Genesis 1–2*, 7–34.

———. "Reading the Torah in a Better Way: Unity and Diversity in Text, Genre, and Compositional History." In *Paradigm Change in Pentateuchal Research*, edited by Matthias Armgardt, Benjamin Kilchör, and Markus Zehnder, 21–43. Beihefte zur Zeitschrift für altorientalische und biblische Rechtsgeschichte. Wiesbaden: Harrassowitz Verlag, 2019.

———. "Responses to Chapter Three." In Charles, *Reading Genesis 1–2*, 94.

Ayala, Francisco J., Ananías Escalante, Colm O'Huigin, and Jan Klein. "Molecular Genetics of Speciation and Human Origins." *Proceedings of the National Academy of Sciences* 91, no. 15 (July 1994): 6787–94. http://doi.org/10.1073/pnas.91.15.6787.

Baaren, Th. P. van. "The Flexibility of Myth." In Dundes, *Sacred Narrative*, 217–24.

Baker, D. W. "Arts and Crafts." In Alexander and Baker, *Dictionary of the Old Testament*, 49–53.

Baker, Mark C., and Stewart Goetz, eds. *The Soul Hypothesis: Investigations into the Existence of the Soul.* London: Continuum, 2011.

Barham, Lawrence S. "Possible Early Pigment Use in South-Central Africa." *Current Anthropology* 39, no. 5 (1998): 703–10.

Barr, James. *Fundamentalism.* Philadelphia: Westminster, 1978.

———. "The Meaning of 'Mythology' in Relation to the Old Testament." *Vetus Testamentum* 9, no. 1 (1959): 1–10.

Barras, Colin. "First Stone-Tipped Spear Thrown Earlier Than Thought." *New Scientist*, November 15, 2012. http://www.newscientist.com/article/dn22508-first-stone-tipped-spear-thrown-earlier-than-thought/.

Barrett, Matthew, and Ardel B. Caneday. "Adam, to Be or Not to Be?" In Barrett and Caneday, *Four Views on the Historical Adam*, 13–36.

———, eds. *Four Views on the Historical Adam.* Counterpoints. Grand Rapids: Zondervan, 2013.

Barrick, William D. "A Historical Adam: Young-Earth Creation View." In Barrett and Caneday, *Four Views on the Historical Adam*, 197–227.

Bascom, William. "The Forms of Folklore: Prose Narratives." In Dundes, *Sacred Narrative*, 5–25.

Bauckham, Richard J. *Jude, 2 Peter*. Word Biblical Commentary 50. Waco: Word, 1983.

Båve, Arvid. "A Deflationary Theory of Reference." *Synthèse* 169 (2009): 51–73.

Beall, Todd. "Reading Genesis 1–2: A Literal Approach." In Charles, *Reading Genesis 1–2*, 45–59.

Beckwith, Martha. *Hawaiian Mythology*. New Haven: Yale University Press, 1940.

Berger, Arno, and Theodore P. Hill. "Benford's Law Strikes Back: No Simple Explanation in Sight for Mathematical Gem." *Mathematical Intelligencer* 33 (2011): 85–91. https://digitalcommons.calpoly.edu/cgi/viewcontent.cgi?article=1074&context=rgp_rsr.

Bickerton, Derek. *Adam's Tongue: How Humans Made Language, How Language Made Humans*. New York: Hill & Wang, 2009.

BioLogos Editorial Team. "Adam, Eve, and Human Population Genetics." *BioLogos* (blog), November 12, 2014. https://biologos.org/articles/series/genetics-and-the-historical-adam-responses-to-popular-arguments/adam-eve-and-human-population-genetics.

Blocher, Henri. *Original Sin: Illuminating the Riddle*. Grand Rapids: Eerdmans, 1997.

Boë, Louis-Jean, Pierre Badin, Lucie Ménard, Guillaume Captier, Barbara Davis, Peter MacNeilage, Thomas R. Sawallis, and Jean-Luc Schwartz. "Anatomy and Control of the Developing Human Vocal Tract: A Response to Lieberman." *Journal of Phonetics* 41, no. 5 (2013): 379–92. http://doi.org/10.1016/j.wocn.2013.04.001.

Boë, Louis-Jean, Jean-Louis Heim, Kiyoshi Honda, and Shinji Maeda. "The Potential Neandertal Vowel Space Was as Large as That of Modern Humans." *Journal of Phonetics* 30, no. 3 (2002): 465–84. https://doi.org/10.1006/jpho.2002.0170.

Bond, Helen K. "What Are the Gospels? And Why Does It Matter?" Paper presented at the Annual Meeting of the Society of Biblical Literature, Synoptic Gospels Section, Denver, CO, November 17, 2018.

Bonnette, Dennis. *Origin of the Human Species*. Value Inquiry Book Series 106. Amsterdam: Rodopi, 2001.

Broadfield, Douglas, Michael Yuan, Kathy Schick, and Nicholas Toth, eds. *The Human Brain Evolving: Paleoneurological Studies in Honor of Ralph L.*

Holloway. Stone Age Institute Publication Series 4. Gosport, IN: Stone Age Institute Press, 2010.

Bromage, Timothy G., and M. Christopher Dean. "Re-evaluation of the Age at Death of Immature Fossil Hominids." *Nature* 317, no. 6037 (October 10, 1985): 525–27.

Brooks, Alison S., John E. Yellen, Richard Potts, Anna K. Behrensmeyer, Alan L. Deino, David E. Leslie, Stanley H. Ambrose, et al. "Long-Distance Stone Transport and Pigment Use in the Earliest Middle Stone Age." *Science* 360, no. 6384 (April 6, 2018): 90–94.

Buggs, Richard. "Adam and Eve: A Tested Hypothesis?" *Ecology & Evolution* (blog). October 28, 2017. https://natureecoevocommunity.nature.com/channels/522-journal-club/posts/22075-adam-and-eve-a-tested-hypothesis.

Bultmann, Rudolf. "Adam and Christ according to Romans 5." In *Current Issues in New Testament Interpretation*, edited by William Klassen and Graydon F. Snyder, 143–65. London: SCM, 1962.

Burridge, Richard A. *What Are the Gospels? A Comparison with Graeco-Roman Biography*. 2nd ed. Waco: Baylor University Press, 2018.

Burstein, Stanley Mayer, ed. *The "Babyloniaca" of Berossus*. Sources from the Ancient Near East 1/5. Malibu, CA: Undena, 1978.

Carson, D. A. "Adam in the Epistles of Paul." In *In the Beginning . . . : A Symposium on the Bible and Creation*, edited by N. M. de S. Cameron, 28–43. Glasgow: Biblical Creation Society, 1980.

Cassuto, Umberto. *A Commentary on the Book of Genesis*, part 1, *From Adam to Noah*. Translated by Israel Abrahams. Skokie, IL: Varda Books, 2005.

Castellino, G. "The Origins of Civilization according to Biblical and Cuneiform Texts." In Hess and Tsumura, *"I Studied Inscriptions from before the Flood,"* 75–95.

Cavigneaux, Antoine. "Les oiseaux de l'arche." *Aula Orientalis* 25, no. 2 (2007): 319–20.

Charles, J. Daryl, ed. *Reading Genesis 1–2: An Evangelical Conversation*. Peabody, MA: Hendrickson, 2013.

Chen, L., A. B. Wolf, W. Fu, L. Li, and J. M. Akey. "Identifying and Interpreting Apparent Neanderthal Ancestry in African Individuals." *Cell* 180, no. 4 (January 2020): 677–87.e16.

Childs, Brevard S. *Introduction to the Old Testament as Scripture*. Philadelphia: Fortress, 1979.

———. *Myth and Reality in the Old Testament*. 2nd ed. Studies in Biblical Theology, 1st ser., 27. 1962. Reprint, Eugene: Wipf & Stock, 2009.

Clifford, Richard J. *Creation Accounts in the Ancient Near East and in the Bible*. Catholic Biblical Quarterly Monograph Series 26. Washington, DC: Catholic Biblical Association of America, 1994.

Clines, David J. A. *The Theme of the Pentateuch*. 2nd ed. Journal for the Study of the Old Testament Supplement Series 10. Sheffield: Sheffield Academic Press, 1997.

Collins, C. John. "Adam and Eve as Historical People, and Why It Matters." *Perspectives on Science and Christian Faith* 62, no. 3 (September 2010): 147–65.

———. *Did Adam and Eve Really Exist? Who They Were and Why You Should Care*. Wheaton: Crossway, 2011.

———. *Reading Genesis Well: Navigating History, Poetry, Science, and Truth*. Grand Rapids: Zondervan, 2018.

———. "Response from the Old Earth View." In Barrett and Caneday, *Four Views on the Historical Adam*, 126–33.

———. "Responses to Chapter Four." In Charles, *Reading Genesis 1–2*, 137.

Collins, Robin. "Evolution and Original Sin." In Miller, *Perspectives on an Evolving Creation*, 469–501.

Conner, Samuel R., and Don N. Page. "*Starlight and Time* Is the Big Bang." *Creation Ex Nihilo Technical Journal* 12, no. 2 (1998): 174–94.

Cooke, Gary A. "Reconstruction of the Holocene Coastline of Mesopotamia." *Geoarchaeology* 2, no. 1 (1987): 15–28.

Copan, Paul, and Douglas Jacoby. *Origins: The Ancient Impact and Modern Implications of Genesis 1–11*. New York: Morgan James, 2019.

Cornford, F. M. *The Unwritten Philosophy and Other Essays*. Cambridge: Cambridge University Press, 1950.

Craig, William Lane. *Atonement and the Death of Christ: An Exegetical, Historical, and Philosophical Exploration*. Waco: Baylor University Press, 2020.

———. *God and Abstract Objects: The Coherence of Theism; Aseity*. Berlin: Springer, 2017.

———. "'No Other Name': A Middle Knowledge Perspective on the Exclusivity of Salvation through Christ." In *The Philosophical Challenge of Religious Diversity*, edited by Philip L. Quinn and Kevin Meeker, 38–53. Oxford: Oxford University Press, 2000.

Craig, William Lane, and Erik J. Wielenberg. *A Debate on God and Morality: What Is the Best Account of Objective Moral Values and Duties?* Edited by Adam Lloyd Johnson. Abingdon, UK: Routledge, 2020.

Currid, John D. *Ancient Egypt and the Old Testament*. Grand Rapids: Baker Books, 1997.

———. "Theistic Evolution Is Incompatible with the Teachings of the Old Testament." In *Theistic Evolution: A Scientific, Philosophical, and Theological Critique*, edited by J. P. Moreland, Stephen C. Meyer, Christopher Shaw, Ann K. Gauger, and Wayne Grudem, 839–78. Wheaton: Crossway, 2017.

Curtis, Edward. "Man as the Image of God in Light of Ancient Near Eastern Parallels." PhD diss., University of Pennsylvania, 1984.

Dalley, Stephanie, ed. *Myths from Mesopotamia: Creation, the Flood, Gilgamesh, and Others*. Rev. ed. Oxford: Oxford University Press, 2000.

D'Anastasio, Ruggero, Stephen Wroe, Claudio Tuniz, Lucia Mancini, Deneb T. Cesana, Diego Dreossi, Mayoorendra Ravichandiran, et al. "Micro-Biomechanics of the Kebara 2 Hyoid and Its Implications for Speech in Neanderthals." *PLoS One* 8, no. 12 (2013): e82261. http://doi.org/10.1371/journal.pone.0082261.

Davis, Jud. "Unresolved Major Questions: Evangelicals and Genesis 1–2." In Charles, *Reading Genesis 1–2*, 207–36.

Day, John. *From Creation to Babel: Studies in Genesis 1–11*. Library of the Hebrew Bible/Old Testament Studies 592. London: Bloomsbury, 2013.

———. "The Serpent of the Garden of Eden: A Critique of Some Recent Proposals." Paper presented at the Annual Meeting of the Society of Biblical Literature, Denver, CO, November 18, 2018.

Dean, Christopher, Meave G. Leakey, Donald Reid, Friedemann Schrenk, Gary T. Schwartz, Christopher Stringer, and Alan Walker. "Growth Processes in Teeth Distinguish Modern Humans from *Homo erectus* and Earlier Hominins." *Nature* 414, no. 6864 (December 6, 2001): 628–31.

Dediu, Dan, and Stephen C. Levinson. "Neanderthal Language Revisited: Not Only Us." *Current Opinion in Behavioral Sciences* 21 (2018): 49–55.

DeGusta, David, W. Henry Gilbert, and Scott P. Turner. "Hypoglossal Canal Size and Hominid Speech." *Proceedings of the National Academy of Sciences* 96, no. 4 (February 16, 1999): 1800–1804. http://doi.org/10.1073/pnas.96.4.1800.

Delitzsch, Friedrich. *Babel und Bibel: Ein Vortrag*. Leipzig: Hinrichs, 1902.

D'Errico, Francesco. "The Invisible Frontier: A Multiple Species Model for the Origin of Behavioral Modernity." *Evolutionary Anthropology* 12, no. 4 (August 5, 2003): 188–202. https://doi.org/10.1002/evan.10113.

D'Errico, Francesco, and Chris B. Stringer. "Evolution, Revolution or Saltation Scenario for the Emergence of Modern Cultures?" *Philosophical Transactions of the Royal Society B* 366, no. 1567 (April 12, 2011): 1060–69. http://doi.org/10.1098/rstb.2010.0340.

Domning, Daryl P. "Evolution, Evil and Original Sin." *America*, November 12, 2001. http://www.americamagazine.org/issue/350/article/evolution-evil-and-original-sin.

Doty, William G. *Myth: A Handbook*. Tuscaloosa: University of Alabama Press, 2004.

Du, Andrew, and Zeresenay Alemseged. "Temporal Evidence Shows *Australopithecus sediba* Is Unlikely to Be the Ancestor of *Homo*." *Science Advances* 5 (May 2019): eaav9038. http://doi.org/10.1126/sciadv.aav9038.

Dundes, Alan. "Earth-Diver: Creation of the Mythopoeic Male." In Dundes, *Sacred Narrative*, 270–94.

———. "Introduction." In Dundes, *Sacred Narrative*, 1–4.

———, ed. *Sacred Narrative: Readings in the Theory of Myth*. Berkeley: University of California Press, 1984.

Dunn, James D. G. *Romans 1–8*. Word Biblical Commentary 38A. Grand Rapids: Zondervan, 1988.

Durvasula, Arun, and Sriram Sankararaman. "Recovering Signals of Ghost Archaic Introgression in African Populations." *Science Advances* 6, no. 7 (February 12, 2020): eaax5097. https://doi.org/10.1126/sciadv.aax5097.

Eliade, Mircea. *Myth and Reality*. Translated by Willard R. Trask. New York: Harper & Row, 1963.

Ellis, E. Earle. *Paul's Use of the Old Testament*. Grand Rapids: Baker Books, 1981. Reprint, Eugene: Wipf & Stock, 2003.

Enns, Peter. "*Adam and the Genome*: Responses; Some Thoughts from Pete Enns." *Biologos* (blog), January 30, 2017: http://biologos.org/articles/adam-and-the-genome-responses.

———. *The Evolution of Adam: What the Bible Does and Doesn't Say about Human Origins*. Grand Rapids: Brazos, 2012.

Erho, Ted, Frederic Krueger, and Matthias Hoffmann. "Neues von Pharaos Zauberern." *Welt und Umwelt der Bibel* 2 (2016): 70–72.

Etz, Donald V. "The Numbers of Genesis V 3–31: A Suggested Conversion and Its Implications." *Vetus Testamentum* 43, no. 2 (1993): 171–89.

Fee, Gordon D. *The First Epistle to the Corinthians*. New International Commentary on the New Testament. Grand Rapids: Eerdmans, 1987.

Fiddes, I. T., G. A. Lodewijk, M. Mooring, C. M. Bosworth, A. D. Ewing, G. L. Mantalas, A. M. Novak, et al. "Human-Specific *NOTCH2NL* Genes Affect Notch Signaling and Cortical Neurogenesis." *Cell* 173, no. 6 (May 31, 2018): 1356–69.e22. http://doi.org/10.1016/j.cell.2018.03.051.

Firth, Raymond. "The Plasticity of Myth: Cases from Tikopia." In Dundes, *Sacred Narrative*, 207–16.

Fisher, Simon E. "Evolution of Language: Lessons from the Genome." *Psychonomic Bulletin and Review* 24, no. 1 (2017): 34–40. http://doi.org/10.3758/s13423-016-1112-8.

Fitzmyer, Joseph A. *Romans*. Anchor Yale Bible 33. New Haven: Yale University Press, 1993.

Fleagle, John G. "Beyond Parsimony." *Evolutionary Anthropology* 6, no. 1 (1997): 1.

Florio, M., T. Namba, S. Pääbo, M. Hiller, and W. B. Huttner. "A Single Splice Site Mutation in Human-Specific *ARHGAP11B* Causes Basal Progenitor Amplification." *Science Advances* 2, no. 12 (December 7, 2016): e1601941. https://doi.org/10.1126/sciadv.1601941.

Foley, Robert. "Striking Parallels in Early Hominid Evolution." *Trends in Ecology and Evolution* 8, no. 6 (June 1993): 196–97.

Fortey, Richard. *Life: An Unauthorized Biography*. London: Folio Society, 2008.

Fowler, Alastair. "The Life and Death of Literary Forms." In *New Directions in Literary History*, edited by Ralph Cohen, 77–94. London: Routledge & Kegan Paul, 1974.

Fox, William Sherwood. *Greek and Roman*. Vol. 1 of *The Mythology of All Races*, edited by Louis Herbert Gray and John Arnott MacCulloch. New York: Cooper Square, 1964.

Frankfort, Henri, and H. A. Frankfort. "The Emancipation of Thought from Myth." In Frankfort, Frankfort, Wilson, Jacobsen, and Irwin, *The Intellectual Adventure of Ancient Man*, 363–88.

———. "Myth and Reality." In Frankfort, Frankfort, Wilson, Jacobsen, and Irwin, *The Intellectual Adventure of Ancient Man*, 3–27.

Frankfort, H., H. A. Frankfort, John A. Wilson, Thorkild Jacobsen, and William A. Irwin. *The Intellectual Adventure of Ancient Man: An Essay on Speculative Thought in the Ancient Near East*. Chicago: University of Chicago Press, 1946.

Frazer, James G. "The Fall of Man." In Dundes, *Sacred Narrative*, 72–97.

Freedman, R. David. "The Dispatch of the Reconnaissance Birds in Gilgamesh XI." *Journal of the Ancient Near Eastern Society of Columbia University* 5 (1973): 123–29.

Fuentes, Agustín. *The Creative Spark: How Imagination Made Humans Exceptional*. New York: Dutton, 2017.

Gaster, Theodor H. "Myth and Story." In Dundes, *Sacred Narrative*, 110–36.

George, Andrew R. *The Babylonian Gilgamesh Epic: Introduction, Critical Edition, and Cuneiform Texts*. 2 vols. Oxford: Oxford University Press, 2003.

———. "Shattered Tablets and Tangled Threads: Editing Gilgamesh, Then and Now." *Aramazd* 3, no. 1 (2008): 7–30. https://eprints.soas.ac.uk/7497/.

Gertz, Jan Christian. "The Formation of the Primeval History." In *The Book of Genesis: Composition, Reception, and Interpretation*, edited by Craig A. Evans, Joel N. Lohr, and David L. Petersen, 107–36. Supplements to Vetus Testamentum 152. Leiden: Brill, 2012.

Gray, Louis Herbert, and John Arnott MacCulloch, eds. *The Mythology of All Races*. 13 vols. 1916–33. Reprint, New York: Cooper Square, 1964.

Green, William Henry. "Primeval Chronology." *Bibliotheca Sacra* (1890): 285–303.

Gundry, Robert H. Sōma *in Biblical Theology: With Emphasis on Pauline Anthropology*. Cambridge: Cambridge University Press, 1976.

Gunkel, Hermann. *The Legends of Genesis: The Biblical Saga and History*. Translated by W. H. Carruth. New York: Schocken Books, 1964.

Halton, Charles, ed. *Genesis: History, Fiction, or Neither? Three Views on the Bible's Earliest Chapters*. Grand Rapids: Zondervan, 2015.

Hamilton, Victor P. *The Book of Genesis: Chapters 1–17*. New International Commentary on the Old Testament. Grand Rapids: Eerdmans, 1990.

Hardy, B. L., M. H. Moncel, C. Kerfant, M. Lebon, L. Bellot-Gurlet, and N. Mélard. "Direct Evidence of Neanderthal Fibre Technology and Its Cognitive and Behavioral Implications." *Scientific Reports* 10, no. 4889 (2020). http://doi.org/10.1038/s41598-020-61839-w.

Harlow, Daniel C. "After Adam: Reading Genesis in an Age of Evolutionary Science." *Perspectives on Science and Christian Faith* 62, no. 3 (2010): 179–95.

Hasel, Gerhard F. "The Polemic Nature of the Genesis Cosmology." *Evangelical Quarterly* 46 (1974): 81–102.

Hasker, William. *The Emergent Self*. Ithaca, NY: Cornell University Press, 1999.

Hauser, Marc D. *The Evolution of Communication*. Cambridge, MA: MIT Press, 1996.

Hauser, M. D., C. Yang, R. C. Berwick, I. Tattersall, M. J. Ryan, J. Watumull, N. Chomsky, and R. C. Lewontin. "The Mystery of Language Evolution." *Frontiers in Psychology* 5 (May 7, 2014). http://doi.org/10.3389/fpsyg.2014.00401.

Hays, Christopher M., and Stephen Lane Herring. "Adam and the Fall." In *Evangelical Faith and the Challenge of Historical Criticism*, edited by Christopher M. Hays and Christopher B. Ansberry, 24–54. Grand Rapids: Baker Academic, 2013.

Heide, M., C. Haffner, A. Murayama, Y. Kurotaki, H. Shinohara, H. Okano, E. Sasaki, and W. B. Huttner. "Human-Specific *ARHGAP11B* Increases Size and Folding of Primate Neocortex in the Fetal Marmoset." *Science* 369, no. 6503 (July 31, 2020): 546–50. https://doi.org/10.1126/science.abb2401.

Heidel, Alexander. *The Babylonian Genesis: The Story of Creation.* 2nd ed. Chicago: University of Chicago Press, 1951.

Hendel, Ronald. "Genesis 6:1–4 in Recent Interpretation." Paper presented at the Annual Meeting of the Society of Biblical Literature, Genesis Section/Pentateuch Section, San Diego, CA, November 24, 2019.

Hess, Richard S. "The Genealogies of Genesis 1–11 and Comparative Literature." In Hess and Tsumura, *"I Studied Inscriptions from before the Flood,"* 58–72.

———. *Israelite Religions: An Archaeological and Biblical Survey.* Grand Rapids: Baker Academic, 2007.

Hess, Richard S., and David Toshio Tsumura, eds. *"I Studied Inscriptions from before the Flood": Ancient Near Eastern, Literary, and Linguistic Approaches to Genesis 1–11.* Sources for Biblical and Theological Studies 4. Winona Lake, IN: Eisenbrauns, 1994.

Hill, Carol A. "Making Sense of the Numbers in Genesis." *Perspectives on Science and Christian Faith* 55, no. 4 (2003): 239–51.

Hill, Theodore P. "The Significant-Digit Phenomenon." *American Mathematical Monthly* 102, no. 4 (April 1995): 322–27.

Hirsch, E. D., Jr. *Validity in Interpretation.* New Haven: Yale University Press, 1967.

Hoffmann, Dirk L., Diego E. Angelucci, Valentín Villaverde, Josefina Zapata, and João Zilhão. "Symbolic Use of Marine Shells and Mineral Pigments by Iberian Neandertals 115,000 Years Ago." *Science Advances* 4, no. 2 (February 2018): eaar5255. https://doi.org/10.1126/sciadv.aar5255.

Hoffmann, D. L., C. D. Standish, M. García-Diez, P. B. Pettitt, J. A. Milton, J. Zilhão, J. J. Alcolea-González, et al. "U-Th Dating of Carbonate Crusts Reveals Neandertal Origin of Iberian Cave Art." *Science* 359, no. 6378 (February 23, 2018): 912–15. https://doi.org/10 .1126/science.aap7778.

Hoffmann, Paul. *Die Toten in Christus: Eine religionsgeschichtliche und exegetische Untersuchung zur paulinischen Eschatologie.* 3rd ed. Neutestamentliche Abhandlungen 2. Münster: Aschendorff, 1978.

Hoffmeier, James K. "Genesis 1–11 as History and Theology." In Halton, *Genesis,* 23–58.

———. "Some Thoughts on Genesis 1 & 2 and Egyptian Cosmology." *Journal of the Ancient Near Eastern Society of Columbia University* 15, no. 1 (1983): 39–49.

Holloway, Ralph L. “The Human Brain Evolving: A Personal Retrospective.” In Broadfield, Yuan, Schick, and Toth, *The Human Brain Evolving*, 1–14.

Honko, Lauri. “Der Mythos in der Religionswissenschaft.” *Temenos* 6 (1970): 36–67.

———. “The Problem of Defining Myth.” In Dundes, *Sacred Narrative*, 41–52.

Hornung, Erik. *Conceptions of God in Ancient Egypt: The One and the Many*. Translated by John Baines. Ithaca, NY: Cornell University Press, 1982.

Horowitz, Wayne. *Mesopotamian Cosmic Geography*. Winona Lake, IN: Eisenbrauns, 2011.

Hössjer, Ola, and Ann Gauger. “A Single-Couple Human Origin Is Possible.” *BIO-Complexity* 2019, no. 1 (October 2019): 1–20.

Hublin, J. J., A. Ben-Ncer, S. E. Bailey, S. E. Freidline, S. Neubauer, M. M. Skinner, I. Bergmann, et al. “New Fossils from Jebel Irhoud, Morocco and the Pan-African Origin of *Homo sapiens*.” *Nature* 546, no. 7657 (June 8, 2017): 289–92. http://doi.org/10.1038/nature22336.

“Humans’ Big Brains May Be Partly Due to Three Newly Found Genes.” *Genetic Engineering and Biotechnology News*, June 1, 2018. https://www.genengnews.com/topics/omics/humans-big-brains-may-be-partly-due-to-three-newly-found-genes/.

Humphrey, Louise, and Chris Stringer. *Our Human Story*. London: Natural History Museum, 2018.

Humphreys, D. Russell. *Starlight and Time: Solving the Puzzle of Distant Starlight in a Young Universe*. Green Forest, AR: Master Books, 1996.

Hurd, James P. “Hominids in the Garden?” In Miller, *Perspectives on an Evolving Creation*, 208–33.

Hurowitz, Victor. *I Have Built You an Exalted House: Temple Building in the Bible in Light of Mesopotamian and North-West Writings*. Library of Hebrew Bible/Old Testament Studies 115. Sheffield: JSOT, 1992.

Irwin, William A. “The Hebrews: God.” In Frankfort, Frankfort, Wilson, Jacobsen, and Irwin, *The Intellectual Adventure of Ancient Man*, 223–54.

Jacobsen, Thorkild. “The Eridu Genesis.” In Hess and Tsumura, *“I Studied Inscriptions from before the Flood,”* 129–42.

———. “Mesopotamia: The Cosmos as a State.” In Frankfort, Frankfort, Wilson, Jacobsen, and Irwin, *The Intellectual Adventure of Ancient Man*, 125–84.

———. *The Sumerian King List*. Assyriological Studies 11. Chicago: University of Chicago Press, 1939.

Jaubert, J., S. Verheyden, D. Genty, M. Soulier, H. Cheng, D. Blamart, C. Burlet, et al. “Early Neanderthal Constructions Deep in Bruniquel Cave in Southwestern France.” *Nature* 534, no. 7605 (May 25, 2016): 111–14.

Johansson, Sverker. “Language Abilities in Neanderthals.” *Annual Review of Lin-*

guistics 1 (2015): 311–32. http://doi.org/10.1146/annurev-linguist-030514-124945.

Kaiser, Walter C., Jr. "The Literary Form of Genesis 1–11." In *New Perspectives on the Old Testament*, edited by J. Barton Payne, 48–65. Waco: Word, 1970.

Kalebic, N., C. Gilardi, M. Albert, T. Namba, K. R. Long, M. Kostic, B. Langen, and W. B. Huttner. "Human-Specific *ARHGAP11B* Induces Hallmarks of Neocortical Expansion in Developing Ferret Neocortex." *eLife* 7 (November 28, 2018): e41241.

Kay, R. F., M. Cartmill, and M. Balow. "The Hypoglossal Canal and the Origin of Human Vocal Behavior." *Proceedings of the National Academy of Sciences* 95, no. 9 (April 28, 1998): 5417–19. http://doi.org/10.1073/pnas.95.9.5417.

Keel, Othmar, and Silvia Schroer. *Creation: Biblical Theologies in the Context of the Ancient Near East*. Translated by Peter T. Daniels. Winona Lake, IN: Eisenbrauns, 2015.

Kemp, Kenneth W. "Science, Theology, and Monogenesis." *American Catholic Philosophical Quarterly* 85, no. 2 (2011): 217–36. https://doi.org/10.5840/acpq201185213.

Kennett, Douglas J., and James P. Kennett. "Early State Formation in Southern Mesopotamia: Sea Levels, Shorelines, and Climate Change." *The Journal of Island and Coastal Archaeology* 1 (2006): 67–99.

Kilchör, Benjamin. "Challenging the (Post-) Exilic Dating of P/H: The Most Important Issues." Paper presented at the Annual Meeting of the Society of Biblical Literature, San Diego, CA, November 22, 2019.

Kirk, G. S. *Myth: Its Meaning and Functions in Ancient and Other Cultures*. Sather Classical Lectures 40. Cambridge: Cambridge University Press, 1970.

———. "On Defining Myths." In Dundes, *Sacred Narrative*, 53–61.

Kissel, Marc, and Agustín Fuentes. "'Behavioral Modernity' as a Process, Not an Event, in the Human Niche." *Time and Mind* 11, no. 2 (April 3, 2018): 163–83. http://doi.org/10.1080/1751696X.2018.1469230.

Kitchen, K. A. *On the Reliability of the Old Testament*. Grand Rapids: Eerdmans, 2003.

Klein, Richard G. "The Stone Age Prehistory of Southern Africa." *Annual Review of Anthropology* 12 (1983): 25–48.

Koslicki, Kathrin. *The Structure of Objects*. Oxford: Oxford University Press, 2008.

Kramer, Samuel Noah. "The 'Babel of Tongues': A Sumerian Version." In Hess and Tsumura, *"I Studied Inscriptions from before the Flood,"* 278–82.

———. Review of *The Intellectual Adventure of Ancient Man: An Essay on Speculative Thought in the Ancient Near East*. *Journal of Cuneiform Studies* 2, no. 1 (1948): 39–70.

———. *Sumerian Mythology: A Study of Spiritual and Literary Achievement in the Third Millennium B.C.* Rev. ed. New York: Harper & Row, 1961.

Labuschagne, C. J. "The Life Spans of the Patriarchs." In *New Avenues in the Study of the Old Testament*, edited by A. S. van der Woude, 121–27. Leiden: Brill, 1989.

Laland, Kevin N. *Darwin's Unfinished Symphony: How Culture Made the Human Mind*. Princeton: Princeton University Press, 2017.

Lambeck, Kurt. "Shoreline Reconstructions for the Persian Gulf Since the Last Glacial Maximum." *Earth and Planetary Science Letters* 142, nos. 1–2 (1996): 43–57.

Lambert, W. G. "Mesopotamian Creation Stories." In *Imagining Creation*, edited by Markham J. Geller and Mineke Schipper, 15–59. IJS Studies in Judaica 5. Leiden: Brill, 2007.

———. "A New Look at the Babylonian Background of Genesis." *Journal of Theological Studies*, n.s., 16, no. 2 (1965): 287–300.

Lamoureux, Denis O. *Evolution: Scripture and Nature Say Yes!* Grand Rapids: Zondervan, 2016.

———. "No Historical Adam: Evolutionary Creation View." In Barrett and Caneday, *Four Views on the Historical Adam*, 37–65.

Leffler, E. M., Z. Gao, S. Pfeifer, L. Ségurel, A. Auton, O. Venn, R. Bowden, et al. "Multiple Instances of Ancient Balancing Selection Shared between Humans and Chimpanzees." *Science* 339, no. 6127 (March 29, 2013): 1578–82. http://doi.org/10.1126/science.1234070.

Legarreta-Castillo, Felipe de Jesús. *The Figure of Adam in Romans 5 and 1 Corinthians 15: The New Creation and Its Ethical and Social Reconfiguration*. Minneapolis: Fortress, 2014.

Levering, Matthew. *Engaging the Doctrine of Creation: Cosmos, Creatures, and the Wise and Good Creator*. Grand Rapids: Baker Academic, 2017.

Levison, John R. *Portraits of Adam in Early Judaism: From Sirach to 2 Baruch*. Journal for the Study of the Pseudepigrapha Supplement Series 1. Sheffield: JSOT Press, 1988.

Lewin, Roger, and Robert A. Foley. *Principles of Human Evolution*. 2nd ed. Oxford: Blackwell, 2004.

Li, Heng, and Richard Durbin. "Inference of Human Population History from Individual Whole-Genome Sequences." *Nature* 475, no. 7357 (2011): 493–96.

Lieberman, Daniel E. *The Evolution of the Human Head*. Cambridge, MA: Harvard University Press, 2011.

Lieberman, Philip. "Current Views on Neanderthal Speech Capabilities: A Reply to Boe et al. (2002)." *Journal of Phonetics* 35, no. 4 (2007): 552–63.

———. "On Neanderthal Speech and Human Evolution." *Behavioral and Brain Sciences* 19, no. 1 (1996): 156–57.

———. "Vocal Tract Anatomy and the Neural Bases of Talking." *Journal of Phonetics* 40, no. 4 (July 2012): 608–22.

Lieberman, Philip, and Edmund S. Crelin. "On the Speech of Neanderthal Man." *Linguistic Inquiry* 11, no. 2 (1971): 203–22.

Lindly, J. M., G. A. Clark, O. Bar-Yosef, D. Lieberman, J. Shea, Harold L. Dibble, Phillip G. Chase, et al. "Symbolism and Modern Human Origins." *Current Anthropology* 31, no. 3 (June 1990): 233–61.

Loke, Andrew. *The Origin of Humanity: Science and Scripture in Conversation*. Forthcoming.

Longman, Tremper, III. *Genesis*. The Story of God Bible Commentary. Grand Rapids: Zondervan, 2016.

———. "Responses to Chapter Two." In Charles, *Reading Genesis 1–2*, 67.

———. "What Genesis 1–2 Teaches (and What It Doesn't)." In Charles, *Reading Genesis 1–2*, 103–28.

Longman, Tremper, III, and John H. Walton. *The Lost World of the Flood: Mythology, Theology, and the Deluge Debate*. Downers Grove, IL: IVP Academic, 2018.

Loose, Jonathan J., Angus J. L. Menuge, and J. P. Moreland, eds. *The Blackwell Companion to Substance Dualism*. Oxford: Wiley-Blackwell, 2018.

Lorente-Galdos, B., O. Lao, G. Serra-Vidal, G. Santpere, L. F. K. Kuderna, L. R. Arauna, K. Fadhlaoui-Zid, et al. "Whole-Genome Sequence Analysis of a Pan African Set of Samples Reveals Archaic Gene Flow from an Extinct Basal Population of Modern Humans into Sub-Saharan Populations." *Genome Biology* 20, no. 1 (April 26, 2019): 77. https://doi.org/10.1186/s13059-019-1684-5.

Lowe, E. J. *Personal Agency: The Metaphysics of Mind and Action*. Oxford: Oxford University Press, 2008.

MacCulloch, John Arnott. *Eddic*. Vol. 2 of *The Mythology of All Races*, edited by Louis Herbert Gray and John Arnott MacCulloch. New York: Cooper Square, 1964.

MacLarnon, A. M., and G. P. Hewitt. "The Evolution of Human Speech: The Role of Enhanced Breathing Control." *American Journal of Physical Anthropology* 109, no. 3 (1999): 341–63.

Maddy, Penelope. "Believing the Axioms I." *Journal of Symbolic Logic* 53, no. 2 (1988): 481–511.

———. "Believing the Axioms II." *Journal of Symbolic Logic* 53, no. 3 (1988): 736–64.

———. *Defending the Axioms: On the Philosophical Foundations of Set Theory.* Oxford: Oxford University Press, 2011.

Malinowski, Bronislaw. "The Role of Myth in Life." In Dundes, *Sacred Narrative*, 193–206.

Mania, Dietrich. "Wer waren die Jäger von Schöningen?" In Thieme, *Die Schöninger Speere*, 222–24.

Marshall, I. Howard. *The Gospel of Luke*. New International Greek Testament Commentary. Grand Rapids: Eerdmans, 1978.

Mathews, Kenneth A. *Genesis 1–11:26*. The New American Commentary 1A. Nashville: Broadman & Holman, 1996.

Maudlin, Tim. "The Tale of Quantum Logic." In *Hilary Putnam*, edited by Yemima Ben-Menahem, 156–87. Contemporary Philosophy in Focus. Cambridge: Cambridge University Press, 2005.

McBrearty, Sally, and Alison S. Brooks. "The Revolution That Wasn't: A New Interpretation of the Origin of Modern Human Behavior." *Journal of Human Evolution* 39, no. 5 (November 2000): 453–563. https://doi.org/10.1006/jhev.2000.0435.

McGee, David. "Creation Date of Adam from the Perspective of Young-Earth Creationism." *Answers Research Journal* 5 (2012): 217–30.

McKnight, Scot. "*Adam and the Genome*: Responses; Some Thoughts from Scot McKnight." *BioLogos* (blog), January 30, 2017. http://biologos.org/articles/adam-and-the-genome-responses.

Mellars, Paul. "Cognitive Changes and the Emergence of Modern Humans in Europe." *Cambridge Archaeological Journal* 1, no. 1 (1991): 63–76.

Menuge, Angus. "Is Downward Causation Possible? How the Mind Can Make a Physical Difference." *Philosophia Christi* 11, no. 1 (2009): 93–110. https://doi.org/10.5840/pc20091117.

———. "Why Not Physicalism?" Paper presented at the Annual Meeting of the Society of Biblical Literature, Evangelical Philosophical Society Panel, San Francisco, CA, November 19, 2011.

Métraux, Alfred. "The Guaraní." In *Handbook of South American Indians*, vol. 3, *The Tropical Forest Tribes*, edited by Julian H. Steward, 69–94. Washington, DC: Smithsonian Institution and United States Government Printing Office, 1948.

———. "The Guarayú and Pauserna." In *Handbook of South American Indians*, vol. 3, *The Tropical Forest Tribes*, edited by Julian H. Steward, 430–38. Washington, DC: Smithsonian Institution and United States Government Printing Office, 1948.

Meyer, M., J. L. Arsuaga, C. de Filippo, S. Nagel, A. Aximu-Petri, B. Nickel, I. Martínez, et al. "Nuclear DNA Sequences from the Middle Pleistocene

Sima de los Huesos Hominins." *Nature* 531, no. 7595 (March 2016): 504–7. http://doi.org/10.1038/nature17405.

Middleton, J. Richard. *The Liberating Image: The* Imago Dei *in Genesis 1*. Grand Rapids: Brazos, 2005.

Millard, A. R. "A New Babylonian 'Genesis' Story." In Hess and Tsumura, *"I Studied Inscriptions from before the Flood,"* 114–28.

Miller, Keith B., ed. *Perspectives on an Evolving Creation.* Grand Rapids: Eerdmans, 2003.

Moo, Douglas J. *The Letter to the Romans.* 2nd ed. New International Commentary on the New Testament. Grand Rapids: Eerdmans, 2018.

Moreland, J. P., and William Lane Craig. *Philosophical Foundations for a Christian Worldview*. 2nd ed. Downers Grove, IL: InterVarsity Press, 2017.

Movius, Hallam L., Jr. "A Wooden Spear of Third Interglacial Age from Lower Saxony." *Southwestern Journal of Anthropology* 6, no. 2 (1950): 139–42.

Müller, W. Max. *Egyptian Mythology*. Vol. 12 of *The Mythology of All Races,* edited by Louis Herbert Gray and John Arnott MacCulloch. New York: Cooper Square, 1964.

Musil, Rudolf. "Die Pferde von Schöningen: Skelettreste einer ganzen Wildpferdherde." In Thieme, *Die Schöninger Speere*, 136–40.

Neubauer, S., J. J. Hublin, and P. Gunz. "The Evolution of Modern Human Brain Shape." *Science Advances* 4 (2018): eaao5961.

Neugebauer, Otto. *The Exact Sciences in Antiquity*. 2nd ed. New York: Dover, 1969.

Northup, Lesley A. "Myth-Placed Priorities: Religion and the Study of Myth." *Religious Studies Review* 32, no. 1 (2006): 5–10.

Numazawa, K. "The Cultural-Historical Background of Myths on the Separation of Sky and Earth." In Dundes, *Sacred Narrative*, 182–92.

Nuttle, X., G. Giannuzzi, M. H. Duyzend, J. G. Schraiber, I. Narvaiza, P. H. Sudmant, O. Penn, et al. "Emergence of a *Homo sapiens*–Specific Gene Family and Chromosome 16p11.2 CNV Susceptibility." *Nature* 536, no. 7615 (August 3, 2016): 205–9. http://doi.org/10.1038/nature19075.

Ortlund, Gavin R. *Retrieving Augustine's Doctrine of Creation: Ancient Wisdom for Current Controversy*. Downers Grove, IL: IVP Academic, 2020.

Osawa, Koji. "Jannes and Jambres: The Role and Meaning of Their Traditions in Judaism." *Frankfurter Judaistische Beiträge* 37 (2011): 55–73.

Otzen, Benedikt. "The Use of Myth in Genesis." In *Myths in the Old Testament*, by Benedikt Otzen, Hans Gottlieb, and Knud Jeppesen, and translated by Frederick Cryer, 22–61. London: SCM, 1980.

Pannenberg, Wolfhart. "The Doctrine of Creation and Modern Science." In *To-*

ward a Theology of Nature: Essays in Science and Faith, edited by Ted Peters, 29–49. Louisville: Westminster John Knox, 1993.

Pettazzoni, Raffaele. "The Truth of Myth." In Dundes, *Sacred Narrative*, 98–109.

Pietersma, Albert, ed. and trans. *The Apocryphon of Jannes and Jambres the Magicians*. Religions in the Graeco-Roman World 119. Leiden: Brill, 1994.

Plantinga, Alvin. "Materialism and Christian Belief." In *Persons: Human and Divine*, edited by Peter van Inwagen and Dean W. Zimmerman, 99–141. Oxford: Oxford University Press, 2007.

———. *Where the Conflict Really Lies: Science, Religion, and Naturalism*. Oxford: Oxford University Press, 2011.

Plantinga, Cornelius, Jr. *Not the Way It's Supposed to Be: A Breviary of Sin*. Grand Rapids: Eerdmans, 1995.

Popper, Karl R., and John C. Eccles. *The Self and Its Brain: An Argument for Interactionism*. New York: Springer, 1977.

Poythress, Vern S. "Rain Water versus a Heavenly Sea in Genesis 1:6–8." *Westminster Theological Journal* 77 (2015): 181–91.

Pritchard, James B., ed. *The Ancient Near East: An Anthology of Texts and Pictures*. Princeton: Princeton University Press, 2011.

Prosee, Reinier. "The Mutation That Allowed Our Brain to Grow." *Science Breaker*, August 24, 2017. http://thesciencebreaker.org/breaks/evolution-behaviour/the-mutation-that-allowed-our-brain-to-grow.

Prüfer, K., F. Racimo, N. Patterson, F. Jay, S. Sankararaman, S. Sawyer, A. Heinze, et al. "The Complete Genome Sequence of a Neanderthal from the Altai Mountains." *Nature* 505, no. 7481 (January 2014): 43–49. http://doi.org/10.1038/nature12886.

Rad, Gerhard von. *Genesis: A Commentary*. Rev. ed. Old Testament Library. Louisville: Westminster John Knox, 1972.

Rasmussen, M. D., M. J. Hubisz, I. Gronau, and A. Siepel. "Genome-Wide Inference of Ancestral Recombination Graphs." *PLOS Genetics* 10, no. 5 (May 15, 2014): e1004342. http://doi.org/ 10.1371/journal.pgen.1004342.

Reich, David. *Who We Are and How We Got Here: Ancient DNA and the New Science of the Human Past*. New York: Pantheon Books, 2018.

Richelle, Matthieu. "La structure littéraire de l'Histoire Primitive (Genèse 1,1–11,26) en son état final." *Biblische Notizen* 151 (2011): 3–22.

Richter, D., R. Grün, R. Joannes-Boyau, T. E. Steele, F. Amani, M. Rué, P. Fernandes, et al. "The Age of the Hominin Fossils from Jebel Irhoud, Morocco, and the Origins of the Middle Stone Age." *Nature* 546, no. 7657 (June 8, 2017): 293–96. http://doi.org/10.1038/nature22335.

Rieder, Hermann. "Zur Qualität der Schöninger Speere als Jagdwaffen—aus der Sicht der Sportwissenschaften." In Thieme, *Die Schöninger Speere*, 159–62.

Rightmire, G. Philip. "Human Evolution in the Middle Pleistocene: The Role of *Homo heidelbergensis*." *Evolutionary Anthropology* 6, no. 6 (December 7, 1998): 218–27. https://doi.org/10.1002/(sici)1520-6505(1998)6:6<218::aid-evan4>3.0.co;2-6.

Rochberg, Francesca. *Before Nature: Cuneiform Knowledge and the History of Science*. Chicago: University of Chicago Press, 2016.

———. *The Heavenly Writing: Divination, Horoscopy, and Astronomy in Mesopotamian Culture*. Cambridge: Cambridge University Press, 2004.

Rogerson, J. W. *Myth in Old Testament Interpretation*. Beiheft zur Zeitschrift für die alttestamentliche Wissenschaft 134. Berlin: de Gruyter, 1974.

———. "Slippery Words: Myth." In Dundes, *Sacred Narrative*, 62–71.

Rosas, A., L. Ríos, A. Estalrrich, H. Liversidge, A. García-Tabernero, R. Huguet, H. Cardoso, et al. "The Growth Pattern of Neandertals, Reconstructed from a Juvenile Skeleton from El Sidrón (Spain)." *Science* 357, no. 6357 (September 22, 2017): 1282–87.

Rose, Jeffrey I. "New Light on Human Prehistory in the Arabo-Persian Gulf Oasis." *Current Anthropology* 51, no. 6 (2010): 849–83.

Rosen, Gideon, and John P. Burgess. "Nominalism Reconsidered." In *The Oxford Handbook of Philosophy of Mathematics and Logic*, edited by Stewart Shapiro, 515–35. Oxford: Oxford University Press, 2005.

Rosenberg, Alex. *The Atheist's Guide to Reality: Enjoying Life without Illusions*. New York: Norton, 2011.

Ross, Allen P. *Creation and Blessing: A Guide to the Study and Exposition of Genesis*. Grand Rapids: Baker Books, 1998.

Ross, Hugh. *Navigating Genesis: A Scientist's Journey through Genesis 1–11*. Covina, CA: Reasons to Believe, 2014.

Sailhamer, John H. *Genesis: Text and Exposition*. Expositor's Bible Commentary 2. Grand Rapids: Zondervan, 1990.

———. *Genesis Unbound: A Provocative New Look at the Creation Account*. Sisters, OR: Multnomah, 1996.

Salamon, Hagar, and Harvey E. Goldberg. "Myth-Ritual-Symbol." In *A Companion to Folklore*, edited by Regina F. Bendix and Galit Hasan-Rokem, 119–35. Oxford: Wiley-Blackwell, 2012.

Sandmel, Samuel. "Parallelomania." *Journal of Biblical Literature* 81, no. 1 (1962): 1–13.

Sanford, Ward E. "Thoughts on Eden, the Flood, and the Persian Gulf." *Newsletter of the Affiliation of Christian Geologists* 7 (1999): 7–10.

Sarfati, Jonathan D. *The Genesis Account: A Theological, Historical, and Scien-*

tific Commentary on Genesis 1–11. Powder Springs, GA: Creation Book Publishers, 2015.

Sarna, Nahum M. *Genesis*. JPS Torah Commentary. Philadelphia: Jewish Publication Society, 1989.

Sauer, James. "The River Runs Dry." *Biblical Archaeology Review* 22, no. 4 (1996): 52–64.

Savage-Rumbaugh, Sue, and William Mintz Fields. "Rules and Tools: Beyond Anthropomorphism." In Toth and Schick, *The Oldowan*, 223–41.

Schilbrack, Kevin. "Introduction: On the Use of Philosophy in the Study of Myths." In *Thinking through Myths: Philosophical Perspectives*, edited by Kevin Schilbrack, 1–17. London: Routledge, 2002.

Schoenemann, P. Tom. "The Meaning of Brain Size: The Evolution of Conceptual Complexity." In Broadfield, Yuan, Schick, and Toth, *The Human Brain Evolving*, 37–50.

Schwartz, Jeffrey H., and Ian Tattersall. "Defining the Genus *Homo*." *Science* 349, no. 6251 (August 28, 2015): 931–32.

Seely, Paul H. "The Firmament and the Water Above, Part I: The Meaning of *raqia'* in Gen 1:6–8." *Westminster Theological Journal* 53, no. 2 (1991): 227–40.

———. "The Firmament and the Water Above, Part II: The Meaning of 'the Water above the Firmament' in Gen 1:6–8." *Westminster Theological Journal* 54, no. 1 (1992): 31–46.

Segal, Robert A. "Myth as Primitive Philosophy: The Case of E. B. Tylor." In *Thinking through Myths: Philosophical Perspectives*, edited by Kevin Schilbrack, 18–45. New York: Routledge, 2002.

———. *Myth: A Very Short Introduction*. 2nd ed. Oxford: Oxford University Press, 2015.

Seymour, R. S., V. Bosiocic, E. P. Snelling, P. C. Chikezie, Q. Hu, T. J. Nelson, B. Zipfel, and C. V. Miller. "Cerebral Blood Flow Rates in Recent Great Apes Are Greater Than in *Australopithecus* Species That Had Equal or Larger Brains." *Proceedings of the Royal Society B* 286, no. 1915 (November 13, 2019): 20192208. https://doi.org/10.1098/rspb.2019.2208.

Skelton, Randall R., and Henry M. McHenry. "Evolutionary Relationships among Early Hominids." *Journal of Human Evolution* 23 (1992): 309–49.

Smith, Benjamin D., Jr. *Genesis, Science, and the Beginning*. Eugene: Wipf & Stock, 2018.

Soressi, Marie, and Francesco d'Errico. "Pigments, gravures, parures: les comportements symboliques controversés des Néandertaliens." In *Les Néandertaliens: Biologie et cultures*, edited by Bernard Vandermeersch and Bruno Maureille, 297–309. Paris: Éditions du CTHS, 2007.

Sousa, A. M. M., K. A. Meyer, G. Santpere, F. O. Gulden, and N. Sestan. "Evolution of the Human Nervous System Function, Structure, and Development." *Cell* 170, no. 2 (July 13, 2017): 226–47. http://doi.org/10.1016/j.cell.2017.06.036.

Sparks, Kenton L. "Genesis 1–11 as Ancient Historiography." In Halton, *Genesis*, 110–39.

———. "Response to James K. Hoffmeier." In Halton, *Genesis*, 63–72.

Speiser, E. A. "The Rivers of Paradise." In Hess and Tsumura, *"I Studied Inscriptions from before the Flood,"* 175–82.

Steiner, V. J. "Literary Structure of the Pentateuch." In Alexander and Baker, *Dictionary of the Old Testament*, 544–56.

Sterelny, Kim. "From Hominins to Humans: How *sapiens* Became Behaviourally Modern." *Philosophical Transactions of the Royal Society B* 366, no. 1566 (March 27, 2011): 809–22. https://doi.org/10.1098/rstb.2010.0301.

Stringer, Chris. "A Comment on the 'Early Neanderthal Constructions Deep in Bruniquel Cave in Southwestern France' Paper Published in *Nature*." Press release. Natural History Museum, London. May 25, 2016. https://www.nhm.ac.uk/press-office/press-releases/comment-on-early-neanderthal-constructions-in-brunique-cave.html.

———. "The Status of *Homo heidelbergensis* (Schoetensack 1908)." *Evolutionary Anthropology* 21, no. 3 (May 2012): 101–7.

Stringer, Chris, and Peter Andrews. *The Complete World of Human Evolution*. 2nd ed. New York: Thames & Hudson, 2012.

Swamidass, S. Joshua. *The Genealogical Adam and Eve: The Surprising Science of Universal Ancestry*. Downers Grove, IL: IVP Academic, 2019.

———. "Heliocentric Certainty against a Bottleneck of Two?" *Peaceful Science* (blog), December 31, 2017. https://discourse.peacefulscience.org/t/heliocentric-certainty-against-a-bottleneck-of-two/61.

———. "Reworking the Science of Adam." *Peaceful Science* (blog), March 22, 2018. http://peacefulscience.org/reworking-Adam/.

———. "Three Stories on Adam." *Peaceful Science* (blog), August 5, 2018. http://peacefulscience.org/three-stories-on-adam/.

Swinburne, Richard. "Authority of Scripture, Tradition, and the Church." In *The Oxford Handbook of Philosophical Theology*, edited by Thomas P. Flint and Michael C. Rea, 11–29. Oxford: Oxford University Press, 2011.

———. *Mind, Brain, and Free Will*. Oxford: Oxford University Press, 2013.

Tattersall, Ian. *The Fossil Trail: How We Know What We Think We Know about Human Evolution*. 2nd ed. Oxford: Oxford University Press, 2009.

———. "The Genus *Homo*." *Inference* 2, no. 1 (February 2016). http://inference-review.com/article/the-genus-homo.

Teixeira, Pedro. *The Travels of Pedro Teixeira*. Edited by William F. Sinclair and Donald Ferguson. London: Hakluyt Society, 1902.

Teller, J. T., K. W. Glennie, N. Lancaster, and A. K. Singhvi. "Calcareous Dunes of the United Arab Emirates and Noah's Flood: The Postglacial Reflooding of the Persian (Arabian) Gulf." *Quaternary International* 68–71 (2000): 297–308.

Thieme, Hartmut, ed. *Die Schöninger Speere: Mensch und Jagd Vor 400 000 Jahren*. Stuttgart: Theiss, 2007.

———. "Der grosse Wurf von Schöningen: Das neue Bild zur Kultur des frühen Menschen." In Thieme, *Die Schöninger Speere*, 224–28.

———. "Lower Paleolithic Hunting Spears from Germany." *Nature* 385, no. 6619 (February 27, 1997): 807–10.

———. "Überlegungen zum Gesamtbefund des Wild-Pferd-Jagdlagers." In Thieme, *Die Schöninger Speere*, 177–90.

Thompson, Stith. *Motif-Index of Folk-Literature: A Classification of Narrative Elements in Folktales, Ballads, Myths, Fables, Mediaeval Romances, Exempla, Fabliaux, Jest-Books, and Local Legends*. Rev. ed. 6 vols. Bloomington: Indiana University Press, 1955.

Tigay, Jeffrey H. *The Evolution of the Gilgamesh Epic*. Philadelphia: University of Pennsylvania Press, 1982.

Tomasello, Michael. *Becoming Human: A Theory of Ontogeny*. Cambridge, MA: Belknap Press of Harvard University Press, 2019.

———. *A Natural History of Human Thinking*. Cambridge, MA: Harvard University Press, 2014.

Toth, Nicholas, and Kathy Schick. "Hominin Brain Reorganization, Technological Change, and Cognitive Complexity." In Broadfield, Yuan, Schick, and Toth, *The Human Brain Evolving*, 293–312.

———, eds. *The Oldowan: Case Studies into the Earliest Stone Age*. Stone Age Institute Publication Series 1. Gosport, IN: Stone Age Institute Press, 2006.

Toth, Nicholas, Kathy Schick, and Sileshi Semaw. "A Comparative Study of the Stone Tool-Making Skills of *Pan*, *Australopithecus*, and *Homo sapiens*." In Toth and Schick, *The Oldowan*, 155–222.

Tsumura, David Toshio. *Creation and Destruction: A Reappraisal of the* Chaoskampf *Theory in the Old Testament*. Winona Lake, IN: Eisenbrauns, 2005.

———. "The Earth in Genesis 1." In Hess and Tsumura, *"I Studied Inscriptions from before the Flood,"* 310–28.

———. "Genesis and Ancient Near Eastern Stories of Creation and Flood: An Introduction." In Hess and Tsumura, *"I Studied Inscriptions from before the Flood,"* 27–57.

Turner, L. A. "Genesis." In Alexander and Baker, *Dictionary of the Old Testament*, 350–59.

University of Copenhagen, the Faculty of Health and Medical Sciences. "Oldest Ever Human Genetic Evidence Clarifies Dispute over Our Ancestors." *Science Daily*, April 1, 2020. http://www.sciencedaily.com/releases/2020/04/200401111657.htm.

Upton, John. "Ancient Sea Rise Tale Told Accurately for 10,000 Years." *Scientific American*, January 26, 2015. http://www.scientificamerican.com/article/ancient-sea-rise-tale-told-accurately-for-10-000-years/.

Vallender, Eric J., and Bruce T. Lahn. "Study of Human Brain Evolution at the Genetic Level." In Broadfield, Yuan, Schick, and Toth, *The Human Brain Evolving*, 107–18.

Van De Mieroop, Marc. *Philosophy before the Greeks: The Pursuit of Truth in Ancient Babylonia*. Princeton: Princeton University Press, 2016.

Venema, Dennis R. "Adam—Once More, with Feeling." *Jesus Creed* (blog), November 4, 2019. http://www.patheos.com/blogs/jesuscreed/2019/11/04/adam-once-more-with-feeling/.

———. "Genesis and the Genome: Genomics Evidence for Human-Ape Common Ancestry and Ancestral Hominid Population Sizes." *Perspectives on Science and Christian Faith* 62, no. 3 (2010): 166–78.

Venema, Dennis R., and Scot McKnight. *Adam and the Genome: Reading Scripture after Genetic Science*. Grand Rapids: Brazos, 2017.

Veyne, Paul. *Did the Greeks Believe in Their Myths? An Essay on the Constitutive Imagination*. Translated by Paula Wissing. Chicago: University of Chicago Press, 1988.

Von Hendy, Andrew. *The Modern Construction of Myth*. Bloomington: Indiana University Press, 2002.

Walton, John H. "Creation." In Alexander and Baker, *Dictionary of the Old Testament*, 155–68.

———. "Eden, Garden of." In Alexander and Baker, *Dictionary of the Old Testament*, 202–7.

———. *Genesis 1 as Ancient Cosmology*. Winona Lake, IN: Eisenbrauns, 2011.

———. "A Historical Adam: Archetypal Creation View." In Barrett and Caneday, *Four Views on the Historical Adam*, 89–118.

———. *The Lost World of Adam and Eve: Genesis 2–3 and the Human Origins Debate*. Downers Grove, IL: IVP Academic, 2015.

———. *The Lost World of Genesis One: Ancient Cosmology and the Origins Debate*. Downers Grove, IL: IVP Academic, 2009.

———. "Response from the Archetypal View." In Barrett and Caneday, *Four Views on the Historical Adam*, 66–71.

———. "Responses to Chapter One." In Charles, *Reading Genesis 1–2*, 43.

Walton, Kendall L. *Mimesis as Make-Believe: On the Foundations of the Representational Arts*. Cambridge, MA: Harvard University Press, 1990.

Wasserman, Nathan. *The Flood: The Akkadian Sources*. Leuven: Peeters, 2020.

Waters, Guy Prentiss. "Theistic Evolution Is Incompatible with the Teachings of the New Testament." In *Theistic Evolution: A Scientific, Philosophical, and Theological Critique*, edited by J. P. Moreland, Stephen C. Meyer, Christopher Shaw, Ann K. Gauger, and Wayne Grudem, 879–926. Wheaton: Crossway, 2017.

Watts, Ian, Michael Chazan, and Jayne Wilkins. "Early Evidence for Brilliant Ritualized Display: Specularite Use in the Northern Cape (South Africa) between ~500 and ~300 Ka." *Current Anthropology* 57, no. 3 (June 2, 2016): 287–310. https://doi.org/10.1086/686484.

Welker, F., J. Ramos-Madrigal, P. Gutenbrunner, M. Mackie, S. Tiwary, R. Rakownikow Jersie-Christensen, C. Chiva, et al. "The Dental Proteome of *Homo antecessor*." *Nature* 580, no. 7802 (April 1, 2020): 235–38. https://doi.org/10.1038/s41586-020-2153-8.

Wenham, Gordon J. "Genesis 1–11 as Protohistory." In Halton, *Genesis*, 73–97.

———. *Genesis 1–15*. Word Biblical Commentary 1. Grand Rapids: Zondervan, 1987.

———. "Response to James K. Hoffmeier." In Halton, *Genesis*, 59–62.

Werner, Alice. "African Mythology." In *Armenian and African*, vol. 7 of *The Mythology of All Races*, edited by Louis Herbert Gray and John Arnott MacCulloch. Boston: Marshall Jones, 1925.

Westermann, Claus. *Genesis 1–11: A Continental Commentary*. Translated by John J. Scullion. Minneapolis: Fortress, 1994.

———. "Sinn und Grenze religionsgeschichtlicher Parallelen." *Theologische Literaturzeitung* 90, no. 7 (1965): 489–96.

Wheeler, Brandon C., and Julia Fischer. "The Blurred Boundaries of Functional Reference: A Response to Scarantino & Clay." *Animal Behaviour* 100 (2015): e9–e13.

———. "Functionally Referential Signals: A Promising Paradigm Whose Time Has Passed." *Evolutionary Anthropology* 21, no. 5 (September 2012): 195–205. http://doi.org/10.1002/evan.21319.

Whiting, Kai, Leonidas Konstantakos, Greg Sadler, and Christopher Gill. "Were Neanderthals Rational? A Stoic Approach." *Humanities* 7, no. 2 (2018): 39. http://doi.org/10.3390/h7020039.

Wilcox, David. "Finding Adam: The Genetics of Human Origins." In Miller, *Perspectives on an Evolving Creation*, 234–53.

———. "Updating Human Origins." *Perspectives on Science and Christian Faith* 71, no. 1 (2019): 37–49.

Wilkins, J., B. J. Schoville, K. S. Brown, and M. Chazan. "Evidence for Early Hafted Hunting Technology." *Science* 338, no. 6109 (November 16, 2012): 942–46. https://doi.org/10.1126/science.1227608.

Wilkins, Jayne, and Michael Chazan. "Blade Production ~500 Thousand Years Ago at Kathu Pan 1, South Africa: Support for a Multiple Origins Hypothesis for Early Middle Pleistocene Blade Technologies." *Journal of Archaeological Science* 39, no. 6 (2012): 1883–1900.

Wilson, John A. "Egypt: The Nature of the Universe." In Frankfort, Frankfort, Wilson, Jacobsen, and Irwin, *The Intellectual Adventure of Ancient Man*, 31–122.

Wilson, Robert R. *Genealogy and History in the Biblical World*. New Haven: Yale University Press, 1977.

———. "Genealogy, Genealogies." In *Anchor Bible Dictionary*, edited by David Noel Freedman, 2:929–32. New York: Doubleday, 1992.

Wiseman, D. J. "Genesis 10: Some Archaeological Considerations." In Hess and Tsumura, *"I Studied Inscriptions from before the Flood,"* 254–65.

Wittgenstein, Ludwig. *Philosophical Investigations*. Edited by G. E. M. Anscombe and R. Rhees. Translated by G. E. M. Anscombe. Oxford: Blackwell, 1953.

Wright, J. Stafford. "The Place of Myth in the Interpretation of the Bible." *Journal of the Transactions of the Victorian Institute* 88 (1956): 18–30.

Young, Davis A. "The Antiquity and Unity of the Human Race Revisited." *Christian Scholar's Review* 24, no. 4 (1995): 380–96.

Young, Dwight Wayne. "The Influence of Babylonian Algebra on Longevity among the Antediluvians." *Zeitschrift für die Alttestamentliche Wissenschaft* 102 (1990): 321–35.

———. "On the Application of Numbers from Babylonian Mathematics to Biblical Life Spans and Epochs." *Zeitschrift für die Alttestamentliche Wissenschaft* 100 (1988): 331–61.

Younger, K. Lawson, Jr., ed. *The Context of Scripture*. Vol. 4, *Supplements*. Leiden: Brill, 2017.

INDEX OF NAMES AND SUBJECTS

INDEX OF SCRIPTURE AND OTHER ANCIENT TEXTS

Greco-Roman Literature

Ancient Near Eastern Works